# Classical Logic

## and Its Rabbit-Holes

## A First Course

# Classical Logic
## and Its Rabbit-Holes

## A First Course

## Nelson P. Lande

Hackett Publishing Company, Inc.
Indianapolis/Cambridge

20  19  18  17      2  3  4  5  6  7  8

For further information, please address
  Hackett Publishing Company, Inc.
  P.O. Box 44937
  Indianapolis, Indiana 46244-0937

  www.hackettpublishing.com

Cover design by Deborah Wilkes
Interior design by Elizabeth L. Wilson
Composition by William Hartman

**Library of Congress Cataloging-in-Publication Data**

Lande, Nelson P.
      Classical logic and its rabbit-holes : a first course / Nelson P. Lande.
        pages cm
      Includes index.
      ISBN 978-1-60384-948-7 (pbk.) — ISBN 978-1-60384-949-4 (cloth)
      1. Logic—Textbooks. I. Title.
      BC108.L25 2013
      160—dc23                                              2013016243

The paper used in this publication meets the minimum requirements of American
National Standard for Information Sciences—Permanence of Paper for Printed
Library Materials, ANSI Z39.48–1984.

# Contents

# Chapter Two – Propositional Logic: A Formal Language, Part Two

# Chapter Three – Propositional Logic: A Deductive Apparatus, Part One

# Chapter Four – Propositional Logic: A Deductive Apparatus, Part Two

## Chapter Five – Predicate Logic: A Formal Language, Part One

# Chapter Six – Predicate Logic:
# A Formal Language, Part Two

# Chapter Seven – Predicate Logic:
## A Deductive Apparatus, Part One

# Chapter Eight – Predicate Logic:
## A Deductive Apparatus, Part Two

Sample anwers to selected exercises can be found on this volume's title support page at www.hackettpublishing.com. Any corrections noted will also be posted on that page.

To Maydee

# Acknowledgments

There are many people to whom I am greatly indebted with respect to the writing and the publication of this book, and whom I very much wish to thank.

Michael Meyer read an earlier version in its entirety. He wrote extensive and detailed comments on each of the chapters. He replied in great depth to each of the many queries—technical, philosophical, and pedagogical—that I frequently put to him. Without exception, his comments displayed immense logical acuity and thus were invaluable.

A number of individuals read one or more early versions of one or more chapters of this book during its development, and provided insights, comments, and criticisms that were most helpful. The effort that they expended in their individual critiques attests to their generosity: Mark Balaguer, Craig Delancey, Robert Fitzgibbons, Hans Halvorson, Steven Levy, Robert May, Matthew Moore, Steven Nelson, Jonah N. Schupbach, Daniel J. Singer, Robin Smith, and Michael Titelbaum.

My former students Greg Brogan, Joey Jebari, Rosalie Sard, and Lily Silverstein read a version of the section that ultimately became the final appendix to Chapter 8. Their comments and suggestions, unsurprisingly, were very sharp. My former student Ceci Judge was sufficiently gracious (and stubborn) to insist on reading an earlier version of the manuscript in its entirety. She caught *scads* of slips of indentation, numbering, punctuation, spelling, and typography.

It is to my logic students—and in particular it is to the seriousness with which they have approached logic and to the enthusiasm with which they have grappled with it—that I owe an immense part of the immense pleasure that I have derived over the years from the teaching of logic.

The responsibility for any flaws which may appear in the book, or any of its shortcomings, is of course entirely mine. In particular, it does not lie with those who were kind enough to read and comment on earlier versions.

Leslie Connor, my copyeditor, was hawk-eyed in her attention to detail—indispensably so—and in thereby spotting infelicities of punctuation, spelling, and style. She was indefatigable in checking the correctness/incorrectness of each of my many internal chapter and section cross-references.

Liz Wilson, the director of production, presided over the entire production process. She ensured that every conceivable detail, from the macroscopic (e.g., the formatting of the text and the design of the pages) to the microscopic, was addressed properly. She was a master of generating both rigorous schedules and gentle but firm reminders of looming deadlines. She supervised and reviewed the copyediting, and contributed crucial stylistic recommendations.

Deborah Wilkes, my editor/publisher, is incontrovertibly the *ne plus ultra* of editors/publishers. While writing the book, I was exceedingly fortunate to be the beneficiary of her support, her wry wit, her flexibility, and her impeccable judgment about matters strategic and pedagogical.

My greatest debt is to my wife, Maydee G. Lande. Where the writing of a logic textbook is concerned, I have benefited immeasurably from her incomparable sense of style (both literary and otherwise). And I have benefited immeasurably from her unending encouragement throughout the entire writing process. Over the years she had asked me repeatedly why I didn't write a logic textbook of my own. *Classical Logic and Its Rabbit-Holes* is my answer to her question.

# Note to the Reader

The past half century has seen the publication of a very considerable number of logic textbooks, many of them first-rate and some of them outstanding.

Obvious question: So why yet *another* logic textbook?

Answer: This logic text differs from other logic texts, I believe, in two fundamental respects. One has to do with its style and one has to do with its substance. In my view—others, of course, will disagree—each of these differences is for the better.

Its style is atypical for a logic text: I wrote the book in the second person, addressing the reader directly and thus informally. Why in the second person? Because I wrote the book for exactly *one* person: the individual who would be reading it. And I wrote it not simply *for* him or her: I wrote it *to* him or her. There is a method to this madness. . . .

I imagined this individual to be a serious student who would approach logic as any serious individual approaches any arduous undertaking: with equal measures of trepidation and curiosity. Taking a logic course is a little like trekking at high altitude. The air is thin. The footpath is narrow and uneven. All too often, a wall of rock rises vertically to one's right and falls off precipitously to one's left. A single misstep would have most unwelcome consequences. The trek is demanding, exhausting, and terrifying. But it can also be fun—and even exhilarating.

And so it is with a course in logic. A good logic course is at once demanding, exhausting, and terrifying. But it too can also be fun—and even exhilarating. A good logic teacher is like a good trekking guide. Such a teacher knows the path, knows the topography, knows the whereabouts of each and every slip and pitfall, and most importantly, knows just how far to push his or her students. The trick of the trek is to make sure that there are as many committed trekkers present at sundown as there were at sunrise. And so it is with a course in logic.

And so it is with a logic text. A good logic text complements a good logic teacher. It provides the student with all the resources necessary to make the trek as painless—and as pleasant—as possible. No trek—no logic course—can be entirely pain-free. And no trek—no logic course—can be endlessly pleasant. But by approaching the reader as a trekking guide approaches a novice trekker, I have endeavored to do my part to make material that is by its very nature intimidating, as unintimidating as possible. Of necessity, such an approach calls for an informal style. One doesn't expect one's trekking guide to be warm and fuzzy—but one does expect him or her to be recognizably *human*. One should expect no less from a logic text. Being recognizably human entails having a *personality*. The instructions to IRS Form 1040 lack a personality. For better or for worse, this book is not the instructions to IRS Form 1040: it has a distinctive personality

Its substance, like its style, is also atypical for a logic text. Every logic text, of course, is a *how-to* text, but the focus of many logic texts seems to be almost exclusively *how-to*. At first glance, this book appears to be one of them. But only at first glance.

The first glance reveals that I walk the student, in excruciating detail, through, among other things, translation after translation and proof after proof. I try to anticipate the most common slips and pitfalls; I warn the student about them; and I show the student how to avoid them. So much one expects of any logic text.

The second glance, however, reveals that I elaborate, at considerable length, on a good many points, and I provide detailed explanations and justifications of others. *Just why is this slip a slip, and just why is this pitfall a pitfall?* I elaborate; I explain; and I justify—much more so, I believe, than is common in current logic texts. There are four reasons why I do so.

First, it seems to me that curious students want to know more than simply how to master the techniques of classical logic. They also want to know why *this*, say, isn't one of our derivation rules, or, more generally, why we have fewer derivation rules than their pals have in *their* logic courses. To answer such questions, sometimes one must elaborate; sometimes one must explain; and sometimes one must justify.

The second reason for my detailed elaborations, explanations, and justifications has to do with my understanding of what it is to understand logic. Logic is *not* a monkey-see-monkey-do course. Too often a student completes a first logic course with a virtuoso's mastery of the skills involved in executing translations and in constructing proofs—but with little or no understanding of, or appreciation for, the conceptual underpinnings of the whole enterprise. Typically, these conceptual underpinnings are also conceptual speed bumps that bedevil the student once he or she thinks twice about them. Many such speed bumps come to mind: the truth-table definition of the arrow (or, as it appears in many logic textbooks, the horseshoe); the equivalence of 'if-then' to 'only if'; the justification for the legitimacy of conditional proofs; and the thousand and one restrictions that attach to the various Predicate Logic/Quantification Theory derivation rules. It's obviously not sufficient that the student be able to follow all the prescribed procedures. In addition, he or she must grasp, and be able to articulate, the justification for them.

Take the classical truth-functional account of the arrow/horseshoe as an example. No logic student worth his or her salt is likely to take this account lying down. To be sure, the typical logic student is fairly quick to master the arrow's truth-table definition. (Anyone, after all, can memorize an array of four Ts and Fs.) But that same logic student would be hard pressed to spell out the underlying *rationale* for the arrow's truth-table definition. Logic teachers, the present writer not excepted, have a way of bullying their students into submission over just such points—and understandably so. The explanation is long; the course is short; time is precious; and essay questions in logic courses, designed to assess the student's grasp of certain concepts, are rare. Nevertheless, it's obviously important for logic students to understand why they are doing what they are doing; why this procedure is legitimate and that one isn't; why some logicians permit such-and-such a procedure and others don't; and so on.

And this leads directly into the third reason. It happens on occasion that one logician's restriction is another logician's laissez-faire. In the course of elaborating, explaining, and justifying a particular restriction, one sometimes finds oneself touching on rival accounts that simply ignore the restriction. And touching on these rival accounts is just how it should be. If we've learned anything from John Stuart Mill, it's that by examining views at odds with our own, we acquire a deeper understanding of our own views.

Indeed, this third reason has to do with the title of this book. Not for nothing does the term "rabbit-hole" appear in it. As far back as I can remember, I have seen philosophy as a matter of one's falling down a rabbit-hole, finding oneself in a *very* strange realm as a consequence, and striving to work one's way back above ground. It all starts with an innocuous question, e.g., "What are numbers?" and before you know it you're poking about in Plato's realm of abstract entities that lie outside of space and time.

By contrast, so it always seemed, there was nothing rabbit-hole-ish about logic. No siree. Logic, unlike philosophy, always seemed so cut-and-dried. And most students today, I suspect, emerge from logic courses with just this view, i.e., that there's nothing Alice-in-Wonderland-ish about logic. Quite the contrary: their view at the beginning, middle, and end of the course is that logic, like school mathematics, is cut-and-dried. But logic isn't school mathematics, and it's disingenuous to pretend that it's all so cut-and-dried. Reasonable philosophers are capable of disagreeing about almost everything under the sun within philosophy, and reasonable logicians are capable of disagreeing about almost everything under the sun within logic. It would be criminal—a capital offense, really—to teach Plato's ontology as though it had no rivals; and it would be criminal—albeit perhaps not a capital offense— to teach classical logic as though *it* had no rivals.

No one is suggesting that the tipping point is in sight. No one is suggesting that the founders of classical logic, from the late nineteenth to the mid-twentieth century, are in danger of being purged, or expelled from the pantheon. Nor is anyone suggesting that classical logic will soon be waging a defensive, rearguard battle. Nevertheless, it's obvious from the current literature that there is a variety of competing views of what logic should look like, and in good conscience one can't simply sweep them under the rug. But nor can one expose students to them without elaborating, explaining, and justifying.

The fourth reason is to point the student in the direction of a second logic course. Students who like logic typically want to know what comes next. Therefore, from time to time in this book, I point the reader in the direction(s) of what comes next. Not only that: I walk him or her through the beginning of what comes next, i.e., through the shallow end of the life-after-introductory-logic pool.

For all sorts of reasons, there will be all sorts of logic teachers who will be unhappy with the prolixity that my approach entails. Perhaps they teach on the quarter system, where time is *really* at a premium, and there's nowhere near enough of it to spend on anything other than the bare bones, the nuts and bolts. Others will be unhappy because, although a small number of their students will find the elaborations, explanations, and justifications of interest, most of their students won't. Most will want the bare bones and nothing but the bare bones. I am not *entirely* unsympathetic to such concerns.

Enter the shaded areas and the appendices. Throughout the text, I have shaded some patches of the text and I have incorporated other patches into appendices at the end of many of the chapters. These are the patches that are, strictly speaking—I fear that I am about to contradict everything that I've written in the past half-dozen or so paragraphs—dispensable. They contain more by way of the *challenging* sorts of elaborations, explanations, and justifications. Logic teachers may wish to encourage, but not require, their students to read the shaded patches and the appendices. The electric sign in Hesse's *Steppenwolf* aptly characterizes what lies in store here:

MAGIC THEATER
ENTRANCE NOT FOR EVERYBODY
FOR MADMEN ONLY!

Think of the shaded patches and the appendices as the magic theater, drawing in those who, before the semester is over, will have been bitten by the logic bug, and who, as a consequence, will become logic fanatics.

Question: So what exactly does this logic text cover?

Answer: It covers everything that *I* aspire—or rather, that I *aspire*—to cover during the semester. My aspirations are fairly conventional, I believe, although no doubt some instructors will wish that I had covered more material; and others, that I had covered less. *Sic vita est.*

Semantically, the emphasis is primarily on translations and the Truth-Table Method of showing validity/invalidity. Syntactically, it's primarily on natural deduction proofs/derivations. The text draws upon two formal systems: one for Propositional Logic and one for Predicate Logic/Quantification Theory. I discuss the formal language of Propositional Logic in Chapters One and Two, the derivation/inference rules of Propositional Logic in Chapters Three and Four, the formal language of Predicate Logic/Quantification Theory in Chapters Five and Six, and the derivation/inference rules of Predicate Logic/Quantification Theory in Chapters Seven and Eight.

In the nature of things, an introductory logic course is a challenging, i.e., a demanding, i.e., a difficult, course. Indeed it has been my experience that for many undergraduates an introductory logic course will be one of the most demanding courses they will encounter as undergraduates. This does not strike me as even *slightly* bizarre: human nature being what it is, and logic being what it is, it's simply a matter of fact that logic is a difficult subject. A logic course, therefore, albeit introductory, will reflect and embody this difficulty. At some level, logic is all about *rigor*—and the road to rigor, as it were, lies through *difficulty.*

In the course of rebuking "the popular leaders of the [French] National Assembly" during the French Revolution, Edmund Burke went on to extol the virtues of *difficulty.* The French Revolutionaries were guilty, he contended, of constructing the sort of state that they were constructing precisely "to evade and slip aside from *difficulty*":

> Difficulty is a severe instructor, set over us by the supreme ordinance of a parental Guardian and Legislator, who knows us better than we know ourselves, as he loves us better, too. *'Jove himself decreed that the cultivator's way should not be easy.'* He that wrestles with us strengthens our nerves and sharpens our skill. Our antagonist is our helper. This amicable conflict with difficulty obliges us to an intimate acquaintance with our object and compels us to consider it in all its relations. *It will not suffer us to be superficial.*[1]

I would like to think that the difficulty of a semester's engagement with this logic book "will not suffer us to be superficial"—and *that,* I would like to think, would be no mean accomplishment.

I have been teaching classical logic every semester (and many summer semesters) for over three decades, i.e., since the fall of 1979. Over this period, I have taught Richard Jeffrey's *Formal Logic: Its Scope and Limits,* Irving M. Copi's *Symbolic Logic,* W. V. Quine's *Methods of Logic,* E. J. Lemmon's *Beginning Logic,* and R. L. Simpson's *Essentials of Symbolic Logic.* Over this same period, I have also taught, once every other year or so, and in a more advanced course on logical metatheory, Geoffrey Hunter's *Metalogic: An Introduction to the Metatheory of Standard First Order Logic.* The imprint, the very *deep* imprint, of each of these earlier—and utterly superb—texts will be apparent—indeed, blindingly obvious—throughout this logic text. Although I never studied under any of the authors of these texts, I regard them as my logic teachers. What I have learned about logic I have learned first and foremost from them, and I am, and shall always be, immensely grateful to each of them for this. I am, and shall always be, in their debt.

---

1. Edmund Burke, *Reflections on the Revolution in France* (Indianapolis: Hackett Publishing Company, 1987), pp. 146–47. Burke's quotation is from Virgil, *Georgics,* I, 120.

# Chapter One

# Propositional Logic:
# A Formal Language, Part One

## 1. Introduction: What Logic Is

It is said that logic is "the science of what follows from what." This is exactly right. Indeed, you may well consider this a first attempt to nail down our subject matter. Obviously the characterization is imprecise, but imprecision in this matter will be unavoidable at the outset of a course in logic—but only at the outset. Logic is indeed a *science*: it is *rigorous*; it is *systematizable*; and (above all else) it is *objective*. In saying that it is objective, one is saying (at a minimum) that there is a solid core of logic with which all rational individuals ought to agree, and that this solid core is immune to our subjective impressions, our intuitions, our gut instincts about what exactly follows from what.

So logic is the science of what follows from what. What are we to make of these 'whats'? Just what is the *what* that is said to follow, and just what is the *what* from which it is said to follow?

Down the rabbit-hole you are about to pop. Be forewarned: your thinking will never be the same.

Imagine that you're trekking in North Zedmenistan with your trusty guide Ardbeg. And imagine that you're resting outside your tent in the early evening, scribbling in your diary and contemplating tomorrow's ascent to the Zompadong Pass. Suddenly you spot a dzo lumbering past you! The high altitude is getting to you and you are tempted to leap onto its back and gallop up to the Zompadong Pass. Ardbeg races over to caution you to do no such thing:

(1) If you leap onto the dzo's back then you'll be dead within the hour.

(2) But you *won't* leap onto the dzo's back!

∴ (3) You *won't* be dead within the hour.

In this context, the horizontal line beneath (2) serves to distinguish the *premises* of Ardbeg's argument—all the sentences above the horizontal line, i.e., (1) and (2)—from the *conclusion*—the single sentence beneath it, i.e., (3). The three dots in triangular formation—'∴'—serve the same purpose as the horizontal line, and as such they are overkill. They simply mean 'therefore'. They indicate that what follows them is the conclusion of the argument and, by implication, that what precedes them are its premises.

Now Ardbeg may be a first-rate trekking guide, but he isn't a first-rate logician. Logic is the science of what follows from what—and Ardbeg's conclusion simply doesn't follow from his premises. It is logic, understood as a science, that will enable you to see why his conclusion doesn't follow. You are just now setting out on this logic trek, so don't worry if you don't yet see why your first-rate trekking guide Ardbeg isn't a first-rate logician.

A second argument. It is the eve of the Great Race, and your nemesis, the evil Egvalt, whispers in your ear:

(1) If you run a sub-2:15 marathon tomorrow then you'll beat me.

(2) But (ha-*ha!*) you *won't* run a sub-2:15 marathon tomorrow!

∴ (3) You *won't* beat me.

Now here's what's interesting about these two arguments: if the conclusion of Ardbeg's argument follows from *its* premises, then the conclusion of Egvalt's argument follows from *its* premises—and vice versa. So if the conclusion of Ardbeg's argument *doesn't* follow from *its* premises—and it doesn't—then the conclusion of Egvalt's argument *doesn't* follow from *its* premises. Why so? Because in logic what follows from what is a function of *form* (or *structure*)—and these two arguments have the exact same *form* (or *structure*), even though they don't have the same *subject matter* (or *content*).

Behold their common form:

> (1) If *zappo* then *zooey*.
> (2) But not-*zappo*.
> _____
> ∴ (3) Not-*zooey*.

Alternatively (letting '△' designate any sentence whatsoever, and letting 'O' designate any sentence whatsoever):

> (1) If △ then O.
> (2) But not-△.
> _____
> ∴ (3) Not-O.

In logic, form has *everything* to do with *everything*, and unsurprisingly, this book is devoted to *formal* logic. It's all about form.

It should strike you as quite obvious that, in Ardbeg's argument, even if both premises were true you might still be dead within the hour. Nothing in the premises rules out this possibility. Indeed nothing in the premises rules out the possibility that in North Zedmenistan *anything* can happen within the hour. By the same token, it should strike you as equally obvious that, in Egvalt's argument, even if both premises were true you might still beat Egvalt. Nothing in the premises rules out the possibility that you might run a 2:18 marathon and Egvalt might run a 2:20. Even though each of the premises of each of these arguments might be true, each of its conclusions might nevertheless be false: it's in precisely this sense that neither of the conclusions of either of these two arguments follows from its premises.

Now suppose that you and Ardbeg are locked in a struggle to the death over whether *this* sentence really follows from *those* sentences. You claim that it does; he claims that it doesn't. Just what are the two of you supposed to do? You have a choice. One alternative is to resort to your (merely) subjective impressions to settle the issue. Subjective impressions being what they are, however, i.e., merely *subjective*, the two of you may never discover whether *this* sentence really does follow from *those* sentences. And in that case, you and Ardbeg may never resolve your disagreement. Not today. Not tomorrow. Not ever.

Another alternative is to draw upon the tools bequeathed to posterity by your logician ancestors, but especially by Aristotle (Greek, 384–322 BCE), who established logic as a science in the ancient world, and by Gottlob Frege (German, 1848–1925), who revolutionized logic in the modern world. In this book, and in this course, you will learn how to use these tools, and in one of your next logic courses you will learn just how powerful they are.

We shall begin our first chapter with definitions, and we shall end our last chapter with definitions: scads and scads of definitions. Definitions, you might think, are vile and loathsome things, abominations that you have to *memorize*. Yes, you do have to commit them to memory, but no, they aren't the unlovely things that you might take them to be. By the end of this course, you will appreciate the clarity that good definitions yield. And you will also come to appreciate that clarity, precisely because it leads to understanding, is next to godliness.

# 2. Arguments: Valid and Invalid; Sound and Unsound

So just what is an *argument*? It's impossible to talk about an argument without talking about its *premises* and its *conclusion*. Think of the premises as the *reasons* that are given for accepting a particular conclusion.

Definition:    An *argument* is a string of sentences; one of the sentences is the conclusion and the others are the premises.

Definition:    The *conclusion* of an argument is the sentence whose truth is to be established.

Definition:    A *premise* of an argument is a sentence that is said, or that is thought, or that appears, to play a role in establishing the truth of the conclusion.

In everyday life we sometimes think of an argument as consisting of premises and a conclusion, and we sometimes think of an argument as consisting of premises alone. Suppose that Ardbeg, in the midst of a heated debate with Bobo, lets loose with a jumble of sentences. It would be entirely appropriate for an exasperated Bobo to exclaim: "Ardbeg! I haven't the faintest idea what the premises are of your argument! Worse yet, I haven't the faintest idea what its conclusion is!" Here Bobo is clearly thinking of an argument as consisting of both the premises and the conclusion.

Sometimes, however, in everyday life we think of an argument as consisting of just the premises. Suppose that an incredulous Coco, while debating with Dagbar the nature of animal intelligence, exclaims: "Dagbar! Do you really believe that Fido wishes that he too could study logic? You need to advance an argument to support that belief!" In distinguishing the argument from its conclusion, Coco is clearly thinking of an argument as consisting of only the premises that lead to the conclusion.

In logic we typically adopt the former view: we think of an argument as consisting of both the premises and the conclusion.[1]

Arguments come in two flavors—inductive and deductive. The difference between inductive and deductive arguments lies in the nature of the relationship between the premises and the conclusion of the given argument. Taking a quick look at this difference will further help us to nail down our subject matter.

Suppose that Coco delivers the Presidential Address at the annual meeting of A.N.Z.A., the Association of North Zedmenistan Actuaries. She informs her audience that the legendary dzo-wrestler Dagbar just celebrated his ninetieth birthday; that he has never been gored by a dzo; and that 90 percent of dzo-wrestlers are gored at some point during their careers. "It follows," says Coco, "that the probability is greater than 70 percent that poor old Dagbar will be gored within the year."

Coco's argument is an *inductive*, i.e., a *probabilistic*, one. In such an argument, the premises support the conclusion *to a greater or lesser extent*,

---

1. See page xxi in the Note to Readers for an explanation of these shaded patches.

i.e., to a greater or lesser degree of probability. Sometimes the relationship between the premises and the conclusion is formulated with numerical precision (as with Coco's argument, above); and sometimes it is formulated in general, but non-numerical, terms. Thus Coco might well have said, "The probability is *high* (or *very* high or *alarmingly* high) that in light of the facts that I have just cited, poor old Dagbar will be gored within the year."

In an inductive argument, everything hinges on the degree of the probability that the truth of the premises lends to the truth of the conclusion. It may be high, or very high, or low, or very low, or just so-so. We characterize inductive arguments accordingly, as ranging from very strong to very weak. Whatever its strength, such an argument is typically known as an *inductive* argument.

The relationship between the premises and the conclusion of a *deductive* argument, on the other hand, is *all-or-nothing*. In a deductive argument, either the conclusion follows from the premises, or it doesn't. If it does, the argument is *valid*; and if it doesn't, the argument is *invalid*. Whether valid or invalid, such an argument is typically known as a *deductive* argument.

Question: How is a deductive argument all-or-nothing?

Answer: Unlike an inductive argument, which admits of varying degrees of strength, a deductive argument doesn't admit of degrees of validity; it's *either-or*: either it's valid or it's invalid. The focus of this book will not be on inductive arguments. It will be only on deductive arguments. From this point on, and unless otherwise noted, all references to arguments will be to deductive arguments.

The goal now is to shed light on the all-or-nothing notion of a *valid* argument. Consider the following pair of arguments:

> (1) All princes dine daily on peas, parsnips, plums, and pita.
> (2) Ardbeg is a prince.
> _____
> ∴ (3) Ardbeg dines daily on peas, parsnips, plums, and pita.

> (1) Some princes dine daily on peas, parsnips, plums, and pita.
> (2) Ardbeg is a prince.
> _____
> ∴ (3) Ardbeg dines daily on peas, parsnips, plums, and pita.

Note that the only difference between these two arguments is the first word of the first premise of each argument: 'All' *vs.* 'Some'. Note next what's remarkable about these two arguments. There is a sense of 'follows from' in accordance with which the conclusion of the first argument really *does* follow from its premises, and the conclusion of the second really does *not* follow from its premises. The question is: 'In *what* sense?' At this point it's too early to say. At the moment, I shall simply count on your intuitive grasp of what the words 'follows from' mean. In a moment, I shall count on your intuitive grasp of what various other words mean. Midway through Chapter 3, it will become perfectly clear what all these words mean.

Now partial clarity, of course, isn't perfect clarity. Nevertheless, it's better than no clarity. Moreover, partial clarity with respect to the meaning of 'follows from', and therefore with respect to the meaning of 'valid', is attainable even now. Consider the following argument:

(1) If Ardbeg is a traitor then he will be shot.

(2) Ardbeg is a traitor.

(3) If Ardbeg is shot, either Bobo or Coco (but not both of them) will join the rebels.

(4) Bobo won't join the rebels.

(5) If Coco joins the rebels then Dagbar will return from exile.

∴ (6) Dagbar will return from exile.

So what do you think: does the conclusion of this argument follow from the premises? If so, the argument of course is valid. You are about to see that yes, the conclusion does follow from the premises.

From (1) and (2) it clearly follows that Ardbeg will be shot. From the discovery that Ardbeg will be shot, along with (3), it clearly follows that either Bobo or Coco (but not both of them) will join the rebels. From the discovery that either Bobo or Coco (but not both of them) will join the rebels, along with (4), it clearly follows that Coco will join the rebels. From the discovery that Coco will join the rebels, along with (5), it clearly follows that (6) Dagbar will return from exile. So what do you now know? You now know that (6), the conclusion of this argument, *follows from* its premises. You know, in other words, that the argument is a *valid* argument.

So the conclusion *follows from* the premises insofar as it was ultimately *generated* by them. The conclusion was generated by one or more sentences, which in turn were generated by one or more sentences, which in turn were generated by one or more sentences, . . . , which in turn were generated by one or more premises. So yes, you have now attained partial clarity with respect to the meaning of 'follows from'. It's only *partial*, of course, because at the moment you're only partially clear with respect to what 'generates' means in this context. (*Observing* the process of generation, whereby some sentences generate other sentences, isn't quite the same as *grasping* the very nature of the process of generation.)

There's another way to capture what it means to say that an argument is valid. Either the truth of the premises *guarantees* the truth of the conclusion or it doesn't. To say that the truth of the premises *guarantees* the truth of the conclusion is to say that it's a matter of *necessity*, rather than a matter of *probability*, that if the premises were true the conclusion would also be true. If the truth of the premises does guarantee the truth of the conclusion, the argument is valid; and if it doesn't, the argument is invalid. Furthermore, if the argument is valid, the premises are said to *imply* the conclusion; and if the argument is invalid, the premises are said to fail to imply the conclusion. Once again, whether valid or invalid, such an argument is typically known as a *deductive* argument.

Consider, in this regard, the last argument once again, the one whose conclusion is that Dagbar will return from exile. It's a matter of *necessity*—although at this point it may not be self-evident—that if the premises were true, then yes, the conclusion would also be true. (Alternatively, it would be *impossible* for the premises to be true and the conclusion to be false.) So the truth of the premises does guarantee the truth of the conclusion. So, once again, the argument is valid.

Thus it appears that there are at least two ways to capture the idea of a valid argument. One focuses on the question of whether the argument's conclusion follows from, i.e., is generated by, its premises. The other focuses on the question of whether it's a matter of necessity that if the argument's premises were true then its conclusion would also be true.

Question: Are these two ways of capturing the idea of a valid argument really different—or are they, in some sense, one and the same?

Evasive answer: They *aren't* one and the same; they *are* different. Nonetheless they *are* related to one another: each captures a different aspect of what we're looking for. The former draws upon the idea that sentences can *generate* other sentences, in such a way that the premises of some arguments—valid arguments—ultimately generate their own conclusions. The latter draws upon the ideas of *truth* and *necessity* in such a way that of necessity, if the premises of some arguments—valid arguments—were true then their conclusions would also be true. It will be clear by the end of Chapter 4 that these two ways of capturing the idea of a valid argument are really two sides—two *distinct* sides—of the same coin.

As a prelude to plunging into more definitions, it will be useful to introduce the expression '*iff*'. Logicians and mathematicians both use it frequently. It means 'if and only if'. Consider the sentence '*n* is an even number *iff n* is divisible by 2 without remainder.' It means that if *n* is an even number then *n* is divisible by 2 without remainder, and vice versa: if *n* is divisible by 2 without remainder then *n* is an even number. Thus consider any two sentences, '△' and 'O'. '△ *iff* O' simply means 'If △ then O, and (vice versa) if O then △'.

| | |
|---|---|
| Tentative Definition: | An argument is *valid iff* either<br>1. its conclusion *follows from* its premises, or<br>2. *of necessity*, if its premises were true then its conclusion would also be true; i.e., it would be *impossible* for its premises to be true and for its conclusion to be false. |
| Tentative Definition: | An argument is *invalid iff* it isn't *valid*; i.e., *iff* either<br>1. its conclusion does *not* follow from its premises, or<br>2. it would be *possible* for its premises to be true and for its conclusion to be false. |

Now here's the rub. (Actually, here's the first of *two* rubs.) You haven't much more than the faintest idea what the key terms in these tentative definitions really mean—and that's why these tentative definitions are merely tentative. Intuitively you have no problem with these terms in ordinary contexts, but you wouldn't much relish the prospect of being required to write a paper with the following opening sentence: "In this paper, I shall produce a knock-down definition of the following terms: 'follows from', 'of necessity', 'impossible', and 'possible'." Consider just 'impossible', and consider the following sentences:

> (1) It's *impossible* for Ardbeg to run a 2:08 marathon.
>
> (2) It's *impossible* for a triangle to have four sides.
>
> (3) It's *impossible* for the sentences 'All goddesses are immortal' and 'Coco is a goddess' to be true, and for the sentence 'Coco is immortal' to be false.

Each of these sentences illustrates a different sense of 'impossible'. (1) illustrates *physical* impossibility; i.e., it is by virtue of Ardbeg's physical constitution—Ardbeg is a middle-aged couch potato—that it's impossible for him to run a 2:08 marathon. (2) illustrates *definitional* impossibility; i.e., it's by virtue of the definition of a triangle (as 'a three-sided, plane, closed figure') that it's impossible for a triangle to have four sides. (3) illustrates *logical* impossibility; i.e., it's by virtue of the *logical form* (or *structure*) of the first two sentences that they *imply* the third.

By the end of Chapter 2 you'll know what these terms mean (at least where logic is concerned): 'follows from', 'of necessity', 'impossible', and 'possible'. By then you will have been introduced to new definitions of 'valid argument' and 'invalid argument' that will supplant the above tentative definitions. Until then (but only until then), these tentative definitions will have to do.

Now for the *second* rub. For an argument to be valid, it isn't necessary—repeat (with emphasis!): *it isn't necessary*—that the premises actually be true. Nor is it necessary that the conclusion actually be true. All that's necessary—repeat: *all* that's necessary—is that *if* the premises were true, *then* the conclusion would also be true. *If* the premises were true: *if, if, if, if, if. . . .*

In this regard, consider the following three arguments, each of which is valid. Only the first, however, is *obviously* valid.

> (1) All even numbers are multiples of two.
>
> (2) Four is an even number.
> _____
>
> ∴ (3) Four is a multiple of two.

Here, as it so happens, the premises are obviously true and so is the conclusion. Now consider the following argument, which is also valid:

> (1) All logicians are magicians.
> (2) Coco is a logician.
> ∴ (3) Coco is a magician.

Here, as it so happens, the premises are false and so is the conclusion. You know *perfectly well* that not all logicians are magicians. (Ask your logic instructor to perform the sugar-cube-through-the-handkerchief trick.) Coco, in any case, is *neither* a logician *nor* a magician. As you know, she's the president of the Association of North Zedmenistan Actuaries. Where the question of the argument's *validity* is concerned, however, it matters not a whit that the premises and the conclusion are all false. All that matters is that *if if if if if* the premises were true—they *aren't* true, but it doesn't matter that they aren't true; just suppose that they *were* true—*then* the conclusion would also be true. Just ask yourself the following (key) question: *If* the premises *were* true, *what then*: could the conclusion *possibly* be false? (The answer is "No. Of course not.")

Here's how to think about validity. Suppose—just suppose—that you just now *popped* into existence. An instant ago you didn't exist, and then *poof!*—here you are; you just popped in! You're endowed with the ability to think logically and you're endowed with a perfect command of the English language, but—and here's what's crucial—you know *nothing* about the world. You're in possession of *no* empirical facts. You don't know *who* the president of the United States is, and for that matter, you don't even know *what* the United States is (or are). In short, you know diddly-squat about diddly-squat. And then a stranger (of course a stranger—you just popped into existence) sidles up to you and tries to strike up a conversation. "Hello, Friend," he says. "I have a question for you." Your ears perk up. You're interested. You should be: it's your first-ever conversation. The stranger continues, and you find yourself listening to your first-ever argument. "All logicians are magicians, and Coco is a logician—so Coco is a magician. Right?"

You know just what to reply. "See here," you say, "I haven't the faintest idea whether all logicians are magicians. Moreover I haven't the faintest idea whether Coco is a logician. But if it really were true that all logicians are magicians, and if it also really were true that Coco is a logician, then of course it would follow that Coco is a magician." And your reply is exactly right: of necessity, *if* the premises of the stranger's argument were true—*if if if if if*—it doesn't matter whether they are or they aren't—*then* the conclusion too would be true. Moral of the story: you can determine whether an argument is valid or invalid without actually knowing whether or not its premises are true.

But now suppose that the stranger's argument had been different by a single word: the first word. Suppose that he had begun, "*Some* logicians are magicians, etc." You would still have known just how to reply, yes? You would have said, "I haven't the faintest idea whether some logicians are magicians. Moreover I haven't the faintest idea whether Coco is a logician. But even if it were true that some logicians are magicians, and even if it were true that Coco is a logician, it wouldn't follow that Coco is a magician. So I must confess that from your premises I know nothing about Coco except that you claim that she's a logician. In particular, I haven't the faintest idea whether she's a magician. Maybe she is and maybe she isn't. The premises of your argument are silent on that score. So even if the conclusion were true, it wouldn't *follow* from the premises. It would just be a coincidence that the premises and the conclusion all happened to be true." And once again your reply would have been exactly right; it's certainly possible for the premises of the second version of the stranger's argument to be true and for the conclusion to be false. Moral of the story: once again, you can determine whether an argument is valid or invalid without actually knowing whether or not its premises are true.

Finally consider one last argument, which—notwithstanding that we are about to sink into verbal nonsense—would certainly be valid *if its respective terms were meaningful*:

> (1) All glmphs are spudzoids.
> (2) Egvalt is a glmph.
> _____
> ∴ (3) Egvalt is a spudzoid.

All three of these arguments have something crucial in common. Obviously it's not their *subject matter*. Nor, obviously, is it the actual *truth* of their premises and conclusions. Indeed, it's only the first of the above three arguments whose premises and conclusion are actually true. The premises and conclusion of the two other arguments *may* be true, but they are not *obviously* true. (Note that I did not say that they are obviously *not* true.)

What all three arguments have in common is their *form*. Indeed they all have (more or less) the following form:

(1) All △s are Os.
(2) *x* is a △.
_____
∴ (3) *x* is a O.

Notice that none of the latter three 'sentences' has any *meaning* or *content* or *subject matter*. None of them is *about* anything. Each of them has merely the *form* of a sentence—and as such, each of them is purely *formal*. Thus you may call it a *sentence-form* or a *sentence-schema* (plural: *schemata*). If you wish, you can transform each of these sentence-forms (or schemata) into an actual sentence by 'pouring' content into it. Thus if you replace '△' with 'logician'; if you replace 'O' with 'magician'; and if you replace '*x*' with 'Coco', then you end up with the second of the above arguments. With different replacements, you end up with the other arguments.

Notice too that this last 'argument'—'All △s are Os, etc.'—isn't really an argument. We can—and indeed we shall—*call* it an argument, but strictly speaking it's merely the *form* of an argument. It is, as they say, an *argument-form* or an *argument-schema*. Any argument that has the same form as this argument-form is a valid argument. And this is the moral of the story: *validity is a purely formal notion: it is entirely about form; it has nothing, nothing, nothing to do with the content (or the subject matter) of the sentences that constitute the argument.* You not only don't have to know whether the sentences are true, you don't even have to know what they mean.

Do you really know what the sentence 'All glmphs are spudzoids' means? Of course not! But that doesn't prevent you from grasping the validity of the 'argument' in which the 'sentence' appears. (All right! All right! The words 'glmphs' and 'spudzoids' aren't real, i.e., genuine English, words. Therefore the 'sentences' in which they appear aren't real sentences. And therefore the 'argument' in which they appear isn't a real argument. All this is true—but just suppose that 'glmphs' and 'spudzoids' *were* real words, whose meaning you simply didn't happen to know. What then? Wouldn't the argument in which these words appear be a perfectly valid argument?)

If you're unhappy with the account of validity that I've been discussing, it's probably because what you are *really* seeking is an account of *soundness*:

Definition:    An argument is *sound iff*
(1) it is valid, and
(2) each of its premises is true.

It is soundness with which you are concerned in every course that you ever take—with one exception, the one exception being Logic. And it is soundness with which you are concerned in life and in the real world. (Careful: This doesn't mean that you needn't be concerned with validity. Reread the definition of 'sound': being valid is an essential component of being sound.)

The reason why you are concerned with soundness in the real world is because normally you wish to know not simply whether a particular conclusion would be true *if* the premises were true, but whether indeed the conclusion actually *is* true. Suppose that you have an argument, any argument, with $n$ premises (where $n$ is any finite number) and, of course, a conclusion:

$$P_1$$
$$P_2$$
$$P_3$$
$$.$$
$$.$$
$$.$$
$$\underline{P_n}$$
$$\therefore C$$

Suppose that the argument is *sound*; i.e., suppose both that the argument is valid and that $P_1$ through $P_n$ are true. What do you now know about the conclusion? You know, given the first condition of soundness, that *if* the premises were true, *then* the conclusion would be true. You also know, given the second condition of soundness, that the premises *are* true. Therefore you know (by elementary logical reasoning) that the conclusion is also true. But this argument represents *any* sound argument. Therefore you know that the conclusion of *every* sound argument is true.

Now suppose that the conclusion of some argument, *any* argument, is false. What else do you know about the argument? As a starter, you know that the argument is *unsound*—but what does that tell you? Do *not* say that you know the argument to be *invalid*; you know *nothing of the sort*! And do *not* say that you know at least one of the premises to be false; again, you know *nothing of the sort*! What you *do* know is that *either* the argument is invalid *or* that at least one of its premises is false. And now your work is cut out for you. You examine the argument for validity. If it passes muster then you know that at least one of the premises is false—and you begin to examine the premises one by one. Alternatively, if you're convinced that each of the premises is true, then you know that the argument is invalid, i.e., that its reasoning is flawed somewhere—and you begin to hunt for the flaw.

This is a course in *formal logic*. By now you should have some sense, however rudimentary, of what each of these words—'formal' and 'logic'—means.

# Exercises

True or False? Defend your answer.

1. If an argument is unsound then it's invalid. *False*
2. If an argument is valid then its premises are true. *False*
3. If an argument is valid then its conclusion is true. *False*
4. If the premises of a given argument are true and the conclusion is also true then the argument is valid. *False*
5. The following is a valid argument:

    (1) If Ardbeg is a spy for South Zedmenistan then Ardbeg is disloyal to North Zedmenistan.

    (2) Ardbeg is disloyal to North Zedmenistan.
    
    ∴ (3) Ardbeg is a spy for South Zedmenistan. *False*

# 3. Sentences/Statements/Propositions: Bearers of Truth-Value

You know now what an *argument* is; you know now what a *deductive* argument is; you know now what a *valid* argument is; and you know now what a *sound* argument is. But what about the bits and pieces of which arguments are composed? What about sentences (or statements or propositions)? What exactly are *they*?

Definition:    A *sentence* (or *statement* or *proposition*) is a bearer of truth-value.

Definition:    A *bearer of truth-value* is something that is either true, on the one hand, or false, on the other.

*Strictly speaking*, it is only *declarative* sentences that, in this book, we shall call *sentences*. We shall *not* refer to *interrogative* sentences (*questions*) or *imperative* sentences (*commands*) or *exclamatory* sentences (*exclamations*) as sentences. The reason is that it is only *declarative* sentences that are either true or false. Consider the following:

(1) The Moon is made of pink fluff.
(2) Who betrayed Ardbeg?
(3) Shoot the mad dogs!
(4) Down with the king!

Of the four, (1) is the only bearer of truth-value: it's something that is either true or false. (Contemporary astronomy suggests that it's false.) (2) is a question. The *answer* to (2) may well be either true or false, but (2) itself is neither-nor. (3) is a command. The *reasons* for issuing it may well be either true or false, but (3) itself is neither-nor. (4) is an exclamation. Given the circumstances, (4) may or may not be an *appropriate* exclamation, but (4) itself is neither true nor false.

Philosophy in general, and the philosophy of language in particular, treats the terms 'sentence,' 'statement,' and 'proposition' as having radically different meanings. In logic, however, the philosophical differences are inconsequential. Accordingly I shall be treating these terms—'sentence,' 'statement,' and 'proposition'—as synonymous, and therefore I shall be using them interchangeably throughout this book.

A brief digression. First I shall convince you that sentences are indeed distinct from statements. Suppose that in my logic class I turn to my students and utter the sentence, "If the world comes to an end in the next fifteen minutes, then you won't get credit for this course." To be sure, I have *uttered* (and indeed have *used*) the *sentence*, "you won't get credit for this course." But nobody in his or her right mind would suggest that I have actually *asserted*, i.e., made the *statement*, that my students won't get credit for this course.

Moreover, suppose that in the same logic class I am illustrating the notion of what follows from what. I utter the sentence, "All traitors will be shot," and I immediately ask, "And what follows from this sentence vis-à-vis Ardbeg?" (The answer for which I'm looking, i.e., the correct answer, is 'If Ardbeg is a traitor then he'll be shot.') Once again, I have *uttered* (and indeed have *used*) the sentence 'All traitors will be shot,' but it would be utterly mad to charge me with having *asserted*, or made the *statement*, that all traitors will be shot. I'm using the sentence to shed light on a central notion in logic, and not to inform or convince or warn anyone of the fact (if it really is a fact) that all traitors will be shot.

It follows that whatever they are, sentences are one sort of thing, whereas statements, whatever *they* are, are quite another sort of thing.

Now I shall convince you that propositions are yet a third sort of thing. Consider the French sentence "Le ciel est toujours bleu." It has the same *meaning* as the English sentence "The sky is always blue." You're looking at *two* sentences—but they have only *one* meaning. Two sentences that have the same meaning (or express the same content or thought) are said to express, or instantiate, or be tokens of, the same *proposition*. A proposition is the *meaning* of a sentence, and as such it's an *abstract* sort of thing. Unlike a particular sentence, or a particular statement, which is *perceivable*—you can see it or hear it—and which is expressed in one language or another, a proposition—a meaning—is neither perceivable nor rooted in any language. It's one thing to see or to hear a sentence or a statement. It's another thing to grasp its meaning. The meaning is something *abstract* that you grasp *with your intellect*; it's not something *perceivable* that you grasp with one or more of your five senses. (In particular, it's not something that you *see* and it's not something that you *hear*.) A proposition is, once again, what you grasp when you grasp the meaning of a sentence or a statement.

Imagine an English-speaker who knows no French and a French-speaker who knows no English. Imagine that the English-speaker says, "The sky is always blue," and that the French-speaker says, "*Le ciel est toujours bleu.*" Both speakers are expressing *the very same proposition*. The two sentences have *the exact same meaning*. Insofar as neither speaker understands the other's language, it follows that the proposition itself— the *meaning* that the two sentences share, or the content or thought that the two sentences express—must itself be a non-linguistic sort of thing.

Perhaps you disagree. Consider then how you would answer the following question: "In which language is the proposition that both sentences express: 'The sky is always blue' and '*Le ciel est toujours bleu*'?" If you answer "English," then you're forced to concede that the French-speaker, who, by hypothesis, doesn't understand English, does understand English. And if you answer "French," then you're forced to concede that the English-speaker, who, by hypothesis, doesn't understand French, does understand French.

As with sentences, so with arguments. Consider the following:

> (1) All logicians are magicians.
> (2) Coco is a logician.
> _____
> ∴ (3) Coco is a magician.

> (1) Tous les logiciennes sont des magiciennes.
> (2) Coco est une logicienne.
> _____
> ∴ (3) Coco est une magicienne.

The second argument's first premise, second premise, and conclusion are direct translations, respectively, from English into French, of the first argument's first premise, second premise, and conclusion. Imagine that an English-speaker advances the first argument and that a French-speaker advances the second. Note that the English-speaker and the French-speaker have advanced *the exact same argument*. By parity of reasoning therefore, arguments, just like propositions, must be non-linguistic, abstract sorts of things. There are the *concrete instances*, the *manifestations*, the *tokens* of the abstract argument—and then there is the abstract argument itself.

Question: So a proposition is 'an abstract sort of thing', eh? And an argument is 'an abstract sort of thing' too? Tell me: Just what exactly is 'an abstract sort of thing'?

Answer: At a minimum, it's a non-perceivable sort of thing; i.e., it's not the sort of thing that you can perceive by means of one or more of your five senses. Unlike a sentence or a statement or a concrete instance of an argument, it's to be found neither in space nor in time. The concrete instances, or tokens, unlike the abstract argument itself of which they are concrete instances, or tokens, are to be found rolling off one's tongue or scribbled on a blackboard. ("*When* and *where* did Bobo utter (or scribble) that sentence or that argument-token?") And unlike a sentence or a statement or an argument-token, the abstract argument itself didn't come into existence at a particular place and at a particular point of time, and it won't go out of existence at a particular place and at a particular point of time. As such, it's outside of space and outside of time; i.e., it's both non-spatial and atemporal. . . . Enough for now. Who would have thought that topics in logic would have mutated into topics in metaphysics? Now go and register for any philosophy course that addresses topics in metaphysics.

# 4. The Artificial Language $L_1$: Propositional Symbols and Connectives

It's high time that we left the English language behind us. Indeed, it's now time to construct what is known as an *artificial* language. Our artificial language stands in contrast to a *natural* language—the sort of language that you grew up speaking—like English or Farsi or Mandarin or Swahili or Tamil or whatever. Our artificial language contains *propositional symbols*, *connectives*, and *parentheses*. In this section the focus will be only on propositional symbols and connectives.

# A. Propositional Symbols: Constants and Variables

Propositional symbols are uppercase letters from the English alphabet, e.g., 'A', 'B', 'C', etc., and they are divisible into two sorts: propositional *constants* and propositional *variables*.

Definition:        A *propositional constant* is a propositional symbol that designates (or represents or stands for) a specific (i.e., exactly one) proposition.

Thus 'A', 'B', and 'C' could be the propositional constants designating the propositions 'Ardbeg drowns', 'Bobo drowns', and 'Coco drowns', respectively.

Definition:        A *propositional variable* is a propositional symbol that designates (or represents or stands for) any proposition whatsoever.

The difference between propositional constants and propositional variables is identical to the difference in mathematics between numerical constants (or numerals, e.g., '1,' '2,' '3,' etc.), on the one hand, and numerical variables (e.g., '$x$,' '$y$,' '$z$'), on the other. A numerical constant designates *exactly one* number, whereas a numerical variable designates *any* number whatsoever. Thus '4' is a numerical constant that designates the number 4, and '$x$' is a numerical variable that designates any number. (You remember how, in your first week of middle school algebra, one of your fellow students insisted on knowing exactly which number '$x$' stands for. You knew immediately that for that student in that class, the game was over.) Just as in mathematics '$x$' (like '$y$' and like '$z$') stands for no particular number but rather for any number whatsoever, so in logic 'P' (like 'Q' and like 'R') stands for no particular proposition but rather for any proposition whatsoever.

As a matter of convention, we shall treat the uppercase letters 'A' through 'O' as propositional *constants*, and the uppercase letters 'P' through 'Z' as propositional *variables*. If we need more propositional symbols (i.e., more than twenty-six), we can simply add numerical subscripts to any given symbol: '$P_1$,' '$P_2$,' . . . , '$Q_2$,' '$Q_3$,' . . . , etc.

More on abstract entities. The *numeral* '4' that you write in your notebook is *not* the *number* 4; it's merely a *symbol* for—a *name* of—the number 4. 'IV' is another name of the number 4. You can *see* the symbol '4'. You can't *see* the number 4. Nor can you *collide* with it. You can *erase* the symbol '4'. You can't *erase* the number 4.

Think of it like this: Suppose that you're a student of mine and suppose that it's the first day of the semester and suppose that I write my name—'Lande'—on the blackboard. Suppose that the door to the classroom flies open and a deranged student appears in the doorway, shrieking, "*Where is Lande?*" What do you do? Do you point to the *name* 'Lande' on the blackboard? Obviously a *name* is one thing, and the *thing* that the name names (or designates) is something else altogether, a thing of a completely different sort.

A numeral is a name, and a propositional constant is a name. The number that the numeral names is an abstract entity—here we go again—and the proposition that a propositional constant names is an abstract entity. *Platonism*, also known as *realism*, is the view that reality comprises not merely bats and cats and hats and rats, but also numbers and propositions and arguments. For the platonist/realist, numbers and propositions and arguments are *real* things; i.e., they *exist*, and their existence isn't dependent on the human (or on any other) mind.

## B. Connectives: New Sentences Out of Old

In formal logic, as they say, paraphrasing George Orwell, all words are created equal but some words are created more equal than others. In Propositional Logic, the *connectives* are the words that are more equal than others—they are the aristocrats of words—and they include such words as 'not', 'and', 'or', 'if-then', and 'if and only if'. It is from these words that we construct propositions of increasingly greater complexity.

A connective is *not* what you think it is: it is *not* something that *connects* two or more sentences!

Definition:  A *connective* is a device (or an operator) that operates on one or more sentences in order to generate
a new sentence.

Consider the two sentences 'Ardbeg howls' and 'Bobo howls.' Now consider the single new sentence 'Ardbeg howls *and* Bobo howls.' This latter new sentence was generated out of the two previous old sentences, and it was the word 'and' that did the generating. Alternatively, the word 'and' *operated* on the two old sentences in order to generate the new sentence.

Consider next the old sentence 'Ardbeg howls.' Now consider the new sentence 'It is not the case that Ardbeg howls'. This latter new sentence was generated out of the previous old sentence. Notice that 'It is not the case that . . .' does *not* connect two or more sentences. Once again, a connective is *not* something that *connects* two or more sentences. Rather, it is (once again) a device that operates on one or more sentences in order to generate a new sentence.

Sentences come in two flavors: atomic and molecular.

Definition:     An *atomic* (or *simple*) sentence is a sentence without any connectives.

Definition:     A *molecular* (or *compound*) sentence is a sentence containing at least one connective.

'Ardbeg howls' is a sentence without any connectives—and as such, it's an atomic sentence (or, more briefly, an atomic). On the other hand, 'Ardbeg howls and Bobo howls' is a sentence containing at least one connective—and as such, it's a molecular sentence (or, more briefly, a molecular).

We shall make do, in our artificial language $L_1$, with five connectives. In what follows in the next five paragraphs, interpret 'A' to mean 'Ardbeg howls' and 'B' to mean 'Bobo howls'.

(1) '—' is the dash. Its closest English equivalent is 'It is not the case that . . .', or 'It is false that . . .'. It operates on a given sentence to create the *negation* of that sentence. '—A' represents the sentence 'It is not the case that Ardbeg howls' or 'It is false that Ardbeg howls' or (simply) 'Ardbeg doesn't howl'.

(2) '∧' is the caret. Its closest English equivalent is 'and'. It operates on any two sentences to create the *conjunction* of those sentences. 'A ∧ B' represents the sentence 'Ardbeg howls and Bobo howls'. 'A', the sentence immediately to the left of the caret, is the left *conjunct*, and 'B', the sentence immediately to the right of the caret, is the right *conjunct*.

(3) '∨' is the wedge. Its closest English equivalent is 'or' (or 'either-or'). It operates on any two sentences to create the *disjunction* of those sentences. 'A ∨ B' represents the sentence 'Either Ardbeg howls or Bobo howls'. 'A', the sentence immediately to the left of the wedge, is the left *disjunct*, and 'B', the sentence immediately to the right of the wedge, is the right *disjunct*.

(4) '→' is the arrow. Its closest English equivalent is 'if-then'. It operates on any two sentences to create the *conditional* of those sentences. 'A → B' represents the sentence 'If Ardbeg howls then Bobo howls'. 'A', the sentence immediately to the left of the arrow, is the *antecedent* of the conditional, and 'B', the sentence immediately to the right of the arrow, is the *consequent* (and not the *consequence*).

(5) '↔' is the double-arrow. Its closest English equivalent is 'if and only if' ('*iff*'). It operates on any two sentences to create the *bi-conditional* of those sentences. 'A ↔ B' represents the sentence 'Ardbeg howls if and only if Bobo howls'. There is no distinctive name for either 'A' or 'B', i.e., for either the sentence immediately to the left of the double-arrow or the sentence immediately to its right.

## C. Summary

| Connective | Name | English Equivalent | Generated Sentence |
|---|---|---|---|
| (1) — | dash | 'it is not the case that' | negation |
| (2) ∧ | caret | 'and' | conjunction |
| (3) ∨ | wedge | 'or' | disjunction |
| (4) → | arrow | 'if-then' | conditional |
| (5) ↔ | double-arrow | 'if and only if' | bi-conditional |

| Corresponding $L_1$-Sentence | Corresponding English Sentence |
|---|---|
| (1) —A | (1) It is not the case that Ardbeg howls. |
| (2) A ∧ B | (2) Ardbeg howls and Bobo howls. |
| (3) A ∨ B | (3) Ardbeg howls or Bobo howls. |
| (4) A → B | (4) If Ardbeg howls then Bobo howls. |
| (5) A ↔ B | (5) Ardbeg howls if and only if Bobo howls. |

How else might we interpret (or understand) the $L_1$ sentences?

(1) —A
_____
    a.   Ardbeg doesn't howl.
    b.   Ardbeg fails to howl.


(2) A ∧ B
_____
    a.   Both Ardbeg and Bobo howl.
    b.   Ardbeg and Bobo both howl.
    c.   Ardbeg howls; moreover (or: furthermore, or: in addition), Bobo howls.
    d.   Referring to Ardbeg and Bobo: both of them howl.
    e.   Referring to Ardbeg and Bobo: each of them howls.


(3) A ∨ B
_____
    a.   Either Ardbeg or Bobo howls.
    b.   Ardbeg or Bobo howls.
    c.   Referring to Ardbeg and Bobo: at least one of them howls.
    d.   Ardbeg howls unless Bobo howls. (Don't worry about this one for the time being; it's not at all self-evident. To be explained presently. . . .)


(4) A → B
_____
    a.   Bobo howls if Ardbeg howls. (Puzzled? Consider the sentence 'You'll pass if you work hard.' Obviously this means the same as the sentence 'If you work hard then you'll pass.' In *Loglish*—a halfway house between purely logical notation and English—this sentence would look like this: 'You work hard → you'll pass.' Moral of the story: what comes after the word 'if' is normally, but not always, the antecedent of the conditional. The exception arises when the word 'only' is glued to 'if', as in the sentence, 'Bobo howls *only if* Ardbeg howls.')
    b.   Ardbeg howls only if Bobo howls. (Don't worry about this one for the time being; it too is not at all self-evident. To be explained presently. . . .)

(5) A ↔ B

----

a.  If Ardbeg howls then Bobo howls, and if Bobo howls
    then Ardbeg howls.
b.  If Ardbeg howls then Bobo howls, and if Ardbeg
    doesn't howl then Bobo doesn't howl.
c.  Either Ardbeg and Bobo both howl or neither of
    them howls.

# 5. More on the Wedge

In English, the word 'or' is ambiguous; i.e., it has two senses—the *exclusive* sense and the *inclusive* sense. Suppose that your somewhat tightfisted Auntie Bobo takes you out for dinner. It's time for dessert, and, looking at the menu and knowing your passion for chocolate, she turns to you and says, "You may have *either* the chocolate soufflé *or* the tiramisu." It's quite clear that what Auntie means here is that you may have one or the other—*but not both*. This is the *exclusive* sense of the word 'or', whereby 'P exclusive-or Q' means 'P or Q *but not both* P and Q'.

On the other hand, there is the *inclusive* sense of the word 'or'. Suppose that I announce in class that you will receive an A in the course if either you receive an A on the final exam or you receive an A on each of the weekly quizzes. Now suppose that you receive an A on *both* the final exam *and* each of the weekly quizzes. What do you think: Do you receive an A in the course? Suppose that I turn to you after the fact and say, "Terribly sorry. What I *really* meant was that you would receive an A in the course if *either* you received an A on the final exam *or* you received an A on each of the weekly quizzes—*but not both*." You would think that I'm utterly mad—and you would be quite right. In ordinary English, it would be perfectly natural to presume that I had the *inclusive* sense of the word 'or' in mind (and perfectly *unnatural* to presume otherwise), whereby 'P inclusive-or Q' means 'P or Q and *possibly* both P and Q'.

If we wished to do so, we could have one connective for 'exclusive-or' and a distinct connective for 'inclusive-or'. Instead of having five connectives in our family of connectives, we would then have six. It's unnecessary to add an 'exclusive-or' connective, however. William of Ockham (or Occam, English, c.1287–c.1347), is credited with having said, "Don't multiply entities beyond necessity." We shall adhere to his injunction, known as Ockham's Razor, and shall not multiply connectives (too much) beyond necessity. (At the end of Chapter 2, you will see what I mean by "too much." It will then be clear that where our connectives are concerned, we are far from being good card-carrying, parsimonious Ockhamites.)

Accordingly, you are to treat the wedge as the sign for 'inclusive-or'. It's clear that you don't need a new connective for 'exclusive-or'. If you wanted to translate 'P exclusive-or Q' into logical notation, you could easily do so by means of our basic five connectives alone, as '(P ∨ Q) ∧ —(P ∧ Q)': 'Either P or Q—but not both P and Q'.

From this point on and forevermore in this course, you must treat *all* English-language uses of 'or' (or 'either-or') as 'inclusive-or'—*regardless of how strained it might seem*. In this context, consistency and utility trump all countervailing considerations.

# 6. Truth-Tables: Definitions

Logic, you will recall, is a science. Rigor is an essential feature of any science. It is now time to give a rigorous definition of each of our connectives.

Definitions:   (1) The sentence '—P' is true *iff* 'P' is false.
(2) The sentence 'P ∧ Q' is true *iff* 'P' is true and 'Q' is true.
(3) The sentence 'P ∨ Q' is false *iff* 'P' is false and 'Q' is false.
(4) The sentence 'P → Q' is false *iff* 'P' is true and 'Q' is false.
(5) The sentence 'P ↔ Q' is true *iff* either 'P' and 'Q' are both true or 'P' and 'Q' are both false.

Another way to give a rigorous definition of each of our connectives is by means of a truth-table. A truth-table shows all possible combinations of truth-value that a given sentence can have. Think of a sentence as a coin. When you flip a single coin, it can land either heads-up or tails-up; there's no other possibility. (Assume, for the sake of this discussion, that it can't land on its edge.) When you flip two coins—call one 'the first' and the other 'the second'—they can land either both heads-up, or both tails-up, or the first heads-up and the second tails-up, or the first tails-up and the second heads-up. Notice that there are no other possibilities; these four scenarios exhaust all the possibilities.

As with coins, so with sentences. With a single sentence, there are exactly two possibilities: it can be true or it can be false, period. This is Aristotle's Law of the Excluded Middle: there is no *third* possibility, i.e., no *third* truth-value. At the same time, we invoke Aristotle's Law of Contradiction—sometimes referred to, curiously, as Aristotle's Law of *Non*-Contradiction—and assume that no sentence can be *both* true *and* false. A would-be sentence that *appears* to be both true and false, e.g., 'Kabul is the nation's capital,' is *ambiguous*. (If, by 'the nation', we were to have Afghanistan in mind, it would be true. On the other hand, if, by 'the nation', we were to have the United States in mind, it would be false.) Such an ambiguous string of words isn't a sentence *strictly speaking*: it has the *form* of a sentence, but it's lacking in the determinate *content* or *meaning* that a sentence must also possess.

> Definition:     A string of words is *ambiguous* *iff* it possesses more than one meaning, such that it's an instance of more than one proposition.

Thus the string of words, 'Kabul is the nation's capital', is not a genuine sentence because it's not a bearer of truth-value. However, if the context makes it clear that the nation in question is Afghanistan, the string is (obviously) a true sentence. If the context makes it clear that the nation in question is the United States, the string is (obviously) a false sentence.

Suppose that the context doesn't provide even the *slightest* hint of what the nation in question is. Under these circumstances, the string simply isn't a genuine sentence. Or suppose that the context makes it clear that the nation in question is either Afghanistan or the United States. Under these circumstances, you're faced with a string of words that's an instance of *two* propositions—one of which refers to Afghanistan and one of which refers to the United States—masquerading as an instance of a *single* proposition. Don't for a moment suppose that what you have here is an instance of a *single* proposition that is *both* true *and* false—true when 'nation' refers to Afghanistan and false when it refers to the United States.

With one atomic sentence, as with one coin, there are two possibilities: it can be true or it can be false. With two atomic sentences, as with two coins, there are four possibilities: they can both be true, or they can both be false, or the first can be true and the second false, or the first can be false and the second true. There are no other possibilities. With three atomic sentences, as with three coins, there are eight possibilities. The magic formula for determining the number of possibilities is 2 raised to the $n$th power (where $n$ = the number of atomic sentences that you are considering). With one atomic, therefore, there are 2-raised-to-the-power-of-$n$ possibilities, i.e., 2 raised to the power of 1, i.e., two possibilities. With two atomics, there are four possibilities; and with three atomics, eight possibilities, etc.

In sum: given one atomic, a truth-table will have two rows; given two atomics, four rows; given three atomics, eight rows, etc. The key word here is 'atomic' (or 'atomics').

Consider the atomic 'P' and consider its negation; behold the two-row truth-table definition of the dash. (The *rows* are the horizontal arrays of Ts and Fs; the *columns* are the vertical arrays.) The purpose of highlighting the truth-values in the column beneath the dash is to draw your attention to the truth-values of the *negation* of 'P', given the truth-values of 'P'.

## A. The Truth-Table Definition of the Dash

| P | —P |
|---|-----|
| T | F T |
| F | T F |

What this truth-table reveals, unsurprisingly, is that (in the first row) '—P' is F if 'P' is T, and (in the second row) '—P' is T if 'P' is F. In other words, '—P' is T *iff* 'P' is F.

## B. The Truth-Table Definition of the Caret

Now consider the conjunction of 'P' and 'Q'; i.e., behold the truth-table definition of the caret. The purpose of highlighting the truth-values in the column beneath the caret is to draw your attention to the truth-values of the *conjunction* 'P ∧ Q', given the truth-values of 'P' and 'Q'.

| P Q | P ∧ Q |
|-----|-------|
| T T | T **T** T |
| T F | T **F** F |
| F T | F **F** T |
| F F | F **F** F |

What this truth-table reveals (again, unsurprisingly) is that 'P ∧ Q' is T *iff* 'P' is T and 'Q' is T. In other words, a conjunction is true *iff* both of its conjuncts are true. Alternatively, 'P ∧ Q' is F *iff* either 'P' is F or 'Q' is F or both 'P' and 'Q' are F. In other words, a conjunction is F *iff* at least one of its conjuncts is false.

## C. The Truth-Table Definition of the Wedge

Now consider the disjunction of 'P' and 'Q'; i.e., behold the truth-table definition of the wedge. The purpose of highlighting the truth-values in the column beneath the wedge is to draw your attention to the truth-values of the *disjunction* 'P ∨ Q', given the truth-values of 'P' and 'Q'.

| P Q | P ∨ Q |
|-----|-------|
| T T | T **T** T |
| T F | T **T** F |
| F T | F **T** T |
| F F | F **F** F |

What this truth-table reveals (yet again, unsurprisingly) is that 'P ∨ Q' is T *iff* either 'P' is T or 'Q' is T or both 'P' and 'Q' are T. In other words, a disjunction is true *iff* at least one of its disjuncts is true. Alternatively, 'P ∨ Q' is F *iff* 'P' is F and 'Q' is F. In other words, a disjunction is F *iff* both of its disjuncts are false. Note the curious symmetry between the truth-table definition of the caret and the truth-table definition of the wedge: a conjunction is true *iff* each conjunct is true, whereas a disjunction is false *iff* each disjunct is false.

## D. The Truth-Table Definition of the Arrow

Now consider the conditional 'If P then Q'; i.e., behold the truth-table definition of the conditional. The purpose of highlighting the truth-values in the column beneath the arrow is to draw your attention to the truth-values of the *conditional* 'P → Q', given the truth-values of 'P' and 'Q'.

| P Q | P → Q |
|-----|-------|
| T T | T **T** T |
| T F | T **F** F |
| F T | F **T** T |
| F F | F **T** F |

What this truth-table reveals (*most* surprisingly!) is that 'P → Q' is T *except* when 'P' is T and 'Q' is F. In other words, 'P → Q' is F *iff* 'P' is T and 'Q' is F.

With the exception of its second row, this truth-table is strikingly counterintuitive. Let's begin with the second row, where the antecedent of the conditional is true, the consequent is false, and the conditional itself is false. Take any conditional whatever with a true antecedent and a false consequent: it should strike you immediately that the conditional itself is false. I tell you that if you invest your life savings with me then you'll be a billionaire in ten years. Suppose that you do invest your life savings with me and suppose that you're flat broke in ten years. What then? Clearly my initial statement was false. I tell you that if you leap off the top of the Empire State Building you'll glide ever so gently to the ground. Suppose that you *do* leap off the top of the Empire State Building and suppose that you *don't* glide ever so gently to the ground. Once again, my original statement was false.

Moral of the story: where any conditional is concerned, it's obvious that if the antecedent is true and the consequent is false, the conditional is false. The second row of the truth-table for the arrow is, once again, a perfectly obvious row. It's also the *only* perfectly obvious row.

Consider the fourth row: 'If Ardbeg prays to the tooth fairy then all of Ardbeg's dreams will come true.' Both the antecedent and the consequent turn out to be false: Ardbeg *doesn't* pray to the tooth fairy and *not* all of Ardbeg's dreams come true. So what about the conditional itself? Is it true or is it false?

Now consider the third row: 'If Socrates despised philosophy then Plato revered him.' The antecedent is obviously false: Socrates did *not* despise philosophy. (Read Plato's *Apology*.) And the consequent is obviously true: Plato *did* revere Socrates. (Read the very end of Plato's *Phaedo*.) So once again: What about the conditional itself? Is it true or is it false?

Finally consider the first row: 'If you smoke three packs a day then you'll live to a hundred.' Suppose that both the antecedent and the consequent turn out to be true: you *do* smoke three packs a day and you *do* live to a hundred. So one last time: What about the conditional itself? Is it true or is it false?

If your intuitions are spinning in rows one, three, and/or four, that's how it should be. If it strikes you as odd that in these three rows the conditional comes out true, it's because it *is* odd that in these three rows the conditional comes out true. However, 'odd' doesn't mean 'unwarranted', much less 'absurd'. I shall now defend (at rather some length) the decision to treat conditionals in this way.

Conditionals are not homogeneous. There is a considerable variety of *kinds* of conditionals. Some are *causal*. Each of the three examples above illustrates a causal conditional. Over each of the three speakers' heads is a distinct bubble, and inside each of the three bubbles is a distinct thought. 'If Ardbeg prays to the tooth fairy then all of Ardbeg's dreams will come true.' The thought in the bubble? The belief that Ardbeg's praying to the tooth fairy will *cause* all of Ardbeg's dreams to come true. 'If Socrates despised philosophy then Plato revered him.' The thought in the bubble? The belief that Plato revered Socrates *because* Socrates despised philosophy. 'If you smoke three packs a day then you'll live to a hundred.' The thought in the bubble? The belief that smoking three packs a day promotes longevity (or at least *your* longevity).

Some conditionals are *definitional*, e.g., 'If Bobo is a widow then Bobo is a woman.' The claim here is not that Bobo's being a widow is the *cause* of Bobo's being a woman; the claim is rather that given that Bobo is a widow then *by definition* Bobo is a woman. (A man who was once married and whose wife died while they were married is not a *widow*. He is, rather, a *widower*.)

Some conditionals are *logical*, e.g., 'If it was either Ardbeg or Bobo who betrayed Coco, and it wasn't Ardbeg, then it was Bobo.' The claim here is *not* that the state of affairs that the antecedent describes is the *cause* of the state of affairs that the consequent describes. *Nor* is the claim here that the state of affairs that the consequent describes is what it is *by definition* of the state of affairs that the antecedent describes. Rather, the claim here is that the consequent follows from the antecedent *as a matter of purely logical implication.*

Now comes the pickle. You need a connective that will do justice to *all* kinds of conditionals, i.e., to each of these three different senses of 'if-then'—as well as to any other kind of conditionals that you may encounter. In other words, you need a sense of 'if-then' that doesn't require the consequent to follow from the antecedent either causally or definitionally or logically, etc. In short, you need a sense of 'if-then' that is common to all of the many senses of 'if-then' but that isn't distinctive of (or unique to) any one of them.

Question: When you drain the notion of 'if-then' of all causal import, of all definitional import, and of all logical import, what are you left with? I.e., what's the bare-bones minimum that characterizes each of these various senses or uses of 'if-then'? I.e., what's common to every 'if-then' sentence and yet isn't distinctive of any one of them?

Answer: To say 'If P then Q' is to say, "If you have the state of affairs 'P' then you have the state of affairs 'Q'." And to say this is to say, "You don't have the state of affairs 'P' without thereby having the state of affairs 'Q'." But to say *this* is to say, "It isn't the case that you have the state of affairs 'P' and *don't* have the state of affairs 'Q'." And to say *this* is simply to say the following: '−(P ∧ −Q)'. It follows that to say 'If P then Q' is simply to say '−(P ∧ −Q)'; i.e., the two sentences have the exact same meaning. That being the case, their truth-tables must be identical. Therefore, to *discover* the truth-table for the former sentence, 'If P then Q', all that you need to do is *construct* the truth-table for the latter:

| P Q | −(P ∧ −Q) |
|-----|-----------|
| T T | T T F F T |
| T F | F T T T F |
| F T | T F F F T |
| F F | T F F T F |

The purpose of highlighting the truth-values in the column beneath the leftmost dash is to draw your attention to the truth-values of the *negation of the conjunction of 'P' and 'Q'*, given the truth-values of 'P' and 'Q'. The highlighting, in other words, draws your attention to the circumstances under which the sentence as a whole—the *negation* of '(P ∧ −Q)'—is true and the circumstances under which the sentence as a whole is false.

If you compare this truth-table with the truth-table of the arrow, you'll discover (unsurprisingly, in light of the argument in the second-to-last paragraph) that the columns of truth-values under the main connectives are *identical*. In other words, if the (obviously) correct understanding of '−(P ∧ −Q)' is T, F, T, T, then the (obviously?) correct understanding of 'P → Q' will also be T, F, T, T. In other words, our original truth-table definition of the arrow was perfectly correct. Q.E.D.

'Q.E.D.' is an abbreviation of the Latin *'quod erat demonstrandum'* which simply means 'that which was to have been demonstrated'—the implication being that now it's been demonstrated.

Suppose that you're unhappy with this argument. I shall now provide you with another, very different sort of approach to the same problem. Consider the following argument; I hope that you 'see' it as valid:

> Either Ardbeg howls or Bobo howls.
> ─────────────────────────────
> ∴ If Ardbeg doesn't howl then Bobo howls.

We can schematize it in the obvious way as follows:

$$\frac{A \lor B}{\therefore -A \to B}$$

Now assume that Ardbeg howls but that Bobo doesn't howl; i.e., assume that 'A' is true but that 'B' is false. Focus first on the premise of the argument. It follows from the first assumption (i.e., that Ardbeg howls but that Bobo doesn't) that the premise is true. (Remember: a disjunction with at least one true disjunct is true.)

Focus next on the conclusion. You assumed 'A' to be true, and therefore '−A', the antecedent of the conditional, must be false. You assumed 'B', which happens to be the consequent of the conditional, to be false. Therefore the conclusion is a conditional whose antecedent and whose consequent are both false.

Remember, however, that the argument is a *valid* argument. Now here's what's crucial (in light of our tentative definition of 'valid'): *of necessity*, because this argument is valid and because its premise is true, its conclusion must also be true. But the conclusion is a conditional whose antecedent and whose consequent are both false. If such a conditional could be false, then the argument's premise would be *true* and its conclusion would be *false*. In that case, the argument would be *invalid*. But you've already acknowledged that it's *valid*. Therefore such a conditional—i.e., one with a *false* antecedent and a *false* consequent— *must* be true.

It follows, therefore, that any conditional with a false antecedent and a false consequent *must* be true. In other words, the fourth row of the truth-table that defines the arrow is *perfectly* correct. By the *exact* same reasoning, we could also (and easily) show that the first and third rows of the truth-table that define the arrow are perfectly correct. The second row, as we saw, is uncontroversial. Therefore (once again) our original truth-table definition of the arrow is perfectly correct. Q.E.D. once again.

## E. The Truth-Table Definition of the Double-Arrow

Think of a bi-conditional as a conditional that points in both directions: from left to right and from right to left. 'P ↔ Q', i.e., 'P *iff* Q', thus means 'If P then Q and if Q then P'. Accordingly the truth-table for 'P ↔ Q' must be identical to the truth-table for 'If P then Q and if Q then P'. Behold the truth-table for '(P → Q) ∧ (Q → P)'. The purpose of highlighting the truth-values in the column beneath the caret is to draw your attention to the truth-values of the *conjunction* '(P → Q) ∧ (Q → P)', given the truth-values of 'P' and 'Q'.

| P Q | (P → Q) ∧ (Q → P) |
|-----|-------------------|
| T T | T T T **T** T T T |
| T F | T F F **F** F T T |
| F T | F T T **F** T F F |
| F F | F T F **T** F T F |

Accordingly the truth-table for 'P ↔ Q' must be identical. The purpose of highlighting the truth-values in the column beneath the double-arrow is to draw your attention to the truth-values of the *bi-conditional* 'P ↔ Q', given the truth-values of 'P' and 'Q'.

| P Q | P ↔ Q |
|-----|-------|
| T T | T T T |
| T F | T F F |
| F T | F F T |
| F F | F T F |

What this truth-table reveals is that 'P ↔ Q' is T *iff* either 'P' and 'Q' are both true or 'P' and 'Q' are both false, i.e., *iff* 'P' and 'Q' have the same truth-value.

# 7. Translating 'But'

Some English-language connectives are now familiar to you; i.e., you know the logical connectives to which they correspond. Thus 'and' corresponds to the caret, 'or' to the wedge, and so on. Now suppose that you encounter an unfamiliar English-language connective. Suppose that you're unsure to which of our five logical connectives, if any, it corresponds: the dash, the caret, the wedge, the arrow, or the double-arrow. Your goal should be to construct a truth-table that serves to define the unfamiliar English-language connective. Suppose that its truth-table is identical to the truth-table for one of our five logical connectives. It follows that the unfamiliar English-language connective corresponds to—and thus is translatable by means of—that particular logical connective.

Consider the sentence 'Ardbeg walks *but* Bobo runs'. Ask yourself the circumstances under which it would be true and the circumstances under which it would be false. There are exactly four possibilities. It would be true if Ardbeg walks and Bobo runs. It would be false, however, if Ardbeg walks and Bobo doesn't run, or if Ardbeg doesn't walk although Bobo does run, or if Ardbeg doesn't walk and Bobo doesn't run.

Let 'A' designate the proposition that Ardbeg walks and let 'B' designate the proposition that Bobo runs. Accordingly, the truth-table for 'Ardbeg walks but Bobo runs' would look just like this:

| A B | A but B |
|-----|---------|
| T T | T  T  T |
| T F | T  F  F |
| F T | F  F  T |
| F F | F  F  F |

You've seen this truth-table before, of course. It's the truth-table for the caret, and so you should now feel free to translate 'but' by means of the caret. (Ditto for 'however', 'furthermore', and 'moreover'.) You now know that because both 'and' and 'but' are translatable via the caret, 'and' and 'but' have the same *meaning*. It's quite true that in everyday conversation, 'and' and 'but' perform different functions. However, where the *truth-values* of 'and' sentences and 'but' sentences are concerned, 'and' and 'but' are indistinguishable.

So once again: whenever you encounter an unfamiliar English-language connective, simply construct a truth-table that corresponds to it, i.e., one that serves to define it. If the truth-table is identical to the truth-table for one of our five logical connectives, then that particular logical connective will serve to translate the unfamiliar English-language connective. Bingo! You will have discovered just what you've been looking for.

# 8. Parentheses and Interpretations

Interpret 'A' to mean 'Ardbeg howls', 'B' to mean 'Bobo howls', and 'C' to mean 'Coco howls'. Now consider the following *would-be* sentence (or sentence wannabe):

> (1) 'A ∧ B ∨ C', i.e., 'Ardbeg howls and Bobo howls or Coco howls.'

As it stands, our would-be sentence is ambiguous. It might mean:

(1a) 'A ∧ (B ∨ C)', i.e., 'Ardbeg howls, and either Bobo or
Coco howls.'

Alternatively, it might mean:

(1b) '(A ∧ B) ∨ C', i.e., 'Either Ardbeg and Bobo howl, or
Coco howls.'

Now suppose that 'A' is false and 'C' is true. (Assign any truth-value you like to 'B'; in this example it makes no difference whether 'B' is true or false.) Notice that (1a) comes out false: any conjunction with a single false conjunct—'A' in this case—automatically comes out false. Notice too that (1b) comes out true: any disjunction with a single true disjunct—'C' in this case—automatically comes out true. It is precisely because (1a) and (1b) have opposite truth-values *under the exact same circumstances* (i.e., 'A' false, 'B' either true or false, and 'C' true), that we deem our would-be sentence—'A ∧ B ∨ C'—*ambiguous*. Hence the need for *parentheses* (or something comparable). Hence the need to transform (1) into either (1a) or (1b).

Note that (1a) is a conjunction (whose right conjunct is a disjunction). Note too that (1b) is a disjunction (whose left disjunct is a conjunction). You might have thought that parentheses were trivial. Quite the contrary: it should now be apparent that they are *far* from trivial; *their purpose*—and a rather noble purpose it is—*is to disambiguate otherwise ambiguous, would-be sentences.* Thanks to parentheses, you (like Midas and Rumpelstiltskin) are able to transform meaningless garbage into gold.

As the number of pairs of parentheses in a given sentence proliferates, ease of reading suggests that we supplement round parentheses with pairs of square brackets, i.e., '[' and ']', and pairs of curly braces, i.e., '{' and '}'. Consider the sentence '−(P → (−Q → −(R ∧ (−S ∨ −T))))'. It may require a bit of effort to determine which left-parenthesis corresponds to which right-parenthesis. By adhering to the convention that round parentheses are to be enclosed within square brackets, which in turn are to be enclosed within curly braces, it takes no effort to determine which left-punctuation sign corresponds with which right-punctuation sign. *In extremis*, we can simply repeat the pattern: round parentheses within square brackets within curly braces within round parentheses within square brackets, and so on. And so the punctuationally monstrous sentence '—(P → (—Q → —(R ∧ (—S ∨ —T))))' becomes the punctuationally manageable sentence '—(P → {—Q → —[R ∧ (—S ∨ —T)]})'.

I began this section with the word 'interpret'. You might well wonder what an interpretation is—especially since you'll be running into the notion of an interpretation quite frequently from this point on. You should know at the outset that the word 'interpretation' is itself variously interpretable; i.e., it's ambiguous; i.e., it has a variety of meanings. Normally, however, the context will make clear which meaning is intended.

Sometimes the object of the interpretation is a propositional *symbol*, and sometimes the object of the interpretation is a *proposition*.

Your logic instructor might well say, referring to various propositional *constants*, e.g., 'A' and 'B': "Interpret 'A' to designate the proposition that Ardbeg howls, and interpret 'B' to designate the proposition that Bobo howls." He or she might then pose the question: "How would you translate into logical notation the proposition that if Ardbeg doesn't howl then either Ardbeg or Bobo doesn't howl?" (The answer, of course, is '—A → (—A ∨ —B)'.) So understood, an interpretation is an assignment to a propositional *symbol*—in this instance a propositional *constant*—of a particular *proposition*.

Definition:     A *propositional interpretation* of a *propositional symbol* is an assignment to the symbol of a particular proposition such that the symbol now designates that proposition.

Alternatively, your logic instructor might well say, referring to a particular *proposition*, e.g., '—(P ∧ Q)': "Interpret 'P' to designate any true proposition and interpret 'Q' to designate any true proposition. For example, consider the interpretation that assigns T to 'P' and T to 'Q'. Question: For this interpretation, what truth-value does the proposition as a whole, i.e., '—(P ∧ Q)', have?" (Answer: F.) Your instructor might then continue: "Now consider the interpretation that assigns T to 'P' and F to 'Q'. Question: For *this* interpretation, what truth-value does '—(P ∧ Q)' have?" (Answer: T.) So understood, an *interpretation* is an assignment to a proposition of a particular truth-value.

Definition:     A *truth-value interpretation* of a *proposition* is an
                assignment of truth-values to the atomics that
                constitute the proposition.

It may be helpful to elaborate briefly on this latter notion of an interpretation. Consider (1b): '(A ∧ B) ∨ C' once again, and in particular,
consider just two interpretations. For the interpretation that each of the
atomics is true, the entire sentence comes out true:

(A ∧ B) ∨ C
T TT T T

For the interpretation that each of the atomics is false, the entire
sentence comes out false:

(A ∧ B) ∨ C
F F F F F

Knowing a given interpretation, and knowing the truth-table definitions of the five connectives, you can quickly determine the truth-
value of any sentence, however complex its logical structure. So if one
function of truth-tables is to provide rigorous definitions of the connectives, another function is to determine when (i.e., the truth-conditions
for which) a sentence is true and when (i.e., the truth-conditions for
which) it's false.

In what follows, we shall use the term 'interpretation' to refer both
to propositional interpretations and to truth-value interpretations. The
context will make it clear which sense is intended.

# Exercises

Determine the truth-values of the following propositions if (1) you
assign T to 'P', F to 'Q', T to 'R', and F to 'S'; and (2) you assign F to
'P', T to 'Q', F to 'R', and T to 'S'. Show all your work. Place a truth-
value under each atomic and under each connective.

1. $(-P \wedge -Q) \vee -R$
2. $-P \wedge (-Q \vee -R)$
3. $(P \rightarrow Q) \rightarrow R$
4. $P \rightarrow (Q \rightarrow R)$
5. $-(-P \leftrightarrow -R)$
6. $P \leftrightarrow [Q \rightarrow (R \wedge S)]$
7. $-(P \vee Q) \wedge (-R \leftrightarrow S)$
8. $-[P \leftrightarrow (Q \vee -R)]$
9. $-\{[(P \rightarrow -Q) \rightarrow (R \wedge -S)] \rightarrow -P\}$
10. $[P \rightarrow (Q \leftrightarrow R)] \rightarrow -\{(-P \wedge -S) \vee -[(P \vee -R) \rightarrow Q]\}$

# 9. Logically Equivalent Propositions

Suppose that Ardbeg and Bobo are close friends of yours. Further suppose that their ship went down at sea. Which of the following sentences would you *most* like to hear, and which would you *least* like to hear? (Remember: they are close friends of yours.)

(1) Neither Ardbeg nor Bobo drowned.
(2) Ardbeg didn't drown and Bobo didn't drown.
(3) Referring to Ardbeg and Bobo: not both of them drowned.
(4) Either Ardbeg didn't drown or Bobo didn't drown.

If it strikes you that (1) has the same meaning as, or says the same thing as, (2), it's because (1) does indeed have the same meaning as, or says the same thing as, (2). By the same token, if it strikes you that (3) has the same meaning as, or says the same thing as, (4), it's because (3) does indeed have the same meaning as, or says the same thing as, (4).

But note, and note well: it should strike you that (1) and (3) have radically different meanings. (1) and (2) entail that you'll have *both* of your pals back. (3) and (4) entail only that you'll have *at least one* of them back. (1) and (2) guarantee that *neither* of your pals drowned. (3) and (4) guarantee only that *at least one* of your pals *didn't* drown. They leave open the possibility that one of them *may* have drowned.

They don't affirm that one of them drowned, but they don't deny it either. By contrast, (1) and (2) deny it.

A *neither-nor* sentence, like (1), is the negation of an *either-or* sentence. Interpret 'A' to mean 'Ardbeg drowned' and interpret 'B' to mean 'Bobo drowned'. The either-or sentence that (1) is negating is 'Either Ardbeg drowned or Bobo drowned', i.e., 'A ∨ B'. As its negation, therefore, (1) goes over into logical notation as '—(A ∨ B)'. Since (1) means the same as (2), it follows that *the negation of a disjunction has the same meaning as the conjunction of two negations*. If you were to construct a truth-table of these two sentences, you would discover that they come out true, and they come out false, for the same interpretations, i.e., in the exact same rows of the truth-table:

| A B | —(A ∨ B) | —A ∧ —B |
|-----|----------|---------|
| T T | F T T T  | F T F F T |
| T F | F T T F  | F T F T F |
| F T | F F T T  | T F F F T |
| F F | T F F F  | T F T T F |

(3) is the negation of a conjunction; in particular, it's the negation of the sentence, 'Both Ardbeg and Bobo drowned', i.e., 'Ardbeg drowned and Bobo drowned', i.e., 'A ∧ B'. As its negation, therefore, (3) goes over into logical notation as '—(A ∧ B)'. (4) is a straightforward disjunction: '—A ∨ —B'. Since (3) means the same as (4), it follows that *the negation of a conjunction has the same meaning as the disjunction of two negations*. If you were to construct a truth-table of these two sentences, you would discover that they come out true, and they come out false, for the same interpretations, i.e., in the exact same rows of the truth-table.

We may now define 'logically equivalent propositions':

Definition:    Two propositions are *logically equivalent iff* they are true for the same interpretations.

Obviously if two propositions are true for the same interpretations then they must be false for the same interpretations. Less concisely, therefore (i.e., redundantly but nonetheless accurately), we may offer a second definition of 'logically equivalent propositions':

Definition:     Two propositions are *logically equivalent iff* they are true for the same interpretations and they are false for the same interpretations.

It will be convenient to have a symbol for logical equivalence: '⇔'. To say that '△' is logically equivalent to 'O', simply write '△'⇔'O'.

Assign whichever truth-values you like to the atomics of which each of two logically equivalent propositions is composed: either both propositions will come out true or both propositions will come out false. Indeed, at this point in the book, saying that two propositions are logically equivalent is tantamount to saying that they come out true (or false) in the exact same truth-table rows.

It is immensely tempting to think that (1) and (3) have the same meaning, and that (2) and (4) have the same meaning. Banish this thought from your mind this very instant and forevermore! They don't have the same meaning. They never did. And they never will. The temptation to think otherwise must be resisted.

You are indebted to the logician/mathematician Augustus De Morgan (English, 1806–1871) for rendering explicit what nowadays we refer to as De Morgan's Laws of Equivalence (i.e., his two laws of logical equivalence):

(5) '—(△ ∨ O)' ⇔ '—△ ∧ —O'
(6) '—(△ ∧ O)' ⇔ '—△ ∨ —O'

So (5) and (6) reaffirm what you have just learned. (5) reminds you that the negation of a disjunction is logically equivalent to the conjunction of two negations; and (6) reminds you that the negation of a conjunction is logically equivalent to the disjunction of two negations.

Now consider two other propositions: '△' and '— —△'. Obviously the two are logically equivalent to each other. Why 'obviously'? Because if '△' is true, then, by the truth-table definition of the dash, '—△' is false, in which case, by the truth-table definition of the dash once again, '— —△' is true. So if '△' is true then '— —△' is also true. And if '△' is false, then, by the truth-table definition of the dash, '—△' is true, in which case, by the truth-table definition of the dash once again, '— —△' is false. So if '△' is false then '— —△' is also false.

So if '△' is true then '— —△' is true, and if '△' is false then '— —△' is false. So '△' and '— —△' come out true and come out false for the same interpretations. They are, therefore, logically equivalent propositions, and the statement of their logical equivalence is typically known as Double Negation:

(7) '△' ⇔ '——△'

Interpret 'A' and 'B' to designate the propositions, respectively, that Ardbeg showed up and that Bobo showed up. Now consider the proposition (referring to Ardbeg and Bobo), 'Not both of them failed to show up'; i.e., 'Ardbeg and Bobo didn't both fail to show up'. It's the negation of 'Both of them—Ardbeg and Bobo—failed to show up'. So you translate it into logical notation first by writing 'Both Ardbeg and Bobo failed to show up—'—A ∧ —B'—and then by enclosing that sentence in parentheses and negating it:

(8) —(—A ∧ —B)

Now (8) has eight symbols (counting the parentheses). Suppose that you wished to simplify it, i.e., to transform it into a logically equivalent sentence with the fewest possible number of symbols. (8) is the negation of a conjunction. Invoking (6)-left, therefore—itself the negation of a conjunction—you would 'De Morganize' (8) as follows:

(9) ——A ∨ ——B

Thanks to De Morgan, therefore, you know that (8) and (9) are logically equivalent:

(10) '—(—A ∧ —B)' ⇔ '——A ∨ ——B'.

Puzzled? Look at (6) and look at (8). (6) is the negation of a conjunction of a triangle and a circle. (8) is the negation of a conjunction of '—A' and '—B'. Question: What in (8) corresponds to the triangle in (6)? Answer: The *negation* of 'A', i.e., '△A'. And what in (8) corresponds to the circle in (6)? Answer: The *negation* of 'B', i.e., '(—B)'. Note that in (6), De Morgan ensures that the negation of a conjunction of a triangle with a circle becomes a disjunction of a negated triangle with a negated circle. Correspondingly, in (8) the negation of a conjunction of a triangle, i.e., '△A', with a circle, i.e., '(—B)', becomes a disjunction of a negated triangle, i.e., '—△A', with a negated circle, i.e., '—(—B)'. In other words, —(△A ∧ (—B)) becomes —△A ∧ —(—B).

Now go back to (9). If you apply Double Negation twice, first to '− −A' and then to '− −B', you'll end up with a sentence with only three symbols:

(11) A ∨ B

Simplification does have its rewards. By simplifying (8), 'Not both Ardbeg and Bobo failed to show up', you haven't merely produced a sentence with fewer symbols, you've also produced a sentence whose meaning is much simpler to grasp: 'Either Ardbeg or Bobo (or both) showed up'.

It's crucial that De Morgan's Laws of Equivalence, not to mention Double Negation, become second nature to you ASAP. Second nature, in this context, means that when you look at, say, '−(−△ ∨ −O)', you immediately *see* '− −△ ∧ − −O' and then '△ ∧ O'. By the same token, second nature, in this context, also means that when you look at '−(−△ ∧ −O)', you immediately *see* '− −△ ∨ − −O' and then '△ ∨ O'.

# 10. Translations

Consider the following interpretations:

'A' = Ardbeg claps
'B' = Bobo claps
'C' = Coco sings
'D' = Dagbar sings

How would you translate into logical notation the proposition that Ardbeg and Bobo clap if Coco sings? Notice that the connective 'if' isn't to be found in its standard spot, i.e., at the beginning of the proposition.

You actually know the answer to this question. Earlier, while learning the truth-table definition of the arrow, you saw that '△ if O' is logically equivalent to 'If O then △'. So 'Ardbeg and Bobo clap if Coco sings' is logically equivalent to 'If Coco sings then Ardbeg and Bobo clap': 'C → (A ∧ B)'. Play it out with any other proposition. As you also saw earlier, 'You'll pass if you work hard' obviously means 'If you work hard then you'll pass'. Moral of the story: what comes after the word 'if' is typically the *antecedent* of the conditional. The exception, as I noted earlier, is when the word 'only' is glued to the word 'if', as in 'Ardbeg and Bobo clap *only if* Coco sings'. (You'll learn how to translate such a sentence by and by.)

Now, how would you translate into logical notation the proposition that either Ardbeg or Bobo fails to clap if Coco and Dagbar don't both sing? The first step is to come up with a proposition that has the same meaning as this one, but in which 'if' appears in its standard spot at the beginning of the proposition: 'If Coco and Dagbar don't both sing then either Ardbeg or Bobo fails to clap'. The sentence as a whole is a *conditional*. When you first look at it, therefore, what you should see is simply a conditional: '△ → O'. Never mind that the antecedent of the conditional, '△', is a molecular; and never mind that the consequent of the conditional, 'O', is also a molecular. Just write down the arrow on your sheet of paper. There's ample time to worry about what to put to its left and what to put to its right.

Suppose that you start with the antecedent: 'Coco and Dagbar don't both sing'. It's obviously the negation of 'Coco and Dagbar both sing'. So first you translate the latter—'C ∧ D'—and then you negate it: '—(C ∧ D)'.

Question: Would it have made any difference if, instead of introducing parentheses around 'C ∧ D', you had written down the following: '—C ∧ D'?

Answer: It would have made an enormous difference! The latter, '—C ∧ D', does *not* mean 'Coco and Dagbar don't both sing'. It means 'Coco doesn't sing but Dagbar sings'—and this is quite different from the original denial that both of them sing. Think for a moment: If you know only that not both of them sing, are you really entitled to infer that Coco doesn't but Dagbar does?

Now suppose that you turn to the consequent: 'Either Ardbeg or Bobo fails to clap'. It's a disjunction. Specifically, it's a disjunction of two negations, the negation of 'A' with the negation of 'B'. Accordingly, the left disjunct is '—A'; the right disjunct is '—B'; and the disjunction as a whole is '—A ∨ —B'.

You are now ready to translate, in its entirety, the proposition that either Ardbeg or Bobo fails to clap if Coco and Dagbar don't both sing: '—(C ∧ D) → (—A ∨ —B)'.

# Exercises

Using the following interpretations, translate the sentences below into logical notation:

A = Ardbeg howls
B = Bobo howls
C = Coco howls
D = Dagbar growls
E = Egvalt growls

1.  Ardbeg and Bobo howl if Coco howls.    $C \to (A \land B)$
2.  Neither Ardbeg nor Bobo howls.    $-(A \lor B)$
3.  Neither Ardbeg nor Bobo fails to howl.    $-(-A \lor -B) = A \land B$
4.  If Ardbeg fails to howl, then if Bobo fails to howl Coco fails to howl.    $-A \to (-B \to -C)$
5.  If Ardbeg fails to howl if Bobo fails to howl, then Coco fails to howl.    $(-B \to -A) \to -C$
6.  Ardbeg and Bobo do not both howl; furthermore, Dagbar and Egvalt do not both growl.    $-(A \land B) \land -(D \land E)$
7.  Ardbeg and Bobo do not both fail to howl.    $-(-A \land -B) = A \lor B$
8.  Either Ardbeg howls and neither Dagbar nor Egvalt growls, or Bobo howls and Dagbar and Egvalt do not both growl.

    $[A \land -(D \lor E)] \lor [B \land -(D \land E)]$

9.  Dagbar and Egvalt both fail to growl.

    $-(A \lor -B)$

10. If both Ardbeg and Bobo howl if and only if Coco doesn't howl, and if Dagbar growls if and only if Egvalt doesn't growl, then either Ardbeg howls and Coco doesn't howl, or Dagbar growls and Egvalt doesn't growl.

    $\{[(A \land B) \leftrightarrow -C] \land [D \leftrightarrow -E]\} \to [(A \land -C) \lor (D \land -E)]$

11. If either Ardbeg howls or Bobo fails to howl, and if either Dagbar growls or Egvalt fails to growl, then if Ardbeg and Bobo both howl Coco howls.

    $[(A \lor -B) \land (D \lor -E)] \to [(A \land B) \to C]$

12. Ardbeg and Bobo howl if and only if Coco fails to howl; nevertheless, Coco, but not Bobo, howls.    $[(A \land B) \leftrightarrow -C] \land C$

    $(A \land B) \leftrightarrow -C \land (C \land -B)$

13. If and only if Ardbeg fails to howl does Bobo fail to howl; however, Coco howls if and only if Dagbar doesn't growl.

    $(-A \leftrightarrow -B) \land (C \leftrightarrow -D)$

14. Neither does Ardbeg howl nor does Bobo fail to howl.
15. It's untrue that Ardbeg fails to howl if and only if Egvalt fails to growl.

    $-(-A \leftrightarrow -E)$

# Chapter Two

# Propositional Logic:
## A Formal Language, Part Two

## 1. Connectives: Truth-Functional and Non-Truth-Functional

Consider the word 'because'. It's obviously a *connective*: it's a device that operates on one or more sentences in order to generate a new sentence.

Question: By means of which of our five connectives would you translate it into logical notation? (Alternatively: Does it call for a sixth connective?)

Your task is to construct a truth-table that corresponds to 'because'. Consider the sentence 'Ardbeg wept *because* Bobo lost everything'. By determining the circumstances under which this sentence comes out true, and the circumstances under which it comes out false, you'll be able to construct the truth-table for 'because'. So all that you have to do is fill in the blanks in the following (unfinished) truth-table. Let 'A' designate the proposition that Ardbeg wept, and let 'B' designate the proposition that Bobo lost everything.

| A B | A | because | B |
|-----|---|---------|---|
| T T | T | ? | T |
| T F | T | ? | F |
| F T | F | ? | T |
| F F | F | ? | F |

Suppose that you start with the fourth row. 'A' is false and 'B' is false: Ardbeg didn't weep and Bobo didn't lose everything. Obviously the sentence 'Ardbeg wept because Bobo lost everything' is false. Now consider the third row. 'A' is false and 'B' is true: Ardbeg didn't weep although Bobo lost everything. Once again the sentence 'Ardbeg wept because Bobo lost everything' is false. Now consider the second row. 'A' is true and 'B' is false: Ardbeg wept but Bobo didn't lose everything. Yet once again the sentence 'Ardbeg wept because Bobo lost everything' is false. So here's how the truth-table looks so far:

| A B | A because B | | |
|-----|------|---|---|
| T T | T | ? | T |
| T F | T | F | F |
| F T | F | F | T |
| F F | F | F | F |

Only one row to go—the first. In the first row 'A' is true and 'B' is true: Ardbeg *did* weep and Bobo *did* lose everything. Six easy questions:

1. 'Ardbeg wept because Bobo lost everything' is *true*, yes?
2. It's *obviously* true, yes?
3. So once you put a T under 'because' in the first row, you'll have the complete truth-table for the 'because' connective, yes?
4. It'll be TFFF, the very same truth-table that captures the caret, yes?
5. So 'because' and 'and' have the very same meaning, yes?
6. So whenever you bump up against the connective 'because' in any sentence, you can simply yank it out and plug in the caret, yes?

Now put this book down for a moment and contemplate all of this. If you smell a rat, you're to be commended for your heightened sense of smell.

Six easy questions and six easy answers. But in truth the questions aren't all that easy and, in any event, each of the six 'suggested' answers—'yes', 'yes', 'yes', 'yes', 'yes', and 'yes'—is wrong. Dead wrong.

There's nothing wrong with the last three rows of the truth-table. The rat is to be found in the first row. It may well be true that Ardbeg wept, and it may well be true that Bobo lost everything. Does it really follow, however, that Ardbeg wept *because* Bobo lost everything? Maybe he wept because Bobo lost everything. But maybe he wept because *he* lost everything. Or maybe he wept because he had been drinking *very* hot mulligatawmy soup, and *very* hot mulligatawmy soup makes him weep. The point is that you haven't the *foggiest* idea why he wept. Not the foggiest. 'A because B' is true *iff* 'A' is true (which, in the first row, it is), and 'B' is true (which, in the first row, it is), *and* the 'B' event—Bobo's having lost everything—is the *cause* of the 'A' event—Ardbeg's having wept. And there's the rub: determining whether the 'B' event is the *cause* of the 'A' event in this instance is a matter for observation, and not for logic, to decide. It's an empirical matter, and as such it lies outside the bounds of logic.

Welcome to the distinction between *truth-functional* connectives and *non-truth-functional* connectives. Clearly, 'because' is a connective. However, unlike the dash, the caret, the wedge, the arrow, and the double-arrow, it's not a *truth-functional* connective. It's a *non-truth-functional* connective.

> **Definition:** A connective is *truth-functional iff* it generates a truth-functional sentence.

Sound circular? It is. Hold on. . . .

> **Definition:** A sentence is *truth-functional iff* its truth-value is determined exclusively by (i.e., is entirely a function of) the truth-values of its atomics.

Consider once again the sentence 'Ardbeg walks but Bobo runs'. The connective here—'but'—is truth-functional because the sentence is truth-functional. The sentence is truth-functional because its truth-value is *entirely* a function of the truth-values of its atomics. If the atomic 'Ardbeg walks' is true, and if the atomic 'Bobo runs' is also true, then the molecular, 'Ardbeg walks but Bobo runs', *must* be true. On the other hand, if either of the atomics is false then the molecular is false.

Now consider the 'because' connective. It's obviously (once again) a *connective*: it's a device that operates on one or more sentences in order to generate a new sentence. But it's not a truth-functional connective. You know that it's not a truth-functional connective because of the first row of its truth-table. In that row each atomic is true. If 'because'

were a truth-functional connective, then knowing that each atomic is true, you'd immediately know the truth-value of the molecular. But you *don't* know the truth-value of the molecular—not without making observations of the empirical world. Therefore 'because' isn't a truth-functional connective.

Examples of non-truth-functional connectives abound: 'at the same time that' (e.g., 'Coco was attacked by killer ants *at the same time that* Dagbar was attacked by killer spiders'), 'in the same place that' (e.g., 'Coco was attacked by killer ants *in the same place that* Dagbar was attacked by killer spiders'), 'under the same circumstances that', 'an hour after', etc.

Lest you think that 'because' always connotes causality in our *ordinary* sense of causality, think again. Consider the two following uses of 'because', neither of which is *causal* in the ordinary sense. If you wish, you may think of the first as causal *definitionally* and the second as causal *logically*: 'ABC is a triangle *because* ABC is a three-sided, rectilinear, plane, closed figure' and 'The silver dollar must be in your left hand *because* either it's in your right hand or it's in your left hand, and clearly it's not in your right hand'. Neither of these two uses of 'because' is truth-functional. Try to explain why. (Hint: Think of a definitional 'because' that relies on a misdefinition; and think of a logical 'because' where the conclusion simply doesn't follow.)

Propositional Logic, the branch of logic that is the focus of the first half of this book, is also known, appropriately, as 'Truth-Functional Logic'—the logic of truth-functions. Indeed, in this book as a whole, truth-functional connectives are the *only* connectives with which we shall be concerned.

# 2. Translating 'Only If'

Be prepared in this section to run up against your first conceptual speed bump. (If you aren't *fully* alert, don't read on; take a nap instead.) Consider the following sentence:

(1) Bobo is a widow only if Bobo is a woman.

Suppose that we dispense with propositional symbols just this once, for the sake of clarity. Interpret 'WIDOW' to mean 'Bobo is a widow', and interpret 'WOMAN' to mean 'Bobo is a woman'. Translating (1) into *Loglish*—our halfway house (once again) between purely logical notation and English—yields the following:

> (2) WIDOW only if WOMAN

Translating (1) and (2) into *full-blown* logical notation is a bit tricky. No doubt your first inclination may be to translate it as follows:

> (3) WOMAN → WIDOW

But (3) *can't* be right; i.e., it can't *possibly* capture what (1) and (2) are claiming. Think of what (3) says: 'If Bobo is a woman then Bobo is a widow'. (1) and (2) are *truths*: if you know *nothing* about Bobo and I tell you that Bobo is a widow, you *immediately* know that Bobo is a woman. Why? Because being a woman is a *necessary* condition of being a widow: you can't be a widow unless you're a woman. (Once again: a man in a comparable position is a *widower*, not a *widow*.) (3), however, is a *falsehood*: if, once again, you know nothing about Bobo and I tell you that Bobo is a woman, you know nothing about her marital status. The claim that if she's a woman then she's a widow is simply false. So if (1) and (2) are truths and (3) is a falsehood, then (3) *must* be a mistranslation of (1) and (2). So then how do you translate (1) and (2)?

It turns out that, your intuitions to the contrary, 'Bobo is a widow only if Bobo is a woman' has the very same meaning as 'If Bobo is a widow then Bobo is a woman'—in which case the correct translation of (1) and (2) is the converse (the very opposite) of (3):

> (4) WIDOW → WOMAN

In the following paragraph, I shall write *very* loosely—so that you'll have an easier time grasping what's at issue. In the paragraph following the following paragraph, I'll express the same thought without the looseness.

The loose version first. All of the following statements have the *exact* same meaning; i.e., it should strike you that (6) has the same meaning as (5), that (7) has the same meaning as (6), etc.

(5) P only if Q.

(6) You have 'P' only if you have 'Q'.

(7) You have to have 'Q' in order to have 'P'.

(8) You can't have 'P' without 'Q'.

(9) It's not the case that you have 'P' without 'Q'; i.e., $-(P \wedge -Q)$.

(10) If you have 'P' then you have 'Q'.

(11) If 'P' is true then 'Q' is true.

(12) If P then Q.

(13) P → Q.

So (5) has the same meaning as (12); i.e., 'P only if Q' has the same meaning as 'If P then Q'. Therefore because we translate 'If P then Q' as 'P → Q', we translate 'P only if Q' as 'P → Q'.

The non-loose version next. All of the following statements, (14) through (19), have the *exact* same meaning; i.e., it should strike you that (15) has the same meaning as (14), that (16) has the same meaning as (15), etc.

(14) P only if Q.

(15) The truth of 'Q' is necessary for the truth of 'P'.

(16) It's not the case that 'P' is true and that 'Q' is not true; i.e., $-(P \wedge -Q)$.

(17) If 'P' is true then 'Q' is true.

(18) If P then Q.

(19) P → Q.

Once again, we see that 'P only if Q' has the same meaning as 'If P then Q'. And (once again) because we translate 'If P then Q' as 'P → Q', it follows that we translate 'P only if Q' as 'P → Q'.

If you're still unconvinced then it's time to beat a dead horse. . . . Notice first that the sentence 'If P then Q' amounts to the following two claims:

(20) If 'P' is true then 'Q' is true; i.e., the truth of 'P' *guarantees* (i.e., is *sufficient* for) the truth of 'Q'.

(21) If 'Q' is not true then 'P' is not true; i.e., the truth of 'Q' is *necessary* for the truth of 'P'.

Notice next that the sentence 'P only if Q' amounts to the following two claims:

(22) If 'Q' is not true then 'P' is not true; i.e., the truth of 'Q' is *necessary* for the truth of 'P'.
(23) If 'P' is true then 'Q' is true; i.e., the truth of 'P' *guarantees* (i.e., is *sufficient* for) the truth of 'Q'.

Of course, (20) simply is (23), and (21) simply is (22). It should come as no surprise, therefore, that 'If P then Q' and 'P only if Q' have the same meaning. Accordingly, because the correct translation of 'If P then Q' is 'P → Q', the correct translation of 'P only if Q' must also be 'P → Q'.

The obvious question: Why do our intuitions have to be dragged kicking and screaming before they will acknowledge that 'If P then Q' and 'P only if Q' have the exact same meaning?

The non-obvious answer: In the course of using conditionals in everyday conversation, we presume that the speaker (or writer) believes that there is a *connection* of some sort between the state of affairs to which the antecedent of the conditional refers and the state of the affairs to which the consequent refers. For example, the connection might be of the causal sort, of the definitional sort, or of the logical sort—and the context will normally make clear exactly which sort of conditional the speaker (or writer) is using.

Suppose that a dog-walker reprimands you: "If you pull Old Fido's tail one more time then he'll bite you." Your presumption is that the dog-walker believes that there is a *causal connection* between the former state of affairs—your pulling Old Fido's tail—and the latter state of affairs—Old Fido's biting you—such that the former will be the *cause* of the latter. But here's the crucial point: Your *presumption*, as well as the dog-walker's *belief*, are distinct from the *meaning* of the conditional sentence itself. The *meaning* of the conditional sentence itself is what it shares with *all* typical conditionals. Because a reference to causality doesn't characterize the other sorts of conditionals, a reference to causality can be no part of its own meaning.

Its *meaning*—what it shares (once again) with all typical conditionals—is precisely this: *It isn't the case that its antecedent is true and its consequent isn't true.* Once you abandon the belief that there is a *connection* of some sort between the state of affairs to which the antecedent of the conditional refers and the state of affairs to which the consequent refers, then you should have no difficulty seeing that the *meaning* of a conditional consists exclusively in its not being the case that its antecedent is true and its consequent is not true.

Think of a conjunction. Suppose that on the first day of the semester, your instructor had walked into your class and said, "This is a course in formal logic and I shall now be taking roll." You would have found that entirely unsurprising. Suppose instead that on the first day of the semester your instructor had walked into your class and said, "This is a course in formal logic, and Lenin suffered his first stroke in May 1922." You would have found this more than a bit odd. Suppose that a short while later in the same class your instructor had then gone on to say, "There will be a quiz every other week, and Alexandria, Egypt, is named after Alexander the Great." At this point you would have begun to feel a bit uneasy and you would have looked around at the other students. Suppose finally that somewhat later, your instructor had then gone on to say, "The final exam will count for one-third of your course grade, and Euclid is credited with the proof that the square root of 2 is an irrational number." My guess is that at that point you and your fellow classmates would have started tiptoeing toward the exit. The collective bubble over all of your heads would have read: "What does the one thing have to do with the other? What's the *connection* between the *first* half of each of this instructor's sentences and the *second* half?" Or (if on that day you had known the terminology) your collective bubble would have read: "In each of the preceding conjunctions the two conjuncts have no *relation* to one another. Why, then, is this instructor conjoining such conjuncts?"

Your unease, however, would have concerned *psychology* (your instructor's) and not *logic* as such. Your confusion concerned not the *meaning* of your instructor's statements but rather your instructor's *reasons* for uttering them. The point is that you understood each of the sentences and you could have determined their truth-values without too much difficulty. Consider the sentence 'This is a course in formal logic, and Lenin suffered his first stroke in May 1922'. Had you known that each conjunct is true, you would have known in a jiffy that the entire conjunction is true. Whether the sentence is true or false is one thing; whether it's appropriate or inappropriate (i.e., bizarre) to utter it is another thing altogether. In logic our concern is exclusively with truth and falsehood, rather than with appropriateness and inappropriateness.

It simply doesn't matter—at least where the truth-value of the sentence is concerned—whether there's any connection between the left conjunct and the right conjunct in the conjunction 'This is a course in formal logic, and Lenin suffered his first stroke in May 1922'. By the same token, it simply doesn't matter—again, at least where the truth-value of the sentence is concerned—whether there's any connection between the antecedent and the consequent in the conditional 'If Fido wrote the *Iliad* then the Moon is made of pink fluff'.

Once you divest yourself of the view that there *has* to be a connection, it should become somewhat easier to see that there's no difference either meaning-wise or truth-value-wise between the sentence '*If* Fido wrote the Iliad *then* the Moon is made of pink fluff' and the sentence 'Fido wrote the *Iliad only if* the Moon is made of pink fluff'. Each of these sentences has the exact same meaning as the sentence 'It is not the case both that Fido wrote the *Iliad* and that the Moon is *not* made of pink fluff'. Now, since *this* sentence is true—Fido did *not* write the *Iliad*—each of the two former sentences is true as well. And once you see *that*, it should become easy-ish to see that there's no difference *truth-value-wise* between the sentence 'If you work hard next semester then you'll pass' and the sentence 'You'll work hard next semester only if you'll pass'. They both mean that it's not the case that you'll work hard and yet that you *won't* pass.

# 3. Translating 'Unless'

Translating 'unless' sentences from *Loglish* into logical notation is also a bit tricky, but the translation piggybacks rather nicely onto 'if-then' sentences. There's a mechanically complicated, but perfectly intuitive, way to translate 'unless', and there's a mechanically simple, but slightly less intuitive, way to translate it. We begin with the former.

Whenever you're faced with an English-language sentence containing an unfamiliar connective, and you're unsure how to translate it into logical notation, there are two useful strategies that you might employ. You're already familiar with the first of them, from our discussion of 'but'.

Try to construct a truth-table for the unfamiliar connective, in order to determine whether it corresponds to any of our five basic connectives. If it corresponds to one of them, then replace the unfamiliar connective that appears in the English-language sentence with whichever one of our basic five connectives it corresponds to, and translate the latter sentence into logical notation.

Suppose, however, that the unfamiliar connective doesn't correspond to any one of our basic five connectives. In that case, try to construct the simplest possible English-language sentence that incorporates the unfamiliar connective. Then construct a sentence in logical notation that has the same meaning as the English-language sentence, but that contains—instead of the unfamiliar connective—either the dash and the caret, the dash and the wedge, or the dash and the arrow. Finally, and based on what you have just done, try to develop a purely mechanical procedure for translating all future sentences containing that unfamiliar connective into sentences in logical notation. The latter will contain, in place of the unfamiliar connective, either the dash and the caret, the dash and the wedge, or the dash and the arrow.

Consider the sentence, 'You'll die unless you have the surgery'. This goes over into *Loglish* as 'D unless S'. The most promising candidates, in light of the second strategy, are the following:

(1) S → —D
(2) —S → D

What exactly is your surgeon saying when she says that you'll die unless you have the surgery? Note what she is *not* saying. She is *not* saying, "If you have the surgery then you *won't* die." After all, she could easily add on the qualification, "And by the way, if you *do* have the surgery, you might *still* die. *Anything*, alas, could go wrong: the surgery itself might be unsuccessful, or there might be postsurgical complications, or a mad dog might work his way into the I.C.U. and maul you to death."

(1), unlike (2), is a promise of eternal life, and while your surgeon is promising you *something*, she is *not* promising you eternal life. She is promising you what (2) affirms; i.e., that if you *don't* have the surgery then you *will* die. Hence '—S → D'. Alternatively, she is promising you that if you *don't* die then you will have had the surgery; i.e., '—D → S'. Unsurprisingly, '—S → D' and '—D → S' are logically equivalent to each other.

Conclusion: 'You will die unless you have the surgery' goes over into logical notation as either '—S → D' or '—D → S'. Notice the purely mechanical rule that you may extract from this:

1.  Replace 'unless' with the arrow.
2.  Place either of the sentences that flanks the word 'unless'—it doesn't matter which—to the left of the arrow, and place the other sentence to its right.
3.  Prefix a dash to the sentence that you placed to the left of the arrow. Done.

Earlier, I mentioned that there is a mechanically simple, but slightly less intuitive, way to translate 'unless' sentences. Consider once again the sentence 'You will die unless you have the surgery'. This amounts to 'Either you will have the surgery or you will die—and possibly both (i.e., you may have the surgery and still die).' Notice that—because the wedge operates as the '*inclusive*-or'—this is a straightforward 'either-or' sentence: 'S ∨ D'. Now the order of disjuncts in a disjunction has no bearing on the truth-value of the sentence as a whole: '△ ∨ O' is logically equivalent to 'O ∨ △'. (The same, of course, holds true of the order of conjuncts in a conjunction.) Therefore you could just as well write 'S ∨ D' as 'D ∨ S'. Here the mechanical principle that allows you to translate 'unless' sentences into logical notation is a snap: replace 'unless' with the wedge. Done.

So you have two procedures for translating 'unless' sentences into logical notation. One procedure renders '△ unless O' as either '—△ → O' or '—O → △'. The other procedure renders it as either '△ ∨ O' or 'O ∨ △'. The four sentences that the two procedures generate are, of course, logically equivalent to each another.

# Exercises

Using the following interpretations, translate the sentences below into logical notation:

A = Ardbeg howls
B = Bobo howls
C = Coco howls
D = Dagbar growls
E = Egvalt growls

1. Ardbeg howls unless Bobo and Coco howl. $-A \rightarrow (B \wedge C)$
2. Ardbeg doesn't howl only if Bobo doesn't howl. $-A \rightarrow -B$
3. Unless Bobo and Coco howl, Ardbeg howls. $-(B \wedge C) \rightarrow A$
4. If Ardbeg howls only if Bobo doesn't howl, then Dagbar growls. $(A \rightarrow -B) \rightarrow D$
5. Ardbeg doesn't howl unless it so happens both that Bobo howls and that Coco fails to howl. $--A \rightarrow (B \wedge -C)$
6. Ardbeg doesn't howl unless either Bobo or Coco fails to howl; in any case, either Dagbar or Egvalt fails to growl. $-A \vee (-B \vee -C) \wedge (-D \vee -E)$
7. If Egvalt growls only if neither Ardbeg nor Bobo howls, then either Coco howls or Coco doesn't howl. $(E \rightarrow -(A \vee B)) \rightarrow (C \vee -C)$
8. Neither Ardbeg nor Bobo fails to howl, unless Dagbar growls. $-D \rightarrow -(A \vee B)$
9. Only if either Bobo or Coco howls does Dagbar fail to growl. $(B \vee C) \rightarrow -D$
10. Ardbeg and Bobo do not both howl unless either Dagbar or Egvalt fails to growl. $-(-D \vee -E) \rightarrow -(A \wedge B)$
11. Referring to Dagbar and Egvalt: exactly one of them fails to growl. $(-D \vee -E) \wedge -(-D \wedge -E)$
12. If Ardbeg howls unless Dagbar growls, then Bobo and Coco do not both howl. $(-A \rightarrow D) \rightarrow -(B \wedge C)$
13. Referring to Dagbar and Egvalt: only one of them fails to growl. $(-D \vee -E) \wedge -(-D \wedge -E)$ or $(-D \vee -E) \wedge (D \vee E)$
14. If Ardbeg howls then, unless Dagbar growls, Egvalt growls. $A \rightarrow (-E \rightarrow D)$
15. Referring to Dagbar and Egvalt: at most one of them growls. $-(D \wedge E)$

16. Unless Bobo and Coco each fails to howl, Egvalt growls. $(-B \wedge -C) \vee E$
17. Referring to Ardbeg, Bobo, and Coco: exactly one of them howls. $[A \vee (B \vee C)] \wedge -(A \wedge B) \wedge -(B \wedge C) \wedge -(A \wedge C)]\}$
18. Only if Ardbeg howls does Bobo fail to howl; moreover Dagbar growls unless Egvalt doesn't growl. $(A \rightarrow -B) \wedge (-E \rightarrow D)$
19. Referring to Ardbeg Bobo, and Coco: at least two of them howl. $(A \wedge B) \vee [(B \wedge C) \vee (A \wedge C)]$
20. Referring to Ardbeg, Bobo, and Coco: exactly two of them howl.

$\{(A \wedge B) \vee [(B \wedge C) \vee (A \wedge C)]\} \wedge -[A \wedge (B \wedge C)]$

# 4. Truth-Tables: Valid and Invalid Arguments

As you know, truth-tables perform a variety of functions, several of which you are already familiar with. One such function involves providing rigorous definitions of our connectives. A second is to determine the circumstances (the *interpretation* or *interpretations*) under which a given sentence is true and the circumstances under which it is false. A third is to determine whether two sentences are logically equivalent to one another. (They *are*, you will recall, *iff* they are true for the same interpretations—and thus are false for the same interpretations.) A fourth function of truth-tables is to determine whether a given argument is valid or invalid. It is this fourth function that we shall now examine.

You will recall that once upon a time we said that an argument is valid *iff* it would be *impossible* for its premises to be true and its conclusion to be false. You will recall that I noted that you would be quite hard-pressed to come up with an adequate definition of 'impossible'. You will recall that we defined an *interpretation* as an assignment of truth-values to the atomics of which a sentence is composed. We are now in a position to illuminate, at least to some extent and in this context, the notion of *impossibility*. To say that it is *impossible* for the premises of an argument to be true and for its conclusion to be false is simply to say that there is no interpretation that makes each of its premises true and its conclusion false. And thus you have a brand new definition of 'valid argument', onto which you may piggyback the notion of implication:

Definition:    An argument is valid *iff* there is no interpretation that makes each of its premises true and its conclusion false.

Definition:    The premises of an argument *imply* its conclusion *iff* the argument is valid.

In *this* branch of logic, i.e., in Propositional Logic, this amounts to saying that an argument is valid just in case there is no truth-table row in which every premise is true and the conclusion is false. So all that you have to do is look at each truth-table row. If, in the premises columns and in the conclusion column, you *ever* see the following pattern, then you know that the argument is *invalid*:

| Premise 1 | Premise 2 | ... | Premise n−1 | Premise n | Conclusion |
|:---:|:---:|:---:|:---:|:---:|:---:|
| T | T | | T | T | F |

If, on the other hand, you *never* see this pattern—even if you see quite literally any pattern other than this one—then the argument is *valid*. And the argument is *valid* because if you *fail* to see this pattern, then you know that there's no interpretation—no assignment of truth-values to the atomics—such that every premise is true and the conclusion is false.

Note that the assignments of truth-values to the atomics in a truth-table represent all *possible* assignments of truth-values to the atomics. It follows, therefore, that if there is no row in which every premise is true and the conclusion is false, it is *impossible* for the premises to be true and the conclusion to be false. You just learned what the word 'impossible' means in this context. Now 'necessary' and 'impossible' are inter-definable; i.e., the sentence "It is *impossible* that 'P' is true" means the same as the sentence "*Of necessity* 'P' is not true". So you have also just learned what the word 'necessary' means in this context.

It might strike you as odd that where a valid argument is concerned, any truth-table row other than T T T ... T F is compatible with the argument's being valid. But think of why this is so. In the case of a valid argument, we do *not* require that the premises actually be true. *Nor* do we require that the conclusion be true. All that we require is that there be no interpretation, no assignment of truth-values to the atomics, no truth-table row, no case, where every premise is true and the conclusion is false. Consider the following argument:

> (1) Washington is the capital of the United States and Boston is the capital of Afghanistan.
> _____
> ∴ (2) Washington is the capital of the United States.

Is the premise of this argument false? Of course it is. Is the conclusion true? Of course it is. So it's possible for a truth to follow from a falsehood? Of course it is—and that's perfectly OK. To be sure, it's not possible for a falsehood to follow from a truth (or from truths). The claim here is simply that in the case of a valid argument—such as this one is—*if, if, if* the premises were true—it's irrelevant whether in fact they are or they aren't true—then the conclusion also would be true. The word 'if' is the crucial word here.

Two last comments on our newly acquired conception of validity. First, consider the following argument:

> (3) Fido is the author of the *Iliad*.
> (4) Fido is not the author of the *Iliad*.
> _____
> ∴ (5) The Moon is made of pink fluff.

So what do you think? Valid or invalid? (Put the book down for five minutes and ponder.)

The crucial hint, of course, is that the premises contradict each other; i.e., there's no interpretation that makes each of them true. Therefore there's no interpretation that makes each of the premises true and the conclusion false. Therefore the argument is valid. Perfectly, perfectly valid. (Before you start gnashing your teeth, you may console yourself with the knowledge that such an argument is of course *unsound*. Remember: to be sound, it's not sufficient that an argument be *valid*; in addition, each of its premises must be *true*.)

The moral of the story is both interesting and important. From a contradiction (e.g., from (3) and (4)), anything whatsoever (e.g., (5))

follows. That being the case, it is crucial to weed out contradictions from your theories (whether they be theories within mathematics or physics or biology or whatever). If you fail to do so, anything whatsoever will follow from them—and a theory from which quite literally *anything whatsoever* follows isn't worth two cents.

Finally, consider the following argument:

> (6) Fido is the author of the *Iliad*.
> _____
> ∴ (7) Either the Moon is made of pink fluff or the Moon isn't made of pink fluff.

So what do you think of *this* one? Valid or invalid? (Put the book down—for three minutes this time—and ponder. You don't need five minutes for this one.)

The crucial hint, of course, is that there's no interpretation that makes the conclusion *false*. Therefore there's no interpretation that makes each of the premises *true* and the conclusion *false*. Therefore the argument is valid. Perfectly, perfectly valid once again. Moral of *this* story: a sentence that is true for every interpretation (e.g., (7)) follows from any sentence(s) whatsoever (e.g., (6)).

## A. Truth-Tables: Examples

Consider the following argument:

> (1) Either Ardbeg or Bobo fails to howl.
> (2) If Bobo doesn't howl then Coco doesn't howl.
> _____
> ∴ (3) Ardbeg and Coco do not both howl.

In logical notation, the argument looks as follows:

> (4) $-A \lor -B$
> (5) $-B \rightarrow -C$
> _____
> ∴ (6) $-(A \land C)$

Now consider the following truth-table:

| A B C | −A ∨ −B | −B → −C | −(A ∧ C) |
|---|---|---|---|
| T T T | F T F F T | F T T F T | F T T T |
| T T F | F T F F T | F T T T F | T T F F |
| T F T | F T T T F | T F F F T | F T T T |
| T F F | F T T T F | T F T T F | T T F F |
| F T T | T F T F T | F T T F T | T F F T |
| F T F | T F T F T | F T T T F | T F F F |
| F F T | T F T T F | T F F F T | T F F T |
| F F F | T F T T F | T F T T F | T F F F |

Is it clear how we constructed this truth-table? There are three initial columns off to the left, one for each of the three atomics that appears in the premises and the conclusion: 'A', 'B', and 'C'. (The rows, once again, are the *horizontal* arrays of Ts and Fs, and the columns are the *vertical* arrays.) There are *eight* rows in our truth-table, precisely because there are *three* atomics. (The magical formula for determining the number of rows, you will recall, is 2 raised to the power of *n*, where *n* is the number of atomics. In this case, then, where there are three atomics, the number of rows in our truth-table will be 2 raised to the power of 3, i.e., 8.)

Take a look at the first premise column—the '−A ∨ −B' column. If you were constructing this truth-table from scratch, where do you suppose that you'd begin entering your Ts and Fs? Under the first dash? Under the 'A'? Under the wedge? Under the second dash? Or under the 'B'?

*Not* in each of the rows of the 'wedge' column; you don't know the truth-value that a disjunction takes on in each row until you know the truth-value that each of its disjuncts takes on in that row. So before you can determine the truth-value that '−A ∨ −B' takes on in each row, you must first determine the truth-values that the disjuncts '−A' and '−B' take on in that row.

Nor would you begin entering your Ts and Fs in each of the rows of the two 'dash' columns: you don't know the truth-value that a negation takes on in each row until you know the truth-value that that which is being negated takes on in that row. So before you can determine the truth-values that '—A' and '—B' take on in each row, you must first determine the truth-values that 'A' and 'B' take on in that row.

And so you begin by entering your Ts and Fs in each row of the 'A' column and in each row of the 'B' column. (The order here—whether you begin with the 'A' column or the 'B' column—is irrelevant.) Next you enter truth-values in each row of the '—A' column, i.e., under the dash of '—A', and in each row of the '—B' column, i.e., under the dash of '—B'. (Once again, the order here—whether you begin with the '—A' column or the '—B' column—is irrelevant.) Finally you enter truth-values in each row of the '—A ∨ —B' column, i.e., under the wedge. Done.

The same reasoning applies to the '—B → —C' column. You don't know the truth-value of a conditional until you first know the truth-values of its antecedent and its consequent. In this instance, the antecedent is the negation of an atomic and so is the consequent. And you don't know the truth-value of the negation of an atomic until you first know the truth-value of the atomic being negated. So the first step is to enter Ts and Fs in the 'B' column and the 'C' column. The second step is to enter the '—B' truth-values under the first dash, i.e., in the first dash column, and the '—C' truth-values under the second dash, i.e., in the second dash column. (Again, it doesn't matter which of these, the '—B' column or the '—C' column, you address first.) The final step is to enter the '—B → —C' truth-values under the arrow, i.e., in the arrow column.

Obviously the same reasoning applies to the '—(A ∧ C)' column too. You don't know the truth-value of the negation of a conjunction until you first know the truth-value of the conjunction. And you don't know the truth-value of a conjunction until you first know the truth-values of its conjuncts. So the first step is to enter Ts and Fs in the 'A' column and the 'C' column. The second step is to enter the 'A ∧ C' truth-values under the caret, i.e., in the caret column. The final step is to enter the '—(A ∧ C)' truth-values under the dash, i.e., in the dash column.

Now what do you discover about this argument? As it turns out, there are four rows—the fourth, fifth, sixth, and eighth—where every premise is true. In each of these rows, however, the conclusion is also true. In other words, there is *no* row (i.e., no interpretation, i.e., no assignment of truth-values to the atomics) where every premise is true and the conclusion is false. Therefore, by the definition of 'valid', the argument is a *valid* argument.

Suppose that we tinker with this argument ever so slightly. Suppose that we add a dash to 'C' in the conclusion. The argument would then look as follows:

$$(7) -A \lor -B$$
$$(8) -B \to -C$$
$$\therefore (9) -(A \land -C)$$

Its resulting truth-table would then look like this:

| A B C | —A ∨ —B | —B → —C | —(A ∧ —C) |
|-------|---------|---------|-----------|
| T T T | F T F F T | F T T F T | T T F F T |
| T T F | F T F F T | F T T T F | F T T T F |
| T F T | F T T T F | T F F F T | T T F F T |
| T F F | F T T T F | T F T T F | F T T T F |
| F T T | T F T F T | F T T F T | T F F F T |
| F T F | T F T F T | F T T T F | T F F T F |
| F F T | T F T T F | T F F F T | T F F F T |
| F F F | T F T T F | T F T T F | T F F T F |

Notice the fourth row: in that row each of the premises is true and the conclusion is false. This means that there is at least one interpretation for which every premise is true and the conclusion is false. *This* argument, therefore, is invalid.

Definition:     A *counterexample* is an interpretation that makes every premise true and the conclusion false.

Obviously every invalid argument has at least one counterexample. Equally obviously, no valid argument has a counterexample. We list the counterexamples—the assignments of truth-values to the atomics that show that the argument is invalid—as follows:

| A | B | C |
|---|---|---|
| T | F | F |

From a *theoretical* point of view, truth-tables are quite miraculous: they provide us with a perfectly *mechanical* method for determining whether an argument is valid or invalid. (Remember this in Chapters 3 and 4, when you are struggling with *non-mechanical* derivations of conclusions from premises.) 'Mechanical' means, of course, that we could (effortlessly) program a computer to answer the question 'Is this argument valid or invalid?' In other words: no thought required.

From a *practical* point of view, however, truth-tables are a bit of a nuisance: they require a good deal of time, ink, and paper. Try to imagine constructing a truth-table with *four* atomics (sixteen rows) or more. Moreover their very mindlessness—a *theoretical* virtue, to be sure—is a *practical* curse: you don't want your neurons to go flabby on you while you're studying logic.

# Exercises

For each of the following arguments, construct a truth-table to show whether it is valid or invalid. Place either a T or an F under each atomic, as well as under each connective. If the argument is valid, write 'Valid' next to it. If it is invalid, write 'Invalid' next to it, and list each counterexample.

1.  P → (Q ∧ R)
    −Q ∨ −R
    ──────────
    ∴ −P

2.  P → Q
    −(Q ∧ −R)
    ──────────
    ∴ −R ∨ P

3.  −P ∨ Q
    − −Q → − −R
    ──────────
    ∴ −(P ∧ −R)

4.    $\dfrac{-(P \wedge -P) \wedge Q}{\therefore P \leftrightarrow -Q}$

5.    $P \leftrightarrow (Q \leftrightarrow R)$
      $\underline{\quad Q \leftrightarrow (P \leftrightarrow R) \quad}$
      $\therefore R \leftrightarrow (P \leftrightarrow Q)$

6.    $\dfrac{-(P \vee Q) \rightarrow (-P \wedge R)}{\therefore (--P \vee -R) \rightarrow -(-P \wedge -Q)}$

7.    $\dfrac{-P \wedge (-Q \vee -R)}{\therefore -(P \vee Q) \vee -(P \vee R)}$

8.    $-(P \leftrightarrow -Q)$
      $(P \wedge Q) \rightarrow -R$
      $\underline{\quad -P \vee -Q \quad}$
      $\therefore -(P \wedge R)$

9.    $(P \wedge Q) \vee [(-P \wedge R) \vee (Q \wedge -R)]$
      $P \rightarrow -Q$
      $\underline{\quad -(-P \wedge R) \quad}$
      $\therefore -(-Q \vee -R)$

10.   $P \rightarrow (Q \rightarrow R)$
      $\underline{\quad -[(-Q \vee R) \wedge -P] \quad}$
      $\therefore -(-P \wedge Q)$

# B. The Short Method

Enter the Short Method. The Short Method is indeed a *short* method *iff* one of the following is the case. (1) The argument is valid. (2) It's invalid; you want to know what the counterexamples are; and there are at most two counterexamples. (3) It's invalid; you want to know only whether it's valid or invalid; i.e., you don't care about how many counterexamples there are or indeed what they are.

Consider the last of the arguments in the previous section:

$$(7)\ -A \lor -B$$
$$(8)\ -B \to -C$$
$$\therefore (9)\ -(A \land -C)$$

Using the Short Method, your goal is to discover *the* (or at least *a*) counterexample. If you succeed, you know that the argument is invalid. If you fail, you know that it's valid. After all, failing to produce a counterexample means that there is no interpretation, i.e., no assignment of truth-values to the atomics, that makes the premises true and the conclusion false. So the argument must be valid.

To discover the (or a) counterexample you try to come up with an interpretation that makes the premises true and the conclusion false. First you place a 'T' under the main connective of each of the premises (i.e., under the wedge in the first premise and under the arrow in the second), and then you place an 'F' under the main connective of the conclusion (i.e., under the leftmost dash). At the end of (a very brief) Round One, the argument should look like this:

$$-A \lor -B$$
$$\text{T}$$

$$-B \to -C$$
$$\text{T}$$

$$-(A \land -C)$$
$$\text{F}$$

Consider the first premise: there are *three* ways to make a disjunction come out true. Move on. (You want to enter, to the extent that it's possible to do so, *only* those truth-values that you are *forced* to enter, rather than those that you *choose* to enter.) Consider the second premise: there are *three* ways to make a conditional come out true. Move on. Consider the conclusion: there's only *one* way to make a negation come out false. No choice here. Begin here. Place an 'F' under the dash.

The conclusion is the negation of a conjunction. For the negation of a conjunction to be *false*, the conjunction that is being negated must be *true*. Place a 'T' under the caret. For the conjunction 'A ∧ −C' to be true, 'A' has to be true and '−C' has to be true. Place a 'T' under the 'A' and place another 'T' under the dash. For '−C' to be true, 'C' must be false. Place an 'F' under the 'C'. At the end of Round Two, the argument should look like this:

-A ∨ −B
   T

-B → −C
   T

−(A ∧ −C)
F  T T T F

You now know that for the conclusion to be false, 'A' has to be true and 'C' has to be false. If 'A' has to be true in the conclusion, it has to be true in the first premise. Place a 'T' under 'A' in the first premise. Therefore '−A' in the first premise has to be false. Place an 'F' under the dash of '−A' in the first premise. You are trying to make the first premise come out true. For a disjunction to come out *true* when its left disjunct, '−A', is *false*, its right disjunct, '−B', has to be *true*. Place a 'T' under the dash of '−B' in the first premise. Therefore 'B' has to be *false*. Place an 'F' under 'B' in the first premise. At the end of Round Three, the argument should look like this:

-A ∨ −B
F T T TF

-B → −C
   T

−(A ∧ −C)
F  TT TF

If 'B' has to be false in the first premise, it has to be false in the second premise. Place an 'F' under 'B' in the second premise. Therefore '−B'

has to be true. Place a 'T' under the dash of '—B' in the second premise.
If 'C' has to be false in the conclusion, it has to be false in the second
premise. Place an 'F' under 'C' in the second premise. Therefore '—C'
has to be true. Place a 'T' under the dash of '—C' in the second premise. Obviously, if '—B' is true and '—C' is true, then '—B → —C' must
also be true. You have just succeeded in making the second premise
true. At the end of Round Four, the argument should look like this:

$$—A \lor —B$$
$$F\,T\ T\ T\ F$$

$$—B \rightarrow —C$$
$$T\,F\ T\ \ T\ F$$

$$—(A \land —C)$$
$$F\ T\ T\ T\ F$$

Question: Is the argument valid or invalid?

Preliminary answer: It's invalid if there's at least one counterexample; otherwise it's valid.

Follow-up question: Is there at least one counterexample?

Final answer: Of course there is. If 'A' is true, if 'B' is false, and if
'C' is false, the premises come out true and the conclusion comes out
false. In other words, there's at least one interpretation—indeed, in this
case there's *exactly* one interpretation—that makes the premises true
and the conclusion false. Therefore the argument is invalid. You list the
counterexample as follows:

| A | B | C |
|---|---|---|
| T | F | F |

Now suppose that you focus on the first argument in the previous
section:

$$(7)\ —A \lor —B$$
$$(8)\ —B \rightarrow —C$$
$$\overline{\phantom{(8)\ —B \rightarrow —C}}$$
$$\therefore (9)\ —(A \land C)$$

At the end of Round One, the argument looks like this:

$$—A \lor —B$$
$$T$$

$$—B \to —C$$
$$T$$

$$—(A \land C)$$
$$F$$

At the end of Round Two, it looks like this:

$$—A \lor —B$$
$$T$$

$$—B \to —C$$
$$T$$

$$—(A \land C)$$
$$F \quad T \ T \ T$$

At the end of Round Three it looks like this:

$$—A \lor —B$$
$$F \ T \ T \ T \ F$$

$$—B \to —C$$
$$T$$

$$—(A \land C)$$
$$F \quad T \ T \ T$$

Midway through Round Four, it looks either like this:

$$—A \lor —B$$
$$F \ T \ T \ \ T \ F$$

$$-B \rightarrow -C$$
$$\text{TF } \text{ T}$$

$$-(A \wedge C)$$
$$\text{F } \text{T T T}$$

or like this:

$$-A \vee -B$$
$$\text{F T T T F}$$

$$-B \rightarrow -C$$
$$\text{T F T}$$

$$-(A \wedge C)$$
$$\text{F T T T}$$

Suppose the former alternative. The second premise is a conditional that you are trying to make come out true. Its antecedent is true. Therefore its consequent, '−C', had better come out true. Place a 'T' under the dash, and therefore place an 'F' under 'C'. The argument should look like this:

$$-A \vee -B$$
$$\text{F T T T F}$$

$$-B \rightarrow -C$$
$$\text{TF T TF}$$

$$-(A \wedge C)$$
$$\text{F T T T}$$

Question: Have you succeeded in discovering a counterexample?

Answer: Well, yes and no. It turns out that to make the premises come out true and the conclusion come out false, you were forced to make at least one of the atomics—'C' in this instance—come out *both* true (in the conclusion) *and* false (in the second premise). In other words, if this argument is invalid, one of its atomics must be both true and false. But no atomic—indeed, no sentence—can be *both* true *and* false. Therefore this argument *isn't* invalid. Therefore it's *valid*.

Now suppose the second alternative. The second premise, once again, is a conditional that you are trying to make come out true. Its consequent is false. Therefore its antecedent, '—B', has to be false. Place an 'F' under the dash, and therefore place a 'T' under 'B'. The argument should look like this:

> —A ∨ —B
> F T T T F
>
> —B → —C
> F T T  F T
>
> —(A ∧ C)
> F  T T T

Once again you find yourself in a pickle—a different pickle, to be sure, but a pickle nonetheless. A moment ago, it was 'C' that you were forced to make both true and false. Now it's 'B'. No matter. The point is this: the *only* way to make the premises of this argument come out true, and the conclusion come out false, is by making at least *one* of the atomics that appears in the argument *both* true *and* false. And that, of course, is simply too high a price to pay; *no* proposition is both true and false. Conclusion: there is no counterexample, and therefore the argument is valid.

## Exercises

For each of the following arguments, use the Short Method—and *not* truth-tables—to show, whether it is valid or invalid. Place either a 'T' or an 'F' under each atomic, as well as under each connective. If the argument is valid, circle one occurrence of the atomic to which you were *forced* to assign a 'T', and circle one occurrence of the same atomic to which you were *forced* to assign an 'F'. Write 'Valid' next to the argument. If the argument is invalid, write 'Invalid' next to it, and list each counterexample.

1.   $\dfrac{P \wedge (Q \vee R)}{\therefore (P \vee Q) \wedge (P \vee R)}$

2.   $\dfrac{-(P \wedge Q)}{\therefore P \rightarrow -Q}$

3.   $\dfrac{P \rightarrow (Q \wedge R)}{\therefore -(Q \wedge R) \rightarrow -P}$

4.   $\dfrac{P \leftrightarrow (Q \wedge R)}{\therefore -[P \wedge (Q \wedge R)]}$

5.   $\dfrac{(P \vee -Q) \rightarrow (P \wedge -R)}{\therefore (-P \wedge -R) \rightarrow (--P \vee -Q)}$

6.   $\dfrac{-P \vee (-Q \wedge -R)}{\therefore -(P \wedge Q) \vee -(P \wedge R)}$

7.   $\begin{array}{l} -(-P \leftrightarrow Q) \\ (P \wedge Q) \rightarrow -R \\ \underline{-(P \wedge -Q)} \\ \therefore -P \vee -R \end{array}$

8.   $\begin{array}{l} (P \wedge Q) \vee [(-P \wedge -R) \vee (-Q \wedge R)] \\ P \rightarrow -Q \\ \underline{-(-P \wedge R)} \\ \therefore -Q \rightarrow -R \end{array}$

9.   $\begin{array}{l} P \wedge (Q \rightarrow R) \\ \underline{-[(-Q \wedge R) \vee -P]} \\ \therefore -(-P \wedge Q) \end{array}$

10.   $\begin{array}{l} -(P \wedge -Q) \leftrightarrow (R \vee -P) \\ \underline{-(Q \vee R) \leftrightarrow -R} \\ \therefore Q \rightarrow P \end{array}$

# 5. Tautologies, Contradictions, and Contingent Sentences

Like connectives and like ice cream, sentences come in a variety of flavors. Unlike connectives and unlike ice cream, sentences (at least where truth-tables are concerned) come in exactly three flavors: tautologies, semantic contradictions, and contingent sentences.

Definition:    A *tautology* is a sentence that is true for every interpretation.

First consider the sentence, 'Either Ardbeg will be hanged at dawn or Ardbeg won't be hanged at dawn.' A truth-table would show this sentence to be a tautology:

| A | A ∨ −A |
|---|--------|
| T | T T F T |
| F | F T T F |

If you were to spend the whole of your life uttering nothing but tautologies, you could never be charged with lies or even with mere falsehoods. "The weather tomorrow? Oh, either it'll rain or it won't." "The stock market tomorrow? Oh, either it'll go up or it won't." "The North Zedmenistanis? Oh, either they'll invade tomorrow or they won't."

You'd pay a stiff price, however, for *never ever* getting it wrong: your sentences would be entirely *uninformative*; they would be entirely *void of all content*; they would say *nothing*. Even though tautologies, in ordinary conversation, are generally without value, in logic they occupy a rather exalted status. They constitute one species of *logical truth*. We shall bump up against them again in Chapter 4, and we shall bump up against a second species of logical truth in Chapter 6.

Definition:    A *semantic contradiction* is a sentence that is false for every interpretation.

Consider the sentence 'Ardbeg will be hanged at dawn and Ardbeg will not be hanged at dawn.' A truth-table would show this sentence to be a semantic contradiction:

| A | A ∧ −A |
|---|--------|
| T | T F FT |
| F | F F TF |

**Definition:**  A *contingent* sentence is a sentence that is true for at least one interpretation and that is false for at least one interpretation.

Consider the sentence 'Ardbeg will be hanged at dawn.' A truth-table would show this sentence to be a contingent sentence:

| A | A |
|---|---|
| T | T |
| F | F |

A contingent sentence is called a *contingent* sentence because its truth-value, unlike the truth-value of a tautology or a semantic contradiction, is *contingent* on, i.e., is *dependent* on, the way the world is. Notice that there's at least one interpretation that makes 'A' come out true: see the first row of its truth-table. Notice too that there's at least one interpretation that makes 'A' come out false: see the second row of its truth-table.

If you wish to know the *actual* truth-value of a contingent sentence, you can't simply examine its truth-table. You have to examine the world, and to do this you have to use one or more of your five senses. You wish to determine the truth-value of the sentence 'It's raining'? What do you do? You *peer* out the door of your tent or you *listen* for the telltale pitter-patter sound on the roof of your tent. On the other hand, it should be obvious that, in order to determine the truth-value of either the sentence 'It's raining *or* it's not raining', or the sentence 'It's raining *and* it's not raining', you don't have to examine the world. You don't search for empirical evidence. You don't use your five senses. And in particular, you don't listen for the telltale pitter-patter sound on the roof of your tent. Almost all of the declarative sentences that you utter in ordinary conversation are of the contingent sort.

Definition:   A *consistent* sentence is a sentence that is true for at least one interpretation.

Don't think of a *consistent* sentence as a *fourth* kind of sentence: it's nothing more than a sentence that isn't a semantic contradiction.

Just when you thought that you were getting it, you're now a bit confused. "What's the difference," you ask, "between a *contingent* sentence and a *consistent* sentence?" Well, a contingent sentence comes out true for at least one interpretation, *and it comes out false for at least one interpretation*. A consistent sentence, on the other hand, comes out true for at least one interpretation, *period*. All contingent sentences are consistent, but not all consistent sentences are contingent. Think of a tautology. It comes out true for *every* interpretation, and therefore (obviously) it comes out true for *at least one* interpretation. As such, a tautology is a *consistent* sentence. A tautology, however, does *not* come out false for *any* interpretation—and as such, a tautology is not a *contingent* sentence.

The Short Method is a convenient instrument for quickly categorizing sentences as tautologous, contradictory, consistent, or contingent. If you smell a tautology, plug in truth-values so as to *falsify* it, i.e., so as to make it come out *false*. If you can't make it come out false, i.e., if there's no interpretation for which it comes out false, then it must come out true for every interpretation—in which case it's a tautology.

If you smell a semantic contradiction, try to make it come out *true*. If you can't make it come out true, i.e., if there's no interpretation for which it comes out true, then it must come out false for every interpretation—in which case it's a semantic contradiction.

If you smell a contingent sentence, try to make it come out true. If you succeed, then try to make it come out false. If you succeed again, then you know that there's at least one interpretation for which it comes out true, and that there's at least one interpretation for which it comes out false; i.e., you know that it's a contingent sentence.

A warning. Suppose that you smell a tautology. Suppose that you try to make it come out *true*. Suppose that it *does* come out true. What are you now entitled to conclude? Only that it's not a *semantic contradiction*.

But you haven't the foggiest idea whether it's a *tautology*, on the one hand, or a *contingent* sentence, on the other. So now you have to try to make it come out false. If you succeed, you know that it's contingent; if you fail, you know that it's a tautology. Moral of the story: if you smell a tautology, don't waste your time by first trying to make it come out *true* and by then trying to make it come out *false*. Simply try to make it come out *false*—and if you fail then you know that it's a tautology. By the same token, if you smell a semantic contradiction, don't try to make it come out *false*; try to make it come out *true*—and if you fail then you know that it's a semantic contradiction.

# Exercises

For each of the following, use the Short Method, and *not* truth-tables, to show that the first four are tautologies, the next four are semantic contradictions, and the final two are contingent sentences.

1. $[P \lor (Q \land R)] \to [(P \lor Q) \land (P \lor R)]$
2. $P \to [--Q \to (P \lor P)]$
3. $(P \to -Q) \to -(P \land Q)$
4. $[P \to (Q \to R)] \to [(P \to Q) \to (P \to R)]$
5. $-(P \to Q) \land -(P \land -Q)$
6. $-(P \lor Q) \land (-P \to Q)$
7. $(-P \to P) \land (P \to -P)$
8. $-[(P \land Q) \lor (P \to -Q)]$
9. $(P \lor P) \to -(P \lor P)$
10. $(-P \to -Q) \leftrightarrow (-Q \to -P)$

# 6. A Formal System

The following discussion will strike you as dry, abstract, boring, and tedious. From a theoretical point of view, however, it is very important.

The title of this section says it all: "A *Formal* System." Never mind that you don't yet know what a *system* is, much less a *formal* system. You know this much: the focus will be on the *forms* of things, rather than on their *content*.

Imagine that this isn't a *logic* book. Imagine that it's a book about *games*. Think of chess. One of the first things that you learn in chess is how each of the pieces moves. You don't learn what each of the pieces *represents* or *stands for*—and that's because none of the chess pieces *represents* or *stands for* anything. The bishop is simply a piece that moves diagonally—but only diagonally. And the rook is simply a piece that moves forward, backward, or sideways—but not diagonally. Chess is a game without *content*. There are rules that determine how you may move each of the pieces, but under normal circumstances, when you make one move rather than another, the move doesn't *mean* or *signify* anything; i.e., you aren't conveying to anyone any information about the world beyond the chessboard.

Of course you could easily imagine a context where you would be conveying such information. You could imagine two spies 'playing chess' at a dingy hotel bar in a war zone at the edge of nowhere. One move might signify an impending air strike; another move might signify a thwarted kidnapping. Under such circumstances, however, such a game wouldn't really be a *game* at all. Either the spies would merely be pretending to play chess, or they would be playing chess, but the play would be secondary to the real work of conveying secret information to one another. Logic isn't like *fake* chess. Logic is *formal*, i.e., void of content. Logic is like *real* chess.

You are about to witness the construction of a formal system.

Definition:     A *formal system* consists of two components—
                a formal language and a deductive apparatus.

Definition:     A *deductive apparatus* consists of either a set of
                axioms and a set of derivation rules, or (merely)
                a set of derivation rules.

If you want to have *some* idea of what an *axiomatic* formal system would look like, think of your high school geometry course, and then think of Euclid's axioms and the vast number of theorems that you cranked out of those axioms. Mercifully, the deductive apparatus in *this* book consists of only a set of derivation rules. You are thereby spared the unimaginable challenge that operating with axiomatic systems of logic involves. Derivation rules, the focus of the next chapter, are rules that allow you to proceed from premises to conclusion, step by step by *logical* step.

> Definition:    A *formal language* consists of both a set of symbols and a set of formation rules.

We shall call our formal language, the language of Propositional Logic, $L_1$.

# A. The Symbols of $L_1$

The set of symbols of $L_1$ consists of mere squiggle-marks that we shall simply call 'propositional symbols', 'numerical subscripts', 'connectives', and 'parentheses'. The following are the symbols/squiggle-marks of $L_1$:

1. Any of the uppercase letters of the English alphabet, 'A' through 'Z', with or without a numerical subscript, is a *propositional symbol.*
2. '—' is the *dash.*
3. '∧' is the *caret.*
4. '∨' is the *wedge.*
5. '→' is the *arrow.*
6. '↔' is the *double-arrow.*
7. '(' and ')' are the *left parenthesis* and the *right parenthesis,* respectively. (For reasons of convenience, we shall supplement these with square brackets and curly braces: '[', ']', '{', '}'.)
8. '$_1$', '$_2$', '$_3$', ... are *numerical subscripts*. If we run out of propositional symbols, we can add numerical subscripts to them as follows: '$A_1$', '$A_2$', '$A_3$', etc.

It's a bit misleading to use the word 'symbols', and to call these the *symbols* of $L_1$, the language of Propositional Logic. After all, symbols *symbolize*—and, at least at *this* stage of the game, our 'symbols' do nothing of the sort. You mustn't think that any of them *stands for* something or (for that matter) *does* anything. In particular you mustn't think that a propositional symbol *stands for* a proposition, or that a connective *operates* on one or more sentences. $L_1$ is (once again) a *formal* language, and so in this section, these 'symbols' are merely uninterpreted squiggle-marks.

Eventually, of course, they *will* do exactly what you would expect them to do. Eventually we shall use the propositional symbols as bona fide symbols that really do symbolize, i.e., stand for, propositions. And eventually we shall use the connectives as devices that really do operate on propositions, etc. While we are constructing a purely *formal* language, however, we want to keep the squiggle-marks from being contaminated, as it were, by any suggestion that they might actually *mean* something or *do* something. In this section, therefore, you are to think of them as every bit as meaningless as the chess pieces in chess.

## B. The Formation Rules of $L_1$

Some strings of symbols in the English language (e.g., letters of the alphabet, numerals, and punctuation marks) constitute grammatically correct sentences, and some don't. Likewise, some strings of symbols in $L_1$ constitute well-formed formulas and some don't.

### The Definition of a Formula of $L_1$

Definition:    A *formula* of $L_1$ is any string of symbols of $L_1$.

Unsurprisingly, the following are all formulas of $L_1$:

$P_1 \rightarrow Q_2$
$(P \rightarrow Q)$
$(P \rightarrow Q) \wedge -R_3$

Surprisingly or not, the following are all formulas of $L_1$ as well:

$(P \rightarrow Q$
$P \wedge\vee Q$
$)P- \vee QR$
$(_1(_2$

After all, each of the above is indeed a sequence (or string) of symbols of $L_1$—and therefore, by definition, each is a formula of $L_1$. The following, however, are *not* formulas of $L_1$:

P or Q

P, Q, ∧ R

Neither 'or' nor 'o' nor 'r' is a symbol of $L_1$. Nor, for that matter, is the comma.

So much for the formulas. Obviously what you really want is to be able to distinguish a formula that you can work with from one that you can't. Your goal, in other words, is to be able to distinguish a grammatically *respectable* formula from a grammatically *unrespectable* formula, i.e., a *well-formed* formula from an *ill-formed* formula. A well-formed formula is known as a *wff*. An ill-formed formula is known simply as either an ill-formed formula or a non-*wff*.

## The Definition of a Well-Formed Formula of $L_1$

Behold the formation rules (the rules of grammar, as it were) of $L_1$. These are the rules that allow you to construct all of $L_1$'s *wffs* and none of its non-*wffs*. As such, they constitute the very definition of a *wff*.

1. Any propositional symbol is a *wff*.
2. Any propositional symbol followed by a numerical subscript is a *wff*.
3. If '△' is a *wff* then '—△' is a *wff*.
4. If '△' is a *wff* and if 'O' is a *wff*, then '(△ ∧ O)' is a *wff*.
5. If '△' is a *wff* and if 'O' is a *wff*, then '(△ ∨ O)' is a *wff*.
6. If '△' is a *wff* and if 'O' is a *wff*, then '(△ → O)' is a *wff*.
7. If '△' is a *wff* and if 'O' is a *wff*, then '(△ ↔ O)' is a *wff*.
8. The Rule of Closure: Nothing is to count as a *wff* unless it has been obtained by one or more applications of Rules 1–7.

Here's how one might apply the rules. In light of the first rule, 'P' is a *wff*. In light of the third rule, '—P' is a *wff*. In light of the first rule once again, 'Q' is a *wff*. In light of the fourth rule, because '—P' is a *wff* and because 'Q' is a *wff*, '(—P ∧ Q)' is a *wff*. In light of the first rule, 'R' is a *wff*. In light of the fifth rule, because '(—P ∧ Q)' is a *wff* and because 'R' is a *wff*, '((—P ∧ Q) ∨ R)' is a *wff*. In light of the third rule, because '((—P ∧ Q) ∨ R)' is a *wff*, '—((—P ∧ Q) ∨ R)' is a *wff*. In light of the first rule, 'S' is a *wff*. In light of the sixth rule, because '—((—P ∧ Q) ∨ R)' is a *wff* and because 'S' is a *wff*, '(—((—P ∧ Q) ∨ R) → S)' is a *wff*. And so on. . . .

In practice, as it turns out, your attitude toward these rules can be somewhat relaxed. First, in practice you won't actually require the numerical subscripts. In practice, in other words, twenty-six propositional symbols will *more* than suffice.

Second, you should feel free to introduce square brackets and curly braces as punctuation devices in addition to parentheses. The problem with using only parentheses is that it's often difficult to see which *left* parenthesis is associated with which *right* parenthesis. In the course of constructing your *wffs*, follow the same order that you've been following thus far. Introduce parentheses first. Surround the parentheses by square brackets. Surround the square brackets by curly braces. Surround the curly braces by parentheses. And so on. Thus you would write the last *wff* in the second-to-last paragraph as follows: '{—[(—P ∧ Q) ∨ R] → S}'.

Third, it is permissible, in practice, to drop *outermost* parentheses. Consider the following formulas:

  (1) (P → Q)
  (2) P → Q

According to the formation rules, (1) is a *wff* but (2) isn't. According to the sixth rule, conditionals, once constructed, must be enclosed within parentheses. Indeed, according to the rules, *every wff,* once constructed, with the exception of atomics and negations, must be enclosed within parentheses.

Question: Is the parentheses requirement *really* necessary?

Answer: Yes and no; i.e., theory-wise, yes; but practice-wise, no. In laying down our formation rules, it *is* necessary to cite outermost parentheses. Here's why. In light of the first rule, 'P' is a *wff*. In light of the first rule once again, 'Q' is a *wff*. In light of the sixth rule, because 'P' is a *wff* and because 'Q' is a *wff*, then '(P → Q)' is a *wff*. Now suppose that the rules *didn't* require outermost parentheses. In that case, 'P → Q' would be a *wff*. Fine. No problem, right? But wait. In light of the first rule, 'R' is a *wff*. In light of the fourth rule, because 'P → Q' is a *wff* and because 'R' is a *wff*, then 'P → Q ∧ R' is a *wff*. But you don't want 'P → Q ∧ R' to be a *wff*; you want it to be an *ill-formed* formula. To prevent this pickle from arising, we introduce the outermost-parentheses requirement so that 'P → Q' is *not* a *wff* but '(P → Q)' *is*.

From a *theoretical* point of view, in other words, i.e., in the course of formulating our formation rules, it *is* necessary to cite outermost parentheses. Otherwise, as you've just seen, the rules would countenance the creation of so-called *wffs* that we would rather treat as non-*wffs*. In actual practice, however, you may relax the rules and drop *outermost* parentheses, so long (of course) as there is nothing to the left of your leftmost parenthesis and nothing to the right of your rightmost parenthesis.

Question: Is it permissible to relax the rules concerning parentheses in other ways as well?

Answer: Yes, there are other contexts in which you may eliminate parentheses. But you may do so only in the course of translating into logical notation—not in the course of constructing either derivations or proofs.

Remember: the whole point of parentheses is to disambiguate. So if you have a *wff* that contains parentheses, and if the *wff* would be unambiguous without the parentheses, then it's fine to eliminate the parentheses. A string of conjuncts, e.g., 'P ∧ Q ∧ R' is unambiguous; i.e., 'P ∧ (Q ∧ R)' is logically equivalent to '(P ∧ Q) ∧ R'. A string of disjuncts, e.g., 'P ∨ Q ∨ R', is also unambiguous; i.e., 'P ∨ (Q ∨ R)' is logically equivalent to '(P ∨ Q) ∨ R'. Finally, a string of *wffs* linked by double arrows, e.g., 'P ↔ Q ↔ R', is also unambiguous; i.e., 'P ↔ (Q ↔ R)' is logically equivalent to '(P ↔ Q) ↔ R'. So in the course of translating into logical notation, it's perfectly fine to eliminate parentheses where these three sorts of *wffs* are concerned.

But it's not fine to eliminate parentheses where a string of *wffs* linked by arrows, e.g., 'P → Q → R', is concerned. 'P → Q → R' is ambiguous: 'P → (Q → R)' is not logically equivalent to '(P → Q) → R'. Nor, of course, is it fine to eliminate parentheses where you have a mishmash of connectives. 'P ∧ Q ∨ R', for example, is obviously ambiguous; i.e., 'P ∧ (Q ∨ R)' is not equivalent to '(P ∧ Q) ∨ R'. So you must disambiguate 'P ∧ Q ∨ R'—and any formula containing a mishmash of connectives—via parentheses.

In practice, you will never (or almost never) actually use these formation rules. In practice, you will rely on your (educated) intuitions about what does, and what doesn't, constitute a *wff*. And in practice, your (educated) intuitions will almost always be spot-on.

Question: So then why all the fuss and bother over these rules?

First answer: The set of symbols, on the one hand, and the formation rules, on the other, constitute the very *essence* of $L_1$. As such, they reveal just how very different the *artificial* language $L_1$ is from any *natural* language, i.e., from the sort of language that you grew up speaking. Do you think that any natural language has a *finite* number of rules that allow you to distinguish grammatically correct from grammatically incorrect strings of words? Of course not—and for at least two reasons. First, the rules of grammar of a particular natural language typically change over time, such that what constitutes a grammatically correct (or incorrect) string of words at one point in time may prove to be a grammatically incorrect (or correct) string of words at a later point in time. Second, even at any given time, grammarians often disagree among themselves about what the correct rules of grammar of a particular natural language actually are. The beauty of $L_1$ consists in the knowledge that with a *finite* number of rules—eight, to be precise—you can construct, in a *finite* number of steps, *all possible wffs* that can be formulated in $L_1$—and no non-*wffs*. So $L_1$ really is radically different from any natural language—and you may find this difference quite interesting.

Second answer: By exhibiting the essence of $L_1$, through its set of symbols and its formation rules, you can then determine just how *powerful* $L_1$ is. In the next section, you will see that its powers of expression are indeed quite extraordinary.

One last question in this section. When I spelled out the eight rules that serve to define what constitutes a well-formed formula, I used the symbols '△' and '○'. Why didn't I simply use 'P' and 'Q'? Consider, for example, the third and the fourth rules:

    3.  If '△' is a *wff* then '—△' is a *wff*.
    4.  If '△' is a *wff* and if '○' is a *wff*, then '(△ ∧ ○)' is a *wff*.

You might think that I *could* have (and perhaps therefore *should* have) expressed these rules respectively as follows:

3a.  If 'P' is a *wff* then '—P' is a *wff.*
4a.  If 'P' is a *wff* and if 'Q' is a *wff*, then '(P ∧ Q)' is a *wff.*

To be sure 'P' and 'Q' are propositional *variables*; i.e., each is a propositional symbol that designates any proposition whatsoever. But now take a second look at 3a. It tells you that if 'P' is a *wff* then '—P' is a *wff*; it does *not* tell you that if, say, 'Q' is a *wff* then '—Q' is a *wff.* Obviously, however, you *do* want to be able to say *exactly* that; namely that if 'Q' is a *wff* then '—Q' is a *wff*, and that if '(R → S)' is a *wff* then '—(R → S)' is a *wff.* By the same token, where 4a is concerned, you want to be able to say that if 'R' is a *wff* and if 'S' is a *wff*, then '(R ∧ S)' is a *wff*, and that if '(P → Q)' is a *wff* and if '(R → S)' is a *wff*, then '((P → Q) ∧ (R → S))' is a *wff.*

The problem is that although a propositional variable like 'P' stands for any *proposition*, it doesn't stand for any *wff.* For example, it doesn't stand for the *wff* 'Q' and it doesn't stand for the *wff* 'P → Q'. But you need a symbol that does *just that*—a symbol that stands *for any wff whatsoever* in the formal language $L_1$. And here's the punch line: if a given symbol stands for *any wff whatsoever* in the formal language $L_1$, then that symbol must itself be in a language *distinct from* the formal language $L_1$.

Hence the need for a distinction between two *languages*, or rather, for a distinction between two different *kinds* of language. The first language (e.g., $L_1$) is the one that comprises our logical terms. The second language (e.g., English) is the one by means of which we discuss the former language. The first is known as the *object language*: it's the object of our focus or discussion. The second is known as the *metalanguage.* (The Greek prefix 'meta' has several meanings, among them 'beyond' and 'about'. Thus the metalanguage is a language *beyond* the object language that enables us to talk *about* the object language.)

If this were an Introductory French (or Latin or Greek) course, French (or Latin or Greek) would be the *object language* and English would be the *metalanguage.* As it is, $L_1$ is our object language, and *English*, enriched by a sprinkling of geometric symbols (like '△' and 'O'), is our metalanguage.

Definition:    The *object language* is the language that is the object of discussion.

Definition:    The *metalanguage* is the language through which the discussion of the object language is conducted.

Just as there's a need to distinguish the object language from the metalanguage, so there's a need to distinguish *wffs* in the object language from expressions in the metalanguage that enable us to talk about these *wffs*. Hence the need for '△' and 'O', etc.—or other meta-language expressions that perform the same function. Think of these expressions as *honorary* members of the English language that enable us to refer to the object language *wffs*, i.e., the *wffs* of $L_1$. An expression like '△' lets us designate *any wff* of $L_1$, e.g., 'P' or '—P' or 'P → Q', etc.

The formation rules of $L_1$ do not appear in $L_1$. They appear in the metalanguage. Each of these expressions—'△', 'O', '△ → O', etc.—is a *meta-wff*, a metalinguistic expression that of course is *not* an expression (much less a *wff*) of $L_1$. And here's the point: not one of them stands for a *proposition*. Rather, each of them stands for one or more of the *wffs* of $L_1$. By means of such *metalinguistic* expressions, i.e., by means of such *meta-wffs,* we can refer in English (enriched, once again, by a sprinkling of geometric symbols) to *all* the *wffs* in $L_1$—which is precisely what we need to do in our formation rules.

# 7. Appendix I: Expressive Completeness: Too Few Connectives?

We approach the end of this chapter with a question, and then a question about the meaning of the question:

1.  'Do we have enough truth-functional connectives?'
2.  'What on Earth does the first question *mean?*'

Now close this book for five minutes (or five hours) and try to answer the second question. . . .

For the remainder of this appendix, and in the interest of brevity, I shall use the term 'connective' when what I really mean is 'truth-functional connective'.

What on Earth does it mean to ask whether we have enough connectives, i.e., whether $L_1$ has enough connectives? Well, suppose that we were all sitting around on the eve of the migrations, some fifty thousand years ago, from what we now know as Africa to what we now know as Eurasia. And suppose that we were all logic students. And suppose that our logic instructor had introduced us to the caret, the wedge, the arrow, and the double-arrow—but *not* to the dash. Just suppose that it had not yet dawned on logicians living in that period that the concept of negation was *crucial* for logic. So there we all are, sitting cross-legged around a campfire, and our logic instructor asks us whether the following argument is valid:

(1) If that blur on the horizon is an elephant, then it has extremely long, curved tusks.
(2) But that blur on the horizon doesn't have extremely long, curved tusks.
_____
∴ (3) That blur on the horizon isn't an elephant.

Intuitively, of course the argument strikes us and our fellow logic students as valid. But then we translate it into logical notation, with the goal of showing its validity via the Short Method:

(1a) B → T
(2a) U
_____
∴ (3a) V

Obvious question: Why did we translate (2) as (2a), i.e., as 'U'—instead of as '—T'? For that matter, why did we translate (3) as (3a), i.e., as 'V'—instead of as '—B'?

Obvious answer to each question: Because—*by hypothesis*—we haven't yet realized the importance of the concept of negation, and therefore it hasn't dawned on us to assign a special symbol to it (e.g., the dash). So we have no choice but to treat (2) and (3) as *atomics*—and therefore to assign new propositional constants to them in (2a) and (3a), respectively.

Now consider the translated version of the argument. Is it valid or invalid? The Short Method will show you rather quickly that it's invalid:

(1a) B → T
     T T T
(2a) U
     T
_____
∴ (3a) V
     F

Notice that I have rather effortlessly produced a counterexample. Actually, I could have produced *three* counterexamples: because (1a) is a conditional, there are three different interpretations that will make it come out true when (2a) is true and (3a) is false. I arbitrarily chose one of these interpretations.

So here's the dilemma. Our intuitions entail that the *English-language* argument is *valid*. The Short Method entails that that argument, *translated into logical notation*, is *invalid*. So either we abandon our intuitions and declare the English-language argument to be *invalid*, or we abandon the Short Method (and with it of course, the Truth-Table Method) and declare the translated argument to be *valid*.

Some intuitions it is wise *not* to give up. Our intuition that the English-language argument is valid is one of them. There is nothing complicated about the argument; we often encounter arguments of the same form; and we always judge such arguments to be valid.

At the same time, the Short Method seems unassailable. It hasn't let us down before now; i.e., it's not as though it declared other arguments to be invalid that we have since deemed to be valid.

Fortunately, the dilemma that confronts us isn't a genuine dilemma. We're *not* compelled to choose between two unpalatable alternatives. There is indeed a third possibility.

The third possibility is that our translation of the English-language argument is insufficiently detailed. (Note that 'insufficiently detailed' doesn't mean 'wrong'. It means 'insufficiently detailed'.) In particular, our translation fails to show enough of the *logical structure* of the English-language argument to display the validity of the latter. The solution to the problem is clear: acknowledge the crucial importance for reasoning of the concept of *negation*, and propose a symbol that expresses it, e.g., the dash.

So where exactly is all this going? Well, we currently have five connectives—the dash, the caret, the wedge, the arrow, and the double-arrow. How do we know that we aren't in the exact same position as our imaginary ancestors of fifty thousand years ago? In particular, how do we know that there aren't some connectives out there in Connectives Land (i.e., in the universe of connectives) that we don't have and that can't be expressed by means of some combination of our five? If there are any such connectives, then there are truth-functional sentences that won't be translatable into $L_1$. And in that case, there may well be valid arguments out there in Valid-Arguments Land that we, with our five connectives, won't be able to show, via either the Truth-Table Method or the Short Method, to be valid.

In other words: *How do we know that we have enough connectives?*

Let's start with a not-so-obvious question: How many connectives are there in the universe of connectives? Think, once again, of what a connective, a *truth-functional* connective, is. It's a device that operates on one or more sentences in order to generate a new sentence, such that the truth-value of the new sentence is *entirely* a function of the truth-values of its atomics. It should strike you that there must be at least one connective for each distinct number of atomics whatsoever, regardless of how many atomics we are operating with. The question is: Just how many such connectives must there be? We know, for instance, that there is at least one connective that operates on a single atomic: the dash. (In fact, there are exactly *four* such connectives. Puzzled? Read on.) We know that there are at least four connectives that operate on two atomics: the caret, the wedge, the arrow, and the double-arrow. (In fact, there are exactly *sixteen* such connectives. Still puzzled? Keep reading on.) So how many connectives are there altogether?

You know that one of the purposes of a truth-table is to *define* a particular connective. Corresponding to any connective there must exist exactly one truth-table, and *corresponding to any truth-table there must exist exactly one connective*. So we shall have an answer to the question 'How many connectives are there?' once we have an answer to the question 'How many truth-tables are there—corresponding to one atomic, to two atomics, and to *n* atomics?' Corresponding to one atomic there are exactly *four* truth-tables, and thus exactly *four* connectives. Consider first the truth-table that defines the dash:

| P | —P |
|---|----|
| T | F T |
| F | T F |

Now consider the truth-table that defines a connective that you've never seen before, the connective '∩':

| P | ∩P |
|---|----|
| T | T T |
| F | T F |

To be sure, the connective '∩' is an odd connective. It generates a *wff* that is true if 'P' is true and that is also true if 'P' is false; i.e., it generates a *wff* that is true no matter what—in short, a tautology. So '∩P' is logically equivalent to, and thus has the same meaning as, 'Either P or not-P'.

Now consider the truth-table that defines another connective that you've never seen before, the connective '‖':

| P | ‖P |
|---|----|
| T | T T |
| F | F F |

The connective '‖' generates a *wff* that is true if 'P' is true and that is false if 'P' is false. This connective simply reaffirms 'P' so that '‖' means 'It is the case that …'. Thus if we interpret 'W' to mean 'Washington is the capital of Afghanistan', then '‖W' simply means 'It is the case that Washington is the capital of Afghanistan'.

Finally, consider the truth-table that defines yet another connective that you've never seen before, the connective '★':

| P | ★P |
|---|----|
| T | F T |
| F | F F |

The connective '★' generates a *wff* that is false if 'P' is true and that is also false if 'P' is false; i.e., this connective generates a *wff* that is false no matter what—in short, a semantic contradiction. So '★P' is logically equivalent to, and thus has the same meaning as, 'P and not-P'.

Instead of constructing each of the *four* truth-tables to illustrate the point that corresponding to one atomic there exist exactly four truth-tables, we could simply have constructed the following table:

| P | ∩P | −P | ‖P | ★P |
|---|-----|-----|-----|-----|
| T | TT | FT | TT | FT |
| F | TF | TF | FF | FF |

It should now be clear that there are exactly *four* truth-tables and thus *four* connectives associated with a *single* atomic *wff* 'P'. One connective performs the tautology-generating operation; one performs the negation-generating operation; one performs the reaffirmation-generating operation; and one performs the semantic-contradiction-generating operation.

Question: How many connectives are associated with *two* atomics, 'P' and 'Q'?

Answer: It turns out that corresponding to two atomics there are exactly *sixteen* truth-tables and thus *sixteen* connectives. Instead of constructing each of the sixteen truth-tables, we can simply construct the following table:

| P Q | 1 | 2 | 3 | 4 | 5 | 6 | 7 | 8 | 9 | 10 | 11 | 12 | 13 | 14 | 15 | 16 |
|-----|---|---|---|---|---|---|---|---|---|----|----|----|----|----|----|----|
| T T | T | F | T | F | T | F | T | F | T | F | T | F | T | F | T | F |
| T F | T | T | F | F | T | T | F | F | T | T | F | F | T | T | F | F |
| F T | T | T | T | T | F | F | F | F | T | T | T | T | F | F | F | F |
| F F | T | T | T | T | T | T | T | T | F | F | F | F | F | F | F | F |

At last we're in a position to answer our original question: 'How many truth-functional connectives are there?' As we have just seen, with one atomic there are four distinct connectives. With two atomics there are sixteen distinct connectives. The magic formula (which I cite *without* proof) is as follows. With $n$ atomics there are 2 raised to the power of $2^n$ connectives. In other words, if $n$ is the number of atomics, then the number of distinct connectives that can operate on $n$ atomics is 2 raised to the power of $2^n$. Moral of the story: because there's no theoretical limit to the number of atomics that constitute a given *wff*, there's no theoretical limit to the number of possible connectives.

Question (once again): How do you know that $L_1$, with its five connectives, has *enough* connectives?

Answer: Read on. . . . Let '⇑' be any arbitrarily chosen connective. Call it the *blappo*, and suppose that it operates on *three* atomics. Is the *blappo* a *real* connective? Of course it's a real connective! From three atomics one could construct 256 (2 raised to the power of $2^3$) distinct truth-tables. Corresponding to three atomics, therefore, there must exist 256 connectives—and *blappo* is simply one of them. It doesn't matter that no one has ever used it, and it doesn't matter that I made up the name. All that matters is that there is a truth-table definition of the *blappo*:

| P Q R | ⇑ P Q R |
|-------|---------|
| T T T | T T T  T |
| T T F | T T T  F |
| T F T | F T F  T |
| T F F | F T F  F |
| F T T | F F T  T |
| F T F | F F T  F |
| F F T | F F F  T |
| F F F | T F F  F |

Note that '⇑PQR' comes out true in rows 1, 2, and 8 of the truth-table.

It's now time for a quick question, an even quicker answer, and a problem with a not-so-quick solution.

First, the quick question: As a connective, is the *blappo dispensable* or *indispensable*?

If the *blappo* were *dispensable*, it would be reducible to, or translatable into, one or more of our basic five connectives. In that case—and because it's an arbitrarily chosen connective—it would follow that *any* connective, and therefore *all* connectives, would be reducible to, or translatable into, one or more of our basic five connectives.

If, on the other hand, the *blappo* were *indispensable*, there would be *wffs* containing it that wouldn't be translatable into *wffs* containing only our basic five connectives. And if there were such non-translatable *wffs*, then (once again) there would be arguments that would be valid and whose validity could be revealed *only* by using *wffs* containing the *blappo*.

Now for the quick answer: The *blappo* connective is indeed a *dispensable* connective—one that's translatable into one or more of our basic five connectives—as you are about to see.

And now for the problem with the not-so-quick solution. Close the book (once again, for five minutes or five hours), and try to show that wherever '⇑PQR' appears, it's translatable into a *wff* lacking any occurrences of the *blappo*, and containing only occurrences of (at least some of) our basic five connectives.

Now pay close attention. Here's what you know about '⇑PQR': the *wff* is true just in case:

1. 'P' is true *and* 'Q' is true *and* 'R' is true (as in the first row of the truth-table), *or*
2. 'P' is true *and* 'Q' is true *and* 'R' is false (as in the second row of the truth-table), *or*
3. 'P' is false *and* 'Q' is false *and* 'R' is false (as in the eighth row of the truth-table).

Another way to express what I have just written is as follows:

'⇑PQR' is true just in case '(P ∧ Q ∧ R) ∨ (P ∧ Q ∧ −R) ∨ (−P ∧ −Q ∧ −R)' is true.

So the two *wffs* are logically equivalent to each other: '⇑PQR' and '(P ∧ Q ∧ R) ∨ (P ∧ Q ∧ −R) ∨ (−P ∧ −Q ∧ −R)'. So '⇑PQR' is translatable into a *wff* lacking the *blappo*, and in which are to be found only the caret, the wedge, and the dash—a subset of our basic five connectives. So the *blappo* is indeed a dispensable connective.

This latter *wff*, '(P ∧ Q ∧ R) ∨ (P ∧ Q ∧ −R) ∨ (−P ∧ −Q ∧ −R)', is said to be the *disjunctive normal form* of '⇑PQR'.

Question: What exactly is a disjunctive normal form?

Answer: Read on.

For any given *wff* there are three possibilities: it's a contingent *wff*; it's a tautology; or it's a semantic contradiction. Whichever it is, there's a purely mechanical procedure for generating its disjunctive normal form. Suppose first that the *wff* in question is either a contingent *wff* or a tautology:

1.  Zero in on the first truth-table row where the *wff* comes out true.
2.  For each atomic that comes out true in that row, if any, write down that atomic.
3.  For each atomic that comes out false in that row, if any, write down the negation of that atomic.
4.  Form the conjunction of each of these atomics and negated atomics, and enclose the conjunction in parentheses. (If what you have written down is an atomic and nothing else, that atomic is what is known as the degenerate case of a conjunction; i.e., it counts as a conjunction with exactly one conjunct. If what you have written down is a negated atomic and nothing else, that negated atomic is also what is known as the degenerate case of a conjunction; i.e., it too counts as a conjunction with exactly one conjunct.)
5.  Proceed to the next truth-table row where the *wff* comes out true, if there is one. If there isn't one, stop; the *wff* that you have just produced simply *is* the disjunctive normal form of the *wff* in question. (It is, as it were, the degenerate case of a disjunction; it's a disjunction with exactly one disjunct, a conjunction.)
6.  If there is another truth-table row where the *wff* comes out true, do unto that row what you did unto the previous row, in (2), (3), and (4), above.
7.  Form the disjunction of the two conjunctions that you have just created.
8.  Proceed to the next truth-table row where the *wff* comes out true, if there is one. If there isn't one, stop; the *wff* that you have just produced simply *is* the disjunctive normal form of the *wff* in question.
9.  If there is another truth-table row where the *wff* comes out true, do unto that row what you did unto the previous row.
10. Form the disjunction of the three conjunctions that you have just created.

11.  Stop once you have done unto the last row where the
     *wff* comes out true what you have done unto each of the
     previous rows where the *wff* comes out true. Form the
     disjunction of all of the conjunctions that you have just
     created. You are now staring at the disjunctive normal
     form of the *wff* in question. (If the *wff* is a contingent *wff*,
     there will be as many disjuncts as there are rows of the
     truth-table in which the *wff* comes out true. If the *wff* is
     a tautology, there will be as many disjuncts as there are
     rows of the truth-table, period.)

Suppose, however, that the *wff* in question is a semantic contradiction. Once again, there's a purely mechanical procedure for generating
its disjunctive normal form:

1.  Take the first atomic that appears in the *wff*; form the
    conjunction of it with its negation; and enclose the
    conjunction in parentheses.
2.  Then take the second atomic that appears in the *wff*; form
    the conjunction of it with its negation; and enclose the
    conjunction in parentheses. If there isn't a second atomic,
    i.e., if the *wff* contains only one atomic, stop; the *wff* that
    you have just produced simply *is* the disjunctive normal
    form of the *wff* in question. (It is, as it were once again,
    the degenerate case of a disjunction; it's a disjunction with
    exactly *one* disjunct, a conjunction.)
3.  Repeat this procedure for each of the atomics that appears
    in the *wff*, forming the conjunction of it with its negation.
4.  Once you have done unto the last atomic what you have
    done unto each of the other atomics, form the disjunc-
    tion of all of the conjunctions that you have just created.
    There will be as many disjuncts as there are atomics. You
    are now staring at the disjunctive normal form of the *wff*
    in question, a disjunction of semantic contradictions.

The *blappo*, you will recall, was an *arbitrarily* chosen connective.
Therefore what holds true of it holds true of *any* truth-functional
connective whatsoever. In other words, any *wff* containing any truth-
functional connective can be translated, using one of the above two
mechanical procedures, into a *wff* that is logically equivalent to it, and
that contains no connectives other than the dash, the caret, and the

wedge. It follows, therefore, that our language $L_1$ does have enough connectives after all. Indeed it has more than enough. We don't even need the arrow or the double-arrow: the double-arrow is collapsible into the arrow and the caret, and the arrow itself is collapsible into the dash and the caret, on the one hand, and the dash and the wedge, on the other hand. Thanks to disjunctive normal forms, we have established that the dash, the caret, and the wedge are sufficient for translating all possible truth-functional *wffs*. The power of $L_1$ is most remarkable indeed.

> **Definition:** A formal language, *L*, is *expressively complete iff* any *wff* containing any truth-functional connective can be translated into a *wff* that is logically equivalent to it, and that contains no connectives other than the connectives of *L*.

Now obviously a formal language containing all possible truth-functional connectives is expressively complete—but only in a trivial, i.e., an uninteresting, sort of way. By contrast, $L_1$ is expressively complete in a non-trivial and an immensely interesting sort of way.

# Exercises

I. Consider once again the table that shows the sixteen truth-tables associated with two atomics:

| P Q | 1 | 2 | 3 | 4 | 5 | 6 | 7 | 8 | 9 | 10 | 11 | 12 | 13 | 14 | 15 | 16 |
|-----|---|---|---|---|---|---|---|---|---|----|----|----|----|----|----|----|
| T T | T | F | T | F | T | F | T | F | T | F  | T  | F  | T  | F  | T  | F  |
| T F | T | T | F | F | T | T | F | F | T | T  | F  | F  | T  | T  | F  | F  |
| F T | T | T | T | T | F | F | F | F | T | T  | T  | T  | F  | F  | F  | F  |
| F F | T | T | T | T | T | T | T | T | F | F  | F  | F  | F  | F  | F  | F  |

I leave it as an interesting exercise (and hardly a taxing one at that) to determine which connective each of the sixteen connectives is that this table defines. Your goal is to produce the simplest possible *wff*, i.e., the *wff* with the fewest number of symbols, that each of the sixteen columns of truth-values defines. For example, one of the columns defines the *wff* '—(P ∧ Q)'; one defines the *wff* '—(P ∨ Q)', etc.

II. Translate the following *wffs* into their respective disjunctive normal forms:

a.   P ∧ Q
b.   P ∨ Q
c.   P → Q
d.   P ↔ Q
e.   P
f.   —P
g.   —(P ↔ Q)
h.   P → P
i.   P ∧ (Q ∨ R)
j.   —[P ∧ (Q ∨ R)]

# 8. Appendix II: Sheffer's Razor: Too Many Connectives?

So these three connectives—the dash, the caret, and the wedge—are jointly *sufficient*. The next obvious question is: 'But are they all *necessary?*' Have we hit rock bottom, as it were, with them, or could we make do with even fewer?

I remind you of Ockham's Razor: 'Don't multiply entities beyond necessity.' Could we express all possible truth-functional *wffs* by means of *wffs* containing just *two* connectives? Or even just *one* connective?

Thanks to De Morgan, you know that you can reduce the dash, the caret, and the wedge to two distinct sets of two: the dash and the caret, on the one hand, and the dash and the wedge, on the other. Any disjunction, '△ ∨ O', is logically equivalent to, and therefore can be replaced by, a *wff* containing only the dash and the caret: '—(—△ ∧ —O)'. Moreover, any conjunction, '△ ∧ O', is logically equivalent to, and therefore can be replaced by, a *wff* containing only the dash and the wedge:

'—(—△ ∨ —O)'. We now have an answer to our first question: All possible truth-functional connectives are collapsible into two distinct sets of two.

In 1913 Henry Sheffer (American, 1882–1964) showed that it's possible to express all possible truth-functional connectives by means of a *single* connective. (C. S. Peirce [American, 1839–1914] had actually shown this in 1880, but his demonstration wasn't published until 1930.) The Sheffer Stroke, ' | ', is definable as follows:

Definition:     '△ | O' ⇔ '—(△ ∧ O)'

In other words, '△ | O' (i.e., '△ Sheffer Stroke O', i.e., '△ Stroke O') simply means 'It's not the case both that △ and that O.' (Thus the sentence 'Ardbeg yawned | Bobo yawned' simply means 'It's not the case both that Ardbeg yawned and that Bobo yawned.')

You've seen that all possible truth-functional connectives are collapsible into the dash, the caret, and the wedge. The trick now is to show that the dash, the caret, and the wedge are collapsible into Sheffer Stroke notation. We begin with the dash:

1.  '△' is logically equivalent to '(△ ∧ △)'. (If '△' is true, '(△ ∧ △)' is true, and if '△' is false, '(△ ∧ △)' is false.)
2.  Therefore '—△' is equivalent to '—(△ ∧ △)'.
3.  By definition of the Sheffer Stroke, '—(△ ∧ O)' is equivalent to '△ | O'.
4.  Therefore '—(△ ∧ △)' is equivalent to '△ | △'.
5.  Therefore, (in light of (2) and (4)), '—△' is equivalent to '△ | △'.

We have successfully translated the dash into Sheffer Stroke notation. Now for the caret:

1.  '△' is logically equivalent to '— —△'.
2.  Therefore '△ ∧ O' is equivalent to '— —(△ ∧ O)'.
3.  By definition of the Sheffer Stroke, '—(△ ∧ O)' is equivalent to '△ | O'.
4.  Therefore '— —(△ ∧ O)' is equivalent to '—(△ | O)'. (I.e., the negation of the first *wff* in 3 is equivalent to the negation of the second *wff* in 3.)

5. We saw above that '$-\triangle$' is equivalent to '$\triangle \mid \triangle$'.
6. Therefore '$-(\triangle \mid \text{O})$' is equivalent to '$(\triangle \mid \text{O}) \mid (\triangle \mid \text{O})$'.
7. We have now established the equivalence of the following wffs:
   a. '$\triangle \wedge \text{O}$'
   b. '$--(\triangle \wedge \text{O})$'
   c. '$-(\triangle \mid \text{O})$'
   d. '$(\triangle \mid \text{O}) \mid (\triangle \mid \text{O})$'
8. Therefore '$\triangle \wedge \text{O}$' is equivalent to '$(\triangle \mid \text{O}) \mid (\triangle \mid \text{O})$'.

We have now successfully translated the caret into Sheffer Stroke notation. Two down and one to go. On to the wedge:

1. '$\triangle \vee \text{O}$' is logically equivalent to '$-(-\triangle \wedge -\text{O})$' (by De Morgan).
2. We saw above that '$-\triangle$' is equivalent to '$\triangle \mid \triangle$'.
3. Therefore '$-(-\triangle \wedge -\text{O})$' is equivalent to '$-[(\triangle \mid \triangle) \wedge (\text{O} \mid \text{O})]$'.
4. By definition of the Sheffer Stroke, however, '$-(\triangle \wedge \text{O})$' is equivalent to '$\triangle \mid \text{O}$'.
5. Therefore '$-[(\triangle \mid \triangle) \wedge (\text{O} \mid \text{O})]$' is equivalent to '$(\triangle \mid \triangle) \mid (\text{O} \mid \text{O})$'.
6. We have now established the equivalence of the following *wffs*:
   a. '$\triangle \vee \text{O}$'
   b. '$-(-\triangle \wedge -\text{O})$'
   c. '$-[(\triangle \mid \triangle) \wedge (\text{O} \mid \text{O})]$'
   d. '$(\triangle \mid \triangle) \mid (\text{O} \mid \text{O})$'
7. Therefore '$\triangle \vee \text{O}$' is equivalent to '$(\triangle \mid \triangle) \mid (\text{O} \mid \text{O})$'.

We have now successfully translated the wedge into Sheffer Stroke notation.

Thanks to disjunctive normal forms, you've seen that all possible truth-functional *wffs* are translatable into *wffs* whose only truth-functional connectives are the dash, the caret, and the wedge. You've now seen that *wffs* containing only the dash, the caret, and the wedge are translatable into *wffs* whose only truth-functional connective is the Sheffer Stroke. It follows that *all possible* truth-functional *wffs* are translatable into *wffs* whose only truth-functional connective is the Sheffer Stroke!

There is no finite limit to the number of truth-functional connectives. However, they are all—*every last one of them*—reducible to, or collapsible into, the Sheffer Stroke. It's possible, therefore, to express any truth-functional *wff* whatsoever using only a *single* truth-functional connective.

# Exercises

I. Translate each of the following *wffs* into logically equivalent *wffs* that contain only the Sheffer Stroke.

1.  $P \rightarrow Q$
2.  $-(P \rightarrow Q)$
3.  $P \wedge (Q \vee R)$
4.  $P \vee (Q \wedge R)$
5.  $P \leftrightarrow Q$

II. Translate each of the following *wffs* into logically equivalent *wffs* that contain only the dash, the caret, the wedge, the arrow, and/or the double-arrow. In each case, produce the simplest possible *wff*, i.e., the *wff* with the fewest number of symbols.

1.  $(P \mid P) \mid (P \mid P)$
2.  $(P \mid P) \mid P$
3.  $(P \mid Q) \mid (P \mid P)$
4.  $(P \mid Q) \mid R$
5.  $[P \mid (P \mid Q)] \mid (P \mid R)$

# 9. Appendix III: Truth-Functional Connectives Reconsidered

A final word (which, of course, isn't *really* a final word) on truth-functional connectives. . . .

If it strikes you now that in logic everything is so very neat and tidy, so cut-and-dried and free of controversy, think again. There are logicians who challenge the claim that each of our five connectives really captures the meaning of its intended natural-language counterpart. Quite the contrary: they would contend that the arrow, the double-arrow, the caret, and the wedge simply fail to capture the meanings of 'if-then', 'if and only if', 'and', and 'or', respectively. They would consider $L_1$, therefore, an artificial language that fails to represent *any* natural language, and that consequently is merely floating unsupported in midair. If they are right, then of course truth-functional logic, i.e., Propositional Logic, is seriously flawed.

You've already seen why one might be tempted to hold that in ordinary conversation 'if-then' is inherently causal, definitional, or logical—in which case it wouldn't be truth-functional. The arrow, of course, *is* truth-functional. Therefore, so the argument goes, the arrow fails to capture the meaning of 'if-then'.

Moreover, there's the problem of the counterfactual sense of 'if-then'. Consider the following counterfactual sentences:

1. 'If the South had won the Civil War then slavery in the South would have continued until the twentieth century.'
2. 'If the South had won the Civil War then slavery in the South would have continued until the twenty-first century.'

Both sentences are if-then sentences. Both have false antecedents. Therefore, on the truth-functional sense of 'if-then', both sentences are true. But while it might well be plausible to think that the first is true, it would be implausible to think so of the second. Therefore, so the argument goes, the arrow fails to capture the counterfactual sense of 'if-then'.

Moreover, if the arrow fails to capture the various meanings of 'if-then' and if the interpretation of the double-arrow piggybacks on the interpretation of the arrow, it follows that the double-arrow fails to capture the corresponding meanings of 'if and only if'.

You might also be tempted to hold that in ordinary conversation 'and' seems to be shorthand for either 'and *then*' or 'and *therefore*'—in which case it too wouldn't be truth-functional. In ordinary conversation, in other words, 'Ardbeg died and Bobo buried him' suggests that Ardbeg's death preceded, and was the cause of, Bobo's having buried him. Suppose, however, that it had been the other way around. Suppose that Bobo's having buried Ardbeg had preceded, and in fact had been the cause of, Ardbeg's death. In that case, you might well view as *false* the sentence, 'Ardbeg died and Bobo buried him'— even though it's a conjunction both of whose conjuncts are true. If deemed truth-functional, however, obviously the conjunction would be true. So whereas the caret is truth-functional, this particular sense of 'and'—the 'and then' sense—isn't. Therefore, so the argument goes, the caret fails to capture the full range of meanings of 'and'.

Matters go from bad to worse when we turn from sentences to arguments. Arguments that are valid on the truth-functional interpretation of 'and' appear to be invalid on the non-truth-functional interpretation.

> (1) Ardbeg died.
> (2) Bobo buried Ardbeg.
> ───────────────────────────
> ∴ (3) Ardbeg died and Bobo buried Ardbeg.

As you've just seen, it may be true that Ardbeg died and it may be true that Bobo buried him, but it may be false that Ardbeg died and that *then* Bobo buried him.

Similarly, you might be tempted to hold that in ordinary conversation 'or' isn't truth-functional. Suppose that I say, "You will apologize this very moment or else I shall leave." You take me seriously and you apologize this very moment. Suppose, however, that even if you *hadn't* apologized this very moment I wouldn't have left. Under such circumstances, it would be natural to view my original utterance, "You will apologize this very moment or else I shall leave," as *false*, as nothing more than a bluff, an idle threat—even though it's a disjunction one of whose disjuncts happens to be *true*. (You did apologize.) If deemed truth-functional, however, obviously the disjunction would be true. So whereas the wedge is truth-functional, this particular sense of 'or' isn't. Therefore, so the argument goes, the wedge fails to capture the full range of meanings of 'or'.

Once again, matters go from bad to worse when we turn from sentences to arguments. Arguments that are valid on the truth-functional interpretation of 'or' appear to be invalid on the non-truth-functional interpretation.

> (3) You will apologize this very moment.
> ─────────────────────────────────────────
> ∴ (4) Either you will apologize this very moment or else
>        I shall leave.

As you've just seen, it may be true that you will apologize this very moment, but it may be false that either you will apologize this very moment or else I shall leave.

So how exactly should one reply to those logicians who view as mistaken the exclusive focus on truth-functional connectives?

The objection to truth-functional logic may be formulated quite succinctly:

1. Truth-functional connectives fail to capture the ordinary, everyday, informal meanings of our connectives.
2. As a result, some arguments that are valid when the connectives are interpreted truth-functionally are invalid when the connectives are interpreted non-truth-functionally, i.e., when they are assigned their ordinary, everyday, informal meanings.
3. Therefore truth-functional logic fails to capture ordinary, everyday, informal reasoning.

There would seem to be four possible responses that you could make toward the objection. You could go for the jugular. You could capitulate. You could simply ignore it. Or you could negotiate a settlement.

Going for the jugular would involve reminding yourself that it's necessary to distinguish the *meaning* of an expression ('if-then', 'if and only if', 'and', or 'or') from the *state of mind* of the person who uses the expression. My *intention* in saying, "If Ardbeg retreats then the game is over," may well be to draw your attention to a *causal* relation that I believe to exist between Ardbeg's retreating and the game's being over. It doesn't follow, however, that the 'if-then' words *themselves* embody a causal claim. Indeed, if they did, then we wouldn't be able to use the words for other, e.g., definitional or logical, purposes. But of course we *do* use the words for such purposes. Thus I might use 'if-then' to make a definitional point: 'If Bobo is a widow then of course Bobo is a woman'. Alternatively, I might use 'if-then' to make a logical point: 'If Ardbeg faints only if Bobo faints, and if Bobo faints only if Coco faints, then Ardbeg faints only if Coco faints'. The arrow, insofar as it's equivalent to '—(P ∧ —Q)', captures the only aspect of 'if-then' that runs through *every* 'if-then' sentence. Indeed, where 'if-then' is concerned, '—(P ∧ —Q)' is the cake, so to speak—and all the rest is icing.

What holds true of 'if-then' holds true as well, *mutatis mutandis* (i.e., making all the relevant changes), of 'if and only if', 'and', and 'or'. When I utter the sentence, "Ardbeg died and Bobo buried him," my intention might well be to use the 'and then' sense of 'and'. By the same token, when I utter the sentence, "You will apologize this very moment or else I shall leave," I might well have in mind the thought that even if you fail to apologize I won't leave. Sometimes, as these examples illustrate, what's in one's mind is one thing, and what the sentence actually means is quite another thing. It's on the latter, of course—on what the sentence *actually* means—that truth-functional logic focuses.

End of story, right? No, not quite. It may well be that the *actual* (or *real*) meaning of each of our connectives is truth-functional; i.e., it may well be that each of our connectives is *inherently* truth-functional. If, however, we seldom use the truth-functional meaning in everyday conversation, then why bother with it? Why bother, in other words, with truth-functional logic? If the connectives that figure in everyday arguments are for the most part non-truth-functional, and if our goal, in this context, is to assess our everyday arguments, then truth-functional logic would seem to have little to do with our goal. Perhaps, then, it's time to capitulate, yes? Capitulating would involve throwing in the towel and declaring the end of truth-functional logic as an important field of study.

To be sure, it would make sense to capitulate only if non-truth-functional uses of the words 'and', 'or', etc., play a *key* role in arguments in ordinary conversation. But what if they don't? What if non-truth-functional uses of the words 'and', 'or', etc., play only a *minor* role in arguments in ordinary conversation? The claim that they play a key role, like the claim that they don't, is of course an empirical claim. As such, whichever claim is to win you over will require strong empirical support. Suppose that the evidence supports the claim that non-truth-functional uses of the words 'and', 'or', etc., *occasionally*, but only *occasionally*, play a key role in arguments in ordinary conversation. In that case, truth-functional logic would be imperfect, but it would be good enough for most purposes; capitulation would be unnecessary; and you could ignore the original objection.

Ignoring the objection would involve sweeping it under the rug and continuing merrily on your truth-functional way. Obviously, you could take this approach if non-truth-functional uses of the words 'and', 'or', etc., seldom played a key role in arguments in ordinary conversation.

Contrariwise, if non-truth-functional uses of these words frequently did play a key role in arguments in ordinary conversation, you might still sweep the objection under the rug. After all, you could dig in your heels and insist that the purpose of truth-functional logic isn't to replicate, or to serve as a prop for, everyday reasoning. Instead, its purpose is to serve as an ideal, a paradigm, of what logical reasoning should aspire to. Accordingly, you would dismiss the non-truth-functional uses of the connectives as simply beside the point, a distraction from the real business at hand: paradigm-construction. And you would think to yourself, "So much the worse for everyday reasoning."

It's difficult to turn your back altogether on everyday reasoning, however. You might think of compromising, of negotiating a settlement. Doing so wouldn't be the end of the world. It would involve acknowledging the legitimacy of *both* truth-functional logic *and* of alternative, non-truth-functional, logics. It would be the context, presumably, that would dictate, in any given instance, your choice of which sort of logic to invoke.

Now keep in mind that this is an *introductory* logic text. You will have ample opportunity to explore this issue in one of your next logic courses.

# Chapter Three

# Propositional Logic:
# A Deductive Apparatus, Part One

## 1. Introduction

Chapters 1 and 2 focused primarily on the *semantics* of logic; Chapters 3 and 4 focus primarily on its *syntax*. These two chapters are all about *derivations* (or *proofs*). In derivations, the goal is to derive a *wff* from any finite number of *wffs*: from one *wff*, from more than one *wff*, or even (as you will see later in the chapter) from no *wffs*.

It is *derivation rules* that allow you to do the deriving. Derivation rules have one overriding purpose: *to justify the assertion of a particular wff.* Different formal systems have different sets of derivation rules. In these two chapters the focus will be on the derivation rules of our formal system, Propositional Logic.

Corresponding to each of our five kinds of molecular *wffs*—conjunctions, disjunctions, conditionals, bi-conditionals, and negations—there are two derivation rules. One rule allows you to destroy, pulverize, or otherwise *eliminate* a particular kind of molecular: ∧E (Conjunction Elimination), ∨E (Disjunction Elimination), →E (Conditional Elimination), ↔E (Bi-conditional Elimination), and − −E (Double Negation Elimination). And one rule allows you to create, generate, or otherwise *introduce* a particular kind of molecular: ∧I (Conjunction Introduction), ∨I (Disjunction Introduction), →I (Conditional Introduction), ↔I (Bi-conditional Introduction), and −I (Negation Introduction). You would think, therefore, that you should end up with exactly ten derivation rules. In fact, you'll end up with exactly eleven. The additional derivation rule, the Rule of Assumptions, or A, allows for the introduction of an assumption, whether it's an assumption that is simply *given,* i.e., a premise, or an assumption that *you yourself* introduce.

Difficulty-wise, the eleven rules are divisible into three categories. Six are perfectly straightforward and simple: ∧E, ∧I, ∨I, →E, ↔E, and ——E. Four are a bit tricky: →I, ↔I, ∨E, and —I. One is a hybrid: A is perfectly straightforward in one respect, and it's a bit tricky in one respect. It's perfectly straightforward when it refers to a *given* assumption, i.e., a premise; and it's a bit tricky when it refers to an assumption that *you yourself* introduce.

We begin with definitions, including a provisional definition that we shall revise in the next chapter. We discuss briefly the two faces of A, the Rule of Assumptions. We discuss, at length, the six straightforward derivation rules; at greater length, the four tricky ones; and at still greater length, derivations. Then we turn to theorems and substitution-instances, and raise the curtain on a potentially unlimited number of 'derived' derivation rules. Just as we concluded the last two chapters with a word about the power of our formal language, so we'll conclude these two chapters with a word about the power of our deductive apparatus, i.e., our set of derivation rules.

**Provisional Definition:**   A *derivation* (or *proof*) is a finite string of *wffs*, each of which is either (1) an assumption or (2) a *wff* that follows from at least one of the *wffs* in the string by one of our derivation rules.

**Definition:**   A *derivation rule* is a rule that serves to justify the assertion of a given *wff* in a derivation.

Question: What exactly are we looking for when we choose a set of derivation rules? Certainly it would be nice if all of our derivation rules were intuitively obvious, i.e., rules such as we use in our everyday reasoning. To be sure, you will find that many, and perhaps most—but certainly not all—of our derivation rules are fairly obvious. The quality of being intuitively obvious, however, is merely the icing on the cake; it isn't the cake itself. What, then, is the cake?

Answer: The cake is the quality of being *truth-preserving*. Being truth-preserving is the only crucial property that each of our derivation rules must possess. Intuitively, to say that derivation rules are truth-preserving is to say that if you start off with truths (or at least *presumed* truths) and you apply our derivation rules to them, you'll end up with nothing but truths; you won't ever end up with falsehoods. In other words, by virtue of being truth-preserving, our derivation rules guarantee that you won't ever derive falsehoods from truths.

> Definition:    Consider any finite set of *wffs*, and consider any *wff*, '△', that follows from the set by a given derivation rule. The derivation rule is *truth-preserving iff* there is no interpretation that makes each *wff* in the set true and that makes '△' false.

The set of *wffs*, like any finite set, might well contain no members—but you needn't concern yourself with such a set until we discuss theorems in the next chapter.

It's hardly a coincidence that our definition of a truth-preserving derivation rule draws upon our definition of validity from Chapter 2: our derivation rules serve to guarantee, and indeed are *designed* to guarantee, that each derivation constitutes a valid argument. Indeed we would never have chosen these derivation rules unless each of them possessed truth as a *hereditary* property. In a derivation, in other words, if each of the 'ancestors', i.e., each of the initial *wffs*, has the property of truth, then so does each of its 'descendants', i.e., each of the later *wffs* (e.g., '△').

# 2. Derivation Rules: The First Seven

## A. The Rule of Assumptions: A

Suppose that you were asked what your justification is for asserting a given *wff*: "Why should anyone believe *that*?" One perfectly appropriate reply would be that it's merely an assumption. There are assumptions that are simply *given* and there are assumptions that *you yourself* introduce. The assumptions that are simply given are *premises*. The difference between the first seven derivation rules and the last four is that the first seven don't require you to introduce any assumptions of your own, whereas the last four do.

## Rule of Assumptions: The Details

1. To the right of any given assumption '△', i.e., any premise, cite only the rule A.
2. To the far left of the assumption, cite the same line number as the line number of the assumption itself.

No doubt item 2 strikes you as gobbledygook. Don't worry: At this point in the text, it *is* gobbledygook; it will become clear once we dive into derivations.

# B. Conjunction Elimination/Caret Elimination: ∧E

## ∧E: The Details

1. From any conjunction '△ ∧ O', it is permissible to derive '△'.
2. From any conjunction, '△ ∧ O', it is also permissible to derive 'O'.
3. To the right of the *wff* that you have derived, i.e., either '△' or 'O', cite the line number of '△ ∧ O', and the rule ∧E.
4. To the far left of the *wff* that you have derived, i.e., either '△' or 'O', cite the line numbers of the assumptions on which it rests, i.e., the line numbers of the assumptions from which it is ultimately derived.

Don't worry about item 4. It falls into the same category as item 2 (above): gobbledygook. It too will become clear once we dive into derivations.

$$\begin{array}{cc} △ ∧ O & △ ∧ O \\ \cdot & \cdot \\ \cdot & \cdot \\ \cdot & \cdot \\ △ & O \end{array}$$

Suppose that the following sentence is true: 'Fitzwilliam won the Gongabong Derby and Fitzhugh won the Clodpeppers'. From that *conjunction* it certainly follows (albeit trivially) that Fitzwilliam won the

Gongabong Derby. Equally, it follows (albeit trivially, once again) that Fitzhugh won the Clodpeppers. In other words, *given any conjunction, you are entitled to derive either of its conjuncts.*

In saying that you are *entitled* to derive either of its conjuncts, what we are saying is that ∧E is truth-preserving. To say that ∧E is truth-preserving is, of course, to say that there's no interpretation that makes the initial conjunction true and the conjunct that you derive from that conjunction, by ∧E, false. A quick application of either the Truth-Table Method or the Short Method should convince you that ∧E is indeed truth-preserving. (Try by either method, in other words, to make '△ ∧ O' true and either '△' or 'O' false: you will *not* succeed.)

## C. Conjunction Introduction/Caret Intro: ∧I

### ∧I: The Details

1. From any *wffs* '△' and 'O', it is permissible to derive the conjunction '△ ∧ O'.
2. To the right of the *wff* that you have derived, i.e., '△ ∧ O', cite the line number of '△' followed by the line number of 'O', and the rule ∧I.
3. From any *wffs* '△' and 'O', it is also permissible to derive the conjunction 'O ∧ △'.
4. To the right of the *wff* that you have derived, i.e., 'O ∧ △', cite the line number of 'O' followed by the line number of '△', and the rule ∧I.
5. To the far left of the *wff* that you have derived, i.e., either '△ ∧ O' or 'O ∧ △', cite the line numbers of the assumptions on which it rests, i.e., the line numbers of the assumptions from which it is ultimately derived.

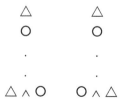

Suppose that the following sentence is true: 'Fitzwilliam is high-spirited.' Suppose that the following sentence is also true: 'Fitzwilliam longs for a Granny Smith.' From the supposed truth of each of these two sentences, the truth of a third sentence follows: 'Fitzwilliam is high-spirited *and* Fitzwilliam longs for a Granny Smith'. Equally, from the supposed truth of each of these two sentences the truth of a variation of the third sentence follows: 'Fitzwilliam longs for a Granny Smith *and* Fitzwilliam is high-spirited.' Notice that ∧I is clearly truth-preserving: when you use it, there is no interpretation that makes each of the initial *wffs* true and the conjunction of these *wffs* false. Notice too that whereas ∧E operates on a *single wff*, ∧I operates on precisely *two wffs*, such that when you perform ∧E, you cite only *one* line number off to the right of your derived *wff*, but when you perform ∧I, you cite *two* line numbers.

# D. Disjunction Introduction/Wedge Intro: ∨I

## ∨I: The Details

1. From any *wff* '△', it is permissible to derive the disjunction '△ ∨ O'.
2. From any *wff* '△', it is also permissible to derive the disjunction 'O ∨ △'.
3. To the right of the *wff* that you have derived, i.e., either '△ ∨ O' or 'O ∨ △', cite the line number of '△' and the rule ∨I.
4. To the far left of the *wff* that you have derived, i.e., either '△ ∨ O' or 'O ∨ △', cite the line numbers of the assumptions on which it rests, i.e., the line numbers of the assumptions from which it is ultimately derived.

```
        △              △

        .              .
        .              .
        .              .

     △ ∨ O          O ∨ △
```

∨I will strike you initially as a most bizarre derivation rule: If '△' and 'O' are any two *wffs*, then if '△' is true it follows that either '△' or 'O' is true. Alternatively, if '△' is true it follows that *either* 'O' ∨ '△' is true. Just think about it for a moment: if it's true that Fitzwilliam longs for a Granny Smith, then it's also true that either he longs for a Granny Smith or he longs for a small batch bourbon. If Aristotle was a Greek then it's also true that either Aristotle was a Greek or he was a Scot. To put the matter slightly differently: *Of necessity*, if '△' is true, then '△ ∨ O', like 'O ∨ △', is true. Why? Because any disjunction with at least one true disjunct *automatically* (i.e., by truth-table definition) comes out true. At the very least, therefore, you have to concede that, however bizarre it might be, ∨I is truth-preserving.

I shall now convince you that ∨I isn't so bizarre after all. Indeed I shall now convince you that you actually make use of ∨I from time to time in the real world. In particular, you make use of it when you wish to be *truthful but uninformative*. Suppose that Egvalt, someone whom you can't stand, asks you what you're doing this evening. You know that you plan to go see *Casablanca* for the umpteenth time. You also know that if you were to say exactly that, Egvalt would ask whether he might join you—and the last thing that you want is for Egvalt to ask whether he might join you!

So you're now in a pickle. You have three goals: you don't want Egvalt to join you; you don't want to hurt his feelings; and you don't want to lie to him. It would appear impossible to achieve all three of your goals. It would appear, in other words, that you won't be able to have your cake and eat it too. . . .

Ah, but you can! You *can* have your cake and eat it too! When Egvalt asks you what you're going to be doing this evening, you simply reply, "Oh, either I'm going to go see *Casablanca* or I'm going to go visit Auntie Coco." You know perfectly well that you're not going to go visit Auntie Coco, but your reply to Egvalt—"Either I'm going to go see *Casablanca* or I'm going to go visit Auntie Coco"—constitutes a *truth*. Never mind that it's a less informative truth than "I'm going to go see *Casablanca*"; no one ever said that the truths that you utter always have to be fully informative. Keep in mind that you have three goals: to be free of Egvalt for the evening, to avoid hurting his feelings, and to be truthful. And you can accomplish all three of these goals simply by communicating less rather than more information to him. If your either-or reply doesn't do the trick, just keep watering down the original, with each reply being less informative than its predecessor:

1. "I'm going to go see *Casablanca*."
2. "Either I'm going to go see *Casablanca* or I'm going to go visit Auntie Coco."
3. "Either I'm going to go see *Casablanca* or I'm going to go visit Auntie Coco or I'm going to memorize the *Iliad*."

Note that ∨I allows you to introduce, either to the left or to the right of the wedge, any *wff* whatsoever, i.e., a *wff* of any length and any complexity. It need not be an atomic; it might well be a molecular thirteen city blocks long. Note too that ∨I operates on a *single wff*—like ∧E and unlike ∧I.

# E. Conditional Elimination/Arrow Elimination/*Modus (Ponendo) Ponens*: →E

## →E: The Details

1. From any conditional '△ → ○' and its antecedent '△', it is permissible to derive its consequent '○'.
2. To the right of the *wff* that you have derived, i.e., '○', cite the line number of '△ → ○' followed by the line number of '△', and the rule →E.
3. To the far left of the *wff* that you have derived, i.e., '○', cite the line numbers of the assumptions on which it rests, i.e., the line numbers of the assumptions from which it is ultimately derived.

$$△ → ○$$
$$△$$
$$.$$
$$.$$
$$○$$

You couldn't survive for more than thirteen seconds on Planet Earth without →E. You make use of it quite literally every moment of the day. 'If the light is red, then I'd better stop. The light *is* red. So I'd better stop.' 'If today is Monday then Monty will be assassinating Fortescue. Today *is* Monday. So Monty will be assassinating Fortescue.' 'If your temperature is above 102, I'm going to call your doctor. Your temperature *is* above 102. So I'm going to call your doctor.' 'If Ardbeg has betrayed Bobo, then Ardbeg is a real scoundrel. Ardbeg *has* betrayed Bobo. So Ardbeg is a real scoundrel.'

Try—*just try*—to come up with an interpretation that makes the premises true and the conclusion false. (Hint: you won't succeed.)

'*Modus Ponendo Ponens*' (the way, or mode, of affirming *by* affirming), or simply '*Modus Ponens*', is the Latinism by which, historically, this derivation rule has been known. Notice what it involves: having affirmed two *wffs*—a conditional along with the antecedent of the conditional—you are entitled to affirm, or derive, a third *wff*—the *consequent* of the conditional.

Notice what →E does *not* permit: from a conditional along with the *consequent* of the conditional, it is *not* permissible to derive the *antecedent* of the conditional. The following, in other words, is a fallacy. It is a fallacy that may often *tempt* you. (It tempted your trekking guide, Ardbeg, at the very beginning of this book.) You must *resist* the temptation *to your last breath*:

To appreciate the fallaciousness of this *so-called* derivation rule, consider the following English-language counterexamples: 'If Fitzwilliam is a horse then Fitzwilliam is a mammal. Fitzwilliam is a mammal. Therefore Fitzwilliam is a horse.' 'If you're a billionaire then you're worth at least ten cents. You're worth at least ten cents. Therefore you're a billionaire.' In each of these two arguments, there is at least one interpretation in which the premises are true and the conclusion is false.

Note once again that in a *genuine* instance of →E you have a conditional; you affirm the *antecedent* of the conditional, and you then derive the *consequent* of the conditional. Note that in an ersatz instance of →E—known (for obvious reasons) as the *Fallacy of Affirming the Consequent*—you have a conditional; you affirm the *consequent* of the conditional, and you then derive the *antecedent* of the conditional. Note, finally, that if you were to elevate the Fallacy of Affirming the Consequent to the status of a derivation rule, the world most assuredly would come to an end. Such a rule would *not* be truth-preserving. It would *not* be a derivation rule for which truth is hereditary.

# F. Bi-conditional Elimination/
# Double-Arrow Elimination: ↔E

### ↔E: The Details

1.  From any bi-conditional '△ ↔ O' it is permissible to derive '(△ → O) ∧ (O → △)'.
2.  To the right of the *wff* that you have derived, i.e., '(△ → O) ∧ (O → △)', cite the line number of '△ ↔ O' and the rule ↔E.
3.  To the far left of the *wff* that you have derived, i.e., '(△ → O) ∧ (O → △)', cite the line numbers of the assumptions on which it rests, i.e., the line numbers of the assumptions from which it is ultimately derived.

$$△ ↔ O$$

$$.$$
$$.$$
$$.$$

$$(△ → O) ∧ (O → △)$$

If →E strikes you as intuitively obvious, then ↔E should strike you as equally so. Think of why a bi-conditional is called a *bi*-conditional. The reason is that it's really *two* conditionals rolled into one: one pointing from left to right and one pointing from right to left. So '*x* is an even number *iff x* is divisible by 2' simply *means*—and therefore obviously *implies*—'If *x* is an even number then *x* is divisible by 2, and contrariwise, if *x* is divisible by 2 then *x* is an even number'. And 'Egvalt is a traitor *iff* Egvalt betrayed his country' also simply *means*—and also therefore *implies*—'If Egvalt is a traitor then he betrayed his country, and contrariwise, if Egvalt betrayed his country then he's a traitor'.

If you remain unconvinced that ↔E is indeed truth-preserving, the Short Method will convince you.

# G. Double Negation Elimination/ Double-Dash Elimination: − −E

### − −E: The Details

1. From any negation of a negation '− −△' it is permissible to derive '△'.
2. To the right of the *wff* that you have derived, i.e., '△', cite the line number of '− −△' and the rule − −E.
3. To the far left of the *wff* that you have derived, i.e., '△', cite the line numbers of the assumptions on which it rests, i.e., the line numbers of the assumptions from which it is ultimately derived.

$$− −△$$

.

.

$$△$$

− −E is obviously truth-preserving. Suppose that the negation of the negation of '△', i.e., '− −△', is true. Then that which is being negated, i.e., the negation of '△', i.e., '−△', must be false. If the negation of '△', i.e., '−△', is false then that which is being negated, i.e., '△' itself, must be true. So, if the negation of the negation of '△', i.e., '− −△', is true, then so is '△'; i.e., − −E is truth-preserving.

Note that − −E allows you to delete exactly *two* dashes at a time—not four, not six, etc. Note too that − −E does *not* allow you to delete *one* dash. Obviously the following derivation rule would *not* be truth-preserving:

Such a derivation rule would guarantee that truths would generate falsehoods and only falsehoods: of necessity, any interpretation that made the premise '—△' true, would make the conclusion '△' false. Interpret '△' to mean 'The Moon is made of pink fluff'. The premise, i.e., 'It's *not* the case that the Moon is made of pink fluff', is obviously true. The conclusion, i.e., 'The Moon *is* made of pink fluff', is obviously false. Moral of the story: don't even *dream* of deleting *one* dash at a time.

You might be tempted to delete any *even* number of dashes at a time, but you should resist the temptation to do so. Consider the following:

In contrast with the previous argument, this one is perfectly valid. "So," you ask, "why exactly isn't this an instance (or application) of — —E?" First, note that the derivation rule doesn't use the expression 'an even number of dashes'. Second, note that strictly speaking it isn't the derivation rule that states that you may delete two dashes at a time; it was *I* who stated that. The derivation rule itself doesn't even use the expression '*two* dashes'. Like our other derivation rules, — —E focuses only on the *forms* or the *structures* of the *wffs* in question. It tells you that when you see a *wff* of one form, i.e., '— —△', it's permissible to derive a *wff* of another form, i.e., '△'.

"But," you reply, "why would it be impermissible to create *additional* derivation rules: one rule that allowed us to delete *four* dashes at a time, another that allowed us to delete *six* dashes at a time, etc.?" The answer is that it would *not* be impermissible to do so. Unlike in the previous case, we wouldn't be violating any of the canons of logic. Indeed the answer has little if anything to do with logic per se. The issue is to some extent an aesthetic/theoretical one and to some extent a practical one.

I begin with the *aesthetic/theoretical* consideration. You remember what your old friend Ockham (of Ockham's Razor fame) is credited with having said: "Don't multiply entities beyond necessity." In this instance, the entities are derivation rules. To paraphrase Ockham: "Don't multiply derivation rules beyond necessity." In other words, from an aesthetic/theoretical point of view, there is something quite appealing about having the smallest possible set of derivation rules. If you can do everything with a small set of derivation rules that you can do with a large set, the former is aesthetically/theoretically preferable. Science in general seeks to discover the smallest possible set of whatevers—fundamental particles, fundamental forces, fundamental laws of nature, etc.—from which everything else can be derived. So it is in logic with our derivation rules.

I conclude with the *practical* consideration. If every time it were permissible to add on a new derivation rule you did so, very soon you'd end up with an unwieldy number of derivation rules. It may seem that I shall be eating these very words in the very next chapter. It may seem that before you know it we shall be piling new derivation rule upon new derivation rule—and indeed we shall be doing *exactly* this. True enough! But we shall always observe the distinction between the rules that we are currently articulating, i.e., our *primitive,* or *basic,* derivation rules, and those that we shall articulate later, i.e., our *derived* derivation rules. By the middle of Chapter 4, in other words, it will be permissible to construct the following derivation rules (among many others)—but they will be *derived*, as distinct from *primitive*, derivation rules:

# 3. From Arguments to Sequents

Several points before you dive into your first derivation. The first point concerns focus. Our concern with arguments in Chapters 1 and 2 was largely (but not exclusively) *semantic*; hence our focus on the truth and falsehood of propositions, and the validity and invalidity of arguments. Our concern in Chapters 3 and 4 is largely (but again, not exclusively) *syntactic*; hence our focus on the purely formal (or structural) aspects of derivations and derivation rules.

I remind you of our definitions of 'argument', 'premise', and 'conclusion':

Definition:    An *argument* is a string of sentences; one of the sentences is the conclusion and the others are the premises.

Definition:    The *conclusion* of an argument is the sentence whose truth is to be established.

Definition:    A *premise* of an argument is a sentence that is said, or that is thought, or that appears, to play a role in establishing the truth of the conclusion.

So arguments are *semantic* sorts of things, defined by reference to premises and conclusions, which in turn are defined by reference to *truth*. I shall now drain the definition of an argument of all reference to truth and falsehood, and thus of all reference to sentences. Exit the *argument* with its truth-bearing sentences. Enter the *sequent*, the syntactic counterpart of an argument, with its *wffs* consisting of uninterpreted squiggle-marks.

Definition:    A *sequent* is a string of *wffs*.

Your goal, now and forevermore, is to derive the last *wff* in a given sequent from the other *wffs* in the sequent (if there are other *wffs* in the sequent!). Indeed, constructing derivations, with a little help from our derivation rules, is about to become your mission in logic-life.

Definition:    A *derivation* is a string of *wffs*, each of which is either an assumption or a theorem or a *wff* that follows, via our derivation rules, from one or more *wffs* in the string.

Don't worry about what a theorem is. You'll have ample opportunity to worry in Chapter 4.

Several points. First, where an *argument* is concerned, the key question is: 'Is it *invalid* or is it *valid*; i.e., is there, or isn't there, a counterexample—an interpretation that makes the premises true and the conclusion false?' This is a *semantic* question. On the other hand, where a *sequent* is concerned, the key question is: 'Is it possible to derive *these* squiggle-marks, i.e., the last *wff* in a given sequent, from *those* squiggle-marks, i.e., the other *wffs* in the sequent (if there are any)?' This is a *syntactic* question.

Second, where an *argument* is concerned, the operative terms are 'show' and 'imply'. You *show* that the argument is either valid or invalid—by means of either the Truth-Table Method or the Short Method. And the premises of a valid argument *imply* the conclusion. On the other hand, where a *sequent* is concerned, the operative terms are 'derive' and 'generate'. You try to *derive* the last *wff* in a given sequent from the other *wffs*—by means of our derivation rules. And the premises of a provable sequent *generate* the conclusion.

*Showing* is a semantic activity in which *you* engage. *Deriving* is a syntactic activity in which *you* engage. *Implying* is a semantic 'activity' in which the *premises* engage. And *generating* is a syntactic 'activity' in which the *premises* engage.

Third, sequents whose last *wff* you are to derive from the initial *wffs* will be expressed horizontally. A given sequent's initial *wffs* (which, for the sake of convenience, we may refer to as its 'premises') will be separated from one another by commas. A single-turnstile will appear to the right of the initial *wffs*. The *wff* to the right of the single-turnstile is the sequent's last *wff* (which, for the sake of convenience once again, we may refer to simply as 'the conclusion'):

$$\triangle_1, \ldots, \triangle_{n-1} \vdash \triangle_n$$

Think of the single-turnstile as serving to affirm that the *wffs* to its left *generate* the *wff* to its right. Alternatively, the *wff* to the right of the turnstile is said to be the *syntactic consequence* of, i.e., *derivable* from, the *wffs* to its left.

Definition:     A *wff* '$\triangle$' is a *syntactic consequence* of a set of *wffs* *iff* there is a derivation of '$\triangle$' from the set.

It's common to use the *double*-turnstile—'⊨'—to affirm that the *wffs* to its left *imply* the *wff* to its right. Alternatively, the *wff* to the right of the double-turnstile is said to be the *semantic consequence* of the *wffs* to its left. The double-turnstile is simply your old friend 'therefore'; it's another way of expressing '∴':

$$\triangle_1, \ldots, \triangle_{n-1} \models \triangle_n$$

Definition:    A *wff* '△' is a *semantic consequence* of a set of *wffs iff* there is no interpretation that makes every *wff* in the set true and that makes '△' false.

In other words, to say that '△' is a *semantic* consequence of a given set of *wffs* is simply to say that '△' is the conclusion of a valid argument.

Once again: the notion of *implication* belongs to semantics, and the notion of *derivation*, with its correlative notion of *generation*, belongs to syntax. Nevertheless, it's common, and entirely unobjectionable, to speak of a *derivation* even where our focus is on a flesh-and-blood *argument* whose premises are natural-language sentences. The fact that our derivation rules arise in the context of *uninterpreted* squiggle-marks doesn't entail that we can't use them in the context of *interpreted* squiggle-marks, i.e., propositions. Indeed, we *can* and, in the very next section, we *shall*.

# 4. Constructing Derivations: The Mechanics and the Strategies

## A. The Mechanics

It's almost time to dive in. . . . In the course of constructing your own derivations, i.e., whenever you derive a *wff* '△' from earlier *wffs* in the string of *wffs* that constitutes the derivation, you must adhere to certain requirements:

1.  To the right of '△', cite the line number(s) of the *wff(s)* from which you have derived '△'. (Obviously you will be doing no such thing in the case of the Rule of Assumptions.)

2.  To the right of the line number(s) that you have just cited, cite the derivation rule that allowed you to derive '△' from the earlier *wff(s)*. (To be sure, in the case of A, i.e., the Rule of Assumptions, you *aren't* deriving '△' from earlier *wffs*. Nevertheless, the derivation rule A, like the other derivation rules, serves to *justify* the assertion of '△'.)

3.  To the left of the line number that is itself to the left of '△', cite the line numbers of all the assumptions—but *only* the assumptions—on which '△' rests, i.e., from which they ultimately derive. Look at the line number(s) that you have just cited to the right of '△'. Ask yourself which *assumptions* the *wffs* corresponding to these line number(s) ultimately derive from. (Don't worry: As Spinoza [1632–1677] once said in a different context, this will soon become clear as the noonday sun.)

## B. The Strategies

There are two strategic approaches that one might adopt in this as in *every* derivation: the Top-Down Approach and the Bottom-Up Approach. The Top-Down Approach works *iff* some of the *wffs* that are staring you in the face are quite literally *begging* you to do something to them, i.e., to operate on them with one or other of the derivation rules. Always oblige them! You have nothing to lose (other than time, ink, and paper), and everything to gain: the proliferation of new *wffs* on your sheet of paper will suggest strategies to you that you might not otherwise have thought of.

The Bottom-Up Approach is the approach to use when the Top-Down Approach is going *nowhere*. Look at the last line of the sequent: the conclusion. Ask yourself which *wff* you would love to have in your *second*-to-last line, i.e., which *wff* is such that from it (along with, perhaps, one of the *wffs* higher up in the string) you could *immediately* derive the conclusion. Now that you have a prospective second-to-last line, play the same game again: ask yourself which *wff* you would love to have in your *third*-to-last line, i.e., which *wff* is such that from it (along with, perhaps, one of the *wffs* higher up in the string) you could *immediately* derive the *wff* in the second-to-last line. Now that you have a prospective third-to-last line, play the same game yet again and again, until you are so close to the initial *wffs* that you can *smell* them.

There is a third possible approach, of course: the Combined Approach. You work *downward* to some extent, and you work *upward* to some extent. Eventually your downward string will fuse with your upward string. You will find that it is the Combined Approach of which you will make the most use.

# 5. A Recapitulation of the First Seven Derivation Rules

## 1. The Rule of Assumptions: A

1.  To the right of any given assumption '$\triangle$', i.e., any premise, cite only the rule A.
2.  To to the assumption's far left, cite the same line number as the line number of the assumption itself.

## 2. $\wedge$E

1.  From '$\triangle \wedge O$', it is permissible to derive either '$\triangle$' or '$O$'.
2.  To the right of either '$\triangle$' or '$O$', cite the line number of '$\triangle \wedge O$', and the rule $\wedge$E.
3.  To the far left of either '$\triangle$' or '$O$', cite the line numbers of the assumptions on which it rests.

$$(m) \quad \triangle \wedge O \qquad\qquad\qquad (m) \quad \triangle \wedge O$$

$$(n) \quad \triangle \qquad m \wedge E \qquad\qquad (n) \quad O \qquad m \wedge E$$

## 3. ∧I

1. From '△' and from 'O', it is permissible to derive either '△ ∧ O' or 'O ∧ △'.
2. To the right of either '△ ∧ O' or 'O ∧ △', cite the line numbers of either '△' and 'O', or 'O' and '△', respectively, and the rule ∧I.
3. To the far left of either '△ ∧ O' or 'O ∧ △', cite the line numbers of the assumptions on which it rests.

| | | | | |
|---|---|---|---|---|
| (*m*) | △ | | (*m*) | △ |
| (*n*) | O | | (*n*) | O |
| | . | | | . |
| | . | | | . |
| (*o*) | △ ∧ O   *m,n* ∧I | | (*o*) | O ∧ △ *n,m* ∧I |

## 4. ∨I

1. From '△', it is permissible to derive either '△ ∨ O' or 'O ∨ △'.
2. To the right of either '△ ∨ O' or 'O ∨ △', cite the line number of '△', and the rule ∨I.
3. To the far left of either '△ ∨ O' or 'O ∨ △', cite the line numbers of the assumptions on which it rests.

| | | | | |
|---|---|---|---|---|
| (*m*) | △ | | (*m*) | △ |
| | . | | | . |
| | . | | | . |
| (*n*) | △ ∨ O   *m* ∨I | | (*n*) | O ∨ △ *m* ∨I |

## 5. →E

1. From '$\triangle \to \bigcirc$' and '$\triangle$', it is permissible to derive '$\bigcirc$'.
2. To the right of '$\bigcirc$' cite the line numbers of '$\triangle \to \bigcirc$' and '$\triangle$', respectively, and the rule →E.
3. To the far left of '$\bigcirc$', cite the line numbers of the assumptions on which it rests.

$(m) \quad \triangle \to \bigcirc$

$(n) \qquad \triangle$

$\cdot$

$\cdot$

$\cdot$

$(o) \qquad \bigcirc \qquad m,n \to E$

## 6. ↔E

1. From '$\triangle \leftrightarrow \bigcirc$' it is permissible to derive '$(\triangle \to \bigcirc) \wedge (\bigcirc \to \triangle)$'.
2. To the right of '$(\triangle \to \bigcirc) \wedge (\bigcirc \to \triangle)$', cite the line number of '$\triangle \leftrightarrow \bigcirc$' and the rule ↔E.
3. To the far left of '$(\triangle \to \bigcirc) \wedge (\bigcirc \to \triangle)$', cite the line numbers of the assumptions on which it rests.

$(m) \qquad \triangle \leftrightarrow \bigcirc$

$\cdot$

$\cdot$

$\cdot$

$(n) \quad (\triangle \to \bigcirc) \wedge (\bigcirc \to \triangle) \qquad m \leftrightarrow E$

## 7. − −E

1. From '$- -\triangle$', it is permissible to derive '$\triangle$'.
2. To the right of '$\triangle$', cite the line number of '$- -\triangle$' and the rule $- -$E.

3. To the far left of '$\triangle$', cite the line numbers of the assumptions on which it rests.

$(m)\ {-}{-}\triangle$

.

.

.

$(n)\quad \triangle \qquad m\ {-}{-}E$

# 6. Constructing Derivations Using Only the First Seven Derivation Rules

It's now time to dive in. Consider the following argument: 'Ardbeg doesn't fail to surrender and Bobo doesn't fail to surrender. If Ardbeg surrenders then Coco will be humiliated. Dagbar will be humiliated if and only if Bobo surrenders and Coco is humiliated. Therefore Dagbar will be humiliated.'

Now suppose that we translate this argument into logical notation, using the obvious interpretations. Expressed in horizontal, sequent notation, it would appear as follows:

S1:        $--A \wedge --B,\ A \rightarrow C,\ D \leftrightarrow (B \wedge C) \vdash D$

1 (1) $--A \wedge --B$          A
2 (2) $A \rightarrow C$          A
3 (3) $D \leftrightarrow (B \wedge C)$          A

.

.

$(n)$ D

The numbers in parentheses are the line numbers—the first line, the second line, etc., with $n$ being the number of the last line. To the left of these numbers are numbers that are *not* in parentheses; these designate the line numbers of the assumptions on which the *wff* on that line rests, i.e., the line numbers of the assumptions from which it is ultimately derived. Look at the *n*th (the last) line in the derivation. Once the derivation is complete, the numbers 1, 2, and 3 should appear to the far left of line *n,* indicating that the conclusion, 'D', rests upon, i.e., is ultimately derived from, the first, second, and third assumptions. These three assumptions, of course, are your three initial *wffs,* your three premises, and you want your conclusion to derive, ultimately, from your initial *wffs.*

Question: So what does it mean for each of the *wffs* in the first three lines—each of the three premises—to rest upon, or derive from, *itself?*

Answer: Patience.

Now somewhere toward the bottom of your sheet of paper, write down 'D', the sequent's last *wff,* its conclusion. Your goal is to construct a string of *wffs* extending from the premises to the conclusion, such that each *wff* in the string is a *syntactic consequence* of, or *follows* from, one or more of the previous *wffs* in the string by means of our derivation rules. Once you're done, then you will know that yes indeed, the sequent's last *wff,* its conclusion, really does *follow* (or *derive*) from the sequent's initial *wffs,* its premises—and you will know this because you will have constructed a derivation of the former from the latter.

You should address this derivation as you should address every derivation: by adopting either or both of the strategic approaches: the Top-Down Approach and the Bottom-Up Approach.

The Top-Down Approach consists in first looking at the *wffs* that you already have, so to speak—as opposed to those that you're trying to generate—and in then asking yourself what these *wffs* are begging you to do.

'— —A ∧ — —B' in line (1) is a conjunction. Like any conjunction, it's begging you to perform ∧E on it. So 'bring down' '— —A' in line (4). To the right of line (4) write '1∧E'—the line number of the *wff* on which you're using the derivation rule, followed by the name of the derivation rule that you're using. To the far left of line (4) write the line number of the assumption on which (1) rests. (1) rests on itself; so you simply write '1' to the far left of line (4).

Now bring down '— —B' in line (5). To the right of line (5) write '1∧E'—once again the line number of the *wff* on which you're using the derivation rule, followed by the name of the derivation rule that you're using. To the far left of line (5) write the line number of the assumption on which (1) rests. (1) rests on itself; so you simply write '1' to the far left of line (5).

Notice that you brought down '− −A' first and '− −B' second. You could just as well have brought down '− −B' first and '− −A' second; the order in which you perform ∧E is irrelevant.

$$
\begin{array}{lll}
1\ (1)\ -\!-A \wedge -\!-B & & A \\
2\ (2)\ A \rightarrow C & & A \\
3\ (3)\ D \leftrightarrow (B \wedge C) & & A \\
1\ (4)\ -\!-A & & 1\ \wedge E \\
1\ (5)\ -\!-B & & 1\ \wedge E \\
\end{array}
$$

'− −A' in line (4) is begging you to perform − −E on it. So write 'A' in line (6). To the right of line (6) write '4 − −E', because you derived the *wff* in line (6) from the *wff* in line (4) via − −E. To the far left of line (6) write the line number of the assumption on which the *wff* in line (4) rests, i.e., '1'.

'− −B' in line (5) is begging you to perform − −E on it. So write 'B' in line (7). To the right of line (7) write '5 − −E', because you derived the *wff* in line (7) from the *wff* in line (5) via − −E. To the far left of line (7) write the line number of the assumption on which the *wff* in line (5) rests, i.e., '1'.

$$
\begin{array}{lll}
1\ (1)\ -\!-A \wedge -\!-B & & A \\
2\ (2)\ A \rightarrow C & & A \\
3\ (3)\ D \leftrightarrow (B \wedge C) & & A \\
1\ (4)\ -\!-A & & 1\ \wedge E \\
1\ (5)\ -\!-B & & 1\ \wedge E \\
1\ (6)\ A & & 4\ -\!-E \\
1\ (7)\ B & & 5\ -\!-E \\
\end{array}
$$

Notice that you performed − −E on '− −A' first and on '− −B' second. You could just as well have performed it on '− −B' first and on '− −A' second; again, the order is irrelevant.

'A → C' in line (2) and 'A' in line (6) are begging you to perform →E on them. So write 'C' in line (8). To the right of line (8) write '2,6 →E', because you derived the *wff* in line (8) from the *wffs* in lines 2 and 6 via →E. To the far left of line (8) write the line numbers of the assumptions on which the *wffs* in lines (2) and (6) rest, i.e., '1' and '2'.

$$1 \ (1) \ {-}{-}A \land {-}{-}B \qquad\qquad A$$
$$2 \ (2) \ A \to C \qquad\qquad A$$
$$3 \ (3) \ D \leftrightarrow (B \land C) \qquad\qquad A$$
$$1 \ (4) \ {-}{-}A \qquad\qquad 1 \ \land E$$
$$1 \ (5) \ {-}{-}B \qquad\qquad 1 \ \land E$$
$$1 \ (6) \ A \qquad\qquad 4 \ {-}{-}E$$
$$1 \ (7) \ B \qquad\qquad 5 \ {-}{-}E$$
$$1,2 \ (8) \ C \qquad\qquad 2,6 \to E$$

You haven't yet operated on 'D ↔ (B ∧ C)' in line (3). It's begging you to perform ↔ on it. So write '[D → (B ∧ C)] ∧ [(B ∧ C) → D]' in line (9) by ↔E from (3). To the far left of line (9) write the line numbers of the assumption on which the *wff* in line (3) rests, i.e., '3'.

(9), in turn, is begging you to perform ∧E on it, so write 'D → (B ∧ C)' in line (10) and '(B ∧ C) → D' in line (11). To the right of both line (10) and line (11) write '9 ∧E', and to their far left write '3'. You won't need 'D → (B ∧ C)', but right now you're doing only what the *wffs* are begging you to do, and in any case, you have nothing to lose by writing it down. '(B ∧ C) → D' is another story, however. It's indispensable—as you're about to see.

You've now gone as far as you can go using the Top-Down Approach. At this point the *wffs* aren't begging you to do anything! No matter: the end, 'D', is in sight. You look at line (11) and you realize that *if* you had 'B ∧ C' then you'd have 'D' by →E, i.e., by performing →E on the *wff* in line (11), '(B ∧ C) → D', and 'B ∧ C'. So how do you generate 'B ∧ C'? Easy: you already have 'B' in line (7) and you already have 'C' in line (8). Presto! Perform ∧I on 'B' and 'C' to generate 'B ∧ C' in line (12). To the right of line (12) write '7,8 ∧I', because you derived the *wff* in line (12) from the *wffs* in lines 7 and 8. To the far left of line (12) write the line numbers of the assumptions on which the *wffs* in lines (7) and (8) rest, i.e., 1 and 2.

$$1 \ (1) \ {-}{-}A \land {-}{-}B \qquad\qquad A$$
$$2 \ (2) \ A \to C \qquad\qquad A$$
$$3 \ (3) \ D \leftrightarrow (B \land C) \qquad\qquad A$$
$$1 \ (4) \ {-}{-}A \qquad\qquad 1 \ \land E$$
$$1 \ (5) \ {-}{-}B \qquad\qquad 1 \ \land E$$
$$1 \ (6) \ A \qquad\qquad 4 \ {-}{-}E$$

| | |
|---|---|
| 1 (7) B | 5 −−E |
| 1,2 (8) C | 2,6 →E |
| 3 (9) [D → (B ∧ C)] ∧ [(B ∧ C) → D] | 3 ↔E |
| 3 (10) D → (B ∧ C) | 9 ∧E |
| 3 (11) (B ∧ C) → D | 9 ∧E |
| 1,2 (12) B ∧ C | 7,8 ∧I |

Perform →E on '(B ∧ C) → D' in line (11) and 'B ∧ C' in line (12) to generate 'D' in line (13). To the right of line (13) write '11,12 →E', because you derived the *wff* in line (13) from the *wffs* in lines (11) and (12) by →E. To the far left of (13) write the line numbers of the assumptions on which the *wffs* in lines (11) and (12) rest on, i.e., 1, 2, and 3. You're done.

| | |
|---|---|
| 1 (1) −−A ∧ −−B | A |
| 2 (2) A → C | A |
| 3 (3) D ↔ (B ∧ C) | A |
| 1 (4) −−A | 1 ∧E |
| 1 (5) −−B | 1 ∧E |
| 1 (6) A | 4 −−E |
| 1 (7) B | 5 −−E |
| 1,2 (8) C | 2,6 →E |
| 3 (9) [D → (B ∧ C)] ∧ [(B ∧ C) → D] | 3 ↔E |
| 3 (10) D → (B ∧ C) | 9 ∧E |
| 3 (11) (B ∧ C) → D | 9 ∧E |
| 1,2 (12) B ∧ C | 7,8 ∧I |
| 1,2,3 (13) D | 11,12 →E |

So what do the numerals at the far left *really* mean? Notice that I wrote the numeral '1' at the far left of line (4). *Syntactically* (where the focus is only on our deductive apparatus), this means that the *wff* in line (4) is ultimately *derivable* from the *wff* in line (1). *Semantically* (where the focus is only on considerations of truth and falsehood), it means that the argument whose premise, so to speak, is the *wff* in line (1), and whose conclusion, so to speak, is the *wff* in line (4), is a *valid* argument: there's no interpretation that makes the *wff* in line (1) true and the *wff* in line (4) false.

Now take a look at line (12). The *wff* in line (12) is derived *immediately* from the *wffs* in lines (7) and (8)—and rests on whatever *wffs* on which the *wffs* in lines (7) and (8) rest. The *wff* in line (7) rests on the *wff* in line (1), and the *wff* in line (8) rests on the *wffs* in lines (1) and (2). So the *wff* in line (12) rests on the *wffs* in lines (1) and (2). To the far left of line (12), therefore, I write the numerals '1' and '2'. *Syntactically*, this means that the *wff* in line (12) is ultimately *derived* from the *wffs* in lines (1) and (2). *Semantically*, this means that the argument whose premises, so to speak, are the *wffs* in lines (1) and (2), and whose conclusion, so to speak, is the *wff* in line (12), is a *valid* argument: there's no interpretation that makes the *wffs* in lines (1) and (2) true and the *wff* in line (12) false.

An aside: From this point on, and on most occasions, instead of using the cumbersome expression, 'the *wff* in line '(*n*)', I shall simply use the expression '(*n*)'. Instead of writing, for example, 'There's no interpretation that makes the *wffs* in lines (1) and (2) true and the *wff* in line (12) false', I shall write, 'There's no interpretation that makes (1) and (2) true and (12) false'.

So far so good. But what about the question that I raised just before launching into this last derivation: "So what does it mean for each of the *wffs* in the first three lines—each of the three premises—to rest upon, or derive from, *itself*?" More generally, what does it mean to say that a *wff*—or rather, every *assumption* but *only* an assumption—rests upon, or derives from, itself?

Answer: Take your first premise as an example. *Syntactically*, the fact that (1) rests on itself means that (1) follows from (1). *Semantically*, it means that there's no interpretation that makes (1) true and that makes (1) false.

Question: Isn't this all rather trivial, i.e., uninformative?

Answer: Perhaps—but that's the whole point of calling (1) an *assumption*. *Syntactically*, you're claiming that in the context of this particular derivation, (1) isn't derived from any other *wffs*. And *semantically*, you're not claiming that (1) is true and you're not claiming that it's false. You're claiming merely that *if* it's true it's true and *if* it's false it's false: that's just what it means for a *wff* to be an *assumption*.

Now for the Bottom-Up Approach. . . . The Top-Down Approach requires *minimal* strategic thinking on your part. The Bottom-Up Approach requires *maximal* strategic thinking. Look at your conclusion,

'D'. Ask yourself which *wffs* you would love to have. Ask yourself, in other words, which *wffs* would enable you to generate 'D'.

You notice that 'D' is the left component of 'D ↔ (B ∧ C)', your line-(3) bi-conditional. Your goal now is to detach it from the rest of the bi-conditional. Through ↔E and then ∧E, you could easily generate '(B ∧ C) → D'. If you could then generate 'B ∧ C', the game would be over—thanks to →E on '(B ∧ C) → D' and 'B ∧ C'. Your new target, of course, is 'B ∧ C'.

Look closely at 'B ∧ C'. Ask yourself what *kind* of a *wff* it is. It's a conjunction, yes? And you know precisely which rule allows you to generate conjunctions: ∧I. To perform ∧I, you need to have each of the two conjuncts that you plan to conjoin to generate 'B ∧ C'. So you need to generate 'B' and you need to generate 'C'.

| | | |
|---|---|---|
| 1 (1) | − −A ∧ − −B | A |
| 2 (2) | A → C | A |
| 3 (3) | D ↔ (B ∧ C) | A |
| 3 (4) | [D → (B ∧ C)] ∧ [(B ∧ C) → D] | 3 ↔E |
| 3 (5) | (B ∧ C) → D | 4 ∧E |
| | . | |
| | . | |
| | . | |
| (?) | B | ? |
| | . | |
| | . | |
| | . | |
| (n−2) | C | ? |
| (n−1) | B ∧ C | ?,n−2 ∧I |
| (n) | D | 5,n−1 →E |

You look at (1) and you immediately see how to generate 'B': first you perform ∧E on '− −A ∧ − −B' in order to generate '− −B' in line (6). Then you perform − −E on '− −B' in order to generate 'B' in line (7).

| | | |
|---|---|---|
| 1 (1) | − −A ∧ − −B | A |
| 2 (2) | A → C | A |
| 3 (3) | D ↔ (B ∧ C) | A |
| 3 (4) | [D → (B ∧ C)] ∧ [(B ∧ C) → D] | 3 ↔E |

3 (5) (B ∧ C) → D                             4 ∧E

1 (6) − −B                                    1 ∧E

1 (7) B                                       6 − −E

.

.

(*n*–2) C                                     ?

(*n*–1) B ∧ C                                 7,*n*–2 ∧I

(*n*) D                                       5,*n*–1 →E

Fine. Now what about 'C'? How do you propose to generate 'C'? You notice 'C' in line (2): it's the consequent of the line-(2) conditional. To generate the consequent of a conditional all you need to do is generate the *wff* that is its antecedent. So all you need to do is generate 'A'. You look back at (1) and you immediately see how to generate 'A'. You perform ∧E on '− −A ∧ − −B' in line (1) in order to generate '− −A' in line (8). Then you perform − −E on '− −A' in order to generate 'A' in line (9). From 'A → C' in line (2) and 'A' in line (9), you now have 'C' in line (10) by →E.

You will recall that your goal was to generate 'B ∧ C' in your second-to-last line. By performing ∧I on 'B' in line (7) and 'C' in line (10), you generate 'B ∧ C' in line (11). You know the rest of the script.

1 (1) − −A ∧ − −B                             A

2 (2) A → C                                   A

3 (3) D ↔ (B ∧ C)                             A

3 (4) [D → (B ∧ C)] ∧ [(B ∧ C) → D]           3 ↔E

3 (5) (B ∧ C) → D                             4 ∧E

1 (6) − −B                                    1 ∧E

1 (7) B                                       6 − −E

1 (8) − −A                                    1 ∧E

1 (9) A                                       8 − −E

1,2 (10) C                                    2,9 →E

1,2 (11) B ∧ C                                7,10 ∧I

1,2,3 (12) D                                  5,11 →I

Quick! Scribble down the premises and conclusion of this last sequent, and try to derive the conclusion from the premises on your own, i.e., without looking at the book. First use the Top-Down Approach and then use the Bottom-Up Approach.

Question: So which approach should you plan on using with derivations in the future: the Top-Down or the Bottom-Up?

Answer: Each one. Often you'll be able to get at least *some* mileage from the Top-Down Approach. The problem is that the more complicated the derivation, the less the likelihood that you'll get sufficient mileage from it alone. The sooner that you accustom yourself to the Bottom-Up Approach—and the strategic thinking that it calls for—the sooner that you'll be doing derivations in your sleep.

Now consider the following argument: 'If either Ardbeg or Bobo surrenders, then either Coco or Dagbar will be humiliated and the evil Egvalt's star will rise. Ardbeg will surrender and the traitor Fortescue will sneak away. If Ardbeg surrenders and the evil Egvalt's star rises then miserable Monty's victory will be secure. So the traitor Fortescue will sneak away and miserable Monty's victory will be secure.'

Now suppose that we translate this argument into logical notation, using the obvious interpretations. Expressed in horizontal, sequent notation, it would appear as follows:

S2:         $(A \lor B) \rightarrow [(C \lor D) \land E], A \land F, (A \land E) \rightarrow M \vdash F \land M$

1 (1) $(A \lor B) \rightarrow [(C \lor D) \land E]$        A
2 (2) $A \land F$        A
3 (3) $(A \land E) \rightarrow M$        A

                .
                .
                .

        ($n$) $F \land M$

The Top-Down Approach is a bit tricky here, and requires some strategic thinking. As a conjunction, your second premise, '$A \land F$', is crying out for $\land$E. $\land$E generates '$A$' and '$F$' separately. Hold '$F$' in reserve for your conclusion, '$F \land M$'.

Your first premise, '$(A \lor B) \rightarrow [(C \lor D) \land E]$', is a conditional. You know that if you had its antecedent, then you'd have its consequent by $\rightarrow$E. Because you now have '$A$', you can generate '$(A \lor B)$' by $\lor$I. $\rightarrow$E on (1), '$(A \lor B) \rightarrow [(C \lor D) \land E]$', and '$A \lor B$' generates '$[(C \lor D) \land E]$'. $\land$E on '$[(C \lor D) \land E]$' generates '$E$'. (It also generates '$C \lor D$', but '$C \lor D$' won't help you generate your conclusion.)

You now have an 'A', an 'E', and an 'F', each waiting to be put to good use. (To be sure, you've already used 'A', but nothing prevents you from using a given *wff* more than once.)

Your third premise, '(A ∧ E) → M', is a conditional. You think to yourself that if you had its antecedent, 'A ∧ E', then you'd have its consequent, 'M', by →E. 'M' is an ideal target insofar as it's one of the conjuncts of your conclusion, 'F ∧ M'. Of course you're within a milli-meter of having 'A ∧ E', insofar as you have each of its conjuncts sepa-rately. ∧I on 'A' and 'E' generates 'A ∧ E'. →E on (3), '(A ∧ E) → M', and 'A ∧ E' generates 'M'. ∧I on 'F'—remember: you held 'F' in reserve a few lines back—and 'M' generates your conclusion 'F ∧ M'. Done.

Now for the Bottom-Up Approach. Your conclusion is the conjunc-tion of 'F' and 'M'. So your goal is to generate either 'F' or 'M' in your second-to-last line, and the other conjunct in some previous line.

$$
\begin{array}{lll}
1 & (1)\ (A \vee B) \rightarrow [(C \vee D) \wedge E] & A \\
2 & (2)\ A \wedge F & A \\
3 & (3)\ (A \wedge E) \rightarrow M & A \\
2 & (4)\ F & 2\ \wedge E \\
\end{array}
$$

$$
\cdot
$$
$$
\cdot
$$

$$
\begin{array}{lll}
(n{-}1) & M & ? \\
(n) & F \wedge M & 4, n{-}1\ \wedge I \\
\end{array}
$$

Generating 'F' in line (4) is a snap, thanks to ∧E on (2). Your goal now is to generate 'M' in your second-to-last line.

'M' is the consequent of your line-(3) conditional, '(A ∧ E) → M'. If you could generate 'A ∧ E' in your third-to-last line, (n–2), you'd have 'M' by →E on lines (3) and (n–2). Your goal now is to generate 'A' and 'E' separately. Generating 'A' is a snap, thanks to ∧E on (2). Your goal now is to generate 'E'.

$$
\begin{array}{lll}
1 & (1)\ (A \vee B) \rightarrow [(C \vee D) \wedge E] & A \\
2 & (2)\ A \wedge F & A \\
3 & (3)\ (A \wedge E) \rightarrow M & A \\
2 & (4)\ F & 2\ \wedge E \\
\end{array}
$$

| | |
|---|---|
| 2 (5) A | 2 ∧E |
| . | |
| . | |
| (*n*–3) E | ? |
| (*n*–2) A ∧ E | 5,*n*–3 ∧I |
| (*n*–1) M | 3,*n*–2 →E |
| (*n*) F ∧ M | 4,*n*–1 ∧I |

So how do you generate your new target, 'E'? Your first premise, '(A ∨ B) → [(C ∨ D) ∧ E]', is a conditional. 'E' appears in the consequent of the conditional. The consequent, '(C ∨ D) ∧ E', is a conjunction, one of whose conjuncts is 'C ∨ D', and one of whose conjuncts is 'E'. You don't need the left conjunct, 'C ∨ D', but you do need the right conjunct, 'E'. So, if you could detach the consequent of your line-(1) conditional from the conditional itself, you could then perform ∧E on '(C ∨ D) ∧ E' to generate 'E'.

Your immediate goal should be clear: you need to generate 'A ∨ B', the antecedent of your line-(1) conditional. Once you have it, then you'll be able to generate '(C ∨ D) ∧ E', its consequent, via →E on the conditional itself and 'A ∨ B', its antecedent.

Question: How do you generate its antecedent?

Answer: 'A ∨ B' is a disjunction. If you had either disjunct, you could generate the disjunction via ∨I. You don't have 'B' but you do have 'A'—in line (5). Game over.

| | |
|---|---|
| 1 (1) (A ∨ B) → [(C ∨ D) ∧ E] | A |
| 2 (2) A ∧ F | A |
| 3 (3) (A ∧ E) → M | A |
| 2 (4) F | 2 ∧E |
| 2 (5) A | 2 ∧E |
| 2 (6) A ∨ B | 5 ∨I |
| 1,2 (7) (C ∨ D) ∧ E | 1,6 →E |
| 1,2 (8) E | 7 ∧E |
| 1,2 (9) A ∧ E | 5,8 ∧I |
| 1,2,3 (10) M | 3,9 →E |
| 1,2,3 (11) F ∧ M | 4,10 ∧I |

Quick! Once again, scribble down the premises and conclusion of this last sequent, and try to derive the conclusion from the premises on your own, i.e., without looking at the book. First use the Top-Down Approach and then use the Bottom-Up Approach.

Now consider the following sequent. Its propositional symbols are variables rather than constants. (Obviously, this won't affect the derivation.)

S3:        $P \rightarrow --(Q \wedge ---R), --(P \wedge S) \vdash -R \wedge S$

Consider first the Top-Down Approach. Notice that the second premise of the sequent is begging you to perform $--$E on it, thereby generating 'P ∧ S' in line (3). Notice that 'P ∧ S' is begging you to perform ∧E on it twice, thereby generating, separately, 'P' in line (4) and 'S' in line (5). 'P' and the first premise together are begging you to perform →E on them in order to generate '$--$(Q ∧ $---$R)' in line (6). '$--$(Q ∧ $---$R)', in turn, is begging you to perform $--$E on it, thereby generating 'Q ∧ $---$R' in line (7). 'Q ∧ $---$R', in its turn, is begging you to perform ∧E on it, thereby generating '$---$R' in line (8). (∧E would also generate 'Q'—but you don't need 'Q'.) '$---$R' is begging you to perform $--$E on it, thereby generating '$-$R' in line (9). You have now derived (among other *wffs*) '$-$R' and 'S' separately. One quick application of ∧I generates '$-$R ∧ S' in line (10) and you're done.

| | | |
|---|---|---|
| 1 | (1) $P \rightarrow --(Q \wedge ---R)$ | A |
| 2 | (2) $--(P \wedge S)$ | A |
| 2 | (3) $P \wedge S$ | $2 --$E |
| 2 | (4) P | 3 ∧E |
| 2 | (5) S | 3 ∧E |
| 1,2 | (6) $--(Q \wedge ---R)$ | 1,4 →E |
| 1,2 | (7) $Q \wedge ---R$ | $6 --$E |
| 1,2 | (8) $---R$ | 7 ∧E |
| 1,2 | (9) $-R$ | $8 --$E |
| 1,2 | (10) $-R \wedge S$ | 9,5 ∧I |

Consider next the Bottom-Up Approach. Your conclusion is a conjunction, so you think ∧I thoughts. You want to generate '$-$R' at

some point and 'S' at some other point. Generating 'S' is the easy part:
——E on your second premise, '——(P ∧ S)', will generate the conjunction 'P ∧ S' in line (3), and ∧E on 'P ∧ S' will generate 'S' in line (4).

Now for the hard part. Your second-to-last line will be '—R'. You
look at your first premise, the conditional 'P → ——(Q ∧ ———R)',
and you see '———R' buried in its consequent. You think to yourself,
"I could generate '—R' in my second-to-last line by ——E if I could
somehow generate '———R' in my third-to-last line. And I could
generate '———R' in my third-to-last line if I could somehow extract
'———R' from my first premise." A second look at your first premise
suggests that if you had 'Q ∧ ———R' in your fourth-to-last line, then
you'd have '———R' in your third-to-last line by ∧E. A third look at
your first premise suggests that if you had '——(Q ∧ ———R)' in your
fifth-to-last line, then you'd have 'Q ∧ ———R' in your fourth-to-last
line by ——E. A fourth look at your first premise suggests that if you
had 'P' in your sixth-to-last line, then you'd have '——(Q ∧ ———R)'
in your fifth-to-last line by →E on line (1) and 'P'. You see 'P' as the
left conjunct of your line-(3) conjunction 'P ∧ S', and you perform ∧E
on line (3) to generate 'P'. The avalanche has begun:

```
   1 (1) P → ——(Q ∧ ———R)      A
   2 (2) ——(P ∧ S)             A
   2 (3) P ∧ S                 2 ——E
   2 (4) S                     3 ∧E
   2 (5) P                     3 ∧E
 1,2 (6) ——(Q ∧ ———R)          1,5 →E
 1,2 (7) Q ∧ ———R              6 ——E
 1,2 (8) ———R                  7 ∧E
 1,2 (9) —R                    8 ——E
1,2 (10) —R ∧ S                9,4 ∧I
```

You know the drill. Try to derive the conclusion from the premises on your own, using first the Top-Down Approach and then the
Bottom-Up Approach.

The penultimate (i.e., the *second*-to-last) sequent in this section is
a bit trickier than the preceding ones. A few words of advice before
you dive in. Just remember: this is neither a battlefield nor a torture
chamber; it's just a derivation in logic. In what follows, do *not* give in

to panic and do *not* despair. (On the other hand, a *little* panic and a *little* despair never hurt anybody!) I am well aware that constructing derivations can be a tricky business. I am also well aware that if you persevere, you'll be able to master this tricky business. Do yourself a favor and don't abandon a derivation through which I am walking you until you have fully grasped it and can do it on your own without sneaking a peek at the text.

S4:          $P \rightarrow (-Q \leftrightarrow R), --P \wedge S, --(P \rightarrow -Q) \vdash R \vee (T \rightarrow U)$

Suppose that you tackle this sequent using the Top-Down Approach. The first premise isn't begging you to do anything. Conditionals by themselves never beg you to do anything—unless you see their antecedents lurking in the vicinity. The second premise is a conjunction. Conjunctions are always begging you to do something: they're begging you to do ∧E. Just do it. As a result, line (4) looks as follows:

1 (1) $P \rightarrow (-Q \leftrightarrow R)$          A
2 (2) $--P \wedge S$          A
3 (3) $--(P \rightarrow -Q)$          A
2 (4) $--P$          2 ∧E

Now (4) is obviously begging you to do −−E. You oblige it and you end up with the following *wff*:

2 (5) P          4 −−E

Now let your eyes sweep up and down the first five lines of the derivation. They—your eyes—should zero in on lines (1) and (5), ripe candidates for →E:

1,2 (6) $-Q \leftrightarrow R$          1,5 →E

Now take a look at the third premise. You haven't yet made use of it. It's the negation of the negation of *zappo*. You use −−E to generate *zappo*:

3 (7) $P \rightarrow -Q$          3 −−E

Notice that (7) and (5) are begging you to do →E. You oblige them accordingly:

2,3 (8) −Q                                              7,5 →E

Notice that (8) is derived from (7) and (5). (7), however, rests on, i.e., is ultimately derived from, (3), whereas (5) rests on, i.e., is ultimately derived from, (2). (8), therefore, rests on, i.e., is ultimately derived from, (2) and (3).

Now look at (6). Immediately, you should have ↔E thoughts:

1,2 (9) (−Q → R) ∧ (R → −Q)     6 ↔E

(9) is a conjunction. Conjunctions are always begging you to do ∧E. It turns out that in this derivation, you don't really need both conjuncts. But if you don't see that immediately, just bring them both down.

1,2 (10) −Q → R                              9 ∧E
1,2 (11) R → −Q                              9 ∧E

Now look at (10) and (8). Immediately, you should have →E thoughts.

1,2,3 (12) R                                          10,8 →E

Thanks to ∨I, you are now within striking distance of the conclusion. Strike!

1 (1) P → (−Q ↔ R)                    A
2 (2) − −P ∧ S                          A
3 (3) − −(P → −Q)                    A
2 (4) − −P                              2 ∧E
2 (5) P                                  4 − −E
1,2 (6) −Q ↔ R                      1,5 →E
3 (7) P → −Q                        3 − −E
2,3 (8) −Q                              7,5 →E
1,2 (9) (−Q → R) ∧ (R → −Q)     6 ↔E
1,2 (10) −Q → R                      9 ∧E

$$1,2 \ (11) \ R \to -Q \qquad\qquad\qquad 9 \ \wedge E$$
$$1,2,3 \ (12) \ R \qquad\qquad\qquad\qquad 10,8 \to E$$
$$1,2,3 \ (13) \ R \vee (T \to U) \qquad\qquad 12 \ \vee I$$

Notice that you could shorten the derivation by one line, had you eliminated line (11). Notice too that the conclusion rests on, i.e., is ultimately derived from, the three premises—which is *exactly* what you want.

Question: When wouldn't a conclusion rest on, i.e., ultimately be derived from, all of the premises?

Answer: When not all of the premises play a role in deriving the conclusion from the premises.

Question: When might that be?

Answer: When you're confronted with either a typo or a curveball.

So much for the Top–Down Approach. What about the Bottom–Up Approach? You start by examining the conclusion and asking your-self what kind of a *wff* it is. Because it's a disjunction, you think ∨I thoughts. If you can generate either the left or the right disjunct, the game will be over.

Look at the right disjunct: 'T → U'. Now look at the premises. Do you see the propositional symbols 'T' or 'U' *anywhere* in the premises? No. Obviously, then, you're not going to be able to generate 'T → U' from the premises. Now look at the left disjunct: 'R'. If you could generate it in your second-to-last line, the game would be over: you'd go from 'R' in your second-to-last line to 'R ∨ (T → U)' in your last line by ∨I. Your new target is 'R'. Suppose that the string of *wffs* in your derivation is exactly *n* lines long. Then 'R' will be on your second-to-last line, i.e., line number $n-1$:

$$1 \ (1) \ P \to (-Q \leftrightarrow R) \qquad\qquad A$$
$$2 \ (2) \ --P \wedge S \qquad\qquad\qquad A$$
$$3 \ (3) \ --(P \to -Q) \qquad\qquad\quad A$$
$$\cdot$$
$$\cdot$$
$$(n-1) \ R \qquad\qquad\qquad\qquad\quad ?$$
$$(n) \ R \vee (T \to U) \qquad\qquad\quad n-1, \ \vee I$$

Which *wff* would you like to see in your third-to-last line, *n*–2; i.e., which *wff* would enable you to generate 'R' in your second-to-last line? Study your premises. Notice the consequent of your line-(1) conditional: '—Q ↔ R'. If you could generate it at some point, then from it you could immediately derive '(—Q → R) ∧ (R → —Q)' by ↔E. From '(—Q → R) ∧ (R → —Q)' you could derive '—Q → R' by ∧E. If somehow you could derive '—Q', then from '—Q → R' and '—Q' you'd have 'R' by →E. With 'R' the game is over, thanks to ∨I.

So here's what you want. You want 'R' in your second-to-last line, '—Q' in your third-to-last line, '—Q → R' in your fourth-to-last line, and '(—Q → R) ∧ (R → —Q)' in your fifth-to-last line. Your work is now cut out for you: you have two targets: '—Q ↔ R' and '—Q'. (Obviously it would make no difference if you were to reverse the order slightly, and generate '—Q → R' in your third-to-last line and '—Q' in your fourth-to-last line.)

$$1 \;(1)\; P \to (—Q \leftrightarrow R) \qquad\qquad A$$
$$2 \;(2)\; ——P \land S \qquad\qquad A$$
$$3 \;(3)\; ——(P \to —Q) \qquad\qquad A$$
.
.
.

$$(n\text{–}5)\; —Q \leftrightarrow R \qquad\qquad 1,? \to E$$
$$(n\text{–}4)\; (—Q \to R) \land (R \to —Q) \qquad ?$$
$$(n\text{–}3)\; —Q \to R \qquad\qquad n\text{–}4 \;\land E$$
$$(n\text{–}2)\; —Q \qquad\qquad ?$$
$$(n\text{–}1)\; R \qquad\qquad n\text{–}3, n\text{–}2 \to E$$
$$(n)\; R \lor (T \to U) \qquad\qquad n\text{–}1 \;\lor I$$

How might you generate '—Q ↔ R'? If you could generate 'P', you could generate '—Q ↔ R' via →E from the first premise, 'P → (—Q ↔ R)', and 'P'. Not only that, if you could generate 'P', you'd also be within a hare's whisker of '—Q'. All you'd have to do is first generate 'P → —Q' from '— —(P → —Q)' in line (3) via — —E, and then generate '—Q' from 'P → —Q' and 'P' via →E. Clearly your new target is 'P': the magic key that opens *all* doors in this derivation.

Look now at line (2) and look no further: from '— —P ∧ S' you can generate '— —P' via ∧E, and from '— —P' you can generate 'P' via — —E.

$$
\begin{array}{lll}
1 & (1)\ P \to (-Q \leftrightarrow R) & A \\
2 & (2)\ --P \wedge S & A \\
3 & (3)\ --(P \to -Q) & A \\
2 & (4)\ --P & 2\ \wedge E \\
2 & (5)\ P & 4\ --E \\
3 & (6)\ P \to -Q & 3\ --E \\
1,2 & (7)\ -Q \leftrightarrow R & 1,5\ \to E \\
1,2 & (8)\ (-Q \to R) \wedge (R \to -Q) & 7\ \leftrightarrow E \\
1,2 & (9)\ -Q \to R & 8\ \wedge E \\
2,3 & (10)\ -Q & 6,5\ \to E \\
1,2,3 & (11)\ R & 9,10\ \to E \\
1,2,3 & (12)\ R \vee (T \to U) & 11 \vee I
\end{array}
$$

Note that where lines (6) and (7) are concerned, the order of the *wffs* in the derivation in the Top-Down Approach was the reverse of the order of the *wffs* in the derivation in the Bottom-Up Approach. There's nothing surprising about this. It's not true that *all* roads lead to Rome—but it is true that *many* roads do—and sometimes, although not in this instance, the roads are radically unlike one another.

You know the drill. Close the book and take out a sheet of clean paper. . . .

One last sequent:

S5:          $P \wedge (Q \wedge R),\ [(R \wedge P) \wedge Q] \to [-S \leftrightarrow (T \wedge V)],$
             $---S \vdash T \vee -(U \wedge V)$

Suppose that you adopt the Top-Down Approach at the outset: just do unto the premises whatever they're imploring you to do unto them:

$$
\begin{array}{lll}
1 & (1)\ P \wedge (Q \wedge R) & A \\
2 & (2)\ [(R \wedge P) \wedge Q] \to [-S \leftrightarrow (T \wedge V)] & A \\
3 & (3)\ ---S & A
\end{array}
$$

The first premise is clearly imploring you to do $\wedge E$ twice to generate (4) and (5); and (3) is clearly imploring you to do '$--E$' to generate (6):

1 (1) P ∧ (Q ∧ R)                                        A
2 (2) [(R ∧ P) ∧ Q] → [−S ↔ (T ∧ V)]    A
3 (3) − − −S                                               A
1 (4) P                                                         1 ∧E
1 (5) Q ∧ R                                                  1 ∧E
3 (6) −S                                                       3 − −E

(5) is imploring you to do ∧E twice, to generate (7) and (8):

1 (7) Q                                                        5 ∧E
1 (8) R                                                        5 ∧E

You haven't yet touched the second premise, '[(R ∧ P) ∧ Q] → [−S ↔ (T ∧ V)]'. It's a conditional. If you had its antecedent, '(R ∧ P) ∧ Q', you'd have its consequent, '−S ↔ (T ∧ V)'. Its antecedent is a conjunction, whose left conjunct is also a conjunction. In two steps of ∧I, first on (8) and (4) to generate (9), 'R ∧ P', and then on (9) and (7) to generate (10), '(R ∧ P) ∧ Q', you'll have its antecedent. Thanks to →E on (2) and (10), you'll have its consequent '−S ↔ (T ∧ V)', in line (11):

1 (9) R ∧ P                                                   8,4 ∧I
1 (10) (R ∧ P) ∧ Q                                         9,7 ∧I
1,2 (11) −S ↔ (T ∧ V)                                   2,10→E

(11), of course, is imploring you to do ↔E to generate (12), '[−S → (T ∧ V)] ∧ [(T ∧ V) → −S]'. ∧E twice on (12) generates '−S → (T ∧ V)' in line (13) and '(T ∧ V) → −S' in line (14). (The latter *wff* won't help you out at all—but you don't know that yet.) You notice '−S' in line (6), and so you operate with →E on (13) and (6) to generate 'T ∧ V' in line (15).

1,2 (12) [−S → (T ∧ V)] ∧ [(T ∧ V) → −S]    11 ↔E
1,2 (13) −S → (T ∧ V)                                      12 ∧E
1,2 (14) (T ∧ V) → −S                                      12 ∧E
1,2,3 (15) T ∧ V                                               13,6 →E

Notice how far you've come without once looking at the conclusion. You've done nothing but take your marching orders from the *wffs* themselves. Now, however, you've hit the wall, and it's time to look at the conclusion, 'T ∨ −(U ∧ V)'. It's a disjunction, of course; and whenever there's a disjunction that you don't *yet* have but are trying to generate, think ∨I thoughts. If you had either 'T' or '−(U ∧ V)' the game would be over. Notice that you have 'V' in line (15). You could bring it down via ∧E and try to derive '−(U ∧ V)' from it— but it's entirely unclear how you might pull that off. Even worse, it's entirely clear that you could *not* pull it off: the argument from 'V' to '−(U ∧ V)' is an *invalid* argument. The Short Method shows you that if you assign T to 'V' and T to 'U', the 'premise', 'V', will be true and the 'conclusion', '−(U ∧ V'), will be false. Our derivation rules, you will recall (for the umpteenth time), are truth-preserving, and so there is no way that they could take you from this 'premise' to that 'conclusion'.

Although 'V' in line (15) doesn't do the trick, 'T' does. Drawing upon it, you can derive the conclusion in two steps:

| | | |
|---|---|---|
| 1 (1) P ∧ (Q ∧ R) | | A |
| 2 (2) [(R ∧ P) ∧ Q] → [−S ↔ (T ∧ V)] | | A |
| 3 (3) − − −S | | A |
| 1 (4) P | | 1 ∧E |
| 1 (5) Q ∧ R | | 1 ∧E |
| 3 (6) −S | | 3 − −E |
| 1 (7) Q | | 5 ∧E |
| 1 (8) R | | 5 ∧E |
| 1 (9) R ∧ P | | 8,4 ∧I |
| 1 (10) (R ∧ P) ∧ Q | | 9,7 ∧I |
| 1,2 (11) −S ↔ (T ∧ V) | | 2,10 →E |
| 1,2 (12) [−S → (T ∧ V)] ∧ [(T ∧ V) → −S] | | 11 ↔E |
| 1,2 (13) −S → (T ∧ V) | | 12 ∧E |
| 1,2 (14) (T ∧ V) → −S | | 12 ∧E |
| 1,2,3 (15) T ∧ V | | 13,6 →E |
| 1,2,3 (16) T | | 15 ∧E |
| 1,2,3 (17) T ∨ −(U ∧ V) | | 16 ∨I |

Game. Set. Match.

Several points are noteworthy about this derivation. First point. You used the Short Method in the previous paragraph to determine that a particular strategy *would not*—because it *could not*—pan out. Making use of the Short Method in this way will save you from hours (if not years) of dead-end attempts to derive a given *wff* from a set of *wffs* from which it simply can't be derived—because the derivation of that *wff* from that set of *wffs* is invalid. Remember: our derivation rules are *truth-preserving*; any interpretation that makes the initial *wffs* true must make true whatever *wff* that you derive from these *wffs*. If you find yourself knocking your head against the wall, trying to derive a *wff* '$\triangle$' from a given set of *wffs*, apply the Short Method to determine whether the argument from the set to '$\triangle$' is a valid argument. If it's valid, by all means keep knocking your head against the wall—but if it's not valid, then go back to square one and try a fresh strategy.

Second point. The numbering to the right of lines (9), (10), and (15) may strike you as a bit odd: Why '8,4' rather than '4,8'; why '9,7' rather than '7,9'; and why '13,6' rather than '6,13'? The answer is simple. In lines (9) and (10) you used ∧I. With ∧I you are creating a conjunction; i.e., you are performing the conjunction operation. The operation consists in first targeting the *wff* that will become the *left* conjunct and then targeting the *wff* that will become the *right* conjunct; hence '8,4' and '9,7', respectively.

In line (15) you used →E. If you return to our initial discussion of →E, you'll notice that the first *wff* to which I drew your attention was the conditional, and the second was its antecedent. In line (15), therefore, first I cited the line where the conditional is to be found, and next I cited the line where its antecedent is to be found, i.e., '13' and '6', respectively.

Question: These considerations don't seem *so* weighty. It doesn't *really* matter whether one writes '4,8' rather than '8,4', or '7,9' rather than '9,7', or '6,13' rather than '13,6', does it?

Answer: No. It doesn't.

Question: Then isn't it a *bit* pedantic to insist on this sort of uniformity?

Answer: It is—but it will make life a bit easier on he or she who grades your derivations.

Suppose that you now try the Bottom-Up Approach to this same sequent:

1 (1) P ∧ (Q ∧ R)                                    A
2 (2) [(R ∧ P) ∧ Q] → [−S ↔ (T ∧ V)]    A
3 (3) − − −S                                          A

.
.

(n) T ∨ −(U ∧ V)

The first question that you should raise is *always*: What sort of a *wff* is the conclusion? In this case it's a disjunction, so you know that if you can derive either disjunct the game will be over. You examine each disjunct. You see the left disjunct, the *wff* 'T', in the second premise. It's buried within a *wff*, '(T ∧ V)', which is itself buried within a *wff*, '−S ↔ (T ∧ V)', which in turn is itself buried within the entire *wff* that constitutes the second premise, '[(R ∧ P) ∧ Q] → [−S ↔ (T ∧ V)]'. At first blush, the prospect of extracting 'T' seems hopeless.

You then turn to the right-hand disjunct of the conclusion, '−(U ∧ V)'. 'U' appears nowhere in the premises. 'V', like 'T', is buried deep within the second premise. At first blush, the prospect of extracting 'V' seems hopeless, as was the case with the prospect of extracting 'T'. Moreover, it's unclear how your extracting 'V' would enable you to generate '−(U ∧ V)'. Drawing upon the Short Method, you discover that even if you were able to extract 'V' from the second premise, you would never succeed in generating '−(U ∧ V)'. You return to the left disjunct, 'T'; you have no choice but to try to generate it. Moral of the story: some first blushes are to be taken *less* seriously than others.

Of necessity, your reasoning now becomes a bit intricate. "If I could generate 'T' in the second-to-last line," you say to yourself, "then I'd have my conclusion by ∨I. If I could generate 'T ∧ V' in the third-to-last line, i.e., if somehow I could extract 'T ∧ V' from (2), then I'd have 'T' by ∧E."

1 (1) P ∧ (Q ∧ R)                                    A
2 (2) [(R ∧ P) ∧ Q] → [−S ↔ (T ∧ V)]    A
3 (3) − − −S                                          A

.
.

$(n-2)$ T ∧ V                                             ?
$(n-1)$ T                                                $n-2$ ∧E
$(n)$ T ∨ −(U ∧ V)                                       $n-1$ ∨I

The trick, of course, is to generate 'T ∧ V'. Notice that 'T ∧ V' is buried deep in (2). It's the right-hand component of the bi-conditional that happens to be the consequent of the line-(2) conditional. The first stage of the extraction project is to generate '(R ∧ P) ∧ Q', the antecedent of the line-(2) conditional. Why so? Because you'll make use of it, along with the conditional itself, '[(R ∧ P) ∧ Q] → [−S ↔ (T ∧ V)]', to generate '−S ↔ (T ∧ V)', the consequent of the conditional, via →E.

Question: And just how is 'T ∧ V' supposed to emerge from '−S ↔ (T ∧ V)'?

Answer: You'll cross that bridge when you get to it; i.e., when you begin the second stage of the extraction process.

1 (1) P ∧ (Q ∧ R)                                        A
2 (2) [(R ∧ P) ∧ Q] → [−S ↔ (T ∧ V)]    A
3 (3) − − −S                                             A
        .
        .

Stage One:
$(m-1)$ (R ∧ P) ∧ Q                                      ?
$(m)$ −S ↔ (T ∧ V)                                       2,$m-1$ →E
        .
        .

Stage Two:
$(n-2)$ T ∧ V                                             ?
$(n-1)$ T                                                $n-2$ ∧E
$(n)$ T ∨ −(U ∧ V)                                       $n-1$ ∨I

Your immediate goal, in Stage One, is to generate '(R ∧ P) ∧ Q', the antecedent of the line-(2) conditional. It's a conjunction whose only atomics are 'P', 'Q', and 'R', and whose left conjunct is also a conjunction. You look up at (1), 'P ∧ (Q ∧ R)', and what do you see? You see a conjunction whose only atomics are 'P', 'Q', and 'R', and whose right conjunct is also a conjunction. Your old pals ∧E and ∧I will help you pull off the transformation of 'P ∧ (Q ∧ R)' into '(R ∧ P) ∧ Q', in lines (4) through (9).

Whenever you're trying to generate a conjunction, think ∧I thoughts. How do you generate '(R ∧ P) ∧ Q'? Obviously by generating 'R ∧ P', on the one hand, and 'Q', on the other. So how do you generate 'R ∧ P'? Obviously by generating 'R', on the one hand, and 'P', on the other. Clearly, then, you generate '(R ∧ P) ∧ Q' by first generating *separately* the three atomics, 'R', 'P', and 'Q', in lines (7), (4), and (6), respectively; next, by conjoining 'R' with 'P' to generate 'R ∧ P' in line (8); and finally, by conjoining 'R ∧ P' with 'Q' to generate '(R ∧ P) ∧ Q' in line (9).

You look again at the line-(1) conjunction, 'P ∧ (Q ∧ R)'. Presto! You see how to generate 'R', 'P', and 'Q' separately. (The order in which you generate them is immaterial.) By several quick applications of ∧E you should be able to incinerate 'P ∧ (Q ∧ R)', the line-(1) conjunction. Out of its ashes, by two quick applications of ∧I, you should be able to re-create it, as '(R ∧ P) ∧ Q', in line (9):

| | |
|---|---|
| 1(1) P ∧ (Q ∧ R) | A |
| 2 (2) [(R ∧ P) ∧ Q] → [−S ↔ (T ∧ V)] | A |
| 3 (3) − − −S | A |
| 1 (4) P | 1 ∧E |
| 1 (5) Q ∧ R | 1 ∧E |
| 1 (6) Q | 5 ∧E |
| 1 (7) R | 5 ∧E |
| 1 (8) R ∧ P | 7,4 ∧I |
| 1 (9) (R ∧ P) ∧ Q | 8,6 ∧I |
| 1,2 (10) −S ↔ (T ∧ V) | 2,9 →E |

.
.

Stage Two:

| | |
|---|---|
| (n−2) T ∧ V | ? |
| (n−1) T | n−2 ∧E |
| (n) T ∨ −(U ∧ V) | n−1 ∨I |

The second, and last, stage of the extraction process—the extraction of 'T ∧ V'—is about to begin. . . . You see your immediate target, 'T ∧ V', buried in the bi-conditional '−S ↔ (T ∧ V)'. It was buried in (2), and it's still buried, to be sure, in (10). But it's not buried quite as deeply in (10) as it was in (2). Little by little, you're succeeding in extracting it.

Now pay *very* close attention to, and make a special point of remembering, what you're about to read. . . . There is only *one* way to extract a *wff* from the bi-conditional in which it's buried: you simply *must* transform the bi-conditional into a conjunction of conditionals by ↔E. At that point there are various possible moves that are open to you. You're now in a position to generate by ∧E, and then to operate on, either or both of the conditionals. Suppose—just *suppose*—that the post-∧E operation that you have in mind is →E in order, say, to detach the consequent of one of the two conditionals from the conditional itself. In that case, the antecedent of the conditional had better be hanging out in the neighborhood.

Performing ↔E on '−S ↔ (T ∧ V)' yields '[−S → (T ∧ V)] ∧ [(T ∧ V) → −S]'. You see 'T ∧ V' in both conjuncts, of course, but it's only its presence in the left conjunct that matters: it's extractable from the left conjunct, but not from the right. (You have no derivation rule that allows you to extract the *antecedent* of a conditional from the conditional.) Once you have '−S → (T ∧ V)' by ∧E, you say to yourself, "If only '−S', the antecedent, were hanging out in the neighborhood, the game would be over." You look up at line (3) and what do you see? You see '−S', ever so slightly disguised, hanging out in the neighborhood. The game is over.

| | | |
|---|---|---|
| 1 (1) | P ∧ (Q ∧ R) | A |
| 2 (2) | [(R ∧ P) ∧ Q] → [−S ↔ (T ∧ V)] | A |
| 3 (3) | − − −S | A |
| 1 (4) | P | 1 ∧E |
| 1 (5) | Q ∧ R | 1 ∧E |
| 1 (6) | Q | 5 ∧E |
| 1 (7) | R | 5 ∧E |
| 1 (8) | R ∧ P | 7,4 ∧I |
| 1 (9) | (R ∧ P) ∧ Q | 8,6 ∧I |
| 1,2 (10) | −S ↔ (T ∧ V) | 2,9 →E |
| 1,2 (11) | [−S → (T ∧ V)] ∧ [(T ∧ V) → −S] | 10 ↔E |
| 1,2 (12) | −S → (T ∧ V) | 11 ∧E |
| 3 (13) | −S | 3 − −E |
| 1,2,3 (14) | T ∧ V | 12,13 →E |
| 1,2,3 (15) | T | 14 ∧E |
| 1,2,3 (16) | T ∨ −(U ∧ V) | 15 ∨I |

Note once again that the order in which you proceeded, the order in which you derived the *wffs* in Top-Down Approach, was slightly different from the order in which you proceeded in the Bottom-Up Approach. Note once again that many roads lead to Rome. (Not *all*—but *many*.)

One last time in this section. . . . You know the drill. First, take out a sheet of clean paper. Next, write down the premises and the conclusion. Third, close the book. Fourth, prove the sequent with the Top-Down Approach. Fifth, prove it with the Bottom-Up Approach.

# 7. A Schematic Recapitulation of the First Seven Derivation Rules

## 1. The Rule of Assumptions: A

To the right of each given assumption, i.e., each premise, cite only the rule A.

## 2. ∧E

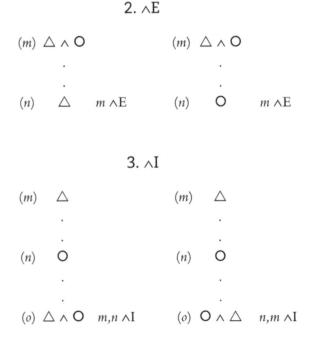

## 4. ∨I

(*m*)   △                    (*m*)   △

. 

.

.

.

(*n*) △ ∨ ○   *m* ∨I        (*n*) ○ ∨ △   *m* ∨I

## 5. →E

(*m*) △ → ○

.

.

(*n*)   △

.

.

(*o*)   ○      *m,n* →E

## 6. ↔E

(*m*)       △ ↔ ○

.

.

(*n*) (△ → ○) ∧ (○ →△)   *m* ↔E

## 7. − −E

(*m*) − −△

.

.

(*n*)   △      *m* − −E

# Exercises

For each of the following sequents, construct a derivation of its conclusion from its premises.

1.  S6: $P \wedge (Q \wedge R) \vdash (P \wedge Q) \wedge R$
2.  S7: $(P \wedge Q) \wedge R \vdash P \wedge (Q \wedge R)$
3.  S8: $P \leftrightarrow (Q \leftrightarrow R), S \rightarrow (P \wedge Q), --S \vdash (R \wedge Q) \vee -(R \vee Q)$
4.  S9: $P \rightarrow [Q \rightarrow (R \wedge S)], --(P \wedge ----Q) \vdash (R \vee -R) \wedge S$
5.  S10: $--P \wedge Q \vdash T \vee \{U \vee [(Q \vee V) \wedge (W \vee P)]\}$
6.  S11: $P \leftrightarrow (Q \wedge R), -Q \wedge --P, (R \wedge Q) \rightarrow S \vdash S \wedge -Q$
7.  S12: $-----[--(P \wedge Q) \wedge (--R \wedge --S)] \vdash (P \wedge R) \wedge (Q \wedge S)$
8.  S13: $(P \wedge --Q) \wedge --(R \wedge --S) \vdash [(S \vee T) \wedge (Q \vee V)] \vee (W \vee P)$
9.  S14: $(P \wedge Q) \rightarrow [(R \wedge S) \rightarrow --T], (P \wedge R) \wedge (Q \wedge S) \vdash U \vee T$
10. S15: $--P \wedge --(---Q \wedge ---R) \vdash (P \wedge -Q) \wedge -R$
11. S16: $[(R \wedge Q) \wedge P] \leftrightarrow S, --[P \rightarrow (Q \rightarrow --R)], P \wedge --Q \vdash S \vee U$
12. S17: $P \rightarrow \{(-Q \wedge -R) \rightarrow [ (S \wedge T) \rightarrow U]\}, [(---R \wedge --P) \wedge (--S \wedge -Q)] \wedge T \vdash (--S \wedge -R) \wedge (-T \vee U)$

# 8. Derivation Rules: The Last Four

Once again: there are assumptions that are simply given (i.e., premises), and there are assumptions that you yourself introduce. In this section you will be focusing on the latter version of rule A, whereby you introduce your own assumptions. No doubt this sounds ridiculously *permissive*. However, you will make use of rule A *only* when making use of the last four derivation rules: →I, ↔I, ∨E, and —I. Once we discuss these four rules, you will come to see just how *non-permissive* A really is: while it's true that you may introduce an assumption whenever you choose to do so, the punch line is that at some point you will have to *discharge* your assumption.

Grasping the mechanics, and understanding the rationale, of each of the final four derivation rules will require a bit of attention. Read on *only if* you are fully alert.

## A. →I: Conditional Introduction/Arrow Intro

Suppose that the *wff* that you are trying to generate is a *conditional*. You don't *yet* have it; it's not one of the given assumptions and it's not (at least it's not yet) a *wff* that you've derived, directly or indirectly, from the assumptions. It's a *wff* that you're trying to *get*. Consider the following argument:

> (1) If Fortescue addresses the mob then there will be blood in the streets and Monty will hang at dawn.
> ———————————————————————————
> ∴ (2) If Fortescue addresses the mob then Monty will hang at dawn.

Translated into logical notation, the sequent looks like this:

S18:          $F \rightarrow (B \wedge M) \vdash F \rightarrow M$

The argument is obviously valid. (If you aren't convinced, the Short Method will convince you.) However, the derivation rules that you currently have won't enable you to derive the conclusion from the premise. Enter Arrow Intro, i.e., →I.

The premise, of course, is a conditional. The problem is that you have no derivation rules that allow you to operate on solo conditionals (other than, of course, ∨I, which allows you to operate on *any wff*, but which would be perfectly useless here). Look, therefore, at the conclusion; as it so happens, it too is a conditional.

Suppose that in the *real world* you were trying to prove to Fortescue and his fellow conspirators that if Fortescue addresses the mob then Monty will hang at dawn. It would be perfectly natural for you to say, "Let's *assume* that Fortescue addresses the mob—and let's see what *follows* from this assumption." You'd then use this assumption, that you yourself have *introduced*, along with any other assumptions which you and Fortescue and his fellow conspirators would treat as simply *given*, to see whether it indeed follows that Monty will hang at dawn. If it turned out that it does follow, then what do you know? You know that from the given assumptions, along with your own additional assumption that Fortescue addresses the mob, it follows that Monty will hang at dawn. And what else do you know? You know that *from the given assumptions alone*, it follows that *if* Fortescue addresses the mob *then* Monty will hang at dawn.

To put the matter a bit abstractly: your goal is to generate a *conditional*, '$\triangle \rightarrow \bigcirc$'. You *assume* its *antecedent*, '$\triangle$'. Your new goal is to generate its *consequent*, '$\bigcirc$', from the given assumptions along with the assumption, '$\triangle$', that *you* introduced. Once you succeed, you know that from the given assumptions *alone*, it follows that *if* '$\triangle$' is the case, *then* '$\bigcirc$' is the case; i.e., '$\triangle \rightarrow \bigcirc$'.

Two points are crucial. First point: Note that the antecedent of the conditional that is the conclusion happens to be the same as the antecedent of the conditional that is the premise. This is strictly a coincidence. There is no reason to think that subsequent sequents will exhibit this same pattern. Your decision to introduce 'F' as an assumption was motivated—or at least it should have been motivated—by the fact that 'F' is the antecedent of the *conclusion*, and *not* by the utterly irrelevant fact that 'F' happens to be the antecedent of the *premise*.

I shall put the matter slightly differently. Suppose that I had prevented you from seeing the *premise* of this sequent. Suppose too that I had simply told you that its conclusion was 'F → M'. Suppose finally that I had then asked you what your first move would be. Without skipping a beat, you should have replied, "Assume 'F'."

On the other hand, suppose that I had prevented you from seeing the *conclusion* of this sequent. Suppose instead that I had simply told you that its *premise* was 'F → (B ∧ M)'. Suppose finally that I had then asked you what your first move would be. This time, without skipping a beat, you should have replied, "Beats me: you haven't given me sufficient information to answer the question."

Second point: Note that because you're introducing an assumption of your own, 'F', you must ultimately *discharge* it. *The final conclusion, in other words, must not rest on any assumption that you introduce.* In this sequent you are given exactly one assumption (one premise), and therefore the conclusion mustn't rest on any other assumption.

Behold the derivation:

$$
\begin{array}{lll}
1 & (1)\ F \rightarrow (B \wedge M) & A \\
2 & (2)\ F & A \\
1,2 & (3)\ B \wedge M & 1,2\ \rightarrow\!E \\
1,2 & (4)\ M & 3\ \wedge\!E \\
1 & (5)\ F \rightarrow M & 2,4\ \rightarrow\!I \\
\end{array}
$$

(3) follows from (1) and (2) by →E, and rests on, i.e., is ultimately derived from, whatever (1) and (2) rest on, i.e., (1) and (2) themselves. (4) follows from (3) by ∧E, and rests on, i.e., is ultimately derived from, whatever (3) rests on, i.e., (1) and (2).

Notice how you discharged your line-(2) assumption at line (5). At line (4), you are still relying on it: hence the reference to (2) to the left of (4). At line (5), however, you are no longer relying on (2): hence the *non*-reference to (2) to the left of (5).

Line (5) is the conceptual speed bump, yes?

Consider the following three approaches for flattening the speed bump.

The first approach. The derivation whose 'premise' is the *wff* in line (2) and whose 'conclusion' is the *wff* in line (4) expresses the following thought *vertically*: "*On the assumption* that 'F' is the case, it *follows* that 'M' is the case." The single *wff* in line (5) expresses the following thought *horizontally*: "*If* 'F' is the case *then* 'M' is the case." It should strike you that the 'two' thoughts are really one and the same. So the conditional conclusion expresses horizontally exactly what the derivation from line (2) to (4) expresses vertically. Think of the (horizontal) line (5) conclusion summarizing, or recording, the (vertical) lines (2) through (4) derivation.

The second approach. What you know at line (4) is that 'M' follows from the first two assumptions. In other words, you know at line (4) that from the first assumption, along with the assumption that 'F' is the case, it follows that 'M' is the case. So you conclude at line (5) that *from the first assumption alone*, it follows that *if* 'F' is the case, *then* 'M' is the case—and that's exactly what line (5) says.

The third approach. If you look very closely beneath the surface of line (4), this is what you should see:

Line (4'):  1,2 $\vdash$ M

To be sure, the numeral '2', to the left of the turnstile, simply designates the *wff* 'F' in line (2); and so if you look very closely beneath the surface of line (4'), this is what you should see:

Line (4"):  1,F $\vdash$ M

Think, for a moment, of what this says:

Line (4'''): Given the first assumption, and given the further assumption that Fortescue addresses the mob, it follows that Monty will hang at dawn.

Now this has the exact same meaning as the following:

Line (5'''): Given the first assumption, it follows that *if* Fortescue addresses the mob *then* Monty will hang at dawn.

And this can obviously be expressed as follows:

Line (5"):  1 $\vdash$ F $\rightarrow$ M

But 'F', once again, is simply the *wff* in the second line of the derivation, and so we have:

Line (5'):  1 $\vdash$ 2 $\rightarrow$ M

In this context, let us say that one string of symbols is equivalent to another if the two strings express the same thought or have the same meaning. Accordingly, because (4') is equivalent to (4"), (4") to (4'''), (4''') to (5'''), (5''') to (5"), and (5") to (5'), it follows that (4') is equivalent to (5'); i.e.,

Line (4'):  1, 2 $\vdash$ M

is equivalent to (i.e., expresses the same thought as, or has the same meaning as)

Line (5'):  1 $\vdash$ 2 → M

In light of their equivalence, it should now strike you that the move from line (4) of our derivation to line (5) is entirely justifiable.

You are now ready for the full statement of the rule of →I.

## →I: The Details

An →I derivation of '△ → O' requires you to adhere to the following conditions:

1. Introduce as an assumption '△', i.e., the antecedent of the conditional that you're trying to generate.
2. From '△', construct a derivation of 'O', i.e., the consequent of the conditional that you're trying to generate.
3. In the course of constructing your derivation, make sure that '△' plays a role in generating 'O'; i.e., make sure that 'O' rests on '△'. ('O' may also rest on other assumptions.)
4. On a line below 'O', write '△ → O'.
5. To the right of '△ → O', cite the line numbers of '△' and 'O', respectively, as well as the rule →I.
6. To the left of the line number of '△ → O', cite the line numbers of each assumption on which 'O' rests, with the exception of the line number of the discharged assumption '△'.

Behold the structure that characterizes every application of →I:

(m)    △          A
         .
         .
(n)    O
(o) △ → O       m,n →I

Two points about the rule are noteworthy, and both pertain to the third clause. The first point has to do with the *wffs* that, along with '△', generate 'O'. In some cases there actually may be *no* such *wffs*: '△' alone may generate 'O'. Under such circumstances, your goal will be to derive a *wff*, 'O', from the assumption, '△', that *you* introduced, but from no *given* assumptions, i.e., from no *premises*. This is an oddity that will serve, in Chapter 4, as the subject matter of the section on *theorems*.

The second point has to do with the requirement that 'O' must rest on '△'. The purpose of this requirement is to ensure that '△', the assumption that you introduce which is the antecedent of the conditional that is your *ultimate* target, actually plays a role in generating 'O', the consequent of that conditional.

Question: Why is it important that '△' play a role in generating 'O'?

Answer: Think of any conditional that you might try to establish in everyday, *informal* reasoning, e.g., 'If Ardbeg sneezes then Bobo will cough' or 'If Bobo coughs then Coco will faint'. In each of these cases, obviously you would *assume* the antecedent of the conditional and you would try to derive the *consequent*. And here's the crucial point: in everyday, *informal* reasoning, you would invariably make use of the assumed antecedent in the course of trying to generate the consequent. It's simply unthinkable that you would do otherwise; i.e., it's unthinkable that you would assume the antecedent and then fail to use it in the course of generating the consequent. Moral of the story: to the extent that you want the rules of *formal* reasoning to reflect, wherever possible, the 'rules' of *informal* reasoning, then you want →I to require that you actually *use* your assumption in the course of generating the consequent of your conditional.

Question: Do all formal systems of Propositional Logic have this →I requirement?

Answer: No. Not all formal systems of Propositional Logic have this →I requirement.

Question: Doesn't this requirement narrow the range of derivations that we can perform within our formal system?

Answer: No. It doesn't narrow the range at all. Whatever conditionals your pals can generate without this requirement, you can generate in spite of the requirement.

Question: Does it follow that our derivations will be trickier to pull off than theirs?

Answer: Yes. Our derivations will be trickier to pull off than theirs. *Not* the end of the world, though. Enough questions for now. . . . If you wish to know more of the details of the rationale for this →I requirement, read Appendix II, "→I and —I Revisited," at the end of Chapter 4.

Question: Doesn't this requirement create a disanalogy between determining the truth-values of conditionals, on the one hand, and constructing proofs of conditionals, on the other? In Chapter 1, we learned that if one wishes to determine the truth-value of a given conditional, it's immaterial whether there's a connection, or relationship, between its antecedent and its consequent. Now it appears that in the context of an →I proof, there *must be* a connection, or relationship, between the assumed antecedent and the derived consequent. In that case, however, there *must* be a connection, or relationship, between the conditional's antecedent and its consequent.

Answer: Yes, this requirement does create a disanalogy between determining the truth-values of conditionals, on the one hand, and constructing proofs of conditionals, on the other—but it's an entirely innocuous disanalogy. The claim is not that the relationship between the antecedent and the consequent is a *causal* one. The claim is not that it's a *definitional* one. The claim is *not* that it's a *logical* one—in the sense that the antecedent *implies* the consequent. The claim is merely that there exists a derivation of the consequent *either* from the antecedent and various other *wffs, or* from the antecedent alone—and that the consequent *rests* on the antecedent. So understood, the relationship is an innocuously *syntactic* one.

Typically '△ → ○' will appear on the line immediately following the line where you generate '○', the consequent of the conditional that you're targeting. 'Typically', however, doesn't mean 'always', as the proof of the following sequent shows:

S19:     $P \rightarrow (Q \wedge R) \vdash (P \rightarrow Q) \wedge (P \rightarrow R)$

| | |
|---|---|
| 1 (1) $P \rightarrow (Q \wedge R)$ | A |
| 2 (2) $P$ | A |
| 1,2 (3) $Q \wedge R$ | 1,2 $\rightarrow$E |
| 1,2 (4) $Q$ | 3 $\wedge$E |
| 1,2 (5) $R$ | 3 $\wedge$E |
| 1 (6) $P \rightarrow Q$ | 2,4 $\rightarrow$I |
| 1 (7) $P \rightarrow R$ | 2,5 $\rightarrow$I |
| 1 (8) $(P \rightarrow Q) \wedge (P \rightarrow R)$ | 6,7 $\wedge$I |

Notice that 'P → Q' in line (6) does not appear on the line immediately following the line where you generated its consequent, 'Q' in line (4). Notice too that 'P → R' in line (7) does not appear on the line immediately following the line where you generated *its* consequent, 'R' in line (5).

To be sure, you could have arranged this proof so as to guarantee that 'P → Q' would immediately follow 'Q', and 'P → R' would immediately follow 'R', but there is no compelling reason why you should do so:

| | |
|---|---|
| 1 (1) $P \rightarrow (Q \wedge R)$ | A |
| 2 (2) $P$ | A |
| 1,2 (3) $Q \wedge R$ | 1,2 $\rightarrow$E |
| 1,2 (4) $Q$ | 3 $\wedge$E |
| 1 (5) $P \rightarrow Q$ | 2,4 $\rightarrow$I |
| 1,2 (6) $R$ | 3 $\wedge$E |
| 1 (7) $P \rightarrow R$ | 2,6 $\rightarrow$I |
| 1 (8) $(P \rightarrow Q) \wedge (P \rightarrow R)$ | 5,7 $\wedge$I |

Notice too that in the first version of this derivation, you discharged your line-(2) assumption in line (6)—and then immediately (albeit implicitly) reintroduced it in line (7): off to the right of line (7), your appeal to line (2) *shows* that you reintroduced it. There is nothing objectionable about this. If you would prefer to reintroduce it explicitly, you may do so, but you will pay a price for doing so: more lines in your proof; hence a greater expenditure of time, ink, and paper—with the resulting depletion of the world's finite resources. Here, in any case, is how your proof would look:

$$
\begin{array}{lll}
1 & (1)\ P \rightarrow (Q \wedge R) & A \\
2 & (2)\ P & A \\
1,2 & (3)\ Q \wedge R & 1,2 \rightarrow E \\
1,2 & (4)\ Q & 3\ \wedge E \\
1 & (5)\ P \rightarrow Q & 2,4 \rightarrow I \\
6 & (6)\ P & A \\
1,6 & (7)\ Q \wedge R & 1,6 \rightarrow E \\
1,6 & (8)\ R & 7\ \wedge E \\
1 & (9)\ P \rightarrow R & 6,8 \rightarrow I \\
1 & (10)\ (P \rightarrow Q) \wedge (P \rightarrow R) & 5,9\ \wedge I
\end{array}
$$

A new twist: Suppose now that your conclusion is a conditional buried within another conditional. Consider the following sequent:

S20:        $(P \wedge Q) \rightarrow R \vdash P \rightarrow (Q \rightarrow R)$

As with any $\rightarrow$I derivation, you assume the antecedent of the conditional that you're trying to derive, and you aim for its consequent:

$$
\begin{array}{lll}
1 & (1)\ (P \wedge Q) \rightarrow R & A \\
2 & (2)\ P & A \\
 & \quad . & \\
 & \quad . & \\
 & \quad . & \\
(n-1) & \ Q \rightarrow R & ? \\
 & (n)\ P \rightarrow (Q \rightarrow R) & 2,n-1 \rightarrow I
\end{array}
$$

Now take a good look at your new target, '$Q \rightarrow R$', and ask yourself what's interesting—indeed, *very* interesting—about *it*? It too, like the original conclusion, is a *conditional*, and it too is a conditional that you're trying to *generate*; it's not one that you already *have*. Whenever there's a conditional that you're trying to *generate*, always think $\rightarrow$I thoughts. In this case, you will assume its antecedent, 'Q', and you will try to generate its consequent, 'R':

```
   1 (1) (P ∧ Q) → R          A
   2 (2) P                    A
   3 (3) Q                    A
                  .
                  .
                  .
 (n–2) R                      ?
 (n–1) Q → R                  3,n–2 →I
   (n) P → (Q → R)            2,n–1 →I
```

Your goal now is *merely* to generate 'R' from the one *given* assumption and *your own* two assumptions. The game is clearly over:

```
       1 (1) (P ∧ Q) → R          A
       2 (2) P                    A
       3 (3) Q                    A
   2,3 (4) P ∧ Q                  2,3 ∧I
 1,2,3 (5) R                      1,4 →E
   1,2 (6) Q → R                  3,5 → I
     1 (7) P → (Q → R)            2,6 → I
```

Note that at line (6) you discharged your line-(3) assumption, the *last* assumption that you introduced, and that at line (7) you discharged your line-(2) assumption, the *first* assumption that you introduced. Where the cost of inventory is concerned, accountants sometimes use the 'FIFO' accounting method—first in, first out—and they sometimes use the 'LIFO' accounting method—last in, first out. Where →I assumptions are concerned, you will generally use the single 'FILO and LIFO' method: first in, last out; and last in, first out. Were you to discharge 'P' before 'Q', here is how life would look:

```
       1 (1) (P ∧ Q) → R          A
       2 (2) P                    A
       3 (3) Q                    A
   2,3 (4) P ∧ Q                  2,3 ∧I
 1,2,3 (5) R                      1,4 →E
   1,3 (6) P → R                  2,5 →I
     1 (7) Q → (P → R)            3,6 →I
```

Now strictly speaking, there's *nothing wrong* with this derivation; i.e., you haven't misused or violated any of the derivation rules. The only problem is that you ended up deriving a *wff* other than the *wff* that you were asked to derive. Had you been asked to prove the sequent '(P ∧ Q) → R ⊢ Q → (P → R)', instead of the sequent '(P ∧ Q) → R ⊢ P → (Q → R)', this last derivation of yours would have been *exactly* what was called for.

## Exercises

I. For each of the following sequents, construct a derivation of its conclusion from its premises.

1.  S21: P → (Q → R) ⊢ (P ∧ Q) → R
2.  S22: P → Q ⊢ P → (Q ∧ Q)
3.  S23: (P ∧ P) → Q ⊢ P → Q
4.  S24: −−−S ∧ −Q, (P ∧ −S) → R ⊢ −−P → (Q ∨ R)
5.  S25: P → Q, R → S ⊢ (Q → R) → (P → S)
6.  S26: [P ∧ (Q ∧ R)] → (S ∧ T) ⊢ P → [Q → (R → S)]
7.  S27: [(P ∧ Q) ∧ (R ∨ −R)] →S⊢R → [P → (Q → S)]
8.  S28: (P ∨ Q) → (R ∧ S), S → T ⊢ P → (T ∨ U)
9.  S29: [(−Q ∧ −R) ∧ P] → −−−−−S ⊢ [(P ∧ −Q) ∧ −R]→[Q ∨ (R ∨ S)]
10. S30: −− [P → −−(Q ∧ R)] ⊢ (R → S) → [P → (Q ∧ S)]
11. S31: P → (−−Q ∧ R), Q →−−[S ∧ (T ∧ U)] ⊢ P → (R ∧ U)
12. S32: P → [Q → (R → S)] ⊢ R → [Q → (P → S)]
13. S33: P → {Q → [R → (S → T)]} ⊢ R → {P → [S → (Q → T)]}
14. S34: P → [Q → (R ∧ S)] ⊢ Q → [P → (R ∨ S)]
15. S35: (P → S) ∧ (S → Q) ⊢ [(P → Q) → R] →R

II. Explain in your own words why →I is a legitimate derivation rule; i.e., explain why it's truth-preserving.

# B. ↔I: Bi-conditional Introduction/
## Double-Arrow Intro

After →I, ↔I will be a snap. Just recall what a bi-conditional is and why it's called a *bi-conditional*. '△ ↔ O' simply *means* '(△ → O) ∧ (O → △)'. Just as '△ ↔ O' generates '(△ → O) ∧ (O → △)' via ↔E, so '(△ → O) ∧ (O → △)' generates '△ ↔ O' via ↔I. To generate a bi-conditional, therefore, all that you have to do is to generate the conjunction of the two corresponding conditionals.

Consider the following sequent:

S36:        P ↔ Q, Q ↔ R ├ P ↔ R

Each of the premises is begging you to do ↔E. The conclusion is begging you to do ↔I. To do ↔I (i.e., to generate 'P ↔ R') you need to generate 'P → R' and you need to generate 'R → P'. Obviously, therefore, you will assume 'P' and try to generate 'R', and then you will assume 'R' and try to generate 'P'.

|          |                                    |           |
|----------|------------------------------------|-----------|
| 1 (1)    | P ↔ Q                              | A         |
| 2 (2)    | Q ↔ R                              | A         |
| 1 (3)    | (P → Q) ∧ (Q → P)                  | 1 ↔E      |
| 2 (4)    | (Q → R) ∧ (R → Q)                  | 2 ↔E      |
| 5 (5)    | P                                  | A         |
| 1 (6)    | P → Q                              | 3 ∧E      |
| 1,5 (7)  | Q                                  | 6,5 →E    |
| 2 (8)    | Q → R                              | 4 ∧E      |
| 1,2,5 (9)| R                                  | 8,7 →E    |
| 1,2 (10) | P → R                              | 5,9 →I    |
| 11 (11)  | R                                  | A         |
| 2 (12)   | R → Q                              | 4 ∧E      |
| 2,11 (13)| Q                                  | 12,11 →E  |
| 1 (14)   | Q → P                              | 3 ∧E      |

1,2,11 (15) P                                    14,13 →E
   1,2 (16) R → P                                11,15 →I
   1,2 (17) (P → R) ∧ (R → P)          10,16 ∧I
   1,2 (18) P ↔ R                                17 ↔I

## ↔I: The Details

A ↔I derivation of '△ ↔ O' requires you to adhere to the following conditions:

1. Construct a derivation of '△ → O'.
2. Construct a derivation of 'O → △'.
3. On a line below both '△ → O' and 'O → △', form the conjunction '(△ → O) ∧ (O → △)'.
4. On a line below '(△ → O) ∧ (O → △)', write '△ ↔ O'.
5. To the right of '△ ↔ O', cite the line number of '(△ → O) ∧ (O → △)' as well as the rule ↔I.
6. To the left of the line number of '△ ↔ O', cite the line numbers of each assumption on which '(△ → O) ∧ (O → △)' rests.

Behold the structure that characterizes every application of ↔I:

| | | |
|---|---|---|
| (*m*) | △ | A |
| | . | |
| | . | |
| | . | |
| (*n*) | O | |
| (*o*) | △ → O | *m,n* →I |
| (*p*) | O | A |
| | . | |
| | . | |
| | . | |
| (*q*) | △ | |
| (*r*) | O → △ | *p,q* →I |
| (*s*) | (△ → O) ∧ (O → △) | *o,r* ∧I |
| (*t*) | △ ↔ O | *s* ↔I |

# Exercises

I. For each of the following sequents, construct a derivation of its conclusion from its premises.

1.  S37: $Q \rightarrow P \vdash - -(P \rightarrow Q) \rightarrow (P \leftrightarrow Q)$
2.  S38: $P \leftrightarrow Q \vdash Q \leftrightarrow P$
3.  S39: $P \rightarrow R, R \rightarrow Q, R \rightarrow P \vdash (P \wedge Q) \leftrightarrow R$
4.  S40: $(P \leftrightarrow Q) \wedge (Q \leftrightarrow R) \vdash P \leftrightarrow R$
5.  S41: $P \rightarrow [(Q \rightarrow R) \wedge (R \rightarrow Q)], [(Q \rightarrow R) \wedge (R \rightarrow Q)] \rightarrow P \vdash P \leftrightarrow (Q \leftrightarrow R)$

II. Explain in your own words why $\leftrightarrow$I is a legitimate derivation rule; i.e., explain why it's truth-preserving.

## C. ∨E: Disjunction Elimination/Wedge Elimination

Suppose that either Egvalt sneers or Fortescue smirks. Suppose that you can prove that if Egvalt sneers then Monty will hang at dawn. Suppose that you can also prove that if Fortescue smirks then Monty will hang at dawn. What do you now know? You know that *whether* Egvalt sneers *or* Fortescue smirks, Monty will hang at dawn. In other words, you know that the conclusion that Monty will hang at dawn follows from the initial disjunction *by itself* (i.e., from the disjunction that *either* Egvalt sneers *or* Fortescue smirks), along with, of course, any assumptions that you use in the course of deriving the conclusion.

Alternatively, suppose that either Ardbeg's hotel room has rats or it has roaches. Suppose that you can prove that if it has rats then Ardbeg will be checking out immediately. Suppose that you can also prove that if it has roaches then Ardbeg will be checking out immediately. You now know that *whether* his hotel room has rats *or* it has roaches, Ardbeg will be checking out immediately. In other words, you know that the conclusion that he will be checking out immediately follows from the initial disjunction *by itself* (i.e., from the disjunction that *either* his hotel room has rats *or* it has roaches), along with (once again) any assumptions that you have used in the course of deriving the conclusion.

When do you use ∨E? Whenever there's a disjunction that you *already* have—as opposed to one that you're trying to derive. (In the latter case, of course, typically you will use ∨I.) The disjunction that you *already* have may be an assumption or it may be a *wff* that you've already derived from your assumptions.

How do you use ∨E? Suppose that you have a disjunction '△ ∨ O'. Suppose too that you are trying to derive a *wff* '□'. Your goal is to prove that *whether* '△' is the case *or* 'O' is the case, '□' is the case. Your first goal is to prove that if '△' is the case then '□' is the case: '△ → □'. And how do you do *this*? You think →I thoughts: you assume '△' and aim to generate '□'. Your second goal is to prove that if 'O' is the case then '□' is the case: 'O → □'. And how do you do *this*? You think →I thoughts once again: you assume 'O' and aim to generate the *exact same wff* '□'.

So here's what you now know. Either '△' is the case or 'O' is the case. If '△' is the case then '□' is the case. If 'O' is the case then '□' is the case. Conclusion: '□' is the case.

So '□' follows from three *wffs*: '△ ∨ O', '△ → □', and 'O → □', and it rests upon whatever assumptions these *wffs* rest upon.

## ∨E: The Details

A ∨E derivation from '△ ∨ O', a disjunction that already appears in your derivation, to a *wff* '□', requires you to adhere to the following conditions:

1. Construct a derivation of '△ → □'.
2. Construct a derivation of 'O → □'.
3. On a line below both '△ → □' and 'O → □', write '□'.
4. To the right of '□', cite the line numbers of '△ ∨ O', '△ → □', and 'O → □', respectively, as well as the rule ∨E.
5. To the left of the line number of '□', cite the line numbers of each assumption on which '△ ∨ O', '△ → □', and 'O → □' rest.

Behold the structure that characterizes every application of ∨E:

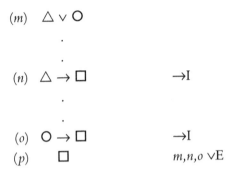

(m)  △ ∨ ○

 .

 .

(n)  △ → □                  →I

 .

 .

(o)  ○ → □                  →I
(p)    □                    m,n,o ∨E

In order to generate the two conditionals that are part of every ∨E proof, first you'll have to assume their respective antecedents and then you'll have to generate their respective consequents. Consequently, you may prefer to think of ∨E's structure as follows:

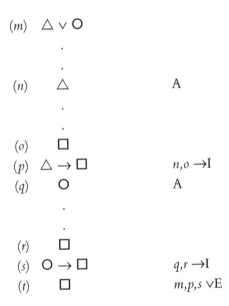

(m)  △ ∨ ○

 .

 .

(n)    △                    A

 .

 .

(o)    □
(p)  △ → □                  n,o →I
(q)    ○                    A

 .

 .

(r)    □
(s)  ○ → □                  q,r →I
(t)    □                    m,p,s ∨E

The following points about ∨E, some of which I have already made explicitly, are noteworthy. First, the initial disjunction is one that is staring you in the face. In other words, it's one that you already *have*; it's *not* one that you're trying to *generate*. As such, it may or may not be a premise.

Second, you will be executing two →I derivations within your ∨E derivation—in order to generate your two conditionals. Indeed the primary purpose of actually generating each of the two conditionals is to allow you to discharge, via →I, each of the two assumptions that you introduce—the first assumption being the left disjunct of your disjunction, and the second assumption being the right disjunct.

Third, you will be deriving your target *three* times: first, from your left-disjunct assumption; second, from your right-disjunct assumption; and third, from the disjunction as a whole. (See lines *o*, *r*, and *t*, above.)

Fourth, when you wrap up the ∨E part of your derivation, you will be citing three lines off to the right: first, the line where the disjunction appears that motivated your use of ∨E; second, the line where you derived your first conditional; and third, the line where you derived your second conditional.

Fifth, in case you're wondering why this rule is called 'Disjunction (or Wedge) Elimination', wonder no longer. . . . Although (as I just noted) it's the presence of a disjunction that *motivates* your use of this rule, you don't actually *use* the disjunction. You *eliminate* it, as it were, by operating instead with each of its disjuncts.

Let's dive in. Consider the following sequent:

S42:          − −P ∨ − −Q ⊢ P ∨ Q

| | | |
|---|---|---|
| 1 (1) − −P ∨ − −Q | A | |
| 2 (2) − −P | A | |
| 2 (3) P | 2 − −E | |
| 2 (4) P ∨ Q | 3 ∨I | |
| (5) − −P → (P ∨ Q) | 2,4 →I | |
| 6 (6) − −Q | A | |
| 6 (7) Q | 6 − −E | |
| 6 (8) P ∨ Q | 7 ∨I | |
| (9) − −Q → (P ∨ Q) | 6,8 →I | |
| 1 (10) P ∨ Q | 1,5,9 ∨E | |

Perhaps you find the absence of numbers to the left of lines (5) and (9) puzzling. Their absence means, of course, that the *wffs* on lines (5) and (9) rest on no assumptions whatsoever. "So what does *this* mean?"

you wonder. Well, in a formal system of logic the only *wffs* that rest on no assumptions whatsoever are *logical truths*. Logical truths are true regardless of what else is (or isn't) true; i.e., their truth is entirely independent of all other truths, empirical or otherwise. It should be unsurprising, therefore, that some of the *wffs* that appear in derivations rest on no assumptions: these will be, once again, logical truths. In Propositional Logic, all such truths, of course, are *tautologies*.

Suppose that I'm trying to convince you that Ardbeg once played mumblety-peg with Pythagoras. *Obviously*, I'll have to defend my claim via an argument in which I invoke various other claims that I expect you to accept. At the end of the day, if my argument is successful, the claim that Ardbeg once played mumblety-peg with Pythagoras will rest on these other claims. But now suppose that I'm trying to convince you that *either* Ardbeg once played mumblety-peg with Pythagoras *or* he didn't. Do I *really* need to invoke any other claims in order to convince you? Of course not. The truth of the *tautological* claim that *either* Ardbeg once played mumlbety-peg with Pythagoras *or* he didn't is independent of all other claims—and as such, it doesn't need to be justified by reference to any of them. Its truth, in short, rests on no assumptions.

So it is with the *wffs* in lines (5) and (9): they are true *no matter what*. Their truth is independent of any truths whatsoever. And that's exactly why they rest on *no* assumptions.

Don't think that it will always be this way in ∨E proofs; i.e., don't think that your two conditionals will always rest on no assumptions. Consider, for example, the following sequent:

S43:        P ∧ (Q ∨ R) ⊢ (P ∧ Q) ∨ (P ∧ R)

| | | |
|---|---|---|
| 1 (1) | P ∧ (Q ∨ R) | A |
| 1 (2) | P | 1 ∧E |
| 1 (3) | Q ∨ R | 1 ∧E |
| 4 (4) | Q | A |
| 1,4 (5) | P ∧ Q | 2,4 ∧I |
| 1,4 (6) | (P ∧ Q) ∨ (P ∧ R) | 5 ∨I |
| 1 (7) | Q → [(P ∧ Q) ∨ (P ∧ R)] | 4,6 →I |
| 8 (8) | R | A |
| 1,8 (9) | P ∧ R | 2,8 ∧I |

1,8 (10) (P ∧ Q) ∨ (P ∧ R)                    9 ∨I
   1 (11) R → [(P ∧ Q) ∨ (P ∧ R)]          8,10 →I
   1 (12) (P ∧ Q) ∨ (P ∧ R)                  3,7,11 ∨E

Notice that each of the *wffs* in lines (7) and (11) *does* rest on a particular assumption: the line-(1) *wff*. There's nothing surprising about this: the *wffs* in lines (7) and (11) simply aren't tautologies.

You might be tempted to conclude your derivation at line (6). "After all," you wonder, "isn't '(P ∧ Q) ∨ (P ∧ R)' my target? Isn't it the conclusion of the sequent?" Indeed it *is* your target—but at line (6) it would be premature to think that it's time to call it quits. Notice what the *wff* in line (6) rests on: the *wffs* in lines (1) *and* (4). By the time you've reached line (6), in other words, you've derived your target from (1) and (4). The problem is that you were required to derive your target from (1) *alone*—and you won't succeed in this objective until line (12), i.e., until you've derived your target *both* from 'Q' in line (4)—the left disjunct of your line-(3) disjunction, *and* from 'R' in line (8)—the right disjunct of your line-(3) disjunction.

Think, for a moment, about why this is so. Suppose that you are trying to prove that whether Egvalt sneers or Fortescue smirks, Monty will hang at dawn. Suppose that you're able to prove that if Egvalt sneers, Monty will hang at dawn. Are you now entitled to conclude that *whether* Egvalt sneers or Fortescue smirks, Monty will hang at dawn? Of course not! Before you're entitled to draw *that* conclusion, you must also go on to prove that if Fortescue smirks, Monty will hang at dawn. In other words, you have to crank your target out of *each* of the disjuncts separately, and then derive your two conditionals.

# Exercises

I. For each of the following sequents, construct a derivation of its conclusion from its premises.

    1.  S44: P ∨ Q ⊢ Q ∨ P
    2.  S45: − −P ∨ − −P ⊢ P
    3.  S46: (P ∧ − −Q) ∨ (P ∧ − −R) ⊢ P ∨ R

4.  S47: $(P \wedge -- -Q) \vee (R \wedge - - - -S)$, $Q \to (T \wedge U)$, $-S \to (-T \wedge V) \vdash (-R \vee T) \vee -T$

5.  S48: $P \to (Q \vee R)$, $(S \vee R) \to (U \wedge T)$, $(S \vee Q) \to (T \wedge U) \vdash P \to (T \vee U)$

6.  S49: $[(Q \vee S) \vee R] \to T \vdash \{[(Q \vee R) \vee S] \to T\}$

7.  S50: $P \vee (Q \wedge R) \vdash (P \vee Q) \wedge (P \vee R)$

8.  S51: $(P \vee Q) \wedge (P \vee R) \vdash P \vee (Q \wedge R)$

9.  S52: $(P \leftrightarrow Q) \vee (P \leftrightarrow R) \vdash P \to (Q \vee R)$

10. S53: $P \vee (Q \vee R) \vdash (P \vee Q) \vee R$

11. S54: $(P \vee Q) \vee R \vdash P \vee (Q \vee R)$

12. S55: $(P \wedge Q) \vee (P \wedge R) \vdash P \wedge (Q \vee R)$

13. S56: $P \vee [Q \vee (R \vee S)] \vdash [P \vee (Q \vee R)] \vee S$

14. S57: $S \to [(U \wedge V) \wedge W]$, $(P \wedge -R) \to (S \vee T)$, $P \to (Q \wedge -R)$, $T \to (V \wedge W) \vdash P \to W$

15. S58: $Q \to (R \wedge S)$, $-R \to (S \wedge T) \vdash [(Q \vee -R) \to S]$

16. S59: $[S \vee (R \vee P)] \to T \vdash [(R \vee S) \to T]$

II. Explain in your own words why ∨E is a legitimate derivation rule; i.e., explain why it's truth-preserving.

# D. —I: Negation Introduction/Dash Intro/*Reductio ad Absurdum*

We begin with terminology and two definitions. First the terminology. Because each of our derivation rules (with the exception of the Rule of Assumptions) is either an introduction rule or an elimination rule, it would be *logically* natural to refer to Negation Introduction as Negation Introduction. Because historically the rule has been referred to as *Reductio ad Absurdum* it would be *historically* natural to refer to it as *Reductio ad Absurdum*. I shall defer to the constraints of logic, history, and brevity. I shall refer to the rule itself, when I cite it in the course of a derivation, as 'Negation Introduction', '—I'. I shall refer to the strategy of employing the rule as a *Reductio ad Absurdum* strategy, or, for short, simply as a *Reductio* strategy.

Definitions next:

**Definition:** A set of *wffs* is *satisfiable iff* there is at least one interpretation that makes each member of the set true.

**Definition:** A set of *wffs* is *unsatisfiable iff* it is not satisfiable, i.e., *iff* there is no interpretation that makes each member of the set true.

Consider the following set of *wffs*: {P ∨ Q, −P ↔ Q, −P → R}. A pair of curly braces, i.e., '{' and '}', typically denotes a *set*, and whatever the curly braces enclose are the *members* of the set. There are exactly *three* members of this set; i.e., there are exactly three *wffs* in the set, separated from one another by two commas. You might think that the atomics 'P', 'Q', and 'R' are members of the set—but you would be mistaken. To be sure, these three atomics are elements of the *wffs* that are the members of the set, but none of these three atomics is a *wff* in the set. Therefore none of them is a member of the set.

If you were to construct an eight-row truth-table, you would discover that there are exactly *three* interpretations that make each of the members of the set, each of these *wffs*, come out true:

| P | Q | R |
|---|---|---|
| T | F | T |
| T | F | F |
| F | T | T |

Clearly the set is satisfiable.

Next consider the following set of *wffs*: {P, −R, P → Q, −P → −Q, Q → −R}. There are exactly *five* members of this set; i.e., there are exactly five *wffs* in the set, separated from one another by four commas. You might think, once again, that the atomics 'P', 'Q', and 'R' are members of the set—but you would be only one-third right: 'P' is a member of the set, but neither 'Q' nor 'R' is a member. And 'P' is a member of the set simply because in constructing the set, I stipulated that it be a member.

If you construct an eight-row truth-table once again, you will discover that there is at least one interpretation—in this instance, indeed, there happens to be *exactly one* interpretation—that makes each member of the set true:

P  Q  R
T  T  F

Once again, the set is satisfiable.

Actually, you could have determined that the set is satisfiable quite quickly, without having to construct a truth-table. If you're trying to come up with an interpretation which makes each *wff* that is a member of the set true, then 'P', being a *wff* that is a member of the set, obviously must be true. '—R', being one of the *wffs* that is a member of the set, must also be true—in which case 'R' must be false. Given that 'P' (as you have just seen) must be true, then 'P → Q' is true just in case 'Q' is true. If (once again) 'P' must be true and 'Q' must be true, then '—P → —Q' must be true. If 'Q' must be true and 'R' must be false then 'Q → —R' must be true. Clearly our set of *wffs* is satisfiable.

Finally consider the following set of *wffs*: {P, P → Q, Q → R, —R}. Notice that this set has exactly *four* members. It should strike you as obvious that this set is *unsatisfiable*: 'P' is either true or false. If 'P' is true, then 'Q' must be true; otherwise, 'P → Q' would be false. If 'Q' is true, then 'R' must be true; otherwise, 'Q → R' would be false. If 'R' is true, however, then '—R' must be false. So if 'P' is true, not all four of the *wffs* in the set are true. If, on the other hand, 'P' is false, then, once again, not all four of the *wffs* in the set are true. So whether 'P' is true or false, not all four of the *wffs* are true. Therefore this set is *unsatisfiable*.

Now take a deep breath and pay *very* close attention. Suppose that there's an interpretation that makes three of the members of this unsatisfiable set true: What do you automatically know about the fourth member of the set, on this interpretation? It *has* to be false. (Remember, this is an *unsatisfiable* set; there is *no* interpretation that makes *each* member true.) Fine. So if there's *any* interpretation that makes *three* of the members of this set true, it must make the *fourth* member *false*. In that case if there's any interpretation that makes three of the members of this set true, it must make the *negation* of the fourth member *true*.

We may generalize. Suppose that you're examining an *unsatisfiable* set of *wffs*. Suppose that the set has *n* members. Suppose that there's an interpretation that makes *n*–1 members true. It follows that the *n*th member must be *false*. On this interpretation, therefore the *negation* of the *n*th member must be *true*. Behold two definitions followed by the secret of *Reductio* proofs.

Definition:      The *negation* of '△' is '—△', i.e., '△' preceded by a dash.

Definition:      The *opposite* of '△' is '—△'; the *opposite* of '—△' is '△'.

Accordingly, the *negation* of 'P' is '—P'; the *negation* of '—P' is '— —P'; and the *negation* of '— —P' is '— — —P'. On the other hand, the *opposite* of 'P' is '—P'; the *opposite* of '—P' is 'P'; and the *opposite* of '— —P' is '—P'.

And now for the how-to and the why-so of *Reductio* proofs. With a *Reductio* proof you introduce as an assumption the *opposite* of your targeted *wff*, and you add it to the string of *wffs*, if any, currently in your derivation. Note that your targeted *wff*, whose opposite you are about to add to the string of *wffs*, may be your final conclusion; alternatively, it may simply be some *wff* that will help you derive your final conclusion.

Note too that the string of *wffs* may consist of given assumptions, i.e., premises, and/or assumptions that you yourself have introduced, and/or theorems (Chapter 4), and/or *wffs* that you have derived from any of the preceding *wffs*. Whatever the string of *wffs* consists of, your goal is to derive a syntactic contradiction—*any syntactic contradiction whatsoever*—from this *enhanced* string of *wffs*, i.e., from the string that you have enhanced by adding to it the *wff* that is the opposite of your targeted *wff*.

Definition:      A *syntactic contradiction* is a conjunction, '△ ∧ —△', whose left conjunct is any *wff*, '△', and whose right conjunct is the negation of that *wff*, '—△'.

Suppose that you're examining a string of *wffs* from which you'd like to derive another *wff*. Take the *opposite* of this latter *wff*, your targeted *wff*, and call it *zappo*. Add *zappo* to the string. Now consider the *enhanced* string of *wffs* consisting of the original *wffs* along with *zappo*. Your goal is to try to derive a contradiction, 'O ∧ —O'—a contradiction that *must* rest on *zappo* and that *may* rest as well on other *wffs* in the string. (And remember: 'O ∧ —O' may be *any contradiction whatsoever*.)

Once you reach your goal, i.e., once you generate your contradiction, 'O ∧ —O', look at the set of assumptions upon which 'O ∧ —O' rests. One of the assumptions in this set will be *zappo*, the opposite of your targeted *wff*. What do you know about this set of assumptions? Keep in mind that our derivation rules are *truth-preserving*. You know, therefore, that any interpretation that makes true all the assumptions in the set must make true any *wff* that you derive from them. Therefore any interpretation that makes true all the assumptions in the set must make true 'O ∧ —O', which (once again) rests upon them. But (obviously) *no* interpretation can make a contradiction true! Therefore *no* interpretation makes true *all* the assumptions in the set upon which 'O ∧ —O' rests. *Therefore the set is unsatisfiable.*

Now one of the assumptions in the set is *zappo*, the opposite of your targeted *wff*. Therefore there's no interpretation that makes true all the assumptions in the set other than *zappo* and that also makes *zappo* true. Therefore there's no interpretation that makes true all the assumptions in the set other than *zappo* and that makes the *opposite* of *zappo* false. Therefore the argument whose premises are all the assumptions in the set other than *zappo*, and whose conclusion is the opposite of *zappo*, is a valid argument. Now the opposite of *zappo* is simply your targeted *wff*. So the argument whose premises are all the assumptions in the set other than *zappo*, and whose conclusion is your targeted *wff* is a valid argument.

Miraculous? Yes, quite miraculous. . . .

Alternatively, consider the set of assumptions upon which 'O ∧ —O' rests. There are two possibilities: Either there's at least one interpretation that makes every assumption in this set other than *zappo* true or there isn't.

Suppose first that there *is* such an interpretation. On that interpretation, *zappo* must be false. Why so? Remember that the set is unsatisfiable, and so there's no interpretation that makes *every* assumption in the set true. So any interpretation that makes every assumption in the set other than *zappo* true must make *zappo* false. So any such interpretation must make the *opposite* of *zappo* true; i.e., any such interpretation must make your targeted *wff* true. It follows that the argument whose premises are all the assumptions in the set other than *zappo*, and whose conclusion is the opposite of *zappo*, i.e., whose conclusion is your targeted *wff*, is a valid argument.

Suppose now that there's *no* interpretation that makes every assumption in the set other than *zappo* true. In that case, then, there's no interpretation that makes every assumption in the set other than *zappo* true—and yet makes your targeted *wff* false. So it follows once again that the argument whose premises are all the assumptions in the set other than *zappo*, and whose conclusion is the opposite of *zappo*, i.e., whose conclusion is your targeted *wff*, is a valid argument.

So whether there is or there isn't at least one interpretation that makes every assumption in the set other than *zappo* true, there's no interpretation that makes every assumption in the set other than *zappo* true and yet makes your targeted *wff* false. So the argument whose premises are all the assumptions in the set other than *zappo*, and whose conclusion is your targeted *wff*, is a *valid* argument.

Moral of the story: with a *Reductio* proof, you add the opposite of your targeted *wff* to the string of *wffs* in the derivation that you're constructing. From this enhanced set of *wffs* you try to derive a contradiction—a contradiction that will rest on your *Reductio* assumption along with, perhaps, other assumptions. *Any* contradiction will do; it may be an atomic and its negation, or it may be a *wff* thirteen city blocks long and *its* negation. Once you have your contradiction, the game is over: you know that your original argument is valid.

A crucial question: How do you know when to start a *Reductio* proof?

Answer: When all else fails; i.e., when there is literally *nothing* else that you can do.

In some ways *Reductio*, i.e., Negation Introduction, is the most *powerful* derivation rule in your arsenal of derivation rules. As it turns out, moreover, it's a derivation rule that mathematicians have been using since at least the time of Euclid (Greek, c. 325–c. 265 BCE). When you're about to despair, *don't!* When you're about to throw in the towel, *don't!* When you're about to think that it's the end of the world, *think again!* Begin a *Reductio* proof: *Reductio* will *never* let you down. Long after your significant other has betrayed you; long after your friends and family have abandoned you; long after your beloved Fido has taken up permanent residence next door—*Reductio* will be there for you, at your side, loyal to the bitter end. . . .

Consider what follows in this paragraph a summary of the *Reductio* procedure. You begin a *Reductio* proof when all else fails. You begin every *Reductio* proof by *assuming* the *opposite* of your targeted *wff*. Add this new *assumption* to the string of *wffs* that you currently have in the derivation. What you have just added to these *wffs*—the opposite of your targeted *wff*—is simply another *wff*; it's not itself a premise, and you aren't to think of it as a premise. Don't even think of the premises themselves as premises any longer! Think of them, along with any other *wffs* in the string, along with the opposite of your targeted *wff*, as simply constituting an interesting *set of wffs*. Your goal is *not* to derive a conclusion from a set of premises; your goal is merely (merely!) to derive a contradiction—a *syntactic* contradiction—from a set of *wffs*.

Question: How does a *syntactic* contradiction differ from a *semantic* contradiction?

Answer: You will recall the definition of 'syntactic contradiction' from just a few pages ago, and you will recall the definition of 'semantic contradiction' from Chapter 2. (Strictly speaking, I defined 'semantic contradiction' in Chapter 2 by reference to a 'sentence' rather than a 'wff'—but that was only because I had not yet introduced the notion of a *wff*.)

Definition:   A *syntactic contradiction* is a conjunction, '$\triangle \wedge -\triangle$', whose left conjunct is any *wff*, '$\triangle$', and whose right conjunct is the negation of that *wff*, '$-\triangle$'.

Definition:   A *semantic contradiction* is a *wff* that is false for every interpretation.

A *syntactic* contradiction differs from a *semantic* contradiction. The notion of a syntactic contradiction is a purely *formal* notion, referring only to the *structural* features of a *wff*. The notion of a semantic contradiction makes no such reference, but instead refers to *truth* and *falsehood*. In our formal system, every syntactic contradiction is a semantic contradiction, but not every semantic contradiction is a syntactic contradiction: Both 'P ∧ −−−P', on the one hand, and '−(P ∨ −P)', on the other, are semantic contradictions. Each is false for every interpretation. But neither one is a syntactic contradiction: neither one has the form 'Δ ∧ −Δ'.

## −I: The Details

Consider any *wff* that you're targeting. Either it is, or it isn't, a negation; i.e., either it does, or it doesn't, have a dash as its main connective. Accordingly, there are *two* versions of −I:

### i. The First Version of −I: Your Targeted *Wff* Is a Negation

A −I derivation of '−Δ', i.e., a *wff* that *does* have a dash as its main connective, requires you to adhere to the following conditions:

1. Introduce an assumption, 'Δ', i.e., the opposite of the *wff* at which you're aiming.
2. From 'Δ', construct a derivation of any contradiction, 'O ∧ −O'.
3. In the course of constructing your derivation, make sure that 'Δ' plays a role in generating 'O ∧ −O'; i.e., make sure that 'O ∧ −O' rests on 'Δ'. ('O ∧ −O' may also rest on other assumptions.)
4. On a line below 'O ∧ −O', write '−Δ'.
5. To the right of '−Δ', cite the line numbers of 'Δ' and 'O ∧ −O', respectively, as well as the rule −I.
6. To the left of the line number of '−Δ', cite the line numbers of each assumption on which 'O ∧ −O' rests, with the exception of the line number of the discharged assumption, 'Δ'.

Behold the structure that characterizes every application of the *first* version of −I:

$$(m) \quad Δ \qquad\qquad A$$

$$\cdot$$

$$\cdot$$

$$(n) \quad O ∧ −O$$
$$(o) \quad −Δ \qquad\qquad m,n \; −I$$

## ii. The Second Version of −I: Your Targeted *Wff* Isn't a Negation

A −I derivation of '△', i.e., a *wff* that *doesn't* have a dash as its main connective, requires you to adhere to the following conditions:

1. Introduce an assumption, '−△', i.e., the opposite of the *wff* at which you're aiming.
2. From '−△', construct a derivation of any contradiction, 'O ∧ −O'.
3. In the course of constructing your derivation, make sure that '−△' plays a role in generating 'O ∧ −O'; i.e., make sure that 'O ∧ −O' rests on '−△'. ('O ∧ −O' may also rest on other assumptions.)
4. On a line below 'O ∧ −O', write '− −△'.
5. To the right of '− −△', cite the line numbers of '−△' and 'O ∧ −O', respectively, as well as the rule −I.
6. To the left of the line number of '− −△', cite the line numbers of each assumption on which 'O ∧ −O' rests, with the exception of the line number of the discharged assumption, '−△'.
7. On a line below '− −△', write '△'.
8. To the right of '△', cite the line number of '− −△', as well as the rule − −E.
9. To the left of the line number of '△', cite the line numbers of each assumption on which '− −△' rests.

Behold the structure that characterizes every application of the second version of −I:

$$(m) \quad −△ \qquad\qquad\qquad A$$

$$.$$

$$.$$

$$(n) \quad O ∧ −O$$
$$(o) \quad − −△ \qquad\qquad\qquad m,n \;\; −I$$
$$(p) \quad △ \qquad\qquad\qquad\quad o \;\; − −E$$

Three points about each version of the rule are noteworthy. The first two pertain to the third clause, and both will remind you of corresponding points pertaining to the rule for →I. The first point has to do with the *wffs* that, along with '△' (or '—△'), generate your contradiction, 'O ∧ —O'. In some cases there actually may be no such *wffs*: '△' (or '—△') alone may generate 'O ∧ —O'. Under such circumstances, your goal will be to derive 'O ∧ —O' from no *given* assumptions, i.e., from no *premises*. Rather, your goal will be to derive 'O ∧ —O' from no *wffs* other than the *Reductio* assumption that you introduce. Once again, this is an oddity that will serve as the subject matter of the section on theorems in Chapter 4.

The second point has to do with the requirement that your *Reductio* assumption, '△' or '—△', must play a role in generating your contradiction, 'O ∧ —O'. In other words, your contradiction must rest on your *Reductio* assumption. This requirement is analogous to the →I requirement that your →I assumption, the antecedent of the conditional that is your ultimate target, must play a role in generating your consequent. In other words, your consequent must rest on your →I assumption. If you wish to know the details of the rationale for both the →I requirement and the —I requirement, read Appendix II, "→I and —I Revisited," at the end of Chapter 4.

The third point pertains to the fourth clause, and is the requirement that when you generate your contradiction, 'O ∧ —O', you subsequently write down the *negation* of your *Reductio* assumption, i.e., your *Reductio* assumption preceded by a dash. This is so even when your *Reductio* assumption is itself a negation. In other words, if your *Reductio* assumption is '—△', you write down '— —△' beneath 'O ∧ —O', rather than what you would be inclined to write down, i.e., '△'. There are two reasons for this requirement. One reason is that in both cases, i.e., whether your *Reductio* assumption is, or isn't, a negation, by negating it once you generate your contradiction, you're asserting *explicitly* that the *Reductio* assumption is *not* the case. And this is *exactly* what you want to assert after you've shown that your *Reductio* assumption leads to a contradiction. The other reason is to keep the fourth clause of the rule to be followed when your *Reductio* assumption *is* a negation, i.e., '—△', identical to the fourth clause of the rule to be followed when your *Reductio* assumption *isn't* a negation, i.e., '△'.

Now consider the following sequent, an ideal candidate for a *Reductio* proof:

S60:          $P \rightarrow Q, -Q \vdash -P$

Notice that there's nothing that you can do with your first premise; there's nothing that you can do with your second premise; and there's nothing that you can do with the two premises together. *When all else fails, do a* Reductio *proof*. Take the *opposite* of your conclusion and add it—as an assumption—to the current string of *wffs*:

    1 (1) P → Q                A
    2 (2) −Q                   A
    3 (3) P                    A

You are now to aim for a contradiction; and for the *umpteenth* time, *any contradiction whatsoever*—just as long, of course, as it rests on your *Reductio* assumption:

    1 (1) P → Q                A
    2 (2) −Q                   A
    3 (3) P                    A
    1,3 (4) Q                  1,3 →E
    1,2,3 (5) Q ∧ −Q           4,2 ∧I

Look closely at line (5), and think about what it says: "There's no interpretation that makes (1), (2), and (3) true, and that makes 'Q ∧ −Q' false." Why should you believe what line (5) says? Because of the crucial property of our derivation rules: they're all *truth-preserving*. If you start off with truths and apply our derivation rules correctly, you'll end up with truths—and only with truths. In other words, there's no interpretation that makes all the *wffs* in a given set of *wffs* true, and that makes a *wff* that you derive from these *wffs* via our derivation rules *false*. So there's no interpretation that makes (1), (2), and (3) true, and that makes (5), 'Q ∧ −Q', false. But course 'Q ∧ −Q' *is* false—and indeed it's false for *every* interpretation. Therefore there's no interpretation that makes (1), (2), and (3) true. So the set of *wffs* consisting of (1), (2), and (3) is *unsatisfiable*.

Therefore there's no interpretation that makes (1) and (2) true and
that also makes (3) true. Therefore there's no interpretation that makes
(1) and (2) true and that also makes the *negation* of (3) false. But (1)
and (2) just happen to be the premises of the original argument, and
the negation of (3) just happens to be the conclusion of the original
argument. So there's no interpretation that makes the premises of the
original argument true and that makes the conclusion of the original
argument false. So the original argument is a valid argument. You wrap
up your derivation as follows:

| | |
|---|---|
| 1 (1) P → Q | A |
| 2 (2) −Q | A |
| 3 (3) P | A |
| 1,3 (4) Q | 1,3 →E |
| 1,2,3 (5) Q ∧ −Q | 4,2 ∧I |
| 1,2 (6) −P | 3,5 −I |

A little repetition never hurt anyone. . . . Look closely once again
at line (5): any interpretation that makes (1), (2), and (3) true makes
'Q ∧ −Q' true. Therefore there's no interpretation that makes (1), (2),
and (3) true. Therefore there's no interpretation that makes (1) and
(2) true, and that also makes (3) true. Therefore there's no interpretation that makes (1) and (2) true, and that also makes the *negation* of (3)
false. But (3) is 'P', and '−P' is its negation. So the numbers to the far
left of line (5) tell you that there's no interpretation that makes (1) and
(2) true, and that also makes '−P' false. Now look at line (6): it says
the very same thing! What it says is that there's no interpretation that
makes true (1) and (2)—the *premises* of our argument—and that also
makes false '−P'—the *conclusion* of our argument. The numbers to the
far left of (6), together with (6), show that the argument is valid; and
the numbers to the far left of (5), together with (5), explain why.

Notice how you discharged your line-(3) *Reductio* assumption at line
(6): the *wff* in line (5) rests on it; the *wff* in line (6) doesn't.

A brief aside: it so happens that the *sequent* that you have just proved
is actually a derivation rule in many other logic textbooks, i.e., in many
other formal systems. It's often paired with →E. In many other logic
textbooks, as I have already mentioned, →E is known as '*Modus Ponens*'
(or '*Modus Ponendo Ponens*'). In these same logic textbooks, this derivation rule ('P → Q, −Q ⊢ −P') is known as '*Modus Tollendo Tollens*'

(the way, or mode, of denying *by* denying), or simply '*Modus Tollens*'. With both of these derivation rules, you have a *conditional*. With *Modus Ponens* you have, in addition to the conditional, the *antecedent* of the conditional, and you end up deriving the *consequent* of the conditional. With *Modus Tollens*, you have, in addition to the conditional, the *negation* of the *consequent* of the conditional, and you end up deriving the *negation* of the *antecedent* of the conditional.

Question: Your pals in their logic courses may well have *Modus Tollens* as one of their derivation rules; why don't *you*?

Two answers, one practical and one theoretical: you've encountered each of them before—in the context of the same question with respect to our *connectives*. The *practical* answer is that if every time it were convenient to add on a new derivation rule we actually did so, we would soon end up with an *unwieldy* number of derivation rules. The *theoretical* answer is that there is something aesthetically, as well as philosophically, pleasing about operating with the *smallest possible set*—or at least a *reasonably small set*—of derivation rules. (As with our connectives, so with our rules.) Whatever your pals in their other logic courses can derive within *their* formal systems, we can derive within *our* formal system—with fewer derivation rules.

Consider next the following sequent:

S61:        P ⊢ – –P

Remember that –E allows you to *subtract* two dashes at a time; it doesn't allow you to *add* two dashes at a time. You have no derivation rule that allows you to add two dashes at a time.

        1 (1) P                                    A

At this point you're stuck. There's *nothing* that you can do with your premise. (Strictly speaking, once again, that's not true: as you know, there's always *something* that you can do with *any wff*: ∨I. It should be obvious, however, that in this instance it serves no strategic purpose to use ∨I at this point.) When all else fails, do a *Reductio* proof. . . . In line (2), you assume the opposite of your conclusion:

        1 (1) P                                    A
        2 (2) –P                                   A

Notice that you now have a contradiction.

    1 (1) P                         A

    2 (2) —P                        A

  1,2 (3) P ∧ —P             1,2 ∧I

Think of what line (3) says: "If there were any interpretation that made (1) and (2) true, it would also make 'P ∧ —P' true." But there's *no* interpretation that makes 'P ∧ —P' true. Therefore there's no interpretation that makes (1) and (2) true. Therefore if there were any interpretation that made (1) true, it would make (2) *false*; i.e., it would make the *negation* of (2) *true*—and this is *exactly* what line (4) says:

    1 (1) P                         A

    2 (2) —P                        A

  1,2 (3) P ∧ —P             1,2 ∧I

    1 (4) — —P               2,3 —I

Consider now a somewhat more difficult sequent, a close cousin of De Morgan. (Strictly speaking, the De Morgan variation would have been: '—(—P ∧ —Q) ⊢ — —P ∨ — —Q'.)

S62:       —(—P ∧ —Q) ⊢ P ∨ Q

    1 (1) —(—P ∧ —Q)        A

Suppose that your strategy is to aim for 'P' in your second-to-last line, and then make the move to your conclusion via ∨I. Suppose that after a dozen or so hours of frustration, it occurs to you that *maybe* the argument whose premise is '—(—P ∧ —Q)' and whose conclusion is 'P' is an *invalid* argument. You make use of the Short Method and what do you discover? You discover that if 'P' is false and 'Q' is true, '—(—P ∧ —Q)' is true and 'P' is false. Better late than never, you abandon your strategy of trying to generate 'P' from '—(—P ∧ —Q)'.

At this point, (2) is a no-brainer. None of your derivation rules allows you to operate on negated conjunctions. So there's nothing that you can do with (1), apart from ∨I, which obviously isn't going to be helpful here.

When all else fails, do a *Reductio* proof. Assume the opposite of what you're aiming for; hence (2):

```
1 (1) —(—P ∧ —Q)              A
2 (2) —(P ∨ Q)                A
```

Your goal now is to generate a contradiction—*any* contradiction. If you could generate '—P ∧ —Q', the opposite of (1), the game would be over. Ditto if you could generate 'P ∨ Q', the opposite of (2). We shall follow the former strategy here; *you* will follow the latter strategy in the sixteenth exercise at the end of this section.

Your target, '—P ∧ —Q', is a conjunction. To generate it, you will generate first one conjunct and then the other. Suppose that you begin by aiming for '—P'. Notice that there's nothing that you can do with (1), and there's also nothing that you can do with (2). When all else fails, do a *Reductio* proof. Your new target, once again, is '—P'; assume its opposite, 'P', and aim for a contradiction. Notice that you're now beginning a *Reductio* proof *within the scope* of another *Reductio* proof; i.e., you're about to introduce a *Reductio* assumption within the scope of another *Reductio* assumption:

```
  1 (1) —(—P ∧ —Q)                 A
  2 (2) —(P ∨ Q)                   A
  3 (3) P                          A
  3 (4) P ∨ Q                      3 ∨I
2,3 (5) (P ∨ Q) ∧ —(P ∨ Q)        4,2 ∧I
  2 (6) —P                         3,5 —I
                .

                .

  (n−3) —P ∧ —Q                    6,? ∧I
  (n−2) (—P ∧ —Q) ∧ —(—P ∧ —Q)    n−3,1 ∧I
  (n−1) — —(P ∨ Q)                 2,n−2 —I
    (n) P ∨ Q                      n−1 — —E
```

You're halfway home. Your target, in line (*n*−3), is the conjunction '—P ∧ —Q'. You already have the left conjunct in line (6), so your goal is to generate the right conjunct,'—Q'. Assume 'Q' and aim for a contradiction. The next four lines of your derivation, (7) through (10), will be the mirror image of the previous four lines, (3) through (6).

$$
\begin{array}{lll}
1 \ (1) & -(-P \wedge -Q) & A \\
2 \ (2) & -(P \vee Q) & A \\
3 \ (3) & P & A \\
3 \ (4) & P \vee Q & 3 \vee I \\
2,3 \ (5) & (P \vee Q) \wedge -(P \vee Q) & 4,2 \wedge I \\
2 \ (6) & -P & 3,5 -I \\
7 \ (7) & Q & A \\
7 \ (8) & P \vee Q & 7 \vee I \\
2,7 \ (9) & (P \vee Q) \wedge -(P \vee Q) & 8,2 \wedge I \\
2 \ (10) & -Q & 7,9 -I \\
2 \ (11) & -P \wedge -Q & 6,10 \wedge I \\
1,2 \ (12) & (-P \wedge -Q) \wedge -(-P \wedge -Q) & 11,1 \wedge I \\
1 \ (13) & --(P \vee Q) & 2,12 -I \\
1 \ (14) & P \vee Q & 13 --E \\
\end{array}
$$

Done.

Now consider the reverse of this sequent:

S63:          $P \vee Q \vdash -(-P \wedge -Q)$

Your given assumption, 'P ∨ Q', is a disjunction, so you naturally think ∨E thoughts. Assume 'P', the left disjunct, in line (2), and then (somewhat later) assume 'Q', the right disjunct. From 'P' you will be trying to derive '−(−P ∧ −Q)', and from 'Q' you will be trying to derive '−(−P ∧ −Q)'. So your immediate task is to get from 'P' to '−(−P ∧ −Q)'. How to proceed? No idea? When all else fails, think *Reductio* thoughts and assume the opposite of what you're aiming for; i.e., assume '−P ∧ −Q' in line (3).

$$
\begin{array}{lll}
1 \ (1) & P \vee Q & A \\
2 \ (2) & P & A \\
3 \ (3) & -P \wedge -Q & A \\
& \quad . & \\
& \quad . & \\
\end{array}
$$

$(m{-}2)$ O $\wedge$ $-$O                          ?
$(m{-}1)$ $-(-$P $\wedge$ $-$Q$)$                  3,$m{-}2$ $-$I
$\quad(m)$ P $\rightarrow$ $-(-$P $\wedge$ $-$Q$)$  2,$m{-}1$ $\rightarrow$I
$(n{-}?)$ Q                                         A

.

.

$(n{-}2)$ $-(-$P $\wedge$ $-$Q$)$                  ?
$(n{-}1)$ Q $\rightarrow$ $-(-$P $\wedge$ $-$Q$)$   $n{-}?$,$n{-}2$ $\rightarrow$I
$\quad(n)$ $-(-$P $\wedge$ $-$Q$)$                  1,$m$,$n{-}1$ $\vee$E

Having introduced a *Reductio* assumption in line (3), your goal is to generate a contradiction. If you look at the *wffs* in lines (2) and (3), you should see how to generate it. The rest of the derivation should unfold naturally enough, with the second half of the derivation, beginning at line (8), constituting a mirror image of the first half. Behold the derivation as a whole:

1 (1) P $\vee$ Q                                   A
2 (2) P                                            A
3 (3) $-$P $\wedge$ $-$Q                           A
3 (4) $-$P                                         3 $\wedge$E
2,3 (5) P $\wedge$ $-$P                            2,4 $\wedge$I
2 (6) $-(-$P $\wedge$ $-$Q$)$                      3,5 $-$I
(7) P $\rightarrow$ $-(-$P $\wedge$ $-$Q$)$        2,6 $\rightarrow$I
8 (8) Q                                            A
9 (9) $-$P $\wedge$ $-$Q                           A
9 (10) $-$Q                                        9 $\wedge$E
8,9 (11) Q $\wedge$ $-$Q                           8,10 $\wedge$I
8 (12) $-(-$P $\wedge$ $-$Q$)$                     9,11 $-$I
(13) Q $\rightarrow$ $-(-$P $\wedge$ $-$Q$)$       8,12 $\rightarrow$I
1 (14) $-(-$P $\wedge$ $-$Q$)$                     1,7,13 $\vee$E

Done!

We'll conclude this section with a derivation that involves the use of $-$I, $\leftrightarrow$I, and $\rightarrow$I:

S64:        $P \leftrightarrow Q \vdash --Q \leftrightarrow --P$

Your premise is begging you to perform $\leftrightarrow$E on it: you will duly oblige it. Your conclusion is a bi-conditional, so you will have to generate both the left-to-right conditional and the right-to-left conditional. Suppose that you try first to generate '$--Q \rightarrow --P$', and then to generate '$--P \rightarrow --Q$'. (The order of generation, of course, doesn't matter.) To generate '$--Q \rightarrow --P$' you'll assume '$--Q$', and your target will be '$--P$'. Accordingly, once you've gotten as much mileage out of the premise as you can get, you'll assume '$--Q$' as an $\rightarrow$I assumption in line (5):

| | | |
|---|---|---|
| 1 | (1) $P \leftrightarrow Q$ | A |
| 1 | (2) $(P \rightarrow Q) \wedge (Q \rightarrow P)$ | 1 $\leftrightarrow$E |
| 1 | (3) $P \rightarrow Q$ | 2 $\wedge$E |
| 1 | (4) $Q \rightarrow P$ | 2 $\wedge$E |
| 5 | (5) $--Q$ | A |
| 5 | (6) $Q$ | 5 $--$E |
| 1,5 | (7) $P$ | 4,6 $\rightarrow$E |

You've generated 'P' from the *wffs* in lines (1) and (5)—but you need, of course, to generate '$--P$'. How do you do so? Well, you just *did* so: Re-visit the proof of S61 (above), '$P \vdash --P$'. All you have to do now is to replicate those steps. You are about to perform a *Reductio* proof within the larger proof. You're aiming for '$--P$', so assume the opposite of what you're aiming for:

| | | |
|---|---|---|
| 8 | (8) $-P$ | A |
| 1,5,8 | (9) $P \wedge -P$ | 7,8 $\wedge$I |
| 1,5 | (10) $--P$ | 8,9 $-$I |
| 1 | (11) $--Q \rightarrow --P$ | 5,10 $\rightarrow$I |

You're halfway done. To generate '$--P \rightarrow --Q$' you'll assume '$--P$' and your target will be '$--Q$'.

| | | |
|---|---|---|
| 12 | (12) $--P$ | A |
| 12 | (13) $P$ | 12 $--$E |
| 1,12 | (14) $Q$ | 3,13 $\rightarrow$E |

From 'Q' you need to derive '——Q'. Once again, assume the opposite of what you're aiming for:

| | | |
|---|---|---|
| 15 (15) —Q | | A |
| 1,12,15 (16) Q ∧ —Q | | 14,15 ∧I |
| 1,12 (17) ——Q | | 15,16 —I |
| 1 (18) ——P → ——Q | | 12,17 →I |
| 1 (19) (——Q → ——P) ∧ (——P → ——Q) | | 11,18 ∧I |
| 1 (20) ——Q ↔ ——P | | 19 ↔I |

Done—in a paltry twenty lines.

# 9. A Recapitulation of the Last Four Derivation Rules

## 1. →I

The →I derivation of '△ → O' requires you to adhere to the following conditions:

1. Introduce as an assumption, '△', i.e., the antecedent of the conditional that you're trying to generate.
2. From '△', construct a derivation of 'O', the consequent of the conditional that you're trying to generate.
3. In the course of constructing your derivation, make sure that '△' plays a role in generating 'O'; i.e., make sure that 'O' rests on '△'. ('O' may also rest on other assumptions.)
4. On a line below 'O', write '△ → O'.
5. To the right of '△ → O', cite the line numbers of '△' and 'O', respectively, as well as the rule →I.
6. To the left of the line number of '△ → O', cite the line numbers of each assumption on which 'O' rests, with the exception of the line number of the discharged assumption, '△'.

(m)    △                        A

          .

          .

(n)    O
(o) △ → O                  m,n →I


## 2. ↔I

The ↔I derivation of '△ ↔ O' requires you to adhere to the following conditions:

1. Construct a derivation of '△ → O'.
2. Construct a derivation of 'O → △'.
3. On a line below both '△ → O' and 'O → △', form the
   conjunction,'(△ → O) ∧ (O → △)'.
4. On a line below '(△ → O) ∧ (O → △)', write '△ ↔ O'.
5. To the right of '△ ↔ O', cite the line number of
   '(△ → O) ∧ (O → △)' as well as the rule ↔I.
6. To the left of the line number of '△ ↔ O', cite
   the line numbers of each assumption on which
   '(△ → O) ∧ (O → △)' rests.


(m)            △                    A

                .

                .

(n)            O
(o)        △ → O              m,n →I
(p)            O              A

                .

                .

(q)            △
(r)        O → △              p,q →I
(s) (△ → O) ∧ (O → △)         o,r ∧I
(t)        △ ↔ O              s ↔I

## 3. ∨E

The ∨E derivation from '△ ∨ O', a disjunction that already appears in your derivation, to a *wff* '□', requires you to adhere to the following conditions:

1. Construct a derivation of '△ → □'.
2. Construct a derivation of 'O → □'.
3. On a line below both '△ → □' and 'O → □', write '□'.
4. To the right of '□', cite the line numbers of '△ ∨ O', '△ → □', and 'O → □', respectively, as well as the rule ∨E.
5. To the left of the line number of '□', cite the line numbers of each assumption on which '△ ∨ O', '△ → □', and 'O → □' rest.

$(m)$  △ ∨ O

    .
    .
    .

$(n)$    △          A

    .
    .
    .

$(o)$    □
$(p)$  △ → □     $n,o$ →I
$(q)$    O       A

    .
    .
    .

$(r)$    □
$(s)$  O → □     $q,r$ →I
$(t)$    □      $m,p,s$ ∨E

## 4a. —I (First Version)

The —I derivation of '—$\triangle$', i.e., a *wff* that *does* have a dash as its main connective, requires you to adhere to the following conditions:

1.  Introduce an assumption, '$\triangle$', i.e., the opposite of the *wff* at which you're aiming.
2.  From '$\triangle$', construct a derivation of any contradiction, 'O $\wedge$ —O'.
3.  In the course of constructing your derivation, make sure that '$\triangle$' plays a role in generating 'O $\wedge$ —O'; i.e., make sure that 'O $\wedge$ —O' rests on '$\triangle$'. ('O $\wedge$ —O' may also rest on other assumptions.)
4.  On a line below 'O $\wedge$ —O', write '—$\triangle$'.
5.  To the right of '—$\triangle$', cite the line numbers of '$\triangle$' and 'O $\wedge$ —O', respectively, as well as the rule —I.
6.  To the left of the line number of '—$\triangle$', cite the line numbers of each assumption on which 'O $\wedge$ —O' rests, with the exception of the line number of the discharged assumption, '$\triangle$'.

$$(m) \quad \triangle \qquad\qquad\qquad A$$

$$\cdot$$
$$\cdot$$

$$(n) \quad O \wedge -O$$
$$(o) \quad\; -\triangle \qquad\qquad\qquad m,n \; -I$$

## 4b. —I (Second Version)

The —I derivation of '$\triangle$', i.e., a *wff* that *doesn't* have a dash as its main connective, requires you to adhere to the following conditions:

1.  Introduce an assumption, '—$\triangle$', i.e., the opposite of the *wff* at which you're aiming.
2.  From '—$\triangle$', construct a derivation of any contradiction, 'O $\wedge$ —O'.

3. In the course of constructing your derivation, make sure that '$-\triangle$' plays a role in generating 'O $\wedge$ $-$O'; i.e., make sure that 'O $\wedge$ $-$O' rests on '$-\triangle$'. ('O $\wedge$ $-$O' may also rest on other assumptions.)

4. On a line below 'O $\wedge$ $-$O', write '$--\triangle$'.

5. To the right of '$--\triangle$', cite the line numbers of '$-\triangle$' and 'O $\wedge$ $-$O', respectively, as well as the rule $-$I.

6. To the left of the line number of '$--\triangle$', cite the line numbers of each assumption on which 'O $\wedge$ $-$O' rests, with the exception of the line number of the discharged assumption, '$-\triangle$'.

7. On a line below '$--\triangle$', write '$\triangle$'.

8. To the right of '$\triangle$', cite the line number of '$--\triangle$', as well as the rule $--$E.

9. To the left of the line number of '$\triangle$', cite the line numbers of each assumption on which '$--\triangle$' rests.

| | | |
|---|---|---|
| *(m)* | $-\triangle$ | A |
| | . | |
| | . | |
| | . | |
| *(n)* | O $\wedge$ $-$O | |
| *(o)* | $--\triangle$ | *m,n* $-$I |
| *(p)* | $\triangle$ | *o* $--$E |

# Exercises

I. For each of the following sequents, construct a derivation of its conclusion from its premises.

1. S65: $P \rightarrow Q \vdash -Q \rightarrow -P$

2. S66: $(P \rightarrow S) \wedge (S \rightarrow Q), (-Q \rightarrow -P) \rightarrow R \vdash R$

3. S67: $(P \rightarrow S) \wedge (-Q \rightarrow -S), -R \rightarrow -(-Q \rightarrow -P) \vdash R$

4. S68: $-(P \wedge Q), P \vdash -Q$

5. S69: $P \wedge Q \vdash -(-P \vee -Q)$

6. S70: $-P \vee -Q \vdash -(P \wedge Q)$

7. S71: $-(P \wedge Q) \vdash -P \vee -Q$

8. S72: $P \to Q \vdash -P \vee Q$
9. S73: $-P \vee Q \vdash P \to Q$
10. S74: $-(P \wedge -Q) \vdash P \to Q$
11. S75: $P \to Q \vdash -(P \wedge -Q)$
12. S76: $-(P \wedge -Q) \vdash -P \vee Q$
13. S77: $P \wedge -Q \vdash -(P \to Q)$
14. S78: $-(P \to Q) \vdash P \wedge -Q$
15. S79: $(P \wedge P) \to Q, (P \to Q) \to R \vdash (-P \to -R) \to Q$

(Note: Construct the following derivation, S62, by aiming for '$(P \vee Q) \wedge -(P \vee Q)$' as your final contradiction. Your derivation had better look substantially different from our earlier proof of the same sequent.)

16. S62: $-(-P \wedge -Q) \vdash P \vee Q$
17. S80: $P \to (-Q \to -R) \vdash -(R \to Q) \to -P$
18. S81: $-(P \vee Q) \vdash -P \wedge -Q$
19. S82: $-P \wedge -Q \vdash -(P \vee Q)$
20. S83: $-(P \to Q) \vdash P$
21. S84: $-(-P \wedge -Q), P \to S, Q \to S \vdash S$
22. S85: $-P \vee Q, -(Q \wedge -R) \vdash P \to R$

II. Explain in your own words why $-$I is a legitimate derivation rule; i.e., explain why it's truth-preserving.

III. Let '$A$' with a numerical subscript designate an assumption, and let '$C$' with a numerical subscript designate a conclusion. Suppose the following: $A_1, A_2, \ldots, A_m \vdash C_1$; $C_1 \vdash C_2$; $\ldots$; $C_{n-1} \vdash C_n$. It follows (obviously) that $A_1, A_2, \ldots, A_m \vdash C_n$. Call such a string of sequents a *transitive* string. Question: Which of the above sequents, from S65 through S85, constitute a transitive strings of sequents?

# Chapter Four

# Propositional Logic: A Deductive Apparatus, Part Two

## 1. Theorems

Consider the following theorem

T1: $\vdash --P \rightarrow P$

If it strikes you as a bit odd, it's because it *is* a bit odd. It's a conclusion that has no premises—a premise-less conclusion. Think of that for a moment. Behold your first theorem.

> **Definition:** A *theorem* is a conclusion, resting on no assumptions, of a provable sequent.

Because, as you are about to see, '$- -P \rightarrow P$' is the conclusion of a sequent resting on no assumptions *and* because the sequent is provable, '$- -P \rightarrow P$' is a theorem. To be sure, in the course of proving '$- -P \rightarrow P$', *you* will introduce one or more assumptions—but there are no *given* assumptions, and in any case you will eventually *discharge* the assumption(s) that you introduce.

$$1\ (1)\ --P \qquad\qquad A$$
$$1\ (2)\ P \qquad\qquad\qquad 1\ --E$$
$$(3)\ --P \rightarrow P \qquad\quad 1,2 \rightarrow I$$

First look at line (1). You know *exactly* what it says. It says (syntactically) that '$--P$' rests on, or is derived from, the *wff* in line (1), i.e., from '$- -P$' itself; and it says (semantically) that there is no interpretation that makes the *wff* in line (1), i.e., '−−P', true and that makes the *wff* in line (1), i.e., '−−P', false.

Now look at line (2). You know *exactly* what it too says: it says (syntactically) that 'P' rests on, or is derived from, the *wff* in line (1), i.e., from '−−P', and it says (semantically) that there is no interpretation that makes the *wff* in line (1), i.e., '−−P', true and that makes the *wff* in line (2), i.e., 'P', false.

Finally look at line (3). Line (3) says (syntactically) that '−−P → P' rests on, or is derived from, *no* assumptions; it rests on, or is derived from *nothing*; it emerges, as it were, from thin air, or (as a student of mine once put it) from the *void*. Line (3) says (semantically) that there is no interpretation that makes '−−P → P' false, *period*. And think of it: in our formal system, how could you *possibly* derive a *wff ex nihilo* (i.e., from diddly-squat) unless that *wff* were true *no matter what*, i.e., unless that *wff* were a logical truth? In saying that '−−P → P' is true *no matter what*, you are saying that its truth is not contingent on *any* assumptions whatsoever. No matter which sentences about the world are true and no matter which are false, '−−P → P' is true, *period*. To establish its truth it is unnecessary to derive it from any truths about the world, and certainly it is not itself inconsistent with any truths about the world. Therefore you shouldn't expect any line numbers to appear to the left of '(3)' in line (3).

Now consider the following theorem:

T2:          $\vdash (-Q \rightarrow -P) \rightarrow (P \rightarrow Q)$

Because it's a conditional, you will assume its antecedent, '−Q → −P', in line (1), and you will aim to derive its consequent, 'P → Q'. Because your new target, 'P → Q', is itself a conditional, you will assume *its* antecedent, 'P', in line (2), and you will aim to derive *its* consequent, 'Q'. Because there is *nothing* that you can do, either individually or collectively, with your first two assumptions, '−Q → −P' and 'P', you will assume the opposite of your new target, 'Q', and aim for a contradiction. Hence your *Reductio* assumption of '−Q' in line (3):

    1 (1) −Q → −P                    A
    2 (2) P                          A
    3 (3) −Q                         A

$$\begin{array}{lll}
1,3 & (4) & -P & & 1,3 \to E \\
1,2,3 & (5) & P \wedge -P & & 2,4 \wedge I \\
1,2 & (6) & --Q & & 3,5 -I \\
1,2 & (7) & Q & & 6 -E \\
1 & (8) & P \to Q & & 2,7 \to I \\
& (9) & (-Q \to -P) \to (P \to Q) & & 1,8 \to I
\end{array}$$

One last theorem:

T3:         ⊢ P ∨ −P

I begin by pointing out how *not* to proceed:

$$\begin{array}{lll}
1 & (1) & P & & A \\
1 & (2) & P \vee -P & & 1 \vee I
\end{array}$$

If you think that this derivation is perfectly correct, think again. Indeed, think for a moment before reading on. . . .

Question: What *must* be true of every theorem?

Answer: It must rest on *no* assumptions. (Does the *wff* in line (2) rest on *no* assumptions?)

What exactly have you demonstrated here? You have indeed demonstrated *something*—but you haven't demonstrated what you were supposed to have demonstrated. You've demonstrated that 'P ∨ −P' is derivable from the assumption 'P'. The only problem is that you were required to demonstrate that 'P ∨ −P' is derivable from *no* assumptions. It's as though you had said, "I'm not so keen to prove *your* sequent: '⊢ P ∨ −P'. I'd rather prove *my* sequent: 'P ⊢ P ∨ −P'." *Yours*, of course, is a much easier one to prove: much, *much* easier. . . . Now obviously, in the course of proving *my* sequent, you're going to have to introduce assumptions of your own, but the trick is to discharge each of those assumptions until you're left with exactly *none*. How to proceed? When all else fails, think *Reductio* thoughts. . . .

Your line-(1) assumption is a no-brainer: '−(P ∨ −P)'. You need a contradiction. If you could generate the opposite of your line-(1) assumption *from* your line-(1) assumption, then you'd have a contradiction: i.e., if you could generate 'P ∨ −P' from '−(P ∨ −P)' then you'd have a contradiction '(P ∨ −P) ∧ −(P ∨ −P)'. The trick is to ensure that 'P ∨ −P' rests on (1), i.e., on '−(P ∨ −P)', and on (1) i.e., on '−(P ∨ −P)', alone. "How on Earth," you ask, "can one generate 'P ∨ −P' from '−(P ∨ −P)'?" Easy: the latter *wff* is self-contradictory, and from a contradiction, as you will see by the end of this chapter, one can generate *anything*; ergo. . . .

So how do you generate 'P ∨ −P'? *This wff*—your new target—is a disjunction. If you could generate either disjunct, the game would be over. Aim for 'P' or aim for '−P'—it makes no difference—and then, by ∨I, add on either '−P' or 'P', respectively.

Suppose that you aim for '−P'. Assume 'P' in line (2) and go for a contradiction.

| | | |
|---|---|---|
| 1 | (1) −(P ∨ −P) | A |
| 2 | (2) P | A |
| 2 | (3) P ∨ −P | 2 ∨I |
| 1,2 | (4) (P ∨ −P) ∧ −(P ∨ −P) | 3,1 ∧I |
| 1 | (5) −P | 2,4 −I |
| 1 | (6) P ∨ −P | 5 ∨I |
| 1 | (7) (P ∨ −P) ∧ −(P ∨ −P) | 6,1 ∧I |
| | (8) −−(P ∨ −P) | 1,7 −I |
| | (9) P ∨ −P | 8 −−E |

Notice that '(P ∨ −P)', at least in its second incarnation, i.e., in line (6), rests on (1) alone. This is exactly what you want—for the sake of your final, i.e., line (7), contradiction. Notice too that the conclusion, like *every* theorem, rests on *no* assumptions. You have just proved that either it's raining or it's not; either the Moon is made of pink fluff or it's not; either Bobo is a spy for North Zedmenistan or she's not.

Question: Is there a *strategic* secret involved in deriving theorems?

Answer: Yes-ish, i.e., yes and no. Behold the secret—such as it is:

1. If the theorem is a negation, think −I thoughts. Introduce as a *Reductio* assumption the theorem's opposite, i.e., the opposite of the negation, and try to derive a contradiction, *any* contradiction, that rests only on your initial *Reductio* assumption.
2. If the theorem is a disjunction, think −I thoughts once again. Introduce as a *Reductio* assumption the theorem's opposite, i.e., the opposite of the disjunction, and try to

derive a contradiction, *any* contradiction, that rests only on your initial *Reductio* assumption.

3.  If the theorem is a conditional, think →I thoughts. Introduce as an →I assumption the antecedent of the conditional at which you are aiming, and try to derive its consequent. The consequent must rest only on your →I assumption.

4.  If the theorem is a bi-conditional, think ↔I thoughts. Your immediate target will be two conditionals: the left-to-right conditional of the bi-conditional and the right-to-left conditional. Once you have generated the two conditionals, you will conjoin them so as to generate your ultimate target, the bi-conditional. Introduce as your first →I assumption the antecedent of the first conditional at which you're aiming, and try to derive, from this →I assumption alone, its consequent. Then introduce as your second →I assumption the antecedent of the second conditional at which you're aiming, and try to derive, from this →I assumption alone, its consequent.

5.  If the theorem is a conjunction, each of its conjuncts *must* be a theorem in its own right. Think of why this must be so: in Propositional Logic, every theorem (as you will prove in one of your next logic courses) is a tautology. For a conjunction to be a tautology, each of its conjuncts must be a tautology. (Otherwise, one of them will come out false for some interpretation or other—and for that interpretation, the entire conjunction will come out false.) Since each of its conjuncts must be a tautology, and since (as you will also prove in one of your next logic courses) every tautology is a theorem, each of its conjuncts must be a theorem. Aim to derive each of its conjuncts separately, such that the last step of your derivation will be ∧I. Look at the left conjunct: it must be either a negation (in which case, proceed as in (1) above); or a disjunction (in which case, proceed as in (2) above); or a conditional (in which case, proceed as in (3) above); or a bi-conditional (in which case, proceed as in (4) above); or a conjunction (in which case, proceed as you proceeded vis-à-vis the original conjunction). Now look at the right conjunct, and proceed as you proceeded vis-à-vis the left conjunct. Now that you have each conjunct, conjoin them. Done!

# Exercises

Construct a proof of each of the following theorems.

1. T4:   $\vdash -(P \wedge -P)$
2. T5:   $\vdash -[P \wedge -(-Q \vee P)]$
3. T6:   $\vdash (-P \rightarrow Q) \rightarrow (-Q \rightarrow P)$
4. T7:   $\vdash [P \rightarrow (Q \rightarrow R)] \rightarrow [(P \rightarrow Q) \rightarrow (P \rightarrow R)]$
5. T8:   $\vdash -(-Q \rightarrow -P) \rightarrow (P \wedge -Q)$
6. T9:   $\vdash -[P \wedge -(Q \rightarrow P)]$
7. T10:   $\vdash \{(P \vee Q) \wedge [(-R \rightarrow -P) \wedge (-R \rightarrow -Q)]\} \rightarrow R$
8. T11:   $\vdash P \leftrightarrow P$
9. T12:   $\vdash (P \leftrightarrow Q) \rightarrow (-P \leftrightarrow -Q)$
10. T13:   $\vdash (P \wedge Q) \rightarrow (P \leftrightarrow Q)$

# 2. Derived Derivation Rules: The First Two

Much as you may not wish to do so, it is salutary to revisit your high school geometry course every now and then. . . . It is now *now-and-then*.

There are many sublime aspects of Euclidean geometry. One of them is the way that everything hangs together. The theorems don't grow willy-nilly, i.e., without rhyme or reason, i.e., without any relation to one another. On the contrary, the later theorems emerge out of (i.e., are derived from, or rest upon) the earlier ones. As in geometry, so in logic.

The focus of this section will be the first two of four new derivation rules. Each of the four is a *derived* derivation rule; i.e., it piggybacks on the earlier eleven—the *primitive*—derivation rules. In other words, none of these *derived* rules is necessary: whatever you can accomplish *with* them, you can accomplish *without* them, i.e., with the *primitive* rules alone. "How odd!" you think. "Why bother incorporating such derivation rules—such *superfluous* derivation rules—into our system at all?" There are two reasons for doing so: first, to shorten (and thereby simplify) our derivations; and second, to reveal the links between new derivations and old ones.

## A. TI: Theorem Introduction

The *derived* derivation rule Theorem Introduction, TI, allows you to introduce, at any point in a derivation, any previously proved theorem, i.e., any theorem that either I proved previously for you in the text or that you yourself proved previously in the exercises. You must cite the rule TI and the number of the previously proved theorem, e.g., T3 (in the case of 'P ∨ −P') or T4 (in the case of '−(P ∧ −P)', the first of the above exercises).

### TI: The Details

1.  Let '△' be any previously proved theorem.
2.  It is permissible to introduce '△' at any point in a derivation.
3.  To the right of '△', cite the rule TI and the theorem's number.
4.  To the far left of '△', cite no line numbers whatsoever.

Now consider the following sequent:

S86:        P → Q, −P → R ⊢ Q ∨ R

A moment's reflection might convince you that deriving this conclusion from these premises will be an insuperable challenge. Theorem Introduction, however, might convince you otherwise—a *challenge*, yes; an *insuperable* challenge, no.

    1 (1) P → Q         A
    2 (2) −P → R       A
      (3) P ∨ −P       TI T3

| | |
|---|---|
| 4 (4) P | A |
| 1,4 (5) Q | 1,4 →E |
| 1,4 (6) Q ∨ R | 5 ∨I |
| 1 (7) P → (Q ∨ R) | 4,6 →I |
| 8 (8) —P | A |
| 2,8 (9) R | 2,8 →E |
| 2,8 (10) Q ∨ R | 9 ∨I |
| 2 (11) —P → (Q ∨ R) | 8,10 →I |
| 1,2 (12) Q ∨ R | 3,7,11 ∨E |

Theorem Introduction plays the key role in this derivation. At line (3), I introduced T3, the last theorem that I proved in the previous section. (T3 is known as the Law of the Excluded Middle: Either 'P' is the case or it isn't. There's no third possibility, no middle ground.)

The obvious question: How on Earth did I think of the *relevance* to this sequent of T3?

The non-obvious answer: By reflecting on the fact that the antecedents of the conditionals that constitute (1) and (2) are 'P' and '—P', respectively—the two disjuncts of the Law of the Excluded Middle.

Notice that (3), i.e., 'P ∨ —P', rests on no assumptions by virtue of its status as a theorem. Notice too that I wasn't *compelled* to introduce the Law of the Excluded Middle in line (3): I could have reproduced its earlier proof in its entirety instead. Had I done so, however, I would have added eight lines to the derivation. Think of Theorem Introduction as a promissory note, an IOU: by invoking it, you're promising to reproduce, on demand, and insert, the proof of the original theorem.

You will recall that a provisional definition of a derivation/proof appeared early on in Chapter 3. It's now time to revise that definition, to take account of theorems.

**Definition:**     A *derivation* of a *wff*, '△', from a set of given assumptions, is a finite string of *wffs*, the last of which is '△'. Each of the *wffs* in the string is either (1) a member of the set of given assumptions, or (2) an introduced assumption, or (3) a theorem, or (4) a *wff* that follows from at least one of the *wffs* in the string by one of our derivation rules.

Definition:  A *proof* of a *wff*, '△', is a finite string of *wffs*, the last of which, '△', is a theorem. Each of the *wffs* in the string is either (1) an introduced assumption, or (2) a theorem, or (3) a *wff* that follows from at least one of the *wffs* in the string by one of our derivation rules.

There's a major *syntactic* difference between a *derivation* of '△' and a *proof* of '△'. In the case of a *derivation*, '△' rests on at least one assumption, whereas in the case of a *proof*, '△' rests on no assumptions.

There's also a major *semantic* difference. In the case of a *derivation*, the given assumptions guarantee the truth of '△' if and only if they are *all* true. On the other hand, in the case of a *proof*, '△' is true unconditionally; i.e., its truth is independent of the truth or falsehood of any other *wffs*.

From an *epistemic* point of view, i.e., from the point of view of someone concerned with what we are justified in believing, the difference is that in the case of a *derivation*, we are fully justified in believing '△' to be true if and only if we are fully justified in believing to be true all of the assumptions (in at least one of the sets of assumptions) from which '△' is derived. On the other hand, in the case of a proof, we are fully justified in believing '△' to be true, period.

Having distinguished derivations from proofs, I shall now backtrack. . . . In many contexts it's common to use the term 'proof' where, strictly speaking, only the term 'derivation' would be appropriate. Indeed I shall so use (some would say *misuse*) the term 'proof' myself in the very next paragraph and, occasionally, in what follows: I have been speaking, and shall continue to speak, of *proving* a sequent, when what I *really* mean is constructing a *derivation* of the sequent's last *wff* from its initial *wffs*. It's unobjectionable to defer to common usage from time to time and conflate two terms, so long as you keep in mind the underlying conceptual distinction. As Bishop Berkeley (Irish, 1685–1753) once put it, albeit in a different context, "[W]e ought to think with the learned, but speak with the vulgar."

# B. SI: Sequent Introduction

The *derived* derivation rule Sequent Introduction, SI, allows you, subject to a single condition, to introduce, at any point in a derivation, the conclusion of any previously proved sequent, i.e., any sequent that either I proved previously in the text or that you yourself proved previously in the exercises. The one condition is that the premises of the original sequent must appear already in the current derivation. (They needn't appear there *as premises*—although, of course, they *may* do so.) You must cite the line numbers of the *wffs* that you'e invoking, the rule 'SI', and the number of the previously proved sequent, e.g., 'S71' (in the case of '$-(P \wedge Q) \vdash -P \vee -Q$') or 'S72' (in the case of '$P \rightarrow Q \vdash -P \vee Q$').

## SI: The Details

1. Let '$\triangle_1$, ... , $\triangle_n$' be the premises, and let '$\triangle_{n+1}$' be the conclusion, of any previously proved sequent.
2. Let '$\triangle_1$, ... , $\triangle_n$' be any *wffs* that appear (not necessarily in that order) in your derivation.
3. It is permissible to introduce '$\triangle_{n+1}$' at any point in the derivation after the appearance of the *wffs* '$\triangle_1$, ... , $\triangle_n$'.
4. To the right of '$\triangle_{n+1}$', cite the line numbers of the *wffs* '$\triangle_1$, ... , $\triangle_n$', the rule SI, and the sequent's number.
5. To the left of the line number of '$\triangle_{n+1}$', cite the line number of each assumption on which the *wffs* '$\triangle_1$, ..., $\triangle_n$' rest.

What all this means is the following. Suppose that you're midway through a derivation, and suppose that at some point you're staring at the following *wffs*:

.

.

.

$(m) \ P \rightarrow Q$

.

.

.

$(n) \ -Q$

Suppose too that your immediate target is '$-$P'. Earlier you saw a proof of S60: 'P $\rightarrow$ Q, $-$Q $\vdash$ $-$P'. The first clause of the rule for SI tells you that in the previously proved S60, 'P $\rightarrow$ Q' was '$\triangle_1$'; '$-$Q' was '$\triangle_2$', i.e., '$\triangle_2$'; and '$-$P' was '$\triangle_{n+1}$', i.e., '$\triangle_3$'. As it turns out, '$\triangle_1$', i.e., 'P $\rightarrow$ Q', and '$\triangle_n$', i.e., '$\triangle_2$', i.e., '$-$Q', both appear in your current derivation. So the second and third clauses of the rule for SI allow you to derive '$\triangle_{n+1}$', i.e., '$\triangle_3$', i.e., '$-$P', from them *immediately*, i.e., without reproducing the earlier derivation of '$-$P' from 'P $\rightarrow$ Q' and '$-$Q':

.
.
.

($m$) P $\rightarrow$ Q ('$\triangle_1$')

.
.

($n$) $-$Q ('$\triangle_n$', i.e., '$\triangle_2$')

.
.

($o$) $-$P ('$\triangle_{n+1}$', i.e., '$\triangle_3$')                    $m,n$ SI S60

An illustration. . . . Suppose that once again you're midway through a derivation, and suppose that you've generated '(P $\wedge$ Q) $\rightarrow$ R'. Further suppose that you're trying to generate 'P $\rightarrow$ (Q $\rightarrow$ R)'. It would be rather silly to run through the derivation all over again: you've already derived the latter *wff* from the former *wff*. Simply write down the latter *wff* on any line below the line on which the former *wff* appears, and cite SI and S20.

S87:          $--\{[(P \wedge Q) \rightarrow R] \wedge S\} \vdash [P \rightarrow (Q \rightarrow R)] \vee T$

    1 (1) $--\{[(P \wedge Q) \rightarrow R] \wedge S\}$          A
    1 (2) $[(P \wedge Q) \rightarrow R] \wedge S$          1 $--$E
    1 (3) $(P \wedge Q) \rightarrow R$          2 $\wedge$E
    1 (4) $P \rightarrow (Q \rightarrow R)$          3 SI S20
    1 (5) $[P \rightarrow (Q \rightarrow R)] \vee T$          4 $\vee$I

# 3. Interlude: Substitution-Instances

Each theorem and each sequent manifests itself in an infinite variety of what are known as *substitution-instances*—first in its original incarnation, and then in an infinite number of subsequent incarnations, each of which preserves the *form* (or *structure*) of the original theorem or sequent. In this section you will learn about substitution-instances; and in the next section you will make use of substitution-instances in order to be able to generate completely new (derived) derivation rules on your own.

You may not be familiar with the *term* 'substitution-instance', but, as you are about to see, you are already familiar with the *notion* (or *concept*) of a substitution-instance. We may speak of the substitution-instance of a particular *wff*, and we may speak of the substitution-instance of a particular *sequent*.

Consider first the substitution-instance of a particular *wff*, rather than that of a particular sequent, and in particular consider 'P ∨ −P'. Intuitively, you should have no problem identifying the following *wffs* as exhibiting the exact same *form* as, and thereby as constituting *instances* (or *manifestations*) of, 'P ∨ −P':

(1) Q ∨ −Q
(2) (P → Q) ∨ −(P → Q)
(3) (R ∧ −R) ∨ −(R ∧ −R)

Now consider the substitution-instance of a particular *sequent*, and in particular consider your old pal →E: 'Δ → O, Δ ⊢ O'. Intuitively, you should have no problem recognizing each of the following sequents as exhibiting the exact same *form* as, and thereby as constituting *instances* (or *manifestations*) of, →E, i.e., of 'Δ → O, Δ ⊢ O':

(1) −P → −Q, −P ⊢ −Q
(2) −Q → −(R ↔ S), −Q ⊢ −(R ↔ S)
(3) −−R → (S ∨ T), −−R ⊢ S ∨ T

In the course of constructing a substitution-instance, whether of a *wff* or of a sequent, you're playing dentist, engaging in the dual processes of *extracting* and *implanting*. First you *extract*, from the original *wff*, each occurrence of a given *atomic*—and 'atomic' really is the key word here. And then, wherever in the *wff* that atomic had occurred, you *implant* one and the same *wff*—and it makes no difference whether this latter *wff* is itself an atomic or a molecular thirteen city blocks long.

N.B.; i.e., *nota bene;* i.e. note well: Every connective and every set of parentheses in the original *wff* or the original sequent must re-appear in its substitution-instance. (To be sure, as you'll see presently, round parentheses may be upgraded to square brackets, square brackets to curly braces, or curly braces to round parentheses, etc.)

The process of generating a new *wff* or a new sequent out of an old *wff* or an old sequent is purely mechanical. The key instrument in the process is the *substitution-instance-generator,* or *S.I.-generator*—a table that provides the *recipe* for generating the new *wff* or the new sequent out of the old *wff* or the old sequent.

Consider the following (old) *wff*:

$$P \rightarrow (Q \rightarrow P)$$

Now consider the following S.I.-generator:

| P | Q |
|---|---|
| —Q | (R ∨ S) |

This S.I.-generator instructs you to replace each occurrence of the atomic 'P' in 'P → (Q → P)'—there are two such occurrences— with the *wff* '—Q', and to replace each occurrence of the atomic 'Q' in 'P → (Q → P)'—there is only one such occurrence—with the *wff* '(R ∨ S)'. Out comes the first 'P' in 'P → (Q → P)' and in goes '—Q'. The first arrow in 'P → (Q → P)' reappears in the substitution-instance. The opening parenthesis, the '(', in 'P → (Q → P)' reappears in the substitution-instance, albeit upgraded to an opening square bracket, '['. Out comes 'Q' and in goes '(R ∨ S)'. The second arrow in 'P → (Q → P)' reappears in the substitution-instance. Out comes the second 'P' in 'P → (Q → P)' and in goes '—Q'. The closing parenthesis, ')', in 'P → (Q → P)' reappears in the substitution-instance—albeit upgraded to a closing square bracket, ']'. Presto! You now have your substitution-instance: by starting with 'P → (Q → P)' and by following the recipe, you end up generating the following (new) *wff*:

$$-Q \rightarrow [(R \vee S) \rightarrow -Q]$$

Note, once again, that the S.I.-generator tells you to replace *atomics* in the original *wff*—but *only* atomics—with *wffs* that can be *either* atomics *or* moleculars. In the previous example, you saw an illustration of the replacement of the atomic 'P' with the molecular '—Q', and of the replacement of the atomic 'Q' with the molecular 'R ∨ S'.

Consider next the following (old) *wff*:

$$(-P \land Q) \rightarrow -P$$

Now consider the following S.I.-generator:

| P | Q |
|---|---|
| —(S ∧ T) | [U → —(V ∧ W)] |

The opening parenthesis in '(—P ∧ Q) → —P', reappears in the substitution-instance, although after you've replaced the first 'P' with '—(S ∧ T)', and 'Q' with '[U → —(V ∧ W)]', the opening parenthesis will be upgraded to an opening curly brace, '{'. The first dash in '(—P ∧ Q) → —P' reappears in the substitution-instance. Wherever 'P' appears in '(—P ∧ Q) → —P' you replace it with '—(S ∧ T)'. Out comes the first 'P' in '(—P ∧ Q) → —P'; in goes '—(S ∧ T)'. The '∧' in '(—P ∧ Q) → —P' reappears in the substitution-instance. Out comes 'Q' in '(—P ∧ Q) → —P'; in goes '[U → —(V ∧ W)]'. (Note the necessity for the square brackets: the '[' and the ']'. Hence the necessity for the curly braces.) The closing parenthesis in the antecedent of '(—P ∧ Q) → —P' reappears in the substitution-instance, albeit upgraded to a closing curly brace, '}'. The '→' in '(—P ∧ Q) → —P' reappears in the substitution-instance, and the second dash in '(—P ∧ Q) → —P' reappears in the substitution-instance. Out comes the second 'P' in '(—P ∧ Q) → —P'; in goes '—(S ∧ T)'. Presto once again! You now have your substitution-instance. By starting with '(—P ∧ Q) → —P' and by following the recipe, you end up generating the following (new) *wff*:

$$\{--(S \land T) \land [U \rightarrow -(V \land W)]\} \rightarrow --(S \land T)$$

Question: Is it clear why '—(S ∧ T)' in this latter *wff*, the substitution-instance, is preceded by a dash in each of its two occurrences?

Answer: Because the original *wff*, once again, is '(−P ∧ Q) → −P'; so when you extract both the first and the second occurrence of 'P', the dash that precedes 'P' in each of its two occurrences must reappear—*like each of the connectives in the original wff*—in the substitution-instance. It so happens that the implant—the *wff* that replaces the extracted atomic 'P'—has a dash as its main connective. Therefore you will end up with the implanted *wff*, with a dash as its main connective, preceded by the dash that, by governing the extracted atomic 'P', had been part of the structure of the original *wff*.

The substitution-instance, whether it be a generated *wff* or a generated sequent, always replicates and retains the *structure* of the original—and in Propositional Logic, the connectives and the punctuation—the parentheses, brackets, and curly braces—play a crucial role in determining the structure. The new structure may constitute an *embellishment* of the original—but the original structure must always be discernible within the new one.

Consider the notion of a substitution-instance where a single *wff* is concerned, and in particular, consider the following *wffs*. Before reading further, ask yourself which of them are substitution-instances of (1).

(1) − −(P → −Q)
(2) − −(Q → −P)
(3) − −[(R ∨ S) → − −T]
(4) − −(P ∧ −Q)
(5) P → −Q

(2) is a substitution-instance of (1): to generate it, you simply replace 'P' in (1) with 'Q' in (2), and you replace 'Q' in (1) with 'P' in (2). The structure of (2) is *identical to* the structure of (1): (2), like (1), is the negation of the negation of a conditional whose consequent is a negated *wff*.

(3) is also a substitution-instance of (1): to generate it, you simply replace 'P' in (1) with 'R ∨ S' in (2), and you replace 'Q' in (1) with '−T' in (2). (3) preserves the structure of (1)—and *adds* to, or *enhances*, or *embellishes* its structure, thereby exhibiting a more complex structure. Indeed (3) retains the structure of (1) within its, (3)'s, more complex structure. In both instances, you're looking at the negation of the negation of a conditional whose consequent is a negation. It's immaterial

that the antecedent of the conditional that is buried in (1) is an *atomic*, whereas the antecedent of the conditional that is buried in (3) is a *molecular*, a disjunction. It's also immaterial that the consequent of the conditional that is buried in (1) is the negation of an atomic, whereas the consequent of the conditional that is buried in (3) is the negation of the negation of an atomic. It's in these latter respects that the structure of (3) constitutes an *embellishment* of the structure of (1).

(4) is clearly *not* a substitution-instance of (1): it fails to preserve the structure of (1); there's no way that an S.I.-generator could generate (4) from (1). (1) is the negation of the negation of a *conditional* whose consequent is a negation, whereas (4) is the negation of the negation of a *conjunction* whose right conjunct is a negation.

Nor is (5) a substitution-instance of (1): it too fails to preserve the structure of (1). There's no way that an S.I.-generator could generate (5) from (1). (1), once again, is the negation of the negation of a conditional; (5) is not the negation of the negation of *anything*. (5) *subtracts* from the structure of (1), by eliminating the two initial dashes, and thus exhibits *less* structural complexity than (1). To be sure, (5) is *semantically* identical to (1): they are true for the same interpretations and false for the same interpretations. Their semantic identity is irrelevant, however; where substitution-instances are concerned, *syntax* (i.e., form or structure) counts for *everything*, and *semantics* counts for *nothing*.

The substitution-instance of a sequent is in principle no different from the substitution-instance of a *wff*. Consider the sequent '(P ∨ Q) ∨ R, −P ∧ −Q ⊢ −−R', and consider the following S.I.-generator:

| P | Q | R |
|---|---|---|
| −(P ∨ Q) | (S ∧ T) | (S → S) |

The sequent consists of three *wffs*. By producing the substitution-instance of each *wff*, you'll thereby produce the substitution-instance of the sequent:

$$[-(P \vee Q) \vee (S \wedge T)] \vee (S \rightarrow S), --(P \vee Q) \wedge -(S \wedge T) \vdash$$
$$--(S \rightarrow S)$$

You're now ready for two definitions—one that captures the very essence of a substitution-instance of an individual *wff*, and one that captures the very essence of a substitution-instance of a sequent. You are *not* to panic at the sight of these definitions and their illustrations. Just read them slowly and then, if necessary, reread them several times. It's *not* the end of the world if you find this business rather painful. It *is* rather painful.

**Definition:**

1. Let '$\triangle$' be any *wff*.
2. Let '$p_1$', '$p_2$', ... , '$p_n$' be the atomics that occur in '$\triangle$'.
3. Let '$q_1$', '$q_2$', ... , '$q_n$' be any *wffs* whatsoever (either atomic or molecular).
4. In '$\triangle$', replace each occurrence of '$p_1$' with '$q_1$', each occurrence of '$p_2$' with '$q_2$', ... , and each occurrence of '$p_n$' with '$q_n$'.
5. Let '$O$' be the resulting *wff*.
6. Accordingly, '$O$' is a *substitution-instance* of '$\triangle$'.

Here's an illustration of what all of this means.

1. Let '$\triangle$' be the *wff* '$(P \rightarrow Q) \rightarrow (-Q \rightarrow -P)$'.
2. Let '$p_1$' be 'P', and let '$q_1$' be 'R ∧ S'.
3. Let '$p_2$' be 'Q', and let '$q_2$' be 'T ∨ U'. (Because there are two atomics in the original *wff*, $n = 2$; therefore '$p_n$' is '$p_2$'; i.e., the $n$th atomic in the original *wff* is '$p_2$'.)
4. In '$\triangle$', replace each occurrence of '$p_1$' (i.e., each occurrence of 'P') with '$q_1$' (i.e., with 'R ∧ S').
5. In '$\triangle$', replace each occurrence of '$p_2$' (i.e., each occurrence of 'Q') with '$q_2$' (i.e., with 'T ∨ U').
6. The resulting *wff*, '$O$', is a substitution-instance of the *wff* '$\triangle$'.
7. In other words, the *wff* '$[(R \wedge S) \rightarrow (T \vee U)] \rightarrow [-(T \vee U) \rightarrow -(R \wedge S)]$' is a substitution-instance of the *wff* '$(P \rightarrow Q) \rightarrow (-Q \rightarrow -P)$'.

The definition of the substitution-instance of a sequent draws upon the above definition of the substitution-instance of a *wff*:

**Definition:**    1. Let '$\triangle_1$,' … , '$\triangle_{m-1}$,' and '$\triangle_m$' be any *wffs*.
2. Let '$\triangle_1$, … , $\triangle_{m-1} \vdash \triangle_m$' be any sequent.
3. Let '$p_1$,' '$p_2$,' … , '$p_n$' be the atomics that occur in the sequent '$\triangle_1$, … , $\triangle_{m-1} \vdash \triangle_m$.'
4. Let '$q_1$,' '$q_2$,' … , '$q_n$' be any *wffs* whatsoever (either atomic or molecular).
5. In '$\triangle_1$, … , $\triangle_{m-1} \vdash \triangle_m$,' replace each occurrence of '$p_1$' with '$q_1$,' each occurrence of '$p_2$' with '$q_2$,' … , and each occurrence of '$p_n$' with '$q_n$.'
6. Let the result of replacing each occurrence of '$p_1$,' '$p_2$,' … , '$p_n$' with '$q_1$,' '$q_2$,' … , '$q_n$,' respectively, in '$\triangle_1$,' … , '$\triangle_{m-1}$,' and '$\triangle_m$' be '$O_1$,' … , '$O_{m-1}$,' and '$O_m$,' respectively.
7. Let '$O_1$, … , $O_{m-1} \vdash O_m$' be the resulting sequent.
8. Accordingly, '$O_1$, … , $O_{m-1} \vdash O_m$' is a *substitution-instance* of '$\triangle_1$, … , $\triangle_{m-1} \vdash \triangle_m$.'

Here's an illustration of what all of this means. (Once again, it's *not* the end of the world if you find this rather difficult.)

1. Let '$\triangle_1$, … , $\triangle_{m-1} \vdash \triangle_m$' be the sequent 'P → Q, Q → R ⊢ P → R.' ('$\triangle_1$' is 'P → Q'; '$\triangle_2$,' i.e., '$\triangle_{m-1}$,' is 'Q → R'; and '$\triangle_3$,' i.e., '$\triangle_m$,' is 'P → R.')
2. Let '$p_1$' be 'P', and let '$q_1$' be 'S ∨ T'.
3. Let '$p_2$' be 'Q', and let '$q_2$' be '—U'.
4. Let '$p_3$' be 'R' and let '$q_3$' be 'R'. (Two points. . . . First, nothing prevents the implanted *wff* from being identical to the extracted atomic that it's replacing. Second, because there are three atomics in the original *wff*, $n = 3$; therefore '$p_n$' is '$p_3$'; i.e., the $n$th atomic in the original wff is '$p_3$'.)
5. Replace each occurrence of $p_1$ in the sequent (i.e., each occurrence of 'P') with $q_1$ (i.e., with 'S ∨ T').

6. Replace each occurrence of '$p_2$' in the sequent (i.e., each occurrence of 'Q') with '$q_2$' (i.e., with '–U').
7. Replace each occurrence of '$p_3$' in the sequent (i.e., each occurrence of 'R') with '$q_3$' (i.e., with 'R').
8. The resulting sequent, '$O_1$, ... , $O_{m-1}$ ⊢ $O_m$', is a substitution-instance of the sequent '$\Delta_1$, ... , $\Delta_{m-1}$ ⊢ $\Delta_m$'.
9. In other words, the sequent '(S ∨ T) → –U, –U → R ⊢ (S ∨ T) → R' is a substitution-instance of the sequent 'P → Q, Q → R ⊢ P → R'.

# Exercises

I. For each of the following *wffs*, (1) indicate each *wff* in the column, if any, that is a substitution-instance of it, and (2) provide the S.I.-generator.

1.  [(P ∨ P) ∨ –(P ∨ P)] ∧ –(P ∨ P)
2.  [(P ∧ Q) ∨ –(P ∧ Q)] ∧ – –(Q ∧ –R)
3.  P ↔ –(Q ∧ –R)
4.  –[(P ∧ P) ∨ (S ∧ –T)]
5.  P
6.  [(P → Q) ∧ (P ∧ Q)] ∨ [(P → Q) ∧ (Q → P)]
7.  –{[(P ↔ Q) ∧ (P ↔ Q)] ∨ [–(P ↔ Q) ∧ – – –(P ↔ Q)]}
8.  [P → (P → P)] → (P → P)
9.  [(R → S) ∧ (R → S)] ∨ [(R → S) ∧ (R → S)]
10. (Q ∨ –P) ∧ –S
11. [(R → S) ∧ (R → S)] ↔ –[(R → S) ∧ – –(R → S)]
12. [(P ∨ Q) ∨ –(P ∨ Q)] ∧ –(P ∨ Q)
13. (P ∧ Q) ∨ (R ∧ S)
14. –P
15. (P → Q) → R

II. For each of the following sequents, (1) indicate each sequent in the column, if any, that is a substitution-instance of it, and (2) provide the S.I.-generator.

1.  $P \to (Q \to R), Q \wedge P \vdash R$
2.  $-(-P \wedge -Q) \vdash --P \vee --Q$
3.  $-[-(P \wedge -P) \wedge -P], -P \vee P \vdash ---(P \wedge -P) \to ---P$
4.  $P \vdash Q \vee -Q$
5.  $-(P \to Q) \vdash P \wedge -Q$
6.  $-P \to -Q, R \to ---P \vdash Q \to -R$
7.  $(-P \to P) \to [(-P \to P) \to (-P \to P)], [(-P \to P) \wedge (-P \to P)] \vdash -P \to P$
8.  $--P \vee --Q \vdash P \vee --Q$
9.  $(P \vee -P) \wedge -(P \vee -P) \vdash Q \vee -Q$
10.  $--(P \wedge Q) \to \{-[-P \vee (Q \wedge -R)] \to -(P \to Q)\} \vdash [--(P \wedge Q) \wedge (P \to Q)] \to [-P \vee (Q \wedge -R)]$
11.  $-[(P \vee -P) \to (P \vee -P)] \vdash (P \vee -P) \wedge -(P \vee -P)$
12.  $-(P \wedge -Q), -Q \vee R \vdash --P \to --R$
13.  $-(P \wedge -P) \to -(P \wedge -P), -(P \wedge -P) \to ---(P \wedge -P) \vdash (P \wedge -P) \to ---(P \wedge -P)$
14.  $-(Q \wedge P) \vdash -Q \vee -P$
15.  $-P \to (-Q \to -R) \vdash (-P \wedge R) \to Q$

III. Using the atomics 'P', 'Q', and 'R', construct five syntactically distinct *wffs*. Now construct a *distinct* S.I.-generator for each of the five *wffs*, and show the substitution-instance that the S.I.-generator generates for each of the five *wffs*.

IV. Using the atomics 'P', 'Q', and 'R', construct five syntactically distinct *wffs*. Now construct *one and the same* S.I.-generator for each of the five *wffs*, and show the substitution-instance that the S.I.-generator generates for each of the five *wffs*

# 4. Derived Derivation Rules: The Last Two

So! Now that you've slogged your way through the notational muck of Section 3, you're asking yourself, "What on Earth did I do to deserve *this*? What could *possibly* be so interesting about the notion of a substitution-instance as to compensate for the slog through the muck? What's the payoff—what's the cash value—of all this talk of substitution-instances?"

## A. TISI: Theorem Introduction Substitution-Instance

Suppose that you're asked to prove that '$(R \to -S) \lor -(R \to -S)$' is a theorem. You have three choices.

First, you can try to pull off the derivation from scratch. But why bother reinventing the derivation-wheel? Your derivation of '$(R \to -S) \lor -(R \to -S)$' will be a *mirror image* of your derivation of T3, '$P \lor -P$', except that wherever you had '$P$' in the original derivation, you'll have '$(R \to -S)$' in your derivation of '$(R \to -S) \lor -(R \to -S)$'.

Second, you can return to your original derivation of '$P \lor -P$' and go through it line by line, replacing each occurrence of '$P$' in each line of that derivation with '$(R \to -S)$'—a process that is purely mechanical, to be sure (i.e., one requiring no real thought on your part), but that would be rather time-consuming, yes?

Third—and this, of course, is the punch line—you can simply write down the *wff*, '$(R \to -S) \lor -(R \to -S)$', and be done with it. Off to the right you cite the new, derived derivation rule, TISI (Theorem Introduction Substitution-Instance), and the number of the theorem that you're invoking, T3.

TISI, in other words, allows you to introduce, at *any* point in a derivation, *any* substitution-instance of *any* previously proved theorem. You must cite both the rule, TISI, and the number of the theorem in its original incarnation.

## TISI: The Details

1. Let '△' be any previously proved theorem.
2. Let 'O' be any substitution-instance of '△'.
3. It is permissible to introduce 'O' at any point in a derivation.
4. To the right of 'O', cite the rule 'TISI' and the theorem's number.
5. To the left of the line number of 'O', do not cite any line numbers of any assumptions.

What does it mean to say that one derivation is (or isn't) a *mirror image* of another derivation? In particular, what would it mean to say that the derivation of 'O' is a mirror image of the derivation of '△'? Consider the following three theorems:

T14: $\vdash ----P \to P$

T15: $\vdash ----(P \to P) \to (P \to P)$

T16: $\vdash P \to P$

The second theorem is clearly a substitution-instance of the first; the third is clearly not. Crucially, the derivation of the second theorem is a mirror image of the derivation of the first; crucially, the derivation of the third theorem is not.

| T14: | 1 (1) $----P$ | A |
| | 1 (2) $--P$ | 1--E |
| | 1 (3) P | 2--E |
| | (4) $----P \to P$ | 1,3 →I |

| T15: | 1 (1) $----(P \to P)$ | A |
| | 1 (2) $--(P \to P)$ | 1--E |
| | 1(3) P $\to$ P | 2--E |
| | (4) $----(P \to P) \to (P \to P)$ | 1,3 →I |

T16:    1 (1) P                                      A
        (2) P → P                                    1,1→I

Notice the fundamental respect in which the second derivation is a mirror image of the first: on any given line, the operation that you perform in the second derivation is identical to the operation that you perform in the first. Think of what this entails. First, the two derivations are of equal length. Second, on any given line, the derivation rules that you cite to the right in the second derivation are identical to those that you cite to the right in the first. Third, on any given line, the line numbers that you cite to the right in the second derivation are identical to those that you cite to the right in the first. And fourth, on any given line, the assumption numbers that you cite to the left in the second derivation are identical to those that you cite to the left in the first. In none of these latter respects is the third derivation a mirror image of the first.

Because T15 is a substitution-instance of T14, you can shrink our four-line derivation of the former into a one-line derivation:

T15:    (1) −−−−−(P →P) → (P → P)          TISI T14

You can make effective use of substitution-instances not only to prove *theorems* but also to prove *sequents*. In the course of proving various sequents, you may now appeal to substitution-instances of previously proved theorems. Consider the following sequent:

S88:        (−−R → R) → (−S → −T) ⊢ T → S

Notice that in the proof of this sequent we invoke the notion of a substitution-instance twice when we appeal to previously proved theorems—once in line (2) and once in line (4):

        1 (1) (−−R → R) → (−S → −T)      A
          (2) −−R → R                    TISI T1
        1 (3) −S → −T                    1,2 →E
          (4) (−S → −T) → (T → S)        TISI T2
        1 (5) T → S                      4,3 →E

## B. SISI: Sequent Introduction Substitution-Instance

What applies to previously proved theorems applies, obviously, to previously proved sequents. Consider the following sequent, commonly known as 'Hypothetical Syllogism':

S89:          $P \rightarrow Q, Q \rightarrow R \vdash P \rightarrow R$

| | |
|---|---|
| 1 (1) $P \rightarrow Q$ | A |
| 2 (2) $Q \rightarrow R$ | A |
| 3 (3) P | A |
| 1,3 (4) Q | 1,3 $\rightarrow$E |
| 1,2,3 (5) R | 2,4 $\rightarrow$E |
| 1,2 (6) $P \rightarrow R$ | 3,5 $\rightarrow$E |

Thanks to your new pal Sequent Introduction, whenever you come across 'P → Q' and 'Q → R' in the course of a derivation, you may immediately write down 'P → R'. Off to the right you write (as you would expect to do) the line numbers of 'P → Q' and 'Q → R', along with the name of the rule, 'SI' ('Sequent Introduction'), and the number of the previously proved sequent.

Now, whenever you come across a single substitution-instance of 'P → Q' and 'Q → R' in the course of a derivation, you may subsequently write down the corresponding substitution-instance of 'P → R'. Off to the right you write (as you would expect to do) the line numbers of the substitution-instances of 'P → Q' and 'Q → R', along with the name of the derived derivation rule, 'SISI' ('Sequent Introduction Substitution-Instance'), and the number of the previously proved sequent.

SISI, in other words, allows you to introduce a *wff* at any point in a derivation, so long as the *wff* itself, and other *wffs* that already appear in the derivation, constitute a substitution-instance of a previously proved sequent. (Clearly, there must be an S.I.-generator that generates, in the derivation on which you're working, the substitution-instance of the premises and the conclusion of the original derivation.) Suppose, in other words, the following:

1. You've proved a given sequent Sm, e.g., S89:
   $P \rightarrow Q, Q \rightarrow R \vdash P \rightarrow R$.
2. There exists a sequent Sn, e.g., 'A $\rightarrow$ B,
   B $\rightarrow$ C $\vdash$ A $\rightarrow$ C', that happens to be a substitution-instance of Sm.
3. In the derivation on which you're currently working, you've already generated every *wff* in Sn except for its conclusion; i.e., you've already generated 'A $\rightarrow$ B' and 'B $\rightarrow$ C'—but not 'A $\rightarrow$ C'.
4. The conclusion of Sn, i.e., 'A $\rightarrow$ C', is exactly what you're aiming for.

Under these conditions, SISI allows you to derive the conclusion of Sn *immediately* from all of the other *wffs* of Sn. In other words, you're free to write down the conclusion of Sn, i.e., 'A $\rightarrow$ C', on a line beneath all of the other *wffs* of Sn, i.e., beneath 'A $\rightarrow$ B' and 'B $\rightarrow$ C'. You must cite the rule, SISI, the number of the sequent in its original incarnation, and the line numbers of the *wffs* that you're invoking.

Note that the *wffs* that constitute Sn may appear as *wffs* of *any* sort in the current derivation, and not necessarily as its premises or its final conclusion.

## SISI: The Details

1. Let '$\triangle_1$', ..., '$\triangle_n$' be the premises, and let '$\triangle_{n+1}$' be the conclusion, of any previously proved sequent.
2. Let '$O_1$', ..., '$O_n$' be any *wffs* that already appear in your derivation, and let '$O_{n+1}$' be a *wff* that you're aiming for.
3. Let the sequent '$O_1$, ..., $O_n \vdash O_{n+1}$' be a substitution-instance of the sequent '$\triangle_1$, ..., $\triangle_n \vdash \triangle_{n+1}$'.
4. It is permissible to introduce '$O_{n+1}$' at any point in your derivation below '$O_1$, ..., $O_n$'.
5. To the right of '$O_{n+1}$', cite the line numbers of the *wffs* '$O_1$', ..., '$O_n$', the rule 'SISI', and the sequent number of the previously proved sequent, '$\triangle_1$, ..., $\triangle_n \vdash \triangle_{n+1}$'.
6. To the left of the line number of '$O_{n+1}$', cite the line number of each assumption on which the *wffs* '$O_1$', ..., '$O_n$' rest.

Now consider the following three sequents. The first two are snaps; the third is a nightmare.

S90:          $P \rightarrow Q, Q \rightarrow R, R \rightarrow S, S \rightarrow T, T \rightarrow U \vdash P \rightarrow U$

If you construct the derivation by using only our primitive rules, the derivation will run twelve lines. (Try this on your own and see for yourself.) On the other hand, if you appeal to the previously proved sequent, S89, you can knock three lines off the derivation:

| | | |
|---|---|---|
| 1 (1) $P \rightarrow Q$ | | A |
| 2 (2) $Q \rightarrow R$ | | A |
| 3 (3) $R \rightarrow S$ | | A |
| 4 (4) $S \rightarrow T$ | | A |
| 5 (5) $T \rightarrow U$ | | A |
| 1,2 (6) $P \rightarrow R$ | | 1,2 SI S89 |
| 1,2,3 (7) $P \rightarrow S$ | | 6,3 SISI S89 |
| 1,2,3,4 (8) $P \rightarrow T$ | | 7,4 SISI S89 |
| 1,2,3,4,5 (9) $P \rightarrow U$ | | 8,5 SISI S89 |

Of course, you should now feel perfectly free to draw upon S90:

S91:          $-P \rightarrow -Q, -Q \rightarrow -R, -R \rightarrow -S, -S \rightarrow -T,$
              $-T \rightarrow -U, -U \rightarrow -V \vdash -P \rightarrow -V$

| | | |
|---|---|---|
| 1 (1) $-P \rightarrow -Q$ | | A |
| 2 (2) $-Q \rightarrow -R$ | | A |
| 3 (3) $-R \rightarrow -S$ | | A |
| 4 (4) $-S \rightarrow -T$ | | A |
| 5 (5) $-T \rightarrow -U$ | | A |
| 6 (6) $-U \rightarrow -V$ | | A |
| 1,2,3,4,5 (7) $-P \rightarrow -U$ | | 1,2,3,4,5 SISI S90 |
| 1,2,3,4,5,6 (8) $-P \rightarrow -V$ | | 7,6 SISI S89 |

S92:          $-S \rightarrow -R, -(--R \wedge -S) \rightarrow T \vdash T$

| | |
|---|---|
| 1 (1) $-S \rightarrow -R$ | A |
| 2 (2) $-(--R \wedge -S) \rightarrow T$ | A |
| (3) $(-S \rightarrow -R) \rightarrow (R \rightarrow S)$ | TISI T2 |
| 1 (4) $R \rightarrow S$ | 3,1 $\rightarrow$I |
| 1 (5) $-R \vee S$ | 4 SISI S72 |
| 1 (6) $-(--R \wedge -S)$ | 5 SISI S63 |
| 1,2 (7) T | 2,6 $\rightarrow$E |

## C. A Brief Recapitulation

It should now be clear what the moral is of the substitution-instances story. Any substitution-instance of a theorem is itself a theorem, and any substitution-instance of a provable sequent is itself a provable sequent. So, having proved a single theorem or a single sequent, you have thereby proved an *unlimited* number of theorems or sequents, i.e., each of the substitution-instances of the theorem or sequent in question. Hence you needn't bother to construct a derivation of the substitution-instance: you need only cite the number of the theorem or sequent in its original incarnation.

Consider a *wff* that is the substitution-instance of a previously proved *theorem*. In saying that the substitution-instance is also a theorem, what you are really saying is that there exists a derivation of it that is *identical* to the derivation of the original theorem—subject only to the qualification that wherever a given atomic appears in the original derivation, the atomic is replaced with the *wff* that the S.I.-generator calls for. It is for this reason that you are now free to insert, at any point in a derivation, any substitution-instance of any previously proved theorem.

Consider too a sequent that is the substitution-instance of a previously proved *sequent*. In saying that there exists a proof of the substitution-instance, what you are really saying is that there exists a derivation of its conclusion from its premises that is *identical* to the derivation of the conclusion of the original sequent from *its* original premises—subject only to the qualification that wherever a given atomic appears in the original derivation, the atomic is replaced with the *wff* that the S.I.-generator calls for. It is for this reason that you are now free to insert, at any point in a derivation, any substitution-instance of any previously proved sequent.

You saw in Section 2 of this chapter, that you are free to insert, at any point in a derivation, any previously proved theorem or sequent. You see now that you are also free to insert, at any point in a derivation, any substitution-instance of any previously proved theorem or sequent. In other words, at any point in a derivation, you are free to insert:

1. any previously proved theorem (by TI), or
2. any previously proved sequent (by SI), or
3. any substitution-instance of any previously proved theorem (by TISI), or
4. any substitution-instance of any previously proved sequent (by SISI).

As you know, our formal system has eleven *primitive*, or *basic*, derivation rules. You are now free to draw upon an unlimited number of new, *derived* derivation rules—a new, derived derivation rule corresponding to each previously proved theorem or sequent, as well as to each substitution-instance of each previously proved theorem or sequent.

Where *primitive* derivation rules are concerned, Ockham reigns and his razor prevails: the fewer the derivation rules the better. Where *derived* derivation rules are concerned, on the other hand, the sky's the limit.

# 5. A Tricky Sequent—and the *Reductio* Assumption Revisited

It's time to turn up the heat. Logic, like life, can become rather warm, i.e., rather complicated, rather quickly. Consider the following sequents:

S93:        $P, -P \vdash Q$

S94:        $P \vee Q, -P \vdash Q$

The validity of the first sequent may not be self-evident (although we did discuss it in Chapter 2). Consider: 'Ardbeg is a double agent. Ardbeg isn't a double agent. Therefore Bobo is a double agent.' Because there's no interpretation for which all the premises are true, there's no interpretation for which all the premises are true and the conclusion is false. So of course the argument is valid.

The validity of the second sequent, on the other hand, is self-evident: 'Either Ardbeg is a double agent or Bobo is. Ardbeg isn't. Therefore Bobo is.' (You may quickly assure yourself of the validity of each of these sequents, self-evident or not, via either truth-tables or the Short Method.)

There are two features of each of the two sequents that render them of interest. First, each is devilishly tricky to prove. Doubtless you will wish to prove each on your own. Your wish will be granted in the very next set of exercises—at least with respect to a variation on the second of the two sequents, S94. In what follows, I shall be dragging you, step by painful step, through S93, and much of what I have to say about S93 is also relevant to S94.

Second, it becomes apparent quite early on in the game that in the course of trying to prove either of the two sequents, you find yourself caught up in trying to prove the other. Here is how life looks just before you embark on your proof of S93:

$$1 \ (1) \ P \qquad\qquad\qquad A$$
$$2 \ (2) \ -P \qquad\qquad\qquad A$$
$$.$$
$$.$$
$$.$$
$$Q$$

And here is how life looks the instant after you dip your toe into the proof of S94, with the *wff* in line (3) serving as a ∨E assumption:

$$1 \ (1) \ P \lor Q \qquad\qquad\qquad A$$
$$2 \ (2) \ -P \qquad\qquad\qquad A$$
$$3 \ (3) \ P \qquad\qquad\qquad A$$
$$.$$
$$.$$
$$.$$
$$Q$$

Notice the crucial feature that the two sequents have in common. Each of them is such that from two *wffs*, 'P' and '—P', one of which is the negation of the other, you're trying to generate a third *wff*, 'Q', that is entirely unrelated to either of the two *wffs*.

S93:          P, —P ⊢ Q

I begin by focusing on how *not* to begin. The following derivation is *dead* wrong. It will be most instructive to see both *that* and *why* it is dead wrong.

```
1 (1) P                      A
2 (2) —P                     A
3 (3) —Q                     A
1,2 (4) P ∧ —P               1,2 ∧I
1,2 (5) — —Q                 3,4 —I      XXX
1,2 (6) Q                    5 — —E
```

The *source* of the problem here (as distinct from the *actual* problem) is line (4). Strictly speaking, there's nothing wrong with line (4): you haven't violated any of the derivation rules in the move to line (4), and therefore you don't lose any points at line (4). You do lose points at line (5), however, where there is something terribly wrong—hence the three red Xs. Even so, line (4) is the *source* of the problem. Notice that the line-(4) contradiction rests on the *wffs* in lines (1) and (2)—and not at all on the line-(3) *Reductio* assumption. The line-(3) *Reductio* assumption, in other words, plays no role in generating the line-(4) contradiction. Nevertheless, it's clear that in line (5), off to the right, the line-(3) *Reductio* assumption is being *blamed,* as it were, for generating the contradiction.

The numbers to the left of '(4)' in line (4), like the numbers to the far left of *any* contradiction, say everything. They tell you that the *wffs* in lines (1) and (2) generate the line-(4) contradiction. They tell you, therefore, that the *wffs* in lines (1) and (2) cannot both be true. But they tell you absolutely nothing—they are perfectly silent— about the line-(3) *Reductio* assumption. *Because the line-(3) Reductio assumption plays no role in generating the line-(4) contradiction—because it is not one of the assumptions upon which the line-(4) contradiction rests—it is illegitimate to pin the contradiction on it.*

If you think that there's no requirement that the contradiction rest on the *Reductio* assumption, reread the third condition of each of the two versions of −I (Chapter 3, Section 8, Subsection D). If you think that such a requirement is *unwarranted*, proceed *posthaste* to the second appendix, "→I and −I Revisited," at the end of this chapter. Otherwise, read on.

Your task, when you tackle these sequents, will be to resist the temptation of this *most* improper use of the *Reductio ad Absurdum* rule, −I. The same temptation will arise again in this derivation, as you will soon see.

It should be clear how you are *not* to proceed with the sequent 'P, −P ⊢ Q'. How, then, *should* you proceed? You will recall that I noted earlier that the derivation is actually quite tricky. You will find yourself zigging and zagging en route to your destination.

Your line-(3) *wff* is a no-brainer. It's a *Reductio* assumption that you introduce because all else has failed; i.e., there is simply nothing else that you can do. The problem is that having made the *Reductio* assumption, you're *stuck*; it's *entirely* unclear what to do next. You know that you need to generate a contradiction; the problem is that you don't know *which* contradiction to aim for.

|   |   |
|---|---|
| 1 (1) P | A |
| 2 (2) −P | A |
| 3 (3) −Q | A |
| . | |
| . | |
| (n−1) − −Q | 3,? −I |
| (n) Q | n−1 − −E |

Suppose that in line (4) you were to conjoin '−P' and '−Q'. Why? Simply because it's something that you *can* do, and in addition, because the sight of '−P ∧ −Q' *might* suggest something useful. So now you have '−P ∧ −Q'. Remember: you've embarked on a *Reductio* proof. If you could derive the opposite of '−P ∧ −Q', i.e., '−(−P ∧ −Q)', you'd have your contradiction. Your new target is '−(−P ∧ −Q)'.

You look at the *wff* in line (1): 'P'. You think to yourself that you could disjoin 'Q' to it to generate 'P ∨ Q' in line (5). Why would you *want* to do that? A quick stroll down memory lane serves to remind you, from Chapter 1, that by one of the versions of your old pal De Morgan, 'P ∨ Q' is logically equivalent to '—(—P ∧ —Q)'—and '—(—P ∧ —Q)' simply happens to be your new target. '—(—P ∧ —Q)' is the very *wff* that, in conjunction with '—P ∧ —Q' in line (4), will generate your contradiction in line (n–2), below. It follows, therefore, that if you could simply (*simply!*) transform 'P ∨ Q' in line (5) into '—(—P ∧ —Q)'—i.e., if you could simply derive the latter *wff* from the former *wff*—then you'd have your contradiction and the game would be over.

| | | |
|---|---|---|
| 1 (1) P | | A |
| 2 (2) —P | | A |
| 3 (3) —Q | | A |
| 2,3 (4) —P ∧ —Q | | 2,3 ∧I |
| 1 (5) P ∨ Q | | 1 ∨I |

. 

.

| | | |
|---|---|---|
| 1 (n–3) —(—P ∧ —Q) | | ? |
| 1,2,3 (n–2) (—P ∧ —Q) ∧ —(—P ∧ —Q) | | 4,n–3 ∧I |
| 1,2 (n–1) —  —Q | | 3,n–2 —I |
| 1,2 (n) Q | | n–1 —  —E |

A second quick stroll down memory lane serves to remind you that we've *already* proved the sequent 'P ∨ Q ⊦ —(—P ∧ —Q)'; see S63. The game is over; i.e., the hard part of the derivation, the part that calls for strategic insight, is over.

You now have a choice of strategies. You may *either* reinvent the wheel and reconstruct a derivation of '—(—P ∧ —Q)' from 'P ∨ Q', *or* appeal to the previously proved sequent S63 in the move from line (5) to line (n–3). Most surprisingly, I shall pursue *each* strategy: first I shall prove the sequent by reinventing the wheel, and then I shall prove it by invoking SI S63. Why bother to reinvent the wheel? Because proving *one* sequent, 'P ∨ Q ⊦ —(—P ∧ —Q)', within the larger context of proving *another*, 'P, —P ⊦ Q', while relying only on *primitive* derivation rules, compels us to come to terms, once again, with our *Reductio* requirement.

I shall now proceed to reinvent the wheel. 'P ∨ Q' in line (5) is a disjunction, so you naturally think ∨E thoughts. Assume 'P', the left disjunct, in line (6), and then, somewhat later, assume 'Q', the right disjunct.

Question: What will you be targeting with each of these disjuncts; i.e., what will you be trying to derive from each of them?

Hint: Your ∨E target is your line-(n–3) *wff*: '—(—P ∧ —Q)'.

Your immediate task is to get from 'P' to '—(—P ∧ —Q)', in order to generate 'P → —(—P ∧ —Q)' via →I. How to proceed? No idea? When all else fails, you know *exactly* what to do. You think *Reductio* thoughts and you assume the opposite of what you're aiming for; i.e., assume '—P ∧ —Q' below in line (7), and aim (somehow) for a contradiction. The contradiction will enable you to zap your line-(7) *Reductio* assumption, '—P ∧ —Q'. Soon thereafter you'll assume 'Q' and repeat the same procedure, so to speak.

In what follows, I have divided the overall strategy into four components. Each component corresponds to how you might think strategically about the derivation.

## First Component

$$
\begin{array}{lll}
1\ (1)\ P & & A \\
2\ (2)\ -P & & A \\
3\ (3)\ -Q & & A \\
2,3\ (4)\ -P \wedge -Q & & 2,3\ \wedge I \\
1\ (5)\ P \vee Q & & 1\ \vee I \\
\end{array}
$$

## Second Component

$$
\begin{array}{lll}
6\ (6)\ P & & A \\
7\ (7)\ -P \wedge -Q & & A \\
\end{array}
$$

.

.

$$
\begin{array}{lll}
(?_1)\ O_1 \wedge -O_1 & & ? \\
(?_2)\ -(-P \wedge -Q) & & 7,?_1\ -I \\
(?_3)\ P \to -(-P \wedge -Q) & & 6,?_2\ \to I \\
\end{array}
$$

**Third Component**

$(?_4) \; Q$ \hfill A

$(?_5) \; -P \wedge -Q$ \hfill A

.

.

$(n-6) \; O_2 \wedge -O_2$ \hfill ?

$(n-5) \; -(-P \wedge -Q)$ \hfill $?_5, (n-6) \; -I$

$(n-4) \; Q \rightarrow -(-P \wedge -Q)$ \hfill $?_4, (n-5) \rightarrow I$

**Fourth Component**

$(n-3) \; -(-P \wedge -Q)$ \hfill $5, ?_3, (n-4) \; \vee E$

$(n-2) \; (-P \wedge -Q) \wedge -(-P \wedge -Q)$ \hfill $4, (n-3) \; \wedge I$

$(n-1) \; --Q$ \hfill $3, (n-2) \; -I$

$(n) \; Q$ \hfill $(n-1) \; --E$

Question: Why bother introducing '$-P \wedge -Q$' as a *Reductio* assumption in line (7), when you already have '$-P \wedge -Q$' in line (4)?

There are two answers—one short and one long. . . .

The short answer: '$-P \wedge -Q$' in line (4) isn't an *assumption*. (A moment ago, you were a *bit* perplexed. Now you're *quite* perplexed.)

The long answer: Your $\vee$E target in line $(n-3)$ is '$-(-P \wedge -Q)$'. You know that to reach your target, you'll need to generate a contradiction twice—once from each $\vee$E assumption. Because you're employing a *Reductio* strategy (twice) within the scope of your $\vee$E derivation, the contradiction that's your immediate target will have to rest on an *assumption*. (Repeat: an *assumption*.) And indeed, it's an assumption that you'll choose precisely because it's the opposite of the *wff* that you're trying to generate.

To be sure, '$-P \wedge -Q$' in line (4) is indeed the opposite of the *wff* that you're trying to generate. It's not an *assumption*, however. Therefore it will be impossible to pin the contradiction on it. Instead, you'll have to pin the contradiction on one of the *assumptions* on which the contradiction rests. On the other hand, not only is '$-P \wedge -Q$' in line (7) the opposite of the *wff* that you're trying to generate, it's also an *assumption*. Hence the necessity for '$-P \wedge -Q$' in line (7).

Suppose that you thought otherwise. Suppose that you thought that you could get sufficient mileage out of '−P ∧ −Q' in line (4), rendering the assumption of '−P ∧ −Q' in line (7) unnecessary. No doubt your derivation would then proceed as follows:

| | | |
|---|---|---|
| 1 (1) P | | A |
| 2 (2) −P | | A |
| 3 (3) −Q | | A |
| 2,3 (4) −P ∧ −Q | | 2,3 ∧I |
| 1 (5) P ∨ Q | | 1 ∨I |
| 6 (6) P | | A |
| 2,3 (7) −P | | 4 ∧E |
| 2,3,6 (8) P ∧ −P | | 6,7 ∧I |

So now you have a contradiction in line (8), and you're grinning from ear to ear. The problem, however, is this: your line-(8) contradiction rests on the *wffs* in lines (2), (3), and (6), i.e., on '−P', '−Q', and 'P'. Presumably, then, your next line will be the negation of one of *these wffs*. But you don't need the negation of *any* of these *wffs*! You don't need either '− −P' or '− −Q' or '−P'. You need '−(−P ∧ −Q)'.

Moral of the story: the *only* way to generate '−(−P ∧ −Q)' is to introduce '−P ∧ −Q', its opposite, as an *assumption*—a *Reductio* assumption. This is so even if (as in this instance) you already happen to have '−P ∧ −Q', insofar as you derived it, in line (4), from other *wffs*.

Behold the derivation as a whole:

| | | |
|---|---|---|
| 1 (1) P | | A |
| 2 (2) −P | | A |
| 3 (3) −Q | | A |
| 2,3 (4) −P ∧ −Q | | 2,3 ∧I |
| 1 (5) P ∨ Q | | 1 ∨I |
| 6 (6) P | | A |
| 7 (7) −P ∧ −Q | | A |
| 7 (8) −P | | 7 ∧E |
| 6,7 (9) P ∧ −P | | 6,8 ∧I |
| 6 (10) −(−P ∧ −Q) | | 7,9 −I |
| (11) P → −(−P ∧ −Q) | | 6,10 →I |

| | |
|---|---|
| 12 (12) Q | A |
| 13 (13) —P ∧ —Q | A |
| 13 (14) —Q | 13 ∧E |
| 12,13 (15) Q ∧ —Q | 12,14 ∧I |
| 12 (16) —(—P ∧ —Q) | 13,15 —I |
| (17) Q → —(—P ∧ —Q) | 12,16 →I |
| 1 (18) —(—P ∧ —Q) | 5,11,17 ∨E |
| 1,2,3 (19) (—P ∧ —Q) ∧ —(—P ∧ —Q) | 4,18 ∧I |
| 1,2 (20) — —Q | 3,19 —I |
| 1,2 (21) Q | 20 — —E |

Checkmate.

Notice that having discharged your line-(7) *Reductio* assumption, '—P ∧ —Q', in line (10)—(9) rests upon it but (10) doesn't—you *explicitly* reintroduced it in line (13) and then discharged it again in line (16). Strictly speaking, it was unnecessary for you to have reintroduced it *explicitly* in line (13). Instead you could have omitted line (13) and reintroduced '—P ∧ —Q' *implicitly* in your *new* line (13) as follows, thereby shaving a line off your derivation:

.
.
.

| | |
|---|---|
| 12 (12) Q | A |
| 7 (13) —Q | 7 ∧E |
| 7,12 (14) Q ∧ —Q | 12,13 ∧I |
| 12 (15) —(—P ∧ —Q) | 7,14 —I |
| (16) Q → —(—P ∧ —Q) | 12,15 →I |
| 1 (17) —(—P ∧ —Q) | 5,11,16 ∨E |

Notice that by *appealing* to your line-(7) *wff* at the far left of line (13), i.e., as a *wff* on which your line-(13) *wff* rests, you are thereby showing that you have *implicitly* reintroduced '—P ∧ —Q', your line-(7) *wff*.

In your zeal to shave off a line here, a line there, you could also have omitted 'P', your line-(6) ∨E assumption: After all, you already have 'P' in line (1)—*also* as an assumption. To be sure, you would be discharging 'P', your line-(1) assumption, in the course of generating

'P → −(−P ∧ −Q)'—and it's obviously a bit odd when you find yourself discharging a *given* assumption. However, you would end up (implicitly) reintroducing 'P' in the course of wrapping up your ∨E proof. How so? To the right of '−(−P ∧ −Q)', your ∨E conclusion, you would cite your line-(5) disjunction 'P ∨ Q'. At the same time, and off to the far left of '−(−P ∧ −Q)', you would cite the *wff* on which 'P ∨ Q' rests—and *that wff* is, of course, 'P', your line-(1) assumption. And so it is that you would end up reintroducing 'P', your line-(1) assumption, precisely then.

A twenty-one-line derivation (or its slightly shaved counterpart) is nothing to sneeze at—but now, thanks to Sequent Introduction, you can *really* shrink it. Simply appeal to the previously proved sequent 'P ∨ Q ⊢ −(−P ∧ −Q)'. You are about to eliminate lines (6) through (17) (above):

| | | |
|---|---|---|
| 1 | (1) P | A |
| 2 | (2) −P | A |
| 3 | (3) −Q | A |
| 2,3 | (4) −P ∧ −Q | 2,3 ∧I |
| 1 | (5) P ∨ Q | 1 ∨I |
| 1 | (6) −(−P ∧ −Q) | 5 SI S63 |
| 1,2,3 | (7) (−P ∧ −Q) ∧ −(−P ∧ −Q) | 4,6 ∧I |
| 1,2 | (8) − −Q | 3,7 −I |
| 1,2 | (9) Q | 8 − −E |

Having proved the sequent that you just proved, 'P, −P ⊢ Q', you are now in a *most* enviable position: you are now free to conjure rabbits out of hats! Any time that you generate a contradiction, you're entitled to write down *any wff whatsoever*. To its right, of course, your write down 'SI' (or 'SISI') and 'S93'—the rabbits-out-of-hats sequent.

As an illustration of SI S93, consider the second of the two sequents that (as I noted earlier) are quite tricky—S94: 'P ∨ Q, −P ⊢ Q'. In many logic texts, this counts as a *primitive* derivation rule, typically known as 'Disjunctive Syllogism'. For us, of course, it's nothing of the sort; instead, it will count as a *derived* derivation rule:

S94:          $P \vee Q, -P \vdash Q$

| | |
|---|---|
| 1 (1) P ∨ Q | A |
| 2 (2) −P | A |
| 3 (3) P | A |
| 2,3 (4) Q | 3,2 SI S93 |
| 2 (5) P → Q | 3,4 →I |
| 6 (6) Q | A |
| (7) Q → Q | 6,6 →I |
| 1,2 (8) Q | 1,5,7 ∨E |

As one last illustration in this chapter of the thesis that many roads lead to Rome, not to mention one last illustration in this chapter of Sequent Introduction, consider the following proof of the same sequent:

| | |
|---|---|
| 1 (1) P ∨ Q | A |
| 2 (2) −P | A |
| 3 (3) −Q | A |
| 2,3 (4) −P ∧ −Q | 2,3 ∧I |
| 1 (5) −(−P ∧ −Q) | 1 SI S63 |
| 1,2,3 (6) (−P ∧ −Q) ∧ −(−P ∧ −Q) | 4,5 ∧I |
| 1,2 (7) −−Q | 3,6 −I |
| 1,2 (8) Q | 7 −−E |

# 6. A Schematic Recapitulation of the Last Four Derivation Rules

## 1. →I

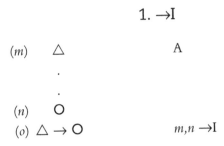

| | | |
|---|---|---|
| (m) | △ | A |
| | . | |
| | . | |
| (n) | ○ | |
| (o) | △ → ○ | m,n →I |

## 2. ↔I

| | | |
|---|---|---|
| (*m*) | △ | A |

$$\vdots$$

| | | |
|---|---|---|
| (*n*) | ○ | |
| (*o*) | △ → ○ | *m,n* →I |
| (*p*) | ○ | A |

$$\vdots$$

| | | |
|---|---|---|
| (*q*) | △ | |
| (*r*) | ○ → △ | *p,q* →I |
| (*s*) | (△ → ○) ∧ (○ → △) | *o,r* ∧I |
| (*t*) | △ ↔ ○ | *s* ↔I |


## 3. ∨E

| | | |
|---|---|---|
| (*m*) | △ ∨ ○ | |
| (*n*) | △ | A |

$$\vdots$$

| | | |
|---|---|---|
| (*o*) | □ | |
| (*p*) | △ → □ | *n,o* →I |
| (*q*) | ○ | A |

$$\vdots$$

| | | |
|---|---|---|
| (*r*) | □ | |
| (*s*) | ○ → □ | *q,r* →I |
| (*t*) | □ | *m,p,s* ∨E |

## 4a. −I (First Version)

$(m)$     $\triangle$                          A

.

.

.

$(n)$  $\bigcirc \wedge -\bigcirc$

$(o)$    $-\triangle$                          $m,n$ −I

## 4b. −I (Second Version)

$(m)$    $-\triangle$                          A

.

.

.

$(n)$  $\bigcirc \wedge -\bigcirc$

$(o)$   $--\triangle$                          $m,n$ −I

$(p)$     $\triangle$                           $o$ −−E

# Exercises

For each of the following sequents, construct a derivation of its conclusion from its premises. Use either the primitive derivation rules alone
or both the primitive and the derived derivation rules.

1. S95: $P \vee Q, -Q \vdash P$
   (Do *not* replicate the structure of the proof of S94; you
   want a *bit* of a challenge.)
2. S96: $P \vdash Q \rightarrow P$
3. S97: $(P \wedge Q) \vee (-P \wedge -Q) \vdash P \leftrightarrow Q$
4. S98: $P \leftrightarrow Q \vdash (P \wedge Q) \vee (-P \wedge -Q)$
5. S99: $-(-P \vee -Q) \vdash P \wedge Q$
6. S100: $-P \vdash P \rightarrow Q$
   (Produce three different short proofs of this sequent, each
   one invoking a different derived rule.)
7. S101: $P \vdash (P \wedge Q) \vee (P \wedge -Q)$

8.  S102: $-Q \rightarrow -(Q \vee -R)$, $(R \wedge -Q) \rightarrow S \vdash --Q \vee S$
9.  S103: $P \wedge -P \vdash Q$
    (Prove this sequent using a strategy radically different
    from the one that I used above in proving S93. Your fifth
    line should be 'P $\wedge$ $-$Q'. Plan on using SI twice. Your
    proof should be much shorter than my proof of S93.)
10. S104: $-(-P \wedge -Q) \vdash -P \rightarrow Q$

# 7. The Cheat Sheet

Question: How is it possible to remember *every* previously proved
sequent and *every* previously proved theorem that are useful for the
derivations/proofs in this book?

Answer: It's not. Hence the following cheat sheet. It contains only
a single theorem, but a rather formidable number of sequents. By now,
however, you should be familiar with a proof of the theorem as well as
a proof of each of the sequents. A proof of the theorem—T3, the Law
of the Excluded Middle—already appears in the text, along with proofs
of many of the sequents. You yourself have proved the remainder of the
sequents.

## A. Theorem Introduction (TI)

T3:        $\vdash \triangle \vee -\triangle$                    Excluded Middle (EM)

## B. Sequent Introduction (SI)

S81:    $-(\triangle \vee \square) \vdash -\triangle \wedge -\square$              De Morgan (DM)

S82:    $-\triangle \wedge -\square \vdash -(\triangle \vee \square)$              De Morgan (DM)

S71:    $-(\triangle \wedge \square) \vdash -\triangle \vee -\square$              De Morgan (DM)

S70:     $-\triangle \vee -\square \vdash -(\triangle \wedge \square)$          De Morgan (DM)

S63:     $\triangle \vee \square \vdash -(-\triangle \wedge -\square)$          De Morgan (DM)

S62:     $-(-\triangle \wedge -\square) \vdash \triangle \vee \square$          De Morgan (DM)

S69:     $\triangle \wedge \square \vdash -(-\triangle \vee -\square)$          De Morgan (DM)

S99:     $-(-\triangle \vee -\square) \vdash \triangle \wedge \square$          De Morgan (DM)

S101:    $\triangle \vdash (\triangle \wedge \square) \vee (\triangle \wedge -\square)$          Expansion (EN)

S20:     $(\triangle \wedge \square) \rightarrow O \vdash (\triangle \rightarrow (\square \rightarrow O))$          Exportation (EX)

S21:     $\triangle \rightarrow (\square \rightarrow O) \vdash (\triangle \wedge \square) \rightarrow O$          Importation (IM)

S93:     $O, -O \vdash \triangle$          Rabbits out of Hats (RH)

S100:    $-O \vdash O \rightarrow \triangle$          Rabbits out of Hats (RH)

S96:     $O \vdash \triangle \rightarrow O$          Conditional from Consequent (CC)

S94:     $\triangle \vee \square, -\triangle \vdash \square$          Disjunctive Syllogism (DS)

S95:     $\triangle \vee \square, -\square \vdash \triangle$          Disjunctive Syllogism (DS)

S89:     $\triangle \rightarrow \square, \square \rightarrow O \vdash \triangle \rightarrow O$   Hypothetical Syllogism (HS)

S72:     $\triangle \rightarrow \square \vdash -\triangle \vee \square$          Material Implication (MI)

S73:     $-\triangle \vee \square \vdash \triangle \rightarrow \square$          Material Implication (MI)

S75:     $\triangle \rightarrow \square \vdash -(\triangle \wedge -\square)$          Material Implication (MI)

S74:     $-(\triangle \wedge -\square) \vdash \triangle \rightarrow \square$          Material Implication (MI)

S78:     $-(\triangle \rightarrow \square) \vdash \triangle \wedge -\square$          Negation Implication (NI)

S77:     $\triangle \wedge -\square \vdash -(\triangle \rightarrow \square)$          Negation Implication (NI)

S53:     $\triangle \vee (\square \vee \bigcirc) \vdash (\triangle \vee \square) \vee \bigcirc$          Association (AS)

S54:     $(\triangle \vee \square) \vee \bigcirc \vdash \triangle \vee (\square \vee \bigcirc)$          Association (AS)

S6:      $\triangle \wedge (\square \wedge \bigcirc) \vdash (\triangle \wedge \square) \wedge \bigcirc$          Association (AS)

S7:      $(\triangle \wedge \square) \wedge \bigcirc \vdash \triangle \wedge (\square \wedge \bigcirc)$          Association (AS)

S50:     $\triangle \vee (\square \wedge \bigcirc) \vdash (\triangle \vee \square) \wedge (\triangle \vee \bigcirc)$          Distribution (DS)

S51:     $(\triangle \vee \square) \wedge (\triangle \vee \bigcirc) \vdash \triangle \vee (\square \wedge \bigcirc)$          Distribution (DS)

S43:     $\triangle \wedge (\square \vee \bigcirc) \vdash (\triangle \wedge \square) \vee (\triangle \wedge \bigcirc)$          Distribution (DS)

S55:     $(\triangle \wedge \square) \vee (\triangle \wedge \bigcirc) \vdash \triangle \wedge (\square \vee \bigcirc)$          Distribution (DS)

S60:     $\triangle \rightarrow \square, -\square \vdash -\triangle$          *Modus (Tollendo) Tollens* (MT)

S65:     $\triangle \rightarrow \square \vdash -\square \rightarrow -\triangle$          Contraposition (CN)

# Exercises

I. For each of the following sequents, construct a derivation of its conclusion from its premises. Use either the primitive derivation rules alone or both the primitive and the derived derivation rules.

1. S105: $-(P \rightarrow Q) \vdash P$
2. S106: $-(P \rightarrow Q) \vdash -Q$
3. S107: $-(P \leftrightarrow Q) \vdash (P \wedge -Q) \vee (-P \wedge Q)$
4. S108: $(P \wedge -Q) \vee (-P \wedge Q) \vdash -(P \leftrightarrow Q)$

5. S109: $-P \leftrightarrow Q \vdash P \leftrightarrow -Q$
6. S110: $P \leftrightarrow -Q \vdash -P \leftrightarrow Q$
7. S111: $-(P \leftrightarrow Q) \vdash -P \leftrightarrow Q$
8. S112: $-P \leftrightarrow Q \vdash -(P \leftrightarrow Q)$

Deriving the conclusion from the premise of each of the following two sequents is not for the faint of heart. Be creative in your use of TI and/or SI. Be immensely pleased with yourself if either of your two derivations is fewer than forty or fifty lines in length.

9. S113: $P \leftrightarrow (Q \leftrightarrow R) \vdash (P \leftrightarrow Q) \leftrightarrow R$
10. S114: $(P \leftrightarrow Q) \leftrightarrow R \vdash P \leftrightarrow (Q \leftrightarrow R)$

II. Construct a proof of each of the following theorems. Use either the primitive derivation rules alone or both the primitive and the derived derivation rules.

1. T17: $\vdash [P \rightarrow (Q \land -Q)] \rightarrow -P$
2. T18: $\vdash [-P \rightarrow (-Q \rightarrow -R)] \rightarrow [(-P \land R) \rightarrow Q]$
3. T19: $\vdash P \rightarrow (Q \rightarrow P)$
4. T20: $\vdash -(P \rightarrow Q) \rightarrow -(-P \lor Q)$
5. T21: $\vdash (-P \lor Q) \lor -(P \rightarrow Q)$
6. T22: $\vdash -(P \lor P) \rightarrow -P$
7. T23: $\vdash -\{[P \lor (Q \rightarrow R)] \land -[(Q \rightarrow P) \lor R]\}$
8. T24: $\vdash -(P \leftrightarrow P) \rightarrow Q$
9. T25: $\vdash [P \lor (-Q \rightarrow R)] \rightarrow [(-P \rightarrow Q) \lor R]$
10. T26: $\vdash [(-P \rightarrow Q) \lor R] \rightarrow [P \lor (-Q \rightarrow R)]$
11. T27: $\vdash [P \land -(-Q \land -R)] \rightarrow [-(P \rightarrow -Q) \lor$
    $-(P \rightarrow -R)]$
12. T28: $\vdash [-(P \rightarrow -Q) \lor -(P \rightarrow -R)] \rightarrow$
    $[P \land -(-Q \land -R)]$
13. T29: $\vdash P \rightarrow (P \rightarrow P)$
14. T30: $\vdash (-P \leftrightarrow -Q) \rightarrow (P \leftrightarrow Q)$
15. T31: $\vdash -(P \lor Q) \lor [(R \rightarrow S) \rightarrow (P \lor Q)]$
16. T32: $\vdash [P \lor (P \lor Q)] \leftrightarrow (P \lor Q)$

# 8. Appendix I: Deductive Completeness: A Next Logic Course

There was a crucial question that we addressed at some length in Appendix I of Chapter 2: How do you know that you have enough connectives? The answer to that question was a bit (but only a bit) tricky. There is an analogous, and equally crucial, question that we shall address now, at the end of Chapter 4: How do you know that you have enough *derivation rules*? The answer to *this* question, alas, is not only *tricky*, it is *very* tricky. It is *so* tricky, indeed, that its answer will have to await one of your *next* logic courses.

Even so, it's possible to say a few words here by way of introduction to the question, and thereby (perhaps) whet your appetite to take a second logic course. What would it mean for you *not* to have enough derivation rules? It would mean that there were arguments out there, in Arguments Land, that are *valid*, and that you can *show* to be valid (via either the Truth-Table Method or the Short Method), but that you cannot *prove* to be valid (via our derivation rules).

Suppose that you've been working on a sequent for an hour or so. Suppose that you keep running up against dead ends. What do you conclude? Either the argument is valid or it isn't. (The Truth-Table Method and/or the Short Method will tell you which it is.) Suppose that it *isn't* valid. In that case—because our derivation rules are truth-preserving—the sequent *can't* be proved. Maybe you miscopied; maybe there's a typo; or maybe whoever assigned the sequent was throwing you a curve ball.

Alternatively, suppose that the argument *is* valid. In that case either you haven't demonstrated sufficient insight, imaginativeness, and/or perseverance, or—and this is the *real* nightmare—you don't have a sufficient number of derivation rules to *prove* that it's valid. In this latter scenario you would suffer from operating within an impoverished formal system, one whose formal language may be up to snuff but whose deductive apparatus certainly isn't.

So if the argument is *valid*, and if you're unable to *prove* that it's valid, how on Earth will you be able to determine whether your inability to prove that it's valid is a function of your own limitations, on the one hand, or the limitations of your deductive apparatus, on the other? (A most interesting question, yes?) For all that you know, in other words, your deductive apparatus might not contain a sufficient number of derivation rules.

And here's another interesting question: If you *did* have a sufficient number of derivation rules in your deductive apparatus, how could you possibly ever *prove* that you had a sufficient number? Note how you could *not* prove it: you could *not* prove it by pointing out that with your current set of derivation rules, you've been able to prove valid every valid argument that you've ever tried to prove valid. *So what* if you haven't yet bumped up against a valid argument that you couldn't prove to be valid? The key word here is 'yet'. Just because you haven't *yet* bumped up against such an argument, it doesn't follow that you won't bump up against one in the future.

And here's yet another interesting question: If you *didn't* have a sufficient number of derivation rules, how would you know whether the addition of any *finite* number of rules would ever do the trick? What if it could be demonstrated that *every* deductive apparatus of *every* formal system of logic with a finite number of derivation rules suffered from a comparable deficiency, i.e., lacked a sufficient number of derivation rules? If such were the case, the very notion of a proof, and the very notion of a formal system, would suffer from a *devastating* limitation.

As it turns out, however, in our formal system we *do* have a sufficient number of derivation rules. Indeed it can be *proved* that every valid argument that can be expressed in the formal language of our formal system is *provable* within the system, i.e., by means of the derivation rules of the system. And in one of your next logic courses, you'll work your way through the development of just such a proof (albeit in a different formal system).

Definition:     A formal system is *deductively complete iff* every valid argument that can be expressed in the formal language of the system is provable within the system.

Because our formal system *is* deductively complete, it follows that if you stumble upon a valid argument that you can't prove, you now know why you can't prove it. It's not because your derivation rules aren't up to the task at hand. It's because you haven't demonstrated sufficient insight, imaginativeness, and/or perseverance. . . . Back to the drawing board you go.

# 9. Appendix II: →I and —I Revisited

Suppose that you're unhappy with the →I requirement that in the course of proving '△ → O', you are to derive 'O' from '△' in such a way that 'O' *rests on* '△'. (See Chapter 3, Section 8, Subsection A, Clause 3.) Suppose too that you're unhappy with the —I requirement that in the course of proving '—△'/'△', you are to derive your contradiction 'O ∧ —O' from your *Reductio* assumption '△'/'—△' in such a way that 'O ∧ —O' *rests on* '△'/'—△'. (See Chapter 3, Section 8, Subsection D, Clause 3 of each of the two versions of —I.)

You may take comfort in learning that you're not alone in your unhappiness. Not only that, but you're in *very* good company indeed. Many (and perhaps most) logicians would be entirely sympathetic to your unhappiness. Indeed, it is for this reason that both →I and —I admit of rival versions—versions from which the above requirements are conspicuously absent. In this appendix, I'll discuss three rival versions, and against them I'll defend the versions that I formulated in Chapter 3, Sections 8A and 8D, respectively.

The first involves taking a rather permissive approach to these rules. The second involves using a sneaky ploy to avoid being charged with taking a rather permissive approach to the rules. The third involves dispensing with the rules altogether, i.e., giving them the boot, as it were.

## A. The Permissive Approach

Consider first the following →I derivation of 'P → Q' from 'Q':

```
1 (1) P                    A
2 (2) Q                    A
2 (3) P → Q                1,2 →I    !!!
```

Two noteworthy points: first, the argument is clearly *valid*; and second, the derivation is clearly *odd*.

The argument is *clearly* valid. I remind you for the umpteenth time: 'P → Q' simply expresses the bare-bones thought that it's not the case that 'P' is true and that 'Q' is false. And obviously, if you assume in lines (1) and (2) that 'P' and 'Q' are both true, then *of course* it's not the case in line (3) that 'P' is true and that 'Q' is false. So, on the assumptions that (1) and (2), i.e., 'P' and 'Q', are both true, then (3), i.e., 'P → Q', *must* be true.

The derivation is *clearly* odd. (Hence the three exclamation marks to the far right of line (3).) 'P', the line-(1) *wff* that is the *antecedent* of the conditional at which you're aiming, plays *no* role in generating 'Q', the line-(2) *wff* that is the *consequent* of the conditional at which you're aiming. This is hardly surprising. (2), after all, is an *assumption*: it rests on itself and not on (1). As an assumption, therefore, *of course* (2) won't be generated by any other *wff*.

Question: So how do you avoid such counterintuitive derivations?

Answer: By adhering to the third condition on →I that emerged in Chapter 3, Section 8A: the *wff* that will become the consequent of your targeted conditional must rest on the *wff* that will become the antecedent of your targeted conditional. Accordingly, the *wff* that will become the antecedent of your targeted conditional must play a role in generating the *wff* that will become the consequent of your targeted conditional.

Consider next the following —I derivation of 'Q' from 'P' and '—P':

```
    1 (1) P                 A
    2 (2) —P                A
    3 (3) —Q                A
1,2 (4) P ∧ —P          1,2 ∧I
1,2 (5) — —Q            3,4 —I      !!!
1,2 (6) Q               5 — —E
```

It's not uncommon for logicians to permit the sort of move to line (5) that I disallowed in Chapter 3, Section 8D. On purely *semantic* grounds, to be sure, there's no reason to disallow it. After all, there's no interpretation that makes 'P' in line (1) and '—P' in line (2) both true. Therefore there's no interpretation that makes 'P' in line (1) and '—P' in line (2) both true and that also makes '— —Q' in line (5) false. Therefore the argument whose premises are 'P' and '—P' and whose conclusion is '— —Q' in line (5) and 'Q' in line (6) is certainly a *valid* argument.

By the exact same token, because there's no interpretation that makes 'P' true in line (1), '—P' true in line (2), and '— —Q' false in line

(5), obviously there's no interpretation that makes 'P' true in line (1), '—P' true in line (2), '—Q' true in line (3), and '——Q' false in line (5). Therefore the argument whose premises are 'P' and '—P', whose *Reductio* assumption is '—Q', and whose conclusion is '——Q', is certainly a *valid* argument. Once again, it follows on purely *semantic* grounds that there's no reason to disallow the move to line (5).

Where proofs are concerned, however, *syntactic*—and not merely *semantic*—considerations should count for *something*. And on *syntactic* grounds, the move to '——Q' in line (5) is rather *fishy*: there is simply no *syntactic* link between the *wffs* in lines (3) and (4). This becomes clear once you realize that the line-(3) *Reductio* assumption plays no role in generating the line-(4) contradiction; i.e., the line-(4) contradiction doesn't rest on the line-(3) *Reductio* assumption. (Take a look at the numbers both to the right and to the left of the line-(4) contradiction: there's no reference to line (3).) Therefore it's misleading to say— as the numbers to the right of line (5) do *seem* to say—that the line-(4) contradiction *follows* from the line-(3) *Reductio* assumption; i.e., that there's a *derivation* of the line-(4) contradiction from the line-(3) *Reductio* assumption.

## B. The Sneaky Ploy

To be sure, you could *contrive* to have the *wff* that is the *antecedent* of the conditional at which you're aiming in your →I derivation play a role in generating the *wff* that is the *consequent* of the conditional at which you're aiming. And you could also *contrive* to have the *Reductio* assumption in your —I derivation play a role in generating the contradiction at which you're aiming. In other words, you could *conjure up* the relevant syntactic links that are missing in the above two derivations. As the following derivations make clear, however, the maneuver is artificial and the link is slippery.

```
    1 (1) P                A
    2 (2) Q                A
  1,2 (3) P ∧ Q            1,2 ∧I
  1,2 (4) Q                3 ∧E
    2 (3) P → Q            1,4 →I
```

Notice the move from (1) and (2) to (3): it's a *bit* slippery, no? Its sole purpose is to ensure that 'P', the →I assumption and the antecedent of your targeted conditional, plays a role in generating 'Q', the consequent of your targeted conditional. *Slyly*, you accomplish this goal by conjoining 'P' with 'Q' in (3)—so that (3) rests on both (1) and (2). And you want (3) to rest on both (1) and (2) so that in (4), 'Q'—the target that you're trying to derive from 'P'—will now rest on both (1) and (2).

An analogous maneuver lends itself to the —I derivation as well:

        1 (1) P                              A
        2 (2) —P                             A
        3 (3) —Q                             A
        1,2 (4) P ∧ —P                       1,2 ∧I
        1,2,3 (5) —Q ∧ (P ∧ —P)              3,4 ∧I
        1,2,3 (6) P ∧ —P                     5 ∧E
        1,2 (7) — —Q                         3,6 —I
        1,2 (8) Q                            7 — —E

Here, of course, your line-(6) contradiction, 'P ∧ —P', *does* rest on your line-(3) *Reductio* assumption. It should strike you, however, that the moves from (4) to (5), and then from (5) to (6), are problematical, albeit (as in the →I derivation) very clever in a *sneaky* sort of way. Your line-(4) contradiction rests only on the *wffs* in lines (1) and (2). In line (5), however, you conjoin '—Q', your line-(3) *Reductio* assumption, to 'P ∧ —P', your line-(4) contradiction, for the *sole* purpose of ensuring that your line-(6) contradiction will rest upon your line-(3) *Reductio* assumption, i.e., for the sole purpose of *manufacturing* a role for your line-(3) *Reductio* assumption to play in generating your line-(6) contradiction. At line (4), however, you *already* generated a contradiction—indeed, the very same contradiction—without using '—Q', your line-(3) *Reductio* assumption. And so you already knew that you could generate a contradiction without using '—Q'. Hence the disingenuousness of blaming '—Q' for your line-(6) contradiction.

Question: What is one to make of such derivations—those that involve the sneaky versions of →I and —I?

Answer: They may well conform to the *letter* of the law, i.e., to the conditions that must be satisfied before one may perform either →I or

—I, but they hardly conform to its *spirit*. Of course, if you were a real stickler, you could try to amend the law to rule out such sneaky ploys. Without going into the details, I shall simply note that the attempt to formulate such an amendment is far more challenging than it might seem.

Now obviously it's possible to derive 'P → Q' from 'Q' in a *non-sneaky* sort of way. Obviously, too, it's possible to derive 'Q' from 'P' and '—P' in a *non*-sneaky sort of way. In each case, the only problem is a *practical* one: it's normally trickier, i.e., more challenging, i.e., more difficult, to do so.

Question: So why bother?

Answer: Because it's desirable that our formal system, and thus our derivation rules, and thus the conditions that attach to the implementation of *each* of our derivation rules, be in sync with our *intuitive/commonsensical/everyday* inference rules to the greatest extent possible.

Question: And *why* is this desirable?

Answer: Read through to the end of this appendix.

## C. The Boot

It's clear why you might be drawn to either or both versions of the 'Sneaky Ploy'. After all, on purely *semantic* grounds, any *wff* whatsoever *does* imply the conditional that happens to have that particular *wff* as its consequent. And on purely *semantic* grounds, a contradiction *does* imply any *wff* whatsoever. Accordingly, in order to capture these curious facts about conditionals and contradictions, respectively, it might be tempting to give the boot to →I and —I, and to introduce two entirely new primitive derivation rules in their place.

In one fell swoop, each of the proposed new rules would do away with the charade of requiring the introduction of an assumption that, on occasion, masquerades as either an →I assumption or a —I assumption, but that is really neither. Such an assumption simply doesn't do what an →I or a —I assumption is supposed to do: it doesn't actually generate, either alone or with other assumptions, the consequent of a targeted conditional, on the one hand, or a targeted contradiction, on the other. Indeed, it's simply an *impostor.* The proposed new rules would eliminate the charade by eliminating the very requirement that there *be* →I and —I assumptions.

The proposed new version of →I—suppose that we call it 'Conditional from Consequent', i.e., 'CC'—would authorize you to write down any conditional, '△ → O', whose consequent, 'O', is *any wff whatsoever* that you already have. This would be so even if 'O' didn't rest on '△':

$(m)$     O

.

.

$(n)$ △ → O                      $m$ CC

Accordingly, the following would be a perfectly fine derivation:

1(1) Q ∧ R                  A
1(2) Q                     1 ∧E
1(3) P → Q                2 CC

Notice that 'Q' in line (2) quite obviously doesn't rest on 'P'.

The proposed new version of —I—suppose that we call it (for obvious reasons) 'Rabbits out of Hats', i.e., 'RH'— would authorize you to write down *any wff '△' whatsoever* once you strike gold, i.e., once you generate a contradiction, 'O ∧ —O'. This would be so even if 'O ∧ —O' didn't rest on the opposite of '△':

$(m)$ O ∧ —O

.

.

$(n)$     △                      $m$ RH

Accordingly, the following would be a perfectly fine derivation:

1 (1) P                     A
2 (2) —P                    A
1,2 (3) P ∧ —P           1,2 ∧I
1,2 (4) Q                  3 RH

Notice that 'P ∧ —P' in line (3) quite obviously doesn't rest on '—Q'.

Two objections to both CC and RH come to mind: one pedagogical and one philosophical.

*Pedagogically*, the proposed new primitive rules seem a *bit* odd. After all, there was a time in your life when it would have taken quite some work to convince you that—*regardless* of the truth-value of 'P'—if 'Q' is true then so is 'P → Q'. And indeed it did take quite some work in Chapter 2 to convince you that the argument whose premise is 'P ∧ —P' and whose conclusion is 'Q' is a *valid* argument.

*Oddness*, to be sure, is no disqualification for our derivation rules. Nevertheless, if you are to succeed in mastering a formal system of logic, it seems that, *ceteris paribus* (i.e., all other things' being equal), rules—*primitive* rules—that are intuitively appealing have a considerable edge over those that aren't. And primitive rules that are intuitively appealing have even more of an edge over those that are plainly counterintuitive. It seems desirable, in other words, from *your* standpoint—i.e., from the standpoint of someone who is *learning* formal logic—for the primitive derivation rules that constitute our formal system to replicate, as much as possible, the inference rules on which we rely in our everyday lives. Needless to say, neither CC nor RH replicates any such rule.

*Philosophically*, you shouldn't want too much of a gap between the reasoning in which you engage *inside* a logic course—*formal* reasoning, with its strict adherence to derivation rules—and the reasoning in which you engage *outside* a logic course—*informal* reasoning. Consider the extreme case, where the ties between the two are tenuous to nonexistent, such that they come to constitute two quite different sorts of entities. Logic then turns out to be something of a *game*, with few roots in, and little relevance to, either everyday-life reasoning, on the one hand, or the reasoning that takes place within the various other intellectual disciplines, including philosophy, on the other hand. In this extreme case, it's only a matter of time before the skeptic raises the disquieting question, "Why even bother to study logic?"

The skeptic is quite right about *one* thing: if logic *were* a mere game, it isn't at all clear why you *should* bother to study it. But is *formal* reasoning really so very different from *informal* reasoning? Our *primitive* derivation rules are quite commonsensical in a great many ways, and therefore logic-course logic *isn't* a mere game. However, the proposed new primitive derivation rules, CC and RH, *aren't* commonsensical—and this is why they would make very bad *primitive* derivation rules indeed.

What, then, is the moral of this story? We exclude CC and RH from our primitive derivation rules. We insist on →I assumptions and we insist on —I assumptions— and we require them to behave like *good* →I and —I assumptions, respectively. A good →I assumption, like a good —I assumption, must be a good team player; it mustn't be lazy and let other *wffs* do all the work required to generate the targeted *wffs*.

Question: Does this mean that we must reject the proposed new rules altogether?

Answer: No. Quite the contrary. . . . Insofar as we can derive CC and RH from our primitive derivation rules—and of course we can—it follows that each is anchored, ultimately and solidly, in our common-sense intuitions. And at the end of the day, that's all that matters. There-fore we should welcome the proposed new rules as *derived*, but only as *derived*, derivation rules.

*Of course* the relatively commonsensical/intuitive nature of the *primitive* rules should capture the commonsensical/intuitive nature of our informal reasoning. There's no reason to think, however, that the same holds true of the *derived* rules. Most of Euclid's axioms and postulates are quite commonsensical. Few of his theorems are.

# Chapter Five

# Predicate Logic:
# A Formal Language, Part One

## 1. Introduction

Consider the following argument:

(1) All tyrants are clowns.
(2) Ardbeg is a tyrant.

∴ (3) Ardbeg is a clown.

A valid argument? Obviously. Easily provable? Of course. Fire away: the derivation, like the translation, is a no-brainer, yes? Suppose, then, that you formulate it as follows:

1 (1) T → C          A
2 (2) A → T          A
1,2 (3) A → C        2,1 SISI 89 HS

Easy as pie, eh? A piece of cake, yes? Nothing to it, right? There's only one problem. Each of these *wffs—each* of them—is a total and complete *mis*translation of its corresponding original, English-language sentence. How so? Take a look at 'T'. What on Earth is the sentence that it designates? 'Tyrants'? Since when is 'Tyrants' a *sentence*? Do you remember from Chapter 1 the definition of a proposition (or sentence or statement)? A proposition (or sentence or statement) is a *bearer of truth-value*; i.e., it's something that is either true or false.

Question: What is the truth-value of 'Tyrants'?

Obvious answer: It has none; it's neither true nor false.

Moral of the story: you're eyeballing a complete mistranslation of our three initial sentences.

Back to square one. The problem was that you treated each of the three sentences as though it were a *molecular*. If you look at each of them closely, though, you should see *atomics* and not moleculars. You don't see the words 'not', 'and', 'or', 'if-then', or 'if and only if' in any of them—nor indeed any equivalent words that might serve as connectives. You have no choice, therefore, but to assign a single atomic letter—a single propositional constant—to each of the premises and to the conclusion. Moreover, because each of the three sentences is different from the others, you'll need three different propositional constants:

$$1 \; (1) \; \text{T} \qquad\qquad\qquad\qquad \text{A}$$
$$2 \; (2) \; \text{A} \qquad\qquad\qquad\qquad \text{A}$$

. 

. 

$$1,2 \; (n) \; \text{C} \qquad\qquad\qquad\qquad ?$$

It's derivation time once again. Fire away once again. Which *wff* do you write down in your third line? '—C' as a *Reductio* assumption because all else has failed, i.e., because there's nothing else that you *can* do, yes? Fine. Now which *wff* do you write down in your fourth line? Not quite sure? Feeling a tad uneasy? I'll spare you the pain: the sequent 'T, A ⊢ C' is obviously unprovable. Why? Because it's obviously invalid. Try either the Truth-Table Method or the Short Method. Can you make 'T' true, 'A' true, and 'C' false? Yes, of course you can: you just did.

Life has now become most interesting. According to your intuitions, the following argument is *valid*:

> (1) All tyrants are clowns.
> (2) Ardbeg is a tyrant.
> ――――――――――――――――
> ∴ (3) Ardbeg is a clown.

According to both the Truth-Table Method and the Short Method, however, the following argument is *invalid*:

(1) T
(2) A
—————
∴ (3) C

What to do? *What to do?* There seem to be two possibilities. You could give up a deep conviction of yours and declare the former argument, the English-language argument, *invalid.* Alternatively, you could give up the Truth-Table Method and the Short Method and declare the latter argument, the logical notation argument, *valid.* I *dare* you—I *defy* you—to do either. In logic, as in life, you should think twice (and then some) before you give up a deeply held conviction. And you should think twice (and then some) before you give up the instruments of classical logic.

Perhaps—just *perhaps*—there is a *third* possibility. When you reach an impasse, you might wish to rethink the assumptions that led you to the impasse. In this instance, it's unclear which assumptions are the culprits, because you haven't made all of your assumptions *explicit.* Nevertheless you have been relying on two crucial, albeit *implicit,* assumptions. The first assumption is that by translating the above English-language argument into the formal language of Propositional Logic, and then by using either the Truth-Table Method or the Short Method, you'd be able to show that the argument is valid. The second assumption is that by using the derivation rules of Propositional Logic, you'd be able to derive the conclusion of the sequent, 'T, A ⊢ C', from its premises.

Now these assumptions may seem innocent enough, but they aren't. As it turns out, Propositional Logic simply isn't up to the tasks at hand. First, its *formal* language isn't sufficiently rich to capture enough of the logical texture, enough of the logical details, of the sentences of the above *English-language* argument *so as to show its validity.* Hence the need for a new and much more *detailed* formal language, one that brings out the logical bits and pieces, as it were, of which *the atomics themselves* are constructed.

Moreover, the deductive apparatus of Propositional Logic isn't sufficiently rich *so as to permit the derivation of the conclusion of the above sequent from its premises.* Hence the need for a new deductive apparatus that contains additional derivation rules to operate on the *wffs* of the new formal language. We shall develop the new formal language in this chapter and the next one, and the new deductive apparatus in the final two chapters.

$L_1$, the formal language of Propositional Logic, takes atomics as fundamental: they are its basic units of analysis. (Hence our choice of the term 'atomic', the Greek word 'atom' meaning 'that which cannot be cut'.) It is now atom-cutting time.

Welcome to a brand-new formal system, Predicate Logic, also known as Quantification Theory, first formulated by Gottlob Frege (German, 1848–1925). Its formal language, $L_2$, includes $L_1$, the language of Propositional Logic, within itself, but goes beyond it by introducing a new set of symbols and a new set of formation rules. By the same token, its deductive apparatus includes within itself the derivation rules of Propositional Logic, but goes beyond it by introducing a new set of derivation rules. As such, Predicate Logic/Quantification Theory is said to be an *extension* of Propositional Logic.

Definition:    A formal system, $S_2$, is an *extension* of a formal system, $S_1$, *iff* $S_2$ contains within itself the formal language and the deductive apparatus of $S_1$.

Like a high-powered microscope, $L_2$, the language of Predicate Logic/Quantification Theory will allow us to peer into the logical structure of atomics themselves, in order to discover the subatomic particles, as it were, of which the atomics are composed.

# 2. Things and Properties: Proper Names and Predicates

Consider the second premise of our argument: 'Ardbeg is a tyrant.' The sentence is about a particular individual, Ardbeg, and it ascribes (or assigns or attributes or imputes) to Ardbeg a particular *property* (or feature or characteristic)—the property of being a tyrant.

Now we need new items in our formal language. We need *proper names* (or *individual constants*) to designate particular *individuals/objects/ things*. (I shall use the three terms—'individual', 'object', and 'thing'— interchangeably. In some contexts, one term will seem more natural, and in other contexts another term will seem so.) And we need *predi- cates* to designate both the *properties* that are ascribed (or assigned or attributed or imputed) to these individuals and the *relations* that they stand in with respect to one another. We shall use the italicized, lower-case letters, 'a' through 't' as proper names, and the italicized, upper-case letters 'A' through 'Z' as predicates. Let 'a' be the proper name of Ardbeg, and let 'T' be the predicate that designates the property of being a tyrant. Accordingly, we translate 'Ardbeg is a tyrant' as 'Ta'. You may also read 'Ta' as 'a has the property of being a T' or simply as 'a is a T'.

Definition:     A *proper name* is a symbol that designates (or denotes or stands for) an individual thing (or object).

Definition:     A *predicate* is a symbol that designates (or denotes or stands for) a property or relation.

In all that follows, I shall use the word 'thing' or 'object' to designate a person or a place, as well as a thing/object. It may not be possible to *define* what an individual thing/object is. (Try to do so in a *non-circular* way, i.e., without referring, explicitly or implicitly, to the very notion of a *thing/object*.) Nevertheless, it is certainly possible to give *examples* of individual *things/objects* and at least some of their proper names: Ardbeg, Bobo, Amsterdam Avenue, the Boston Common, Chandni Chowk, North Zedmenistan, your Lamborghini, the dog Dagbar, your gall bladder (as yet unnamed—but you could easily give it a name, e.g., 'Egvalt'), last night's nightmare about the killer-kangaroos (also unnamed—but again, you could easily give it a name, e.g., 'Flaubert'), the Marine Corps, the number 13 (a thing with many names, two of which are the numerals '13' and 'XIII'), the square root of minus 1 ($i$), Coco's soul (if she has one), your birthday, the midpoint between any two points, the headache (or heartache or heartbreak) that your significant other has just caused you, your wish to study logic forever and ever, etc. Thus you could say of your gall bladder, "Egvalt is acting up again," just as you could say of last night's nightmare about the killer-kangaroos, "Flaubert went on and on, and was utterly *terrifying*."

By the same token, whether it's possible to define what a property is—any such definition, of course, must refer to an individual *thing*—it's certainly possible to give *examples* of properties: being a traitor, being a suitor, being a petitioner, feeling stuffed, feeling blue, feeling old, sliding into third base, sliding down a glacier, sliding into oblivion, barking, coughing, pacing, being divisible by two, etc.

In the real world you would never confuse an individual thing with a property. Things *have* properties; properties don't *have* things. You can pat, feed, or frighten Dagbar; you can't pat, feed, or frighten barking. (If you're keen to dive into the metaphysical underpinnings of this distinction between things and their properties, start with Aristotle's brief but dense *Categories,* chapters 2–5.)

In logic, as in life, you should never confuse an individual thing with a property; i.e., you should never symbolize an individual thing by means of a predicate, or uppercase letter; and likewise you should never symbolize a property by means of a proper name, or lowercase letter.

Consider the following English sentences and their respective translations in $L_2$:

| English Sentence | $L_2$ Translation |
|---|---|
| Ardbeg is a tyrant. | $Ta$ |
| Bobo is a tyrant. | $Tb$ |
| Ardbeg is a lunatic. | $La$ |
| Ardbeg isn't a Spinozist. | $-Sa$ |
| Neither Bobo nor Coco is a tyrant. | $-(Tb \lor Tc)$ |

Now go back to the original argument:

(1) All tyrants are clowns.
(2) Ardbeg is a tyrant.
_____
∴ (3) Ardbeg is a clown.

If you translate the second premise as '$Ta$', you obviously translate the conclusion as '$Ca$'. What, then, about the first premise? Welcome to the universal quantifier.

# 3. The Universal Quantifier

Unlike the second premise, 'Ardbeg is a tyrant', and unlike the conclusion, 'Ardbeg is a clown', the first premise, 'All tyrants are clowns', does *not* involve the ascription of a property to a particular object. Do you think otherwise? Do you think that it involves the ascription to *Ardbeg* of the property of being a clown? Not by itself it doesn't, i.e., not unless it's taken in conjunction with some other sentence, such as the second premise, 'Ardbeg is a tyrant'. *All by itself,* the sentence 'All tyrants are clowns' is utterly *silent* with respect to whether Ardbeg—or for that matter, *anyone or anything*—is either a tyrant or a clown.

Alternatively, consider the sentence 'All tyrants who burn logic books are clowns'. Suppose that there are no tyrants who burn logic books. The sentence is perfectly meaningful—yet it's clearly not about any particular object.

The sentence 'Ardbeg is a tyrant' is *about* the particular object Ardbeg: it ascribes to him the property of being a tyrant. By contrast, the sentence 'All tyrants are clowns' isn't *about*—it doesn't say anything *about*—any *particular* object. It doesn't ascribe to any particular object either the property of being a tyrant or the property of being a clown.

However, the sentence 'All tyrants are clowns' *is* about—it *does* say something about— each and every object *that happens to be a tyrant.* The sentence says of *that* particular object that he, she, or it is a clown. It ascribes to *that* particular object the property of being a clown.

In other words, the sentence 'All tyrants are clowns' says *of any particular object* that *if* he, she, or it is a tyrant *then* he, she, or it is a clown. As such, the sentence is indeed about—it says something about—*each and every object in the universe!* It ascribes to each such object a *conditional* property: the property of being such that *if* it's a tyrant *then* it's a clown. (In the interest of brevity, I shall treat the word 'it' as shorthand for 'he, she, or it'—even if, as here, the object under discussion is clearly a *person.*)

Thus the sentence 'All tyrants are clowns' really boils down to this: 'Given any object *x,* if it's a tyrant then it's a clown'. And this in turn boils down to two logically distinguishable elements: 'Given any object *x*', and 'if it's a tyrant then it's a clown'.

How might the first element, 'Given any object *x*', be expressed in logical notation? We obviously need new notation. First, we need what is known as the universal quantifier, '$\forall$', to articulate in $L_2$ the expression, 'Given any object'. Next, we need a new type of variable: we need variables that apply to, or *range over,* a set of particular objects. In $L_1$ we have *propositional* variables: 'P', 'Q', and 'R', etc., each of which refers to any *proposition* whatsoever. In $L_2$ we need variables, each of which refers to any *object* whatsoever (or, for that matter, whomsoever): '*u*', '*v*', '*w*', '*x*', '*y*', and '*z*', with or without numerical subscripts. (Notice that I surreptitiously introduced you to the variable '*x*' in the last paragraph. You weren't, and you shouldn't have been, one bit puzzled by it.)

So the expression '∀*x*' (pronounced 'universal quantifier *x*' or simply 'universal *x*') will be shorthand for, and is thus equivalent to, 'Given any object *x*', or 'Every object *x* is such that'. (Obviously, '∀*x*' isn't a *wff* in its own right, any more than 'Given any object *x*' is a sentence in its own right. Obviously, '∀*x*' is merely a fragment of a *wff*, just as 'Given any object *x*' is merely a fragment of a sentence.)

So if you express the first element of our sentence, 'Given any object *x*', as '∀*x*', how might you express the second element, 'if it's a tyrant then it's a clown'? It's obviously a conditional, but it's a problematical conditional. The antecedent is 'it's a tyrant' and the consequent is 'it's a clown'—and the problem has to do with the word 'it'. You don't yet know how to translate it; i.e., you don't yet know how to translate 'it'. (No, I did *not* just repeat myself here. And no, I am *not* guilty of a misprint either.)

In English the word 'it', like the words 'he' or 'she', functions as a *pronoun*. A pronoun is a word that refers to the same object to which a particular noun refers. Typically, but not necessarily, the pronoun and the noun appear in the same sentence. Typically, but not necessarily, the pronoun appears after the noun. Consider the following:

> (1) While old Ardbeg was tickling the rat, it bit him.
>
> (2) Old Ardbeg was tickling the rat. Suddenly it bit him.
>
> (3) Just as he was tickling it, old Ardbeg was bitten by the rat.

(1) is an example of a single sentence in which the pronouns 'it' and 'him' refer to the same objects to which their corresponding nouns— 'rat' and 'Ardbeg', respectively— refer. It is also an example of a sentence in which the pronouns appear *after* their corresponding nouns. (2), by contrast, is an example of two sentences in which the pronouns 'it' and 'him' appear in a sentence different from the sentence in which their corresponding nouns—'rat' and 'Ardbeg', respectively—appear. (3), like (1), is an example of a single sentence in which the pronouns 'he' and 'it' refer to the same objects to which their corresponding nouns—'Ardbeg' and 'rat', respectively—refer. However, (3), unlike (1), is an example of a sentence in which the pronouns appear *before* their corresponding nouns.

You're now ready to translate, step by step, from the English original into $L_2$:

1.  'All tyrants are clowns'.
2.  'Given any object $x$, if it's a tyrant then it's a clown'.

Clearly, the two occurrences of the pronoun 'it' refer to the same object that the expression 'object $x$' refers to, namely, the object $x$. The following makes this sameness of reference explicit:

3.  'Given any object $x$, if it, i.e., $x$, is a tyrant then it, i.e., $x$, is a clown'.

Here it's quite obvious that the two occurrences of the pronoun 'it' refer to the same object that the expression 'object $x$' refers to: all three expressions refer to the object $x$, whatever the object $x$ happens to be. In this sentence, therefore, if you eliminate the pronoun 'it' and replace it with the variable '$x$', you end up with the following:

4.  'Given any object $x$, if $x$ is a tyrant then $x$ is a clown'.

As you now know, the first part of this sentence, the phrase 'Given any object $x$', goes over into logical notation as '$\forall x$'. It seems reasonable to translate the second part, 'if $x$ is a tyrant then $x$ is a clown', as '$Tx \rightarrow Cx$'. So the original sentence, 'All tyrants are clowns', fully translated into $L_2$, becomes:

5.  '$(\forall x)(Tx \rightarrow Cx)$'

There are many equivalent ways to read, i.e., to understand, this *wff*, '$(\forall x)(Tx \rightarrow Cx)$'. Among them are the following:

1.  'Given any object $x$, if it's a tyrant then it's a clown'.
2.  'Given any object $x$, if $x$ is a tyrant then $x$ is a clown'.
3.  'Every object $x$ is such that if it's a tyrant then it's a clown'.
4.  'Every object $x$ is such that if $x$ is a tyrant then $x$ is a clown'.

Question: How should you think of the variable '$x$' as it appears *not* in the complete, quantified sentence 'Given any object $x$, if $x$ is a tyrant then *x* is a clown', but *rather* in the incomplete, unquantified sentence fragment 'if *x* is a tyrant then *x* is a clown'?

Answer: *Exactly* as you think of the word 'it' in the expression 'if *it* is a tyrant then *it* is a clown'. *On its own*, i.e., in isolation from a phrase like 'Given any object whatsoever', the word 'it' fails to function as a pronoun. In particular, it fails to refer to whatever its corresponding noun refers—precisely because in the expression 'if *it* is a tyrant then *it* is a clown' there *is* no corresponding noun.

On the other hand, when the word 'it' appears in its *normal* habitat, i.e., when it's clear what the noun is to which the word 'it' is attached, then the word 'it' serves to designate the very same object that the noun designates. So it is with a variable. 'Given any object *x*, e.g., given Ardbeg, if *x*, i.e., Ardbeg, is a tyrant then *x*, i.e., Ardbeg (once again), is a clown.'

You might think that the variable '*x*' functions as a rather bizarre kind of name. It certainly does *not* function as a *proper* name: you don't know too many people who have the name '*x*'. (But even if you did, their names would be, and function as, proper names, and not as variables.) Perhaps you think that the variable '*x*' functions as the *temporary* (or *ad hoc*) name of whatever object you happen to be considering: '*x*' is the name that, like '*u*', '*v*', '*w*', '*y*', or '*z*', you *arbitrarily* assign to a particular object on a particular occasion and for a limited period of time, for the sole purpose of referring to *that* object and to no other.

And it's certainly true that in this respect '*x*' does sometimes function as a name. Suppose that as luck would have it, you had been robbed earlier today. You might well find yourself saying, "I had my sack of *deadly hot* chili peppers with me when I got onto the subway this morning, and I didn't have it when I got off. I was standing and I put it down for *just* an instant. When I went to pick it up, it was *gone*. All of a sudden I heard someone—call her *x*—shout at the top of her lungs, 'Stop that thief!' But we had just pulled into the station, and the thief—call him *y*—leaped off of the train and onto the platform. *x* and I tore after *y*, but to no avail. In two seconds *y* had rounded a corner and had quite disappeared into the crowd. I thanked *x* for her efforts. And I assured her that if ever I bump into *y* in the future, I'll give him a thrashing and a throttling that he won't soon forget!"

So yes, there are contexts where variables appear namelike. But even in these contexts, the variable is still functioning, at bottom, as a pronoun. In the previous paragraph, the variable '*x*' is shorthand for the *implicit* noun phrase, 'the woman who came to my assistance'—and functions like the pronoun 'she' to designate the same woman whom this latter noun phrase designates. Similarly, the variable '$y$' is simply shorthand for the *implicit* noun phrase, 'the person who stole my sack of chilis'—and functions like the pronoun 'he' or 'she' to designate the same person whom this latter noun phrase designates. Variables are namelike only in the way in which pronouns are namelike: they refer to objects only indirectly, i.e., via their corresponding nouns or noun phrases.

You're always free to say, "Let $x$ be Ardbeg", and then to raise the question, "So is it true that $x$ is a tyrant?" By the same token you're always free to say, "Let $x$ be the number 3," and then to raise the question, "So is it true that $x$ is divisible by 2 without remainder?"

In general though, it's best *not* to think of variables as namelike. In '$Tx \rightarrow Cx$', interpreted as 'if $x$ is a tyrant then $x$ is a clown', '$x$' isn't, and doesn't even appear to be, functioning as a name—not even as a bizarre kind of name. Ditto with respect to each occurrence of '$x$' in '$(\forall x)(Tx \rightarrow Cx)$'.

It's flashback time: The variables '$u$', '$v$', '$w$', '$x$', '$y$', and '$z$' function in Predicate Logic/Quantification Theory almost exactly as they did in your high school algebra course. (The one difference—and it's a trivial one—is that in your high school algebra course the only objects to which the variables referred were *numbers*, whereas in logic they refer to *any* objects whatsoever.) Consider the algebraic identity '$x^2 = x \cdot x$'. It's really a universally quantified sentence, albeit a disguised one. What it *really* means—what it's shorthand for—is '$(\forall x)(x^2 = x \cdot x)$', where the variable $x$ after the universal quantifier ranges over the set of numbers, so that you would read the sentence as either

1.  'Given any number $x$, that number squared is identical to, i.e., *equals*, itself multiplied by itself'; or as
2.  'Given any number $x$, $x^2$ is identical to $x$ multiplied by $x$'.

One last point—a warning—before we leave this section. It's a common mistake for logic students to translate universally quantified sentences as universally quantified *conjunctions* rather than as universally quantified *conditionals*. Suppose that you thought that the correct translation of 'All tyrants are clowns' is '$(\forall x)(Tx \land Cx)$'. It's clear how you would read this sentence in English: 'Given any object $x$, it's a tyrant *and* it's a clown.' Now think of what this really means: it means that whoever utters this sentence in earnest is committed to the view that you can point to any object whatsoever and infer that it's both a tyrant and a clown. This lizard, that locust, Ardbeg, or the number 13: each of these objects is both a tyrant and a clown! Obviously, whoever takes 'All tyrants are clowns' seriously isn't committed to such nonsense— whereas whoever takes '$(\forall x)(Tx \wedge Cx)$' seriously is committed to just such nonsense. Therefore '$(\forall x)(Tx \wedge Cx)$' must be a mistranslation of 'All tyrants are clowns'—although it's a perfectly correct translation of the obviously false sentence 'Everything whatsoever is both a tyrant and a clown'.

A universally quantified conjunction is a very strange animal indeed. In uttering it, one is ascribing *two* properties to each and every object in the universe—to people, dreams, hiccups, itches, numbers, minds, photons, black holes, katydids, bacteria, memories, etc. Now just try to come up with *two* properties that are ascribable to *each and every* object in the universe. It's not clear that you (or anyone else, for that matter) can do so. It's not clear that you could even come up with *one* such property.

# 4. The Existential Quantifier

Unlike the sentence 'All tyrants are clowns', the sentence 'Some tyrants are clowns' comes with a red flag attached to it: the word 'some' is *numerically* imprecise (or inexact). In some contexts, numerical precision matters considerably; in others, it matters somewhat; and in still others, it matters not at all. If you tell your florist that you'd like to order *one* orchid, or *two* orchids, or *all* of the orchids in the shop, she knows exactly what to do. But if you tell her that you'd like to order either *some* orchids or *some of* the orchids in the shop, she'll want to know *precisely* how many you have in mind. Here numerical precision matters. At the other extreme, if your dinner host asks you whether you'd like some peas, and you reply that yes, you would like some, you don't expect your host's next question to be, "And *precisely* how many would you like?" Here numerical precision is entirely out of place.

In the physical sciences, in mathematics, and in logic, precision matters considerably. Therefore logicians attach a precise meaning to the otherwise imprecise word 'some'. Henceforth you are to take 'some' to mean 'There exists at least one'. Enter the existential quantifier, '∃', to capture this notion. The expression '(∃x)' (pronounced 'existential quantifier x' or simply 'existential x' or even just 'E–x') is shorthand for, and thus equivalent to, 'There exists at least one object x which is such that' or 'At least one object x is such that' or 'Some object x is such that'.

Thus the sentence 'Some tyrants are clowns' is true *iff* at least one tyrant is a clown; i.e., *iff* there *exists* at least one tyrant who is a clown; i.e., *iff* there exists at least one object that has two properties: the property of being a tyrant and the property of being a clown.

You're now ready to translate, step by step, from the English original into $L_2$:

1.  'Some tyrants are clowns'.
2.  'There exists at least one object which is such that it's a tyrant and it's a clown'.
3.  'There exists at least one object x which is such that it, i.e., x, is a tyrant and it, i.e., x, is a clown'.
4.  'There exists at least one object x which is such that x is a tyrant and x is a clown'.
5.  '(∃x)(Tx ∧ Cx)'.

There are many equivalent ways to read, i.e., to understand, the *wff* '(∃x)(Tx ∧ Cx)'. Among them are the following:

1.  'There exists at least one object x which is such that it's a tyrant and it's a clown'.
2.  'There exists at least one object x which is such that x is a tyrant and x is a clown'.
3.  'At least one object x is such that it's a tyrant and it's a clown'.
4.  'At least one object x is such that x is a tyrant and x is a clown'.
5.  'Some object x is such that it's a tyrant and it's a clown'.
6.  'Some object x is such that x is a tyrant and x is a clown'.

Question: Isn't it arbitrary to define 'some' as 'at least one'?

Answer: It may be a bit odd, but it isn't arbitrary. In English, to be sure, 'some' typically implies a plurality. It might be odd to utter the sentence, 'Some tyrants are clowns' if only *one* tyrant were a clown. Indeed, if only one tyrant were a clown, some people might well view the sentence not simply as odd but actually as false. Whether you view the sentence as odd but true or odd and false, we can probably agree that there is no consensus on how to treat such a sentence.

It doesn't follow, however, that our choice of 'at least one' is an *arbitrary* choice. Quite the contrary: we have a very *good* reason for defining 'some' as 'at least one'. By so doing, we acquire the ability, as you will see in Chapter 6, to translate, *with perfect precision*, sentences containing numerical adjectives, i.e., sentences containing such expressions as 'at least one', 'exactly one', 'at most one', 'at least two', 'exactly two', 'at most two', 'at least three', etc. This pragmatic consideration trumps the oddness consideration of our definition of 'some'.

Questions: We translate 'All tyrants are clowns' via a universally quantified *conditional*, but 'Some tyrants are clowns' via an existentially quantified *conjunction*. Why the discrepancy? Don't the two sentences have the exact same grammatical structure? Don't they both consist of an adjective denoting quantity ('all' or 'some'), followed by a plural noun ('tyrants'), followed by a copula ('are'), followed by another plural noun ('clowns')? Shouldn't their *logical* structure reflect their *grammatical* structure? Shouldn't, therefore, 'Some tyrants are clowns' be translated as '$(\exists x)(Tx \rightarrow Cx)$'?

The quick answers to these questions are that *yes*, the two sentences do have the same *grammatical* structure, but *no*, it doesn't follow thereby that they have the same *logical* structure—and indeed they *don't* have the same logical structure.

Think for a moment of how you would actually establish the truth of the sentence 'Some tyrants are clowns'. You would have to find some individual with *two* properties: the property of being a tyrant *and* the property of being a clown. Now ask yourself how you would establish the truth of the sentence 'Some clowns are tyrants'. You would have to find some individual with *two* properties: the property of being a clown *and* the property of being a tyrant.

Now surely there is *no* difference between an individual with the property of being a tyrant and the property of being a clown, on the one hand, and an individual with the property of being a clown and the property of being a tyrant, on the other hand. In other words, the two sentences come out true under the *exact* same conditions; i.e., the sentence 'Some tyrants are clowns' is true *iff* the sentence 'Some clowns are tyrants' is true. Therefore the two sentences are logically equivalent to one another.

So, where *these* two sentences are concerned, the order of terms, 'tyrants' and 'clowns', i.e., the order of predicates, is *reversible*. On the other hand, where *conditionals* are concerned, the order of terms is *irreversible*. The sentence 'All tyrants are clowns' is *not* equivalent to the sentence 'All clowns are tyrants', any more than the (true) sentence 'All camels are animals' is equivalent to the (false) sentence 'All animals are camels'. Therefore, even though the sentences 'All tyrants are clowns' and 'Some tyrants are clowns' share the same *grammatical* structure, they don't share the same underlying *logical* structure. Therefore there's *no* reason to think that what follows the quantifier in the one case should be identical to what follows the quantifier in the other case. Therefore there's no reason to think that an existentially quantified *conditional* is what's called for here.

Moreover there *is* reason—indeed, there's *sufficient* reason—to think that an existentially quantified conditional is exactly what's *not* called for here. Suppose that you thought otherwise. Suppose that you thought that the correct translation of 'Some tyrants are clowns' is '$(\exists x)(Tx \rightarrow Cx)$'. Now this sentence affirms that there exists at least one object which is such that *if* it's a tyrant *then* it's a clown. (In this respect, it's radically unlike '$(\exists x)(Tx \wedge Cx)$' which affirms [once again] that there exists at least one object which is such that it *is* a tyrant and it *is* a clown.) In other words, '$(\exists x)(Tx \rightarrow Cx)$' is true *iff* there exists at least one object $x$ which is such that if $x$ is a tyrant then $x$ is a clown. Now consider any object $x$ that *isn't* a tyrant. So for this particular object $x$, '$Tx$' is *false*. So for this particular object $x$, the conditional '$Tx \rightarrow Cx$' is *true*. (Remember: Any conditional with a false antecedent is automatically true.) But if, for this particular object $x$, the conditional '$Tx \rightarrow Cx$' is *true*, then the existential quantification of this conditional, i.e., '$(\exists x)(Tx \rightarrow Cx)$', must also be true. Why so? Because it merely affirms the existence of at least one object that satisfies the terms of the conditional '$Tx \rightarrow Cx$'—and $x$, as you've just seen, is just such an object; i.e., it does indeed satisfy the terms of the conditional. In other words, the existence of at least one object $x$ that isn't a tyrant *guarantees* the truth of '$(\exists x)(Tx \rightarrow Cx)$'. But the existence of at least one object $x$ that isn't a tyrant *hardly* guarantees the truth of 'Some tyrants are clowns'. So '$(\exists x)(Tx \rightarrow Cx)$' can't *possibly* be the correct translation of 'Some tyrants are clowns'.

To see that an existentially quantified *conjunction* is exactly what *is* called for here, remind yourself how you would establish the truth of the sentence 'Some tyrants are clowns'. Once again: You would have to find some individual with *two* properties—the property of being a tyrant *and* the property of being a clown. The key word here is 'and'; hence the caret and not the arrow in our translation.

# 5. The Square of Opposition

It was once thought that what is known as the Square of Opposition captured all logically significant sentences, as well as their mutual relations. Although the Square of Opposition fails to do justice to the complexity of the sentences that you will soon be encountering, it provides you with a structure that is actually quite helpful for translating increasingly complex sorts of English sentences into logical notation.

<table>
<tr><td>A: All tyrants are clowns.</td><td>E: No tyrants are clowns.</td></tr>
<tr><td>$(\forall x)(Tx \rightarrow Cx)$</td><td>$(\forall x)(Tx \rightarrow -Cx)$</td></tr>
<tr><td>Universal-Affirmative</td><td>Universal-Negative</td></tr>
<tr><td>I: Some tyrants are clowns.</td><td>O: Some tyrants are not clowns.</td></tr>
<tr><td>$(\exists x)(Tx \wedge Cx)$</td><td>$(\exists x)(Tx \wedge -Cx)$</td></tr>
<tr><td>Particular/Existential-<br>Affirmative</td><td>Particular/Existential-<br>Negative</td></tr>
</table>

A word about logical structure. The A-proposition is *universal*: it's about *each and every* object *x* insofar as it claims that if *x* is a tyrant then *x* is a clown. It's also *affirmative*, insofar as it *affirms* the property of being a clown of each and every tyrant. The E-proposition is also *universal*. Unlike the A-proposition, however, it's *negative*, insofar as it *denies* the property of being a clown of each and every tyrant. The I-proposition is *particular* (or *existential*): it's about *at least one* (and not necessarily *every*) object *x*, insofar as it claims that *x* is both a tyrant and a clown; and it's obviously affirmative. The O-proposition is also *particular* (or *existential*), and it's obviously *negative*.

It is said that the names of the affirmative A- and I-propositions derive from the first two vowels in the Latin word 'affirmo'—'I affirm'; and that the names of the negative E- and O-propositions derive from the only two vowels in the Latin word 'nego'—'I deny (or negate)'.

A word or two about logical relations. There are two pairs of propositions that are related to each other *diagonally*, as it were: the A- and the O-propositions are so related, as are the E- and the I-propositions. Consider first the A- and the O-propositions. Suppose that the A-proposition is *true*; what do you know about the corresponding O-proposition? Suppose, in other words, that the sentence 'All tyrants are clowns' is *true*. What do you now know about the sentence 'Some tyrants are not clowns'? Obviously it must be *false*. Now suppose that the A-proposition is *false*; i.e., suppose that *not* all tyrants are clowns. What do you now know about the corresponding O-proposition, 'Some tyrants are not clowns'? Obviously it must be *true*. It follows that the A- and the O-propositions are *semantic contradictories*: they can't both be true and they can't both be false. Alternatively, if the first is true, the second is false, and if the first is false, the second is true. Such propositions are said to be *semantic contradictories*.

> **Definition:**  Two propositions are semantic contradictories *iff* there is no interpretation that makes both of them true and there is no interpretation that makes both of them false; i.e., they have opposite truth-values for every interpretation. (Informally, this means that the two propositions can't both be true and they can't both be false.)

*Semantic* contradictories, you'll recall, are distinct from *syntactic* contradictories. The definition of the former refers to truth and falsehood, and not to form. The definition of the latter refers to form, and not to either truth or falsehood. The *wffs* '△' and '—△' are *syntactic* contradictories insofar as the two are formally or structurally identical, except that one has a dash as its main connective.

> **Definition:**  Two *wffs* '△' and '—△' are *syntactic contradictories iff* the latter is the negation of the former, i.e., *iff* the latter is the former preceded by a dash.

All *syntactic* contradictories are *semantic* contradictories; i.e., the two *wffs* cannot both be true and cannot both be false. But not all *semantic*

contradictories are *syntactic* contradictories; e.g., '$(\forall x)(Tx \rightarrow Cx)$' and '$(\exists x)(Tx \wedge -Cx)$' are *semantic*, but not *syntactic*, contradictories. The syntactic contradictory of '$(\forall x)(Tx \rightarrow Cx)$' is '$-(\forall x)(Tx \rightarrow Cx)$', and the syntactic contradictory of '$(\exists x)(Tx \wedge -Cx)$' is '$-(\exists x)(Tx \wedge -Cx)$'.

Consider now the E- and the I-propositions. Suppose that the E-proposition is *true*; what do you know about the corresponding I-proposition? Suppose, in other words, that the sentence 'No tyrants are clowns' is *true*. What do you now know about the sentence 'Some tyrants are clowns'? Obviously it must be *false*. Now suppose that the E-proposition is *false*; i.e., suppose that it's not the case that *no* tyrants are clowns. What do you now know about the corresponding I-proposition 'Some tyrants are clowns'? Obviously it must be *true*. It follows that the E- and the I-propositions are also *semantic contradictories*.

There are two pairs of propositions that are related to each other *horizontally*, as it were: the A- and the E-propositions are so related, as are the I- and the O-propositions. Consider first the A- and the E-propositions. Can they both be true? Can it be true both that all tyrants are clowns and that no tyrants are clowns? Obviously not. (But be forewarned: what's obvious at this moment won't be quite so obvious later in Chapter 6, Section 4 ["The Square of Opposition Revisited"]). Well, then, can the A- and the E-propositions both be false? Can it be false both that *all* tyrants are clowns and that *no* tyrants are clowns? Of course it can be. Suppose a world of three tyrants: Ardbeg, Bobo, and Coco. If Ardbeg *isn't* a clown, then the sentence 'All tyrants are clowns' is false; and if both Bobo and Coco *are* clowns then the sentence 'No tyrants are clowns' is false. The A- and the E-propositions—like any two propositions that *can't* both be true but *can* both be false—are said to be *contraries*.

> Definition:     Two propositions are *contraries iff* there is no inter-
>                 pretation that makes both of them true but there is
>                 at least one interpretation that makes both of them
>                 false.

Consider now the A- and the I-propositions. Obviously, if the sentence 'All tyrants are clowns' is true, so is the sentence 'Some tyrants are clowns; i.e., there exists at least one tyrant who is a clown'. We may call this *vertical* relationship between the A- and the I-propositions the relationship of *downward implication*. On the other hand, the truth of the sentence 'Some tyrants are clowns' hardly guarantees the truth of the sentence 'All tyrants are clowns'. So we have *downward implication*, but we don't have *upward implication*. (But be forewarned once again: what's obvious at this moment won't be quite so obvious later in Chapter 6, Section 4.)

Consider now the E- and the O-propositions. Obviously if the sentence 'No tyrants are clowns' is true, so is the sentence 'Some tyrants are not clowns; i.e., there exists at least one tyrant who is not a clown'. We may also call this *vertical* relationship between the E- and the O-propositions the relationship of *downward implication*. On the other hand, the truth of the sentence 'Some tyrants are not clowns' hardly guarantees the truth of the sentence 'No tyrants are clowns'. So once again we have *downward implication*, but we don't have *upward implication*. (But be forewarned for the third time: what's obvious at this moment won't be quite so obvious later in Chapter 6, Section 4.)

Consider now the I- and the O-propositions. Can they both be true? Can it be true both that some tyrants are clowns and that some tyrants are not clowns? Yes, of course it can be. Well, then, can the I- and the O-propositions both be false? Can it be false both that some tyrants *are* clowns and that some tyrants are *not* clowns? Ponder the answer to this question for a moment, before reading on.

If you are hesitant about answering, it's probably because your intuitions are now spinning in your head. It's unsurprising when our intuitions start spinning over seemingly *complicated* matters; what is surprising, though, is when they start spinning over seemingly *simple* matters—as is now happening. Fortunately, we don't have to rely on our intuitions to answer the question of whether the I- and the O-propositions can both be false. We can rely on logical reasoning instead—even though at bottom logical reasoning itself rests on *other* intuitions of ours.

Suppose that the I-proposition is false. By the diagonal relationship of semantic contradiction, the corresponding E-proposition must be true. By the vertical relationship of downward implication, the O-proposition must also be true. Therefore, if the I-proposition is false, the O-proposition must be true.

Now suppose that the O-proposition is false. By the diagonal relationship of semantic contradiction, the corresponding A-proposition must be true. By the vertical relationship of downward implication, the I-proposition must also be true. Therefore, if the O-proposition is false, the I-proposition must be true.

It follows that if the I-proposition is false, the O-proposition is true, and if the O-proposition is false, the I-proposition is true. Obviously, therefore, the I- and the O-propositions cannot both be false. (But be forewarned a fourth time: what's obvious at this moment won't be quite so obvious later in Chapter 6, Section 4.) It follows that the I- and the O-propositions—like any two propositions that *can* both be true but *can't* both be false—are said to be *subcontraries*.

> Definition:    Two propositions are *subcontraries iff* there is no interpretation that makes both of them false but there is at least one interpretation that makes both of them true.

One last word vis-à-vis the Square of Opposition: Do *not* suppose for an instant that the subcontraries, the I- and the O-propositions, imply one another. 'Some of the apples *are* rotten' does *not* imply 'Some of the apples *aren't* rotten'. There you are, turning over the apples one by one. "Hmm," you say, after having examined the first half dozen or so, each of which is rotten. "Some of the apples are rotten." And then you *immediately* add, "But I haven't yet examined the rest. I have *no* idea whether they're rotten as well." Suppose that 'Some of the apples are rotten' really *did* imply—and suppose too that everyone knew that it really *did* imply—'Some of the apples aren't rotten'. In that case, you couldn't very well say, "Some of the apples are rotten, but I have no idea whether the rest are rotten as well." But of course you *can* very well say this. So 'Some of the apples *are* rotten' does *not* imply 'Some of the apples *aren't* rotten'.

By the very same token, 'Some of the apples *aren't* rotten' doesn't imply 'Some of the apples *are* rotten'.

Moral of the story: the I- and the O-propositions simply don't imply one another.

Alternatively, suppose that you ask your logic instructor after an exam, "Well, how did the class do?" And suppose that your logic instructor turns to your class and says, "Quite nicely; some of the students received As." In ordinary conversation, it might well be common for you to infer that some of the students *didn't* receive As. *Strictly speaking,* however, your inference would be illegitimate. After all, although your instructor's statement doesn't *imply* the statement that *all* the students received As, it's certainly *consistent* with it. Hence the illegitimacy of inferring from the I-proposition, 'Some of the students received As', the O-proposition, 'Some of the students didn't receive As'.

By the very same token, 'Some of the students *didn't* receive As' doesn't imply 'Some of the students *did* receive As'.

Upshot: we adopt the minimalist take on 'some': it means, once again, 'at least one'—period.

# Exercises

Using the following interpretations, translate the sentences below into logical notation:

$Dx = x$ is a dragon
$Rx = x$ is rabid
$Sx = x$ is silly
$Tx = x$ is treacherous
$Ux = x$ is a unicorn
$Vx = x$ is vicious
$m$ = Monty
$n$ = Nicole
$o$ = Oedipus
$p$ = Pogdor

1. Neither Monty nor Nicole is treacherous.
2. Oedipus isn't a vicious unicorn.
3. Neither Pogdor nor Monty is a silly unicorn.
4. Even though Nicole is a silly unicorn, some unicorns aren't silly.
5. Either Oedipus or Pogdor isn't vicious unless Monty is vicious.
6. All dragons are vicious.
7. All silly dragons are treacherous.
8. Some unicorns are treacherous.
9. Some vicious unicorns are treacherous.
10. No unicorns are silly.

11. No treacherous unicorns are silly.
12. At least one dragon isn't vicious.
13. At least one silly dragon isn't vicious.
14. At least one silly but non-treacherous dragon isn't vicious.
15. Every unicorn that's either silly or treacherous is vicious.
16. Not every unicorn that's either silly or treacherous is vicious.
17. Not every vicious unicorn is both silly and treacherous.
18. Not a single unicorn is vicious.
19. Not a single silly unicorn is vicious.
20. Not a single rabid, silly, and treacherous unicorn is vicious.
21. Anything that's vicious is treacherous.
22. Anything that's rabid and vicious is treacherous.
23. Anything that's vicious is either a dragon or a unicorn.
24. Anything that's rabid, silly, and treacherous is either a dragon or a unicorn.
25. Silly unicorns are treacherous.
26. Treacherous dragons aren't silly.
27. Unicorns don't exist.
28. If unicorns don't exist then vicious unicorns don't exist.
29. Some dragons are neither silly nor non-silly.
30. Some dragons that are rabid are neither silly nor non-silly.
31. Some dragons that are either rabid or vicious are neither silly nor non-silly.
32. No rabid dragons that are silly are treacherous but not vicious.
33. Unicorns are vicious but not rabid.
34. Unicorns are vicious; unicorns are treacherous; and unicorns are rabid.
35. Neither dragons nor unicorns are either vicious or treacherous.
36. Only dragons are silly.
37. Nothing that's rabid, silly, and treacherous is either a dragon or a unicorn.
38. If unicorns are vicious then so are dragons.
39. Rabid dragons and rabid unicorns are vicious.
40. There exists no object which is both vicious and non-vicious.

# 6. Free and Bound Variables, Open and Closed *Wffs*, and Quantifier Scope

A tiny roadmap. . . . In this section you will be acquiring the notions of free and bound variables, open and closed *wffs*, and quantifier scope. I begin with examples—designed to appeal to your intuitions—and I end with definitions. You may wish to re-read the section in light of the definitions.

## A. Free and Bound Variables

Consider '(∃x)Tx'. It's a *wff*, and with a suitable interpretation—'There exists at least one tyrant'—it's a bearer of truth-value. (It's true.) Significantly, each of the two occurrences of the variable 'x' in '(∃x)Tx' is said to be *bound*—bound by the existential quantifier '∃'.

Now consider 'Tx'. It too is a *wff*, but even with a suitable interpretation—'He, she, or it is a tyrant'—it's *not* a bearer of truth-value. Significantly, the one occurrence of the variable 'x' in 'Tx' is said to be *free*—free of being bound by any quantifier.

To be a *wff* a string of symbols has to satisfy certain *syntactic* criteria, and to be a bearer of truth-value it has to satisfy certain *semantic* criteria. 'Tx' satisfies the syntactic criteria for being a *wff*, but it doesn't satisfy the *semantic* criteria for being a bearer of truth-value. It's neither true nor false, and so it's a *wff* that doesn't represent a proposition/statement/sentence.

First question: How does one know that 'Tx' is a *wff*?

Answer: One *doesn't*. At least not yet. All that one knows now is that I've *declared* it to be a *wff*. Be patient. In Chapter 6 you'll learn the formation rules that determine what is, and what isn't, a *wff* in Predicate Logic/Quantification Theory.

Second question: How does one know that 'Tx' has no truth-value?

Answer: Read on.

Interpret 'Tx' to mean, once again, 'x is a tyrant' or 'he, she, or it is a tyrant'. Suppose that it's a Friday afternoon in summertime and that you're heading out of Boston, north on Route 1, up toward Maine. You spot a huge billboard containing *only* the words 'He's a tyrant'.

Your significant other turns to you and asks, "So what do you think? That sentence—'He's a tyrant'—is it true or not?" What do you reply? Assume that there's neither a photograph nor a painting nor a sketch of anyone on the billboard. Assume that there's no other billboard for miles around. Assume that there haven't been, and aren't about to be, any accusations in the press about the tyrannical ambitions of this or that politician. What, then, do you reply to your significant other when he/she asks you about the truth-value of 'He's a tyrant'?

The problem is *not* that the referent of the word 'he' is *knowable* but that you, in your ignorance, simply don't know who the individual is to whom the word 'he' refers. Nor is the problem that you haven't tried hard enough to discover who the individual is to whom the word 'he' refers. The problem is that in this instance the word 'he' fails to do what a pronoun is designed to do: it simply fails to refer; i.e., it has no referent. It's for this reason that our *wff* fails to represent a *proposition*. As such, it's neither true nor false: it has no truth-value.

It's very much like the algebraic equation '$x + 9 = 13$'. What would you say if someone asked you whether *it* were true or false? As it stands, it's *neither-nor*. If I were to say, "Let $x$ be the number 3", the equation would now have a truth-value: it would be *false*. If I were to say, "Let $x$ be the number 4", once again the equation would have a truth-value: this time, however, it would be *true*. If I were to universally quantify the sentence—'$(\forall x)(x + 9 = 13)$'—the resulting sentence would be false, and if I were to existentially quantify it—'$(\exists x)(x + 9 = 13)$'—the resulting sentence would be true. But once again, as it stands, '$x + 9 = 13$' is neither true nor false.

In '$x + 9 = 13$', just as in '$Tx$', the variable '$x$' is *free*—free of any quantifier to which it's bound. By contrast, in both '$(\forall x)(x + 9 = 13)$', and '$(\exists x)(x + 9 = 13)$', just as in '$(\exists x)Tx$', each occurrence of '$x$' is *bound*—bound to a particular quantifier.

Interpret '$Tx$' and '$Cx$', yet again, to mean '$x$ is a tyrant' and '$x$ is a clown', respectively.

Question: What about '$Tx \rightarrow Cx$'? And what about '$(\forall x)Tx \rightarrow Cx$'? What's the status of these two *wffs* in this regard?

Answer: Like '$Tx$', each of these is a *wff*. And each suffers from the same semantic disease, as it were, that '$Tx$' suffers from; i.e., neither is a bearer of truth-value. You would translate the former, '$Tx \rightarrow Cx$', either as 'If $x$ is a tyrant then $x$ is a clown', or as 'If *it* is a tyrant then *it* is a clown'. And you would translate the latter, '$(\forall x)Tx \rightarrow Cx$', either as

'If each and every object is a tyrant then *x* is a clown', or as 'If each and every object is a tyrant then it is a clown', or simply as 'If everything is a tyrant then it is a clown'. Note that in each of these translations, as is the case with '*Tx*', neither the variable '*x*' nor the pronoun 'it' refers to any object at all. (And therefore, in the sentence 'If each and every object is a tyrant then it is a clown', there's *no* reason to suppose that the word 'it' refers to each and every object.)

## B. Open and Closed *Wffs*

*Wffs* like '*Tx*', '*Tx* → *Cx*', and '($\forall x$)*Tx* → *Cx*', stand on one side of the *open-wff/closed-wff* divide. *Wffs* like '($\exists x$)*Tx*' and '($\forall x$)(*Tx* → *Cx*)' stand on the other side.

Each of the *wffs* '*Tx*', '*Tx* → *Cx*', and '($\forall x$)*Tx* → *Cx*', contains at least one occurrence of a free variable. In '*Tx*', as you know, '*x*' is free, i.e., free of any quantifier. Likewise, in '*Tx* → *Cx*', each of the two occurrences of '*x*' is free. In '($\forall x$)*Tx* → *Cx*', the third occurrence of '*x*' is free, although each of the first two occurrences of '*x*' is bound, i.e., bound by a quantifier—in this instance, the universal quantifier. Because each of these *wffs* contains at least one occurrence of a free variable, each is said to be an *open wff*.

Neither of the *wffs* '($\exists x$)*Tx*' and '($\forall x$)(*Tx* → *Cx*)' contains any occurrence of a free variable. In each of them, every occurrence of '*x*' is bound by a quantifier. As such, each of these *wffs* is a *closed wff*. Subject to qualifications that I shall discuss at the end of this section, closed *wffs* possess truth-value—they're either true or false, whereas open *wffs* lack truth-value—they're neither true nor false.

## C. Quantifier Scope

Another divide: the *unlimited/limited quantifier-scope* divide. A *wff* like '($\forall x$)(*Tx* → *Cx*)' stands on one side of the quantifier-scope divide. A *wff* like '($\forall x$)*Tx* → *Cx*' stands on the other side. '($\forall x$)(*Tx* → *Cx*)' is a universally quantified conditional. '($\forall x$)*Tx* → *Cx*', on the other hand, is nothing of the sort: instead, it's a conditional whose antecedent is universally quantified.

In '$(\forall x)(Tx \rightarrow Cx)$', each of the three occurrences of '$x$' is said to fall within the *scope* of the universal quantifier. In other words, the universal quantifier is said to *operate* on each of them. In '$(\forall x)Tx \rightarrow Cx$', on the other hand, only the first two occurrences of '$x$' are said to fall within the *scope* of the universal quantifier. In other words, the universal quantifier is said to *operate* both on the first occurrence of '$x$' and on the second, but not on the third.

Take another look at '$(\forall x)(Tx \rightarrow Cx)$'. Look, in particular, at the second set of parentheses, the ones that surround '$Tx \rightarrow Cx$'. The presence of these parentheses ensures that the universal quantifier operates on the *whole* of the *wff*. In other words, the universal quantifier's scope extends over the *whole* of '$(Tx \rightarrow Cx)$', and thus its scope is *unlimited*. Now take another look at '$(\forall x)Tx \rightarrow Cx$. The *absence* of parentheses immediately to the right of '$(\forall x)$' ensures that the scope of the universal quantifier doesn't extend to the right of '$Tx$'. As such, its scope is *limited*: it stops dead with the second of the three occurrences of the variable $x$ in the *wff*—the variable '$x$' in '$Tx$'. In other words, the third occurrence of the variable '$x$' in the *wff*—the variable '$x$' in '$Cx$'—lies *outside* the universal quantifier's scope. Therefore the universal quantifier doesn't *operate* on it or *govern* it. As such, it's not *bound* to that quantifier. Nor is it bound to any other quantifier. It is said to be, as you know full well by now, a *free* variable.

A few last words on the vast difference between '$(\forall x)(Tx \rightarrow Cx)$' and '$(\forall x)Tx \rightarrow Cx$'—two *wffs* that it's so tempting to confuse with one another. '$(\forall x)(Tx \rightarrow Cx)$' is (once again) a universally quantified conditional. It's *not* a conditional. If it were a conditional, the scope of the arrow would take precedence over the scope of the universal quantifier. A quantified conditional—whether universally or existentially quantified—is no more a conditional than a negated conditional is a conditional. '$(\forall x)Tx \rightarrow Cx$', on the other hand, is (once again) a conditional. It's *not* a universally quantified conditional. If it were a universally quantified conditional, the scope of the universal quantifier would take precedence over the scope of the arrow. It's not even a universally quantified *wff* of *any* sort. It's simply a conditional whose antecedent happens to be a universally quantified *wff*, and whose consequent, containing a free variable, lacks truth-value.

The first words out of your mouth when you start to translate into English the universally quantified conditional '$(\forall x)(Tx \rightarrow Cx)$' are the words 'All' or 'Each and every' or 'Given any object $x$'—and *not* the word 'If'. By contrast, the first word out of your mouth when you start to translate into English the conditional '$(\forall x)Tx \rightarrow Cx$' *is* the word 'If'.

One last time. . . . '$(\forall x)(Tx \rightarrow Cx)$' has truth-value: it's either true or false. You and I may not know *which* it is—true or false—but we know that it's one or the other. Not so with '$(\forall x)Tx \rightarrow Cx$'. It's not that you and I don't *know* what its truth-value is; it's rather that it has none.

So! At this point, the notions of a *free* variable, a *bound* variable, an *open wff*, a *closed wff*, and the *scope* of a quantifier should be fairly clear. But 'fairly clear' isn't good enough. Hence the following series of definitions, each of which leads quite naturally into its successor. By rendering explicit what, by now, with any sort of luck, you will have grasped implicitly, the definitions should serve to dissipate whatever residual fog may be hovering over these various notions.

## D. Definitions

Note that in this section '**x**' appears in bold font. The reason is that in this context, i.e., in the context of a definition, '**x**' isn't a variable. It's a meta-variable; i.e., it's functioning as a proxy for any variable whatsoever. As such, it stands for any of the actual variables '$u$', '$v$', '$w$', '$x$' itself, '$y$', or '$z$'.

Definition:  If '$\triangle$' is a *wff* and if '$(\forall x)\triangle$' is a *wff*, then the *scope* of the universal quantifier '$\forall$' is '$(\forall x)\triangle$', i.e., the *wff* in its entirety.

In light of this definition it should be clear what it means for a *wff* to fall within the scope of a universal quantifier:

Definition:  If '$\triangle$' is a *wff* and if '$(\forall x)\triangle$' is a *wff*, then '$\triangle$' *falls within the scope* of the universal quantifier '$\forall$'.

Obviously there are comparable definitions where existentially quantified *wffs* are concerned.

> **Definition:**    If '△' is a *wff* and if '(∃*x*)△' is a *wff*, then the *scope* of the existential quantifier '∃' is '(∃*x*)△', i.e., the *wff* in its entirety.

And in light of this definition it should be clear what it means for a *wff* to fall within the scope of an existential quantifier:

> **Definition:**    If '△' is a *wff* and if '(∃*x*)△' is a *wff*, then '△' *falls within the scope* of the existential quantifier '∃'.

Note that where both universally and existentially quantified *wffs* are concerned, '△' is the *wff* immediately to the right of '(∀*x*)' and '(∃*x*)', respectively. Obviously, therefore, where the *quantified conditional* '(∀*x*)(*Tx* → *Cx*)' is concerned, '△'—as the *wff* immediately to the right of '(∀*x*)'—is '(*Tx* → *Cx*)'. Less obviously, where the *unquantified conditional* '(∀*x*)*Tx* → *Cx*' is concerned, '△'—as the *wff* immediately to the right of '(∀*x*)'—is '*Tx*', rather than '*Tx* → *Cx*'. Why so? Because '*Tx* → *Cx*' doesn't count as a *wff* in $L_2$! Why not? Because it's not enclosed in parentheses, and to count as a *wff*, a conditional, e.g., '*Tx* → *Cx*', has to be enclosed in parentheses. To be sure, it's permissible to drop outermost parentheses—but only if there's *nothing*, i.e., no quantifier and no connective, to the left of the leftmost parenthesis, and *nothing*, i.e., no connective, to the right of the rightmost parenthesis. (You will learn this as soon as you dive into the formation rules for $L_2$ in Chapter 6. In the meantime, just recall the analogous formation rule for conditionals—not to mention, conjunctions, disjunctions, and bi-conditionals—in $L_1$.)

As you know, it's not merely *wffs* that fall within the scope of quantifiers. Variables too fall within their scope.

> **Definition:**    A variable '*x*' falls within the scope of a given quantifier *iff* either '*x*' appears immediately to the right of the quantifier, or '*x*' appears in a *wff* that itself falls within the scope of the quantifier.

In '$(\forall x)(Tx \rightarrow Cx)$', the first of the three occurrences of '$x$' appears immediately to the right of '$\forall$', the quantifier, and therefore falls within its scope. Moreover, as you know, '$(Tx \rightarrow Cx)$' is a *wff* that itself falls within the scope of the quantifier. Therefore each occurrence of '$x$' in '$(Tx \rightarrow Cx)$' appears in a *wff* that itself falls within the scope of the quantifier. Therefore each occurrence of '$x$' in '$(Tx \rightarrow Cx)$' falls within the scope of the quantifier.

The notion of a variable's falling within the *scope* of a given quantifier is quite different from the notion of its being *bound* by a given quantifier. In order to get a better sense of what it means for a variable to be *bound* by a given quantifier, consider the *wffs*—your first multiply quantified *wffs*—'$(\forall x)[Wx \rightarrow (\exists y)Ly]$' and '$(\forall x)[Wx \rightarrow (\exists x)Lx]$'. Suppose that the domain of objects on which we're focusing consists of race-horses. Interpret '$Wx$' to mean '$x$ is a winner' and '$Lx$' to mean '$x$ is a loser'. So interpreted, the natural reading of '$(\forall x)[Wx \rightarrow (\exists y)Ly]$' is identical to the natural reading of '$(\forall x)[Wx \rightarrow (\exists x)Lx]$': 'If any horse is a winner then at least one horse is a loser'.

Is it clear which variables fall within the *scope* of which quantifier(s)? And is it clear which variables are *bound* by which quantifier(s)? (Try to answer each of these questions on your own, before you continue reading.)

It shouldn't be too difficult at this point to determine which variables fall within the *scope* of which quantifier(s). In the first *wff*, '$(\forall x)[Wx \rightarrow (\exists y)Ly]$', each of the two occurrences of '$x$' and each of the two occurrences of '$y$' falls within the scope of the universal quantifier; however, only the third and fourth occurrences of '$y$' also fall within the scope of the existential quantifier. In the second *wff*, '$(\forall x)[Wx \rightarrow (\exists x)Lx]$', each of the four occurrences of '$x$' falls within the scope of the universal quantifier; however, only the third and fourth occurrences of '$x$' also fall within the scope of the existential quantifier.

On the other hand, it might still be a bit difficult determining which variables are *bound* by which quantifier(s). Vis-à-vis the first *wff*, '$(\forall x)[Wx \rightarrow (\exists y)Ly]$', your intuitions are urging you to say that each occurrence of '$x$' is bound by the universal quantifier, and that each occurrence of '$y$' is bound by the existential. Your intuitions in this instance are spot-on. Vis-à-vis the second *wff*, '$(\forall x)[Wx \rightarrow (\exists x)Lx]$', you may be less sure. Nevertheless, your intuitions are urging you, however weakly, to say that the first two occurrences of '$x$' are bound, once again, by the universal quantifier, and that the last two occurrences of '$x$'—here's where you're less sure—are bound by the existential.

Given the formation rules that you will encounter in Chapter 6, your intuitions are spot-on once again. So what exactly does it mean to say, vis-à-vis the second *wff*, that the last two occurrences of '*x*' are bound by the existential quantifier?

On the natural reading once again of the two *wffs*—'If any horse is a winner then at least one horse is a loser'—there's no reason to suppose that any horse that's a winner is also a loser. I.e., there's no reason to suppose that the last two occurrences of '*x*' in '$(\forall x)[Wx \rightarrow (\exists x)Lx]$' are bound by the universal quantifier. Nor does anything change if you use pronouns in your translation: 'Given any horse, if *it* is a winner then there exists at least one horse which is such that *it* is a loser.' It would be utterly perverse to infer that the two instances of the pronoun 'it' in this sentence must refer to one and the same horse. They *might* do so—but the point is that they *needn't* do so. And yet they *would* do so if the last two occurrences of '*x*' were bound by the universal quantifier. It's the second quantifier—the existential—that blocks the inference that the two instances of 'it' must refer to the same horse. It's the existential quantifier, in other words, that prevents you from treating the last two occurrences of '*x*' in '$(\forall x)[Wx \rightarrow (\exists x)Lx]$' as being bound by the universal quantifier rather than by the existential quantifier itself.

Thanks to your intuitions, you're now capable of distinguishing variables that are bound by a given quantifier from those that aren't. The following definitions are designed to serve as a foundation for these intuitions. The second definition is a bit complicated, however— and it wouldn't be the end of the world if you ended up relying on your intuitions instead of the definition.

---

**Definition:**     A quantifier $\mathbf{Q}_1$ falls within the scope of a quantifier $\mathbf{Q}_2$ *iff* $\mathbf{Q}_1$ appears in a *wff* that itself falls within the scope of $\mathbf{Q}_2$.

---

Thus, in the *wff* '$(\forall x)[Wx \rightarrow (\exists x)Lx]$' the existential quantifier '∃' appears in a *wff*, '$(\exists x)Lx$', that itself falls within the scope of the universal quantifier '∀'. As such, the quantifier '∃' may be said to fall within the scope of the quantifier '∀'. On the other hand, the universal quantifier '∀' does *not* appear in a *wff* that itself falls within the scope of the existential quantifier '∃'. As such, the quantifier '∀' may *not* be said to fall within the scope of the quantifier '∃'.

**Definition:** A variable '$x$' is *bound*, or *governed*, by a quantifier $Q_1$ iff

(1) '$x$' falls within the scope of the quantifier $Q_1$;

(2) an occurrence of the same variable '$x$' appears immediately to the right of the quantifier $Q_1$; and

(3) if there's another quantifier $Q_2$ within whose scope '$x$' also falls, and that also has an occurrence of '$x$' immediately to its right, then the quantifier $Q_1$ falls within the scope of the quantifier $Q_2$.

It follows from (3) that '$x$' is located closer, so to speak, to the quantifier $Q_1$ than to the quantifier $Q_2$.

The point of (3) is to address the following state of affairs. Suppose that conditions (1) and (2) are satisfied; i.e., suppose (1) that '$x$' falls within the scope of a quantifier $Q_1$, and that (2) an occurrence of the same variable '$x$' appears immediately to the right of the quantifier $Q_1$. Suppose too that there *is* another quantifier $Q_2$ within whose scope '$x$' also falls, and that also has an occurrence of '$x$' immediately to its right. Accordingly—and this is the thrust of (3)—the former occurrence of '$x$' isn't bound by $Q_1$ *unless* $Q_1$ falls within the scope of $Q_2$.

For instance, consider '$(\forall x)[Wx \rightarrow (\exists x)Lx]$' one last time, and consider in particular the last two occurrences of '$x$'. Suppose that you thought that each of them were bound by the universal quantifier. It's certainly true that (1) each of the last two occurrences of '$x$' falls within the scope of the universal quantifier. Moreover, it's certainly true that (2) an occurrence of '$x$' appears immediately to the right of the universal quantifier. Now it just so happens that (3) there's another quantifier within whose scope each of the two occurrences of '$x$' also falls, i.e., the existential quantifier. And it also just so happens that the existential quantifier has an occurrence of '$x$' immediately to its right. It would be false, however, to suppose that the universal quantifier falls within the scope of the existential. Quite the contrary: It is the existential quantifier that falls within the scope of the universal. Clearly, then—in light of (3)—neither of the last two occurrences of '$x$' is bound by the universal quantifier.

So, is each of them bound by the existential? It's certainly true that (1) each of the last two occurrences of 'x' falls within the scope of the existential quantifier. Moreover, it's certainly true that (2) an occurrence of 'x' appears immediately to the right of the existential quantifier. And it so happens once again that (3) there's another quantifier within whose scope 'x' also falls, i.e., the universal quantifier, and that also has an occurrence of 'x' immediately to its right. In this instance, however, the existential quantifier does indeed fall within the scope of the universal. Clearly, then—in light of (3)—each of the last two occurrences of 'x' is bound by the existential quantifier.

The remaining definitions should inspire a sense of déjà-vu.

The definition of a free variable piggybacks on the definition of a bound variable:

**Definition:**    A variable is *free iff* it isn't bound, or governed, by any quantifier.

The definition of an open *wff* piggybacks on the definition of a free variable:

**Definition:**    A *wff* is *open iff* it contains at least one occurrence of a free variable.

And the definition of a closed *wff* piggybacks on the definition of an open *wff*:

**Definition:**    A *wff* is *closed iff* it isn't open; i.e., *iff* it contains no occurrence of a free variable.

## E. Odds and Ends

In '$(\forall x)(Tx \rightarrow Cx)$', not only does each of the three occurrences of 'x' fall within the scope of the universal quantifier; in addition, each is bound by it. In '$(\forall x)Tx \rightarrow Cx$', on the other hand, each of the first two occurrences of '$x$' falls within the scope of the universal quantifier and is bound by it, but the third occurrence of '$x$' is free: it doesn't fall within the quantifier's scope and therefore it isn't bound by it.

Consider, and look closely at, the following *wff*: '$(\forall x)(Tx \to Cy)$'. You would translate it as 'If anything (or *anyone*—assuming that only people were our focus) is a tyrant then $y$ is a clown'. Notice that each of the two occurrences of '$x$', as well as the one occurrence of '$y$', falls within the *scope* of the universal quantifier. Only the two occurrences of '$x$', however, are *bound* by that quantifier; '$y$' is free. Puzzled? Reread Clause 2 of the definition of a bound variable: '$y$' simply isn't the same variable as the one immediately to the right of the quantifier.

Question: What about the *wff* '$(\forall x)Tx \to Cy$'? Where does it stand with respect to the *wff* '$(\forall x)(Tx \to Cy)$'?

Answer: '$(\forall x)Tx \to Cy$' differs both semantically and syntactically from '$(\forall x)(Tx \to Cy)$'. From a semantic perspective, they have quite different meanings. You would translate '$(\forall x)Tx \to Cy$' as 'If *everyone* is a tyrant then $y$ is a clown'. You would translate '$(\forall x)(Tx \to Cy)$' as 'If *anyone* is a tyrant then $y$ is a clown'.

From a syntactic perspective, they have quite different structures. '$(\forall x)Tx \to Cy$' is a conditional whose antecedent happens to be a universally quantified *wff*. '$(\forall x)(Tx \to Cy)$', on the other hand, is a universally quantified conditional.

Question: What about the *wff* '$(\forall x)Tx \to Cx$'? Where does it stand with respect to the *wff* '$(\forall x)Tx \to Cy$'?

Answer: Semantically, they are indistinguishable. You could happily read each one as 'If everyone is a tyrant then *bzzz* is a clown'. (Think of the two algebraic equations '$x + 9 = 13$" and '$y + 9 = 13$': they have the exact same meaning.)

Syntactically, however, they are quite different from one another. Watch what happens if you extend the scope of each of the universal quantifiers. The open *wff* '$(\forall x)Tx \to Cx$' becomes the new and *closed wff* '$(\forall x)(Tx \to Cx)$'. The third occurrence of '$x$' now falls within the scope of the universal quantifier *and* is bound by it. The open *wff* '$(\forall x)Tx \to Cy$', on the other hand, becomes the new but still *open wff* '$(\forall x)(Tx \to Cy)$'. And once again: '$y$' now falls within the scope of the universal quantifier but is *not* bound by it.

Note that you can always transform an open *wff* into a closed *wff*; i.e., you can always eliminate each of its free variables. Simply substitute a proper name for each of its free variables, in which case, for example, the open *wff* 'Tx', 'x is a tyrant', becomes the closed *wff* 'Ta', 'Ardbeg is a tyrant' or 'Tb', 'Bobo is a tyrant'. Alternatively, simply quantify the *wff* so as to bind each of its free variables, in which case the open *wff* 'Tx' becomes the closed *wff* '(∀x)Tx', 'Everyone is a tyrant', or '(∃x)Tx', 'There exists at least one tyrant'. Alternatively, substitute proper names *and* quantify, in which case the open *wff* 'Tx → Cy' becomes '(∀x)(Tx → Ca)', 'If anyone is a tyrant then Ardbeg is a clown'.

## F. Open and Closed Wffs Revisited

A last, albeit lengthy, word. . . . It is tempting to think that *no* open *wff* is a bearer of truth-value, and that *every* closed *wff* is a bearer of truth-value. Tempting, perhaps—but mistaken.

Consider first the claim that no open *wff* is a bearer of truth-value. In the abstract, 'Tx' is neither true nor false and '—Tx' is neither true nor false. It would be natural to think that a molecular, whose atomics are neither true nor false, must itself be neither true nor false. Not so, however. Consider the following *wffs*: 'Tx ∨ —Tx', 'Tx → Tx', 'Tx ↔ Tx', '—(Tx ∧ —Tx)', and 'Tx → (Cx → Tx)', etc. Each of these is an open *wff* whose atomics are neither true nor false, yet each of these is itself a logical truth. No matter how you interpret each predicate, and no matter which object in the universe you substitute for 'x', each *wff* will come out true. By the very same token, of course, the negation of each of these open *wffs* is a semantic contradiction, a logical falsehood. So much for the view that *no* open *wff* is a bearer of truth-value.

In general, however, i.e., with the exception of logical truths and logical falsehoods, no open *wff* is a bearer of truth-value.

Consider next the claim that every closed *wff* is a bearer of truth-value. Consider '(∃x)Zx'. It's obvious that it's a closed *wff*. If every closed *wff* is a bearer of truth-value, then it too must be a bearer truth-value.

Question: So what's the truth-value of '(∃x)Zx'?

Answer: Obviously, until you assign an interpretation to 'Z' (or 'Zx'), '(∃x)Zx' is neither true nor false, and thus has no truth-value.

Question: If '(∃x)Zx', uninterpreted, has no truth-value, how is it any different from an open *wff* like 'Zx'?

Answer: Once you assign an interpretation to each of the predicates of $L_2$, and in particular to 'Z', then '$(\exists x)Zx$' will be either true or false. For example, if you interpret 'Z' to mean 'is a zebra' (or '$Zx$' to mean '$x$ is a zebra'), then '$(\exists x)Zx$' will be true. And if you interpret 'Z' to mean 'is a zombie' (or '$Zx$' to mean '$x$ is a zombie'), then '$(\exists x)Zx$' will be false.

Question: So once again, until we assign an interpretation to 'Z' (or '$Zx$'), '$(\exists x)Zx$' is neither true nor false, right?

Answer: Right. Uninterpreted, '$(\exists x)Zx$' is still a *wff*, but it's not a bearer of truth-value. The notion of a *wff* is a purely *syntactic* notion, whereas the notion of a bearer of truth-value is a purely *semantic* notion. You could have raised a similar question in $L_1$ about the propositional variable 'P'. It's obviously a *wff*, but until you assign an interpretation to it, it too is neither true nor false.

Question: So, if '$Zx$' and '$(\exists x)Zx$' are both *wffs*, and if, uninterpreted, neither one is a bearer of truth-value, just what *are* the differences between them?

Answer: Syntactically, they are as different as night and day. '$Zx$' is a *wff* containing at least one occurrence (in fact, exactly one occurrence) of a free variable, and as such it's an open *wff*. '$(\exists x)Zx$' is a *wff* containing no occurrence of a free variable, and as such it's a closed *wff*.

Semantically, too, they are as different as night and day. Once you assign an interpretation to the predicate 'Z', the closed *wff* '$(\exists x)Zx$' acquires a truth-value. But even if you assign an interpretation to the predicate 'Z', the open *wff* '$Zx$' still fails to acquire a truth-value.

There are two morals of this story: one semantic and one syntactic.

Semantic moral of the story: if you wave a semantic wand over an uninterpreted, semantically lifeless, i.e., truth-value-less, closed *wff*, e.g., '$(\exists x)Zx$', it comes to life. By assigning an interpretation to 'Z', you thereby bring the *wff* to life. But if you wave a semantic wand over an uninterpreted, semantically lifeless, i.e., truth-value-less, open *wff*, e.g., '$Zx$', it remains as lifeless as ever.

So to guarantee that each of the *closed wffs* of $L_2$ is a bearer of truth-value, all that you have to do is assign an interpretation to each of the predicates in $L_2$.

# Exercises

True or false? Defend your answer *iff* it is 'False'.

1. (a) '(∃x)[Tx ∧ (∃y)Cy]' is a conjunction, and (b) '(∃x)Tx ∧ (∃y)Cy' is an existentially quantified *wff*.
2. By bringing a free variable within the scope of a given quantifier, you thereby transform an open *wff* into a closed *wff*.
3. Semantically, '(∃x)(Tx ∧ Cx)' is indistinguishable from '(∃x)Tx ∧ Cx'.
4. Syntactically, '(∃x)(Tx ∧ Cx)' is indistinguishable from '(∃x)Tx ∧ Cx'.
5. Semantically, '(∃x)(Tx ∧ Cx)' is indistinguishable from '(∃x)(Tx ∧ Cy)'.
6. Syntactically, 'Tx ↔ Cx' is indistinguishable from 'Cx ↔ Tx'.
7. Semantically, '(∀x)(Tx → Cy)' is indistinguishable from '(∀x)Tx → Cy'.
8. Syntactically, '(∀x)Tx → Cx' is indistinguishable from '(∀x)Tx → Cy'.
9. Any variable that falls within the scope of a given quantifier is bound by that quantifier.
10. A variable that is bound by a given quantifier doesn't necessarily fall within the scope of that quantifier.

# 7. Translations

Back to the Square of Opposition! For our purposes, the payoff of the Square of Opposition is the role that it plays in translating from English into logical notation. When translating into the formal language of Quantification Theory, proceed as follows:

1. Determine whether the proposition is universal or particular/existential.
2. Determine whether it's affirmative or negative.

3. If it's universal and affirmative then it's an A-proposition, in which case you want a universally quantified conditional whose consequent isn't a negation.

4. If it's universal and negative then it's an E-proposition, in which case you want a universally quantified conditional whose consequent is a negation.

5. If it's particular/existential and affirmative then it's an I-proposition, in which case you want an existentially quantified conjunction whose right conjunct isn't a negation.

6. If it's particular/existential and negative then it's an O-proposition, in which case you want an existentially quantified conjunction whose right conjunct is a negation.

Are there exceptions to these rules? Yes, of course there are. Not every quantified proposition is either an A- or an E- or an I- or an O-proposition. Consider the following example: 'Each and every object whatsoever is both a tyrant and a clown.' This proposition is (implausibly) ascribing two properties to each and every object, namely, the property of being a tyrant and the property of being a clown. Hence the correct translation would be as follows: '$(\forall x)(Tx \land Cx)$'. Notice that this is a universally quantified *conjunction* (rather than either a universally quantified *conditional* or an *existentially* quantified conjunction.) As such, it's neither an A- nor an E- nor an I- nor an O-proposition.

Consider a second example: 'There exists at least one object which is such that if it's a tyrant then it's a clown.' This proposition is *not* asserting the existence of *either* tyrants *or* clowns. Instead, it's asserting the existence of something which is such that *if* it's a tyrant *then* it's a clown. Hence the correct translation would be as follows: '$(\exists x)(Tx \rightarrow Cx)$'. Notice that this is an existentially quantified *conditional* (rather than either an existentially quantified *conjunction* or a *universally* quantified conditional). As such, it's neither an A- nor an E- nor an I- nor an O-proposition.

Consider four last examples, none of which is either an A-, E-, I-, or O-proposition. 'Each and every object is a tyrant', i.e., '$(\forall x)Tx$', is universal and affirmative, but it's not a universally quantified *conditional* whose consequent isn't a negation. 'Nothing is a tyrant', i.e., '$(\forall x)-Tx$', is universal and negative, but it's not a universally quantified *conditional* whose consequent is a negation. 'There exists at least one tyrant', i.e.,

'$(\exists x)Tx$', is particular/existential and affirmative, but it's not an existentially quantified *conjunction* whose right conjunct isn't a negation. 'There exists at least one object that isn't a tyrant', i.e., '$(\exists x)-Tx$', is particular/existential and negative, but it's not an existentially quantified *conjunction* whose right conjunct is a negation.

Clearly there are many propositions that are of neither the A, E, I, nor O type. It is useful nevertheless to focus on these four types. Many, if not most, of the quantified propositions that you will be encountering are of these four types. Imposing the grid of universal-affirmative, universal-negative, particular-affirmative, and particular-negative, on the vast array of quantified *wffs* serves to impose a *bit* of order on the otherwise chaotic, unwieldy, and fragmented array.

Now let's get to work and do some translations. Consider the following interpretations:

> $Bx = x$ is bloodthirsty
> $Cx = x$ is a clown
> $Dx = x$ is doomed
> $Jx = x$ is jolly
> $Tx = x$ is a tyrant

Consider the sentence 'All bloodthirsty tyrants are jolly clowns.' It's a universal-affirmative sentence, i.e., an A-proposition, i.e., a universally quantified conditional. A promising first step into *Loglish*, the halfway house between English and $L_2$, would be the following: 'Given any object $x$, if $x$ is a bloodthirsty tyrant then $x$ is a jolly clown'. Obviously, this is tantamount to 'Given any object $x$, if $x$ is a tyrant and $x$ is bloodthirsty, then $x$ is a clown and $x$ is jolly'. Behold the universally quantified conditional: '$(\forall x)[(Tx \wedge Bx) \rightarrow (Cx \wedge Jx)]$'.

Consider next the sentence, 'No doomed clowns are either bloodthirsty or jolly'. It's obviously a universal-negative sentence, i.e., an E-proposition, i.e., a universally quantified conditional whose consequent is a negation. A first step into *Loglish* yields 'Given any object $x$, if $x$ is a clown and $x$ is doomed, then $x$ is neither bloodthirsty nor jolly': '$(\forall x)[(Cx \wedge Dx) \rightarrow -(Bx \vee Jx)]$'.

How else might you translate this proposition? Notice that it has the same meaning as the proposition 'There doesn't exist a single doomed clown who is either bloodthirsty or jolly'. Notice too that this latter proposition isn't one of your basic four; it's rather the *negation* of one of your basic four. It's the negation of the following I-proposition: 'There exists at least one doomed clown who is either bloodthirsty or jolly'. So first you translate the latter and then you prefix a dash to it.

What kind of a proposition is 'There exists at least one doomed clown who is either bloodthirsty or jolly'? It's existential-affirmative; therefore it's an I-proposition; therefore it's an existentially quantified conjunction: '$(\exists x)[(Cx \wedge Dx) \wedge (Bx \vee Jx)]$'. With the dash prefixed to it, it becomes '$-(\exists x)[(Cx \wedge Dx) \wedge (Bx \vee Jx)]$', and this latter sentence has the *exact* same meaning as '$(\forall x)[(Cx \wedge Dx) \rightarrow -(Bx \vee Jx)]$'. Each is a perfectly respectable translation of 'No doomed clowns are either bloodthirsty or jolly'.

This should be unsurprising. Think of the Square of Opposition, and think of the 'diagonal' propositions—the A and the O, on the one hand, and the E and the I, on the other. Because the I is the semantic contradictory of the E, if you negate the I—i.e., if you prefix a dash to it—you'll produce a proposition that is semantically equivalent to the E—and that's exactly what we just did. By the same token, if you negate the E you'll produce a proposition that is semantically equivalent to the I. We may generalize: by negating any of the basic four, you thereby generate a *wff* that is logically equivalent to its diagonal contradictory.

Two examples of fairly *long* translations can be disposed of quite quickly. 'Some bloodthirsty tyrants who aren't clowns are jolly but not doomed' is a particular-affirmative sentence, i.e., an I-proposition, i.e., an existentially quantified conjunction whose right conjunct isn't a negation: '$(\exists x)[(Tx \wedge Bx \wedge -Cx) \wedge (Jx \wedge -Dx)]$'. And 'Some jolly but doomed clowns aren't bloodthirsty tyrants' is a particular-negative sentence, i.e., an O-proposition, i.e., an existentially quantified conjunction whose right conjunct is a negation: '$(\exists x)[(Cx \wedge Jx \wedge Dx) \wedge -(Tx \wedge Bx)]$'.

And one example of a short, but slightly tricky, translation *cannot* be disposed of so quickly. 'A tyrant is doomed if and only if he or she is bloodthirsty' is a universal-affirmative sentence, i.e., an A-proposition, i.e., a universally quantified conditional whose consequent isn't a negation: '$(x)[Tx \rightarrow (Dx \leftrightarrow Bx)]$'. Notice that you're ascribing to each and every tyrant the following complex property: 'being doomed *iff* bloodthirsty', i.e., the complex property of being doomed *iff* he or she is bloodthirsty.

You should resist the (quite natural) temptation to translate the sentence as a universally quantified bi-conditional: '$(x)[(Tx \rightarrow Dx) \leftrightarrow Bx)]$'. This latter translation, of course, is equivalent to the following: '$(x)\{[(Tx \rightarrow Dx) \rightarrow Bx] \wedge [Bx \rightarrow (Tx \rightarrow Dx)]\}$'. This, in turn, involves the ascription to every object $x$ of two complex properties: the property conveyed by the open *wff* '$(Tx \rightarrow Dx) \rightarrow Bx$' and the property conveyed by the open *wff* '$Bx \rightarrow (Tx \rightarrow Dx)$'. By Contraposition, the first of these two open *wffs*, '$(Tx \rightarrow Dx) \rightarrow Bx$', is equivalent to '$-Bx \rightarrow -(Tx \rightarrow Dx)$'. By Negation Implication (albeit applied to an open-sentence-fragment), this is equivalent to '$-Bx \rightarrow (Tx \wedge -Dx)$'. So, among other things, the universally quantified bi-conditional '$(x)[(Tx \rightarrow Dx) \leftrightarrow Bx]$' is saying of every object $x$ that if $x$ isn't bloodthirsty then $x$ is a tyrant who isn't doomed. In other words, the universally quantified bi-conditional is saying of *you* that if you're not bloodthirsty, then you're a tyrant who isn't doomed. But the English original—'A tyrant is doomed if and only if he or she is bloodthirsty'—is saying no such thing about you. So much the worse, then, for treating the English original as a universally quantified bi-conditional.

One last point about the sentence 'A tyrant is doomed if and only if he or she is bloodthirsty'. Not every English sentence that begins with the word 'A' is an A-proposition, i.e., a universally quantified conditional whose consequent isn't a negation. Consider the sentence 'A bloodthirsty tyrant will come to power within a year.' Obviously this is an existentially quantified conjunction: it affirms the existence of at least one object $x$ such that $x$ is a tyrant and $x$ is bloodthirsty and $x$ will come to power within a year. The context *should* make perfectly clear exactly which type of proposition is called for: a universally quantified conditional or an existentially quantified conjunction. If the context *fails* to make it perfectly clear, however, you will have to rely on your judgment. (Not the end of the world.)

# Exercises

Using the following interpretations, translate the sentences below into logical notation:

$Bx$ = $x$ is bloodthirsty
$Cx$ = $x$ is a clown
$Dx$ = $x$ is doomed
$Jx$ = $x$ is jolly
$Px$ = $x$ is pompous
$Sx$ = $x$ is sanctimonious
$Tx$ = $x$ is a tyrant
$a$ = Ardbeg
$b$ = Bobo

1. All tyrants who aren't bloodthirsty are either doomed or jolly.
2. Some clowns who are neither bloodthirsty nor jolly are doomed tyrants.
3. No tyrants who aren't clowns are either jolly or bloodthirsty.
4. Some non-clowns who aren't tyrants are not both jolly and doomed.
5. Not all tyrants are bloodthirsty clowns.
6. Ardbeg and Bobo aren't both tyrants.
7. At least one sanctimonious clown isn't a doomed tyrant.
8. If all tyrants are bloodthirsty then no clowns are doomed.
9. If any tyrants are bloodthirsty then they are doomed.
10. Any bloodthirsty tyrant who isn't a clown is doomed.
11. Any tyrant who is bloodthirsty only if he is a clown is doomed.
12. Any sanctimonious tyrant who is bloodthirsty if he is a pompous clown is doomed.
13. Ardbeg and Bobo are not both jolly tyrants.
14. Only tyrants are clowns.
15. No pompous clown who is sanctimonious is a doomed non-tyrant.

16. All clowns are sanctimonious if and only if they are tyrants.
17. Some tyrants are pompous if they are doomed.
18. Any clown who is jolly unless he is doomed is either sanctimonious or pompous.
19. Some pompous tyrants are clowns only if they aren't sanctimonious.
20. Neither Ardbeg nor Bobo is a doomed clown.
21. No tyrants who aren't clowns are bloodthirsty.
22. Ardbeg and Bobo are both sanctimonious clowns, and unless they are tyrants no sanctimonious clowns are tyrants.
23. Some jolly and non-pompous clowns are either sanctimonious tyrants or doomed tyrants.
24. Only tyrants are sanctimonious clowns.
25. Only clowns aren't doomed.
26. Only jolly clowns are doomed. (This is ambiguous. Explain why; give one of the two rival interpretations; and make it clear which of the two rival interpretations it corresponds to.)
27. Only jolly clowns are doomed. (Now provide the other interpretation, and make it clear which of the two rival interpretations it corresponds to.)
28. A tyrant is a pompous and sanctimonious clown who is bloodthirsty.
29. Jolly clowns don't exist.
30. Neither bloodthirsty clowns nor jolly tyrants exist.
31. Only clowns exist. (Careful.)
32. If any tyrant is bloodthirsty then Ardbeg is doomed.
33. If any tyrant is bloodthirsty then Ardbeg is doomed. (Use a different quantifier here from the one you used in the preceding translation.)
34. If every tyrant is bloodthirsty then Ardbeg is doomed.
35. A jolly clown is a tyrant. (This is ambiguous. Explain why and give the two rival translations.)

# Chapter Six

# Predicate Logic:
# A Formal Language, Part Two

## 1. Multiple Quantifiers and Polyadic/Multiplace Predicates

Life in Predicate-Logic Land/Quantification-Theory Land becomes immensely interesting with the introduction of *multiple* quantifiers and *polyadic/multiplace* predicates. Whereas monadic/one-place predicates designate *properties*, polyadic/multiplace predicates designate *relations*. We start with polyadic/multiplace predicates, and then we turn to *wffs* with multiple quantifiers.

Consider our predicates thus far, e.g., 'Cx' or 'Tx'. Each of these is a *monadic* (or one-place) predicate: to the right of the predicate 'C' or the predicate 'T' is a single slot (or place) reserved for exactly *one* proper name or one variable. Another way of putting this is that the property of being a clown or the property of being a tyrant is ascribable to, or predicable of, individuals as individuals. It is not ascribable to, or predicable of, individuals as constituting pairs or trios or quartets, etc., of individuals. If you wish to express the thought that Ardbeg, Bobo, and Coco are clowns, you do so by writing the predicate three times: 'Ca ∧ Cb ∧ Cc'. You *don't* express the same thought by writing 'Cabc'. Why is this? Simply because in our 'dictionary' you were instructed to interpret 'Cx' to mean 'x is a clown'. To be sure, we *could* have defined 'Cxyz' to mean 'x, y, and z are clowns', or that the property of being a clown is ascribable to, or predicable of, each member of the trio consisting of *x*, *y*, and *z*. But then you wouldn't have been able to express either the thought that Ardbeg is a clown or the thought that Ardbeg and Bobo are both clowns.

Consider the following *two*-place predicates: '$Lxy$', e.g., '$x$ loves $y$', '$Oxy$', e.g., '$x$ is older than $y$', or '$Rxy$', e.g., '$x$ is to the right of $y$'. Consider the following English sentences and their translations into $L_2$:

| English Sentence | $L_2$ Counterpart |
|---|---|
| Ardbeg loves Bobo. | $Lab$ |
| Bobo loves Ardbeg. | $Lba$ |
| Bobo doesn't love Ardbeg. | $-Lba$ |
| Ardbeg loves Bobo *iff* Bobo doesn't love Ardbeg. | $Lab \leftrightarrow -Lba$ |
| Ardbeg loves himself. | $Laa$ |
| Ardbeg is older than Bobo and is to her right. | $Oab \wedge Rab$ |
| Ardbeg loves Bobo only if he's neither older than Bobo nor to her right. | $Lab \rightarrow -(Oab \vee Rab)$ |

Consider the following *three*-place predicate: '$Bxyz$', interpretable, for example, as '$x$ is between $y$ and $z$'. (Think of numbers or points on a line or politicians at a press conference or politicians on a left-to-right political spectrum.) You could conceive of four-place, five-place, and six-place, etc., predicates. There's no upper limit on the number of places that a predicate may have

One-place/monadic predicates designate *properties*. Multiplace/polyadic predicates designate *relations*. If you like, you may think of *all* predicates as designating relations—in which case a property would simply constitute the limiting, or degenerate, case of a relation—a relation with exactly *one* term, as it were.

Consider the following interpretations:

$$Px = x \text{ is a person}$$
$$Lxy = x \text{ loves } y$$
$$a = \text{Ardbeg}$$
$$b = \text{Bobo}$$

You would translate 'Ardbeg loves everything as '$(\forall x)Lax$', and you would translate 'Everything loves Ardbeg' as '$(\forall x)Lxa$'. What about 'Ardbeg loves *everyone?*'

Question: What's the difference between 'Ardbeg loves every*thing*' and 'Ardbeg loves every*one*'?

Answer: 'Ardbeg loves every*thing*' implies that, in addition to loving people, Ardbeg loves scorpions, snakes, rats, bats, and locusts. 'Ardbeg loves every*one*', on the other hand, implies that Ardbeg loves every *person*—but it's noncommittal with respect to the question of Ardbeg's loving scorpions, snakes, rats, bats, and locusts. If you peeked into a cave containing *only* scorpions, snakes, rats, bats, and locusts, and if someone were to ask you, "Is *anyone* in that cave?" obviously the truthful answer would be "No." On the other hand, if someone were to ask you, "Is *anything* in that cave?" obviously the truthful answer would be "Yes." All people are things, but not all things are people.

You would translate 'Ardbeg loves everyone' as '$(\forall x)(Px \rightarrow Lax)$'; i.e., 'Given any object $x$, if $x$ is a person then Ardbeg loves $x$.' You would translate 'Everyone loves Ardbeg as '$(\forall x)(Px \rightarrow Lxa)$'; i.e., 'Given any object $x$, if $x$ is a person then $x$ loves Ardbeg.' Notice that each of these is a universal-affirmative proposition, and therefore an A-proposition. So a universally quantified conditional is exactly what you want.

'Someone loves Ardbeg' is particular/existential and affirmative, and therefore it's an I-proposition, an existentially quantified conjunction: '$(\exists x)(Px \wedge Lxa)$'. 'Ardbeg loves someone' is also an I-proposition: '$(\exists x)(Px \wedge Lax)$'.

For the sake of variety, of course, you could have translated any of these English sentences via a *wff* containing the variable '$y$' or the variable '$z$' instead of the variable '$x$'. Thus either of the following would be a perfectly happy translation of 'Ardbeg loves someone': '$(\exists y)(Py \wedge Lay)$' or '$(\exists z)(Pz \wedge Laz)$'.

I raise the temperature ever so slightly. . . .

Question: How should you translate 'If anyone loves Bobo then Bobo loves herself'?

First possible answer: '$(\forall x)[(Px \wedge Lxb) \rightarrow Lbb]$'.

Second possible answer: '$(\exists x)(Px \wedge Lxb) \rightarrow Lbb$'.

*The* answer: *Each* of the above is correct. You would read the first as 'Given any object $x$, if $x$ is a person and $x$ loves Bobo then Bobo loves herself'. And you would read the second as 'If there exists at least one person who loves Bobo then Bobo loves herself'. A moment's thought should convince you that the two are equivalent—notwithstanding that the first is a universally quantified conditional and the second is a conditional whose antecedent is an existentially quantified conjunction.

I now raise the temperature a bit more than ever so slightly. Consider the sentence 'Someone loves everyone'. The first thing that should catch your attention is the presence of *two* quantifier expressions in the same sentence: 'someone' and 'everyone'. To be sure, you already encountered a *multiply quantified* sentence in Chapter 5, Section 6D, but this is your first translation involving both multiple quantifiers and a polyadic/multiplace predicate.

If you translate 'Someone loves everyone' into logical notation one step at a time, i.e., one quantifier at a time, you are much likelier to produce a correct translation than if you try to translate it and its two quantifiers all at once. Suppose that you first tackle the leftmost quantifier as you ascend into *Loglish*:

(1) $(\exists x)(Px \land x$ loves everyone)

Now, how do you translate '*x* loves everyone'? You know how to translate 'Ardbeg loves everyone:

(2) $(\forall x)(Px \rightarrow Lax)$

It should be a simple matter, therefore, to translate '*x* loves everyone', yes? You simply replace '*a*' with '*x*', yes?

(3) $(\forall x)(Px \rightarrow Lxx)$

Alas, (3) does *not* say, as you had wanted it to say, '*x* loves everyone'. '*x* loves everyone' is an *open wff*: it contains a free variable. (3), on the other hand, is a *closed wff*: each occurrence in (3) of the variable '*x*' is bound. What (3) says is that everyone loves himself (or herself).

Back to the drawing board. How might you recast '*x* loves everyone' to ensure that the pre-translation *open wff* remains a post-translation *open wff*? Keep in mind that '*x*' isn't the only show in town—it's not your *only* variable:

(4) $(\forall y)(Py \rightarrow Lxy)$

Now you're almost done. Return to (1) and replace '*x* loves everyone' with (4):

(5) $(\exists x)(Px \land (\forall y)(Py \rightarrow Lxy))$

You will be completely done once you upgrade to square brackets those parentheses in need of upgrading:

(6) $(\exists x)[Px \land (\forall y)(Py \to Lxy)]$

Done! You could translate this back into a somewhat stilted English as follows: 'There exists at least one object which is such that it's a person, and each and every object is such that if *it's* a person then the former object loves the latter object.' Or: 'There exists at least one object x which is such that x is a person, and given any object y, if y is a person then x loves y.' Alternatively, you might simply say, 'Someone loves everyone.'

Now consider the sentence 'Everyone loves someone'. Notice that in 'Someone loves everyone', the love necessarily springs, as it were, from one and the same individual. (There may be more than one such individual, but there must be at least one.) In 'Everyone loves someone', however, the love is *not* necessarily directed at one and the same individual. It *might* be, but it *needn't* be. Imagine a universe of only three people: Ardbeg, Bobo, and Coco. 'Everyone loves someone' would be true, for example, if Ardbeg loved Bobo, if Bobo loved Coco, and if Coco loved herself.

Suppose, once again, that you first tackle the leftmost quantifier as you ascend into *Loglish*:

(7) $(\forall x)(Px \to x$ loves someone$)$

Now, how do you translate 'x loves someone'? This is an *open wff*, and therefore the translation has to reflect this fact. 'There exists at least one object y such that y is a person and x loves y':

(8) $(\exists y)(Py \land Lxy)$

Now return to (7) and replace 'x loves someone' with (8):

(9) $(\forall x)(Px \to (\exists y)(Py \land Lxy))$

Upgrade to square brackets those parentheses in need of upgrading, and you're done:

(10) $(\forall x)[Px \to (\exists y)(Py \land Lxy)]$

Examining the following two pairs of sentences, (11) and (12), on the one hand, and (13) and (14), on the other, is quite instructive. It reveals the striking difference between *proper names*, like 'Ardbeg' and 'Bobo', on the one hand, and non–name, quantifier expressions like 'everyone', 'someone', and 'no one', on the other.

> (11) Ardbeg loves Bobo.
> (12) Bobo is loved by Ardbeg.

> (13) Someone loves everyone.
> (14) Everyone is loved by someone.

On the surface, the first pair, (11) and (12), seems exactly like the second pair, (13) and (14). But only on the surface.

Consider (11) first: 'Ardbeg loves Bobo'. Grammatically, you're looking at a subject-verb-object sentence, with the verb in the active voice. If you flip the subject and object, and also flip the active-voice verb into its passive-voice counterpart, you end up with (12), 'Bobo is loved by Ardbeg'. The two sentences—(11), 'Ardbeg loves Bobo', and (12), 'Bobo is loved by Ardbeg'—obviously have the exact same meaning.

So far so good. Now consider (13): 'Someone loves everyone'. Grammatically, you're looking once again at a subject-verb-object sentence, with the verb once again in the active voice. If you flip the subject and object, and also flip the active-voice verb into its passive-voice counterpart, you end up with (14): 'Everyone is loved by someone'. So these two sentences—(13), 'Someone loves everyone', and (14), 'Everyone is loved by someone'—obviously have the exact same meaning too, yes?

But of course they don't. (13), 'Someone loves everyone', implies (14), 'Everyone is loved by someone', but (14), 'Everyone is loved by someone', doesn't imply (13), 'Someone loves everyone'. (Return to our three-person universe consisting of Ardbeg, Bobo, and Coco. If Ardbeg is loved by Bobo, if Bobo is loved by Coco, and if Coco is loved by herself, then it's true that everyone is loved by someone, but it's false that someone loves everyone.)

Where *ordinary* grammar is concerned, the two pairs of sentences are indeed identical to one another. Where *logical* grammar is concerned, however, the two pairs are quite dissimilar. At this stage of the game, *logical* grammar is what you see when you translate a natural-language sentence into the logical notation of Predicate Logic/Quantification Theory.

Now here's what interesting. If 'everyone' and 'someone' were, or functioned like, proper names, then (13) and (14) would be equivalent to each other. But they aren't. Therefore 'everyone' and 'someone' simply aren't, and don't function as, proper names.

The same holds true of 'no one' as well—not to mention 'everything', 'something', and 'nothing'. Each of these is a quantifier expression, rather than a proper name. When Alice reports to the king, "I passed nobody on the road," the king's reply is telling: "Then nobody walks more slowly than you." His reply shows that this distinction—between a quantifier expression and a proper name—has completely eluded him: he treats a quantifier expression as though it were a proper name.

Moral of the story: don't be like the king! Don't mistake 'everyone' or 'someone' or 'no one' for a proper name. Logical grammar incorporates the insight that unlike 'Ardbeg' and 'Bobo'—which are, and which function as, proper names—'everyone', 'someone', and 'no one' aren't, and don't function as, proper names at all. Hence the necessity for variables and quantifiers (or for something comparable).

So how might you translate 'Everyone is loved by someone'? You begin your ascent into *Loglish*:

(15) $(\forall x)(Px \rightarrow$ there is at least one person who loves $x)$

By now, 'there is at least one person who loves $x$' should be a snap:

(16) $(\exists y)(Py \land Lyx)$

Now return to (15) and replace 'there is at least one person who loves $x$' with (16):

(17) $(\forall x)(Px \rightarrow (\exists y)(Py \land Lyx))$

Upgrade to square brackets those parentheses in need of upgrading, and you're done:

(18) $(\forall x)[Px \rightarrow (\exists y)(Py \land Lyx)]$

It's striking to compare the translation of our two pairs, (11), 'Ardbeg loves Bobo' and (12), 'Bobo is loved by Ardbeg', on the one hand, with (6), 'Someone loves everyone', and (18), 'Everyone is loved by someone', on the other:

| English Sentence | $L_2$ Translation |
|---|---|
| (11) 'Ardbeg loves Bobo.' | $Lab$ |
| (12) 'Bobo is loved by Ardbeg.' | $Lab$ |
| (6) 'Someone loves everyone.' | $(\exists x)[Px \wedge (\forall y)(Py \rightarrow Lxy)]$ |
| (18) 'Everyone is loved by someone.' | $(\forall x)[Px \rightarrow (\exists y)(Py \wedge Lyx)]$ |

Notice that the translations of (11) and (12) are identical. Given that they have the same meaning, this is unsurprising. Notice that the translations of (6) and (18) are radically different. Given that they have quite different meanings, this too is unsurprising. (6) is an existentially quantified conjunction whose right conjunct isn't a negation. As such, it's an I-proposition: it ascribes a complex property—the property of being a person and of loving everyone—to at least one object $x$. (18) is a universally quantified conditional whose consequent is un-negated. As such it's an A-proposition: it ascribes a complex property—the property of being loved by at least one person if one is a person—to every object. The different logical structures of (6) and (18) serve to reveal their different meanings.

It is also striking to compare the translation of (10), 'Everyone loves someone', and (18), 'Everyone is loved by someone':

(10) $(\forall x)[Px \rightarrow (\exists y)(Py \wedge Lxy)]$

(18) $(\forall x)[Px \rightarrow (\exists y)(Py \wedge Lyx)]$

The two sentences have *radically* different meanings, and yet the *only* difference between the two translations is the order of variables of the predicate '$L$'. Ah, what a difference the order of variables makes. . . .

Two last translations, each involving *three* quantifiers: consider first 'Everyone loves at least one person who loves everyone'. Note that in spite of its being rather complicated, it's a straightforward A-proposition. It ascribes to everyone (i.e., to every object that happens to be a person) the property of loving at least one person who loves everyone. As always, you start by knocking off the leftmost quantifier:

(19) $(\forall x)(Px \rightarrow x$ loves at least one person who loves everyone)

Moving from left to right, you knock off the next quantifier:

(20) $(\forall x)[Px \rightarrow (\exists y)(Py \wedge y$ loves everyone $\wedge Lxy)]$

Now it's just a matter of translating '$y$ loves everyone'; of replacing that clause in (20) with its translation; and of upgrading whatever parentheses and square brackets need to be upgraded:

(21) $(\forall x)\{Px \rightarrow (\exists y)[Py \wedge (\forall z)(Pz \rightarrow Lyz) \wedge Lxy]\}$

Done.

Finally, consider 'No one loves anyone who loves no one'. Note that although this is an E-proposition, you might find it easier to translate if you construct the negation of the corresponding I-proposition. First step: Off with the leftmost quantifier!

(22) $-(\exists x)(Px \wedge x$ loves someone who loves no one)

Second step: Off with the next leftmost quantifier!

(23) $-(\exists x)(Px \wedge (\exists y)(Py \wedge y$ loves no one $\wedge Lxy)$

Final step (completed by the customary upgrades to square brackets and curly braces, of course): Off with the sole surviving quantifier!

(24) $-(\exists x)\{Px \wedge (\exists y)[Py \wedge (\forall z)(Pz \rightarrow -Lyz) \wedge Lxy]\}$

# Exercises

Using the following interpretations, translate the sentences below into logical notation.

$Px$ = $x$ is a person
$Rx$ = $x$ is rude
$Bxy$ = $x$ belittles $y$
$Cxy$ = $x$ clobbers $y$
$a$ = Ardbeg
$b$ = Bobo

1. No one belittles either Ardbeg or Bobo.
2. No one belittles Ardbeg but not Bobo.
3. Bobo clobbers anyone who belittles Ardbeg.
4. Ardbeg doesn't belittle anyone.
5. Ardbeg doesn't belittle everyone.
6. There is at least one rude person who both belittles and clobbers Ardbeg.
7. Not everyone belittles either Ardbeg or Bobo.
8. No one who is rude belittles both Ardbeg and Bobo.
9. If everyone clobbers either Ardbeg or Bobo, then everyone is rude.
10. Anyone who clobbers either Ardbeg or Bobo is rude.
11. There is at least one rude person who belittles himself.
12. Everyone who is rude belittles someone.
13. Someone belittles everyone who is rude.
14. No one belittles anyone.
15. No one belittles everyone.
16. Someone is belittled by everyone.
17. No one is belittled by everyone.
18. No one is belittled by anyone.
19. Ardbeg clobbers anyone who belittles Bobo.
20. Someone belittles someone.
21. Someone clobbers everyone who is rude.

22. Anyone who fails to clobber both Ardbeg and Bobo fails to clobber himself.
23. Someone belittles everyone who belittles Ardbeg.
24. No one clobbers everyone who belittles Ardbeg.
25. No one clobbers anyone who belittles Ardbeg.
26. Ardbeg belittles anyone who belittles himself.
27. Anyone who belittles everyone belittles himself.
28. Anyone who belittles Bobo is clobbered by someone.
29. Anyone who belittles everyone is clobbered by someone.
30. There exists at least one person who clobbers everyone who belittles anyone.
31. No one belittles anyone who clobbers anyone.
32. Only rude people clobber Ardbeg. (This sentence is ambiguous, and therefore requires two non-equivalent translations. Produce the first of the two translations here.)
33. Only rude people clobber Ardbeg. (Produce the second translation here.)
34. Some rude people clobber people.
35. Some rude people clobber only people.

# 2. The Formal Language $L_2$

The issue of what does, and what doesn't, constitute a *wff* has been, as they say, the elephant in the living room (indeed, for some time now). Accordingly the formation rules of $L_2$ will serve as the theoretical underpinnings of your intuitions that a particular *wff* really is a *wff*, and that a particular non-*wff* really is a non-*wff*.

As was the case with $L_1$, the *formal language* of Propositional Logic, the *formal language*, $L_2$, of Predicate Logic/Quantification Theory consists of both a set of symbols and a set of formation rules. $L_2$ is itself an extension of—i.e., includes but extends beyond—$L_1$.

# A. The Symbols of $L_2$

1. Any of the lowercase letters '$a$' through '$t$', with a numerical subscript, is a *proper name*.

2. Any of the lowercase letters '$u$' through '$z$', with a numerical subscript, is a *variable*.

3. Any of the italicized uppercase letters '$A$' through '$Z$', with a numerical superscript followed by one or more asterisks, is a *predicate*.

4. Any of the non-italicized uppercase letters 'A' through 'Z', with a numerical subscript and no asterisks, is a *propositional symbol*.

5. '$\forall$' is the *universal quantifier*.

6. '$\exists$' is the *existential quantifier*.

7. '$-$' is the *dash*.

8. '$\wedge$' is the *caret*.

9. '$\vee$' is the *wedge*.

10. '$\rightarrow$' is the *arrow*.

11. '$\leftrightarrow$' is the *double-arrow*.

12. '(' and ')' are the *left parenthesis* and the *right parenthesis*, respectively.

13. '$\star$' is an *asterisk*.

14. '$^1$', '$^2$', '$^3$', ... are *numerical superscripts*.

15. '$_1$', '$_2$', '$_3$', ... are *numerical subscripts*.

Obviously, some of these clauses require a bit of elaboration. The reason for the reference to numerical subscripts in Clauses 1, 2, and 4 is to ensure that we don't run out of proper names, variables, or propositional symbols, respectively. The reason for the reference to asterisks in Clause 3 is to ensure that we don't run out of predicates. The reason for the reference to numerical superscripts in Clause 3 is to indicate the number of places that each predicate has. Thus the superscripts '$^1$', '$^2$', and '$^3$' indicate that the predicates in question are *one*-place, *two*-place, and *three*-place predicates, respectively. So if the predicate is the two-place predicate 'loves' (as in 'Ardbeg loves Bobo'), it will appear as, say, '$L^{2\star}a_1b_1$'.

A point to note with respect to Clause 4: There's a minor, i.e., a notationally trivial, difference between the propositional symbols of $L_2$ and those of $L_1$: those of $L_2$, unlike those of $L_1$, are italicized.

A qualification with respect to Clause 12: As is the case with $L_1$, and for reasons of convenience, we shall supplement the parentheses of the twelfth clause with square brackets and curly braces: '[', ']', '{', '}'.

## B. The Formation Rules of $L_2$

### a. The Definition of a Formula of $L_2$

**Definition:**     A *formula* of $L_2$ is any string of symbols of $L_2$.

So the following, for instance, is a formula of $L_2$:

$$\forall \exists xy(\wedge_1{}^2)$$

The reason why it's a formula of $L_2$ is simply that it's a string of symbols of $L_2$.

On the other hand, the following isn't a formula of $L_2$:

$$(\exists x)(Tx \ \& \ Cx)$$

The ampersand—'&'—isn't a symbol of $L_2$, even though it's a symbol in other formal languages that appear in other logic textbooks.

What you really want to be able to do, of course, is to distinguish *well-formed* from *ill-formed* formulas of $L_2$.

### b. The Definition of a Well-Formed Formula of $L_2$

1. Any propositional symbol is a *wff* and an atomic *wff*.
2. Any predicate with the numerical superscript '*n*', followed by *n* proper names, or *n* variables, or *n* proper names and

variables combined, is a *wff* and an atomic *wff*. (*n* is any number equal to or greater than 1.)

3.  '$(\forall v)\triangle$' is a *wff iff* '$\triangle$' is a *wff* containing at least one free occurrence of the variable '***v***'.

4.  '$(\exists v)\triangle$' is a *wff iff* '$\triangle$' is a *wff* containing at least one free occurrence of the variable '***v***'.

5.  If '$\triangle$' is a *wff* then '$-\triangle$' is a *wff*.

6.  If '$\triangle$' is a *wff* and if 'O' is a *wff*, then '$(\triangle \wedge O)$' is a *wff*.

7.  If '$\triangle$' is a *wff* and if 'O' is a *wff*, then '$(\triangle \vee O)$' is a *wff*.

8.  If '$\triangle$' is a *wff* and if 'O' is a *wff*, then '$(\triangle \rightarrow O)$' is a *wff*.

9.  If '$\triangle$' is a *wff* and if 'O' is a *wff*, then '$(\triangle \leftrightarrow O)$' is a *wff*.

10. Rule of Closure: Nothing is to count as a *wff* unless it has been obtained by one or more applications of Rules 1–9.

In Clauses 3 and 4, '***v***' appears in bold font because it's functioning as a meta-variable. A meta-variable, as you already know, is a proxy for any variable whatsoever. In this instance, '***v***' stands for any of the actual variables '*u*', '*v*' itself, '*w*', '*x*', '*y*', or '*z*'.

Clause 2 lets you know that '$B^{3*}a_1b_1c_1$', '$B^{3*}x_1y_2z_3$', and '$B^{3*}a_2x_4c_6$' are all *wffs*, and that neither '$T^{1*}a_2b_4$' nor '$L^{2*}a_5$' is a *wff*. (The superscript '*1*' in '$T^{1*}a_2b_4$' indicates that '$T$' is a *one*-place predicate. The superscript '*2*' in '$L^{2*}a_5$' indicates that '$L$' is a *two*-place predicate.)

The rules let you know that '$(\forall x_1)(T^{1*}x_1 \rightarrow C^{1*}x_1)$' is a *wff*. How so? By Clause 2, '$T^{1*}x_1$' is a *wff*, and also by Clause 2, '$C^{1*}x_1$' is a *wff*. So, by Clause 8, '$(T^{1*}x_1 \rightarrow C^{1*}x_1)$' is a *wff*. So, by Clause 3, '$(\forall x_1)(T^{1*}x_1 \rightarrow C^{1*}x_1)$' is a *wff*.

The rules also let you know that '$(\exists x_1)(T^{1*}x_1 \wedge C^{1*}y_2)$' is a *wff*. How so? By Clause 2, '$T^{1*}x_1$' is a *wff*, and also by Clause 2, '$C^{1*}y_2$' is a *wff*. So, by Clause 6, '$(T^{1*}x_1 \wedge C^{1*}y_2)$' is a *wff*. So, by Clause 4, '$(\exists x_1)(T^{1*}x_1 \wedge C^{1*}y_2)$' is a *wff*.

The rules let you know that '$(\exists x_1)(\forall y_2)L^{2*}x_1y_2$' is a *wff*. How so? By Clause 2, '$L^{2*}x_1y_2$' is a *wff*. So, by Clause 3, '$(\forall y_2)L^{2*}x_1y_2$' is a *wff*. So, by Clause 4, '$(\exists x_1)(\forall y_2)L^{2*}x_1y_2$' is a *wff*.

The rules let you know that '$(\exists x_1)(T^{1*}x_1 \wedge A_1)$' is a *wff*. How so? Note that '$A_1$' is a non–italicized uppercase letter that has a numerical *subscript*, as opposed to a numerical *superscript*, and that it has *no* asterisks. As such, it's not a predicate; it's a *propositional symbol*. By Clause 2, '$T^{1*}x_1$' is a *wff*. By Clause 1, '$A_1$' is a *wff*. So by Clause 6, '$(T^{1*}x_1 \wedge A_1)$' is a *wff*. And so, by Clause 4, '$(\exists x_1)(T^{1*}x_1 \wedge A_1)$' is a *wff*.

Incidentally, the rules let you know that '$(\exists y_3)T^{1*}x_2$' is *not a wff.* How so? By Clause 2, to be sure, '$T^{1*}x_2$' is a *wff.* By Clause 4, however, '$(\exists y_3)T^{1*}x_2$' would be a *wff* only if the variable to the right of the existential quantifier were identical to the variable to the right of '$T^{1*}$'.

Some other versions of Predicate Logic/Quantification Theory, i.e., alternative formal systems, recognize '$(\exists y_3)T^{1*}x_2$' as a *wff*—and, by the same token, they recognize '$(\exists y_3)(\exists y_3)T^{1*}x_2$' and '$(\exists z_1)(\exists y_3)(\exists y_3)T^{1*}x_2$' as *wffs.* When the variable immediately to the right of the quantifier isn't the same variable as *any* of the free variables in '$\triangle$', the quantifier is said to be a *vacuous,* i.e., an *empty,* quantifier. In other words, it performs no function; it's as though it weren't there. Semantically, there's no difference whatsoever, in these alternative formal systems, between '$(\exists y_3)T^{1*}x_2$' and '$T^{1*}x_2$'; between '$(\exists y_3)(\exists y_3)T^{1*}x_2$', $(\exists y_3)T^{1*}x_2$', and $T^{1*}x_2$'; and between $(\exists z_1)(\exists y_3)(\exists y_3)T^{1*}x_2$', '$(\exists y_3)(\exists y_3)T^{1*}x_2$', '$(\exists y_3)T^{1*}x_2$', and '$T^{1*}x_2$'.

In practice, we shall adopt a fairly relaxed stance toward $L_2$'s formation rules, just as we did toward $L_1$'s. In $L_2$, as in $L_1$, you may eliminate outermost parentheses. In addition, and under normal circumstances, it won't be necessary to use either numerical subscripts or asterisks, and we may dispense with them accordingly. (It's rather unlikely that *in practice,* as opposed to *in theory,* we're in any real danger of running out of either proper names or variables or predicates or propositional symbols, in the absence of numerical subscripts and asterisks.) Numerical superscripts, on the other hand, are another matter: they serve as a salutary reminder that the predicate with which you're operating is *really* an *n*-place predicate. But in the interest of eliminating notational clutter—the elimination of *any* sort of clutter being a *most* noble goal—I'm happy to defer to convention and forgo the numerical superscript requirement.

# 3. Identity

The identity relation plays a key role both in logic and in mathematics. As logicians and mathematicians use the notion of identity, to say that *x* is identical to *y* is to say that *x* and *y* are *literally* one and the same object. Ardbeg's Lamborghini may be very similar to Bobo's Lamborghini, but it isn't *identical* to it. Why not? Because however similar the two Lamborghinis may be, there are still *two* of them: Ardbeg's and Bobo's. The notion of identity that logicians and mathematicians use is the notion of *numerical* identity: to say that $x$ is identical to $y$ is to say that $x$ is $y$.

Close your book; close your eyes; and try to come up with an instance of an $x$ and an instance of a $y$ such that the sentence '$x$ is identical to $y$' is a true sentence. . . .

Lewis Carroll is identical to Charles Dodgson. Mark Twain is identical to Samuel Clemens. Superman is identical to Clark Kent. Lenin is Ulyanov. Trotsky is Bronstein. Stalin is Djugashvili. In each of these cases, there aren't *two* individuals: there is exactly *one* with two names.

We express the identity relation by means of the identity, or equality, sign. The translation of '$x$ is identical to $y$' is '$x = y$'. In grade school you read '$4 + 9 = 13$' as 'Four plus nine *equals* thirteen'—but you could just as well have read it as 'The number that is the sum of four and nine *is identical to* the number thirteen'.

There is a great temptation to treat the identity sign as a truth-functional connective, on a par with the dash, the arrow, etc. This is a temptation that one must resist with *all* of one's might. The identity sign is nothing other than—i.e., it is itself *identical to*—a two-place predicate. Perhaps you would find it easier to resist the temptation by expressing '$x$ is identical to $y$' as '$Ixy$'. If so, by all means do so. (It may be *eccentric* to do so, but you should never sacrifice clarity merely to avoid eccentricity.)

There are several ways to express the *denial* of the identity of two objects. For example, it is permissible to express the denial that Bobo is Coco in any of the following ways:

(1) $b \neq c$
(2) $-(b = c)$
(3) $-b = c$
(4) $-Ibc$

Each has its advantages. (1) shows that the notion of identity that is at stake here is the mathematician's. (2) lets you express the notion of identity without introducing a new negation symbol, e.g., the diagonal intersecting the identity sign in (1). (3) is slightly less cluttered with notation than (2). (4) emphasizes, and thus reminds you, that the identity symbol isn't a connective: it's nothing more than a two-place predicate.

You might think that (3) is ambiguous; you might think that the advantage of (2) over (3) is that (3) suggests that the scope of the dash is '*b*', whereas (2) is explicit that the scope of the dash is the identity as a whole, '(*b* = *c*)'. But the scope of the dash in (3) can't *possibly* be '*b*'. '*b*' is a *proper name*; it isn't a *wff*—and the dash, like any connective, operates *only* on *wffs*. Therefore there's nothing ambiguous about (3).

The identity sign is invaluable. Thanks to it, you can now translate 'except' phrases (e.g., 'Everyone *except* Dagbar shrieked'), numerical adjectives (e.g., 'Ardbeg slew *exactly two* dragons'), and definite descriptions (e.g., '*The* dog that bit Bobo bit Coco').

## A. 'Except' Phrases

One use of the identity sign is to let you translate 'except' phrases—as in 'Everybody *except* Ardbeg' or 'Everybody *other than* Ardbeg' or 'Everybody *but* Ardbeg'. Suppose that a day arrives when Bobo denounces the Platonist trekkers:

(1) "Bah! Every trekker except Ardbeg is a Platonist!"

Consider the following interpretation:

$Px$ = *x* is a Platonist
$Tx$ = *x* is a trekker
$a$ = *Ardbeg*

In order to translate (1) (without 'Bah!', of course) it helps, as always, to ascend into *Loglish*:

(2) $(\forall x)[(Tx \land x$ isn't Ardbeg$) \rightarrow Px]$

It should be clear how to translate '*x* isn't Ardbeg': '$x \neq a$'. Replace '*x* isn't Ardbeg' in (2) with '$x \neq a$', and you're done:

(3) $(\forall x)[(Tx \land x \neq a) \rightarrow Px]$

Question: Are you *really* done? Don't you need to indicate that Ardbeg *isn't* a Platonist? Isn't his *not* being a Platonist implicit in the English-language original? And if so, don't you then have to create (4)—a conjunction of (3) with '−*Pa*'?

$$(4)\ (\forall x)[(Tx \wedge x \neq a) \rightarrow Px] \wedge -Pa$$

Answer: Logicians typically accept (3), and reject (4), as the correct translation of (1). It would be *odd*, and no doubt *misleading*, for Bobo to make the statement, "Every trekker except Ardbeg is a Platonist", if Ardbeg himself were a Platonist. On the other hand, you could well imagine Bobo's making the statement and then adding *sotto voce*, "Ardbeg is *very* secretive; he plays his metaphysical cards close to his vest; he won't say whether or not he's a Platonist; and frankly, I myself have no idea whether or not he is."

Now suppose that the sentence 'Every trekker except Ardbeg is a Platonist' logically *implied* the sentence 'Ardbeg is *not* a Platonist'. In that case, Bobo would be guilty of uttering a sentence that logically implies that Ardbeg is *not* a Platonist at the same time that she is professing ignorance of whether Ardbeg *is* a Platonist. Accordingly, Bobo would be deeply confused. But why think that Bobo is *that* confused? She has a perfect grasp of the meaning and of the implications of the sentence that she is uttering—and, in particular, of its *minimalist sense*. It is in this minimalist sense that (3) is the correct translation of (1). (Hearken back to our discussion of the minimalist sense of 'some' at the end of Section 5 in Chapter 5: 'Some apples are rotten' doesn't imply 'Some apples *aren't* rotten'. 'Some of the students received As' doesn't imply 'Some of the students *didn't* receive As'. As with 'some', so with 'except'. By the same minimalist token, in other words, 'Every trekker except Ardbeg is a Platonist' doesn't imply 'Ardbeg *isn't* a Platonist'. Minimalism here. Minimalism there. Minimalism *everywhere*.

The logician's focus isn't on what the (typically unwritten) conversational rules within a given community allow you to *infer* when someone utters a particular sentence. (These rules may well allow you to infer from Bobo's uttering, "Every trekker except Ardbeg is a Platonist," that Ardbeg isn't a Platonist.) And the logician's focus isn't on whatever happens to be in the bubble over the head of whoever utters the sentence. (In saying what she says, Bobo might well have in mind that Ardbeg isn't a Platonist.) On the contrary, the logician's focus is simply on the bare-bones *meaning* of a sentence—rather than on what a given speaker *means*, i.e., *intends*, by the sentence.

A word of caution. You might be tempted to translate 'Every trekker except Ardbeg is a Platonist' as follows:

(5) $(\forall x)[Tx \rightarrow (Px \wedge x \neq a)]$

Resist the temptation. (5) asserts the following: 'Given any object $x$, if $x$ is a trekker then $x$ is a Platonist and $x$ isn't Ardbeg'. Whence it follows that if Ardbeg is a trekker then Ardbeg isn't Ardbeg. Whence it follows that Ardbeg isn't a trekker. (1), on the other hand, implies no such nonsense. Therefore (5) fails to represent (1).

One more temptation: You might find it irresistible to translate 'Every trekker except Ardbeg is a Platonist' as '$(\forall x)[(Tx \wedge -Px) \rightarrow x = a]$'. By all means succumb to *this* temptation: this *wff* is logically equivalent to (1). (Hint: '$(P \wedge -Q) \rightarrow R$' is logically equivalent to '$(P \wedge -R) \rightarrow Q$'.)

# Exercises

Using the following interpretations, translate the sentences below into logical notation.

$Ax = x$ is an actor
$Bx = x$ is a ballerina
$Cx = x$ is a cabaret singer
$Fx = x$ is famous
$Ux = x$ is unemployed
$Rxy = x$ reveres $y$
$x = y = x$ is (or is identical to) $y$
$m = $ Monty
$n = $ Nicole
$o = $ Oedipus

1. Every actor except Monty is unemployed.
2. No ballerina other than Nicole is famous.
3. Every famous cabaret singer except Oedipus is unemployed.
4. No actors other than both Monty and Oedipus are famous.
5. Every unemployed ballerina except Nicole is famous.
6. At least one cabaret singer reveres every actor except Monty.
7. Every ballerina except Nicole reveres every actor except Oedipus.
8. At least one actor doesn't revere any ballerina other than Nicole.
9. At least one unemployed ballerina—and it's not Nicole—reveres both every actor and every cabaret singer.
10. No famous actor other than either Monty or Oedipus reveres every cabaret singer except Nicole.

## B. Numerical Adjectives

You know how to translate into logical notation the sentence that there exists *at least* one tyrant. How would you translate the following sentence?

(1) 'There exists *exactly* one tyrant'.

The first thing to notice is that this is an I-proposition: it's particular/existential and it's affirmative. So you know that however tricky the translation, ultimately it will be an existentially quantified conjunction.

Question: Under what circumstances would each of the following propositions be true?

(2) 'Bobo is a tyrant'.
(3) 'Coco is a tyrant'.
(4) 'There exists *exactly* one tyrant'.

Answer: Each of the three would be true *iff* Bobo *were* Coco; i.e., *iff* Bobo and Coco were numerically one and the same.

Think of Lewis Carroll and Charles Dodgson. Lewis Carroll wrote *Alice in Wonderland*. Charles Dodgson wrote *Alice in Wonderland*. There is exactly one person who wrote *Alice in Wonderland*. Question: How is this possible? Answer: It's possible if and only if Lewis Carroll *is*—or *is identical to*—Charles Dodgson. Or think of Superman and Clark Kent. Superman flies. Clark Kent flies. There is exactly one natural being who looks like a human being and who flies. Question: How is this possible? Answer: It's possible if and only if Superman *is*—or *is identical to*—Clark Kent.

So, to express in logical notation the sentence 'There exists exactly one tyrant', here's what you do. First you state that there exists *at least* one tyrant *x*. Then you state that if *any* object *y* happens to be a tyrant, then (as with Bobo and Coco, as with Lewis Carroll and Charles Dodgson, and as with Superman and Clark Kent) that object *y* simply *is x*, i.e., *they are numerically one and the same*:

(5) $(\exists x)[Tx \wedge (\forall y)(Ty \rightarrow y = x)]$

Expressing in logical notation that there is exactly one jolly tyrant who loves Bobo involves only *minor* tinkering with (5):

(6) $(\exists x)\{(Tx \wedge Jx \wedge Lxb) \wedge (\forall y)[(Ty \wedge Jy \wedge Lyb) \rightarrow y = x]\}$

On the other hand, expressing in logical notation that there exist exactly *two* tyrants involves *major* tinkering with (5). Always ascend step by step, quantifier by quantifier, into *Loglish*. First you have to say that there exist *at least* two tyrants, and so perhaps this is your first shot:

(7) $(\exists x)Tx \wedge (\exists y)Ty$

Try to think of what's wrong with (7). How does it *fail* to say that there exist at least two tyrants?

(7) says, 'There exists at least one tyrant and there exists at least one tyrant'. If you utter (7), you are simply *repeating* yourself. How, then, do you transform (7) into 'There exist at least two tyrants'? You need to express the thought that there exists at least one tyrant, *x*, and there exists at least one tyrant, *y*, and *y* is *not x*:

(8) $(\exists x)[Tx \wedge (\exists y)(Ty \wedge y \neq x)]$

Pay close attention to the parentheses and square brackets. Without the square brackets, the rightmost occurrence of *x* will be free; i.e., it won't be bound by the existential quantifier '(∃*x*)'.

Having written that there are *at least* two tyrants, you now need to set an upper bound: you need to write that there are *at most* two. It's time to call on Ardbeg, Bobo, and Coco for assistance.

Question: Under what circumstances would each of the following propositions be true?

1. 'There exist exactly two tyrants'.
2. 'Ardbeg is a tyrant'.
3. 'Bobo is a tyrant'.
4. 'Ardbeg isn't Bobo'.
5. 'Coco is a tyrant'.

Answer: Each of the five would be true *iff* either Coco were Ardbeg or Coco were Bobo. You are now ready to complete your translation of 'There exist exactly two tyrants':

$$(9)\ (\exists x)(Tx \wedge (\exists y)\{(Ty \wedge y \neq x) \wedge (\forall z)[Tz \to (z = x \vee z = y)]\})$$

Now I ask you: Is this *not* a work of art? Pause for a moment to reflect on this: you are able to define, using *only* the language of Predicate Logic/Quantification Theory, 'There exists exactly *one* object having such-and-such a property', 'There exist exactly *two* objects having such-and-such a property', etc. Numbers, at least when expressed as *adjectives*—'*one* tyrant', '*two* tyrants', etc.—are *fully* definable in $L_2$. On the other hand, numbers, when expressed as *nouns*—'the number 1', 'the number 2', etc.—are *not* so definable, as you will learn in one of your next logic courses. To define the natural numbers (0, 1, 2, etc.) you need to quantify not only over individual objects but also over *sets* of individual objects—and this, as it turns out, involves a different branch of logic altogether.

# Exercises

Using the following interpretations, translate the sentences below into logical notation.

$Kx$ = $x$ is a kangaroo
$Ox$ = $x$ is orange
$Px$ = $x$ is a person
$Sxy$ = $x$ sings to $y$
  $x = y$ = $x$ is (or is identical to) $y$
  $o$ = Oedipus

1. There exists exactly one orange kangaroo that sings to Oedipus.
2. There exists exactly one orange kangaroo that sings to someone.
3. Oedipus sings to exactly one orange kangaroo.
4. Someone sings to exactly one orange kangaroo.
5. There exist at least two orange kangaroos.
6. There exist exactly two orange kangaroos.
7. There exist exactly two kangaroos and Oedipus sings to them.
8. There exists exactly two kangaroos and someone sings to them.
9. There exist at least three kangaroos.
10. There exist exactly three kangaroos.

## C. Definite Descriptions

Bertrand Russell (British, 1872–1970) published a landmark paper, "On Denoting," in 1905. In the paper he invites us to consider a sentence like 'The present king of France is bald'. (At the time that Russell wrote his paper, there was no longer a king of France.) The sentence certainly appears to be meaningful; i.e., we seem to understand it. Therefore, like any genuine sentence it must be either true or false. However, it would seem odd to view it as *true*. After all, if you were to rattle off a list of all the things in the universe that are bald, you wouldn't find any reference to the present king of France on the list. Surely, therefore, the sentence must be *false*. In that case, however, the sentence 'The present king of France is *not* bald' must be *true*. But that too seems odd: if you were to rattle off a list of all the things in the universe that are *not* bald, you wouldn't find any reference to the present king of France on *this* list either. We seem to be caught in a pickle.

Matters go from bad to worse. Alexius Meinong (Austrian, 1853–1920) had contended that an expression like 'the golden mountain' is obviously meaningful, and therefore must denote *something*. It's quite clear, however, that it doesn't denote anything that exists in the sort of way that ordinary things exist. Therefore, he concluded, such an expression must denote something that exists in a *non-ordinary* sort of way. Therefore there must be two modes of existence, two realms of reality: ours, on the one hand, and on the other hand, another realm that contains such inhabitants as the golden mountain, Russell's present king of France, Santa Claus, and of course the tooth fairy.

Russell deemed such a theory of reality—such an *ontology*—a bit extravagant. The root of the problem, so he insisted, is that the expression 'the present king of France' appears both to be, and to function as, a *proper name*. Now to be sure, he thought, a *genuine* proper name does name (or denote) a particular object. Indeed one might plausibly hold that the *meaning* of a proper name consists *entirely* in the thing, the particular object, that it names (or denotes). From Russell's vantage point, there were three possibilities:

1. Meinong got it completely right: the expression 'the present king of France' is indeed a proper name, and therefore denotes a particular object that exists in a non-ordinary sort of way.
2. Meinong got it half right and half wrong: by the rules of *ordinary* grammar, the expression 'the present king of France' is indeed a proper name. However, because there is no particular object that the expression denotes, it isn't behaving as a proper name is supposed to behave. Therefore any sentence containing such an expression—and in particular, the sentence 'The present king of France is bald'—must be meaningless.

3. Meinong got it completely wrong: by the rules of *logical* grammar (as distinct from *ordinary* grammar) the expression 'the present king of France' simply is *not* a proper name. Therefore there is no reason to suppose that there must exist some object that it names (or denotes). Furthermore, once one subjects the sentence to logical analysis and thereby dissects it, it will become clear that although the sentence purports to be *about* the present king of France, in fact it is *about* no such thing whatsoever. As it turns out, the expression 'the present king of France' is meaningful *not* on its own, but *only* in the context of the sentence in which it appears.

Russell rejected both the first and second possibilities: the first because of its ontological extravagance, and the second because of the counterintuitiveness of the thought that the sentence 'The present king of France is bald' is meaningless. He thereby rejected the views that the expression 'the present king of France' is a proper name, that it is meaningful on its own, and that therefore it must denote a particular object. Instead, and with considerable enthusiasm, he embraced the third possibility.

Enter his theory of definite descriptions. For Russell an expression that zeroes in on exactly one individual, like 'the present king of France', is a 'definite description'. But of course the definite description 'the present king of France' does *not* name (or denote) a particular individual—not in 1905, not today, and not even in 1789 (when Louis XVI was still the king of France). Although the expression has the status of a proper name *from the standpoint of ordinary grammar*, it doesn't have the status of a proper name *from the standpoint of logical grammar*. So just how did Russell conceive of *logical* grammar?

First consider the sentence as a whole:

(1) 'The present king of France is bald.'

Russell noted that in this sentence, the word 'the' implies that there exists exactly *one* object that falls under the *indefinite* description '*a* present king of France'. Now consider the following interpretations:

$Bx = x$ is bald
$Kx = x$ is a present king of France
$x = y = x$ is (or is identical to) $y$

By now, of course, you know how to translate 'There exists exactly one present king of France':

$$(2)\ (\exists x)[Kx \wedge (\forall y)(Ky \rightarrow y = x)]$$

To complete the translation, you need only indicate that the unique object that is the present king of France has the property of being bald:

$$(3)\ (\exists x)\{[Kx \wedge (\forall y)(Ky \rightarrow y = x)] \wedge Bx\}$$

Thus (3) is what emerges once you subject (1), 'The present king of France is bald', to the correct logical analysis. It is (3) that reveals the *logical* grammar implicit in (1).

We may now summarize Russell's position. First, the definite description 'the present king of France' *appears* to denote a specific object, just as the proper name 'Ardbeg' appears to denote Ardbeg. Second, a proper name really *does* denote a specific object, but a definite description really *doesn't*. And third, a definite description has no meaning on its own, unlike a proper name, and instead acquires its meaningfulness only in the context of a sentence, e.g., 'The present king of France is bald'. Fourth, ordinary language generates sentences, like (1), that are ontologically misleading, suggesting the existence, in some non-ordinary sort of way, of objects that don't exist in the ordinary sort of way. Fifth, the logician's task is to subject the sentences of ordinary language, of which (1) is a stellar example, to logical analysis, displaying their underlying *logical* structure. Sixth, the light at the end of the logical-analysis tunnel is the generation of a *logically perfect language*, i.e., one free of the ontologically misleading defects of ordinary language.

Indeed, (3), which, in Russell's view constitutes the correct logical analysis of (1), 'The present king of France is bald', discloses two noteworthy features about (1). First, although meaningful, the sentence is not *about* the present king of France—appearances to the contrary. Thus compare (3), Russell's analysis of (1), with the following translation of 'Ardbeg is bald':

$$(4)\ Ba$$

Now (4) is obviously *about* Ardbeg, but—and this is the *first* noteworthy feature of (3)—(3) is not *about* the present king of France.

From the standpoints of *both* ordinary grammar *and* logical grammar, Ardbeg is the subject of (4), and indeed (4) ascribes to Ardbeg the property of being bald. In contrast, the present king of France may well be the *grammatical* subject of (1), but—as (3) reveals—the present king of France is not the *logical* subject of (1). (How could it be? Unlike (4), (3) isn't a subject-predicate sentence.) Consequently, (3) doesn't ascribe to a particular subject, e.g., the present king of France, the property of being bald. (4) contains a symbol that denotes Ardbeg, namely, the proper name '*a*'. But there is nothing, no symbol, in (3) that denotes any such mysterious object as 'the present king of France'. Instead, (3) is an existentially quantified sentence, and as such, it employs variables and quantifiers to affirm the existence of exactly one object with (in this case) the following three properties: the property of being *a* present king of France, the property of being the *only* present king of France, and the property of being *bald*.

And this brings us to the *second* noteworthy feature of (3). Because there is *no* such object, i.e., no object that happens to have all *three* of these properties, and because (3) affirms the existence of exactly *one* such object, (3) is simply *false*. In Russell's view, *any* sentence is false that contains a definite description, in the event that there is no object that answers to the description. So, for example, the following sentences will all be false: 'The greatest positive integer is greater than the number 13'; 'The unicorn that ate Ardbeg's chili peppers sleeps in Bobo's garden'; and 'The logic student who has memorized Russell's *Principia Mathematica* has a very fine memory indeed'.

Question: If 'The present king of France is bald' is *false*, does it follow that 'The present king of France is *not* bald' is *true*?

Answer: No—as the following translation thereof reveals:

$$(5)\ (\exists x)\{[Kx \wedge (\forall y)(Ky \rightarrow y = x)] \wedge -Bx\}$$

This latter sentence affirms the existence of exactly one object with the following three properties: the property of being *a* present king of France, the property of being the *only* present king of France, and the property of *not* being bald. Since there is no such object that has all three properties, the affirmation is false.

Question: How can *both* sentences—'The present king of France is bald' and 'The present king of France is not bald' *both* be false? Aren't they semantic contradictories of one another?

Answer: Russell's analysis of each sentence shows that they *aren't* semantic contradictories of one another. The semantic contradictory of (3) isn't (5); it's (3) preceded by a dash—which also happens to be the *syntactic* contradictory of (3):

$$(6) \; -(\exists x)\{[Kx \land (\forall y)(Ky \to y = x)] \land Bx\}$$

And (6) is actually a *true* sentence: 'There doesn't exist a single object with the following three properties: the property of being *a* present king of France, the property of being the *only* present king of France, and the property of being *bald*'.

# Exercises

I. The sentences below contain no punctuation errors. Translate them into logical notation, using the following interpretations:

$Dx$ = $x$ is a dragon
$Hx$ = $x$ is a hero
$Px$ = $x$ is a Platonist
$Sxy$ = $x$ slew $y$
  $x = y$ = $x$ is (or is identical to) $y$
  $a$ = Ardbeg
  $b$ = Bobo

1. Ardbeg slew the dragon.
2. The dragon slew Ardbeg.
3. Either Ardbeg slew the dragon or the dragon slew Ardbeg.
4. The hero slew at least one dragon.
5. Ardbeg is a Platonist, and every Platonist other than Ardbeg is a hero.
6. Ardbeg and Bobo are both Platonists, and no Platonists other than Ardbeg and Bobo are heroes.
7. Ardbeg is a Platonist, and every Platonist except Ardbeg slew at least one dragon.

8. Ardbeg is a Platonist and a hero, and every Platonist who's a hero, other than Ardbeg, slew exactly one dragon.
9. The hero slew the dragon.
10. The Platonist who's a hero didn't slay the dragon.
11. The hero who slew the dragon is a Platonist.
12. The hero, who slew the dragon, is a Platonist.
13. Ardbeg slew at least two dragons.
14. Ardbeg slew exactly two dragons.
15. Every Platonist except Bobo slew exactly two Platonist dragons.

II. Using the following interpretations, translate the sentences below into logical notation:

$Ex$ = x is even
$Nx$ = x is a natural number
$Ox$ = x is odd
$Px$ = x is a prime number
$Dxy$ = x is divisible by y
$Gxy$ = x is greater than y
$Lxy$ = x is less than y
$x = y$ = x is (or is identical to) y
$Bxyz$ = x is between y and z
$a$ = the number 0
$b$ = the number 1
$c$ = the number 2
$d$ = the number 3

   (The natural numbers are the numbers 0, 1, 2, 3, etc. A prime number is a natural number divisible only by the number 1 and itself, e.g., the numbers 2, 3, 5, 7, 11, etc.)

1. There is at least one natural number between 1 and 3.
2. There is exactly one natural number between 1 and 3.
3. There is at most one natural number between 1 and 3.
4. Every natural number except 0 is either odd or even, and 0 is neither odd nor even.
5. Not every natural number is greater than some natural number.

6.  There exist at least two natural numbers between 0 and 3.
7.  Any natural number between 0 and 2 is greater than 0 but less than 2.
8.  No natural number greater than 0 but less than 2 is even.
9.  There exist exactly two natural numbers between 0 and 3.
10. Every odd natural number other than 1 is greater than 2.
11. There doesn't exist a natural number less than 0.
12. There doesn't exist a natural number that is greater than all natural numbers.
13. There doesn't exist a natural number than which 0 is greater.
14. If every even natural number is divisible by 2, then there exists at least one even natural number by which every even natural number is divisible.
15. No odd natural numbers are divisible by any even natural numbers, but some even natural numbers are divisible by some odd natural numbers.
16. Given any two distinct prime numbers other than 2 and 3, there exists at least one natural number between them.
17. No natural number is less than itself or greater than itself, but every natural number is identical to itself.
18. Given any two distinct odd natural numbers, there exists at least one even natural number between them.
19. Not every natural number is greater than some natural number (or other), but every natural number is less than some natural number (or other).
20. No odd natural number is divisible by any natural number that is greater than 1 but less than 3.
21. There is only one prime number that is even.
22. Only natural numbers are prime numbers.
23. No prime number except 2 is divisible by an even number.
24. Every prime number is divisible by exactly one natural number between 0 and 3.
25. No prime number other than 2 is divisible by an even number.

# 4. The Square of Opposition Revisited

Question: What does the present king of France tell us about the Square of Opposition? Or rather (since the present king of France doesn't exist and therefore can't tell us anything), what do the *sentences* 'The present king of France is bald' and 'The present king of France is not bald' tell us about the Square of Opposition?

It's clear that 'The present king of France is bald' and 'The present king of France is not bald' aren't *semantic contradictories.* Semantic contradictories can't both be true and they can't both be false. However, because there's no present king of France, each of these two sentences, as you saw in Section 3, is false.

Perhaps, then, they are *subcontraries.* Isn't 'The present king of France is bald' an existentially quantified conjunction whose right conjunct isn't a negation—and isn't it therefore an I-proposition? And isn't 'The present king of France is not bald' an existentially quantified conjunction whose right conjunct is a negation—and isn't it therefore an O-proposition? So they both *seem* to be subcontraries. But they *can't* be subcontraries: they're both *false*—and one of the morals of the Square of Opposition story is that subcontraries can't both be false.

So here's where matters stand. Yes, 'The present king of France is bald' is an I-proposition. And yes again, 'The present king of France is not bald' is its corresponding O-proposition. And yes yet again, one of the morals of the Square of Opposition story is that subcontraries can't both be false. It follows, therefore, that the logical relationship of subcontrariety collapses in the event that the object, $x$, whose existence both the I- and the O-propositions affirm, doesn't actually exist.

From this point on, matters go from *bad* to *bizarre.* . . . Consider another case where there doesn't exist any object, $x$, that has the property that both the I- and the O-propositions ascribe to the object:

A: All unicorns are vicious.          E: No unicorns are vicious.
   $(\forall x)(Ux \rightarrow Vx)$              $(\forall x)(Ux \rightarrow -Vx)$

I: Some unicorns are vicious.          O: Some unicorns are not vicious.
   $(\exists x)(Ux \wedge Vx)$              $(\exists x)(Ux \wedge -Vx)$

Both the I- and the O-propositions ascribe the property of being a unicorn to at least one object, $x$; i.e., they both affirm the existence of at least one unicorn. Unicorns don't exist, of course, and so the property of being a unicorn isn't ascribable to *any* existent object $x$. Therefore both the I- and the O-propositions are false. So much for the logical relationship of subcontrariety.

Because the I- and the O-propositions are both false, their corresponding contradictories, the E- and the A-propositions, respectively, must both be true. In short, because unicorns don't exist, it must be true both that *all* unicorns are vicious and that *no* unicorns are vicious. So much for the logical relationship of contrariety.

Because, in this instance, the A-proposition is true and the I-proposition is false, the A-proposition doesn't imply the I-proposition. And because, in this instance, the E-proposition is true and the O-proposition is false, the E-proposition doesn't imply the O-proposition. So much for the logical relationship of downward implication.

Thus it so happens that if there doesn't exist at least one object that has the property that both the I- and the O-propositions ascribe to that object, then every logical relationship that constitutes the Square of Opposition goes belly-up—with *one* exception. The one exception is the logical relationship of contradiction. Another way of putting this is that we may be willing, *in extremis*, to sacrifice the logical relationships of contrariety, downward implication, and subcontrariety, but we are *never* willing to sacrifice the logical relationship of contradiction.

What would it mean, validity-wise, to sacrifice the logical relationship of contrariety? It would mean that because unicorns don't exist, the following arguments would be *valid*:

| | |
|---|---|
| All unicorns are vicious. | $(\forall x)(Ux \to Vx)$ |
| Unicorns don't exist. | $-(\exists x)(Ux)$ |
| ∴ No unicorns are vicious. | ∴ $(\forall x)(Ux \to -Vx)$ |

| | |
|---|---|
| No unicorns are vicious. | $(\forall x)(Ux \to -Vx)$ |
| Unicorns don't exist. | $-(\exists x)(Ux)$ |
| ∴ All unicorns are vicious. | ∴ $(\forall x)(Ux \to Vx)$ |

And what would it mean, validity-wise, to sacrifice the logical relationship of downward implication? It would mean that because unicorns don't exist, the following arguments would be *invalid*:

| | |
|---|---|
| All unicorns are vicious. | $(\forall x)(Ux \to Vx)$ |
| Unicorns don't exist. | $-(\exists x)(Ux)$ |
| ∴ Some unicorns are vicious. | ∴ $(\exists x)(Ux \wedge Vx)$ |

| | |
|---|---|
| No unicorns are vicious. | $(\forall x)(Ux \to -Vx)$ |
| Unicorns don't exist. | $-(\exists x)(Ux)$ |
| ∴ Some unicorns are not vicious. | ∴ $(\exists x)(Ux \wedge -Vx)$ |

And lastly, what would it mean, validity-wise, to sacrifice the logical relationship of subcontrariety? It would mean that because unicorns don't exist, the following arguments would be *valid*:

| | |
|---|---|
| Some unicorns are vicious. | $(\exists x)(Ux \wedge Vx)$ |
| Unicorns don't exist. | $-(\exists x)(Ux)$ |
| ∴ Some unicorns are not vicious. | ∴ $(\exists x)(Ux \wedge -Vx)$ |

| | |
|---|---|
| Some unicorns are not vicious. | $(\exists x)(Ux \wedge -Vx)$ |
| Unicorns don't exist. | $-(\exists x)(Ux)$ |
| ∴ Some unicorns are vicious. | ∴ $(\exists x)(Ux \wedge Vx)$ |

If we replaced the assumption that unicorns don't exist with the assumption that at least one unicorn does exist, i.e., '$(\exists x)Ux$', then the first two arguments would be *invalid*, the second two would be *valid*, and the third two would be *invalid*—which is exactly what we want.

Where the logical relationship of contradiction is concerned, matters are quite different. We are unwilling to concede that there are *any* circumstances under which 'All unicorns are vicious' and 'Some unicorns are not vicious' might both be true or might both be false. Equally, we are unwilling to concede that there are *any* circumstances under which 'No unicorns are vicious' and 'Some unicorns are vicious' might both be true or might both be false. The existence or non-existence of unicorns is simply irrelevant to the question whether the A- and the O-propositions, on the one hand, and the E- and the I-propositions, on the other hand, are contradictories (and behave as contradictories are supposed to behave). The following arguments, in other words, are valid unconditionally, i.e., *no matter what,* i.e., whether or not unicorns exist:

| | |
|---|---|
| All unicorns are vicious. | $(\forall x)(Ux \rightarrow Vx)$ |
| $\therefore$ It's not the case that some unicorns aren't vicious. | $\therefore -(\exists x)(Ux \wedge -Vx)$ |

| | |
|---|---|
| No unicorns are vicious. | $(\forall x)(Ux \rightarrow -Vx)$ |
| $\therefore$ It's not the case that some unicorns are vicious. | $\therefore -(\exists x)(Ux \wedge Vx)$ |

It must, and it should, strike you as a bit odd that the existence of various *logical* relationships (contrariety, downward implication, and subcontrariety), as well as the validity or invalidity of various arguments, hinges on the *empirical* question whether an object exists that has a particular property (in this instance, the property of being a unicorn). Validity, we emphasized in Chapter 1, is a purely *formal* notion, entirely independent of the content or meaning of the propositions that constitute the argument in question. And yet now it turns out that in Predicate Logic/Quantification Theory, the existence of various Square of Opposition relationships, as well as the validity or invalidity of various arguments, is dependent on the way the world is, i.e., on the existence or non-existence of an object of a particular sort.

One final point. If *nothing at all* were to exist—and I do mean literally *nothing*—then we'd find ourselves in the very same pickle. In particular, various Square of Opposition relationships that should hold wouldn't hold; arguments that should be valid would be invalid; and arguments that should be invalid would be valid.

But the pickle is avoidable: we simply make an implicit assumption in the case of each argument in Predicate Logic/Quantification Theory that at least one object exists, i.e., '$(\exists x)x = x$'.

# 5. Restricted Domains and the (In)dispensability of Quantifiers

Consider the set of objects to which we apply our quantifiers, i.e., the set of objects over which our variables range, i.e., the set of objects on which we're focusing. We refer to this set as our *domain* or our *universe of discourse* or (for short) our *universe*. Normally, there's no restriction on the sorts of objects that might show up in our domain—eels and worms, rats and snakes, minds and mental states, brains and brain states, rational numbers and irrational numbers, Bolsheviks and Mensheviks, points and lines, and so on and so forth. When there's no such restriction, we say that we're operating with an *unrestricted* domain or universe.

Sometimes, however, and sometimes for purely pedagogical reasons, it's convenient to zero in on a particular *kind* of thing—the set of *eels*, say, or the set of *rats*, etc. Under such circumstances, we speak of a *restricted* domain or a *restricted* universe. Under such circumstances, instead of having our variables range over the *domain* or *universe* or *set* of *all* objects (whatever that might mean), we focus instead on one particular set of objects and have our variables range over *it*. In this book, unless I specify otherwise, our domain will be *unrestricted*.

I am now specifying otherwise. Consider a domain restricted to *people*. Accordingly, you would read '$(\forall x)$' and '$(\exists x)$', respectively, as 'Given any *person*, $x$,' and 'There exists at least one *person*, $x$, who is such that'. Suppose that you interpret '$Sx$' to mean '$x$ is a Spinozist'. Accordingly you would translate 'Everyone is a Spinozist' as '$(\forall x)Sx$', and 'Someone is a Spinozist' as '$(\exists x)Sx$'.

Imagine a domain of exactly *one* individual: Ardbeg. Suppose that you wished to translate '*Everyone* is a Spinozist' *without using quantifiers*. How would you do so? Obviously, by writing '$Sa$'. Why so? Because in a one-person domain, where Ardbeg is the one person in the domain, and where *everyone* in the domain is a Spinozist, obviously Ardbeg is a Spinozist. The converse is true as well: in a one-person domain, where Ardbeg is the one person in the domain, and where Ardbeg is a Spinozist, obviously *everyone* is a Spinozist.

Once again, imagine a domain of exactly *one* individual: Ardbeg. Suppose that you wished to translate '*Someone* is a Spinozist' *without using quantifiers*. How would you do so? Obviously, by writing '$Sa$'. Why so? Because in a one-person domain, where Ardbeg is the one person in the domain, and where *someone* in the domain is a Spinozist, obviously Ardbeg is a Spinozist. The converse is true as well: in a one-person domain, where Ardbeg is the one person in the domain, and where Ardbeg is a Spinozist, obviously *someone* is a Spinozist.

Moral of the story: in a one-object domain (but *only* in a one-object domain, as you are about to see) a universally quantified *wff* and its existentially quantified counterpart are logically equivalent to each other.

Now imagine a domain of exactly *two* individuals: Ardbeg and Bobo. Suppose that you wished to translate '*Everyone* is a Spinozist' *without using quantifiers*. How would you do so? Obviously by writing '*Sa* ∧ *Sb*'. Why so? Because in a two-person domain, where Ardbeg and Bobo are the only two people in the domain, and where *everyone* is a Spinozist, obviously *both* Ardbeg *and* Bobo are Spinozists. The converse is true as well: in a two-person domain, where Ardbeg and Bobo are the only two people in the domain, and where *both* Ardbeg *and* Bobo are Spinozists, obviously *everyone* is a Spinozist.

Once again imagine a domain of exactly *two* individuals: Ardbeg and Bobo. Suppose that you wished to translate '*Someone* is a Spinozist' *without using quantifiers*. How would you do so? Obviously by writing '*Sa* ∨ *Sb*'. Why so? Because in a two-person domain, where Ardbeg and Bobo are the only two people in the domain, and where *someone* is a Spinozist, obviously *either* Ardbeg *or* Bobo is a Spinozist. The converse is true as well: in a two-person domain, where Ardbeg and Bobo are the only two people in the domain, and where *either* Ardbeg *or* Bobo is a Spinozist, obviously *someone* is a Spinozist.

It goes without saying that in a three-object domain, consisting of Ardbeg, Bobo, and Coco, '$(\forall x)Sx$' is equivalent to '*Sa* ∧ *Sb* ∧ *Sc*', and '$(\exists x)Sx$' is equivalent to '*Sa* ∨ *Sb* ∨ *Sc*'.

Moral of the story: in any domain containing more than one object, universally quantified *wffs* are disguised *conjunctions* and existentially quantified *wffs* are disguised *disjunctions*.

Question: Why then do we need quantifiers at all? Why can't we simply operate with conjunctions instead of universally quantified *wffs*, and with disjunctions instead of existentially quantified *wffs*?

Four answers. First, suppose that the domain contains a fairly *large*, albeit *finite*, number of objects, each of which currently has a name, e.g., all people currently alive. From a *practical* point of view, it would be rather challenging to list each conjunct or disjunct. Second, suppose that the domain contains a fairly *large*, albeit *finite*, number of objects, not each of which currently has a name, e.g., all microbes that currently make their home in your intestines. From a practical point of view, it would be rather challenging to assign a name to each object in the domain and then, once again, to list each conjunct or disjunct. Third, suppose that the domain contains an *infinite* number of objects, each of which has a name, e.g., the natural numbers. From a *theoretical* point of view, it would be *impossible* to list each conjunct or disjunct. Fourth, suppose that the domain contains an *infinite* number of objects, not each of which has a name, and not each of which *could* have a name, e.g., the real numbers. From a theoretical point of view, it would be *impossible* to list each conjunct or disjunct. (This last point will make perfectly good sense once you have learned Cantor's Diagonal Argument in one of your next logic courses.)

So without quantifiers, some translations will take a good bit of time to perform (e.g., those that refer to all living people or to all microbes in your intestines), and some will be impossible to perform (e.g., those that refer to all natural numbers or to all real numbers). Moral of the story: eliminating quantifiers and replacing them with proper names and predicates, along with either conjunctions or disjunctions, doesn't come cheaply.

# 6. Quantifier Negation (QN)

Definition: A *negated* quantified *wff* is a *wff* whose main operator is a dash and whose main operator, in the absence of the dash, would be a quantifier.

Definition: A *non-negated* quantified *wff* is a quantified *wff* whose main operator is a quantifier.

So a non-negated quantified *wff* may well have a dash buried within it. '$(\forall x)-Sx$' and '$(\exists x)-Sx$' are examples of just such *wffs*.

Some *negated* quantified *wffs* are logically equivalent to other, *non-negated* quantified *wffs*. To fully grasp the meaning of each quantifier, it's useful to examine these equivalences. Consider the following pairs of *wffs*. Suppose that our domain is restricted to people, and further suppose that '*Sx*' means, once again, '*x* is a Spinozist'. (A reminder: I use the symbol '⟺' to denote the logical equivalence of two *wffs*. It is a symbol from our metalanguage and not from our object language.)

(1a) '—$(\forall x)\,Sx$'    ⟺    (1b) '$(\exists x)$—$Sx$'

(2a) '—$(\exists x)\,Sx$'    ⟺    (2b) '$(\forall x)$—$Sx$'

(3a) '—$(\forall x)$—$Sx$'    ⟺    (3b) '$(\exists x)\,Sx$'

(4a) '—$(\exists x)$—$Sx$'    ⟺    (4b) '$(\forall x)\,Sx$'

(1a), 'Not everyone is a Spinozist', obviously has the same meaning as (1b), 'There's at least one person who isn't a Spinozist'. (2a), 'There isn't a single person who is a Spinozist', obviously has the same meaning as (2b), 'No one is a Spinozist'. (3a), 'Not everyone isn't a Spinozist', has the same meaning as (3b) 'There's at least one person who is a Spinozist'. And (4a), 'There isn't a single person who isn't a Spinozist', has the same meaning as (4b) 'Everyone is a Spinozist'. (It may take you a moment or two to see that (3a) is equivalent to (3b), and that (4a) is equivalent to (4b).)

It's customary to refer to these four pairs of equivalent *wffs* as instances of Quantifier Negation (QN).

Note the purely mechanical process that is involved in transforming the *negation* of a quantified *wff* into its logically equivalent *un-negated* quantified counterpart. First, you move the dash from the left side of the quantifier to the right. (If there's already a dash to the right of the quantifier, as in (3a) and (4a), then the two dashes—the old one and the new one—self-destruct, as it were.) Second, the quantifier does a flip-flop: a universal becomes an existential, and an existential becomes a universal.

The parallel here to De Morgan's Laws of Equivalence should be striking. Remember: universally quantified *wffs* are disguised conjunctions, and existentially quantified *wffs* are disguised disjunctions. (1a) and (1b), respectively, illustrate that a negation of a conjunction is equivalent to a disjunction of negations. (2a) and (2b), respectively, illustrate that a negation of a disjunction is equivalent to a conjunction of negations. (3a) and (3b), respectively, illustrate that a negation of a conjunction of negations is equivalent to a disjunction. And (4a) and (4b), respectively, illustrate that a negation of a disjunction of negations is equivalent to a conjunction.

Consider the following pairs of *wffs*, each of which either illustrates, or is a variation on, one of De Morgan's Laws of Equivalence. In a domain of two objects, Ardbeg and Bobo, (1a') is the de-quantified counterpart of (1a); (1b') is the de-quantified counterpart of (1b); etc.

(1a') '$-(Sa \wedge Sb)$'     $\Leftrightarrow$     '(1b') $-Sa \vee -Sb$'

(2a') '$-(Sa \vee Sb)$'     $\Leftrightarrow$     (2b') '$-Sa \wedge -Sb$'

(3a') '$-(-Sa \wedge -Sb)$'  $\Leftrightarrow$     (3b') '$Sa \vee Sb$'

(4a') '$-(-Sa \vee -Sb)$'  $\Leftrightarrow$     (4b') '$Sa \wedge Sb$'

Thanks to Quantifier Negation, you are now able to translate *any* negated quantified *wff* in at least two *syntactically* dissimilar ways. Consider (in an unrestricted domain) 'Not everyone loves someone'. Drawing upon (1a) would yield '$-(\forall x)[Px \rightarrow (\exists y)(Py \wedge Lxy)]$'. Now consider (again, in an unrestricted domain) 'There is at least one person who doesn't love anyone'. Drawing upon (1b) would yield '$(\exists x) [Px \wedge (\forall y)(Py \rightarrow -Lxy)]$'. You can see that these two *wffs* are logically equivalent to each other by transforming each one, step by logically equivalent step, into the other—and back again:

1 (1) $-(\forall x)[Px \rightarrow (\exists y)(Py \wedge Lxy)]$     A
1 (2) $(\exists x)-[Px \rightarrow (\exists y)(Py \wedge Lxy)]$     1 QN
1 (3) $(\exists x)[Px \wedge -(\exists y)(Py \wedge Lxy)]$     2 NI
1 (4) $(\exists x)[Px \wedge (\forall y)-(Py \wedge Lxy)]$     3 QN
1 (5) $(\exists x)[Px \wedge (\forall y)(-Py \vee -Lxy)]$     4 DM
1 (6) $(\exists x)[Px \wedge (\forall y)(Py \rightarrow -Lxy)]$     5 MI

For two reasons, this successive transformation of (1) into (6) does *not* count as a bona fide derivation.

In the first place, we appealed to QN in the moves from lines (1) to (2) and lines (3) to (4). Although QN is a primitive derivation rule in many logic texts, it isn't a primitive derivation rule in *this* text. (Once you prove each of the four versions of QN in Chapter 7, then you may invoke each of the four versions of QN as a *derived* derivation rule.)

In the second place, we operated on *wff fragments* four times: in the moves from lines (2) to (3), (3) to (4), (4) to (5), and (5) to (6). As you know, however, our derivation rules require us to operate only on *wffs* in their totality, and never on fragments of *wffs*. Nevertheless, it should strike you as justifiable, in *informal* reasoning, to replace a *wff* fragment with another *wff* fragment that is logically equivalent to it.

For the fun of it, you might wish to execute the reverse transformation on your own—i.e., from '(∃x)[Px ∧ (∀y)(Py → −Lxy)]' to '−(∀x) [Px → (∃y)(Py ∧ Lxy)]'—without simply reversing the order of steps in the above transformation. (That would be *legitimate* but it wouldn't be *challenging.*) To be sure, you already know that the two *wffs* are logically equivalent to one another. How so? Think of what we were really doing in the above transformation: we showed that (2) is logically equivalent to (1), that (3) is logically equivalent to (2), that (4) is logically equivalent to (3), that (5) is logically equivalent to (4), and that (6) is logically equivalent to (5)—from which it follows—yes?—that (6) is logically equivalent to (1).

Question: And why exactly is each of these *wffs* logically equivalent to its immediate predecessor?

Answer: Because each is *interderivable* with its predecessor. In other words, not only is there a derivation of each of these *wffs* from its immediate *predecessor*, there's also a derivation of each of these *wffs* from its immediate *successor*. And, if there's a derivation of 'O' from 'Δ' and of 'Δ' from 'O', then (because our derivation rules are truth-preserving) there's no interpretation that makes 'Δ' true and 'O' false—*and* there's no interpretation that makes 'O' true and 'Δ' false. So 'Δ' and 'O', being interderivable, are logically equivalent to each other.

One last point. Thanks to QN, you don't need both the universal and the existential quantifier. Either would suffice by itself. Think of '(∃x)Sx': because it's logically equivalent to '−(∀x)−Sx', the existential quantifier is eliminable and replaceable with the universal quantifier and (two occurrences of) the dash. But of course the same applies to '(∀x)Sx': because it's logically equivalent to '−(∃x)−Sx', the universal quantifier is eliminable and replaceable with the existential quantifier and (two occurrences of) the dash. Life is much easier, however, when you have access to both quantifiers. Ease of operations is a *practical* goal, of course. Parsimony, vis-à-vis the number of operators that you have, is a *theoretical* goal. If your passion for parsimony exceeds your passion for ease of operations, you will eliminate one or the other of the two quantifiers. (But really, you needn't be *quite* so parsimonious: one has to draw the line *somewhere.*)

# 7. Invalid Arguments

In Propositional Logic, the Truth-Table Method and the Short Method constitute purely mechanical procedures for determining whether a given argument is valid or invalid. In Predicate Logic/Quantification Theory, a modification of the Short Method constitutes a mechanical procedure for determining whether a given argument is invalid. To be sure, the procedure is cumbersome, time-consuming, resource-depleting, and (above all) *boring*—but it *is* mechanical. As you'll see, however, its scope is limited.

In Predicate Logic/Quantification Theory, as in Propositional Logic, to say that an argument is *valid* is to say that there's no interpretation that makes the premise(s) true and the conclusion false; and to say that an argument is *invalid* is to say that there's at least one interpretation that makes the premise(s) true and the conclusion false.

Where $L_1$, the formal language of Propositional Logic, is concerned, defining an interpretation is easy enough. An interpretation of a given *wff* is simply an assignment of truth-values to the atomics of which the *wff* is composed. Where $L_2$, the formal language of Predicate Logic/Quantification Theory is concerned, however, matters are a bit tricky, and are best postponed until a next logic course. A *part* of what's involved in specifying an interpretation in the language of Predicate Logic/Quantification Theory is the specification of a *domain*, whether it be a domain of people or dreams or musical notes or floral scents or whatever.

## A. Showing Invalidity with Monadic Predicates

Consider the following argument:

> (1) Some philosophers are mad.
> ∴ (2) All philosophers are mad.

Obviously the argument is invalid. Now suppose that we translate it into logical notation:

$$(1a) \ (\exists x)(Px \land Mx)$$

$$\therefore (2a) \ (\forall x)(Px \rightarrow Mx)$$

Consider the following interpretation: a one-object domain consisting only of Ardbeg. On this interpretation, the premise, which asserts that there exists at least one object that has the properties of being a philosopher and of being mad, amounts to the claim that *Ardbeg* has the properties of being a philosopher and of being mad: '*Pa* $\land$ *Ma*'. (Remember: by hypothesis, Ardbeg is the *only* object in the domain.)

The conclusion, which asserts that *every* object is such that if it's a philosopher then it's mad, amounts to the claim that if Ardbeg is a philosopher then Ardbeg is mad: '*Pa* $\rightarrow$ *Ma*'. (Remember once again: by hypothesis, Ardbeg is the *only* object in the domain.) Using the Short Method, your goal is to try to make the premise true and the conclusion false:

$$(1b) \ Pa \ \land \ Ma$$
$$T \ T \ \boxed{T}$$

$$(2b) \ Pa \ \rightarrow \ Ma$$
$$T \ F \ \boxed{F}$$

Clearly, there's no interpretation that will make *this* premise true and *this* conclusion false. *This* argument, in other words, is *valid*. Does this mean that our *original* argument is valid? No, of course not: to show that an argument is *valid*, you have to show that there is *no* interpretation that makes the premise(s) true and the conclusion false. All that you've shown thus far is that there is *one* interpretation, i.e., an interpretation involving a *one-object domain*, that fails to make the premise true and the conclusion false. You may, if you wish, refer to our argument as *one-valid*, i.e., valid in a domain of one object, but it is certainly not valid *unconditionally*. Being *one-valid* doesn't mean that the argument is *valid*: for all you know, there may be some other interpretation that makes the premise true and the conclusion false.

And indeed there is. Consider a new interpretation. Consider a *two-object* domain, consisting of Ardbeg and Bobo. Keeping in mind that

(1a), the premise, is a disguised *disjunction*, and that (1b), the conclusion, is a disguised *conjunction*, you would—or at least you *should*—
produce the *wffs* (1c) and (2c). In a domain of two objects, (1c) is the
de-quantified counterpart of (1a), and (2c) is the de-quantified counterpart of (2a).

     (1c) $(Pa \land Ma) \lor (Pb \land Mb)$
     (2c) $(Pa \rightarrow Ma) \land (Pb \rightarrow Mb)$

    The trick now is to find an interpretation that makes (1c) true and
(2c) false. Notice that there are three different interpretations that will
make (2c) false: first, by making '$(Pa \rightarrow Ma)$' true and '$(Pb \rightarrow Mb)$'
false; second, by making '$(Pa \rightarrow Ma)$' false and '$(Pb \rightarrow Mb)$' true; and
third, by making '$(Pa \rightarrow Ma)$' false and '$(Pb \rightarrow Mb)$' false.

    Ignore the third interpretation: it would land you right back where
you were a moment ago. You would end up replicating (1b) and (2b)
for each conjunct of the conclusion, and the argument would appear
two-valid, which it isn't.

    Suppose that you opt for the second interpretation:

     (1c) $(Pa \land Ma) \lor (Pb \land Mb)$
         T F F T
     (2c) $(Pa \rightarrow Ma) \land (Pb \rightarrow Mb)$
         T F F F   T

    The only interpretation that makes '$Pa \rightarrow Ma$' false also makes
'$Pa \land Ma$' false. Your goal is to make the premise true and the conclusion false. You have already succeeded in making the conclusion false.
To make the premise true—it's a disjunction and its left disjunct is
already false—you have to make the right disjunct true. The right
disjunct, '$Pb \land Mb$', is a conjunction. For it to be true, each conjunct
has to be true.

     (1d) $(Pa \land Ma) \lor (Pb \land Mb)$
         T F F T T T T

     (2d) $(Pa \rightarrow Ma) \land (Pb \rightarrow Mb)$
         T F F F T T T

Using the Short Method, you have shown that the original argument is invalid. Not only is there *a* counterexample in an interpretation with a two-object domain, there are *two* counterexamples. (If you had begun by making '(Pb → Mb)' false and '(Pa ∧ Ma)' true, you would have generated the second counterexample.) In a domain of two objects, the two counterexamples are the following:

| Pa | Ma | Pb | Mb |
|----|----|----|----|
| T  | F  | T  | T  |
| T  | T  | T  | F  |

In other words, in a domain of two objects, Ardbeg and Bobo, there are two interpretations that make 'Some philosophers are mad' true and 'All philosophers are mad' false. One is the interpretation whereby Ardbeg is a non-mad philosopher and Bobo is a mad philosopher. The other is the interpretation whereby Ardbeg is a mad philosopher and Bobo is a non-mad philosopher.

Two points. First, you needn't bother checking to see whether the argument is invalid in a domain of three objects, or four, or five, etc. If an argument is invalid in a domain of two objects, then it's invalid *period.* You have found *an* interpretation that makes each premise true and the conclusion false. Second, it should strike you (intuitively) that if an argument is invalid in a domain of *n* objects, then it's invalid in a domain of *n*+1 objects. This point too awaits proving in one of your next logic courses.

## B. Showing Invalidity with Polyadic/ Multiplace Predicates

Invalidity-wise, the most interesting arguments are the ones with multiple quantifiers and polyadic/multiplace predicates. Consider the following sentence:

(1) Everyone loves someone.

In a domain restricted to people, where '*Lxy*' means '*x* loves *y*', the corresponding *wff* is

(1a) $(\forall x)(\exists y)Lxy$

This, of course, is the *universal* quantification of an *existentially* quantified *wff*. As such, it's a disguised *conjunction* whose conjuncts are existentially quantified *wffs*, i.e., disguised *disjunctions*. Suppose that you wish to produce its de-quantified counterpart in a domain of one object, a domain of two objects, etc. First you produce the *partially* de-quantified, *conjunctional* counterpart of (1a). Then you produce the *fully* de-quantified, *disjunctional* counterpart of each of the conjuncts. The end result will be a fully de-quantified counterpart of (1a).

Consider first a domain of one person: Ardbeg. You delete the universal quantifier, but *only* the universal quantifier, as well as each occurrence of the variable '*x*'. You then replace each occurrence of the variable '*x*' that had followed '$(\forall x)$'—in this instance there's only *one* such occurrence—with the proper name '*a*'. You will thereby produce the *partially* de-quantified, conjunctional counterpart of (1a):

(1b) $(\exists y)Lay$

Yes, yes, I am well aware that this hardly looks like a *conjunction*. But that's because you're operating with a one-object domain. Once you operate with a domain of more than one object, you'll see the conjunction. If you like, you may think of (1b) as the limiting, or degenerate, case of a conjunction, i.e., a conjunction with only one conjunct, so to speak.

Now think of what (1b) says: 'Ardbeg loves someone; i.e., there is someone whom Ardbeg loves'. This, of course, is *exactly* what you want—given that *everyone* loves *someone*, and given, too, that Ardbeg is the *only* person in the domain.

So if there is someone whom Ardbeg loves, and if Ardbeg is the only person in the domain, then obviously Ardbeg must love *himself*. When you produce the de-quantified counterpart of (1b), what you end up with is the fully de-quantified counterpart of (1a) for a domain consisting of just one person, i.e., Ardbeg:

(1c) *Laa*

Now suppose that you have a domain of two people: Ardbeg and Bobo. Your initial *wff*, once again, looks like this:

(1a) $(\forall x)(\exists y)Lxy$

(1a) tells you that *everyone* has a particular property: the property of *loving someone*. Obviously, therefore, Ardbeg must have that property *and* Bobo must have that property. Ardbeg has the property of loving someone *and* Bobo has the property of loving someone. In other words, there is someone whom Ardbeg loves *and* there is someone whom Bobo loves. (1a) is about to lose its universal quantifier and become a conjunction of two existentially quantified *wffs*. The proper name '*a*' replaces each occurrence of the variable '*x*' in the first conjunct (there is only one such variable), and the proper name '*b*' replaces each occurrence of the variable '*x*' (again: there is only one such variable) in the second conjunct. You will thereby produce the *partially* de-quantified, conjunctional counterpart of (1a)—and now you *see* your conjunction:

(1d) $(\exists y)Lay \wedge (\exists y)Lby$

Think of what (1d) says: 'Ardbeg loves someone and Bobo loves someone; i.e., there is someone whom Ardbeg loves and there is someone whom Bobo loves'. Once again, this is *exactly* what you want—given that everyone loves someone, and given, too, that Ardbeg and Bobo are the only objects, i.e., the only people, in the domain.

To de-quantify (1d), you de-quantify each of the two existentially quantified *wffs*. An existentially quantified *wff* is a disguised disjunction. The domain, once again, contains two people, Ardbeg and Bobo. Therefore 'Ardbeg loves someone'—the left conjunct of (1d)—amounts to the disjunction 'Either Ardbeg loves himself or he loves Bobo'. Moreover, 'Bobo loves someone'—the right conjunct of (1d)—amounts to the disjunction 'Either Bobo loves Ardbeg or she loves herself'. (1d) easily becomes (1e), which is the fully de-quantified counterpart of '$(\forall x)(\exists y)Lxy$' for a domain consisting of only Ardbeg and Bobo:

(1e) $(Laa \vee Lab) \wedge (Lba \vee Lbb)$

Finally, suppose, that we have a domain of three people: Ardbeg, Bobo, and Coco. Following the same steps as previously, you will thereby produce the *partially* de-quantified, conjunctional counterpart of (1a):

(1f) $(\exists y)Lay \land (\exists y)Lby \land (\exists y)Lcy$

Given that *everyone* loves someone, (1f) says *exactly* what you want it to say: 'Ardbeg loves someone and Bobo loves someone and Coco loves someone'.

To de-quantify (1f), you de-quantify each of the three existentially quantified *wffs*. An existentially quantified *wff* is a disguised disjunction. The domain contains three people: Ardbeg, Bobo, and Coco. Therefore 'Ardbeg loves someone'—the leftmost conjunct of (1f)—amounts to the disjunction 'Either Ardbeg loves himself or he loves Bobo or he loves Coco'. Moreover, 'Bobo loves someone'—the middle conjunct of (1f)—amounts to the disjunction 'Either Bobo loves Ardbeg or she loves herself or she loves Coco'. Finally, 'Coco loves someone'—the rightmost conjunct of (1f)—amounts to the disjunction 'Either Coco loves Ardbeg or she loves Bobo or she loves herself'. (1f) easily becomes (1g), which is the fully de-quantified counterpart of '$(\forall x)(\exists y)Lxy$' for a domain consisting of only Ardbeg, Bobo, and Coco:

(1g) $(Laa \lor Lab \lor Lac) \land (Lba \lor Lbb \lor Lbc) \land (Lca \lor Lcb \lor Lcc)$

You are now ready to use the Short Method, as amended for Predicate Logic/Quantification Theory, to show that the following argument, a moderately difficult one, is invalid:

(2) Everyone is loved by someone.
_____
∴ (3) Someone loves everyone.

Once you translate (2) and (3), the premise and the conclusion, respectively, into logical notation, you end up with the following:

(2a) $(\forall x)(\exists y)Lyx$
_____
∴ (3a) $(\exists x)(\forall y)Lxy$

Suppose a domain restricted to people. In a domain of one object, Ardbeg, the partial de-quantification of the premise and the conclusion results in the following:

$$\frac{(2b)\ (\exists y)Lya}{\therefore\ (3b)\ (\forall y)Lay}$$

You may now complete the de-quantification as follows:

$$\frac{(2c)\ Laa}{\therefore\ (3c)\ Laa}$$

Quite obviously the argument is *one*-valid; i.e., it's valid in a domain of *one* object, i.e., one person.

In a domain of two people, the partial de-quantification of the premise and the conclusion results in the following:

$$\frac{(2d)\ (\exists y)Lya \wedge (\exists y)Lyb}{\therefore\ (3d)\ (\forall y)Lay \vee (\forall y)Lby}$$

(2d) is a *conjunction* because (2a), the fully quantified version of the premise, is a universally quantified *wff*. (3d) is a *disjunction* because (3a), the fully quantified version of the conclusion, is an existentially quantified *wff*. You may now complete the de-quantification as follows:

$$\frac{(2e)\ (Laa \vee Lba) \wedge (Lab \vee Lbb)}{\therefore\ (3e)\ (Laa \wedge Lab) \vee (Lba \wedge Lbb)}$$

If you were to construct a complete truth-table for this argument, (2e) and (3e), the number of rows would be $2^4$, i.e., 16.

But it's unnecessary to construct a complete truth-table: the Short Method will do the trick. Your goal is to make the premise true and the conclusion false. For the premise—a conjunction—to be true, each conjunct must be true. For the conclusion—a disjunction—to be false, each disjunct must be false.

For the left conjunct of the premise to be true, either 'Laa' or 'Lba' must be true. Start by assigning 'T' to 'Laa' in order to generate your first counterexample. Then start over by assigning 'T' to 'Lba' in order to generate your second counterexample. Only assign a 'T' or an 'F' when you have no choice in your assignment. You're on your own from this point on.

It turns out that there are two counterexamples whereby the premise, (2e), is true and the conclusion, (3e), is false:

| Laa | Lba | Lab | Lbb |
|-----|-----|-----|-----|
| T | F | F | T |
| F | T | T | F |

In the first counterexample, Ardbeg loves himself and Bobo loves herself, but neither one loves the other. So it's true that everyone is loved by someone (i.e., someone or other), but it's false that someone (i.e., one and the same person) loves everyone. In the second counterexample, Bobo loves Ardbeg and Ardbeg loves Bobo, but neither one loves himself or herself. So (once again) it's true that everyone is loved by someone (i.e., someone or other), but it's false that someone (i.e., one and the same person) loves everyone.

## C. Failing to Show Invalidity with Polyadic/Multiplace Predicates

In Propositional Logic, as you know, the Truth-Table Method is a purely *mechanical* (or algorithmic) procedure for determining whether an argument is valid or invalid. Cumbersome, time-consuming, resource-depleting, and (above all) *boring*, to be sure—but *mechanical*. You would expect to find a comparable mechanical procedure in Predicate Logic/Quantification Theory. That there *isn't*, and that there *can't be*, any such procedure was one of the great discoveries of mathematical logic in the first third of the twentieth century.

Question: What exactly does all this *mean*? Answer: It means that it isn't possible for a computer to perform certain tasks that you might have thought that it could easily perform. It means that a computer—or indeed *any* device that relies wholly on mechanical/algorithmic procedures—has a crucial limitation where logic is concerned. It's possible, and not at all difficult, to program a computer to sort the arguments of Propositional Logic into two piles—the Valid Pile and the Invalid

Pile—just as truth-tables enable you to do. It's also possible, and not at all difficult, to program a computer to sort the arguments of *monadic* Predicate Logic into two piles: the Valid Pile and the Invalid Pile. It isn't possible, however—contrary to what you may well have supposed— to program a computer to sort all the arguments of *polyadic/multiplace* Predicate Logic/Quantification Theory into these same two piles: the Valid and the Invalid. (Some of them, yes. All of them, no.) And this *impossibility* is not a function of the state of computer technology: it's inherent in the very nature of mechanical/algorithmic procedures. In the first appendix to Chapter 8 I shall return to this topic and say a few more words about it.

# Exercises

I. Using the following interpretations, translate the arguments below into English:

$Lx = x$ is a logician
$Mx = x$ is a magician
$Nx = x$ is a nihilist
$Rxy = x$ respects $y$

1.    $(\exists x)(Lx \wedge Mx)$
   ∴ $(\forall x)(Lx \rightarrow Mx)$

2.    $-(\forall x)(Lx \rightarrow -Mx)$
   ∴ $-(\exists x)(Lx \wedge -Mx)$

3.    $(\exists x)(Lx \rightarrow Mx)$
      $(\exists y)(My \rightarrow Ny)$
   ∴ $(\forall z)(Lz \rightarrow Nz)$

4.    $(\forall x)(\exists y)Rxy$
   ∴ $(\exists x)(\forall y)Ryx$

5.  $\dfrac{(\forall x)(\exists y)Ryx}{\therefore\ (\forall x)(\exists y)Rxy}$

6.  $-(\forall x)(Lx \wedge -Mx)$
    $\dfrac{-(\forall y)(My \wedge -Ny)}{\therefore\ -(\exists z)-(Lz \to Nz)}$

7.  $\dfrac{-(\exists x)(\forall y)-Rxy}{\therefore\ -(\forall x)(\exists y)-Ryx}$

8.  $\dfrac{-(\exists x)(\forall y)-Ryx}{\therefore\ -(\exists x)(\forall y)-Rxy}$

9.  $\dfrac{(\forall x)-(\forall y)Rxy}{\therefore\ (\forall x)(\forall y)-Rxy}$

10. $\dfrac{(\exists x)-(\forall y)Rxy}{\therefore\ (\forall x)(\exists y)-Rxy}$

II. Show that each of the above is an invalid argument, using the version of the Short Method that we have adapted to Predicate Logic/Quantification Theory. List all counterexamples.

# 8. Appendix I: Logically Valid *Wffs*/Logical Truths

It would be criminal, in an introductory logic course, to say *nothing* about the logically valid *wffs*/logical truths of $L_2$, the language of Predicate Logic/Quantification Theory. However, it would also be criminal—indeed, some might deem it cruel and unusual punishment—to say *much* about them. The topic is important—but a bit digressive for a first logic course.

**Definition:**    A *logically valid* wff/a *logical truth* is a *wff* that is true
for every interpretation.

In $L_1$, the formal language of Propositional Logic, all tautologies are
logically valid *wffs* and all logically valid *wffs* are tautologies. (You may
call a *logically valid wff* simply a *valid wff.*) In $L_2$, the formal language of
Predicate Logic/Quantification Theory, all tautologies are valid *wffs*,
but not all valid *wffs* are tautologies.

Examples of quantificational tautologies are legion. Each of the
following *wffs* is a tautology insofar as it's a substitution-instance of an
$L_1$ tautology, and as such, each is a logically valid *wff*:

(1) $Lx \vee -Lx$
(2) $Lxy \rightarrow Lxy$
(3) $(\forall x)Mx \vee -(\forall x)Mx$
(4) $(\exists x)Lxx \rightarrow (\exists x)Lxx$
(5) $(\exists x)(\forall y)(Px \wedge Lxy) \rightarrow (\exists x)(\forall y)(Px \wedge Lxy)$

On the other hand, each of the following is a valid *wff* even though
none of them is a substitution-instance of an $L_1$ tautology:

(6) $(\forall x)(Mx \rightarrow Mx)$
(7) $(\forall x)(\forall y)Lxy \rightarrow (\forall y)(\forall x)Lxy$
(8) $(\forall x)Lx \rightarrow Ly$
(9) $Lx \rightarrow (\exists y)Ly$
(10) $-(\forall x)Lxy \rightarrow (\exists x)-Lxy$

The problem here starts, as you've already seen, with open *wffs*.
'$Lxy$', for example, is an open *wff*; and as such, it's neither true nor
false. How then can (2), '$Lxy \rightarrow Lxy$', *possibly* be true—and not merely
*true* but logically *valid*, i.e., true for every interpretation? The problem
doesn't stop with open *wffs*. It continues with closed *wffs*, e.g., (6) and
(7), that are not themselves substitution-instances of $L_1$ tautologies. On
the one hand, they certainly *appear* to be valid—and indeed they are.
On the other hand, it's obviously not by means of truth-tables that we
know them to be valid.

Where $L_2$ is concerned, what holds true of logically valid *wffs* holds
true as well of logically valid arguments and of logically equivalent
*wffs*. What could it possibly mean to say that '$(\forall x)Tx \models Tz$' is a valid

argument, when at least one of its *wffs* contains a free variable? And what could it possibly mean to say that two *wffs* are logically equivalent to each other, if each happens to contain a *free* variable, e.g., '*Ex* ∧ (∃*y*)*Oy*' and '(∃*y*)(*Ex* ∧ *Oy*)'? Intuitively, you want to say that the former implies the latter, that the latter implies the former, and that of course, therefore, they're equivalent to each other. As you know, however, two *wffs* are logically equivalent to each other when there's no interpretation that makes one of them *true* and the other *false*. But an open *wff* like '*Ex*' is *neither* true *nor* false. So what could it possibly mean for an interpretation to make '*Ex* ∧ (∃*y*)*Oy*' either true or false, and for an interpretation to make '(∃*y*)(*Ex* ∧ *Oy*)' either true or false?'

Alfred Tarski (Polish and then American, 1901–1983) formulated what is generally regarded as *the* solution to this problem. His solution is a bit too intricate for a first course in logic, however. As a consequence, you're about to receive, instead of the whole shebang, a *sketch* of his solution.

Suppose that we start with *validity*. To be sure, it's a bit odd to start with *validity* and not with *truth*: validity, after all, is defined in terms of truth. But there's something to be said for starting with what's intuitively attractive, and what immediately follows is certainly intuitively attractive.

Consider the open *wff* '*Rxy* → (∃*z*)*Rzy*': 'if *x* stands in the *R*-relation to *y* then *something* stands in the *R*-relation to *y*'. Suppose that the free variable '*x*' designates *any* object *x* in any domain whatsoever of *infinitely* many objects. Suppose that the free variable '*y*' also designates *any* object *y* in the same domain of infinitely many objects. (It makes no difference whether *x* and *y* are *different* objects or the *same* object.) So, regardless of what the domain is, and regardless of which objects in the domain the variables '*x*' and '*y*' designate, and regardless of what the *R*-relation is, if *x* stands in the *R*-relation to *y* then yes indeed, *something* stands in the *R*-relation to *y*. *End of story*: the open *wff* '*Rxy* → (∃*z*)*Rzy*' *must be* true for every interpretation, yes? As such, even though it's an *open wff*, it's a logically *valid wff*.

Consider next the algebraic equation '$x^2 - 6x + 8 = 0$'. As it stands, this equation is the algebraic counterpart of an open *wff*: it's neither true nor false. Your task in the eighth grade was to discover the numbers—2 and 4, as it turns out—that *satisfy* this equation. To say that 2 *satisfies* this equation is to say that when you replace *x* with 2, $2^2 - (6 \times 2) + 8 = $ (i.e., really *does* equal) 0. By the same token, to say that 4 *satisfies* this equation is to say that when you replace *x* with 4, $4^2 - (6 \times 4) +$

$8 = $ (i.e., really *does* equal) 0. On the other hand, to say that 3 *fails* to satisfy this equation is to say that when you replace $x$ with 3, $3^2-(6 \times 3)$ $+ 8 \neq$ (i.e., really does *not* equal) 0.

So what do you know? You know that at least one value of the variable '$x$' *satisfies* the equation '$x^2-6x + 8 = 0$', and at least one value of the variable '$x$' *fails* to satisfy the equation. Note that the equation as it stands, i.e., '$x^2-6x + 8 = 0$', is *neither true nor false*. It is, however, *satisfiable*.

As in algebra, so in logic—at least where the notion of *satisfaction* is concerned. If *logical validity* is definable in terms of *truth*—and of course it is—and if, as Tarski showed (and as you are about to see), *truth* is definable in terms of *satisfaction*, then *logical validity* is definable in terms of *satisfaction*. Consider a very simple open *wff*, e.g., '$Ex$', as a hint, a *mere* hint, of what the notion of satisfaction involves. Assign to the predicate '$E$' the property of being an even number. There are three possibilities where '$Ex$' is concerned. If the domain is, e.g., the even numbers, then *each* object in the domain (i.e., 2, 4, 6, ...) has the property of being an even number; i.e., 2, 4, 6, etc., each *satisfies* '$Ex$'. If the domain is, e.g., the odd numbers, then *no* object in the domain (i.e., 1, 3, 5, ...) has the property of being an even number; i.e., 1, 3, 5, etc., each *fails* to satisfy '$Ex$'. And if the domain is the natural numbers, then at least one object in the domain has the property of being an even number and at least one doesn't; i.e., at least one object in the domain *satisfies* '$Ex$' and at least one *fails* to do so.

In other words, the open *wff* '$Ex$' is true *iff* each value of the variable '$x$', i.e., each object in the domain, satisfies '$Ex$'. And '$Ex$' is false *iff* no value of '$x$', i.e., no object in the domain, satisfies '$Ex$'. And, finally, '$Ex$' is neither true nor false *iff* at least one value of '$x$' fails to satisfy '$Ex$' and at least one value of '$x$' satisfies '$Ex$'.

Truth may now be defined in terms of satisfaction. Consider, once again, an interpretation in which the domain is the even numbers and the property of being an even number is assigned to the predicate '$E$'. Each of the objects in the domain satisfies '$Ex$', and thus '$Ex$' is said to be *true for this interpretation*.

Now consider an interpretation in which the domain is once again the even numbers, but the property of being an odd number is assigned to '$E$'. None of the objects in the domain satisfies '$Ex$', and thus '$Ex$' is said to be *false for this interpretation*.

Finally, consider an interpretation in which the domain is the natural numbers and the property of being an even number is assigned to '*E*'. At least one of the objects in the domain satisfies '*Ex*', and at least one fails to satisfy '*Ex*'. Thus '*Ex*' is said to be *neither true nor false for this interpretation*. For this interpretation, in other words, '*Ex*' is *exactly* like our algebraic equation '$x^2-6x + 8 = 0$'.

Questions: So, in $L_2$, the language of Predicate Logic/Quantification Theory, the notion of an *interpretation* is considerably more complex than it is in $L_1$, yes? It involves both the specification of a domain and the assignment of a property to each predicate, yes?

Answers: Yes and yes. And it also involves even more, e.g., the assignment of an *n*-place relation to each *n*-place predicate, and the assignment of one member of the domain to each proper name.

So a logically valid *wff* is one that is true for *every* interpretation. And a *wff* is true for *every* interpretation *iff* it is satisfied by *every* object in the domain, regardless of which domain you specify, and regardless of how you interpret its predicates. Whence it follows that a logically valid *wff* is a *wff* that is satisfied by *every* object in the domain, regardless of which domain you specify, and regardless of how you interpret its predicates. So validity is definable in terms of truth, and truth is definable in terms of satisfaction. Q.E.D.

'*Lx* ∨ —*Lx*' is a logically valid *wff*. Regardless of which domain you specify and regardless of how you interpret its predicates, *every* object in the domain satisfies it. Therefore it's true for *every* interpretation. And therefore it's logically valid.

Question: Why exactly does *every* object in *every* domain satisfy '*Lx* ∨ —*Lx*'?

Answer: Consider an arbitrarily designated object from any domain whatsoever. Assume that either it satisfies a given *wff* or it satisfies the negation of the *wff*. Assume too that an object satisfies a disjunction *iff* either the object satisfies the left disjunct or it satisfies the right disjunct. So if an arbitrarily designated object satisfies '*Lx*' then it satisfies '*Lx* ∨ —*Lx*'. And if it doesn't satisfy '*Lx*', then it satisfies '—*Lx*'—in which case it satisfies '*Lx* ∨ —*Lx*'. So whether or not an arbitrarily designated object from any domain whatsoever satisfies '*Lx*', it satisfies '*Lx* ∨ —*Lx*'. Therefore *every* object in *every* domain satisfies '*Lx* ∨ —*Lx*'.

It's now possible to give a sketch of what it means for an *argument* to be valid in $L_2$, i.e., for one or more *wffs* to imply another *wff*—even when at least one of the *wffs* is an open *wff*. Consider any valid argument '$\triangle_1$, ..., $\triangle_{n-1}$ ⊨ $\triangle_n$'. In other words, consider any string of *wffs* '$\triangle_1$, ..., $\triangle_{n-1}$, $\triangle_n$' such that '$\triangle_1$, ..., $\triangle_{n-1}$' *imply* '$\triangle_n$'. Accordingly, the argument is *valid iff* for each interpretation, i.e., regardless of which domain you specify, and regardless of how you interpret the predicates that appear in the argument, there are no objects in the domain that satisfy '$\triangle_1$, ..., $\triangle_{n-1}$' and that fail to satisfy '$\triangle_n$'.

For example, the argument whose premise is '*Tx* ∧ *Cx*' and whose conclusion is '*Tx*' is a *valid* argument. Assume that an object satisfies a conjunction *iff* the object satisfies both conjuncts. So, regardless of which domain you specify, and regardless of how you interpret '*T*' and '*C*', there's no object that satisfies '*Tx* ∧ *Cx*' and that fails to satisfy '*Tx*'. On the other hand, the argument whose premise is '*Tx*' and whose conclusion is '*Tx* ∧ *Cx*' is an *invalid* argument: it's hardly a great challenge to specify a domain, an interpretation of '*T*' and '*C*', and an object in the domain, such that the object satisfies '*Tx*' but fails to satisfy '*Tx* ∧ *Cx*'. Suppose that the domain consists only of Ardbeg. Suppose too that Ardbeg is a tyrant but not a clown. Accordingly, Ardbeg satisfies '*Tx*', the premise of the argument: Ardbeg *does* have the property of being a tyrant. But Ardbeg does *not* satisfy '*Tx* ∧ *Cx*', the conclusion of the argument: Ardbeg does *not* have the complex property of being a tyrant *and* being a clown.

It's also possible now to give a sketch of what it means for two *wffs* to be equivalent to each other, even when each is an open *wff*. Accordingly, '$\triangle$' and '**O**' are logically equivalent to each other *iff* '$\triangle$' implies '**O**' and '**O**' implies '$\triangle$'; i.e., *iff* the argument whose premise is '$\triangle$' and whose conclusion is '**O**' is a valid argument, and the argument whose premise is '**O**' and whose conclusion is '$\triangle$' is also a valid argument. The following are examples of open *wffs* that are logically equivalent to each other:

(1) '*Ex*'           ⇔     '− −*Ex*'
(2) '*Ex* ∨ *Ox*'      ⇔     '*Ox* ∨ *Ex*'
(3) '−(*Ex* ∨ *Ox*)'    ⇔     '−*Ex* ∧ −*Ox*'

The following are examples of open *wffs* that aren't logically equivalent to each other:

(4) '*Ex*'           and   '− −*Ey*'
(5) '*Ex* ∨ *Ox*'      and   '*Oy* ∨ *Ey*'
(6) '−(*Ex* ∨ *Ox*)'   and   '−*Ex*'

A few last words on Tarski's solution to the problem of truth and falsehood where open *wffs* are concerned. I remind you that what I've just finished dragging you through in this appendix is but a *sketch* of his solution. I have focused on the satisfaction of a *wff* by an *individual* object. Strictly speaking, however, one should focus, as Tarski himself focused, on the satisfaction of a *wff* by a *sequence*, a *denumerable* sequence, of objects.

"Good grief!" you're thinking. "Why didn't I bail out while there was still time to bail out?"

Too late. You're stuck. But cheer up; it'll be over before you know it. . . .

A *sequence* is any ordering of objects, such that it's clear which is the first object in the sequence, which is the second, etc. Think of the sequence of natural numbers greater than 10 and less than or equal to 20. There are clearly ten objects in the sequence, with 11 being the first, 12 being the second, etc.

A *denumerable* sequence is a sequence that can be placed into a one-to-one correspondence with, i.e., can be paired off with, the *natural* numbers, i.e., the numbers 0, 1, 2, etc. The even natural numbers, for example, constitute a denumerable sequence. How so? Well, suppose that you're a born matchmaker, and suppose that you're trying to pair off the sequence of even numbers with the sequence of natural numbers. So what do you do? You pair off the even number 2 with the natural number 0, the even number 4 with the natural number 1, the even number 6 with the natural number 2, and so on:

| The Evens | | The Naturals |
|:---:|:---:|:---:|
| 2 | – | 0 |
| 4 | – | 1 |
| 6 | – | 2 |
| 8 | – | 3 |
| 10 | – | 4 |

Before you know it, you've paired off the whole sequence of even numbers with the whole sequence of natural numbers. And what do you know? The two sequences stand in a one-to-one correspondence with each other. And so, by definition, the sequence of even numbers is *denumerable*.

Question: And just how does the notion of a denumerable sequence shed light on the notion of satisfaction?

Answer: You really want to know? Read on.

Let our domain be the natural numbers. Let our sequence of variables be '$x_1$', '$x_2$', '$x_3$', etc., such that '$x_1$' is the first variable in the sequence, '$x_2$' is the second, '$x_3$' is the third, etc. Assign to the two-place predicate 'S' the relation 'is the square of'. Accordingly '$Sx_2x_1$' means '$x_2$ is the square of $x_1$'. Let $s_1$ be the denumerable sequence 1, 1, 1, 1, 1, etc. Let $s_2$ be the denumerable sequence 2, 4, 8, 16, 32, etc. Let $s_3$ be the denumerable sequence 1, 2, 3, 4, 5, etc.

Remember: '$x_1$' is the *first* variable in our sequence of variables, and '$x_2$' is the *second*. A denumerable sequence of objects from our domain is said to satisfy the *wff* '$Sx_2x_1$' *iff* the *second* object in the sequence stands in the S-relation to the *first* object in the sequence. (Yes, yes, a denumerable sequence of objects from our domain is said to satisfy the *wff* '$Sx_9x_{13}$' *iff* the *ninth* object in the sequence stands in the S-relation to the *thirteenth* object in the sequence.)

Accordingly, the sequence $s_1$ satisfies '$Sx_2x_1$' because the *second* object in $s_1$, i.e., 1, is the square of the *first* object in $s_1$, i.e., 1. Moreover, the sequence $s_2$ satisfies '$Sx_2x_1$' because the *second* object in $s_2$, i.e., 4, is the square of the *first* object in $s_2$, i.e., 2. By contrast, the sequence $s_3$ does *not* satisfy '$Sx_2x_1$' because the *second* object in $s_3$, i.e., 2, is *not* the square of the *first* object in $s_3$, i.e., 1.

So now you have some idea of what it means to say that a denumerable sequence of objects *satisfies* a *wff*. And now you have an account of *truth*: to say that a *wff* is *true* for a given interpretation is just to say that *every* denumerable sequence of objects from the domain satisfies it.

But perhaps it's best to quit while you're ahead. Don't say that you weren't warned.

In one of your next logic courses, you'll get the whole shebang. You'll get *all* the details of Tarski's account of satisfaction—and with them, the whole of his solution to the problem of truth and falsehood where open *wffs* are concerned.

# 9. Appendix II: Quantifier Shift (QS)

Quantifier Shift (QS) enables you either to broaden or to narrow the scope of a quantifier. It thereby enables you to identify quantificational *wffs* that are logically (or semantically) equivalent to one another, even though syntactically they are quite dissimilar. In order to establish the logical equivalence of two quantificational *wffs*, you will be invoking various laws of logical equivalence from Propositional Logic.

## A. Laws of Equivalence

A reminder: the symbol '⇔' indicates that the two *wffs* flanking it, the one on its left and the one on its right, are logically equivalent to each other. The following thirteen pairs of equivalent *wffs* are all from Propositional Logic. Some you've seen before and some you haven't. Each of them will play a role, however, in establishing various pairs of the equivalences.

(1) Commutation(CM)
  '△ ∨ O'          ⇔  'O ∨ △'
(2) De Morgan(DM)
  '—(△ ∨ O)'       ⇔  '—△ ∧ —O'
(3) De Morgan(DM)
  '—(△ ∧ O)'       ⇔  '—△ ∨ —O'
(4) Association(AS)
  '△ ∨ (O ∨ □)'    ⇔  '(△ ∨ O) ∨ □'
(5) Association(AS)
  '△ ∧ (O ∧ □)'    ⇔  '(△ ∧ O) ∧ □)'
(6) Distribution(DS)
  '△ ∨ (O ∧ □)     ⇔  '(△ ∨ O) ∧ (△ ∨ □)'
(7) Distribution(DS)
  '△ ∧ (O ∨ □)'    ⇔  '(△ ∧ O) ∨ (△ ∧ □)'
(8) ∨-Redundancy(∨R)
  '△ ∨ (O ∨ □ ∨ …)'  ⇔  '(△ ∨ O) ∨ (△ ∨ □)' ∨ …
(9) ∧-Redundancy(∧R)
  '△ ∧ (O ∧ □ ∧ …)'  ⇔  '(△ ∧ O) ∧ (△ ∧ □)' ∧ …

(10) Material Implication (MI)

'$\triangle \rightarrow O$'                    $\Leftrightarrow$   '$-(\triangle \wedge -O)$'

(11) Material Implication (MI)

'$\triangle \rightarrow O$'                    $\Leftrightarrow$   '$-\triangle \vee O$'

(12) Negation Implication (NI)

'$-(\triangle \rightarrow O)$'                 $\Leftrightarrow$   '$\triangle \wedge -O$'

(13) Double Negation (DN)

'$--\triangle$'                    $\Leftrightarrow$   '$\triangle$'

The following two pairs of equivalent *wffs*, unlike the previous thir-teen, are, of course, distinctively quantificational. They are to be used only in *informal* reasoning, as you will soon see.

(14) $\forall$/Conjunction ($\forall/\wedge$)

'$(\forall v)Pv$'                    $\Leftrightarrow$   '$Pa_1 \wedge Pa_2 \wedge Pa_3 \wedge \ldots$'

(15) $\exists$/Disjunction ($\exists/\vee$)

'$(\exists v)Pv$'                    $\Leftrightarrow$   '$Pa_1 \vee Pa_2 \vee Pa_3 \vee \ldots$'

Let '$v$' be any variable. Let '$Pv$' be any *wff* containing at least one free occurrence of '$v$'. Let '$a_1$', '$a_2$', '$a_3$', etc., be proper names. (Note that each of these symbols, '$v$', '$P$', and '$a_1$', '$a_2$', '$a_3$', etc., appears in bold font, to alert you to its metalinguistic status.)

To say that these two pairs of equivalent *wffs*, (14) and (15), are to be used only in *informal* reasoning is simply to acknowledge that neither '$Pa_1 \wedge Pa_2 \wedge Pa_3 \wedge \ldots$' nor '$Pa_1 \vee Pa_2 \vee Pa_3 \vee \ldots$' is a genuine *wff*. The three dots '…' are *not* part of our formal language: they imply that the conjunction/disjunction to the right of '$\Leftrightarrow$' might (although it *needn't*) have an *infinite* number of conjuncts/disjuncts. Obviously no *wff* in our formal language may have an infinite number of conjuncts/disjuncts.

## B. Three Forms: Prenex, Purified, and Mixed

Sometimes you bump up against a quantified *wff* whose quantifiers are lined up neatly and compactly, stacked to the far left, wholly segregated from the rest of the *wff*. Such a *wff* is said to be in *prenex* form, e.g.,

(1) $(\exists x)(\forall y)(\exists z)[Px \wedge (Ly \rightarrow Mz)]$

Sometimes you bump up against a *wff*, at least one of whose components is a quantified *wff*, and none of whose quantifiers lies within the
scope of any of its other quantifiers. Such a *wff* is said to be in *purified*
form, e.g.,

(2) $(\exists x)Px \wedge [(\forall y)Ly \rightarrow (\exists z)Mz]$

And sometimes you bump up against a quantified *wff* that is in
neither prenex nor purified form. Instead, its quantifiers are jumbled
higgledy-piggledy throughout the *wff*. Such a *wff* may be said to be in
*mixed* form, e.g.,

(3) $(\exists x)[Px \wedge (\forall y)(Ly \rightarrow (\exists z)Mz)]$

As it turns out, (1), (2), and (3) are logically equivalent to one other.
Each form has its virtues. There are two reasons why a *wff* in either
its *purified* or its *mixed* form is just what you want. You may wish to
grasp exactly what a particular interpreted *wff means*. Alternatively,
you may be translating from English into logical notation and wish to
maximize the likelihood of a correct translation. On the other hand,
there are two reasons why a *wff* in its *prenex* form is just what you want.
You may wish your *wff* to be maximally tidy and elegant. Moreover (as
you will see in the next chapter), you may wish to be able to use your
quantificational derivation rules in rapid-fire succession, i.e., one right
after the other.

Definition:　　A *wff* is in *prenex* form *iff*
(a) the leftmost quantifier is the *wff*'s main
operator;
(b) the rightmost quantifier has within its scope
the whole of the *wff* to its right; and
(c) between any two quantifiers there are no
connectives.

The following are examples of *wffs* in prenex form:

(4) $(\exists x)Sx$
(5) $(\exists x)(\forall y)-Pxy$
(6) $(\exists x)(\exists y)(\exists z)[Bxyz \wedge (Lxy \vee Lyz \vee Lxz)]$

The following are examples of *wffs* that are *not* in prenex form:

(7) $Px \rightarrow (\exists x)(\exists y)[Px \wedge (Py \wedge Lxy)]$ (It violates (a).)
(8) $-(\forall x)Px$ (Ditto.)
(9) $(\exists x)[(\exists y)(Px \wedge Py) \wedge Lxy]$ (It violates (b).)
(10) $(\exists x)[Px \wedge (\exists y)(Py \wedge Lxy)]$ (It violates (c).)

Definition:     A *wff* is in *purified* form *iff* none of its quantifiers falls within the scope of any of its other quantifiers.

In addition to (8), the following are examples of *wffs* in purified form:

(11) $(\exists x)Lx \wedge (\exists y)My$
(12) $(\exists x)Rxy \wedge (\forall z)(Ryz \rightarrow Mz)$

The following are examples of *wffs* that are *not* in purified form:

(13) $(\exists x)[Lx \wedge (\forall y)My]$
(14) $(\forall x)\{Lx \rightarrow (\forall y)[My \rightarrow (\forall z)Nz]\}$

Note that a *wff* with only one quantifier (but only such a *wff*) might well be in both prenex and purified forms, e.g., (4) '$(\exists x)Sx$'.

Definition:     A *wff* is in *mixed* form *iff* it is in neither prenex nor purified form.

Examples of *wffs* in mixed form are (7), (9), (10), (13), and (14).

At times you will suspect that the *wffs* that you are bumping up against, one of which exhibits one of these forms and one of which doesn't, are logically equivalent to one another. At other times you won't have the foggiest idea whether they are logically equivalent. It would be nice to have a method to establish logical equivalence where quantificational *wffs* are concerned. Enter Quantifier Shift.

# C. Quantifier Shift (QS)

Let '$v$' be any variable. Let '$Pv$' be any *wff* containing at least one free occurrence of '$v$'. And let '$\triangle$' be any *wff* containing no free occurrence of '$v$'.

Thus '$v$', as any variable, is either '$u$' or '$v$' itself or '$w$' or '$x$' or '$y$' or '$z$'.

Instances of '$Pv$', a *wff* containing at least one free occurrence of '$v$', are the following:

    (1) '$Mx$'
    (2) '$Lxy$'
    (3) '$(\forall x)Lxy$'
    (4) '$(\exists x)[(\forall y)Bxyz \rightarrow Mz]$'

In '$Mx$', '$v$' is '$x$'. In '$Lxy$', '$v$' is either '$x$' or '$y$'. In '$(\forall x)Lxy$' '$v$' is '$y$'. And in '$(\exists x)[(\forall y)Bxyz \rightarrow Mz]$', '$v$' is '$z$'.

The restriction on '$\triangle$'—that it contain no free occurrence of the variable '$v$' that occurs free in '$Pv$'—entails that in (1), '$x$' must not appear free in '$\triangle$'; in (2), whichever of the two variables is '$v$' must not appear free in '$\triangle$'; in (3), '$y$' must not appear free in '$\triangle$'; and in (4), '$z$' must not appear free in '$\triangle$'.

Now consider the following eight pairs of *wffs*. The left member of each pair, as you will soon see, is logically equivalent to the right member. Quantifier Shift (QS) consists in the shift either from the left *wff* to the right or from the right *wff* to the left.

    (1a) '$\triangle \vee (\exists v)Pv$'    $\Leftrightarrow$    (1b) '$(\exists v)(\triangle \vee Pv)$'
    (2a) '$\triangle \wedge (\exists v)Pv$'    $\Leftrightarrow$    (2b) '$(\exists v)(\triangle \wedge Pv)$'
    (3a) '$\triangle \rightarrow (\exists v)Pv$'    $\Leftrightarrow$    (3b) '$(\exists v)(\triangle \rightarrow Pv)$'
    (4a) '$\triangle \vee (\forall v)Pv$'    $\Leftrightarrow$    (4b) '$(\forall v)(\triangle \vee Pv)$'
    (5a) '$\triangle \wedge (\forall v)Pv$'    $\Leftrightarrow$    (5b) '$(\forall v)(\triangle \wedge Pv)$'
    (6a) '$\triangle \rightarrow (\forall v)Pv$'    $\Leftrightarrow$    (6b) '$(\forall v)(\triangle \rightarrow Pv)$'
    (7a) '$(\exists v)Pv \rightarrow \triangle$'    $\Leftrightarrow$    (7b) '$(\forall v)(Pv \rightarrow \triangle)$'
    (8a) '$(\forall v)Pv \rightarrow \triangle$'    $\Leftrightarrow$    (8b) '$(\exists v)(Pv \rightarrow \triangle)$'

Note once again that '△' must not contain any free occurrence of '*v*'. If it did, then when you performed QS on a *wff* in the left column and transformed it into its counterpart in the right column—so as to *broaden* the scope of the quantifier—each free occurrence of '*v*' in '△' in the left-column *wff* would be *captured*, i.e., would become *bound*, by the quantifier in the right-column *wff*. By the same token, when you performed QS on a *wff* in the right column and transformed it into its counterpart in the left column—so as to *narrow* the scope of the quantifier—at least one *bound* occurrence of '*v*' in '△' in the right-column *wff* would be *freed* in the left-column *wff*. In each case, as a consequence, the two *wffs* would have quite different meanings.

For example, suppose that '*v*' is free in '△' in the left-column *wff* and bound by the quantifier in the right-column *wff*, as in the following two *wffs*: '$Ex \land (\exists x)Ox$' and '$(\exists x)(Ex \land Ox)$'. Suppose a domain of the natural numbers. Interpret '$Ex$' to mean '*x* is even' and '$Ox$' to mean '*x* is odd'. The former *wff*, '$Ex \land (\exists x)Ox$', means '*x* is even and there exists at least one odd number'. As such, the *wff* is neither true nor false. (It would be true if '*x*' designated 2 or 4 or 6, etc., but it would be false if '*x*' designated 1 or 3 or 5, etc.) The latter *wff*, '$(\exists x)(Ex \land Ox)$', means 'There exists at least one natural number that is both even and odd'— and it's obviously false. Clearly the two *wffs* are not equivalent to each other. Hence the rationale for the restriction that '△' contain no free occurrence of '*v*'.

## D. The Justification for Quantifier Shift (QS)

So how do you establish the logical equivalence of the left member of each of the eight pairs in Subsection C, with the right member?

In what follows, I employ what I shall refer to as the Transformation Method, whereby step by step you transform one quantificational *wff* into another. There are three features of a transformation that distinguish it from a derivation. First, each *wff* in the string of *wffs* isn't simply *implied* by its predecessor: it's *logically equivalent* to it. Second, you're permitted to operate on *wff fragments*; i.e., you're permitted to extract a *fragment* of a *wff* (as long as it is itself a *wff*) and replace it with a logically equivalent *wff*. Third, to justify each step, you cite one of the laws of equivalence listed in Subsection A.

Consider first how you might transform (1a) into (1b):

(1) $\triangle \vee (\exists v)\boldsymbol{Pv}$                                   (1a)

(2) $\triangle \vee (\boldsymbol{Pa_1} \vee \boldsymbol{Pa_2} \vee \boldsymbol{Pa_3} \vee \ldots)$          1 $\exists/\vee$

(3) $(\triangle \vee \boldsymbol{Pa_1}) \vee (\triangle \vee \boldsymbol{Pa_2}) \vee (\triangle \vee \boldsymbol{Pa_3}) \vee \ldots$     2 $\vee$R

(4) $(\exists v)(\triangle \vee \boldsymbol{Pv})$                                 3 $\exists/\vee$

Similar reasoning establishes the logical equivalence of (2a) to (2b). *Fairly* similar reasoning establishes the logical of equivalence of (3a) to (3b):

(1) $\triangle \to (\exists v)\boldsymbol{Pv}$                                   (2a)

(2) $-\triangle \vee (\exists v)\boldsymbol{Pv}$                           1 MI

(3) $-\triangle \vee (\boldsymbol{Pa_1} \vee \boldsymbol{Pa_2} \vee \boldsymbol{Pa_3} \vee \ldots)$        2 $\exists/\vee$

(4) $(-\triangle \vee \boldsymbol{Pa_1}) \vee (-\triangle \vee \boldsymbol{Pa_2}) \vee (-\triangle \vee \boldsymbol{Pa_3}) \vee \ldots$   3 $\vee$R

(5) $(\exists v)(-\triangle \vee \boldsymbol{Pv})$                         4 $\exists/\vee$

(6) $(\exists v)(\triangle \to \boldsymbol{Pv})$                          5 MI

## E. Using Quantifier Shift (QS)

One example. I purify a *wff* that's currently in prenex form. To the far right of each *wff*, I cite the instance of QS that I'm invoking from the beginning of Subsection C. If you'd like an example whereby a *wff* in purified form is transformed into prenex form, simply reverse the order of *wffs* in this transformation.

(1) $(\forall x)(\exists y)(\forall z)[Lx \to (My \to Nz)]$

(2) $(\forall x)(\exists y)[Lx \to (\forall z)(My \to Nz)]$       1QS (6)

(3) $(\forall x)(\exists y)\{Lx \to [My \to (\forall z)Nz]\}$       2QS (6)

(4) $(\forall x)\{Lx \to (\exists y)[My \to (\forall z)Nz]\}$       3QS (3)

(5) $(\forall x)\{Lx \to [(\forall y)My \to (\forall z)Nz]\}$       4QS (8)

(6) $(\exists x)Lx \to [(\forall y)My \to (\forall z)Nz]$       5QS (7)

# Exercises

I. Use the Transformation Method to show that the left member of each of the pairs of *wffs* in Subsection C is logically equivalent to the right member. (No need to do (1a)/(1b) or (3a/3b).

II. Each of the following *wffs* is in mixed form. Use QS to transform each of them, step by step, first into prenex form and then into purified form. Cite by number the instance of QS that you're invoking from the beginning of Subsection C.

1.  $(\exists x)[(Px \wedge Lx) \wedge (\exists y)(Py \wedge Ly) \wedge Mx]$
2.  $(\forall x)\{Px \rightarrow (\forall y)[Ly \rightarrow (\exists z)Mz]\}$
3.  $(\forall x)\{Px \rightarrow (\forall y)[Ly \rightarrow (\exists z)Mz]\}$
4.  $Px \rightarrow (\exists x)\{Px \wedge (\exists y)[(Py \wedge Lxy) \rightarrow (\forall z)(Mz \vee Nz)]\}$
5.  $(\forall x)\ \{[Px \rightarrow (\forall y)My] \rightarrow (\exists z)(Mz \rightarrow Nz)\}$

III. Each of the following *wffs* is in prenex form. Use QS to transform each of them, step by step, into purified form. Cite by number the instance of QS that you're invoking from the beginning of Subsection C.

1.  $(\forall x)(\forall y)(\exists z)[Lx \wedge (Mz \vee Ny)]$
2.  $(\exists z)(\forall x)(\forall y)[Lx \wedge (Mz \vee Ny)]$
3.  $(\forall x)(\forall y)(\exists z)[Lz \rightarrow (Mx \wedge Ny)]$
4.  $(\exists x)(\exists y)(\forall z)[Lx \rightarrow (Mz \rightarrow Ny)]$
5.  $(\exists z)(\exists x)(\forall y)[Lx \vee (Mz \rightarrow Ny)]$

IV. Each of the following *wffs* is in purified form. Use QS to transform each of them, step by step, into prenex form. Cite by number the instance of QS that you're invoking from the beginning of Subsection C.

1.  $(\forall x)Lx \wedge [(\exists y)My \rightarrow (\exists z)Nz]$
2.  $(\forall x)Lx \rightarrow [(\exists y)My \wedge (\exists z)Nz]$
3.  $[(\forall x)Lx \wedge (\exists y)My] \rightarrow (\exists z)Nz$
4.  $(\exists x)Lx \wedge [(\exists y)My \vee (\exists z)Nz]$
5.  $[(\forall x)Lx \rightarrow (\exists y)My] \rightarrow (\exists z)Nz$

# Chapter Seven

# Predicate Logic:
# A Deductive Apparatus, Part One

## 1. Introduction

We return to the scene of the crime, i.e., to the very beginning of Chapter 5. You saw there that the following argument *must* be valid, but that the deductive apparatus of Propositional Logic isn't up to the task at hand, i.e., of enabling you to construct a derivation that will establish its validity.

> (1) All tyrants are clowns.
> (2) Ardbeg is a tyrant.
> _____
> ∴ (3) Ardbeg is a clown.

Just as there are two derivation rules for each Propositional Logic connective—an elimination rule and an introduction rule—so there are two for each of the quantifiers of Predicate Logic/Quantification Theory:

1. Universal Quantifier Elimination, i.e., Universal Elimination, i.e., ∀E;
2. Universal Quantifier Introduction, i.e., Universal Introduction, i.e., ∀I;
3. Existential Quantifier Elimination, i.e., Existential Elimination, i.e., ∃E; and
4. Existential Quantifier Introduction, i.e., Existential Introduction, i.e., ∃I.

Each of these rules comes with a host of restrictions—restrictions that render the construction of derivations rather challenging at times. I shall ease you into the restrictions quite gradually. At the outset, indeed, I shall say precious little about them.

# 2. ∀E: An Introduction to Universal Quantifier Elimination

Suppose that you translate the argument above into logical notation in the obvious sort of way:

S115:          $(\forall x)(Tx \rightarrow Cx)$, $Ta \vdash Ca$

$$1\ (1)\ (\forall x)(Tx \rightarrow Cx) \qquad\qquad A$$
$$2\ (2)\ Ta \qquad\qquad\qquad\qquad A$$
$$\cdot$$
$$\cdot$$
$$1,2\ (n)\ Ca$$

You know from both the second premise and the conclusion that there is an individual in the domain named 'a'. (Indeed, without either the second premise or the conclusion you wouldn't have the foggiest idea whether an individual of such a name existed.) Now focus on the first premise and only the first premise: 'All tyrants are clowns'. What do you know of Ardbeg *in light of this premise and in light of this premise alone*? Ponder. . . .

You do *not* know that Ardbeg is a clown! Banish the thought! In order to know *that*, you'd first have to know both that all tyrants are clowns (i.e., you'd have to know that the first premise is true) *and* that Ardbeg is a tyrant (i.e., you'd have to know that the second premise is also true). In other words, you'd have to be focusing on *both* premises. For the moment, however, I want you to focus only on the first.

From the claim that all tyrants are clowns, you know *this* about Ardbeg: you know that *if* Ardbeg is a tyrant *then* Ardbeg is a clown. Alternatively, think of it as follows. The first premise affirms that every object in the domain has a particular property: the *conditional* property of being such that *if* that object is a tyrant *then* it is a clown. So from this it follows that any particular object in the domain, e.g., Ardbeg, must have that same property, i.e., the property (once again) of being such that *if* it is a tyrant *then* it is a clown. Alternatively and more abstractly: from the claim that *every* object in the domain has a particular property or stands in a particular relation, it follows that *any* object in the domain has that property or stands in that relation. Behold an instance of Universal Quantifier Elimination:

S116:  $(\forall x)(Tx \rightarrow Cx), Ta \vdash Ca$

1 (1) $(\forall x)(Tx \rightarrow Cx)$  A
2 (2) $Ta$  A
1 (3) $Ta \rightarrow Ca$  1 ∀E
1,2 (4) $Ca$  3,2 →E

It should be clear from this derivation, if only in a very *tiny* way, that Predicate Logic/Quantification Theory is an *extension* of Propositional Logic: although at line (3) you used a brand-new, Predicate Logic/ Quantification Theory derivation rule, at line (4) you used one of your old Propositional Logic rules. I remind you of the definition of an extension of a formal system:

Definition:  A formal system $S_2$ is an *extension* of a formal system $S_1$ iff $S_2$ contains both the formal language and the deductive apparatus of $S_1$.

Insofar as Predicate Logic/Quantification Theory incorporates both the formal language and the deductive apparatus (the derivations rules) of Propositional Logic, Predicate Logic/Quantification Theory is an *extension* of Propositional Logic. Whatever you can do in Propositional Logic you can do in Predicate Logic/Quantification Theory—and then some.

# 3. ∃I: An Introduction to Existential Quantifier Introduction

Now suppose an argument with the same premises but a different conclusion:

> (1) All tyrants are clowns.
> (2) Ardbeg is a tyrant.
> _____
> ∴ (3) Someone is a clown.

In a domain restricted to people, the argument would go over into logical notation as follows:

S117:        $(\forall x)(Tx \rightarrow Cx)$, $Ta \vdash (\exists x)Cx$

| | | |
|---|---|---|
| 1 | (1) $(\forall x)(Tx \rightarrow Cx)$ | A |
| 2 | (2) $Ta$ | A |
| | . | |
| | . | |
| 1,2 | (n) $(\exists x)Cx$ | |

Until the very end, you proceed exactly as in the preceding derivation. Your goal is to prove that someone is a clown. Clearly, if *Ardbeg* is a clown then *someone* is a clown. Alternatively and more abstractly: if a particular object in the domain has a particular property, it follows that there exists at least one object in the domain that has that same property. Hence the move from (4) to (5) via Existential Quantifier Introduction:

| | | |
|---|---|---|
| 1 | (1) $(\forall x)(Tx \rightarrow Cx)$ | A |
| 2 | (2) $Ta$ | A |
| 1 | (3) $Ta \rightarrow Ca$ | 1 $\forall$E |
| 1,2 | (4) $Ca$ | 3,2 $\rightarrow$E |
| 1,2 | (5) $(\exists x)Cx$ | 4 $\exists$I |

# 4. ∀I: An Introduction to Universal Quantifier Introduction

So far so good. Time now for Universal Quantifier Introduction. Let's start with an obviously valid argument and an obviously flawed derivation. First the valid argument:

> (1) Everyone is both a tyrant and a clown.
>
> ∴ (2) Everyone is a tyrant.

Now for the flawed derivation. (Assume, once again, a domain restricted to people.)

S118:          $(\forall x)(Tx \wedge Cx) \vdash (\forall x)Tx$

| | |
|---|---|
| 1 (1) $(\forall x)(Tx \wedge Cx)$ | A |
| 1 (2) $Ta \wedge Ca$ | 1 ∀E |
| 1 (3) $Ta$ | 2 ∧E |
| 1 (4) $(\forall x)Tx$ | 3 ∀I |

Once again: the argument is valid but the derivation is flawed. So where's the flaw?

(1) is simply an assumption. Unless it's ill-formed—which it isn't—*it* can't be flawed.

(2) *is* flawed—but intuitively it should strike you that it isn't *fatally* flawed. It's flawed insofar as you haven't the foggiest idea whether there's an individual in the domain named '*a*'. If there is such an individual then (2) is perfectly legitimate; otherwise it's perfectly *illegitimate*. In other words, it isn't legitimate to introduce proper names of individuals if the proper names aren't 'given', i.e., if they don't appear already in the premise(s) and/or the conclusion.

So what does it mean to say that (2) isn't *fatally* flawed? What it means is that if there *had* been another premise containing the proper name '*a*', then the ∀E move at (2) (or wherever) would have been perfectly acceptable—and yet the derivation would remain flawed nonetheless, as you will see presently.

(3) is obviously unobjectionable.

And that, of course, leaves (4)—which, by a process of elimination, *must* be the villain of the piece. And indeed it is: it may well be true that Ardbeg is a tyrant; it doesn't follow that *everyone* is a tyrant. Clearly, what's true of the particular person Ardbeg may *not* be true of *all* people. Hence the illegitimacy of (4).

Question: That being the case, how is it ever possible to derive a universally quantified *wff*?

Answer: Flashback (painful though it may be) to your high school geometry class. . . . Egad! There's the old curmudgeon himself at the blackboard: old Mr. Groats. "Let *ABC* be any triangle," Mr. Groats intones—and proceeds to draw a triangle on the blackboard, labeling the vertices '*A*', '*B*', and '*C*', respectively. Much scribbling with chalk follows, up and down and all over the blackboard, culminating in Mr. Groats' triumphant proclamation: "And so it follows that the angles of *ABC* add up to 180 degrees." But Mr. Groats doesn't stop *there*. He immediately (and ever so casually) draws a *second* conclusion, indeed the *crucial* conclusion: "And so the angles of *every* triangle add up to 180 degrees. Q.E.D."

Now, good logician that you are—and that no doubt you were then as well—what kept you from leaping out of your desk and onto your feet, flailing your arms in the air, and then *smashing* your right fist down on your desk? "*Really now, Mr. Groats! Really!* It may well be true that the angles of *ABC* add up to 180 degrees! You've convinced all of us of that! But it hardly follows that the angles of *every* triangle add up to 180 degrees! Why should what's true of *one* triangle—*ABC*—be true of *every* triangle? It may well be true that *Ardbeg* is a tyrant—but it hardly follows that *everyone* is a tyrant! Where on Earth is the *logic* behind your reasoning, Mr. Groats???"

Now of course Mr. Groats would have had the last word here—and not *merely* because he wielded all the power. There *is* a radical difference between the following two cases:

> Ardbeg is a tyrant.
> _____
> ∴ *Everyone* is a tyrant.

> The angles of *ABC* add up to 180 degrees.
> _____
> ∴ The angles of *every* triangle add up to 180 degrees.

And don't say that the difference here is that the first argument has to do with people and the second has to do with geometric figures! (To be sure, that's true—but it's utterly irrelevant.)

So what's the secret here? Think of how Mr. Groats began the demonstration: "Let $ABC$ be any triangle." Think of that: "Let $ABC$ be *any* triangle. *Any* triangle." *$ABC$ has no characteristics that distinguish it from any other triangle.* It's a three-sided, plane, closed figure, *period.* Mr. Groats made *no special assumption* about $ABC$. Mr. Groats never said, "Assume that $ABC$ is an *equilateral* triangle." Mr. Groats never said, "Assume that it's an *isosceles* triangle." Mr. Groats never said, "Assume that it's a *right-angled* triangle." Mr. Groats treated $ABC$ simply as a *triangle, any* triangle, period.

Alternatively: Mr. Groats treated $ABC$ simply as a *proxy* for any triangle. Indeed he could just as well have called the triangle '$x$'. And having proved something of $x$, he has thereby proved something of *all* triangles—but of course *only* of triangles. Why of *all* triangles? For two reasons. First, because the free variable '$x$' (or '$ABC$') stands for *any* triangle, i.e., for *any* object in the domain of triangles. And second, because Mr. Groats made *no special assumption* about $x$ that might serve to distinguish it from other members of the domain. He never said, "Assume that $ABC$ is *this* sort of triangle or *that* sort of triangle." What-ever is true of $x$, therefore, is true of *every* member of the domain, i.e., of every triangle.

To be sure, if Mr. Groats had begun by saying, "Let $ABC$ be any *isosceles* triangle," his conclusion would have held of all *isosceles* trian-gles—but of course *only* of isosceles triangles. In saying, "Let $ABC$ be any triangle," Mr. Groats was really saying, "Suppose a domain of triangles, and let $ABC$ be *any* object in the domain, i.e., *any* triangle." Hence what holds true of $ABC$ holds true of *any* object in the domain, i.e., of *any* triangle.

We return to our earlier derivation. Suppose that you get rid of the proper name '$a$', and introduce the free variable '$x$' instead:

S119:        $(\forall x)(Tx \wedge Cx) \vdash (\forall x)Tx$

| | | |
|---|---|---|
| 1 (1) | $(\forall x)(Tx \wedge Cx)$ | A |
| 1 (2) | $Tx \wedge Cx$ | 1 ∀E |
| 1 (3) | $Tx$ | 2 ∧E |
| 1 (4) | $(\forall x)Tx$ | 3 ∀I |

Perfecto.

Note that in line (2) you could have introduced *any* variable, e.g., '*u*', '*v*', '*w*', '*x*', '*y*', or '*z*'. (Remember: for our purposes, we are treating the last six letters of the alphabet as variables, and the first twenty letters as proper names. Were we to need either more variables or more proper names, we could simply add numeral subscripts to the relevant letters, e.g., '$x_1$' or '$a_1$'.)

By the way, the following is also perfectly correct:

S120:    $(\forall x)(Tx \wedge Cx) \vdash (\forall z)Tz$

| | | |
|---|---|---|
| 1 (1) | $(\forall x)(Tx \wedge Cx)$ | A |
| 1 (2) | $Ty \wedge Cy$ | 1 $\forall$E |
| 1 (3) | $Ty$ | 2 $\wedge$E |
| 1 (4) | $(\forall z)Tz$ | 3 $\forall$I |

Don't think that because each occurrence of the (bound) variable in line (1) is '*x*', each occurrence of the (free) variable in line (2) must also be '*x*'. Line (1) simply says, 'Given any person, he (or she) is a tyrant and he (or she) is a clown'. Alternatively: 'The property of being a tyrant and the property of being a clown are true of (or are instantiated by) each object in the domain'. It follows from the first premise that no matter which object in the domain you select in line (2), it will have each of these two properties. In S119 you selected *x* at line (2), and in S120 you selected *y*. It makes no difference. In the move from (1) to (2), you are simply lopping off the universal quantifier and replacing the pronoun 'he', 'she', or 'it' with a variable that, once again, functions as a proxy for *any* object in the domain.

So now you know, of course, the answer to the crucial question: What justifies the move from (3) to (4) in both S119 and S120; i.e., what justifies the $\forall$I move? A preliminary (and tentative) answer: What's true of *any* object in the domain is true of *every* object in the domain—*so long as you make no special assumption about that object*. In other words, you must make no assumption that that object has *this* or *that* property—a property that might serve to distinguish it from other objects in the domain. In S119 *x* is indeed *any* object in the domain; and in S120 *y* too is *any* object in the domain. And neither in S119 nor in S120 does what's true of *x* or *y*, respectively, rest on a special *assumption* about *x* or *y*. To be sure, in both S119 and S120 (3) rests on an assumption, of course, but—and here's the crucial point—the assumption makes no reference to $x$ or $y$. Hence what's true of $x$ or $y$ is true of *every* object in the domain. Hence the justification for the ∀I move from (3) to (4) in both S119 and S120.

# 5. ∃E: An Introduction to Existential Quantifier Elimination

Consider the following obviously valid argument:

> There exists at least one mad logician.
> ─────────────────────────────────
> ∴ There exists at least one logician.

How might you prove this argument valid? Suppose that you translate it into logical notation as follows:

> $(\exists x)(Lx \land Mx)$
> ─────────────────
> ∴ $(\exists x)Lx$

Question: How do you derive *this* conclusion from *this* premise?
Wrong answer: By ∧E.
Question: Why is '∧E' the wrong answer?
Answer: Because the premise, $(\exists x)(Lx \land Mx)$, isn't a *conjunction*: it's an *existentially quantified* conjunction. Not being a conjunction, it's not a suitable candidate for ∧E.

Puzzled? Think of it like this: '$(\exists x)(Lx \land Mx)$' is no more of a conjunction than '$-(P \land Q)$' is a conjunction. '$-(P \land Q)$' is a *negated* conjunction: the main operator is the dash. And '$(\exists x)(Lx \land Mx)$' is an *existentially quantified* conjunction: the main operator is the existential quantifier. In neither case is ∧E a legitimate move.

How, then, to proceed? Precisely because the premise is an existentially quantified *wff*, you should think of introducing an assumption. Why so? If the premise asserts that there exists at least one object that has a particular property, then it's perfectly reasonable to entertain the assumption that a *particular* object in the domain has the property in question. To be sure, if all that you know is that there exists at least one object that has the property, i.e., that some object or other has the property, then of course you don't know exactly *which* object has the property. But that's fine: it's perfectly permissible to *assume* that some particular object $x$ (where '$x$' designates *any* object in the domain) has the property in question. The trick now is to see what follows from this assumption.

Alternatively, think of it like this: An existentially quantified *wff*, you'll recall, is a disguised *disjunction*—and, in the course of a derivation from a disjunction, it's natural to introduce two assumptions, each of them a ∨E assumption. The only difference is that in this case you'll be introducing *one* assumption—and it will be an ∃E assumption.

S121:          $(\exists x)(Lx \land Mx) \vdash (\exists x)Lx$

  1 (1) $(\exists x)(Lx \land Mx)$          A
  2 (2) $Lx \land Mx$                      A
  2 (3) $Lx$                            2 ∧E
  2 (4) $(\exists x)Lx$                   3 ∃I
    (5) $(Lx \land Mx) \rightarrow (\exists x)Lx$   2,4 →I
  1 (6) $(\exists x)Lx$                   1,5 ∃E

Notice that when you invoke ∃E in line (6), you cite two *wffs*. The first is the existentially quantified *wff* in line (1) that was the reason for your introducing an ∃E assumption in line (2). The second is the conditional in line (5) whose antecedent is your ∃E assumption and whose consequent is your targeted *wff*.

"Now exactly what's going on here?" you wonder. On the obvious interpretation, (1) says that there exists at least one mad logician. (2) is an assumption: 'Assume that $x$ is a mad logician'. "Who or what is $x$?" you ask. Once again: $x$ is simply an object in the domain. Indeed, $x$ is *any* object in the domain. "But what if $x$ *isn't* a mad logician?" you reply. It doesn't matter whether $x$ is or isn't a mad logician. You're merely *assuming* that $x$ is a mad logician; you're not *asserting* that $x$ is a mad logician. Your goal is simply to see how much mileage you can get out of this assumption, i.e., to see whether from this assumption (along with, perhaps, other assumptions) you're able to generate your targeted *wff*.

Think of it as follows. From (2), the ∃E assumption that $x$ is a mad logician, it follows that (4) *someone* is a logician. Hence (5), the crucial conditional: If $x$ is a mad logician then *someone* is a logician. Whence it follows that if *someone* (i.e., someone or other) is a mad logician then *someone* (i.e., someone or other) is a logician. So given (1), the premise that *someone* is a mad logician, it follows that (6) *someone* is a logician.

Alternatively, think of ∨E: you *assume* first the left and then the right disjunct of your disjunction without *asserting* either one, precisely in order to see how much mileage you can get out of each assumption. Indeed the mileage that you try to get out of your one ∃E assumption is identical to the mileage that you try to get out of each of your two ∨E assumptions. In each instance, you try to generate your targeted *wff* so that you can then derive the conditional whose antecedent is either your ∃E assumption or your ∨E assumption, and whose consequent is your targeted *wff*.

Now you're puzzled. Each disjunction has two disjuncts, and so each ∨E derivation requires you to introduce *two* assumptions, one corresponding to each disjunct. Why, then, do you introduce only *one* assumption in an ∃E derivation?

Take another look at the derivation of S121. Suppose a domain of two objects: Ardbeg and Bobo. The de-quantified version of the S121 premise, '$(\exists x)(Lx \wedge Mx)$', would then be '$(La \wedge Ma) \vee (Lb \wedge Mb)$'; and the derivation, with *this* version of S121's premise and with S121's conclusion, would be as follows:

S122:        $(La \wedge Ma) \vee (Lb \wedge Mb) \vdash (\exists x)Lx$

| | | |
|---|---|---|
| 1 | (1) $(La \wedge Ma) \vee (Lb \wedge Mb)$ | A |
| 2 | (2) $La \wedge Ma$ | A |
| 2 | (3) $La$ | 2 $\wedge$E |
| 2 | (4) $(\exists x)Lx$ | 3 $\exists$I |
| | (5) $(La \wedge Ma) \rightarrow (\exists x)Lx$ | 2,4 $\rightarrow$I |
| 5 | (6) $Lb \wedge Mb$ | A |
| 5 | (7) $Lb$ | 6 $\wedge$E |
| 5 | (8) $(\exists x)Lx$ | 7 $\exists$I |
| | (9) $(Lb \wedge Mb) \rightarrow (\exists x)Lx$ | 6,8 $\rightarrow$I |
| 1 | (10) $(\exists x)Lx$ | 1,5,9 $\vee$E |

Note that the only substantial difference between the S121 derivation and the S122 derivation is the introduction of *one* assumption
in S121—'$Lx \land Mx$'—and *two* assumptions in S122—'$(La \land Ma)$' and
'$(Lb \land Mb)$'. But the *one* assumption in S121 is equivalent to the *two*
assumptions in S122. How so? Read on.

The S121 premise affirms that there exists at least one mad logician. The $\exists$E assumption that you introduce in line (2) is that $x$ is a
mad logician. The variable '$x$' stands for *any* object in the domain. (In
this case, it stands for any *person* whomsoever.) It makes no difference
how many objects are in the domain. Suppose that there were three:
Ardbeg, Bobo, and Coco. You could always de-quantify the line-(1)
premise and proceed with a $\lor$E derivation that would simply be a variation on the S122 derivation. You would end up doing a $\lor$E derivation
within the scope of another $\lor$E derivation. Your derivation, however,
would be quite laborious:

S123:     $(La \land Ma) \lor [(Lb \land Mb) \lor (Lc \land Mc)] \vdash (\exists x)Lx$

| | |
|---|---|
| 1 (1) $(La \land Ma) \lor [(Lb \land Mb) \lor (Lc \land Mc)]$ | A |
| 2 (2) $La \land Ma$ | A |
| 2 (3) $La$ | 2 $\land$E |
| 2 (4) $(\exists x)Lx$ | 3 $\exists$I |
| (5) $(La \land Ma) \to (\exists x)Lx$ | 2,4 $\to$I |
| 6 (6) $(Lb \land Mb) \lor (Lc \land Mc)$ | A |
| 7 (7) $Lb \land Mb$ | A |
| 7 (8) $Lb$ | 7 $\land$E |
| 7 (9) $(\exists x)Lx$ | 8 $\exists$I |
| (10) $(Lb \land Mb) \to (\exists x)Lx$ | 7,9 $\to$I |
| 11 (11) $Lc \land Mc$ | A |
| 11 (12) $Lc$ | 11 $\land$E |
| 11 (13) $(\exists x)Lx$ | 12 $\exists$I |
| (14) $(Lc \land Mc) \to (\exists x)Lx$ | 11,13 $\to$I |
| 6 (15) $(\exists x)Lx$ | 6,10,14 $\lor$E |
| (16) $[(Lb \land Mb) \lor (Lc \land Mc)] \to (\exists x)Lx$ | 6,15 $\to$E |
| 1 (17) $(\exists x)Lx$ | 1,5,16 $\lor$E |

The variable '*x*' in S121 renders unnecessary all of the de-quanti-ficational fussiness of S122 and (especially) S123. The object *x* serves as a proxy for each object in the domain: *x* could be Ardbeg; *x* could be Bobo; and *x* could be Coco. Therefore there's no difference of any consequence between making the ∃E assumption that *x* has a particular property or stands in a particular relation, and making the ∨E assumption that Ardbeg (or Bobo or Coco or any named individual) has that property or stands in that particular relation.

And just as the object *x* serves as a proxy for each object in the domain, so the ∃E assumption '*Lx* ∧ *Mx*' serves as a proxy for each of the ∨E assumptions '*La* ∧ *Ma*', '*Lb* ∧ *Mb*', and '*Lc* ∧ *Mc*'. '*Lx* ∧ *Mx*' could just as well be '*La* ∧ *Ma*' or '*Lb* ∧ *Mb*' or '*Lc* ∧ *Mc*'. Think of an ∃E derivation, in other words, as neither more nor less than a *condensed*—a *streamlined*—version of the corresponding ∨E derivation.

It may be helpful to generalize from the preceding. You want to know why an ∃E proof proves what it claims to prove; i.e., what the reasoning is that underlies, or serves to justify, every ∃E proof. And you also want to know exactly how an ∃E proof is analogous to a ∨E proof.

Let '***P***' be any property or relation; let '***v***' be any variable; and let ***v*** be any object in the domain. (An example: '***P***' might be the complex property that ***v*** has of being a mad logician; alternatively, '***P***' might be the relation in which ***v*** stands with respect to ***w*** of being older than ***w***.)

Suppose that there exists at least one object which has a particular property or stands in a particular relation: '(∃***v***)***Pv***'. Suppose too that *if **v**—any* object in the domain—has that property or stands in that relation *then* '△' is the case: '***Pv*** → △'. It follows from the two preceding propositions, i.e., from '(∃***v***)***Pv***' and '***Pv*** →△', that '△' is the case.

The reasoning here is *identical* to the reasoning underlying ∨E. For simplicity's sake, I'll focus on a domain consisting of only two objects, but everything I say applies, albeit with some modification, to a domain of any number of objects. Let '***P***' designate, once again, any property or relation; let '***a***' and '***b***' designate any proper names; and let ***a*** and ***b*** be the two objects in the domain corresponding to the names '***a***' and '***b***', respectively.

Suppose that either $a$ or $b$ has a particular property or stands in a particular relation: '$Pa \lor Pb$'. Suppose next that *if $a$* has that property or stands in that relation *then* '$\triangle$' is the case: '$Pa \rightarrow \triangle$'. Suppose finally that *if $b$* has that property or stands in that relation *then* '$\triangle$' is the case: '$Pb \rightarrow \triangle$'. It follows from the three preceding propositions that '$\triangle$' is the case.

The reasoning is identical in the two cases—the $\exists E$ case and the $\lor E$ case. Why so? Because in the $\exists E$ derivation, the object $v$ serves as a proxy for each of the objects in the domain; i.e., it could be *any* of them. In particular, $v$ could be the object $a$; alternatively, $v$ could be the object $b$. Therefore there's no difference of any consequence between making the $\exists E$ assumption that $v$ has a particular property or stands in a particular relation, and making the $\lor E$ assumptions that $a$ has that property or stands in that particular relation and that $b$ has that property or stands in that particular relation.

Moreover, the $\exists E$ assumption '$Pv$' serves as a proxy for each of the $\lor E$ assumptions '$Pa$' and '$Pb$'. '$Pv$' could just as well be either '$Pa$' or '$Pb$'. Therefore there's no difference of any consequence between the derived $\exists E$ *wff* '$Pv \rightarrow \triangle$', on the one hand, and the derived $\lor E$ *wffs* '$Pa \rightarrow \triangle$' and '$Pb \rightarrow \triangle$', on the other hand.

So in a two-object domain there's no difference of any consequence between '$(\exists v)Pv$' and '$Pa \lor Pb$'. And there's no difference of any consequence between '$Pv \rightarrow \triangle$', on the one hand, and '$Pa \rightarrow \triangle$' and '$Pb \rightarrow \triangle$', on the other hand. So it should be unsurprising that there's no difference of any consequence between deriving '$\triangle$' by $\exists E$ from '$(\exists v)Pv$' and '$Pv \rightarrow \triangle$', on the one hand, and deriving '$\triangle$' by $\lor E$ from '$Pa \lor Pb$', '$Pa \rightarrow \triangle$', and '$Pb \rightarrow \triangle$', on the other hand. The legitimacy of $\exists E$, in other words, stands or falls with the legitimacy of $\lor E$. But of course the legitimacy of $\lor E$ is beyond doubt, is it not? And so the legitimacy of $\exists E$ should also be beyond doubt.

# 6. Derivations

Before studying the step-by-step details of the following two derivations, each one an instance of Quantifier Negation, try to work your
way through them on your own.

S124:        $(\forall x)-Lx \vdash -(\exists x)Lx$

Your first inclination might be to perform $\forall$E on the premise,
'$(\forall x)-Lx$', thereby generating '$-Lx$'. Your second inclination might
be to perform $\exists$I on '$-Lx$', thereby generating your conclusion, '$-(\exists x)$
$Lx$'. But not so fast. '$-(\exists x)Lx$' isn't an existentially quantified *wff*: it's
the *negation* thereof. $\exists$I on '$-Lx$' generates '$(\exists x)-Lx$'—which you *don't*
need, rather than '$-(\exists x)Lx$'—which you *do* need. . . . Back to square
one.

Suppose that you introduce the opposite of your conclusion as a
*Reductio* assumption in line (2), with the goal, obviously, of generating
a contradiction.

$$1\ (1)\ (\forall x)-Lx \qquad\qquad\qquad A$$
$$2\ (2)\ (\exists x)Lx \qquad\qquad\qquad\ \ A$$
$$.$$
$$.$$
$$(n–1)\ \triangle \wedge -\triangle$$
$$(n)\ -(\exists x)Lx \qquad\qquad\qquad 2,n–1\ -I$$

Your now have to zero in on a *specific* contradiction. The likeliest candidates are either the conjunction of (1) and its opposite, or
the conjunction of (2) and its opposite. Suppose that you aim for the
former, the conjunction of (1) and its opposite, in (n–1). Your target in
(n–2), accordingly, is the opposite of (1), i.e., '$-(\forall x)-Lx$'.

$$1\ (1)\ (\forall x)-Lx \qquad\qquad\qquad A$$
$$2\ (2)\ (\exists x)Lx \qquad\qquad\qquad\ \ A$$
$$.$$
$$.$$

$(n–2) \; –(\forall x)–Lx$

$(n–1) \; (\forall x)–Lx \wedge –(\forall x)–Lx \qquad 1,n–2 \; \wedge I$

$(n) \; –(\exists x)Lx \qquad\qquad\qquad 2,n–1 \; –I$

(2) is an existentially quantified *wff*, so you'll introduce '$Lx$' as an $\exists E$ assumption in line (3). You look up at line (1) and you think $\forall E$ thoughts for line (4). A contradiction is now staring you in the face.

| | | |
|---|---|---|
| 1 | (1) $(\forall x)–Lx$ | A |
| 2 | (2) $(\exists x)Lx$ | A |
| 3 | (3) $Lx$ | A |
| 1 | (4) $–Lx$ | 1 $\forall E$ |
| 1,3 | (5) $Lx \wedge –Lx$ | 3,4 $\wedge I$ |

.

.

$(n–2) \; –(\forall x)–Lx$

$(n–1) \; (\forall x)–Lx \wedge –(\forall x)–Lx \qquad 1,n–2 \; \wedge I$

$(n) \; –(\exists x)Lx \qquad\qquad\qquad 2,n–1 \; –I$

Don't forget that your $\exists E$ target in line ($n$–2) is '$–(\forall x)–Lx$', the opposite of (1). Your line-(5) contradiction rests on both (1), $(\forall x)–Lx$, and (3), $Lx$. You're now able to generate '$–(\forall x)–Lx$' in line (6), by zapping (1). The rest of the derivation should be more or less obvious.

| | | |
|---|---|---|
| 1 | (1) $(\forall x)–Lx$ | A |
| 2 | (2) $(\exists x)Lx$ | A |
| 3 | (3) $Lx$ | A |
| 1 | (4) $–Lx$ | 1 $\forall E$ |
| 1,3 | (5) $Lx \wedge –Lx$ | 3,4 $\wedge I$ |
| 3 | (6) $–(\forall x)–Lx$ | 1,5 $–I$ |
| | (7) $Lx \rightarrow –(\forall x)–Lx$ | 3,6 $\rightarrow I$ |
| 2 | (8) $–(\forall x)–Lx$ | 2,7 $\exists E$ |
| 1,2 | (9) $(\forall x)–Lx \wedge –(\forall x)–Lx$ | 1, 8 $\wedge I$ |
| 1 | (10) $–(\exists x)Lx$ | 2,9 $–I$ |

The following sequent is somewhat trickier.

S125:        $-(\forall x)Lx \vdash (\exists x)-Lx$

There's nothing much that you can do with the premise. As you know, it's not a universally quantified *wff*: it's the *negation* of a universally quantified *wff*. As such, it's not a suitable candidate for ∀E.

Your hands are tied. Much as you may not wish to do a *Reductio* proof—it's not going to be an easy one—you have no choice. The key question is: '*Which Reductio* assumption do you introduce in line (2)? Suppose that you aim for '−Lx' in your second-to-last line, with the intention of doing ∃I from your second-to-last line to your last line. In that case, your *Reductio* assumption in line (2) will be '*Lx*'.

1 (1) $-(\forall x)Lx$        A
2 (2) $Lx$        A

      .

      .

(*n*–1) $-Lx$        ?
  (*n*) $(\exists x)-Lx$        *n*–1 ∃I

The problem is that you're now stuck. You're aiming for a contradiction. Doing ∃I on (2), '*Lx*', to generate '$(\exists x)Lx$', simply won't help you generate a contradiction. Alternatively, doing ∀I on (2) to generate '$(\forall x)Lx$' *would* generate a contradiction, thanks to (1), '$-(\forall x)Lx$'. The problem, though, is that the move from '*Lx*' in line (2) to '$(\forall x)Lx$' is *illegitimate*. You don't yet know this, but it's impermissible to perform ∀I on a *wff* with respect to a variable '*v*' if the *wff* either is, or rests on, an assumption containing a free occurrence of '*v*'. Assume that *x* will be ordering a pound of smoked whitefish tomorrow. Does it follow that *everyone* will be ordering a pound of smoked whitefish tomorrow? (If it *does* follow, then you'd be well advised to buy smoked whitefish futures *immediately*.)

Back to square one. You need a *Reductio* assumption—but (clearly) a different *Reductio* assumption. There's really only one other possibility, and that's the *obvious* candidate: the opposite of your conclusion.

$$1 \ (1) \ -(\forall x)Lx \qquad\qquad A$$
$$2 \ (2) \ -(\exists x)-Lx \qquad\qquad A$$

.

.

$$(n) \ (\exists x)-Lx \qquad\qquad ?$$

So what now? (1), as you know, is the negation of a quantified *wff*—
and so, alas, is (2). Therefore you can't do $\forall$E on (1) and you can't begin
an $\exists$E proof with respect to (2). Therefore there's nothing that you can
do with either of them. What you need to do is come up with another
*Reductio* assumption, in addition to your line-(2) *Reductio* assumption.
But it can't be just any old *Reductio* assumption. You're trying to generate a contradiction, so you should choose a *wff* that will help you generate the contradiction. The two likeliest contenders are the opposite of
(1) and the opposite of (2). Suppose that you aim for the opposite of
(1); i.e., suppose that you aim for '$(\forall x)Lx$'. To generate it, you'll need
'$Lx$'—but *not* as an assumption and *not* as a *wff* resting on any assumption containing a free '$x$'. Obviously your line-(3) *Reductio* assumption
will be '$-Lx$'. Your goal is to generate a contradiction from '$-Lx$', so
that you can then write down first '$--Lx$' and then '$Lx$'. Your hope is
that '$Lx$' won't rest on any assumption containing a free '$x$'.

$$1 \ (1) \ -(\forall x)Lx \qquad\qquad A$$
$$2 \ (2) \ -(\exists x)-Lx \qquad\qquad A$$
$$3 \ (3) \ -Lx \qquad\qquad A$$

.

.

| | |
|---|---|
| $(n-6) \ \triangle \wedge -\triangle$ | $?,? \ \wedge$I |
| $(n-5) \ --Lx$ | $3,n-6 \ -$I |
| $(n-4) \ Lx$ | $n-5 \ --$E |
| $(n-3) \ (\forall x)Lx$ | $n-4 \ \forall$I |
| $(n-2) \ (\forall x)Lx \wedge -(\forall x)Lx$ | $n-3,1 \ \wedge$I |
| $(n-1) \ --(\exists x)-Lx$ | $2,n-2 \ -$I |
| $(n) \ (\exists x)-Lx$ | $n-1 \ --$E |

It's crucial that $(n-2)$ rest on both (1) and (2), so that $(n-1)$ can rest
on just (1). For $(n-2)$ to rest on both (1) and (2), $(n-3)$ has to rest on
(2). $(n-4)$, therefore, also has to rest on (2), as does $(n-5)$. Moral of the

story: whatever contradiction you generate from (3) had better rest on
(2) in addition to whatever other *wff(s)* it happens to rest on. The end
is in sight.

| | | |
|---|---|---|
| 1 | (1) $-(\forall x)Lx$ | A |
| 2 | (2) $-(\exists x)-Lx$ | A |
| 3 | (3) $-Lx$ | A |
| 3 | (4) $(\exists x)-Lx$ | 3 ∃I |
| 2,3 | (5) $(\exists x)-Lx \wedge -(\exists x)-Lx$ | 4,2 ∧I |
| 2 | (6) $--Lx$ | 3,5 −I |
| 2 | (7) $Lx$ | 6 −−E |
| 2 | (8) $(\forall x)Lx$ | 7 ∀I |
| 1,2 | (9) $(\forall x)Lx \wedge -(\forall x)Lx$ | 8,1 ∧I |
| 1 | (10) $--(\exists x)-Lx$ | 2,9 −I |
| 1 | (11) $(\exists x)-Lx$ | 10 −−E |

## Exercises

For each of the following sequents, derive its conclusion from its
premises.

1.   S126: $(\forall x)[Lx \rightarrow (Mx \wedge Nx)] \vdash (\forall x)(Lx \rightarrow Mx)$
2.   S127: $(\exists x)[Lx \wedge (Mx \vee Nx)] \vdash (\exists x)[(Lx \wedge Mx) \vee$
     $(Lx \wedge Nx)]$
3.   S128: $(\forall x)(Lx \rightarrow Mx), (\exists x)(Lx \wedge Nx) \vdash (\exists x)(Mx \wedge Nx)$
4.   S129: $(\forall x)[Lx \rightarrow (Mx \vee Nx)], (\exists x)Lx \vdash$
     $(\exists x)(--Nx \vee --Mx)$
5.   S130: $(\forall x)(Lx \rightarrow Mx) \vdash (\forall x)Lx \rightarrow (\forall x)Mx$
6.   S131: $(\forall x)(Lx \rightarrow Mx), (\forall x)(Mx \rightarrow Nx), (\exists x)-Nx \vdash$
     $(\exists x)-Lx$
7.   S132: $(\exists x)-Lx \vdash -(\forall x)Lx$
8.   S133: $(\exists x)Lx \vdash -(\forall x)-Lx$
9.   S134: $(\forall x)Lx \vdash -(\exists x)-Lx$
10.  S135: $-(\exists x)Lx \vdash (\forall x)-Lx$
11.  S136: $-(\forall x)-Lx \vdash (\exists x)Lx$

12.  S137: $-(\exists x)-Lx \vdash (\forall x)Lx$
13.  S138: $(\exists x)(Lx \wedge -Mx) \vdash -(\forall x)(Lx \rightarrow Mx)$
14.  S139: $(\exists x)(Lx \wedge Mx) \vdash -(\forall x)(Lx \rightarrow -Mx)$
15.  S140: $(\forall x)(Lx \rightarrow -Mx) \vdash -(\exists x)(Lx \wedge Mx)$
16.  S141: $(\forall x)(Lx \rightarrow Mx) \vdash -(\exists x)(Lx \wedge -Mx)$
17.  S142: $-(\forall x)[Lx \rightarrow Mx) \vdash (\exists x)(Lx \wedge -Mx)$
18.  S143: $-(\forall x)(Lx \rightarrow -Mx) \vdash (\exists x)(Lx \wedge Mx)$
19.  S144: $-(\exists x)(Lx \wedge Mx) \vdash (\forall x)(Lx \rightarrow -Mx)$
20.  S145: $-(\exists x)(Lx \wedge -Mx) \vdash (\forall x)(Lx \rightarrow Mx)$

# 7. The Refined Version of the Quantifier Rules: Preliminary Matters

This section will strike you as opaque, perhaps *impenetrably* so. Worse yet (if there *is* anything worse yet), it will strike you as ghastly, monstrous, and tortuous. It will cause you to rue the day that you ever set foot in a logic course! Try, however, to be patient; try to persevere; and try your best to make sense of the difficulty that looms before you. If you succeed, you'll find the subsequent discussion of the refined version of the quantification rules far less painful than you would otherwise find it.

So fasten your seatbelts, as they say; it's going to be a bumpy ride. But don't despair *completely*: bumpy rides are often challenging, and challenges can sometimes be *fun*.

What follows are seven *crucial* definitions. (You should have a sense of déjà vu with respect to some of them.)

First Definition:       '$v$' signifies any free variable.

Second Definition:      '$Pv$' signifies any open *wff* containing both the predicate '$P$' and at least one occurrence of the free variable '$v$'.

Note that '**P**' signifies any *property* of some object *v*, or any *relation* in which *v* is one of the *relata*, i.e., one of the objects related to one or more objects. Note too that '**Pv**' contains at least one occurrence of the free variable '*v*', and as such signifies an *open wff.*

The *open wff* might be an atomic *wff*, i.e., a *wff* that contains no connectives or quantifiers, e.g., '*Lx*' or '*Ayy*', as in rows 1 and 3, respectively, in the table below.

Alternatively, the *open wff* might contain at least one connective but no quantifiers, e.g., '*Lx* → *Mx*', as in row 2 in the table below.

Lastly, the *open wff* might contain at least one quantifier. Thus '**P**' might signify the property of being a magician *and* of being admired by *everyone*, as in row 4; or the property of being a logician if *everyone* is a logician, as in row 5; or the property of being a magician whom *someone* admires, as in row 6; etc.

By providing seven different instances of '**Pv**', the following table should make clear exactly what '**Pv**' means.

| | **Pv** | **P** | **v** |
|---|---|---|---|
| 1 | *Lx* | *L*... | *x* |
| 2 | *Lx* → *Mx* | *L*... → *M*... | *x* |
| 3 | *Ayy* | *A*... ... | *y* |
| 4 | *My* ∧ (∀*x*)*Axy* | *M*... ∧ (∀*x*)*Ax*... | *y* |
| 5 | (∀*x*)*Lx* → *Lx* | (∀*x*)*Lx* → *L* ... | *x* |
| 6 | (∃*x*)(*My* ∧ *Axy*) | (∃*x*)(*M*... ∧ *Ax*...) | *y* |
| 7 | (∀*x*) −(∃*y*) −*Rwxyz* | (∀*x*) −(∃*y*) −*R*...*xy*... | either *w* or *z* |

Two points. First, note that the *wff* in row 7 contains more than one free variable: '*w*' and '*z*'. Remember: '**Pv**' signifies any *wff* that contains at least one occurrence of the free variable '*v*'. So in a case where you have an instance of a *wff* '**Pv**' that contains *more* than one free variable, it will be *your* choice which of the free variables to treat as '*v*'. (This will be a *strategic* choice on your part. The rationale for your choice will become clear once we return to derivations.)

Second, note that '*x*' in row 5 occurs *both* bound (in the first two of its occurrences) *and* free (in the third). In other words, although '*v*' in '**Pv**' must be free in at least *one* of its occurrences, it may well be bound in others. This will be the case, of course, whenever '**Pv**' signifies a *wff* that contains a universally or existentially quantified '*v*' in addition to a free '$v$'—which is *exactly* what you find in row 5. Normally, you would expect the quantifier(s) embedded within the *wff* that '$Pv$' signifies to bind some variable(s) *other than* '$v$', as in rows 4, 6, and 7. As row 5 illustrates, however, the quantifier(s) may *also* bind '$v$' itself in one or more of its occurrences. In either case, of course, '$Pv$' must be free in at least *one* of its occurrences.

| | |
|---|---|
| **Third Definition:** | '$(\forall v)Pv$' signifies any universally quantified *wff*. |
| **Fourth Definition:** | '$(\exists v)Pv$' signifies any existentially quantified *wff*. |

These two definitions are obvious, yes? But note that '$Pv$' signifies the *whole* of the *wff* to the right of '$(\forall v)$' or '$(\exists v)$', as the case may be. Note too that '$v$' is the variable in '$(\forall v)$' or '$(\exists v)$', as the following table illustrates.

| | $(\forall v)Pv$ | $Pv$ | $v$ |
|---|---|---|---|
| 1 | $(\forall x)Lx$ | $Lx$ | $x$ |
| 2 | $(\forall x)(Lx \rightarrow Mx)$ | $(Lx \rightarrow Mx)$ | $x$ |
| 3 | $(\forall y)Lyy$ | $Lyy$ | $y$ |
| 4 | $(\forall y)[(\forall x)My \wedge Axy]$ | $[(\forall x)My \wedge Axy]$ | $y$ |
| 5 | $(\forall x)[(\forall x)Lx \rightarrow Lx]$ | $[(\forall x)Lx \rightarrow Lx]$ | $x$ |
| 6 | $(\exists y)(\exists x)(My \wedge Axy)$ | $(\exists x)(My \wedge Axy)$ | $y$ |
| 7 | $(\forall w)(\forall x)-(\exists y)-Rwxyz$ | $(\forall x)-(\exists y)-Rwxyz$ | $w$ |

Several points. First, notice rows 2, 4, and 5, in the '$Pv$' column. Strictly speaking, the outermost parentheses in 2 and the outermost brackets in 4 and 5 are necessary, given that '$Pv$' signifies 'the whole of the *wff* to the right of '$(\forall v)$'. In practice, however, as you already know, it's always permissible to drop *outermost* parentheses, brackets, and curly braces.

Second, notice row 5. It might strike you that the formula '$(\forall x)[(\forall x)Lx \rightarrow Lx]$' is *ill-formed*. You might think that it's unclear *which* universal quantifier binds *which* variable. Think again. Better yet, re-read the formation rules for $L_2$, i.e., for the language of Predicate Logic/Quantification Theory: they most certainly *do* allow for such a *wff*.

Look at the two universal quantifiers. Call the leftmost quantifier (i.e., the main quantifier) 'Quantifier 1', and call the rightmost quantifier 'Quantifier 2'. Quantifier 1 has within its scope everything within the square brackets that immediately follows it, i.e., '[($\forall x$)$Lx \rightarrow Lx$]'. In particular, Quantifier 1 has within its scope each of the three occurrences of the variable '$x$' within the square brackets. However, although it has each of them within its *scope*, it doesn't *bind* each of them. The first two occurrences of the variable '$x$' within the square brackets are *already* bound. *Within the square brackets,* Quantifier 2 binds the variable $x$ that is glued to it (as it were), and it also binds the variable $x$ in the *leftmost* '$Lx$'. And that's it. Still within the square brackets, Quantifier 2 doesn't bind the third—the rightmost—occurrence of the variable '$x$', the one in the rightmost '$Lx$'. The latter falls *outside* the scope of Quantifier 2, and thus is free *within the square brackets.* As such, it's the *only* variable that's eligible for being captured (i.e., bound) by Quantifier 1. So Quantifier 1 binds—within the square brackets—the rightmost occurrence, and *only* the rightmost occurrence, of the variable '$x$'.

If you're confused, think of it like this. Just remember that what you're looking at *within* the square brackets is a *conditional*: it's *not* a quantified *wff*. The *antecedent* of the conditional, '($\forall x$)$Lx$', is quantified, to be sure, but—*within the square brackets*—the *consequent* of the conditional, the second '$Lx$', is *not* quantified: it's an *open wff* containing a *free* '$x$'. Therefore within the square brackets, it's *only* the third occurrence of the variable '$x$' that's free and that Quantifier 1 could possibly bind.

The bumpy ride is half over. If you're reading these words, then you've survived to *this* point. And if you've survived to *this* point then *by cracky*, you *will* survive!

As you already know, '$Pv$' signifies any *wff* containing at least one occurrence of the free variable '$v$'. Let '$t$' designate *either* an individual constant *or* a variable. (Such an expression is typically called a *term*; if you wish, however, you may call it a *constable*.)

| | |
|---|---|
| **Fifth Definition:** | A *term*, '$t$', is a symbol that signifies either an individual constant or a variable. |
| **Sixth Definition:** | '$Pt/v$' signifies the *wff* that results from '$Pv$' by replacing every *free* occurrence of '$v$' in '$Pv$' with '$t$', as in the following table. |

| | **Pv** | **v** | **t** | **Pt/v** |
|---|---|---|---|---|
| 1 | $Lx$ | $x$ | $y$ | $Ly$ |
| 2 | $Lx \rightarrow Mx$ | $x$ | $z$ | $Lz \rightarrow Mz$ |
| 3 | $Lyy$ | $y$ | $x$ | $Lxx$ |
| 4 | $(\forall x)My \wedge Axy$ | $y$ | $y$ | $(\forall x)My \wedge Axy$ |
| 5 | $(\forall x)Lx \rightarrow Lx$ | $x$ | $z$ | $(\forall x)Lx \rightarrow Lz$ |
| 6 | $(\exists x)(My \wedge Axy)$ | $y$ | $a$ | $(\exists x)(Ma \wedge Axa)$ |
| 7 | $(\forall x) - (\exists y) - Rwxyz$ | $w$ | $x$ | $(\forall x) - (\exists y) - Rxxyz$ |

You might find the fourth row puzzling: '$t$' simply *is* '$v$' and therefore '**Pt/v**' simply *is* '**Pv**'. Think of a dentist who extracts two teeth and then implants *the very same* two teeth in their original locations. In the fourth row, you are that dentist.

Note that in the fifth row you replaced only the *third* occurrence of the variable '$x$' with '$z$'. This is because it's only the *third* occurrence that is *free*. (If you're puzzled, reread the sixth definition above.)

Note that in the sixth row '$t$' doesn't signify a variable: it signifies the individual constant '$a$'.

**Seventh Definition:**     Consider each *free* occurrence of '$v$' in '**Pv**'. '$t$' is *free for* '$v$' in '**Pv**' *iff* when you replace each free occurrence of '$v$' in '**Pv**' with '$t$', '$t$' is free in '**Pt/v**' exactly where '$v$' was free in '**Pv**'.

Here's what this means in (more or less) plain English. Suppose that you have a *wff* '**Pv**' that contains at least one free occurrence of '$v$'. Suppose that you replace each free occurrence of '$v$' in '**Pv**' with '$t$'. The new *wff*, of course, is '**Pt/v**'. Now if every occurrence of '$t$' that you have just implanted into '**Pt/v**' is *free*, then '$t$' *is* free for '$v$' in '**Pv**'. If, however, at least one occurrence of '$t$' becomes captured (or bound) by a quantifier in '**Pt/v**', i.e., by either '$(\forall t)$' or '$(\exists t)$', then '$t$' is *not* free for '$v$' in '**Pv**'. In the previous table, '$t$' is free for '$v$' in '**Pv**' in every row except row 7, where '$w$' in '**Pv**' became '$x$' in '**Pt/v**'—and in its new incarnation as '$x$', it becomes *captured* by '$\forall x$'.

*This* bumpy ride is now over. You have survived the bumps. If you commit to memory each detail of the bumpy ride, the remaining bumps in the text will be *almost* tolerable.

Before we dive into the refined version of each of the four derivation rules of Predicate Logic/Quantification Theory, I shall make two preliminary points. First, in the course of formulating these new rules, I shall be using such metalinguistic expressions as '$(\forall v)Pv$', '$(\exists v)Pv$', and '$Pv$'. By each of these expressions, I shall have in mind a *wff* that is *not* a part of another, larger *wff*—unless, of course, I stipulate otherwise. Thus consider '$(\forall x)(\exists y)Lxy$': it's obviously a universally quantified *wff* and *not* an existentially quantified *wff*. To be sure, there's an existentially quantified *wff* buried within '$(\forall x)(\exists y)Lxy$'—but it's only a *fragment* of the overall *wff*. The main operator, i.e., the main quantifier, i.e., the leftmost quantifier, is the *universal* quantifier. Clearly, therefore, you're looking at an instance of '$(\forall v)Pv$', and not at an instance of '$(\exists v)Pv$'. Accordingly, '$v$' designates the variable immediately to the right of '$\forall$', the *wff*'s main operator and main quantifier. Accordingly, '$v$' designates '$x$', and '$Pv$' designates the whole of the *wff* to the right of '$(\forall v)$', i.e., '$(\exists y)Lxy$'

Second, if you can derive your targeted *wff* *without* using the new derivation rules of Predicate Logic/Quantification Theory, and if you would find it more convenient to do so, then by all means do so. Thus consider the following two sequents:

S146:        $(\forall x)Lx \wedge (\forall y)My \vdash (\forall y)My \vee -(\forall x)Lx$

S147:        $(\forall x)Lx \wedge (\forall y)My \vdash (\forall z)Mz \vee -(\forall x)Lx$

It's obviously *possible* to derive the conclusion of S146 from its premise via the derivation rules of Propositional Logic alone. (Think $\wedge$E followed by $\vee$I.) It's obviously *impossible* to do likewise with S147. (The derivation of '$(\forall z)Mz$' from '$(\forall y)My$' involves a change of variable. Therefore you have no choice but to make use of the new rules of Predicate Logic/Quantification Theory.) Moral of the story: S146 *doesn't* call for $\forall$E followed by $\forall$I; S147 *does*. (To be sure, you *could* use $\forall$E followed by $\forall$I in S146—but it would be *mad*—unless, of course, you had a personal grudge against Ockham—to do so.)

At long last you're ready for the refined version of each of the four derivation rules of Predicate Logic/Quantification Theory. Two questions pertain to each rule: a *when* question—"*When* do you use the rule?"—and a *how* question—"*How* do you use it?"

# 8. ∀E: The Refined Version

## A. When to Use ∀E

You should think ∀E thoughts whenever a universally quantified *wff*, '$(\forall v)Pv$', is staring you in the face; i.e., whenever it already appears in the derivation.

## B. How to Use ∀E

To perform ∀E, it's necessary to perform the following operations:

1. In a line, *n*, below '$(\forall v)Pv$', delete '$(\forall v)$', the leftmost quantifier in '$(\forall v)Pv$', so that only '$Pv$' remains.
2. Let the term '$t$' be either
   a. a variable that is free for '$v$' in '$Pv$' (i.e., that won't become bound by any quantifier in '$Pv$'), or
   b. a constant that already appears either in the sequent's premises or in its conclusion.
3. Convert '$Pv$' in line *n* into '$Pt/v$' in line *n* by replacing, in '$Pv$', each free occurrence of '$v$', and no bound occurrence of '$v$', with '$t$'.
4. Off to the right of '$Pt/v$', cite the line number of '$(\forall v)Pv$', followed by '∀E'.
5. Off to the far left of '$Pt/v$', cite the line number(s) of whatever *wffs* '$(\forall v)Pv$' rests on.

The point of Clause 1 is to ensure that when you perform ∀E on a universally quantified *wff*, it's the *main* universal quantifier that you're lopping off. Consider the following two derivations:

S148:    $(\forall x)(\forall y)[(Px \land Py) \to Lxy] \vdash (\forall y)[(Px \land Py) \to Lxy]$

1(1) $(\forall x)(\forall y)[(Px \land Py) \to Lxy]$    A
1(2) $(\forall y)[(Px \land Py) \to Lxy]$    1∀E

S149:          $(\forall x)(\forall y)[(Px \wedge Py) \rightarrow Lxy] \vdash (\forall x)[(Px \wedge Py) \rightarrow Lxy]$

1(1) $(\forall x)(\forall y)[(Px \wedge Py) \rightarrow Lxy]$          A
1(2) $(\forall x)[(Px \wedge Py) \rightarrow Lxy]$          1∀E          XXX

You're looking at two derivations, one of which, S148, is perfectly *correct*, and one of which, S149, is perfectly *dreadful*. Specifically, the move in S149 to line (2) violates Clause 1. To perform ∀E on a universally quantified *wff*, the rule requires you to lop off the *main*, i.e., the *leftmost*, quantifier. In the premise of S149, as in the premise of S148, it is '$(\forall x)$', rather than '$(\forall y)$', that is the *main*, i.e., the *leftmost*, quantifier.

Clauses 2 and 3 require considerable elaboration. First consider Clause 2. Three points. The first is a general point. It's of course permissible, but not necessary, for '*t*' to be '*v*' itself: '*v*' *is* bound in '$(\forall v)Pv$', but, as you know, there's at least one free occurrence of '*v*' in '$Pv$'. The following are both perfectly fine instances of ∀E. In the first, but only in the first, '*t*' is '*v*' itself.

S150:          $(\forall x)(\exists y)Lxy \vdash (\exists y)Lxy$

1(1) $(\forall x)(\exists y)Lxy$          A
1(2) $(\exists y)Lxy$          1 ∀E

S151:          $(\forall x)(\exists y)Lxy \vdash (\exists y)Lzy$

1(1) $(\forall x)(\exists y)Lxy$          A
1(2) $(\exists y)Lzy$          1 ∀E

Assume a domain restricted to people. Interpret the premise to mean 'Everyone loves someone'. Accordingly, the conclusion of the first sequent asserts that $x$ loves someone, and the conclusion of the second asserts that $z$ loves someone. Of course, $x$ and $z$ are *any* people in the domain: perhaps they're distinct from each other and perhaps they're not. Clearly, if *everyone* loves someone, then *anyone in particular* loves someone. Thus $x$, in the first derivation, loves someone, and $z$, in the second derivation, also loves someone—given that (once again) $x$ and $z$ are *any* people in the domain.

The second point concerns Clause 2a: it's impermissible to choose a variable '*t*' that becomes bound by a quantifier in '*Pv*'. Otherwise you violate Clause 2a and run into pickles of the following sort:

S152:   1(1) $(\forall x)(\exists y)Lxy$          A
        1(2) $(\exists y)Lyy$          1 $\forall$E      XXX

It may well be true that everyone loves someone; it doesn't follow that someone loves himself (or herself). Consider a three-person domain consisting of Ardbeg, Bobo, and Coco. Suppose the following: Ardbeg loves Bobo but not himself; Bobo loves Coco but not herself; and Coco loves Ardbeg but not herself. For this interpretation, the premise is true because everyone *does* love someone. The conclusion, however, is false because *no one* loves himself (or herself). The problem here is that '*t*' was *not* free for '*v*' in '*Pv*': '*t*' became captured by a quantifier in '*Pv*'. In other words, when you replaced each free occurrence of '*v*' in '*Pv*' with '*t*', '*t*' was *not* free in '*Pt/v*' exactly where '*v*' had been free in '*Pv*'. In still other words, when you replaced each free occurrence of '*x*' in '$(\exists y)Lxy$' with '*y*', '*y*' was *not* free in '$(\exists y)Lyy$' exactly where '*x*' had been free in '$(\exists y)Lxy$'. On the contrary, although '*x*' had been free in '$(\exists y)Lxy$', '*y*' became captured by '$(\exists y)$' in '$(\exists y)Lyy$'.

The third point concerns Clause 2b.

Question: Why, in Clause 2b, are you limited in your choice of a constant to one that already appears either in the sequent's premises or in its conclusion?

Answer: Remember our discussion of this point at the beginning of Section 4. Think, once again, of what a constant is: it's the proper name of an object in the domain. Unless the proper names are *given*, however (either in the premises or in the conclusion), you have no way of knowing the names of any of the objects in the domain. In some domains, indeed, either some or all of the objects may be *nameless*. An example of the former is the domain of real numbers. An example of the latter is the domain of rats in Boston's subway system on New Year's Day, 1900.

Now consider Clause 3 of the rule for $\forall$E. There are two aspects to this clause. The first requires you to replace *each* free occurrence of '*v*' in '*Pv*' with '*t*'. The second requires you to replace each *free* occurrence of '*v*' in '*Pv*' with '*t*'. (No, these last two sentences do not contain a typo.)

Behold the first aspect of Clause 3: in constructing '**Pt/v**', you're required to replace *each* free occurrence of '*v*' in '**Pv**' with '*t*'. Question: Why so? Why *each*? Why not simply *at least one*? Consider the following derivation:

S153:   1 (1) *Ma*                          A
      2 (2) (∀x)(Mx → Axx)        A
      2 (3) *Ma → Aax*              2 ∀E     XXX

The move from (2) to (3) violates Clause 3's *each*-free-occurrence requirement. Interpret the first premise to mean that Ardbeg is a magician, and the second to mean that every magician admires himself (or herself). From these two premises it follows that if Ardbeg is a magician, then he admires himself: '*Ma → Aaa*'. Alternatively, from these two premises it follows that Ardbeg has the complex property of admiring himself if he's a magician. It most certainly does *not* follow that Ardbeg has the complex property of admiring *x* if he, Ardbeg, is a magician—where *x* is *anyone in the domain*. By adhering to the *each* free occurrence requirement, you end up with '*Ma → Aaa*' and thus avoid such problems.

In saying that *each and every* individual in the domain has a certain property, you're committed to the view that *any particular individual* has that property—and this is so regardless of how complex the property is. To ensure that you've affirmed that either a *named* individual (e.g., Ardbeg) has that property, or that an *unnamed* individual (e.g., *x*) has it, you must replace *every* occurrence of '*v*' in '**Pv**' with '*t*'. Thus, other perfectly respectable conclusions of S153 would be '*Mx → Axx*', '*My → Ayy*', and '*Mz → Azz*'.

Behold the second aspect of Clause 3: in constructing '**Pt/v**', you're required to disregard, i.e., to leave undisturbed, each *bound* occurrence of '*v*' in '**Pt/v**', if any such there be. In other words, you are *not* to replace any bound occurrence of '*v*' with '*t*'. The following derivation violates this second aspect of Clause 3, and is therefore illegitimate:

S154:       (∀x)[Lxx → (∃x)Axx] ⊢ Lyy → (∃y)Ayy

    1 (1) (∀x)[Lxx → (∃x)Axx]   A
    1 (2) Lyy → (∃y)Ayy         1 ∀E     XXX

Notice that '*Pv*' signifies '$[Lxx \rightarrow (\exists x)Axx]$' and that '*v*' signifies '*x*'. If you wish to replace the free occurrences of '*x*' in '$[Lxx \rightarrow (\exists x)Axx]$' with either '*x*' itself or '*y*' or '*z*', say, then the correct version of '*Pt/v*' in line (2) would be either '$Lxx \rightarrow (\exists x)Axx$' or '$Lyy \rightarrow (\exists x)Axx$' or '$Lzz \rightarrow (\exists x)Axx$', etc. The mistake consisted in tinkering with the *bound* occurrences of '*v*' in '*Pt/v*' (i.e., with the three *bound* occurrences of '*x*' in '$(\exists x)Axx$'—instead of with only the two *free* occurrences of '*x*' in '*Lxx*'.

To the charge that S154 is a *valid* argument, the appropriate reply is "Yes—and *so what?*" ∀E simply doesn't allow the move from (1) to (2)—end of story! Is it possible to derive the *wff* in line (2) from the *wff* in line (1)? Of course it is—but not in a two-line derivation. Should you, then, modify ∀E to allow the move from (1) to (2)? Not unless you're prepared to swear that the modification will remain truth-preserving (it will); not unless you're prepared to modify *each* of the derivation rules whenever it's convenient to do so; and not unless you're prepared to end up with a deluge of derivation rules.

Nor would it be permissible to make the move from the premise of S154, '$(\forall x)[Lxx \rightarrow (\exists x)Axx]$', to '$Lyy \rightarrow (\exists x)Axy$'. Once again, you've replaced at least one *bound* occurrence of '*v*' with '*t*'. (In this instance, you've replaced exactly one such occurrence, whereas previously you replaced three such occurrences.) Unlike its predecessor, this inference is clearly invalid: it may be true that if anyone stands in the '*L*'-relation to himself then someone or other stands in the '*A*'-relation to himself. It hardly follows that if *y* stands in the '*L*'-relation to himself then someone stands in the '*A*'-relation to *y*.

# 9. ∃I: The Refined Version

## A. When to Use ∃I

You should think ∃I thoughts when:

1. you're trying to generate an existentially quantified *wff*, '$(\exists v)Pv$', and
2. a *wff*, '*Pt*', in which '*t*' signifies either a free variable or an individual constant, already occurs in the derivation.

Don't forget that Clause 2 has as its focus a *wff in its entirety*. '*Pt*', in other words, is not a *wff* that is a mere fragment (or component) of some other *wff*. Resist the temptation to perform ∃I on a *wff* fragment:

S155:        $Ma \wedge Lax \vdash Ma \wedge (\exists x)Lax$

          1(1) $Ma \wedge Lax$                    A
          1(2) $Ma \wedge (\exists x)Lax$          1 EI     XXX

'*Pt*' in line (1) signifies the *wff* in its *entirety*, i.e., the entire conjunction '$Ma \wedge Lax$'. Although the move from (1) to (2) is indeed truth-preserving, it's impermissible insofar as it involves a misuse of ∃I. (Unhappy? Reread the penultimate, i.e., (once again) the second-to-last paragraph of the previous section.) The right conjunct of (2) is indeed a *wff*, but it's a mere fragment of the *wff* in its entirety. (You can easily get (2) out of (1)—but not in one step. It should take you four steps beyond (1).)

The reference to *both* free variables *and* individual constants in Clause 2 is to remind you that it doesn't matter whether it's an *unnamed* or a *named* individual that has a particular property or stands in a particular relation to something. In either case it's legitimate to infer that *something* has that property or stands in that relation to something. In other words, '$(\exists x)Lx$'—'Someone is a logician'—follows equally from '$Lx$'—'*x* is a logician'—and from '$La$'—'Ardbeg is a logician'.

## B. How to Use ∃I

To perform ∃I, it's necessary to perform the following operations:

On a line, *n*, below '*Pt*', where '*t*' is either a free variable or an individual constant, construct a *wff* '$(\exists v)Pv$' as follows:

1.  First suppose that '*t*' is a free variable.
    a. Let '*v*' be either the free variable '*t*' itself, or any variable, other than '*t*', that doesn't occur in '*Pt*'.
    b. Convert '*Pt*' into '*Pv*' by replacing, in '*Pt*', at least one free occurrence of '*t*' with '*v*'.

2.  Now suppose that '$t$' is an individual constant.
    a. Let '$v$' be any variable that doesn't occur in '$Pt$'.
    b. Convert '$Pt$' into '$Pv$' by replacing, in '$Pt$', at least one occurrence of '$t$' with '$v$'.
3.  Enclose '$Pv$' within parentheses.
4.  Introduce '$(\exists v)$' to the immediate left of '$(Pv)$'.
5.  Off to the right of '$(\exists v)Pv$', cite the line number of '$Pt$', followed by '$\exists$I'.
6.  Off to the far left of '$(\exists v)Pv$', cite the line number(s) of whatever *wff(s)* '$Pt$' rests on.

The Clause 1a restriction that '$v$' must not occur in '$Pt$', unless '$v$' is '$t$' itself, prevents various sorts of egregious missteps. Consider the following derivation as an illustration of one sort. Let '$Pt$' be '$Lxy$' and let '$t$' be '$x$'. (All that *this* means is that you've chosen to perform $\exists$I on '$x$', rather than on '$y$'. Had you chosen, instead, to perform $\exists$I on '$y$', then '$t$' would have been '$y$'.) Now suppose that you blithely disregard the Clause 1a restriction that '$v$' must not occur in '$Pt$', unless '$v$' is '$t$' itself. So you choose a variable '$v$' ('$y$') that isn't '$t$' ('$x$'), even though that variable '$v$' ('$y$') *does* occur in '$Pt$' ('$Lxy$'). So you replace '$x$' in '$Lxy$' with '$y$'; you prefix '$(\exists y)$' to '$Lyy$'; and you thereby generate '$(\exists y)Lyy$':

S156:   1 (1) $Lxy$                    A
        1 (2) $(\exists y)Lyy$         1 $\exists$I      XXX

Assume a domain restricted to people. It may well be true that (1) a person $x$ loves a person $y$. It doesn't follow that (2) someone loves himself (or herself). Hence the requirement to choose either '$x$' itself as '$v$', or else a *new* variable, e.g., '$z$', that doesn't occur in $Lxy$. Each of the following two derivations adheres to this restriction:

S157:       $Lxy \vdash (\exists x)Lxy$

        1 (1) $Lxy$                    A
        1 (2) $(\exists x)Lxy$         1 $\exists$I

S158:        $Lxy \vdash (\exists z)Lzy$

    1 (1) $Lxy$                     A
    1 (2) $(\exists z)Lzy$          1 ∃I

In each of these two derivations, the inference—and it's an entirely legitimate inference—is that because *x* loves *y*, *someone* loves *y*.

The Clause 1a restriction that '*v*' must not occur in '***Pt***', unless '*v*' is '*t*' itself, also prevents another sort of egregious misstep. Let '***Pt***' be '$(\exists y)Lxy$' and let '*t*' be '*x*'. Now suppose that once again you blithely disregard the Clause 1a restriction that '*v*' must not occur in '***Pt***', unless '*v*' is '*t*' itself. So you choose a variable, '*v*'('*y*') that isn't '*t*'('*x*'), and yet that *does* occur in '***Pt***'('$(\exists y)Lxy$'). So you replace '*x*' in '$(\exists y)Lxy$' with '*y*'; you prefix '$(\exists y)$' to '$(\exists y)Lyy$'; and you thereby generate '$(\exists y)(\exists y)Lyy$':

S159:  1 (1) $(\exists y)Lxy$             A
       1 (2) $(\exists y)(\exists y)Lyy$   1 ∃I     XXX

The problem here is that (2) isn't a *wff*. Using the formation rules of $L_2$, you could never have generated it. But even if the rules were amended to allow for such a *wff*, you wouldn't be home free. The leftmost of the two '$(\exists y)$' quantifiers would perform no function whatsoever: it would be what you already know to be a *vacuous* quantifier. (Ditto if you were to add a third '$(\exists y)$' quantifier to the immediate left of the first two: it too would be a vacuous quantifier.) So the conclusion is equivalent to '$(\exists y)Lyy$'. Assume, once again, a domain restricted to people. It may well be the case that (1) an individual *x* loves someone. It doesn't follow that (2) someone loves himself (or herself). Hence the requirement to choose either '*x*' itself as '*v*', or else a *new* variable, e.g., '*z*', that doesn't occur in '$(\exists y)Lxy$'.

Next consider Clauses 1b and 2b. They allow you, respectively, to replace *at least one* free occurrence of '*t*' (where '*t*' is a variable), and *at least one* occurrence of '*t*'(where '*t*' is a constant), with '*v*'. In other words, in each application of ∃I, as long as you replace *at least one* such occurrence of '*t*' with '*v*', you may replace as few or as many such occurrences as you wish.

Clause 1b, therefore, permits the following derivation:

S160:        $Lxx \vdash (\exists x)(\exists y)Lxy$

$$
\begin{array}{lll}
1 & (1)\ Lxx & A \\
1 & (2)\ (\exists y)Lxy & 1\ \exists I \\
1 & (3)\ (\exists x)(\exists y)Lxy & 2\ \exists I
\end{array}
$$

Obviously, if (1) $x$ loves himself then (2) there is *somebody* whom $x$ loves; i.e., $x$ loves *somebody*. Therefore (3) there is *somebody* who loves *somebody*.

By the same token, Clause 2b permits each of the following derivations, S161, S162, and S163:

S161:        $Laa \vdash (\exists x)Lxx$

$$
\begin{array}{lll}
1 & (1)\ Laa & A \\
1 & (2)\ (\exists x)Lxx & 1\ \exists I
\end{array}
$$

Obviously, if (1) Ardbeg loves himself then (2) somebody loves himself.

S162:        $Laa \vdash (\exists x)(\exists y)Lxy$

$$
\begin{array}{lll}
1 & (1)\ Laa & A \\
1 & (2)\ (\exists y)Lay & 1\ \exists I \\
1 & (3)\ (\exists x)(\exists y)Lxy & 2\ \exists I
\end{array}
$$

Obviously, if (1) Ardbeg loves himself then (2) there is *somebody* whom Ardbeg loves; i.e., Ardbeg loves *somebody*. Therefore (3) there is *somebody* who loves *somebody*.

S163:        $Laa \vdash (\exists y)(\exists x)Lxy$

$$
\begin{array}{lll}
1 & (1)\ Laa & A \\
1 & (2)\ (\exists x)Lxa & 1\ \exists I \\
1 & (3)\ (\exists y)(\exists x)Lxy & 2\ \exists I
\end{array}
$$

Obviously, if (1) Ardbeg loves himself then (2) there is *somebody* who loves Ardbeg; i.e., Ardbeg is loved by *somebody*. Therefore (3) there is *somebody* who is loved by *somebody*.

Finally, consider Clauses 3 and 4. They force you, when performing ∃I, to enclose '*Pv*' within parentheses, and to introduce '(∃*v*)' to the left of '(*Pv*)'. The point is to make sure that the *whole* of '*Pv*' falls within the scope of '(∃*v*)'. The rationale should be clear: as with any introduction rule, the operator that you are introducing—whether it be a connective or, as in this instance, a quantifier—is to become the *main* operator of the *wff*.

Accordingly, in each of the sequents, S164 and S167, the existential quantifier *should be* the main operator in the conclusion—but it *isn't* the main operator in either. The missteps simply arise from a failure to heed Clauses 3 and 4:

First consider S164:

S164:   1 (1) −*Lab*                    A
        1 (2) −(∃*x*)*Lxb*          1 ∃I      XXX

Note first that the argument is clearly invalid. It may be true that (1) *Ardbeg* doesn't love Bobo. (Alas, poor Bobo—but really it's Ardbeg's loss!) It doesn't follow, however, that (2) *nobody* loves Bobo. . . .

Note next that ∃I didn't generate a *wff* in line (2) whose main operator is the existential quantifier; instead, the main operator in (2) is the dash. '(∃*v*)' in (2), i.e., '(∃*x*)', is *not* to the left of '*Pv*', i.e., '−*Lxb*'. And it's not to the left of '(*Pv*)', i.e., '(−*Lxb*)'. And it's certainly not to the *immediate* left of '(*Pv*)', i.e., once again, '(−*Lxb*)'. '*Pt*' in line (1) is '−*Lab*'; so '(*Pt*)' is '(−*Lab*)'; so '(*Pv*)' in line (2) should be '(−*Lxb*)'; and so '(∃*v*)*Pv*' in line (2) should be '(∃*x*)(−*Lxb*)'. But it's not. Introducing '(∃*v*)', i.e., '(∃*x*)', to the immediate *left* of '(*Pv*)', i.e., to the immediate left of '(−*Lxb*)', would have prevented the misstep at line (2):

S165:        −*Lab* ⊢ (∃*x*)(−*Lxb*)

        1(1) −*Lab*                    A
        1(2) (∃*x*)(−*Lxb*)          1 ∃I

Now I am *entirely* sympathetic to anyone who finds the conclusion of S165, i.e., '$(\exists x)(-Lxb)$', much too cluttered with parentheses. Fine. Suppose that '$\boldsymbol{Pv}$' has a dash as its main connective, as it does here, i.e., '$-Lxb$'. Even better, suppose that '$\boldsymbol{Pv}$' is just an atomic *wff*, e.g., '$Lxb$'. In either case, and unless you feel yourself being taken in by, and becoming addicted to, S164-type moves from (1) to (2), you may cheerfully disregard the requirement that '$\boldsymbol{Pv}$' be enclosed within parentheses, as in S166:

S166:       $-Lab \vdash (\exists x) -Lxb$

      1(1) $-Lab$                    A
      1(2) $(\exists x)-Lxb$          1 $\exists$I

'(1) *Ardbeg doesn't love Bobo*; therefore (2) *somebody* doesn't love Bobo': this, of course, is *exactly* what you want.

As S167 illustrates, however, parentheses *are* essential in moleculars other than negations:

S167:  1 (1) $Lab \rightarrow Cb$           A
        1 (2) $(\exists x)Lxb \rightarrow Cb$     1 $\exists$I      XXX

It may be true that (1) if Ardbeg loves Bobo then Bobo will be on cloud nine. Suppose, however, that Ardbeg *doesn't* love Bobo, and that Bobo *isn't* on cloud nine. Suppose that Bobo is, on the contrary, entirely disconsolate. Thus the premise—a conditional with a false antecedent and a false consequent—is true. Now suppose that Dagbar loves Bobo. Then *someone* loves Bobo—in which case the conclusion—a conditional with a *true* antecedent and a *false* consequent (Dagbar's love for her means *nothing* to Bobo)—is false. So the argument is invalid—and the use of $\exists$I here *must* therefore be erroneous.

One correct variation on S167 would be as follows:

S168:       $(Lab \rightarrow Cb) \vdash (\exists x)(Lxb \rightarrow Cb)$

      1 (1) $(Lab \rightarrow Cb)$          A
      1 (2) $(\exists x)(Lxb \rightarrow Cb)$    1 $\exists$I

Strictly speaking, as you know, the formation rules of $L_2$ require that (1) be enclosed within parentheses. *Unstrictly* speaking, however, as you also know, we ignore this particular requirement in practice. In this instance, however, I've included the parentheses in (1) simply to remind you that when you introduce the existential quantifier in line (2), the left parenthesis of '$(Lxb \rightarrow Cb)$' had better appear just to the right of '$(\exists x)$', and the right parenthesis of '$(Lxb \rightarrow Cb)$' had better appear at the very end—at the far right—of the *wff*.

Now the line-(2) *wff* says that someone has the following property: if he or she loves Bobo then Bobo will be on cloud nine. (*Bobo* knows who that someone is, and *you* know (from (1)) who that someone is.) And (2) clearly follows from (1).

# 10. ∀I: The Refined Version

## A. When to Use ∀I

You should think ∀I thoughts whenever you're trying to generate a universally quantified *wff* '$(\forall v)Pv$'.

## B. How to Use ∀I

1.  First generate a *wff*, '$Pt$', such that
    a. '$t$' is any variable that is free in '$Pt$', and
    b. '$Pt$' doesn't rest on any assumption that contains a free occurrence of '$t$'.
2.  In a line below '$Pt$', construct '$(\forall v)Pv$' from '$Pt$' as follows:
    a. Choose any variable, '$v$', that is free for '$t$' in '$Pt$'.
    b. Construct '$Pv/t$' by replacing, in '$Pt$', each free occurrence of '$t$', and no bound occurrence of '$t$', with '$v$', such that '$v$' occurs free in '$Pv/t$' exactly where '$t$' had occurred free in '$Pt$'.
    c. Enclose '$Pv/t$' within parentheses.
    d. Introduce '$(\forall v)$' to the immediate left of '$Pv/t$'.

3.  Off to the right of '$(\forall v)Pv/t$', cite the line number of '$Pt$', followed by '$\forall I$'.
4.  Off to the far left of '$(\forall v)Pv/t$', cite the line number(s) of whatever *wff(s)* '$Pt$' rests on.

Most of these clauses should be self-explanatory. Most—but not all. Several of them require a word of elaboration. Two of them are a bit tricky and thus require more than a word of elaboration.

## a. Clause 1a

Note that although in '$\forall E$' and '$\exists I$', '$t$' may signify either a constant or a variable, in $\forall I$ (as in $\exists E$, below) it signifies only a variable.

## b. Clause 1b

Clause 1b is one of the two tricky $\forall I$ clauses: "'$Pt$' doesn't rest on any assumption that contains a free occurrence of '$t$'."

What follows is an elaboration on what you've already encountered in Section 4. We begin with the preliminaries. Cigars. *Assume* that some unnamed member of the Philosophy Department smokes a cigar a day in his office. Does it follow that *every* member of the department smokes a cigar a day in his or her office? (Obviously this is a rhetorical question, yes?)

Alternatively, *assume* that some unnamed object in the domain of natural numbers, i.e., some unnamed natural number, is even. (The naturals, once again, are the numbers 0, 1, 2, 3, etc.) Does it follow that *every* object in the domain, i.e., *every* natural number, is even? (Obviously, this is another rhetorical question, yes?) In *assuming* that an unnamed natural number is even, you're entitled to infer all sorts of things about *it*, e.g., that *it's* divisible by 2 without remainder, that *its* predecessor is odd, that *its* successor is odd, that *its* square is even, etc. What you are *not* entitled to infer, however, is that each of these things holds true of *every* object in the domain, i.e., of *every* natural number.

Enough with the preliminaries. Now consider the following derivation:

S169:   1(1) $Lx \wedge Mx$             A
        1(2) $Lx$                 1 ∧E
        1(3) $(\forall x)Lx$         2 ∀I    XXX

Suppose a domain of people. You are given an *assumption* in (1) that *an unnamed individual x*—it doesn't matter *who x is*—is both a logician and a magician. Therefore (2) that same individual *x* is a logician. Therefore (3)—here comes the fatal move—*everyone* is a logician!

Question: How could it *possibly* follow from the *assumption* that *an unnamed individual x* is both a logician and a magician that *everyone* is a logician?

Answer: It couldn't and therefore it doesn't.

Question (by way of generalizing): Why on Earth should it follow from the *assumption* that *x* has a particular property that *everyone* has that property?

Answer: It *shouldn't* and indeed it *doesn't*.

It is *assumed* that an unnamed individual *x* is both a logician and a magician. (More power to this individual!) For all you know, the possession of this *assumed* property may *distinguish x* from other individuals in the domain. For all you know, he or she is the *only* individual in the domain who is *both* a logician *and* a magician. Hence it is simply implausible to infer that what's true of *x* is *true of*—or *implies* anything that is true of—*every* individual in the domain.

Question: Doesn't the variable '*x*' stand for *any* individual in the domain? And if so, *why* doesn't it follow that what's true of *x*, i.e., of *any* individual in the domain, is true of *every* member?

Answer: It's certainly true that the variable '*x*' stands for *any* individual in the domain. The problem arises when you *assume* something to be true of *x* that may *not* be true of other individuals in the domain. In this case, it's *assumed* that *x* possesses a given property: the property of being both a logician and a magician. Precisely because (once again) other individuals in the domain may *not* possess this property, it *doesn't* follow that what's true of *x* is true of other individuals in the domain. To be sure, what's true of *any* individual *x* in the domain is true of *every* individual in the domain—but only if no *assumption* is made about the properties that *x* happens to have. Repeat: only if no *assumption* is made about the properties that *x* happens to have. Repeat one last time: only if no *assumption* is made about the properties that *x* happens to have.

Examining another derivation should make this perfectly clear. This derivation is a *legitimate* one, and it bears a superficial, but *only* a superficial, resemblance to the previous one.

S170:     $(\forall x)(Lx \wedge Mx) \vdash (\forall x)Lx$

$$1(1)\ (\forall x)(Lx \wedge Mx) \qquad\qquad A$$
$$1(2)\ Lx \wedge Mx \qquad\qquad\qquad 1\ \forall E$$
$$1(3)\ Lx \qquad\qquad\qquad\qquad 2\ \wedge E$$
$$1(4)\ (\forall x)Lx \qquad\qquad\qquad 3\ \forall I$$

Suppose the same domain and the same interpretation as in S169. You are told in (1) that *everyone* is both a logician and a magician. Therefore (2) *any* individual $x$ is both a logician and a magician. Therefore (3) that same individual $x$ is a logician. Therefore (4) *everyone* is a logician. Indeed, how could it possibly *not* follow from the assumption that *everyone* is both a logician and a magician that *everyone* is a logician? (Hint: it couldn't; i.e., it couldn't *not* follow; i.e., it *must* follow.)

The problem—insofar as there is a problem—is this: the move from (2) to (3) in S169 *looks* identical to the move from (3) to (4) in S170. In each case, the move is from '$Lx$', the *wff from which* you are about to perform $\forall I$—call it the *springboard wff*—to the targeted *wff* '$(\forall x) Lx$'. But the similarity between the two moves is only skin-deep: The numbers on the far left—and in particular, *the wffs to which the numbers point*—tell a rather different story.

Note that in each derivation the springboard *wff* '$Lx$' rests on an assumption. In S169, however, $x$—the variable with respect to which you're contemplating doing $\forall I$—occurs *free* in the assumption, whereas in S170 it doesn't. And this, of course, is precisely the point of Clause 1b. In S169, the claim in (2) that $x$ has the property of being a logician rests on (i.e., derives from) the assumption—the *assumption*—in (1) that $x$ has the property of being both a logician and a magician. But of course (and yet again) there's no reason to think that *every* individual in the domain has this property. And therefore there's no reason to infer from (2) the conclusion (3) that *every* individual in the domain has the property of being a logician.

An assumption, after all, is *just* an assumption. It is simply unreasonable (and therefore impermissible) to infer that the *assumption* that $x$ has a particular property entails that *everything* in the domain has that property.

Think of it this way: When the claim that $x$ has a particular property rests on an *assumption* about $x$, there's *no* reason to think that $x$ *is typical* of, or *representative* of, or *characteristic* of, *each* of the individuals in the domain. Perhaps $x$ is—but then again perhaps $x$ isn't! Perhaps $x$ is the Everyman of the domain, so to speak—but then again perhaps $x$ isn't! Perhaps $x$ is wildly *atypical* of the individuals in the domain. The point is that with no reason to think that $x$ exemplifies *each* of the individuals in the domain, i.e., with no reason to think that $x$ is his, her, or its *proxy*, you aren't warranted in inferring a truth about *each* individual in the domain from a truth that is *assumed* to hold of one particular individual, $x$. This is so even though the one individual, $x$, is assumed to be *any* individual in the domain.

And *therefore* it's impermissible to perform ∀I on a *wff* containing at least one occurrence of a free variable '$x$', with respect to '$x$', when that *wff* rests on an *assumption* that $x$ has a particular property, i.e., on an assumption containing a free '$x$'. Hence the illegitimacy of the move from (2) to (3) in S169.

Now focus on S170. You are told in (1) that *everyone* is both a logician and a magician. Therefore (2) *any* individual $x$ in the domain is both a logician and a magician—irrespective of any *assumptions* about the properties that the individual $x$ happens to have. Therefore (3) $x$ is a logician—*irrespective* (once again) *of any assumptions about the properties that $x$ happens to have*. But $x$ is typical of *each* of the individuals in the domain; i.e., he is indeed the *proxy* of each. Therefore whatever is true of $x$ is true of each of the individuals in the domain. Therefore (4) *everyone* is a logician.

Is it now clear what the difference is between the *illegitimate* move from '$Lx$' to '$(\forall x)Lx$' in S169, and the *legitimate* move from '$Lx$' to '$(\forall x)Lx$' in S170?

I'm afraid that in the course of summarizing, I'm about to beat a dead horse. . . . In each of these two derivations, the springboard *wff*, '$Lx$', rests on an *assumption*. In S169, however, but not in S170, you are required to *assume* that a particular individual $x$ has a particular property: the property of being both a logician and a magician. You are given no reason to think that *any other* individual in the domain has this property. On the other hand, in S170 but not in S169, and in particular because of the first *universally quantified* assumption, you are given every reason to think that *each* individual in the domain has this property.

Accordingly, the difference between the individual *x* in S169 and the individual *x* in S170, is that in the latter, *x* is *typical* of, or *representative* of, or *characteristic* of, *each* of the individuals in the domain: *x* does indeed exemplify *each* of them, and as such is its *proxy*.

In S169, you're *assuming* that one particular individual *x*—again, it doesn't matter *who x* is—has a particular property, whether or not *x actually* has it. Other individuals in the domain may or may not have that property. In S170, however, you're not *assuming* that *x* has that property; you *know* that *x* has it—because *every* individual in the domain has it. It should be unsurprising, therefore, that from the *wff* ‘$Lx \land Mx$’ in S169 it is *impermissible* to go on and draw an inference about *every* individual in the domain. Furthermore, it should be equally unsurprising that from the very same *wff* ‘$Lx \land Mx$’ in S170 it is *permissible* to go on and draw an inference about *every* individual in in the domain.

So one last time: what's the difference between the variable ‘$x$’ in S169 and the variable ‘$x$’ in S170? The variable ‘$x$’ in S169 denotes any individual *x* in the domain that is *assumed* to be both a logician and a magician. By contrast the variable ‘$x$’ in S170 denotes any individual *x* in the domain *period*, i.e., without qualification, i.e., *unconditionally*. As a consequence, any conclusion that you derive from (1) in S169 will be true of any individual in the domain who is *assumed* to be both a logician and a magician—whereas any conclusion that you derive from (1) in S170 will be true of any individual in the domain *period*, i.e., *without qualification*, i.e., *unconditionally*. Hence the legitimacy of ∀I in S170 but not in S169; hence the necessity for Clause 1b.

### c. Clause 2b

Clause 2b is the second of the two tricky ∀I clauses: Why the necessity of "replacing, in ‘$Pt$’, each free occurrence of ‘$t$’ . . . with ‘$v$’"? Why isn't it sufficient to replace *at least one* free occurrence of ‘$t$’ with ‘$v$’?

Consider the following derivation:

S171:       $(\forall x)(x = x) \vdash (\forall x)(\forall y)(x = y)$

   1(1) $(\forall x)(x = x)$          A
   1(2) $x = x$                1 ∀E
   1(3) $(\forall y)(x = y)$          2 ∀I     XXX
   1(4) $(\forall x)(\forall y)(x = y)$       3 ∀I

(1) is an obvious truth: everything is identical to itself. (2) follows from (1), and is another obvious truth: any object $x$ is identical to itself. (3), however, is an obvious falsehood: each object $y$ is such that $x$, the object cited in (2), is identical to $y$. (Rhetorical question: Can you think of *any* object $x$ that is identical to *each and every* object in the domain—no matter *what* the domain is—unless, of course, it's a domain of exactly one object?) (4) is another obvious falsehood: each object $x$ is such that it's identical to *any* object $y$ whatsoever.

The problem obviously arose with the move from (2) to (3). Moral of the story: when performing ∀I on '**P**t', you simply must replace, in '**P**t', *every* free occurrence of '$t$' with '$v$'. Thus, when performing ∀I on '$x = x$' in (2), you must replace *every* free occurrence of '$x$' with one and the same variable in (3). Depending on what you're trying to prove, one possible correct version would be as follows:

S172:       $(\forall x)(x = x) \vdash (\forall y)(y = y)$

   1 (1) $(\forall x)(x = x)$         A
   1 (2) $x = x$               1 ∀E
   1 (3) $(\forall y)(y = y)$         2 ∀I

Alternatively, consider the following derivation:

S173:  1 (1) $(\forall x)(Ex \rightarrow Dx)$        A
       1 (2) $Ex \rightarrow Dx$           1 ∀E
       1 (3) $(\forall y)(Ex \rightarrow Dy)$        2 ∀I     XXX
       1 (4) $(\forall x)(\forall y)(Ex \rightarrow Dy)$     3 ∀I

Suppose a domain of natural numbers. Interpret 'Ex' to mean 'x is even', and interpret 'Dx' to mean 'x is divisible by 2 without remainder', or, for brevity's sake, 'x is divisible by 2'. Accordingly, (1) means 'Each natural number is such that if it's even then it's divisible by 2'. (2) obviously follows from (1): if x—any natural number whatsoever—is even then x is divisible by 2. So far so good. The problem arises at (3): 'Each natural number y is such that if x, the number cited in (2), is even, then y is divisible by 2'. The problem is that it's easy to come up with an interpretation that makes (2) true and (3) false. Suppose that x in both (2) and (3) is the number 4. So (2)—if 4 is even then 4 is divisible by 2—is an obvious truth. But what about (3)? Each number y whatsoever, e.g., the number 5, is such that if 4 is even then 5 is divisible by 2. Well, last I checked, 4 *is* even and 5 is *not* divisible by 2 (without remainder). So there's at least one interpretation that makes (2) true and (3) false. So the move from (2) is (3) is illegitimate.

(4) simply makes a bad situation worse. Reach into the vat of natural numbers and grab any natural number that you like. Now reach into the vat once again, and once again grab any natural number that you like. The number that you grab now might be the same as the first one that you grabbed, or it might be different. (4) involves the assertion that if the first natural number that you grabbed is even, then the second is divisible by 2. Codswallop pure and simple! The problem obviously arose with the move from (2) to (3). Moral of the story once again: when performing ∀I on '*Pt*' you have to replace, in '*Pt*', *every* free occurrence of '*t*' with '*v*'.

So here's what you know: you know that unless you adhere to the *every*-free-occurrence-of-'*t*' restriction, you'll end up constructing derivations that you shouldn't be able to construct. But here's what you don't know (at least not yet and not fully): you don't fully know *why* this is so. After all, ∃I *doesn't* have this restriction! On the contrary, with ∃I, as you know, you can move blithely not only from 'Lxx' to '(∃x)Lxx' or '(∃y)Lyy', say, but also to '(∃y)Lyx' or '(∃y)Lxy'. So what you really want to know is the *reason* why the *every*-free-occurrence-of-'*t*' restriction exists where ∀I is concerned—such that flouting it gets you into hot water—but *not* where ∃I is concerned. It's one thing to know *that* flouting the restriction gets you into hot water. It's another thing to know *why* it gets you into hot water.

Or maybe you *don't* really want to know the reason. . . . If you *do* really want to know, dive into the second appendix to Chapter 8 *immediately*. But if you *don't* really want to know, read on.

# 11. ∃E: The Refined Version

## A. When to Use ∃E

You should think ∃E thoughts whenever an existentially quantified *wff*, '(∃*v*)*Pv*', is staring you in the face; i.e., whenever it already appears in the derivation, and when you wish to use it to generate a *wff*, '☐'.

## B. How to Use ∃E

1. In a line below '(∃*v*)*Pv*', introduce '*Pt/v*' as an assumption as follows:
   - a. Delete '(∃*v*)', the leftmost quantifier in '(∃*v*)*Pv*', so that only '*Pv*' remains.
   - b. Construct '*Pt/v*'; i.e., convert '*Pv*' into '*Pt/v*' by replacing in '*Pv*' each free occurrence, and no bound occurrence, of '*v*' with a variable '*t*'. '*Pt/v*' is subject to two restrictions:
     - i. '*t*' must be free for '*v*' in '*Pv*'; i.e., '*t*' must be a variable that won't become bound by any quantifier in '*Pv*'. In other words, '*t*' must be free in '*Pt/v*' exactly where '*v*' was free in '*Pv*'; and
     - ii. '*t*' must not appear free in any prior assumption.
   - c. Off to the right of '*Pt/v*', write 'A'.
   - d. Off to the left of '*Pt/v*', cite the line number of '*Pt/v*'.
2. Construct a derivation of '*Pt/v* → ☐'.
3. In a line below '*Pt/v* → ☐', write '☐'. '☐' is subject to one restriction: '*t*' must not appear free in it.
4. Off to the right of '☐', cite the line numbers of '(∃*v*)*Pv*' and '*Pt/v* → ☐', followed by '∃E'.
5. Off to the far left of '☐', cite the line number of each assumption on which the *wffs* cited to the right of '☐', i.e., '(∃*v*)*Pv*' and '*Pt/v* → ☐', rest.

Unsurprisingly, several of these clauses require a word of elaboration.

## a. Clause 1b

Note that although in ∀E and ∃I, '$t$' may signify either a constant or a variable, in ∃E (as in ∀I, above) it signifies only a variable.

## b. Clause 1bi

In constructing your ∃E assumption, i.e., '$Pt/v$', Clause 1bi requires you to choose a variable '$t$' that is free for '$v$' in '$Pv$', i.e., a variable that won't become *bound* by any quantifier in '$Pv$'. Otherwise you run into pickles of the following sort:

S174:  1 (1) $(\exists x)(\exists y)Lxy$       A  
       2 (2) $(\exists y)Lyy$          A        X  
       3 (3) $Lzz$              A  
       3 (4) $(\exists z)Lzz$        3 ∃I  
          (5) $Lzz \rightarrow (\exists z)Lzz$     3,4 →I  
       2 (6) $(\exists z)Lzz$        2,5 ∃E  
          (7) $(\exists y)Lyy \rightarrow (\exists z)Lzz$    2,6 →I  
       1 (8) $(\exists z)Lzz$        1,7 ∃E     XXX

It may be true that (1) someone loves someone. It doesn't follow that (8) someone loves himself (or herself). So what went wrong? Take a second look at (1) and (2). '$(\exists v)Pv$' in (1) is, of course, '$(\exists x)(\exists y)Lxy$', and therefore '$Pv$' is '$(\exists y)Lxy$'. The ∃E restriction formulated in Clause 1bi requires that in the course of constructing your ∃E assumption, '$Pt/v$', you choose a variable, '$t$', "that won't become bound by any quantifier in '$Pv$'." The problem with the '$t$' that emerged in (2), i.e., '$y$', is that it *did* become bound by a quantifier in '$Pv$', i.e., in '$(\exists y)Lxy$': instead of being free, the '$y$' that replaced '$x$' became bound by the '$(\exists y)$' quantifier.

Question: But isn't (2), merely an *assumption*—and aren't you permitted to assume whatever you like whenever you like?

Answer: Yes and yes. (2) *is* merely an assumption, and you *are* permitted to assume whatever you like whenever you like. Nevertheless, even though you don't lose points at line (2), it doesn't follow that (2) is the right sort of ∃E assumption. And of course it isn't: it fails to comply with the relevant ∃E restriction. So, while (2) is a perfectly legitimate *assumption*, it's a perfectly illegitimate *Existential Elimination* assumption. Accordingly, you lose points at line (8), when you invoke the ∃E rule. Off to the right you cite lines (1) and (7). The antecedent of (7), of course, is your ∃E assumption, and the consequent is your targeted *wff*. Insofar as your ∃E assumption is an illegitimate ∃E assumption, the antecedent of (7) is an illegitimate antecedent for the purpose of making the ∃E step in line (8). The conditional as a whole, in other words, is not suitable as a *wff* from which to make the ∃E step in line (8). Hence the loss of points, and the three red Xs at line (8). (Consider the *single* red X off to the right of line (2) as a *warning* rather than a *ticket*.)

So what would a respectable line-(2) ∃E assumption look like? '**P*v***' itself is '(∃y)Lxy'—the line-(1) *wff* with the initial existential quantifier deleted. You're free to extract '*x*' ('***v***') from '(∃y)Lxy' and implant, in its place, *any* variable that will remain free, i.e., that won't become bound by any quantifier in '(∃y)Lxy', *and* that adheres to Clause 1bii (see below). The problem with S174, once again, is that the variable newly implanted in line (2) is '*y*'—and '*y*' most certainly *did* become bound by a quantifier in '(∃y)Lxy', i.e., by '∃y' itself. A perfectly respectable line-(2) assumption, on the other hand, would be '(∃y)Lxy' or '(∃y)Lzy' or '(∃y)Lwy', etc.

### c. Clause 1bii

In constructing your '***Pt/v***' ∃E assumption, Clause 1bii also requires you to choose a variable '*t*' that doesn't appear free in any prior assumption. Otherwise you run into pickles of the following sort:

S175:
| | | |
|---|---|---|
| 1 (1) $(\exists x)Sx$ | A | |
| 2 (2) $(\exists x)Cx$ | A | |
| 3 (3) $Sx$ | A | |
| 4 (4) $Cx$ | A | X |
| 3,4 (5) $Sx \land Cx$ | 3,4 $\land$I | |
| 3,4 (6) $(\exists x)(Sx \land Cx)$ | 5 $\exists$I | |
| 3 (7) $Cx \rightarrow (\exists x)(Sx \land Cx)$ | 4,6 $\rightarrow$I | |
| 2,3 (8) $(\exists x)(Sx \land Cx)$ | 2,7 $\exists$E | XXX |
| 2 (9) $Sx \rightarrow (\exists x)(Sx \land Cx)$ | 3,8 $\rightarrow$I | |
| 1,2 (10) $(\exists x)(Sx \land Cx)$ | 1,9 $\exists$E | |

Suppose a domain of two-dimensional Euclidean shapes. Interpret 'Sx' to mean 'x is a square'. Interpret 'Cx' to mean, 'x is a circle'. So (1) says that there exists at least one square, and (2) says that there exists at least one circle. So (1) and (2) are both true for this interpretation. However (10), resting only on (1) and (2), affirms the existence of at least one object that is *both* a square *and* a circle —a *squircle*. But squircles, of course, don't exist. (Why? Because they *can't* exist: the very *notion* of a squircle is self-contradictory.) So for this interpretation (10) is false, even though (1) and (2) are true. The argument, therefore, is invalid and the sequent is unprovable.

So where's the misstep? (If it strikes you that you've *already* read what you're about to read, it's because you've read something *similar*—but not *identical*—in the very last subsection.) It might seem to you that the misstep is to be found in (4), where you assume that the object x— which you assumed in (3) to be a square—is also a circle. But (once again) you're permitted to assume *whatever* you like *whenever* you like, right? Right! However, what you're *not* permitted to do is to treat just *any* old assumption as an ∃E assumption.

The misstep occurs at (8), with the first of the two applications of ∃E. Note the numerals to the left of (8): '2' and '3'. Their presence tells you that (2) and (3) imply (8). In other words, (2) and (3) together— the claim that there exists at least one object that's a circle, and the claim that an object x is a square—*imply* (8): the claim that there exists at least one object that's both a square and a circle. And of course, (2) and (3) imply nothing of the sort; they do *not* imply (8). Hence the loss of points at (8)—and the mere *warning* at (4).

But (2) and (3) *would* imply (8) if it were permissible to assume that the object that we assume to be a circle in (4) is identical to the object that we assume to be a square in (3). But, of course, it isn't permissible: nothing in the premises entails this. In assuming that the 'two' objects are identical to each other—which of course is just what you're doing when you designate the second object by the same variable, 'x', that you used to designate the first object—you're going beyond what the premises imply. Hence the requirement that when you introduce an ∃E assumption, you choose a variable that doesn't appear free in any prior assumption.

Question: If 'x' appears in a prior assumption, and we then adhere to the restriction and introduce 'y' into the next ∃E assumption, aren't we thereby assuming that x is *distinct* from y? And doesn't this too involve going beyond what the premises imply? It's clear that the premises don't imply that the object that is square is *identical* to the object that is circular, but the premises don't imply that the 'two' objects are *distinct* from each other either!

Answer: In introducing '*y*', we are *not* committing ourselves to the existence of two distinct objects. Just as the premises themselves are noncommittal, we too are being noncommittal with respect to the question of whether *x* and *y* are identical or distinct: at no point are we making the claim '*x* = *y*', and at no point are we making the claim '—(*x* = *y*)'.

So how do you avoid the squircles pickle; i.e., how do you comply with Clause 1bii? Easy. Each time that you make an ∃E assumption, make sure that the variable that you introduce doesn't *already* appear free in any assumption.

Question: So what's the correct version of S175?

Answer: There's *no* correct version of S175. Rather, from the same premises it's possible to derive a variety of different conclusions—but not the conclusion of S175. S175 is an unprovable sequent: the argument is an invalid argument and our derivation rules are truth-preserving. No matter how hard you try, therefore, you *shouldn't* (and *won't*) be able to derive its conclusion from its premises. Indeed, whatever conclusion you derive will be different from S175's conclusion. Consider S176 and its conclusion:

S176:        $(\exists x)Sx, (\exists x)Cx \vdash (\exists y)(\exists x)(Sx \wedge Cy)$

| | | |
|---|---|---|
| 1 (1) $(\exists x)Sx$ | | A |
| 2 (2) $(\exists x)Cx$ | | A |
| 3 (3) $Sx$ | | A |
| 4 (4) $Cy$ | | A |
| 3,4 (5) $Sx \wedge Cy$ | | 3,4 ∧I |
| 3,4 (6) $(\exists x)(Sx \wedge Cy)$ | | 5 ∃I |
| 3,4 (7) $(\exists y)(\exists x)(Sx \wedge Cy)$ | | 6 ∃I |
| 3 (8) $Cy \rightarrow (\exists y)(\exists x)(Sx \wedge Cy)$ | | 4,7 →I |
| 2,3 (9) $(\exists y)(\exists x)(Sx \wedge Cy)$ | | 2,8 ∃E |
| 2 (10) $Sx \rightarrow (\exists y)(\exists x)(Sx \wedge Cy)$ | | 3,9 →I |
| 1,2 (11) $(\exists y)(\exists x)(Sx \wedge Cy)$ | | 1,10 ∃E |

There exists at least one square. There exists at least one circle. Conclusion: there exists at least one object $y$ and there exists at least one object $x$, such that $x$ is a square and $y$ is a circle. For all you know, $x$ and $y$ may be identical to each other. And for all you know they may not be. The premises are noncommittal on this issue—and so (correctly) is the conclusion.

## d. Clause 3

In generating your targeted *wff* '□', Clause 3 requires you to ensure that '*t*' doesn't occur free in '□'. There are two closely related reasons for this restriction. One reason is to prevent you from asserting of any object whatsoever that it has a given property simply because some object or other has some property or other. The other reason for this restriction is to prevent you from performing ∀I down the line—in a context that clearly rules out the permissibility of ∀I. The following exemplifies both of these considerations:

S177:   1 (1) $(\exists x)(Lx \wedge Mx)$         A
       2 (2) $Lx \wedge Mx$             A
       2 (3) $Lx$                   2 ∧E
          (4) $(Lx \wedge Mx) \rightarrow Lx$    2,3 →I
       1 (5) $Lx$                   1,4 ∃E      XXX
       1 (6) $(\forall x)Lx$             5 ∀I

Suppose that the premise affirms the existence of at least one logician who's also a magician. At (2) you're *assuming* that an unnamed individual, $x$, is both a logician and a musician.

First problem: At (5) you're making the *assertion* that *any* individual $x$ in the domain is a logician—and you're basing this assertion on (1)—the premise that *someone* is a logician and a magician. Why on Earth are you entitled to make *this* assertion? It's one thing to *assume* at (2) that any individual $x$ in the domain is a logician and a magician. It's quite another thing to *assert* at (5) that any individual $x$ in the domain is a logician. You avoid this first pickle by disallowing any free occurrence of '*t*', i.e., '*x*', in '□', i.e., in the line where you invoke ∃E, i.e., in (5).

Second problem: At (6) you're making the *assertion* that *every* individual *x* in the domain is a logician—and you're basing this assertion too on (1)—the premise that *someone* is a logician and a magician. Notice that the problem here has nothing to do with the move from (5) to (6): that's a *perfectly* legitimate move. After all, '*Lx*' in line (5) rests on no assumption containing the free variable '*x*'. Therefore (5) (once again) amounts to the *assertion* that *any* individual *x* is a logician. Therefore (5) is a perfectly legitimate springboard *wff* for performing ∀I in line (6)—and for thereby generating '(∀x)Lx'. So from the premise that at least one person is both a logician and a magician you conclude that everyone is a logician? No, no, no! The problem here is the very existence of (5) itself. You avoid this second pickle in the same way that you avoid the first pickle: by disallowing any free occurrence of '*t*', i.e., '*x*', in '□', i.e., in the line where you invoke ∃E, i.e., in (5).

Some ∃E assumptions may contain more than one free variable. When they do, you may have a bit of a problem determining which of these free variables mustn't appear free in your targeted ∃E *wff*. The solution? Flag the free variable that you introduce in your ∃E assumption by circling it.

## e. Clause 4

Clause 4 requires you to cite the line numbers of two *wffs* off to the right of '□', your ∃E target: first, the line number of '(∃v)Pv', the existentially quantified *wff* on which '□' rests, and second, '*Pt/v* → □', the conditional whose antecedent is your ∃E assumption and whose consequent, of course, is your ∃E target itself.

Question: How do you identify each of these two *wffs*, '(∃v)Pv' and '*Pt/v* → □'?

Answer: Start with the *second wff*, '*Pt/v* → □'. Its whereabouts are obvious, given that its consequent is '□', the same *wff* as your ∃E target, and given too that it's sandwiched between the two occurrences of '□'.

Now focus on the *first wff*, '(∃v)Pv', the more difficult one to track down: the existentially quantified *wff* on which '□' rests. There might be a slew of existentially quantified *wffs* above '□' on your notebook page, and perhaps you haven't the slightest idea which one to cite.

So here's what you do: You return to the line where '*Pt/v* → □' appears. Off to the right you'll see two numerals. The first of them represents the line number of '$Pt/v$', the conditional's antecedent, and the second represents the line number of the first occurrence of '$\square$', the conditional's consequent. Focus on the first, the line number of '$Pt/v$'. '$Pt/v$' is the $\exists$E assumption that helped to generate the first occurrence of '$\square$'—and '$(\exists v)Pv$' is its existential counterpart. You know how you constructed '$Pt/v$' out of '$(\exists v)Pv$'—and you know, therefore, the nature of the intimate structural relation between the two *wffs*. Once you find '$Pt/v$', '$(\exists v)Pv$' should be a short hop, skip, and a jump away. Look immediately to its left and you'll have your magic line number: the first of the two line numbers that you'll cite off to the right of '$\square$'.

Now consider the following derivation:

S178:          $(\exists x)(\exists y)Lxy \vdash (\exists w)(\exists z)Lwz$

| | | |
|---|---|---|
| 1 (1) | $(\exists x)(\exists y)Lxy$ | A |
| 2 (2) | $(\exists y)Lwy$ | A |
| 3 (3) | $Lwz$ | A |
| 3 (4) | $(\exists z)Lwz$ | 3 $\exists$I |
| (5) | $Lwz \rightarrow (\exists z)Lwz$ | 3,4 $\rightarrow$I |
| 2 (6) | $(\exists z)Lwz$ | 2,5 $\exists$E |
| 2 (7) | $(\exists w)(\exists z)Lwz$ | 6 $\exists$I |
| (8) | $(\exists y)Lwy \rightarrow (\exists w)(\exists z)Lwz$ | 2,7 $\rightarrow$I |
| 1 (9) | $(\exists w)(\exists z)Lwz$ | 1,8 $\exists$E |

What follows is a short string of alternating questions and answers. Try to answer each question on your own before you actually read the answer.

Question: Is it really legitimate to have a free '$w$' in (6), '$(\exists z)Lwz$', your targeted $\exists$E *wff*? After all, in light of Clause 3, '$t$' mustn't appear free in your targeted $\exists$E *wff*; but (6) is your targeted $\exists$E *wff* and '$w$' is certainly free in (6).

Answer: Yes, it's legitimate to have a free '$w$' in (6), '$(\exists z)Lwz$'. The reason is that in (6) '$w$' simply isn't '$t$'—and therefore there's been no violation of the Clause 3 restriction that '$t$' mustn't appear free in your $\exists$E *wff*.

Question: How do we know that '*w*' in (6) *isn't* '*t*'—and just how do we determine *which* is the variable '*t*' that mustn't appear free in (6)?

Answer: Note that (6), '(∃z)Lwz', rests on (2), '(∃y)Lwy'. In other words, the existentially quantified *wff* that generates (6) is (2). Now the ∃E assumption corresponding to (2), and motivated by (2), is (3), '*Lwz*'. And you came up with this assumption by following the script. First you deleted the leftmost (the only) existential quantifier in (2), '(∃y)Lwy', to yield '*Lwy*'. Then you extracted each free occurrence of '*y*' from '*Lwy*' (there's only one). And finally you implanted '*z*' wherever '*y*' had been free in '*Lwy*'. In brief, out came '*y*' from '*Lwy*'; in went '*z*'; and the result was '*Lwz*'. So it's '*z*', the variable that's newly implanted in your ∃E assumption '*Lwz*', that's '*t*' in your ∃E assumption. And therefore it's '*z*' that mustn't appear free in (6), '(∃z)Lwz', your targeted ∃E *wff*. And it doesn't: while '*z*' does *appear* in '(∃z)Lwz', it doesn't appear *free* in '(∃z)Lwz'.

For the slightly more *abstract* version of what's going on here, read on.

What generates '□', your targeted ∃E *wff* '(∃z)Lwz', is '(∃y)Lwy'. So '(∃v)**Pv**' is '(∃y)Lwy'. So '**Pv**'—the whole of '(∃v)**Pv**' to the right of '(∃v)'—is '*Lwy*', the whole of '(∃y)Lwy' to the right of '(∃y)'. So '*v*' is '*y*': the variable immediately to the right of the existential quantifier. And '*t*' is the variable that you *introduced* in the course of transforming '**Pv**' ('*Lwy*') into '**Pt/v**' ('*Lwz*'), your ∃E assumption. So '*t*' in '*Lwz*' must be—and indeed is—'*z*'. And so '*t*' in '**Pt/v**' had better correspond *exactly* to '*v*' in '**Pv**'; i.e., '*t*' ('*z*') had better occur free in '**Pt/v**' ('*Lwz*') exactly where '*v*' ('*y*') occurs free in '**Pv**' ('*Lwy*'). And it does: '*z*', like '*y*', occurs in the second slot to the right of the predicate '*L*'.

Just in case you're not convinced and think that it's '*w*' that's '*t*' in (6), '(∃z)Lwz', think again: You introduced '*w*' in (2) and not in (3), whereas you introduced '*z*' in (3).

Question: And '*w*', therefore, mustn't appear free in which line?

Answer: In (9), '(∃w)(∃z)Lwz'—and it doesn't.

# Exercises

For each of the following sequents, derive its conclusion from its premises.

1. Variations on QN:

S179:  $(\exists x)-Lx \vdash -(\forall x)Lx$
S180:  $(\forall x)-Lx \vdash -(\exists x)Lx$
S181:  $(\exists x)Lx \vdash -(\forall x)-Lx$
S182:  $(\forall x)Lx \vdash -(\exists x)-Lx$

2. Variations on QS:

S183:  $(\forall x)[Lx \wedge (\forall y)My] \vdash (\forall x)Lx \wedge (\forall y)My$
S184:  $(\forall x)Lx \wedge (\forall y)My \vdash (\forall x)[Lx \wedge (\forall y)My]$
S185:  $(\forall x)[Lx \vee (\forall y)My] \vdash (\forall x)Lx \vee (\forall y)My$
S186:  $(\forall x)Lx \vee (\forall y)My \vdash (\forall x)[Lx \vee (\forall y)My]$
S187:  $(\forall x)[Lx \rightarrow (\forall y)My] \vdash (\exists x)Lx \rightarrow (\forall y)My$
S188:  $(\exists x)Lx \rightarrow (\forall y)My \vdash (\forall x)[Lx \rightarrow (\forall y)My]$

# Chapter Eight

## Predicate Logic:
## A Deductive Apparatus, Part Two

### 1. Derivations Involving Multiplace Predicates

Derivations involving multiplace predicates can be challenging. Three such derivations, that also happen to illustrate each of the four quantification rules, may be helpful. I'll walk you through them in some detail.

S189:     $(\forall x)(\exists y)Lxy \vdash -(\exists x)(\forall y)-Lxy$

Suppose that you try a combination of the Top-Down and the Bottom-Up Approaches. Suppose that you start with the Bottom-Up Approach. Your goal is to generate '$-(\exists x)(\forall y)-Lxy$' from '$(\forall x)(\exists y)Lxy$'. You introduce the obvious *Reductio* assumption in line (2): '$(\exists x)(\forall y)-Lxy$'. To be sure, you *could* have begun by first performing $\forall$E on (1). Then you could have followed up by introducing the corresponding $\exists$E assumption in line (3). At that point, however, you'd be stuck, and you'd have to introduce the *Reductio* assumption anyway.

Your goal is to generate a contradiction in your second-to-last line. But *which* contradiction? Two contradictions come to mind. One is the conjunction of (1) and *its* opposite. The other is the conjunction of (2) and *its* opposite. If you derive the opposite of (1) you'll then conjoin it with (1) to generate your contradiction. By the same token, if you derive the opposite of (2) you'll then conjoin it with (2) to generate your contradiction. Only trial and error will decide the issue. Whichever contradiction it is, it had better rest on both (1) and (2), allowing you to *zap* (2) in your last line.

Suppose that you decide to try to generate in your second-to-last line the conjunction of (1) and its opposite. That means that you'll need to generate, in your third-to-last line, the opposite of (1), i.e., '$-(\forall x)(\exists y)Lxy$'. In your second-to-last line, you'll then form the conjunction of (1) with its opposite from your third-to-last line.

$$1 \ (1) \ (\forall x)(\exists y)Lxy \qquad\qquad\qquad\qquad A$$
$$2 \ (2) \ (\exists x)(\forall y)-Lxy \qquad\qquad\qquad\qquad A$$

$$.$$
$$.$$

$$? \ (n\text{--}2) \ -(\forall x)(\exists y)Lxy \qquad\qquad\qquad\qquad ?$$
$$1,2 \ (n\text{--}1) \ (\forall x)(\exists y)Lxy \wedge -(\forall x)(\exists y)Lxy \qquad 1,n\text{--}2 \ \wedge I$$
$$1 \ (n) \ -(\exists x)(\forall y)-Lxy \qquad\qquad\qquad\qquad 2,n\text{--}1 \ -I$$

Obvious question: How do you generate your third-to-last line, '$-(\forall x)(\exists y)Lxy$'? It's time to switch to the Top-Down Approach. Your line-(2) *Reductio* assumption, '$(\exists x)(\forall y)-Lxy$', is itself an *existentially* quantified *wff*. So you launch an $\exists E$ proof within the scope of your $-I$ proof. In line (3), therefore, you introduce an $\exists E$ assumption corresponding to (2): '$(\forall y)-Lxy$', noting (with satisfaction) that the free variable '$x$' doesn't appear free in any prior, undischarged assumption. (How could it? '$x$', as a *free* variable, is making its *debut* in (3).)

You're in the midst of an $\exists E$ derivation. Your goal is to derive '$-(\forall x)(\exists y)Lxy$' twice. Ultimately you want to derive it in your third-to-last line from (2), your existentially quantified *wff*. As with any $\exists E$ derivation, however, first you'll have to derive it from your $\exists E$ assumption—in this instance, (3). Of course, you'll also need a derivation of '$(\forall y)-Lxy \rightarrow -(\forall x)(\exists y)Lxy$' to be sandwiched between these two derivations of '$-(\forall x)(\exists y)Lxy$'. You now know exactly what your fourth-to-last and fifth-to-last lines will look like.

$$1 \ (1) \ (\forall x)(\exists y)Lxy \qquad\qquad\qquad\qquad A$$
$$2 \ (2) \ (\exists x)(\forall y)-Lxy \qquad\qquad\qquad\qquad A$$
$$3 \ (3) \ (\forall y)-Lxy \qquad\qquad\qquad\qquad\qquad A$$

$$.$$
$$.$$

$$3,? \ (n\text{--}4) \ -(\forall x)(\exists y)Lxy \qquad\qquad\qquad\qquad ?$$
$$? \ (n\text{--}3) \ (\forall y)-Lxy \rightarrow -(\forall x)(\exists y)Lxy \qquad 3,n\text{--}4 \ \rightarrow I$$

$$2,? \ (n-2) \ -(\forall x)(\exists y)Lxy \qquad\qquad 2,n-3 \ \exists E$$
$$1,2 \ (n-1) \ (\forall x)(\exists y)Lxy \wedge -(\forall x)(\exists y)Lxy \qquad 1,n-2 \ \wedge I$$
$$1 \ (n) \ -(\exists x)(\forall y)-Lxy \qquad\qquad 2,n-1 \ -I$$

In lines (1) and (3) you now have two *universally* quantified *wffs* that are *crying out* for $\forall E$. First you look at the open *wff* that follows (1)'s string of quantifiers and you see '$Lxy$'. Then you look at the open *wff* that follows (3)'s single quantifier and you see '$-Lxy$'. You see a *contradiction*, in short, and so your goal, quite obviously, is to release '$Lxy$' and '$-Lxy$' from the *wffs* within which they are, respectively, buried. Your goal, as always with *Reductio*, is to make the implicit *explicit*.

It makes no difference which of the two universally quantified *wffs*, (1) or (3), you operate on first. Suppose that you perform $\forall E$ on (1) to generate (4), '$(\exists y)Lxy$'. You now have another *existentially* quantified *wff*. You introduce *its* corresponding $\exists E$ assumption in line (5): '$Lxy$'. It's perfectly legitimate for '$y$' to appear free in (5)—and for the same reason that it's perfectly legitimate for '$x$' to appear free in (3): as a free variable, '$y$' is making its debut in (5); i.e., '$y$' doesn't appear free in any prior assumption.

> A slight digression: Suppose that you had already performed $\forall E$ on '$(\forall y)-Lxy$' in line (3) to generate '$-Lxy$' in an alternative line (4). Even so, you *still* would have been able to introduce your $\exists E$ assumption '$Lxy$' in the very next line. To be sure, '$y$' would have appeared free in the alternative line (4), in '$-Lxy$'—but '$-Lxy$' in the alternative line (4) wouldn't have been an *assumption*. It would have been a *wff* that (once again) you would have *derived* by $\forall E$ from your line-(3) assumption, '$(\forall y)-Lxy$'—and '$y$' is *not* free in that assumption.

You now perform $\forall E$ on '$(\forall y)-Lxy$' in line (3) to generate '$-Lxy$' in line (6). And now you construct your contradiction, '$Lxy \wedge -Lxy$', in line (7).

$$1 \ (1) \ (\forall x)(\exists y)Lxy \qquad\qquad\qquad A$$
$$2 \ (2) \ (\exists x)(\forall y)-Lxy \qquad\qquad\qquad A$$
$$3 \ (3) \ (\forall y)-Lxy \qquad\qquad\qquad\qquad A$$
$$1 \ (4) \ (\exists y)Lxy \qquad\qquad\qquad\qquad 1 \ \forall E$$

$$5 \ (5) \ Lxy \qquad\qquad\qquad\qquad\qquad\qquad\qquad A$$
$$3 \ (6) \ {-}Lxy \qquad\qquad\qquad\qquad\qquad\qquad\ 3 \ \forall E$$
$$3,5 \ (7) \ Lxy \wedge {-}Lxy \qquad\qquad\qquad\qquad\ 5,6 \ \wedge I$$

.

.

$$? \ (n{-}4) \ {-}(\forall x)(\exists y)Lxy \qquad\qquad\qquad\qquad\qquad ?$$
$$? \ (n{-}3) \ (\forall y){-}Lxy \rightarrow {-}(\forall x)(\exists y)Lxy \qquad\quad 3,n{-}4 \rightarrow I$$
$$2,? \ (n{-}2) \ {-}(\forall x)(\exists y)Lxy \qquad\qquad\qquad\quad 2,n{-}3 \ \exists E$$
$$1,2 \ (n{-}1) \ (\forall x)(\exists y)Lxy \wedge {-}(\forall x)(\exists y)Lxy \qquad 1,n{-}2 \ \wedge I$$
$$1 \ (n) \ {-}(\exists x)(\forall y){-}Lxy \qquad\qquad\qquad\qquad 2,n{-}1 \ {-}I$$

It's time to stop and think. Your de-quantifying days are over (at least where this derivation is concerned): you've de-quantified to the *max*, as it were, every quantified *wff* through line (7). You stare at your line-(7) contradiction: whether you realize it or not, it's *terribly* interesting. What makes it so interesting is that it rests on (3) and (5). As always, the numerals off to the left tell the story. (3), of course, is the ∃E assumption corresponding to (2). (5) is the ∃E assumption corresponding to (4)—and (4) rests on (1). So your line-(7) contradiction is linked *ultimately* (albeit *indirectly*) with precisely those *wffs* with which you want it to be linked: (1) and (2).

You now have a choice vis-à-vis line (8). You know that because (3) and (5) together generate a contradiction, (3) generates the negation of (5) and (5) generates the negation of (3). So one possible line-(8) *wff* is '—*Lxy*', the negation of (5), resting on (3). But you already have '—*Lxy*' resting on (3), in line (6)! The only other possible line-(8) *wff* is '—(∀y)—*Lxy*', the negation of (3), resting on (5). A bit apprehensively (*apprehensively*, because you don't really know where you're going with this) you write down '—(∀y)—*Lxy*' in line (8).

Notice that (8) rests only on (5). (5), you'll recall once again, is an ∃E assumption, corresponding to (4). The beauty of (4) is that it rests only on (1). You discharge (5) now by performing →I in (9). You then repeat (8) in (10). (10) rests only on (1), and it's the opposite of (3). (3), of course, is the ∃E assumption corresponding to (2). And (2) is nothing less than your *Reductio* assumption. You are circling (1) and (2), and are closing in on (2). You conjoin (3) with (10) to generate a new contradiction in line (11), resting on (1) and (3).

1 (1) $(\forall x)(\exists y)Lxy$           A
2 (2) $(\exists x)(\forall y)-Lxy$         A
3 (3) $(\forall y)-Lxy$              A
1 (4) $(\exists y)Lxy$               1 $\forall$E
5 (5) $Lxy$                   A
3 (6) $-Lxy$               3 $\forall$E
3,5 (7) $Lxy \wedge -Lxy$      5,6 $\wedge$I
5 (8) $-(\forall y)-Lxy$       3,7 $-$I
   (9) $Lxy \rightarrow -(\forall y)-Lxy$    5,8 $\rightarrow$I
1 (10) $-(\forall y)-Lxy$        4,9 $\exists$E
1,3 (11) $(\forall y)-Lxy \wedge -(\forall y)-Lxy$     3,10 $\wedge$I

      .
      .
      .

? $(n-4)$ $-(\forall x)(\exists y)Lxy$          ?
? $(n-3)$ $(\forall y)-Lxy \rightarrow -(\forall x)(\exists y)Lxy$    3,$n$-4 $\rightarrow$I
2,? $(n-2)$ $-(\forall x)(\exists y)Lxy$      2,$n$-3 $\exists$E
1,2 $(n-1)$ $(\forall x)(\exists y)Lxy \wedge -(\forall x)(\exists y)Lxy$    1,$n$-2 $\wedge$I
1 $(n)$ $-(\exists x)(\forall y)-Lxy$        2,$n$-1 $-$I

From this point on, each *wff* in each of the remaining lines is exactly what you had been consciously aiming for all along.

(12) is '$-(\forall x)(\exists y)Lxy$', the negation of (1), resting on (3). Notice that (12) rests only on (3). (3), you'll recall, is an $\exists$E assumption corresponding to (2). You discharge (3) now via $\rightarrow$I in (13), and then you repeat (12) in (14). (14) rests only on (2), and it's your targeted opposite of (1). You conjoin (1) with (14) to generate the line-(15) contradiction, resting on—Hold your breath!—(1) and (2)! So what do you know? You know that (1) generates the negation of (2). You write down the negation of (2), i.e., '$-(\exists x)(\forall y)-Lxy$', in line (16), resting only on (1). Done. *Ecce*:

1 (1) $(\forall x)(\exists y)Lxy$          A
2 (2) $(\exists x)(\forall y)-Lxy$       A
3 (3) $(\forall y)-Lxy$            A
1 (4) $(\exists y)Lxy$             1 $\forall$E
5 (5) $Lxy$                 A
3 (6) $-Lxy$             3 $\forall$E

3,5 (7) $Lxy \wedge -Lxy$                                5,6 $\wedge$I
   5 (8) $-(\forall y)-Lxy$                               3,7 $-$I
      (9) $Lxy \rightarrow -(\forall y)-Lxy$              5,8 $\rightarrow$I
   1 (10) $-(\forall y)-Lxy$                              4,9 $\exists$E
 1,3 (11) $(\forall y)-Lxy \wedge -(\forall y)-Lxy$      3,10 $\wedge$I
   3 (12) $-(\forall x)(\exists y)Lxy$                    1,11 $-$I
     (13) $(\forall y)-Lxy \rightarrow -(\forall x)(\exists y)Lxy$   3,12 $\rightarrow$I
   2 (14) $-(\forall x)(\exists y)Lxy$                    2,13 $\exists$E
 1,2 (15) $(\forall x)(\exists y)Lxy \wedge -(\forall x)(\exists y)Lxy$   1,14 $\wedge$I
   1 (16) $-(\exists x)(\forall y)-Lxy$                   2,15 $-$I

Now consider the converse of S189:

S190:          $-(\exists x)(\forall y)-Lxy \vdash (\forall x)(\exists y)Lxy$

Notice that you *can't* adopt the Top-Down Approach at the outset: the quantification rules allow you to do *nothing* with the *negation* of a quantified *wff*. So you adopt the Bottom-Up Approach. Your conclusion being a universally quantified *wff*, you try to generate '$(\exists y)Lxy$' in your second-to-last line. You now have two fantasies: a *first* fantasy of trying to generate '$Lxy$' in your third-to-last line, and a *second* fantasy of introducing '$-Lxy$' as a *Reductio* assumption in line (2). You then perform $\forall$I on '$-Lxy$' to generate '$(\forall y)-Lxy$' in line (3). You existentially quantify the latter to generate '$(\exists x)(\forall y)-Lxy$' in line (4). You now have the two halves of your contradiction and are grinning from ear to ear. You can see your destination and you can see *exactly* how to arrive at your destination.

   1 (1) $-(\exists x)(\forall y)-Lxy$                         A
   2 (2) $-Lxy$                                                A
   2 (3) $(\forall y)-Lxy$                                     2 $\forall$I
   2 (4) $(\exists x)(\forall y)-Lxy$                          3 $\exists$I
 1,2 (5) $(\exists x)(\forall y)-Lxy \wedge -(\exists x)(\forall y)-Lxy$   4,1 $\wedge$I
   1 (6) $--Lxy$                                               2,5 $-$I
   1 (7) $Lxy$                                                 6 $--$E
   1 (8) $(\exists y)Lxy$                                      7 $\exists$I
   1 (9) $(\forall x)(\exists y)Lxy$                           8 $\forall$I

There's only one problem here. One *fatal* problem. Take a second look at line (3). The derivation is *impeccable*—except for the move from (2) to (3). (2), you will note, is an *assumption*—and '*y*' appears free in (2). Therefore it's impermissible to perform ∀I with respect to '*y*' in the move from (2) to (3). Back to square one. . . .

You need a more *promising*, a more *robust*, a more *substantial*, *Reductio* assumption than (2). In general, if your *Reductio* assumption is too *skimpy*, you won't get sufficient mileage out of it. If it's too *bulky*, you'll end up with a longer derivation than you need. Even so, better bulky, long, and correct than skimpy, short, and dead wrong.

Suppose that in your second attempt at S190, you proceed initially (but *only* initially) as you proceeded a moment ago. You aim for '$(\exists y)Lxy$' in your second-to-last line. But now you assume, in line (2), the opposite of '$(\exists y)Lxy$', i.e., '$-(\exists y)Lxy$'. Your goal is to derive a contradiction. Once you generate your contradiction, you'll end up with the negation of (2), i.e., '$--(\exists y)Lxy$', in your third-to-last line. Obviously, you'll make the move from your third-to-last line to '$(\exists y)Lxy$' in your second-to-last line via $--$E, and from your second-to-last line to '$(\forall x)(\exists y)Lxy$' in your last line via ∀I.

Question: *Which* contradiction should you aim for in your fourth-to-last line? Suppose that you aim for the conjunction of (1) and its opposite, i.e., '$-(\exists x)(\forall y)-Lxy$' and '$(\exists x)(\forall y)-Lxy$'. That means that in your fifth-to-last line you should aim for '$(\exists x)(\forall y)-Lxy$'. Notice that your new target is an existentially quantified *wff*. Accordingly, in your sixth-to-last line you'll aim for '$(\forall y)-Lxy$' and then, in the move to your fifth-to-last line, you'll existentially quantify the variable '*x*'.

| | | |
|---|---|---|
| 1 (1) $-(\exists x)(\forall y)-Lxy$ | | A |
| 2 (2) $-(\exists y)Lxy$ | | A |
| . | | |
| . | | |
| 2 ($n$–5) $(\forall y)-Lxy$ | | ? |
| 2 ($n$–4) $(\exists x)(\forall y)-Lxy$ | | $n$–5 ∃I |
| 1,2 ($n$–3) $(\exists x)(\forall y)-Lxy \wedge -(\exists x)(\forall y)-Lxy$ | | $n$–4,1 ∧I |
| 1 ($n$–2) $--(\exists y)Lxy$ | | 2,$n$–3 $-$I |
| 1 ($n$–1) $(\exists y)Lxy$ | | $n$–2 $--$E |
| 1 ($n$) $(\forall x)(\exists y)Lxy$ | | $n$–1 ∀I |

The trick now, of course, is to get from '$-(\exists y)Lxy$' in line (2) to '$(\forall y)-Lxy$' in your sixth-to-last line, ($n$–5). (QN thoughts, anyone?) There's nothing that you can do with (1) and (2): each is a negated *wff*. You look at your new target, '$(\forall y)-Lxy$'. You think that if you could just generate '$-Lxy$, then, by $\forall$I, you'd have '$(\forall y)-Lxy$'. So how do you generate '$-Lxy$'? The same way that you generate *any wff* when its generation seems hopeless: you invoke your old pal *Reductio*; you assume '$Lxy$' in line (3); and you aim for a new contradiction.

$$
\begin{array}{lll}
1 & (1)\ -(\exists x)(\forall y)-Lxy & \text{A} \\
2 & (2)\ -(\exists y)Lxy & \text{A} \\
3 & (3)\ Lxy & \text{A} \\
3 & (4)\ (\exists y)Lxy & 3\ \exists\text{I} \\
2,3 & (5)\ (\exists y)Lxy \wedge -(\exists y)Lxy & 4,2\ \wedge\text{I} \\
2 & (6)\ -Lxy & 3,5\ -\text{I} \\
2 & (7)\ (\forall y)-Lxy & 6\forall\text{I} \\
2 & (8)\ (\exists x)(\forall y)-Lxy & 7\ \exists\text{I} \\
1,2 & (9)\ (\exists x)(\forall y)-Lxy \wedge -(\exists x)(\forall y)-Lxy & 8,1\ \wedge\text{I} \\
1 & (10)\ --(\exists y)Lxy & 2,9\ -\text{I} \\
1 & (11)\ (\exists y)Lxy & 10\ --\text{E} \\
1 & (12)\ (\forall x)(\exists y)Lxy & 11\ \forall\text{I} \\
\end{array}
$$

Notice that in your $\forall$I move from (6) to (7), '$y$' does *not* appear free in any assumption upon which (6) rests, i.e., in (2). To be sure, '$x$' appears free in (2), but that's irrelevant: in the move from (6) to (7) you're performing $\forall$I with respect to '$y$' and *not* with respect to '$x$'.

One last derivation before you spread your quantificational wings and fly on your own.

S191:      $(\exists x)(\forall z)(\exists y)Bzxy \vdash (\forall y)-(\forall z)-(\exists x)Byzx$

First I'm going to take you on the Tour to Nowhere. You're going to do *exactly* what seems sensible; you're going to violate *none* of the rules; and you're going to end up as far from your goal at the end as you were at the beginning. The purpose of taking you on this Tour to Nowhere is to teach you how to avoid *ever* signing up for such a tour again.

There are various ways of proceeding. Suppose that you focused on (1) and introduced its corresponding ∃E assumption in (2), and then performed ∀E on (2) to generate (3), and then introduced (3)'s corresponding ∃E assumption in (4).

$$1 \ (1) \ (\exists x)(\forall z)(\exists y)Bzxy \qquad A$$
$$2 \ (2) \ (\forall z)(\exists y)Bzxy \qquad A$$
$$2 \ (3) \ (\exists y)Bzxy \qquad 2 \ \forall E$$
$$4 \ (4) \ Bzxy \qquad A$$

.

.

$$1 \ (n) \ (\forall y)-(\forall z)-(\exists x)Byzx \qquad ?$$

The Top-Down Approach has taken you as far as it can take you, and you begin the Bottom-Up Approach. Because your conclusion is a universally quantified *wff*, a promising candidate for your second-to-last *wff* will be a springboard *wff*, i.e., one on which you will perform ∀I to generate your conclusion, i.e., '−(∀z)−(∃x)Byzx'. Because your second-to-last *wff* is a negation, and because the only rule that *uniformly* generates a negation is −I, you introduce (∀z)−(∃x)Byzx as a *Reductio* assumption in line (5). You then perform ∀E on (5) to generate '−(∃x)Byzx' in (6). You sense that you're on the verge of your contradiction, and so you perform ∃I on (4) to generate in (7) what you hope will be the opposite of (6).

$$1 \ (1) \ (\exists x)(\forall z)(\exists y)Bzxy \qquad A$$
$$2 \ (2) \ (\forall z)(\exists y)Bzxy \qquad A$$
$$2 \ (3) \ (\exists y)Bzxy \qquad 2 \ \forall E$$
$$4 \ (4) \ Bzxy \qquad A$$
$$5 \ (5) \ (\forall z)-(\exists x)Byzx \qquad A$$
$$5 \ (6) \ -(\exists x)Byzx \qquad 5 \ \forall E$$
$$4 \ (7) \ (\exists x)Bzxx \qquad 4 \ \exists I$$

.

.

$$1 \ (n-1) \ -(\forall z)-(\exists x)Byzx \qquad 5,n-2 \ -I$$
$$1 \ (n) \ (\forall y)-(\forall z)-(\exists x)Byzx \qquad n-1 \ \forall I$$

Now of course (6) is *not* the negation of (7). This should be clear *syntactically* when you look at the two quite different strings of variables. And it should be clear *semantically*. There is no interpretation that makes a *wff* and its negation both *true*, and there is no interpretation that makes a *wff* and its negation both *false*. There is at least one interpretation, however, that *does* make both (6) and (7) false. Interpret 'B*xyz*' to mean '*x* is between *y* and *z*', and let the domain be the natural numbers: 0, 1, 2, 3, etc. Accordingly, (6) says that there is no natural number *x* such that *y* is between *z* and it. The truth or falsehood of (6) depends on which natural numbers you substitute for *y* and *z*. If *y* is 1 and *z* is 0, then (6) is false: there *does* exist at least one natural number *x*, e.g., 2, such that 1 is between 0 and 2. (7), however, is false *regardless* of which natural numbers you substitute for *y* and *z*. It is simply false that there is at least one natural number *x* such that *z* is between *x* and *x*.

So what do you know now? You know that (6) and (7) can both be false—and you know therefore, in case you had thought otherwise, that (7) isn't the negation of (6).

So what do you do now? You pause, of course. (What else *can* you do?) You pause and you take the lay of the land and you draw the only possible conclusion that you can draw: *you're stuck*. You're *close* to a contradiction but you're not close enough.

You could try to reshuffle the deck; i.e., you could try proceeding in a different order. For example, you could introduce your *Reductio* assumption at the very outset. Trust me: Reshuffling the deck in this instance just won't work.

So what else *can* you do? De-quantifying *blindly* can be a futile exercise, as it is here. But you don't have to de-quantify *blindly*. When you de-quantify, *you don't have to stick with the same variables*. You're free, subject to the restrictions of the four quantification rules, to *vary the variables*. You need to think strategically vis-à-vis both the *particular* variables that you'll be introducing and the *order* of these variables.

In S191, you want to generate an existentially quantified *wff* with three variables, along with the negation of that *wff*—with the *exact same* variables in the *exact same* order. If you limit yourself to '*x*', '*y*', and '*z*', you won't be able to generate two such *wffs* in this case. Hence the necessity for introducing '*u*', '*v*', and '*w*'.

$$1 \ (1) \ (\exists x)(\forall z)(\exists y)Bzxy \qquad\qquad\qquad A$$
$$2 \ (2) \ (\forall z)(\exists y)Bzuy \qquad\qquad\qquad\qquad A$$
$$2 \ (3) \ (\exists y)Bvuy \qquad\qquad\qquad\qquad\quad 2 \ \forall E$$
$$4 \ (4) \ Bvuw \qquad\qquad\qquad\qquad\qquad\quad A$$
$$5 \ (5) \ (\forall z)-(\exists x)Bvzx \qquad\qquad\qquad A$$
$$5 \ (6) \ -(\exists x)Bvux \qquad\qquad\qquad\quad 5 \ \forall E$$
$$4 \ (7) \ (\exists x)Bvux \qquad\qquad\qquad\qquad 4 \ \exists I$$
$$4,5 \ (8) \ (\exists x)Bvux \land -(\exists x)Bvux \qquad 7,6 \ \land I$$
$$4 \ (9) \ -(\forall z)-(\exists x)Bvzx \qquad\qquad 5,8 \ -I$$
$$(10) \ Bvuw \rightarrow -(\forall z)-(\exists x)Bvzx \qquad 4,9 \ \rightarrow I$$
$$2 \ (11) \ -(\forall z)-(\exists x)Bvzx \qquad\qquad 3,10 \ \exists E$$
$$(12) \ (\forall z)(\exists y)Bzuy \rightarrow -(\forall z)-(\exists x)Bvzx \qquad 2,11 \ \rightarrow I$$
$$1 \ (13) \ -(\forall z)-(\exists x)Bvzx \qquad\qquad 1,12 \ \exists E$$
$$1 \ (14) \ (\forall y)-(\forall z)-(\exists x)Byzx \qquad 13 \ \forall I$$

There are *scads* of points here worthy of your attention. You begin this derivation by utilizing the Top-Down Approach. In lines (2), (3), and (4) you introduce '$u$', '$v$', and '$w$', respectively—three brand-new variables that appear neither in the premise nor in the conclusion. Lines (2) and (4) are $\exists E$ assumptions: obviously, neither '$u$' in (2) nor '$w$' in (4) appears free in any previous assumption.

With line (4), you've squeezed as much juice out of your line-(1) orange as you can. Time for the Bottom–Up Approach. Your conclusion is '$(\forall y)-(\forall z)-(\exists x)Byzx$', a universally quantified *wff*. A promising second-to-last line, therefore, will consist of a springboard *wff*, i.e., a *wff* from which you'll generate your conclusion by $\forall I$. Your conclusion is '$(\forall v)Pv$'. Your second-to-last *wff* will be '$Pt$'.

Crucial question: Which variable will serve as the free variable '$t$' in your second-to-last *wff*?

Answer: '$v$'. Why '$v$'? A hunch. Nothing more than a hunch. You've worked your way down from (1) to (4). The first variable in the string of variables to the right of '$B$' in (4) is '$v$'. Recent experience tells you that you want your variables to line up in those *wffs* destined to spawn the *wffs* that will serve as contradictories of one another. Out of deference, then, to the presence of '$v$' as the first variable in the string of variables to the right of '$B$' in (4), you decide on '$v$' as the first variable in the string of variables to the right of '$B$' in your second-to-last *wff*. Hence '$-(\forall z)-(\exists x)Bvzx$'.

Your second-to-last *wff* being a negation, your only sensible choice now is to introduce a *Reductio* assumption. (5), i.e., '$(\forall z)-(\exists x)Bvzx$', is the *Reductio* assumption that's the opposite of your second-to-last *wff*. You suspect that your contradiction eventually will arise from the ashes of (4), i.e., '$Bvuw$', and (5), i.e., '$(\forall z)-(\exists x)Bvzx$'. You now have two visions.

Your first vision is of *lopping* the '$(\forall z)$' quantifier off of (5), i.e., '$(\forall z)-(\exists x)Bvzx$', and replacing '$z$' with '$u$'. The result of your first vision is '$-(\exists x)Bvux$': your line-(6) *wff*.

Question: Why replace '$z$' with '$u$'?

Answer: You're trying to get all the variables to the right of '$B$' in '$Bvzx$' in your line-(5) *wff* to line up with all the variables to the right of '$B$' in '$Bvuw$' in your line-(4) *wff*. So you let '$u$' occupy the second slot in the string of variables in (6) *precisely because* '$u$' occupies the second slot in the string of variables in (4).

Your second vision is of *adding* an '$(\exists x)$' quantifier onto (4), i.e., '$Bvuw$', with the two goals of binding the third variable in the string of variables to the right of '$B$', and of replacing '$w$' with '$x$'. The result of your second vision is '$(\exists x)Bvux$': your line-(7) *wff*.

Question: Why replace '$w$' with '$x$'?

Answer: You're trying to get all the variables to the right of '$B$' in '$Bvuw$' in your line-(4) *wff* to line up with all the variables to the right of '$B$' in '$Bvux$' in your line-(6) *wff*. So you let '$x$' occupy the third slot in the string of variables in (7) *precisely because* '$x$' occupies the third slot in the string of variables in (6).

And the result of the two visions combined? The *summum bonum*: the creation of your line-(8) contradiction: '$(\exists x)Bvux \wedge -(\exists x)Bvux$'.

In other words, you looked at (5), '$(\forall z)-(\exists x)Bvzx$', and you saw (6), '$-(\exists x)Bvux$'. Then you looked at (4), '$Bvuw$', and you saw (7), '$(\exists x)Bvux$'. Magic? No. Trial and error. Intuitions sharpened by practice and by perseverance. And by more practice and by more perseverance.

If you have followed the reasoning thus far, the remainder of the derivation should strike you as quite straightforward.

Note that it would be *impermissible* to perform $\forall$I on (9), '$-(\forall z)-(\exists x)Bvzx$', to generate your *ultimate* target, i.e., your conclusion, '$(\forall y)-(\forall z)-(\exists x)Byzx$'. (9) is an *illegitimate* springboard *wff* to perform $\forall$I vis-à-vis '$v$', given that '$v$' appears *free* in the line-(4) *assumption* upon which (9) rests.

In line (10), you discharge your line-(4) ∃E assumption via →I. In line (11), you perform your first instance of ∃E. (11) is a perfectly suitable candidate for ∃E, even though '*v*' appears free *both* in it *and* in (4), your ∃E assumption. The point is that you didn't *introduce* '*v*' in (4). It was '*w*' that you introduced in (4). You introduced '*v*' in (3), and (3) isn't an *assumption*, much less an ∃E assumption.

In line (12) you discharge your line-(2) ∃E assumption via →I. In line (13), you perform your second instance of ∃E. '*v*' appears free in (13) but doesn't appear in (2); obviously, therefore, you didn't introduce '*v*' in (2). So, (13) is a perfectly suitable candidate for ∃E.

Note that you *could* have performed ∀I instead of →I at line (12): (11) would have been a perfectly suitable springboard *wff* vis-à-vis '*v*', given that '*v*' doesn't *appear*—and therefore doesn't appear *free*—in the line-(2) assumption upon which (11) rests. Obviously, if you had performed ∀I at line (12), you would have performed your second instance of →I at line (13), and your second instance of ∃E at line (14).

# Exercises

For each of the following sequents, derive its conclusion from its premises.

1. Variations on QS:

S192: $(\forall x)[(\forall y)Ly \rightarrow Mx] \vdash (\forall y)Ly \rightarrow (\forall x)Mx$
S193: $(\forall y)Ly \rightarrow (\forall x)Mx \vdash (\forall x)[(\forall y)Ly \rightarrow Mx]$
S194: $(\exists x)[(\exists y)Ly \rightarrow Mx] \vdash (\exists y)Ly \rightarrow (\exists x)Mx$
S195: $(\exists y)Ly \rightarrow (\exists x)Mx \vdash (\exists x)[(\exists y)Ly \rightarrow Mx]$
S196: $(\exists x)[Lx \rightarrow (\forall y)My] \vdash (\forall y)Ly \rightarrow (\forall x)Mx$
S197: $(\forall x)Ly \rightarrow (\forall y)My \vdash (\exists x)[Lx \rightarrow (\forall y)My]$

2. Variations on QN:

S198: $-(\forall x)Lx \vdash (\exists x)-Lx$
S199: $-(\exists x)Lx \vdash (\forall x)-Lx$
S200: $-(\forall x)-Lx \vdash (\exists x)Lx$
S201: $-(\exists x)-Lx \vdash (\forall x)Lx$

3. Variations on Variations on QN (do each twice: first without QN, and then with it):

S202:  $(\exists x)-(\forall y)Lxy \vdash -(\forall x)(\forall y)Lxy$
S203:  $(\forall x)-(\exists y)Lxy \vdash (\forall x)(\forall y)-Lxy$
S204:  $(\forall x)(\exists y)-Lxy \vdash (\forall x)-(\forall y)Lxy$
S205:  $(\forall x)-(\forall y)Lxy \vdash (\forall x)(\exists y)-Lxy$
S206:  $(\exists x)(\forall y)-Lxy \vdash -(\forall x)(\exists y)Lxy$
S207:  $(\forall x)(\exists y)-Lxy \vdash -(\exists x)(\forall y)Lxy$
S208:  $-(\exists x)(\forall y)Lxy \vdash (\forall x)(\exists y)-Lxy$
S209:  $-(\forall y)-Lxy \vdash (\exists y)Lxy$
S210:  $-(\forall x)(\exists y)Lxy \vdash (\exists x)(\forall y)-Lxy$  (Not for the faint of heart.)

4. Miscellaneous:

S211:  $(\exists x)(\forall y)Lxy \vdash (\forall y)(\exists x)Lxy$
(Does it strike you as counterintuitive that a *universally* quantified *wff* is derivable from an *existentially* quantified *wff*? Produce an interpretation that suggests that the argument is valid after all.)
S212:  $(\forall x)(\forall y)(\forall z)Rxyz \vdash (\forall z)(\forall y)(\forall x)Rxzy$
S213:  $(\exists x)(\exists y)(\exists z)Rxyz \vdash (\exists z)(\exists y)(\exists x)Rxzy$
S214:  $(\exists x)(\forall y)(\exists z)Rzxy \vdash (\forall y)(\exists z)(\exists x)Rzxy$
S215:  $(\exists x)(\forall y)(\exists z)Rxyz \vdash -(\forall x)(\exists y)(\forall z)-Rxyz$
S216:  $(\forall x)(\exists y)(\forall z)Rxyz \vdash -(\exists x)(\forall y)(\exists z)-Rxyz$

# 2. Identity Elimination (=E)

Suppose that Bobo is a spy, and suppose that because of the secretive nature of her work, some people know her as Bobo and others know her as Coco. Bobo, in other words, simply *is*, i.e., *is identical to,*

Coco. It follows (obviously) that Coco is a spy. Welcome to Identity Elimination:

S217:          $Sb, b = c \vdash Sc$

| | | |
|---|---|---|
| 1 (1) $Sb$ | | A |
| 2 (2) $b = c$ | | A |
| 1,2 (3) $Sc$ | | 1,2 =E |

Suppose that Ardbeg betrays Bobo in the course of her work, and suppose, once again, that Bobo is Coco. It follows (again, obviously) that Ardbeg betrays Coco.

S218:          $Bab, b = c \vdash Bac$

| | | |
|---|---|---|
| 1 (1) $Bab$ | | A |
| 2 (2) $b = c$ | | A |
| 1,2 (3) $Bac$ | | 1,2 =E |

Identity Elimination is the first of the two derivation rules involving the notion of identity, and it operates on exactly two *wffs*. First you have a *wff* that affirms that an individual $x$ either has a particular property or stands in a particular relationship with respect to one or more other individuals, $x$, $y$, or $z$, etc. Second, you have another *wff* that affirms that the individual $x$ is really one and the same as the individual $y$. It follows that *for our purposes* (but see Subsection C below) whatever is true of the first individual, $x$, is true of the second, $y$.

Thus, the first premise of S217 affirms that Bobo has the *being-a-spy* property; the second premise affirms that Bobo is the same individual as Coco; hence it follows that *Coco* has the *being-a-spy* property. And the first premise of S218 affirms that Ardbeg and Bobo stand in *the-former-betrays-the-latter* relation; the second premise affirms that Bobo is the same individual as Coco; hence it follows that Ardbeg and *Coco* stand in *the-former-betrays-the-latter* relation.

# A. When to Use =E

You should think =E thoughts under the following circumstances:

1.  A *wff* '$Pv$' appears in the derivation, such that either
    a.  '$P$' is a one–place/monadic predicate, or
    b.  '$P$' is a multiplace/polyadic predicate.
2.  A *wff* '$v = t$', ascribing the identity of $v$ to $t$, also appears in the derivation, such that
    a.  '$v$' is either a variable or a constant, and
    b.  '$t$' is either a variable or a constant.
3.  Your goal is to generate '$Pt$'.

# B. How to Use =E

To perform =E in order to generate '$Pt$', it's necessary to do the following:

1.  In a line below both '$Pv$' and '$v = t$', construct '$Pt$'. '$Pt$' is the *wff* that results from '$Pv$' by replacing, in '$Pv$', at least one free occurrence of '$v$', and no bound occurrence of '$v$', with '$t$'.
2.  Make sure that '$t$' is free for '$v$' in '$Pv$'.
3.  Off to the right of '$Pt$', cite the line numbers of '$Pv$' and '$v = t$', followed by '=E'.
4.  Off to the far left of '$Pt$', cite the number of each assumption on which the two *wffs* cited to the right of '$Pt$', i.e., '$Pv$' and '$v = t$', rest.

Three words of elaboration: two words on Clause (1), and one word on Clause (2). A first word on Clause 1: In many formal systems of logic, Clause 1 (or its equivalent) would be formulated somewhat differently: "In a line below both '$Pv$' and *either* '$v = t$' *or* '$t = v$', construct '$Pt$'." This formulation of Clause 1 allows for the derivation of '$Pt$' from '$Pv$' and *either* '$v = t$' *or* '$t = v$'. However, in keeping with the minimalism— the *reasonable* minimalism—that characterizes *this* system of logic, the latter sort of move is impermissible. If you wish to derive '$Pt$' from '$Pv$' and '$t = v$', first you will have to engage in some fancy footwork. (See S224 below.)

A second word on Clause 1: It's unnecessary to replace *each* occurrence of '$v$', with '$t$'. Consider the following sequent:

S219:       $Sb \wedge Bab, b = c \vdash Sc \wedge Bab$

     1 (1) $Sb \wedge Bab$                    A
     2 (2) $b = c$                          A
     1,2 (3) $Sc \wedge Bab$                 1,2 =E

Assume that (1) Bobo is a spy and Ardbeg betrays Bobo. Assume too that (2) Bobo is Coco. It clearly follows that (3) Coco is a spy and Ardbeg betrays Bobo. (Obviously, '$Sc \wedge Bac$' also follows: 'Coco is a spy and Ardbeg betrays Coco'.)

A word on Clause 2: You must make sure that '$t$' is free for '$v$' in '$Pv$' by making sure that '$t$' isn't captured by a '$(\forall t)$' or '$(\exists t)$' quantifier in '$Pv$'. Here's what you want to avoid:

S220:  1 (1) $(\exists x)Byx$                 A
      2 (2) $y = x$                      A
      1,2 (3) $(\exists x)Bxx$            1,2 =E     XXX

Assume that (1) an unnamed individual $y$ betrays someone. Assume that (2) that same unnamed individual $y$ is identical to an unnamed individual $x$. It follows, of course, that $x$ betrays someone. It hardly follows that (3) someone betrays himself (or herself)—whatever *that* might mean. The problem here is that '$x$' *isn't* free for '$y$' in (1), '$(\exists x)Byx$', and so '$x$' becomes captured by the '$(\exists x)$' quantifier in (3).

Suppose that your goal is to generate from (1) and (2) the conclusion that $x$ betrays someone. You have no choice but to take a rather indirect route—or, if you prefer, either of *two* indirect routes:

S221:       $(\exists x)Byx, y = x \vdash (\exists z)Bxz$

     1 (1) $(\exists x)Byx$                   A
     2 (2) $y = x$                         A
     3 (3) $Byz$                           A
     3 (4) $(\exists z)Byz$                 3 $\exists$I
       (5) $Byz \rightarrow (\exists z)Byz$     3,4 $\rightarrow$I

$$1 \ (6) \ (\exists z) B y z \qquad\qquad 1,5 \ \exists E$$
$$1,2 \ (7) \ (\exists z) B x z \qquad\qquad 6,2 \ =\!E$$

S222:        $(\exists x) B y x, \ y = x \ \vdash \ (\exists z) B x z$

$$1 \ (1) \ (\exists x) B y x \qquad\qquad A$$
$$2 \ (2) \ y = x \qquad\qquad A$$
$$3 \ (3) \ B y z \qquad\qquad A$$
$$2,3 \ (4) \ B x z \qquad\qquad 3,2 \ =\!E$$
$$2,3 \ (5) \ (\exists z) B x z \qquad\qquad 4 \ \exists I$$
$$2 \ (6) \ B y z \to (\exists z) B x z \qquad\qquad 3,5 \to I$$
$$1,2 \ (7) \ (\exists z) B x z \qquad\qquad 1,6 \ \exists E$$

## C. When Not to Use =E

Consider the following pickles.

First pickle: Suppose that Bobo has the property of being believed by Ardbeg to be a spy. Suppose too that Bobo is Coco.

Question: Does it follow that Coco has the *same* property: the property of being believed by Ardbeg to be a spy?

Second pickle: Suppose that it's *Ardbeg* who has a particular property. Suppose that Ardbeg has the property of believing that Bobo is a spy. Suppose too that Bobo is Coco.

Question: Does it follow that Ardbeg has the property of believing that Coco is a spy? Or, for the sake of simplicity: Does it follow that Ardbeg believes that Coco is a spy?

Answer to both questions: It's not at all clear what follows—especially if Ardbeg has *no idea* that Bobo is Coco.

Third pickle: Bobo is *pleased* that Ardbeg *believes* that Coco is a spy. Coco is Bobo.

Question: Does it follow that Bobo is *pleased* that Ardbeg *believes* that she, Bobo, is a spy?

Answer: Once again, it's not at all clear that this follows. Suppose that Bobo *desperately* wants Ardbeg to believe first, that she and Coco are two *distinct* people, and second, that *Coco* is a spy but that *she, Bobo,* isn't.

Fourth pickle: Suppose that Ardbeg *hopes* that Bobo isn't Coco. (He's heard rumors to the effect that they are one and the same individual, but so far he has managed to dismiss the rumors.) In fact Bobo *is* Coco.

Question: Does it follow that Ardbeg *hopes* that Coco isn't Coco?

Answer: Obvious.

All this is a bit puzzling, yes? If Bobo is Coco then whatever is true of Bobo *must* be true of Coco, yes? And if so, then each of the above four conclusions *must* follow, yes? But (once again) it's not at all clear that *any* of them follows. What *is* clear is that there's a pickle here—and if pickles could be *deep* then this would be a very *deep* pickle indeed.

Two options present themselves. First option: we reject =E as one of our derivation rules, on the grounds that it's not *truth-preserving*. Second option: we restrict the contexts in which =E is applicable. The problem with the first option is that, *in general*, =E is both too useful and too intuitively appealing to abandon. So we accept the second option. We distinguish two kinds of contexts: *extensional* and *intensional*.

Classical logic focuses exclusively on *extensional* contexts. If, in an *extensional* context, you pop a proper name out of one sentence and replace the proper name with another proper name of the same individual, the second sentence will have the same truth-value as the first. If the first is true, the second will be true; and if the first is false, the second will be false. (Suppose that Bobo is Coco. First sentence: 'Bobo is a spy.' Second sentence: 'Coco is a spy.' Either both sentences are true or both are false.)

By contrast, if, in an *intensional* context, you pop a proper name out of a sentence and replace the proper name with another proper name of the same individual, it's not at all clear that the two sentences have the same truth-value. (Suppose that Bobo is Coco. First sentence: 'Bobo is believed by Ardbeg to be a spy.' Second sentence: 'Coco is believed by Ardbeg to be a spy.')

Don't expect a definition *here* of 'extensional' and 'intensional'. A *hint* of a definition, yes, but a full-blown definition, no. The *extension* of a term is the *actual thing* that the term *denotes/designates/refers to*, otherwise known as the term's *denotation/referent*. The *intension* of a term is the *meaning* of the term. (You may well grasp the *meaning* of the expression 'the scoundrel who betrays Bobo' without knowing the *referent* of the expression, i.e., without knowing to whom the expression refers.) Much in this discussion turns on the answer to the question whether a proper name is both *intensional* and *extensional*, or whether it's merely *extensional*.

In other words, does the proper name 'Bobo' have both a *meaning* (e.g., 'Ardbeg's pal' or 'the first spy to trek in North Zedmenistan') and a *referent* (i.e., the actual individual *Bobo*)? Or does the proper name 'Bobo' have *only* a *referent*? And what about fictional objects? Obviously, the proper name 'Santa Claus'—if indeed it's a genuine proper name—lacks a *referent*. So does it have a *meaning* and only a *meaning* (i.e., 'the good-natured, roly-poly fellow in the red suit, etc.')? In recent (or at least *fairly* recent) times, it was Frege who started this ball rolling. The ball hasn't stopped rolling.

In Classical Logic, i.e., the logic that you are currently learning, the focus is on *extensional* contexts—and therefore on the *extensions* of proper names and *not* their *intensions*. Various sorts of notions create *intensional* contexts. Two such notions are *epistemic* notions (e.g., '*x* believes that . . .', '*x* knows that . . .', or '*x* wonders whether . . .') and *modal* notions ('It is necessarily the case that . . .' or 'It is possibly the case that . . .').

*All* of the contexts on which we focus in this logic book are of the *extensional* sort. Hence the obvious validity of the following argument:

    1 (1) *Kb*           A
    2 (2) *b* = *c*      A
    1,2 (3) *Kc*      1,2 =E

To say that the argument is valid is to say, of course, that there's no interpretation that makes the premises true and the conclusion false. Now you know *exactly* what's going to happen if you interpret '*Kx*' to mean '*x* is known by Ardbeg to be a spy'. Suppose that the first premise is true. Suppose that the second premise is true. At this point you should be *very* unsure what truth-value to assign to the conclusion. Moral of the story: the validity of this argument (as of each of the arguments that appears in this book) is a function of our interpreting their constituent sentences exclusively in *extensional* contexts.

To dive deeply into this topic, sign up for either a course in the philosophy of language or a course in modal logic (or both).

# 3. Identity Introduction (=I)

Consider the following statements: 'Ardbeg is Ardbeg', 'Bobo is Bobo', and 'Coco is Coco'. Could any of these *possibly* be false? What on Earth would it mean to deny that Ardbeg is Ardbeg?

Question: If '$a = a$', '$b = b$', and '$c = c$' are obvious truths—and they are—what *kind* of truth are they? They aren't $L_1$ *tautologies* like 'P ∨ —P'. They are *atomics*, after all—and no atomic comes out true for *every* interpretation. (Woe unto you if you treat '=' as a connective! It's nothing more than a two-place predicate.) In other words, '$a = a$', '$b = b$', and '$c = c$' aren't the sort of truth on which we focused in Chapter 1.

Nor are they $L_2$ substitution-instances of tautologies. Nor are they *quantificationally valid wffs*, like '$(\forall x)(Lx \rightarrow Lx)$'. Such *wffs*, after all, require *quantifiers*—and while *some* statements of identity involve quantifiers, e.g., '$(\forall x)x = x$', not *all* of them do, e.g., '$a = a$'. In other words, '$a = a$', '$b = b$', and '$c = c$' aren't the sort of truth on which we focused in Chapters 5 and 6.

Furthermore, if '$a = a$', '$b = b$', and '$c = c$' were logical truths of *any* sort, then they'd be true *regardless* of how you interpreted '$x = y$' ('$Ixy$'). Suppose, however, that you interpreted '$x = y$' ('$Ixy$') to mean '$x$ is *taller* than $y$' or '$x$ is *older* than $y$' or '$x$ isn't (i.e., is *distinct from*) $y$'. For any of these interpretations, obviously, '$a = a$' ('$Iaa$'), '$b = b$', and '$c = c$' would be false.

Even on their standard interpretation, however, '$a = a$', '$b = b$', and '$c = c$' are odd truths: their truth is *not* contingent on the way that the world is. Regardless of what the world is like, and regardless of what's true and what's not true of Ardbeg, Bobo, and Coco, on the standard interpretation of the identity symbol, '$a = a$', '$b = b$', and '$c = c$'—'Ardbeg is Ardbeg', 'Bobo is Bobo', and 'Coco is Coco'—are *truths*, period. So they obviously aren't *empirical* truths.

The question remains: What kind of truth are they?

Answer: Consider them *semantic* truths: they're true solely in virtue of the *interpretation* that you assign to '='. Interpret '$x = y$' to mean '$x$ is identical to $y$'—and '$a = a$', '$b = b$', and '$c = c$' are obvious *truths* that, once again, are *not* contingent on the way that the world is. Interpret

'$x = y$' to mean '$x$ is taller than $y$'—and '$a = a$', '$b = b$', and '$c = c$' are obvious *falsehoods* that are *not* contingent on the way that the world is. Interpret '$x = y$' to mean '$x$ thinks highly of $y$'—and '$a = a$', '$b = b$', and '$c = c$' are neither obvious truths nor obvious falsehoods; rather, they *are* contingent for their truth-value on the way that the world is.

In logic we stick with the standard interpretation of the identity symbol: we interpret '$x = y$' to mean '$x$ is identical to $y$'. So understood, '$a = a$' is (once again) a *truth*—a *semantic* truth.

Identity Introduction is a rule that allows you to introduce an identity statement at *any* point in a derivation. If you wish to introduce '$a = a$'—if it will help you arrive at your target—*just introduce it.* And what do you write off to the right; i.e., what *wffs* do you cite by way of justification? (Think for exactly three seconds before answering.) You cite *no* line numbers, *no wffs*! As a semantic *truth*, '$a = a$' needs no justification; it follows from no previous *wffs*. Off to the right you write '=I', period. Off to the far left you write nothing.

## A. When to Use =I

It's appropriate to perform =I in a derivation *iff* there's a *wff* '$v = v$' that you would like to generate, where '$v$' designates any variable or constant.

## B. How to Use =I

To perform =I, it's necessary to do the following.

1. Enter '$v = v$' on any line of a derivation.
2. Off to the right of '$v = v$', cite '=I'.
3. Off to the far left of '$v = v$', leave a *void*; i.e., don't cite the line numbers of *any* assumptions.

## C. Examples

S223:          $a = a \rightarrow (b = b \rightarrow Sc) \vdash Sc$

     1 (1) $a = a \rightarrow (b = b \rightarrow Sc)$          A
        (2) $a = a$          =I
     1 (3) $b = b \rightarrow Sc$          1,2 →E
        (4) $b = b$          =I
     1 (5) $Sc$          3,4 →E

S224:          $a = b \vdash b = a$

     1 (1) $a = b$          A
        (2) $a = a$          =I
     1 (3) $b = a$          2,1 =E

On one level you may find the move to (3) perfectly straightforward. On another level, however, you may find it perfectly confusing. Look at the *wffs* on lines (1) and (2). You are about to perform =E on them. To do so, you first need to know which of them is '$Pv$' and which is '$v = t$'. Because *each* is an identity statement, it may not be immediately clear which is which. You know *this* much, however: you know that in order to construct '$Pt$' from '$Pv$', you'll be extracting at least one free occurrence of '$v$' from '$Pv$', and you'll then be implanting '$t$' wherever you had extracted '$v$'.

Suppose that you treat '$a = b$' as '$Pv$'. Accordingly, you'll have to treat '$a = a$' as '$v = t$'—in which case '$v$' will be '$a$' and '$t$' will *also* be '$a$'! So when you extract '$a$', i.e., '$v$', from '$a = b$' and replace it with the rightmost '$a$', i.e., '$t$', from '$a = a$', '$a = b$' will be completely unchanged! So you don't want to treat '$a = b$' as '$Pv$' and '$a = a$' as '$v = t$'.

Think of it like this: You're trying to construct a new *wff* by extracting at least one constant (or variable) '$v$' from '$Pv$' and implanting in its place a *different* constant (or variable) '$t$'. In other words, '$Pv$' is the *wff* on which you will be performing the extraction and implantation procedures. So of course the extracted '$v$' *must* be different from the implanted '$t$'. So of course, in S224 '$v = t$' must be '$a = b$'—in which case '$Pv$' must be '$a = a$'. '$v$', of course, must be whichever constant (or variable) is to the left of the identity sign in '$v = t$'. Alternatively, '*v*' must be whichever constant (or variable) is *common* to both '**P*v***' and '*v* = *t*'. Now suppose that you extract the *leftmost* '*a*' from '*a* = *a*'. (Remember: Clause 1 of =E authorizes you to replace in '**P*v***' at least *one*, and not necessarily *each*, free occurrence of '*v*' with '*t*'.) Next, suppose that you implant '*b*' in the place vacated by the leftmost '*a*'. (You're authorized to do so by the first premise, which proclaims the *identity* of *a* with *b*.) So what do you end up with? '*b* = *a*'. Done.

Alternatively, suppose that you have *two* identity statements, as you have here. Suppose that you *still* find this confusing. Probably the easiest way to see which *wff* is '**P*v***' and which is '*v* = *t*' is by expressing the one that asserts the identity of an individual to itself as '*Iaa*' or '*Ibb*' or '*Ixx*'. Here's how S224 would look in this notation:

$$
\begin{array}{lll}
1 \ (1) \ a = b & \qquad & A \\
\ \ \ (2) \ Iaa & & =I \\
1 \ (3) \ Iba & & 2,1 \ =E
\end{array}
$$

In other words, if (1) *a* is identical to *b*, and if (2) *a* stands in the is–identical-to relation to itself, i.e., to *a*, then, obviously, (3) *b* stands in the *is-identical-to* relation to *a*.

Next, suppose the following: all spies are traitors; Bobo is a spy; Coco is Bobo. Now prove that Coco is a traitor. Two versions follow.

S225:          $(\forall x)(Sx \rightarrow Tx)$, $Sb$, $c = b \vdash Tc$

$$
\begin{array}{lll}
1 \ (1) \ (\forall x)(Sx \rightarrow Tx) & \qquad & A \\
2 \ (2) \ Sb & & A \\
3 \ (3) \ c = b & & A \\
1 \ (4) \ Sb \rightarrow Tb & & 1 \ \forall E \\
1,2 \ (5) \ Tb & & 4,2 \rightarrow E \\
\ \ \ (6) \ c = c & & =I \\
3 \ (7) \ b = c & & 6,3 \ =E \\
1,2,3 \ (8) \ Tc & & 5,7 \ =E
\end{array}
$$

S226:      $(\forall x)(Sx \rightarrow Tx), Sb, c = b \vdash Tc$

     1 (1) $(\forall x)(Sx \rightarrow Tx)$          A
     2 (2) $Sb$                   A
     3 (3) $c = b$               A
     1 (4) $Sc \rightarrow Tc$          1 $\forall$E
        (5) $c = c$              =I
     3 (6) $b = c$             5,3 =E
    2,3 (7) $Sc$                 2,6 =E
   1,2,3 (8) $Tc$                  4,7 $\rightarrow$E

Now suppose the following: Bobo's a traitor; Coco isn't a traitor. Now prove that Bobo isn't Coco. A *Reductio* assumption will play the key role here.

S227:      $Tb, -Tc \vdash b \neq c$

     1 (1) $Tb$                 A
     2 (2) $-Tc$               A
     3 (3) $b = c$            A
    1,3 (4) $Tc$               1,3 =E
  1,2,3 (5) $Tc \wedge -Tc$       4,2 $\wedge$I
   1,2 (6) $b \neq c$           3,5 $-$I

One last example of a derivation involving the notion of identity. The derivation is obviously a bit long, but it requires only a little by way of commentary.

S228:      $(\exists x)(\exists y)Raxby, c = a \vee c = b \vdash (\exists w)(\exists z)Rcwbz \vee$
                 $(\exists z)(\exists w)Razcw$

The assumptions at lines (3) and (4) are $\exists$E assumptions corresponding to the existentially quantified *wffs* at lines (1) and (3), respectively. The assumptions at lines (5) and (13) are $\vee$E assumptions corresponding to the disjunction at line (2). The rest should be self-explanatory.

1 (1) $(\exists x)(\exists y)Raxby$           A

2 (2) $c = a \lor c = b$           A

3 (3) $(\exists y)Raxby$           A

4 (4) $Raxby$           A

5 (5) $c = a$           A

    (6) $c = c$           =I

5 (7) $a = c$           6,5 =E

4,5 (8) $Rcxby$           4,7 =E

4,5 (9) $(\exists z)Rcxbz$           8 $\exists$I

4,5 (10) $(\exists w)(\exists z)\, Rcwbz$           9 $\exists$I

4,5 (11) $(\exists w)(\exists z)Rcwbz \lor (\exists z)(\exists w)Razcw$           10 $\lor$I

4 (12) $c = a \rightarrow [(\exists w)(\exists z)Rcwbz \lor (\exists z)(\exists w)Razcw]$     5,11 $\rightarrow$I

13 (13) $c = b$           A

    (14) $c = c$           =I

13 (15) $b = c$           14,13 =E

4,13 (16) $Raxcy$           4,15 =E

4,13 (17) $(\exists w)Raxcw$           16 $\exists$I

4,13 (18) $(\exists z)(\exists w)Razcw$           17 $\exists$I

4,13 (19) $(\exists w)(\exists z)Rcwbz \lor (\exists z)(\exists w)Razcw$           18 $\lor$I

4 (20) $c = b \rightarrow [(\exists w)(\exists z)Rcwbz \lor (\exists z)(\exists w)Razcw]$     13,19 $\rightarrow$I

2,4 (21) $(\exists w)(\exists z)Rcwbz \lor (\exists z)(\exists w)Razcw$           2,12,20 $\lor$E

2 (22) $Raxby \rightarrow [(\exists w)(\exists z)Rcwbz \lor (\exists z)(\exists w)Razcw]$     4,21 $\rightarrow$I

2,3 (23) $(\exists w)(\exists z)Rcwbz \lor (\exists z)(\exists w)Razcw$           3,22 $\exists$E

2 (24) $(\exists y)Raxby \rightarrow [(\exists w)(\exists z)Rcwbz \lor (\exists z)(\exists w)$
     $Razcw]$           3,23 $\rightarrow$I

1,2 (25) $(\exists w)(\exists z)Rcwbz \lor (\exists z)(\exists w)Razcw$           1,24 $\exists$E

# Exercises

For each of the following sequents, derive its conclusion from its premises.

S229:  $a = b, b = c \vdash a = c$

S230:  $a = b, c = b \vdash c = a$

S231:  $a = b, b \neq c \vdash a \neq c$

S232:  $a = b, c \neq b \vdash c \neq a$

S234:  $(\exists x)(Px \wedge Lxa), a = b \vee a = c \vdash (\exists x)[Px \wedge (Lxb \vee Lxc)]$

S235:  $Ta \wedge -Tb \vdash a \neq b$

S236:  $(\forall x)(Tx \rightarrow x = a), a \neq b \vdash -Tb$
(The domain is restricted to people. In English: 'If anyone is a traitor, it's Ardbeg. Ardbeg isn't Bobo. So Bobo isn't a traitor.' Note that this does *not* entail that Ardbeg is a traitor.)

S237:  $Ta, -(\exists x)(Tx \wedge x \neq a), (\exists x)(\forall y)(Ty \leftrightarrow Hxy), d \neq a \vdash (\exists z)(Hza \wedge -Hzd)$
(The domain is restricted to people. In English: 'Ardbeg's a traitor. There are no traitors other than Ardbeg. There's at least one person who hangs all traitors and only traitors. Dagbar isn't Ardbeg. So there's at least one person who hangs Ardbeg but doesn't hang Dagbar.')

S238:  $(\forall x)Lax \vee (\forall y)-Lay, d = a \vdash (\exists z)-Ldz \rightarrow -(\exists u)Ldu$
(The domain is restricted to people. In English: 'Either Ardbeg loves everyone or he loves no one. Dagbar is Ardbeg. So if there's at least one person whom Dagbar doesn't love, then Dagbar loves no one.')

S239:  $(\exists x)[Tx \wedge (\forall y)(Ty \rightarrow y = x)], Tb, b \neq c \vdash -Tc$
(The domain is unrestricted. In English: 'There's exactly one traitor. Bobo's a traitor. Bobo isn't Coco. So Coco isn't a traitor.')

S240:  $(\exists x)Baxb, e = a \vee c = b \vdash (\exists w)Bewb \vee (\exists y)Bayc$
(The domain is restricted to people. In English: 'Someone is marching between Ardbeg and Bobo. Either Egvalt is Ardbeg or Coco is Bobo. So either someone is marching between Egvalt and Bobo or someone is marching between Ardbeg and Coco.')

S241:  $(\exists x)(\forall y)(Ty \rightarrow Hxy), Ta \wedge Tb, a = d \vee b = c \vdash (\exists x)(Hxd \vee Hxc)$
(The domain is restricted to people. In English: 'There exists at least one person who hangs every traitor. Ardbeg is a traitor and Bobo is a traitor. Either Ardbeg is Dagbar or Bobo is Coco. So there's at least one person who hangs either Dagbar or Coco.')

S242:   $(\exists x)(\forall y)\{(Px \wedge -Lxc) \wedge [(Py \wedge Lyd) \rightarrow Lyc]\}, d = a \vdash$
       $(\exists z)(Pz \wedge -Lza)$
       (The domain is unrestricted. In English: 'There's at least
       one person who doesn't love Coco, although anyone who
       loves Dagbar loves Coco. Dagbar is Ardbeg. So there's at
       least one person who doesn't love Ardbeg.')

S243:   $(\exists x)\{[Tx \wedge (\forall y)(Ty \rightarrow y = x)] \wedge x = a\}, b \neq a \vdash Ta \wedge -Tb$
       (The domain is unrestricted. In English: 'There exists
       exactly one traitor and it's Ardbeg. Bobo isn't Ardbeg. So
       Ardbeg's a traitor and Bobo isn't.')

S244:   $(\forall x)\{[Mx \wedge -(x = a \vee x = d)] \rightarrow Tx\}, Me \wedge -Te$
       $\vdash a = e \vee d = e$
       (The domain is unrestricted. In English: 'Every magi-
       cian other than Ardbeg and Dagbar is a traitor. Egvalt is
       a magician and Egvalt isn't a traitor. So either Ardbeg is
       Egvalt or Dagbar is Egvalt.')

# 4. Odds and Ends

In this final section, I shall say, where Predicate Logic/Quantification
Theory is concerned, a few words—but only a *very* few words—about
theorems and about the derivation rules Theorem Introduction and
Sequent Introduction. I shall then say a few words—but even *fewer*
words—about substitution-instances and the derivation rules TISI and
SISI. The reason for the fewness of my words is *not* the unimportance
of the topic. Quite the contrary: the topic is a *most* important one. It
is also, where Predicate Logic/Quantification Theory is concerned,
a very *complicated* topic. As such, it lies a bit beyond the scope of this
book.

## A. Theorems

Proving that a given *wff* is a theorem in Predicate Logic/Quantification
Theory is no different, in principle, from proving that a given *wff* is a
theorem in Propositional Logic. Consider the following proofs, most of
which need no commentary.

T33: $\vdash x = x$

(1) $x = x$  =I

Notice that in T33, (1) is a provable *wff* that rests on *no* assumptions, and therefore qualifies as a theorem.

T34: $\vdash (\forall x)x = x$

(1) $x = x$  =I
(2) $(\forall x)x = x$  1 $\forall$I

Notice that in T34, (1) is *not* an assumption. If it *were*, you wouldn't be able to perform $\forall$I on it to generate (2).

T35: $\vdash (\forall x)(Lx \rightarrow Lx)$

1 (1) $Lx$  A
(2) $Lx \rightarrow Lx$  1,1 →I
(3) $(\forall x)(Lx \rightarrow Lx)$  2 $\forall$I

T36: $\vdash (\forall x)(\forall y)Lxy \rightarrow (\forall z)Lzz$

1 (1) $(\forall x)(\forall y)Lxy$  A
1 (2) $(\forall y)Lxy$  1 $\forall$E
1 (3) $Lxx$  2 $\forall$E
1 (4) $(\forall z)Lzz$  3 $\forall$I
(5) $(\forall x)(\forall y)Lxy \rightarrow (\forall z)Lzz$  1,4 →I

T37: $\vdash (\exists x)(\forall y)(Lx \rightarrow My) \rightarrow [(\forall x)Lx \rightarrow (\forall y)My]$

1 (1) $(\exists x)(\forall y)(Lx \rightarrow My)$  A
2 (2) $(\forall x)Lx$  A
3 (3) $(\forall y)(Lx \rightarrow My)$  A
3 (4) $Lx \rightarrow My$  3 $\forall$E

$$2 \ (5) \ Lx \qquad\qquad\qquad\qquad\qquad\qquad\qquad\qquad\quad 2 \ \forall E$$
$$2,3 \ (6) \ My \qquad\qquad\qquad\qquad\qquad\qquad\qquad\qquad\quad 4,5 \to E$$
$$2,3 \ (7) \ (\forall y) My \qquad\qquad\qquad\qquad\qquad\qquad\qquad\quad 6 \ \forall I$$
$$2 \ (8) \ (\forall y)(Lx \to My) \to (\forall y) My \qquad\qquad\qquad 3,7 \to I$$
$$1,2 \ (9) \ (\forall y) My \qquad\qquad\qquad\qquad\qquad\qquad\qquad\quad 1,8 \ \exists E$$
$$1 \ (10) \ (\forall x) Lx \to (\forall y) My \qquad\qquad\qquad\qquad\quad 2,9 \to I$$
$$(11) \ (\exists x)(\forall y)(Lx \to My) \to [(\forall x) Lx \to (\forall y) My] \quad 1,10 \to I$$

## B. TISI and SISI: Drawn from Propositional Logic

In Predicate Logic/Quantification Theory, substitution-instances come in two flavors, one of which is immediately pleasing to the palate, and one of which is an acquired taste. Immediately pleasing to the palate are theorems and sequents in Predicate Logic/Quantification Theory that are (merely) substitution-instances of previously proved theorems and sequents in Propositional Logic. Acquired tastes are theorems and sequents in Predicate Logic/Quantification Theory that are substitution-instances of previously proved theorems and sequents in Predicate Logic/QuantificationTheory that are not themselves substitution-instances of previously proved theorems and sequents in Propositional Logic.

It should strike you that it's fairly straightforward both to spot and to construct a substitution-instance of a Propositional Logic theorem. '$(\forall x)(\exists y) Lxy \lor -(\forall x)(\exists y) Lxy$' and '$Lx \lor -Lx$' are obvious substitution-instances of the Law of the Excluded Middle, the former substitution-instance being a closed *wff* and the latter being an open *wff*. It's equally straightforward to spot or to construct a substitution-instance of a previously proved Propositional Logic sequent. '$-[(\forall x)(\forall y) Lxy \to (\forall z) Mz] \vdash (\forall x)(\forall y) Lxy \land -(\forall z) Mz$' and '$-[(\exists x) Lxy \lor (\exists x) Lxz] \vdash -(\exists x) Lxy \land -(\exists x) Lxz$' are obvious examples of substitution instances of Negation Implication and De Morgan, respectively, the former substitution-instance involving closed *wffs* and the latter open *wffs*.

Consider the two following derivations. The first involves a substitution-instance of a previously proved *theorem* from Propositional Logic:

S245:    $(\forall x)[Lx \rightarrow (Mx \wedge Tx)], (\forall x)[-Lx \rightarrow (Mx \wedge Tx)] \vdash$
         $(\forall x)Mx$

| 1 (1) $(\forall x)[Lx \rightarrow (Mx \wedge Tx)]$ | A |
|---|---|
| 2 (2) $(\forall x)[-Lx \rightarrow (Mx \wedge Tx)]$ | A |
| 1 (3) $Lx \rightarrow (Mx \wedge Tx)$ | 1$\forall$E |
| 2 (4) $-Lx \rightarrow (Mx \wedge Tx)$ | 2$\forall$E |
| (5) $Lx \vee -Lx$ | TISI EM |
| 6 (6) $Lx$ | A |
| 1,6 (7) $Mx \wedge Tx$ | 3,6 $\rightarrow$E |
| 1,6 (8) $Mx$ | 7$\wedge$E |
| 1 (9) $Lx \rightarrow Mx$ | 6,8 $\rightarrow$I |
| 10 (10) $-Lx$ | A |
| 2,10 (11) $Mx \wedge Tx$ | 4,10 $\rightarrow$E |
| 2,10 (12) $Mx$ | 11$\wedge$E |
| 2 (13) $-Lx \rightarrow Mx$ | 10,12 $\rightarrow$E |
| 1,2 (14) $Mx$ | 5,9,13 $\vee$E |
| 1,2 (15) $(\forall x)Mx$ | 14 $\forall$I |

Assume a domain restricted to people. So, if all logicians are both magicians and tyrants, and if all non-logicians are also both magicians and tyrants, then everyone is a magician.

Note the key role played by the Law of the Excluded Middle, the line-(5) theorem: it allows us here (and indeed everywhere) to use $\vee$E effortlessly.

The second derivation involves a substitution-instance of a previously proved *sequent* also from Propositional Logic:

S246:    $(\exists x)(-Lx \wedge Mx) \vdash (\exists y)(Ly \rightarrow Ny)$

| 1 (1) $(\exists x)(-Lx \wedge Mx)$ | A |
|---|---|
| 2 (2) $-Lx \wedge Mx$ | A |
| 2 (3) $-Lx$ | 2 $\wedge$E |
| 2 (4) $-Lx \vee Nx$ | 3 $\vee$I |
| 2 (5) $Lx \rightarrow Nx$ | 4 SISI MI |

$$2 \; (6) \; (\exists y)(Ly \rightarrow Ny) \hspace{3cm} 5 \; \exists I$$
$$(7) \; (-Lx \wedge Mx) \rightarrow (\exists y)(Ly \rightarrow Ny) \hspace{1cm} 2,6 \rightarrow I$$
$$1 \; (8) \; (\exists y)(Ly \rightarrow Ny) \hspace{3cm} 1,7 \; \exists E$$

Notice that in the move from (4) to (5) we drew upon a substitution-instance of Material Implication. We could have shaved a line off the derivation if we had drawn upon a substitution-instance of RH (Rabbits out of Hats) instead. Thereby, we would have made the move from (3), '$-Lx$', to (5), '$Lx \rightarrow Nx$', in a single step.

Moral of the story: it's not so difficult to spot or to construct theorems and sequents in Predicate Logic/Quantification Theory that are substitution-instances of previously proved theorems and sequents of Propositional Logic.

# C. TISI and SISI: Drawn from Predicate Logic/Quantification Theory

On the other hand, it can be quite difficult to spot or to construct theorems and sequents in Predicate Logic/Quantification Theory that are substitution-instances of previously proved theorems and sequents in Predicate Logic/Quantification Theory that are not themselves substitution-instances of previously proved theorems and sequents in Propositional Logic. In spotting or constructing such substitution-instances, you must see to it that the initial connectives and the initial quantifiers remain undisturbed. The connectives and the quantifiers, after all, are the logical constants, or operators, that constitute the logical scaffolding of all *wffs*—and therefore of all previously proved theorems and sequents. Predicates, on the other hand, whether one-place or multiplace, are extractable and implantable, as are variables. But the extraction/implantation process doesn't proceed willy-nilly. It comes hedged with restrictions—and there's the rub. Restrictions in logic, as you have no doubt learned by now, come with a price. The price, of course, is the complexity involved in the construction of such substitution-instances. For once in this book—*just for once*—you are spared having to grapple with complexity. Not everyone, of course, would consider this a blessing. If you're one of the ones who wouldn't, just remember: you're never terribly far from a rabbit-hole.

# Exercises

Prove each of the following theorems. Wherever possible, make use of TISI and SISI, drawing upon previously proved theorems and sequents, respectively, from Propositional Logic.

T38:  $\vdash Lx \rightarrow (\exists z)(Lx \lor Mz)$
T39:  $\vdash (\forall x)Lx \rightarrow (Lz \lor My)$
T40:  $\vdash [(a = b \lor a = c) \land La] \rightarrow (Lb \lor Lc)$
T41:  $\vdash -(\exists x)-(x = x)$
T42:  $\vdash (\forall x)(Lx \lor -Lx)$
T43:  $\vdash (\forall x)-(Lx \land -Lx)$
T44:  $\vdash (\exists x)Sx \lor (\forall x)-Sx$
T45:  $\vdash (-Lb \land -Lc) \rightarrow [(a = b \lor a = c) \rightarrow -La]$
T46:  $\vdash (\exists x)[Lxx \rightarrow (\forall y)Lyy]$
T47:  $\vdash (\forall y)(\exists z)[(\exists w)(\forall x)Lwx \rightarrow Lzy]$
T48:  $\vdash (\exists x)(-Lx \land Mx) \rightarrow (\exists y)(Ly \rightarrow Ny)$
T49:  $\vdash (\forall x)[Tx \rightarrow (Px \land x \neq b)] \rightarrow -Tb$
T50:  $\vdash (\exists x)\{x = a \land (\exists y)[y = b \land (\exists z)z = c]\}$
    (Translate into *colloquial* English and then prove.)

# 5. Appendix I: Undecidability

Propositional Logic, you will recall (from Appendix I of Chapter 4) is *deductively complete*: every valid argument that can be expressed in the formal language of the system is provable within the system.

Question: And what about Predicate Logic/Quantification Theory: is it too deductively complete?

Answer: It is. And the proofs that it is are quite exhilarating. Almost as exhilarating as trekking in North Zedmenistan. You'll master one or two of these proofs in a second logic course, after you master one or two of the proofs of the deductive completeness of Propositional Logic.

Question: Are there other questions that we should be asking about these formal systems—Propositional Logic and Predicate Logic/Quantification Theory?

Answer: Read on.

Predicate Logic/Quantification Theory, as you know, is an extension of, and thus includes, Propositional Logic. As you also know, the range of logical truths (logically valid *wffs*) in Predicate Logic/Quantification Theory includes, but is broader than, the range of logical truths in Propositional Logic. In Propositional Logic the range is restricted to tautologies. Predicate Logic/Quantification Theory includes not only tautologies (or substitution-instances of tautologies), e.g., '$(\forall x)$ $Lx \rightarrow (\forall x)Lx$', but also *wffs* that aren't tautologies. The following are reminders of examples of the latter:

1. '$(\forall x)(Px \rightarrow Tx) \rightarrow -(\exists x)(Px \wedge -Tx)$': 'If everyone is a traitor then there's not a single person who isn't a traitor.
2. '$(\forall x)(Px \rightarrow Tx) \rightarrow (\forall y)(Py \rightarrow Ty)$': 'If everyone is a traitor then everyone is a traitor.' (Note that while the sentence expressed in English is a tautology, the sentence expressed in logical notation isn't: *syntactically*, the conditional's antecedent differs from its consequent.)
3. '$(\forall x)(Tx \rightarrow Tx)$': 'All traitors are traitors.'
4. '$Lxy \rightarrow (\exists z)Lzy$': 'If $x$ loves $y$ then someone loves $y$.'
5. '$(\forall x)(\exists y)Lxy \rightarrow (\exists z)(\exists w)Lzw$': 'If everyone loves someone then someone loves someone.'

Now in Propositional Logic, the Truth-Table Method constitutes a purely *mechanical method*, a *decision procedure*, an *algorithm*, for determining, with respect to each *wff*, whether or not it's a logical truth, i.e., a tautology, and for determining, with respect to each argument, whether or not it's valid. It should strike you as obvious that one could program a computer to sort *wffs* into two piles—the tautological *vs.* the non-tautological—and to sort arguments into another two piles: the valid *vs.* the invalid.

And what about Predicate Logic/Quantification Theory? Obviously there must be a comparable method for sorting *wffs* and arguments into their respective piles: the *wffs* that are logical truths *vs.* the *wffs* that aren't, and the arguments that are valid *vs.* the arguments that aren't. *Obviously* there must be such a method, yes? This, of course, would be a logician's dream: a computer program that would render unnecessary the hard work of deductive reasoning in *both* of these branches of logic.

Alonzo Church (American, 1903–1995) shattered the logician's dream in 1936. He demonstrated, in what is known as Church's

Theorem, the *impossibility* of devising a mechanical method for determining, with respect to each *wff*, whether or not it's a logical truth. It follows from Church's Theorem that it's also impossible to determine, with respect to each *argument*, whether or not it's valid.

These two demonstrations—that in Predicate Logic/Quantification Theory there's no mechanical method for determining, with respect to each *wff*, whether or not it's a logical truth, and for determining, with respect to each argument, whether or not it's valid—are really two sides of the same metalogical coin.

You will tackle Church's Theorem in one of your next logic courses. You are now about to see that, *given* Church's Theorem, there's no mechanical method, no decision procedure, no algorithm, for determining, with respect to each argument, whether or not it's valid.

Suppose the opposite. Suppose that there were a mechanical method for determining, with respect to each argument, whether or not it's valid. In that case, there would be a mechanical method for determining, with respect to each *wff*, whether or not it's a logical truth. As Church proved, however, there is no mechanical method for determining, with respect to each *wff*, whether or not it's a logical truth. Therefore there's no mechanical method for determining, with respect to each argument, whether or not it's valid.

Question: Why does it follow that because there's no mechanical method for determining, with respect to each *wff*, whether or not it's a logical truth, there's no mechanical method for determining, with respect to each argument, whether or not it's valid?

Answer: Read on.

Let '$\triangle$' be any *wff* whatsoever of Predicate Logic/Quantification Theory. It makes no difference whether '$\triangle$' is a logical truth. Construct the one-premise argument whose conclusion is '$\triangle$', and whose premise is the disjunction of '$\triangle$' with its negation, i.e., '$\triangle \lor -\triangle$':

$$\frac{\triangle \lor -\triangle}{\therefore \triangle}$$

Suppose that there were a mechanical method for determining, with respect to *each* argument, whether or not it's valid. Then there would be a mechanical method for determining, with respect to *this* argument, whether or not *it's* valid. Note, however, that this argument is valid *iff* the conclusion, '△', is a logical truth. Why so? Ponder for a few minutes, and try to come up with the answer on your own. . . .

Suppose first that the argument is valid; i.e., suppose that there's no interpretation that makes the premise, '△ ∨ —△', true and the conclusion, '△', false. Because the premise is a tautology, *every* interpretation makes it true. So if there were *any* interpretation that made the conclusion false, for *that* interpretation the premise would be true and the conclusion would be false; i.e., the argument would be *invalid*. By hypothesis, however, the argument is *valid*. Therefore there can be *no* interpretation that makes the conclusion false. So the conclusion, i.e., '△', must be a logical truth. So if the argument is valid, '△' must be a logical truth.

Suppose next that the argument is invalid; i.e., suppose that there's at least one interpretation that makes the premise, '△ ∨ —△', true and the conclusion, '△', false. Because (once again) the premise is a tautology, *every* interpretation makes it true. So there must be at least one interpretation that makes the conclusion false. So the conclusion, i.e., '△', can't be a logical truth. So if the argument is invalid, '△' can't be a logical truth.

So here's what you now know. By hypothesis, '△' is any *wff* whatsoever of Predicate Logic/Quantification Theory. Corresponding to '△' is a unique argument, whose conclusion is '△', and whose premise is the disjunction of '△' with its negation, i.e., '△ ∨ —△'. If there were a mechanical method for determining, with respect to *each* argument, whether or not it's valid, then there would be a mechanical method for determining, with respect to *this* argument, whether or not *it's* valid. In that case, there would be a mechanical method for determining, with respect to '△', whether or not *it's* a logical truth.

By hypothesis once again, however, '△' is *any wff* whatsoever of Predicate Logic/Quantification Theory. So if there were a mechanical method for determining, with respect to each argument whether or not it's valid, there would be a mechanical method for determining, with respect to each *wff* of Predicate Logic/Quantification Theory, whether or not it's a logical truth. By Church's Theorem, however, there is no such method (i.e., for determining, with respect to each *wff* of Predicate Logic/Quantification Theory, whether or not it's a logical truth). Therefore there simply is no mechanical method for determining, with respect to each argument of Predicate Logic/Quantification Theory, whether or not it's valid. *Q.E.D.*

I promised you at the very outset of this book that we would begin with definitions and that we would end with definitions. We are nearing the end.

"More definitions?" you ask—in shock, dismay, bewilderment, and utter disbelief.

Yea, even unto the bitter end . . . *More* definitions . . . *Four more* definitions:

Definition:     A *wff* is *decidable iff* there's a mechanical method for determining whether it's a theorem.

Definition:     A *wff* is *undecidable iff* it's not decidable; i.e., *iff* there's no mechanical method for determining whether it's a theorem.

Definition:     A formal system is *decidable iff* there's a mechanical method for determining, for each *wff* in the formal system, whether it's a theorem.

Definition:     A formal system is *undecidable iff* it's not decidable; i.e., *iff* there's no mechanical method for determining, for each *wff* in the formal system, whether it's a theorem.

So here's what you now know. Each of the *wffs* of Propositional Logic is decidable, and therefore Propositional Logic, as a formal system, is itself decidable. However, some of the *wffs* of Predicate Logic/Quantification Theory are undecidable, and therefore Predicate Logic/Quantification Theory, as a formal system, is itself *undecidable*.

Question: Exactly how many of the *wffs* of Predicate Logic/Quantification Theory are undecidable?

Answer: As many as are decidable: an infinite number.

Kurt Gödel (Austrian and then American, 1906–1978) constructed a mechanical method for enumerating, i.e., generating an ordered list of, all the *wffs* in Predicate Logic/Quantification Theory. Gödel's method entails that it's possible to generate the *first wff* in the list, the *second wff* in the list, and so on. He also proved that it's possible to order all the *strings of wffs* in Predicate Logic/Quantification Theory, such that it's possible to generate the *first* string in the list, the *second* string in the list, and so on.

Now think of a computer endlessly generating string after string of *wffs*. The first string will consist of a *single wff*, an atomic. The second string will also consist of a *single wff*—another atomic. Before too long there will be a string that also consists of a *single wff*, but this time it will be a *molecular*. Eventually there will be a string consisting of *two wffs*, then more (many, many more) strings also containing two *wffs*—and all the strings will be quite different from one another. Before you know it, there will be strings containing *hundreds* of *wffs*, and then *hundreds of thousands* of *wffs*, and then *hundreds of millions* of *wffs*, and so on.

Now consider any one of these strings in general, and the *last wff* in that particular string in particular. Either the string will constitute a proof of its last *wff* from *wffs* preceding it in the string, or it won't. Clearly, there exists a mechanical method for distinguishing a string that constitutes such a proof from a string that doesn't. The last *wff* in a string that constitutes a genuine proof is, of course, either a theorem or the conclusion of a provable sequent—depending on whether the last *wff* rests on *no* assumptions or on *at least one* assumption. So there exists a mechanical method for identifying each *wff* that's a theorem, and each sequent that's provable.

Now it can easily be shown that, where either Propositional Logic or Predicate Logic/Quantification Theory is concerned, every theorem is a logical truth, and every provable sequent is a valid argument. (The fact that our derivation rules are truth-preserving plays the crucial role in showing this.) So there exists a mechanical method for identifying each *wff* that's a logical truth and each argument that's a valid argument.

Given Church's Theorem, however, there's *no* mechanical method for identifying either *wffs* that *aren't* logical truths or arguments that *aren't* valid. So here's the pickle: how could there *possibly* be a mechanical method for identifying the logical truths and the valid arguments, on the one hand, but no mechanical method for identifying the *wffs* that aren't logical truths and the arguments that aren't valid, on the other? This, of course, strikes you as *impossible*—or worse yet, as utterly *mad!*

Return to the scene of the crime. The printer attached to your computer is printing a list—an infinitely long list—of all possible strings of *wffs*. (Forget about arguments for the moment, and focus only on *wffs*.) Next to the printer there are two vats. One vat is for the *wffs* that the computer identifies as theorems—and thus as logical truths. And one vat is for the *wffs* that the computer identifies as non-theorems—and thus as not being logical truths. Suppose that each vat is infinitely deep, so that it can accommodate an infinite number of *wffs*.

Question: Do you have enough vats?

Answer: No. You do *not* have enough vats.

The computer examines a string of *wffs* that it identifies as *not* constituting a proof of the last *wff* in the string. Call this last *wff* '△'. What does the computer then do with '△'? Obviously it doesn't plunk it down into the Vat of Theorems/Logical Truths. So does it plunk it down into the Vat of Non-Theorems? Well, does it? (Think about this for a moment before reading on.)

It's true that *this particular string* doesn't constitute a proof of '△', the last *wff* in the string. It doesn't follow, however, that there won't be a string of *wffs* that will be printed tomorrow, perhaps, or the next day, or the day after that, that *will* constitute just such a proof. If such a string *is* eventually printed, the computer will plunk '△' down into the Vat of Theorems/Logical Truths. And if such a string *isn't* printed tomorrow, or the next day, or the day after that, what then? Well, maybe it'll be printed next year, or the year after that, or. . . .

So what does the computer do? It does what any good, self-respecting computer would do: it demands a *third* vat and it plunks '△' down into it. The computer knows that you need to keep *three* vats next to your printer:

1. one vat for *wffs* that most certainly *are* logical truths,
2. one vat for *wffs* that most certainly are *not* logical truths, and
3. one vat for *wffs* that the computer can't yet assign to either of the first two vats.

So what exactly does the third vat contain? It contains the *wffs* with respect to which the computer thinks to itself, "Hmmm. *This* string of *wffs* doesn't constitute a proof of the last *wff* in the string. But maybe *the very next string*, or *the one after that*, or *the one after that*, or . . . *will* constitute just such a proof. So what do I know now? I know *only* that none of the strings that I've examined *thus far* constitutes such a proof. So I can't conclude that the last *wff* in the string *is* a logical truth and I can't conclude that it *isn't*. Not yet, at any rate." (Now of course computers don't really *think*, and therefore they don't really *think to themselves*, and therefore they don't really think *this* to themselves. But you get the point.)

What holds true of *wffs* holds true, *mutatis mutandis* (i.e., making all the relevant changes), of *arguments*. You'll need three infinitely deep vats next to your printer for arguments:

1. one vat for arguments that the computer recognizes as valid,
2. one vat for arguments that it recognizes as invalid, and
3. one vat for arguments that it doesn't recognize as either valid or invalid.

The story doesn't end here. As you saw in Chapter 6, a modification of the Truth-Table Method yields a purely mechanical method for identifying invalid arguments within Predicate Logic/Quantification Theory. Alas, the method works only with respect to arguments containing *wffs* containing *monadic*/one-place predicates, and/ or a *restricted* range of polyadic/multiplace predicates. It is *not* an adequate method *in general* for quantificational arguments containing *wffs* containing polyadic/multiplace predicates. Indeed, we are left with an *infinite* number of such arguments, whose status as valid or invalid isn't determinable by *any* purely mechanical method. To determine that such arguments are invalid, you must draw upon your powers of insight and imaginativeness to come up with *counterexamples*.

So Propositional Logic is a *decidable* formal system and Predicate Logic/Quantification Theory *isn't*. Note that the claim is *not* the quite modest claim that we haven't yet discovered a mechanical method for distinguishing valid from invalid arguments. The claim is rather the quite radical claim that there can be no such method!

This is an extraordinary discovery. It entails limits to the powers of mechanical methods—and thus limits to the powers of computers and the mechanical-method programs on which they rely. What this means is that the world's smartest possible computer isn't up to the task of distinguishing, where the arguments of Predicate Logic/Quantification Theory are concerned, the valid from the invalid.

Or rather (and once again): it's possible to program a computer to be able to list all the *valid* arguments of Predicate Logic/Quantification

Theory. What it isn't possible to do is to program a computer to list, in addition, all the *invalid* arguments of Predicate Logic/Quantification Theory.

One last point, and not a trivial one at that. You might have expected by this point in the text a definition of 'mechanical method'. There is a very good reason why I have *not* provided you with such a definition: it's not clear that it's *possible* to provide one—at least in a non-circular way. A mechanical method generates its results in a *finite* number of steps. So far, so good. And it's a method of *computing*, of course. But here's the pickle: just how does one define '*computing*'? And in particular, just how does one define it without appealing to the very notion that one is trying to define: the notion of a mechanical method? Perhaps we have no choice here, as the British logician Geoffrey Hunter (1925–2000) suggests, but to rely on our *informal/intuitive/imprecise* understanding of what a mechanical method is.

Now go and take a second logic course.

# 6. Appendix II: ∀I *vs.* ∃I: Restriction *vs.* No Restriction

Question: Why is it that, in performing ∀I, but not ∃I, you have to replace in '***Pt***' *every* free occurrence of '***t***' with '***v***'? The *quick* answer is that if you ignore the restriction where ∀I is concerned, you'll bump up against counterexamples.

The problem with the quick answer is that it generates a new question: Why is it that failing to replace in '***Pt***' *every* free occurrence of '***t***' with '***v***' generates counterexamples where ∀I is concerned—but not where ∃I is concerned?

We begin with the relevant nuts and bolts, the nuts being the objects in the domain, and the bolts being the constants and the variables. Let the objects in the domain be $a_1$, $a_2$, etc. Let the *constants*, i.e., the proper names of the corresponding objects in the domain, be '$a_1$', '$a_2$', etc., such that '$a_1$' is the proper name of $a_1$, '$a_2$' is the proper name of $a_2$, etc. Let the *variables* be '***v***' (without a numerical subscript) and '***t***'. (The variables, of course, range over the domain of the objects $a_1$, $a_2$, etc.)

Throughout this discussion I shall be invoking the notion of *implication*—*semantic* implication. The claim that '$\triangle$' implies, i.e., *semantically* implies, '$O$' is the claim that there is no interpretation that makes '$\triangle$' true and '$O$' false. The claim that '$\triangle$' implies, i.e., *semantically* implies, '$O$' is independent of, and therefore is *silent* with respect to, the *syntactic* claim that there is a *proof* or *derivation* of '$O$' from '$\triangle$'.

Consider $\forall$I first. Three preliminary points. First, let '$Pt$' be any *wff* containing at least *two* occurrences of the free variable '$t$'. (Why at least *two*? If there were only *one* occurrence of '$t$' in '$Pt$', you wouldn't be addressing the problem of why it is that in performing $\forall$I, but not $\exists$I, you have to replace in '$Pt$' *every* free occurrence of '$t$' with '$v$'.) Second, assume that '$Pt$' doesn't rest on any assumption containing the free variable '$t$'; i.e., assume that the object $t$ is a *proxy* for *each* object in the domain. Third, remind yourself of the point that universally quantified *wffs* are disguised *conjunctions*; thus the de-quantified counterpart of '$(\forall v)Pv$' is '$Pa_1 \wedge Pa_2 \wedge Pa_3 \wedge \dots$'.

Now '$Pt$' implies '$(\forall v)Pv$' *iff* '$Pt$' implies the conjunction '$Pa_1 \wedge Pa_2 \wedge Pa_3 \wedge \dots$'. And '$Pt$' implies the conjunction '$Pa_1 \wedge Pa_2 \wedge Pa_3 \wedge \dots$' *iff* '$Pt$' implies *each* conjunct separately, i.e., *iff* '$Pt$' implies '$Pa_1$', *and* '$Pt$' implies '$Pa_2$', *and* '$Pt$' implies '$Pa_3$', etc. You are about to see that if you flout the replace-*every*-free-occurrence-of-'$t$'-with-'$v$' restriction, you'll find yourself in hot water—but if you don't, you won't.

Suppose first that you *do* adhere to the restriction. Let '$Pa_1$' be the *wff* that you construct from '$Pt$' by replacing *every* free occurrence (and no bound occurrence) of '$t$' in '$Pt$' with '$a_1$'. So '$a_1$' occurs in '$Pa_1$' *exactly* where '$t$' occurs free in '$Pt$'. Recall that $t$ serves as a proxy for *each* object in the domain. So $t$ serves as a proxy for $a_1$, $a_2$, $a_3$, etc. Now the sense in which $t$ serves as a proxy for *each* object in the domain is that whatever is true of $t$ is true of each object in the domain. (Remember the Euclidean geometry example: whatever is true of the *proxy* triangle *ABC* is true of *every* triangle.) So any interpretation that makes '$P$' true of $t$ makes '$P$' true of $a_1$, $a_2$, $a_3$, etc. So '$Pt$' implies '$Pa_1$', '$Pa_2$', '$Pa_3$', etc. So '$Pt$' implies '$Pa_1 \wedge Pa_2 \wedge Pa_3 \wedge \dots$'. So '$Pt$' implies '$(\forall v)Pv$'. So adhering to the replace-*every*-free-occurrence-of-'$t$'-with-'$v$' restriction keeps you from getting into hot water where $\forall$I is concerned.

An example: Let '$Lxx$' be any *wff* that rests on *no* assumption in which '$x$' is free. Suppose a domain of people: Ardbeg, Bobo, Coco, etc. Interpret '$Lxy$' to mean that $x$ loves $y$. Your goal is to show that '$Lxx$' implies '$(\forall y)Lyy$'.

Because 'Lxx' rests on *no* assumption in which 'x' is free, x is fit to serve as a proxy for *any* object in the domain. In other words, what's true of x is true of *any* object in the domain. Now, what you know to be true of x is that x loves x. So if x loves x (i.e., if x loves himself or herself) then Ardbeg loves himself *and* Bobo loves herself *and* Coco loves herself, etc. In that case, *everyone* loves himself or herself. In other words, 'Lxx' implies 'Laa ∧ Lbb ∧ Lcc ∧ …'. But of course 'Laa ∧ Lbb ∧ Lcc ∧ …' implies '(∀y)Lyy'. Therefore 'Lxx' implies '(∀y)Lyy'.

Notice that you showed that 'Lxx' implies '(∀y)Lyy' by showing that 'Lxx' implies the de-quantified counterpart of '(∀y)Lyy', i.e., the conjunction 'Laa ∧ Lbb ∧ Lcc ∧ …'. And notice that to show that 'Lxx' implies the conjunction 'Laa ∧ Lbb ∧ Lcc ∧ …', you extracted *each* occurrence of the variable 'x' from 'Lxx' and replaced *each* such occurrence with the proper name of *one and the same* object in the domain to generate the *first* conjunct: 'Laa'. Then you repeated the process and extracted *each* occurrence of 'x' from 'Lxx' and replaced *each* such occurrence with the proper name of *one and the same* object in the domain to generate the *second* conjunct: 'Lbb'. And so on. So by adhering to the replace-*every*-free-occurrence-of-'*t*'-with-'*v*' restriction, you avoided the hot water.

Now suppose that you *flout* the restriction. Suppose that in constructing '**Pa**$_1$' from '**Pt**', you *fail* to replace *every* free occurrence of '*t*' in '**Pt**' with '**a**$_1$'. Suppose instead that you replace in '**Pt**' at least *one* free occurrence (and no bound occurrence) of '*t*' with '**a**$_1$', but that you leave in place in '**Pt**' at least *one* free occurrence of '*t*'. So now, corresponding to each free occurrence of '*t*' that you have left in place in '**Pt**', there will be a free occurrence of '*t*' in '**Pv**'. Obviously, therefore, there is at least one occurrence of '*t*' in '**Pt**' that does *not* correspond to an occurrence of '**a**$_1$' in '**Pa**$_1$'. So the number of free occurrences of '*t*' in '**Pt**' is at least one greater than the number of occurrences of '**a**$_1$' in '**Pa**$_1$'. So there's a *numerical mismatch*, as it were, between the string of '*t*'s in '**Pt**' and the string of '**a**$_1$'s in '**Pa**$_1$'. And this might (and should!) strike you as troubling.

You're looking at two *wffs*: '**Pt**' and '**Pa**$_1$ ∧ **Pa**$_2$ ∧ **Pa**$_3$ ∧ …'. The first *wff*, '**Pt**', has a given number of occurrences of the free variable '*t*'. The second *wff* is a conjunction, none of whose conjuncts is a perfect match of '**Pt**'. Once again: It simply *isn't* the case that *wherever* the free variable '*t*' appears in '**Pt**', the constant '**a**$_1$' appears in the *first* conjunct of the conjunction, and the constant '**a**$_2$' appears in the *second* conjunct of the conjunction, etc. On the contrary, '**Pt**' has *more* occurrences of the free variable '*t*' than either the first conjunct has of '*a₁*', or the second conjunct has of '*a₂*', etc.

Now *t* serves as a proxy for *any* object in the domain. Suppose that *t* is a proxy for the object *a₂*. So any interpretation that makes '*P*' true of *t* makes '*P*' true of *a₂*. So '*Pt*' implies '*Pa₂*'. But here's the catch: '*Pt*' doesn't imply *either* '*Pa₁*' or '*Pa₃*' or '*Pa₄*', etc. Why not? Remember: There are *more* occurrences of the free variable '*t*' in '*Pt*' than there are of the constant '*a₁*' in '*Pa₁*', of the constant '*a₃*' in '*Pa₃*', etc. So all you have to do is conjure up an interpretation that is true of '*Pt*' but false of '*Pa₁*', or false of '*Pa₃*', etc. And once you have your interpretation, you know that even though '*Pa₂*' is true for that interpretation, at least one of the other instances of '*Pa*' (i.e., either '*Pa₁*' or '*Pa₃*' or '*Pa₄*' or ...) is false. And therefore for *that* interpretation the conjunction '*Pa₁* ∧ *Pa₂* ∧ *Pa₃* ∧ ...' will be false. After all, even though one of the conjuncts, '*Pa₂*', is true, at least one of the other conjuncts is false. And therefore '*Pt*' doesn't imply the *conjunction* '*Pa₁* ∧ *Pa₂* ∧ *Pa₃* ∧ ...'. And therefore '*Pt*' doesn't imply '(∀*v*)*Pv*'. So flouting the *every*-free-occurrence-of-*t* restriction gets you into *very* hot water where ∀I is concerned.

For the record: Nothing stands between you and a counterexample *except* a failure of imagination on your part to come up with the magic interpretation. The magic interpretation, of course, is the one that makes '*P*' true of *t* in '*Pt*' but false of *a₁* in '*Pa₁*' or false of *a₃* in '*Pa₃*' or false of *a₄* in '*Pa₄*', etc.

An example: Suppose that you thought that '*Lxx*' implied a *wff* of a form quite different from the form of '(∀*y*)*Lyy*'. Suppose that you really thought that '*Lxx*' implied '(∀*y*)*Lyx*'. Suppose that, to show this, you didn't replace in '*Lxx*' *each* occurrence of '*x*' with the proper name of *one and the same* object in the domain. Suppose that instead you declined to replace *at least one* occurrence of '*x*', and generated the following conjunction instead: '*Lax* ∧ *Lbx* ∧ *Lcx* ∧ ...'. To be sure, this latter conjunction *does* imply '(∀*y*)*Lyx*': if, as the conjunction proclaims, Ardbeg, Bobo, and Coco, etc., *each* loves *x*, then *everyone* loves *x*. So if '*Lxx*' implies '*Lax* ∧ *Lbx* ∧ *Lcx* ∧ ...' then '*Lxx*' implies '(∀*y*)*Lyx*'— but not otherwise. The key question, clearly, is whether '*Lxx*' implies '*Lax* ∧ *Lbx* ∧ *Lcx* ∧ ...'.

The quick and easy answer, of course, is 'No'. Now sometimes the quick and easy answer happens to be the *correct* answer. And indeed this is one of those times. It may well be true that *anyone* in the domain whom you choose loves *himself* or *herself*. It doesn't follow that *everyone* loves *x*—whoever *x* happens to be.

Now here's what's interesting. '*Lxx*' *does* imply *at least one* of the conjuncts of the conjunction '*Lax* ∧ *Lbx* ∧ *Lcx* ∧ …'. But it also implies *at most one* of them. And therefore it doesn't imply the conjunction as a whole. And therefore it doesn't imply '(∀*y*)*Lyx*'. How so? Read on.

Let '*x*' designate *any* of the objects in the domain. Suppose, for example, that '*x*' designates Bobo. Then '*Lxx*' implies *at least one* of the conjuncts in the conjunction '*Lax* ∧ *Lbx* ∧ *Lcx* ∧ …', namely, the conjunct '*Lbx*'. Puzzled? If '*x*' designates Bobo then '*Lxx*' is equivalent to '*Lbb*'. By the same token '*Lbx*' is also equivalent to '*Lbb*'. So of course '*Lxx*' ('*Lbb*') implies '*Lbx*' ('*Lbb*'). And so (once again) if '*x*' designates Bobo then '*Lxx*' implies *at least one* of the conjuncts in the conjunction '*Lax* ∧ *Lbx* ∧ *Lcx* ∧ …'.

But it also implies *at most one* of them. If '*x*' designates Bobo then '*Lxx*' ('*Lbb*') doesn't imply either '*Lax*' ('*Lab*') or '*Lcx*' ('*Lcb*'), etc. Bobo may well love herself; it doesn't follow that Ardbeg and Coco, etc., each loves her (unless, of course, Bobo *is* Ardbeg, and Bobo *is* Coco, etc.— but there's no reason to think that). If '*Lxx*' were to imply '(∀*y*)*Lyx*', it would have to imply the conjunction '*Lax* ∧ *Lbx* ∧ *Lcx* ∧ …', and therefore it would have to imply each conjunct. But it turns out that '*Lxx*' implies *at most one* of the conjuncts. So '*Lxx*' doesn't imply '(∀*y*)*Lyx*'.

Or, to put the matter a bit more abstractly: it may well be true that each object in the domain stands in the '*L*'-relationship to itself; it doesn't follow that there is one object in the domain to which each object in the domain stands in the '*L*'-relationship.

To summarize: '*Lxx*' implies *exactly one* of the conjuncts in the conjunction '*Lax* ∧ *Lbx* ∧ *Lcx* ∧ …'. Therefore '*Lxx*' doesn't imply the conjunction as a whole: '*Lax* ∧ *Lbx* ∧ *Lcx* ∧ …'. Therefore '*Lxx*' doesn't imply '(∀*y*)*Lyx*'. So by flouting the replace-*every*-free-occurrence-of-'*t*'-with-'*v*' restriction, you're not in merely *hot* water, you're in *scalding* water.

Finally, consider ∃I and recall our initial question: Why does this restriction hold with respect to ∀I but not with respect to ∃I? Alternatively: Why is ∃I a horse of a different color?

Three preliminary points once again. First, let '**P*t***' be any *wff* containing at least *two* occurrences of the free variable '*t*'. (Puzzled? See the discussion above of the first of the three corresponding preliminary points.) Second, assume that '**P*t***' *does* rest on an assumption containing the free variable '$t$'. Assume, in other words, that the object $t$ is *not* a proxy for each object in the domain, but rather is merely *one particular* object in the domain. (It's not crucial that you make this assumption. Even if you don't, the same conclusion at which you're aiming will follow *a fortiori*, i.e., all the more so, as it were.) Third, remind yourself of the point that existentially quantified *wffs* are disguised *disjunctions*; thus the de-quantified counterpart of '$(\exists v)Pv$' is '$Pa_1 \lor Pa_2 \lor Pa_3...$'.

Now '$Pt$' implies '$(\exists v)Pv$' *iff* '$Pt$' implies the disjunction '$Pa_1 \lor Pa_2 \lor Pa_3 \lor ...$'. And '$Pt$' implies the disjunction '$Pa_1 \lor Pa_2 \lor Pa_3 \lor ...$' *iff* '$Pt$' implies *at least one* (but not necessarily more than one) of these disjuncts, i.e., *iff* '$Pt$' implies *either* '$Pa_1$' or '$Pa_2$' or '$Pa_3$', etc.

Suppose that you construct '$Pa_1$' from '$Pt$' by replacing in '$Pt$' at *least one* free occurrence (and no bound occurrence) of '$t$' with '$a_1$', but that you leave in place in '$Pt$' at least one free occurrence of '$t$'. So '$t$' occurs in at least one location in '$Pt$' where '$a_1$' doesn't occur in '$Pa_1$'. So the number of free occurrences of '$t$' in '$Pt$' is at least one greater than the number of occurrences of '$a_1$' in '$Pa_1$'. So there's a numerical mismatch, as it were, between the string of '$t$'s in '$Pt$' and the string of '$a_1$'s in '$Pa_1$'. So there's no reason to think that any interpretation that makes '$P$' true of $t$ makes '$P$' true of $a_1$. So '$Pt$' doesn't imply '$Pa_1$'. So far so good. Here, however, you might be tempted to conclude that '$Pt$' doesn't imply '$Pa_1 \lor Pa_2 \lor Pa_3 \lor ...$', and therefore '$Pt$' doesn't imply '$(\exists v)Pv$'. But not so fast. . . .

'$Pt$' may not imply '$Pa_1$', but it *does* imply *one* of these disjuncts. You will recall that $t$ does *not* serve as a proxy for *each* object in the domain; it is rather one particular (unnamed) object. The objects in the domain, once again, are $a_1$, $a_2$, $a_3$, etc. So the variable '$t$' stands for *either $a_1$ or $a_2$ or $a_3$*, etc. Suppose that '$t$' stands for $a_2$. In that case the variable '$t$' stands for the very same object that the individual constant '$a_2$' stands for. So any interpretation that makes '$P$' true of $t$ makes '$P$' true of $a_2$. So '$Pt$' implies '$Pa_2$'. But (thanks to the truth-table definition of the wedge) '$Pa_2$' implies '$Pa_1 \lor Pa_2 \lor Pa_3 \lor ...$'. So '$Pt$' implies '$Pa_1 \lor Pa_2 \lor Pa_3 \lor ...$'. So '$Pt$' implies '$(\exists v)Pv$'. So the replace-*every*-free-occurrence-of-'$t$'-with-'$v$' restriction has no bearing where $\exists$I is concerned.

An example: Suppose that you thought (correctly!) that from '$Lxx$' you could generate a *wff* of a form quite different from the form of '$(\exists y)Lyy$'. Suppose that you thought (also correctly!) that from '$Lxx$' you could generate '$(\exists y)Lyx$'. Suppose that, to accomplish this end, you didn't replace in '*Lxx*' *each* occurrence of '*x*' with the proper name of *one and the same* object in the domain. Suppose that instead you declined to replace *at least one* occurrence of '*x*', and generated the following disjunction instead: '*Lax* ∨ *Lbx* ∨ *Lcx* ∨ …'. Now this latter disjunction *does* imply '(∀y)*Lyx*': if, as the disjunction proclaims, *either* Ardbeg *or* Bobo *or* Coco, etc., loves *x*, then *someone* loves *x*. So if '*Lxx*' implies '*Lax* ∨ *Lbx* ∨ *Lcx* ∨ …' then '*Lxx*' implies '(∃y)*Lyx*'— but not otherwise. The key question, clearly, is whether '*Lxx*' implies '*Lax* ∨ *Lbx* ∨ *Lcx* ∨ …'.

The quick and easy answer, of course, is 'Yes'. Now sometimes (once again) the quick and easy answer happens to be the *correct* answer. And indeed (and once again) this is one of those times. On the assumption that an unnamed individual *x* loves *himself* or *herself*, it most certainly *does* follow that *someone* loves *x*—whoever *x* happens to be.

Now here's what's interesting. '*Lxx*' does imply *at least one* of the disjuncts of the disjunction '*Lax* ∨ *Lbx* ∨ *Lcx* ∨ …'. And therefore it implies the disjunction as a whole. And therefore it implies '(∃y)*Lyx*'. How so? Read on.

Let '*x*' designate *any* of the objects in the domain. Suppose, for example, that '*x*' designates Bobo. Then '*Lxx*' implies *at least one* of the disjuncts in the disjunction '*Lax* ∨ *Lbx* ∨ *Lcx* ∨ …', namely, the disjunct '*Lbx*'. Puzzled? If (once again) '*x*' designates Bobo, '*Lxx*' is equivalent to '*Lbb*', and '*Lbx*' is also equivalent to '*Lbb*'. So of course '*Lxx*' ('*Lbb*') implies '*Lbx*' ('*Lbb*'). And so (yet once again) if '*x*' designates Bobo then '*Lxx*' implies *at least one* of the disjuncts in the disjunction '*Lax* ∨ *Lbx* ∨ *Lcx* ∨ …'. And therefore (thanks, once again, to the truth-table definition of the wedge) '*Lxx*' implies the disjunction '*Lax* ∨ *Lbx* ∨ *Lcx* ∨ …'. And therefore '*Lxx*' implies '(∃y)*Lyx*'.

Or, to put the matter a bit more abstractly: On the assumption that *x*, an unnamed object in the domain, stands in the '*L*'-relationship to itself, i.e., to *x*, it follows that there is at least one object in the domain which stands in the '*L*'-relationship to *x*.

To generalize and to summarize: Regardless of which individual in the domain '*x*' stands for, '*Lxx*' implies *at least one* of the disjuncts in the disjunction '*Lax* ∨ *Lbx* ∨ *Lcx* ∨…'. Therefore '*Lxx*' implies the disjunction as a whole: '*Lax* ∨ *Lbx* ∨ *Lcx* ∨ …'. Therefore '*Lxx*' implies '(∃y)*Lyx*. So (once again) the replace-*every*-free-occurrence-of-'*t*'-with-'*v*' restriction has no bearing where ∃I is concerned.

*Grand* moral of the story: it is precisely because universally quantified *wffs* are disguised *conjunctions* and existentially quantified *wffs* are disguised *disjunctions* that the replace-*every*-free-occurrence-of-*t*-with-*v* restriction holds where ∀I is concerned but *not* where ∃I is concerned. Universally quantified *wffs*, in other words, are true *iff every* conjunct is true, whereas existentially quantified *wffs* are true *iff at least one* disjunct is true. Flouting the restriction, as you have seen, guarantees that *exactly one* conjunct is true, and it also guarantees that *at least one* disjunct is true. One true conjunct, however, doth *not* a true conjunction make (except, trivially, in a one-object domain), whereas one true disjunct *doth* a true disjunction make. Hence the reason why in performing ∀I, but not ∃I, you have to replace, in '*Pt*', *every* free occurrence of '*t*' with '*v*'.

# List of Definitions

Ambiguous:
> A string of words is *ambiguous iff* it possesses more than one meaning, such that it's an instance of more than one proposition.

Argument:
> An *argument* is a string of sentences; one of the sentences is the conclusion and the others are the premises.

Atomic:
> An *atomic* (or *simple*) sentence is a sentence without any connectives.

Bearer of Truth-Value:
> A *bearer of truth-value* is something that is either true, on the one hand, or false, on the other.

Bound (or Governed):
> A variable '*x*' is *bound*, or *governed*, by a quantifier $Q_1$ *iff* (1) '*x*' falls within the scope of the quantifier $Q_1$; (2) an occurrence of the same variable '*x*' appears immediately to the right of the quantifier $Q_1$; and (3) if there's another quantifier $Q_2$ within whose scope '*x*' also falls, and that also has an occurrence of '*x*' immediately to its right, then the quantifier $Q_1$ falls within the scope of the quantifier $Q_2$.

Closed:
> A *wff* is *closed iff* it isn't open; i.e., *iff* it contains no occurrence of a free variable.

Conclusion:
> The *conclusion* of an argument is the sentence whose truth is to be established.

Connective:
> A *connective* is a device (or an operator) that operates on one or more sentences in order to generate a new sentence.

Consistent:
> A *consistent* sentence is a sentence that is true for at least one interpretation.

Contingent:
> A *contingent* sentence is a sentence that is true for at least one interpretation and that is false for at least one interpretation.

Contraries:
Two propositions are *contraries* *iff* there is no interpretation that makes both of them true but there is at least one interpretation that makes both of them false.

Counterexample:
A *counterexample* is an interpretation that makes every premise true and the conclusion false.

Decidable Formal System:
A formal system is *decidable* *iff* there's a mechanical method for determining, for each *wff* in the formal system, whether it's a theorem.

Decidable *Wff*:
A *wff* is *decidable* *iff* there's a mechanical method for determining whether it's a theorem.

Deductive Apparatus:
A *deductive apparatus* consists of either a set of axioms and a set of derivation rules, or (merely) a set of derivation rules.

Deductively Complete:
A formal system is *deductively complete* *iff* every valid argument that can be expressed in the formal language of the system is provable within the system.

Derivation:
A *derivation* is a string of *wffs*, each of which is either an assumption or a theorem or a *wff* that follows, via our derivation rules, from one or more *wffs* in the string.

Derivation of a *Wff*:
A *derivation* of a *wff*, '△', from a set of given assumptions, is a finite string of *wffs*, the last of which is '△'. Each of the *wffs* in the string is either (1) a member of the set of given assumptions, or (2) an introduced assumption, or (3) a theorem, or (4) a *wff* that follows from at least one of the *wffs* in the string by one of our derivation rules.

Derivation Rule:
A *derivation rule* is a rule that serves to justify the assertion of a given *wff* in a derivation.

Expressively Complete:
A formal language, L, is *expressively complete* *iff* any *wff* containing any truth-functional connective can be translated into a *wff* that is logically equivalent to it, and that contains no connectives other than the connectives of L.

Extension:
    A formal system, $S_2$, is an *extension* of a formal system, $S_1$, *iff* $S_2$ contains within itself the formal language and the deductive apparatus of $S_1$.

Falls within the Scope:
    If '$\triangle$' is a *wff* and if '$(\forall x)\triangle$' is a *wff*, then '$\triangle$' *falls within the scope* of the universal quantifier '$\forall$'.
    If '$\triangle$' is a *wff* and if '$(\exists x)\triangle$' is a *wff*, then '$\triangle$' *falls within the scope* of the existential quantifier '$\exists$'.

Falls within the Scope of a Quantifier:
    A quantifier $\mathbf{Q}_1$ falls within the scope of a quantifier $\mathbf{Q}_2$ *iff* $\mathbf{Q}_1$ appears in a *wff* that itself falls within the scope of $\mathbf{Q}_2$.

Formal Language:
    A *formal language* consists of both a set of symbols and a set of formation rules.

Formal System:
    A *formal system* consists of two components: a formal language and a deductive apparatus.

Formula:
    A *formula* of $L_1/L_2$ is any string of symbols of $L_1/L_2$.

Free:
    A variable is *free iff* it isn't bound, or governed, by any quantifier.

Imply:
    The premises of an argument *imply* its conclusion *iff* the argument is valid.

Logically Equivalent:
    Two propositions are *logically equivalent iff* they are true for the same interpretations and they are false for the same interpretations.

Logically Valid:
    A *logically valid wff*/a *logical truth* is a *wff* that is true for every interpretation.

Metalanguage:
    The *metalanguage* is the language through which the discussion of the object language is conducted.

Mixed:
    A *wff* is in *mixed* form *iff* it is in neither prenex nor purified form.

**Molecular:**
A *molecular* (or *compound*) sentence is a sentence containing at least one connective.

**Negated:**
A *negated* quantified *wff* is a *wff* whose main operator is a dash and whose main operator, in the absence of the dash, would be a quantifier.

**Negation:**
The *negation* of '$\triangle$' is '$-\triangle$', i.e., '$\triangle$' preceded by a dash.

**Non-Negated:**
A *non-negated* quantified *wff* is a quantified *wff* whose main operator is a quantifier.

**Object Language:**
The *object language* is the language that is the object of discussion.

**Open:**
A *wff* is *open iff* it contains at least one occurrence of a free variable.

**Opposite:**
The *opposite* of '$\triangle$' is '$-\triangle$'; the *opposite* of '$-\triangle$' is '$\triangle$'.

**Predicate:**
A *predicate* is a symbol that designates (or denotes or stands for) a property or relation.

**Prenex:**
A *wff* is in *prenex* form *iff* (a) the leftmost quantifier is the *wff*'s main operator; (b) the rightmost quantifier has within its scope the whole of the *wff* to its right; and (c) between any two quantifiers there are no connectives

**Proof:**
A *proof* of a *wff*, '$\triangle$', is a finite string of *wffs*, the last of which, '$\triangle$', is a theorem. Each of the *wffs* in the string is either (1) an introduced assumption, or (2) a theorem, or (3) a *wff* that follows from at least one of the *wffs* in the string by one of our derivation rules.

**Proper Name:**
A *proper name* is a symbol that designates (or denotes or stands for) an individual thing (or object).

**Propositional Constant:**
A *propositional constant* is a propositional symbol that designates (or represents or stands for) a specific (i.e., exactly one) proposition.

Propositional Interpretation:

A *propositional interpretation* of a *propositional symbol* is an assignment to the symbol of a particular proposition such that the symbol now designates that proposition.

Propositional Variable:

A *propositional variable* is a propositional symbol that designates (or represents or stands for) any proposition whatsoever.

Premise:

A *premise* of an argument is a sentence that is said, or that is thought, or that appears, to play a role in establishing the truth of the conclusion.

Purified:

A *wff* is in *purified* form *iff* none of its quantifiers falls within the scope of any of its other quantifiers.

Satisfiable:

A set of *wffs* is *satisfiable iff* there is at least one interpretation that makes each member of the set true.

Scope:

If '$\triangle$' is a *wff* and if '$(\forall x)\triangle$' is a *wff*, then the *scope* of the universal quantifier '$\forall$' is '$(\forall x)\triangle$', i.e., the *wff* in its entirety.
If '$\triangle$' is a *wff* and if '$(\exists x)\triangle$' is a *wff*, then the *scope* of the existential quantifier '$\exists$' is '$(\exists x)\triangle$', i.e., the *wff* in its entirety.

Scope of a Variable:

A *variable* '$x$' falls within the scope of a given quantifier *iff* either '$x$' appears immediately to the right of the quantifier, or '$x$' appears in a *wff* that itself falls within the scope of the quantifier.

Semantic Consequence:

A *wff* '$\triangle$' is a *semantic consequence* of a set of *wffs iff* there is no interpretation that makes every *wff* in the set true and that makes '$\triangle$' false.

Semantic Contradiction:

A *semantic contradiction* is a *wff* or sentence that is false for every interpretation.

Semantic Contradictories:

Two propositions are *semantic contradictories iff* there is no interpretation that makes both of them true and there is no interpretation that makes both of them false; i.e., they have opposite truth-values for every interpretation. (Informally, what this means is that the two propositions can't both be true and they can't both be false.)

Sentence:
  A *sentence* (or *statement* or *proposition*) is a bearer of truth-value.

Sequent:
  A *sequent* is a string of *wffs*.

Sheffer Stroke:
  '$\triangle \mid O$' $\Leftrightarrow$ '$-(\triangle \wedge O)$'

Sound:
  An argument is *sound iff* (1) it is valid, and (2) each of its premises is true.

Subcontraries:
  Two propositions are *subcontraries iff* there is no interpretation that makes both of them false but there is at least one interpretation that makes both of them true.

Substitution-Instance of an Individual *Wff*:
  1. Let '$\triangle$' be any *wff*.
  2. Let '$p_1$', '$p_2$', ... , '$p_n$' be the atomics that occur in '$\triangle$'.
  3. Let '$q_1$', '$q_2$', ... , '$q_n$' be any *wffs* whatsoever (either atomic or molecular).
  4. In '$\triangle$', replace each occurrence of '$p_1$' with '$q_1$', each occurrence of '$p_2$' with '$q_2$', ... , and each occurrence of '$p_n$' with '$q_n$'.
  5. Let '$O$' be the resulting *wff*. 6. Accordingly, '$O$' is a substitution-instance of '$\triangle$'.

Substitution-Instance of a Sequent:
  1. Let '$\triangle_1$' ... , '$\triangle_{m-1}$', and '$\triangle_m$' be any *wffs*.
  2. Let '$\triangle_1$, ... , $\triangle_{m-1} \vdash \triangle_m$' be any sequent.
  3. Let '$p_1$', '$p_2$', ... , '$p_n$' be the atomics that occur in the *wffs* '$\triangle_1$, ... , $\triangle_{m-1} \vdash \triangle_m$'.
  4. Let '$q_1$', '$q_2$', ... , '$q_n$' be any *wffs* whatsoever (either atomic or molecular).
  5. In '$\triangle_1$, ... , $\triangle_{m-1} \vdash \triangle_m$', replace each occurrence of '$p_1$' with '$q_1$', each occurrence of '$p_2$' with '$q_2$', ... , and each occurrence of '$p_n$' with '$q_n$'.
  6. Let the result of replacing each occurrence of '$p_1$', '$p_2$', ... , '$p_n$' with '$q_1$', '$q_2$', ... , '$q_n$', respectively, in '$\triangle_1$', ... , '$\triangle_{m-1}$', and '$\triangle_m$' be '$O_1$', ... , '$O_{m-1}$', and '$O_m$', respectively.
  7. Let '$O_1$, ... , $O_{m-1} \vdash O_m$' be the resulting sequent.
  8. Accordingly, '$O_1$, ... , $O_{m-1} \vdash O_m$' is a substitution-instance of '$\triangle_1$, ... , $\triangle_{m-1} \vdash \triangle_m$'.

Syntactic Consequence:

A *wff* '△' is a *syntactic consequence* of a set of *wffs iff* there is a derivation of '△' from the set.

Syntactic Contradiction:

A *syntactic contradiction* is a conjunction, '△ ∧ −△', whose left conjunct is any *wff*, '△', and whose right conjunct is the negation of that *wff*, '−△'.

Syntactic Contradictories:

Two *wffs* '△' and '−△' are *syntactic contradictories iff* the latter is the negation of the former, i.e., *iff* the latter is the former preceded by a dash.

Tautology:

A *tautology* is a sentence that is true for every interpretation.

Theorem:

A *theorem* is a conclusion, resting on no assumptions, of a provable sequent.

Truth Functional:

A connective is *truth-functional iff* it generates a truth-functional sentence. A sentence is *truth-functional iff* its truth-value is determined exclusively by (i.e., is entirely a function of) the truth-values of its atomics.

Truth-Preserving:

Consider any finite set of *wffs*, and consider any *wff*, '△', that follows from the set by a given derivation rule. The derivation rule is *truth-preserving iff* there is no interpretation that makes each *wff* in the set true and that makes '△' false.

Truth-Value Interpretation:

A *truth-value interpretation* of a *proposition* is an assignment of truth-values to the atomics that constitute the proposition.

Undecidable Formal System:

A formal system is *undecidable iff* it's not decidable; i.e., *iff* there's no mechanical method for determining, for each *wff* in the formal system, whether it's a theorem.

Undecidable *Wff*:

A *wff* is *undecidable iff* it's not decidable; i.e., *iff* there's no mechanical method for determining whether it's a theorem

Unsatisfiable:

A set of *wffs* is *unsatisfiable iff* it is not satisfiable, i.e., *iff* there is no interpretation that makes each member of the set true.

Valid:

An argument is *valid iff* there is no interpretation that makes each of its premises true and its conclusion false.

# The following are definitions of metalinguistic expressions that denote symbols and *wffs* of L$_2$

'*v*':

'*v*' signifies any free variable.

'*Pv*':

'*Pv*' signifies any open *wff* containing both the predicate '*P*' and at least one occurrence of the free variable '*v*'.

'$(\forall v)Pv$':

'$(\forall v)Pv$' signifies any universally quantified *wff*.

'$(\exists v)Pv$':

'$(\exists v)Pv$' signifies any existentially quantified *wff*.

'*t*':

A *term*,'*t*', signifies either an individual constant or a variable.
Lande, Classical Logic 1st proof new text additions

'*Pt/v*':

'*Pt/v*' signifies the *wff* that results from '*Pv*' by replacing every *free* occurrence of '*v*' in '*Pv*' with '*t*'.

'*t*' is *free for* '*v*' in '*Pv*':

'*t*' is *free for* '*v*' in '*Pv*' *iff* when you replace each free occurrence of '*v*' in '*Pv*' with '*t*', '*t*' is free in '*Pt/v*' exactly where '*v*' was free in '*Pv*'.

# Index